"EXPANDING
THE FRONTIERS
OF CIVIL RIGHTS"

"EXPANDING
THE FRONTIERS
OF CIVIL RIGHTS"
MICHIGAN, 1948–1968

SIDNEY FINE

WAYNE STATE UNIVERSITY PRESS
DETROIT

GREAT LAKES BOOKS

*A complete listing of the books in this series
can be found at the back of this volume.*

Philip P. Mason, Editor
Department of History, Wayne State University

Dr. Charles K. Hyde, Associate Editor
Department of History, Wayne State University

Library of Congress Cataloging-in-Publication Data

Fine, Sidney, 1920–
   Expanding the frontiers of civil rights : Michigan, 1948–1968 / Sidney Fine.
      p.   cm.—(Great Lakes books)
   Includes bibliographical references (p.   ) and index.
   ISBN 0-8143-2875-X (alk. paper)
   1. Civil rights—Michigan—History—20th century.   I. Title.   II. Series.

KFM4611.F56   2000
342.774'085'09—dc21   00-020935

TO
TERRY AND DARRELL

Contents

PREFACE

Although historians and others have devoted a great deal of attention to the development of U.S. government policy regarding civil rights in the quarter century following World War II, relatively little attention, with the exception of New York State, has been paid to the equally important developments at the state government level. In few states during these years did civil rights policy undergo a more dramatic transformation than in Michigan. In 1948 the Michigan Committee on Civil Rights characterized the state of civil rights in Michigan as presenting "an ugly picture." Twenty years later, however, Michigan was a leader among the states in the protection it accorded the civil rights of its inhabitants.

The Michigan civil rights program embraced not only African Americans, the principal focus of civil rights concern in the nation in the post–World War II era, but also women, the elderly, Native Americans, migrant workers, and the physically handicapped. Three governors—Democrats G. Mennen Williams and John B. Swainson and Republican George Romney—played leadership roles in furthering the civil rights cause in Michigan. All three used their executive power to promote civil rights in the state, but Williams and Swainson, although winning some legislative victories, were largely thwarted by an unsympathetic legislature in securing the civil rights legislation they favored. The major civil rights legislation between 1948 and 1968 was enacted during the Romney governorship, thanks to the civil rights provisions of Michigan's 1963 constitution and Romney's ability to gain bipartisan support for the civil rights legislation he advocated. The growing influence of the civil rights movement in Washington and across the nation while Romney was governor helped to create a climate of opinion that facilitated the enactment of civil rights legislation in Michigan.

My research for this book was facilitated by Francis Blouin, William Wallach, Nancy Bartlett, Anne Frantilla, Karen Jania, and Thomas Powers of the Bentley Historical Library; Margaret Raucher and Michael Smith of the Wayne State University Archives of Labor and Urban Affairs; LeRoy Barnett and Mark E. Harvey of the State Archives of the Michigan History Division; Frederick L. Monhart of the Michigan State University Archives; Janet Whitson of the Burton Historical Collection; Ellen B. McCarthy and Judith L. Brownlee of the Michigan Department of Civil Rights; Richard Harms of the Grand Rapids Public Library; Joellen ElBashir of the Moorland-Spingarn Research Center; Harold L. Miller of the State Historical Society of Wisconsin; and Kerry J. Norce of the Presbyterian Historical Society. I am grateful to Kristen Dombkowski for the expert typing of the manuscript. As always, my wife, Jean Fine, was my indispensable partner in the preparation of this book.

I dealt with some of the issues treated in the book in "A Jewel in the Crown of All of Us": Michigan Enacts a Fair Employment Practices Act," *Michigan Historical Review* 22 (Spring 1996): 19–66; "Michigan and Housing Discrimination," *Michigan Historical Review* 23 (Fall 1997): 81–114; and *Civil Rights and the Michigan Constitution of 1963*, Bentley Historical Library Bulletin No. 43, June 1996. I have received permission from the *Michigan Historical Review* and the Bentley Historical Library to use portions of these items.

1

"AN UGLY PICTURE": Civil Rights in Michigan, 1948

As Milton R. Konvitz has noted, it was state action regarding civil rights that helped prepare the ground for "a comprehensive and far reaching federal law" such as the Civil Rights Act of 1964. At the same time, however, it was the establishment in 1941 by President Franklin D. Roosevelt of the Committee on Fair Employment Practice and the 1947 report of President Harry S. Truman's Committee on Civil Rights that helped to spur state action in the civil rights field.[1]

Under the leadership of Governors G. Mennen Williams, John B. Swainson, and George Romney, Michigan between 1949 and 1968 demonstrated a growing concern for the civil rights of African Americans, Native Americans, women, the elderly, migrant workers, and the physically and mentally handicapped among its inhabitants. Despite gubernatorial commitment and prodding, however, Michigan, because of legislative resistance, initially lagged behind some of the other states in its adoption of civil rights measures. By the end of 1968, however, Michigan was in the forefront among the states in the scope and effectiveness of its civil rights measures.

Michigan's first civil rights legislation was adopted in 1867, when racial segregation in public education was banned in the state. Two years later a Michigan statute prohibited life insurance companies doing business in the state from discriminating on the basis of race, and an 1883 law removed the state's ban on miscegenation. In a key action in 1885, the legislature made racial discrimination in public places of accommodation, amusement, and recreation and in the selection

11

of jurors subject to criminal sanctions. Like the similar laws of most states, the 1885 measure, which was strengthened in 1937, proved to be ineffective. Prosecutors had been reluctant to prosecute under the law and juries to convict, and aggrieved individuals had been disinclined to sue for damages, as the statute provided.

The Michigan state constitution in effect in 1948 contained a section in the document's Declaration of Rights stating, "All political power is inherent in the people. Government is instituted for their equal benefit, security and protection." The language, however, lacked the explicitness of an equal protection guarantee and had been employed after the constitution went into effect in 1908 largely in dealing with "classifi-cations in regulatory legislation based upon the police power." Another section of the Declaration of Rights provided that "the civil and polit-ical rights, privileges and capacities of no person shall be diminished or enlarged on account of his religious belief," but reference to race, color, national origin, ancestry, and gender was notably missing from the section. Although the constitution prohibited the removal or demotion of an individual from the state civil service because of "partisan, racial, or religious considerations," the ban did not apply to appointments, municipal government employees, or employees in private business.[2]

Between 1941 and 1945 fair employment occupied the central place in the national struggle for civil rights. Discrimination in employment, Paul H. Norgren and Samuel E. Hill pointed out in their 1964 study of the subject, was "the driving force behind the Negro protest movement." As they noted, "of all the forms of inequality to which the Negro group . . . [was] subjected, job discrimination . . . [was] the most widely experienced, and its impact most acutely felt." When four thousand dele-gates from thirty-three states met in January 1950 to form the Leadership Conference on Civil Rights, they proclaimed fair employment practice legislation "the most fundamental of the pending civil rights" measures.[3]

By executive order on June 25, 1941, President Roosevelt banned employment discrimination in firms accepting defense contracts as well as in government agencies and job training programs for defense pro-duction. The president established the Committee on Fair Employment Practice (FEPC) to implement his order. In Detroit, the president's order served as a stimulus to "civil rights activists" and led to the formation of both the Metropolitan Detroit Council on Fair Employment Practice (MDFEPC) and, a few months later, the Citizens Committee for Jobs in Industry. At a meeting called in January 1942 by the United Automobile Workers (UAW) Union's Inter-Racial Committee (succeeded in 1944 by the Fair Practices Committee and in 1946 by the Fair Practices and Anti-Discrimination Department), the seventeen persons present con-cluded that discrimination in Detroit against "qualified" minority-group workers was rampant. Since only five officials in the Detroit office of the FEPC dealt with employment discrimination complaints, the Detroit conferees thought it necessary to supplement the federal effort with a local organization. This led in March to the creation of the MDFEPC, with Edward W. McFarland, a Wayne University economics professor, as chairman.

The MDFEPC was an interfaith, interracial federation of some seventy civic organizations and labor unions. Its constitution stated that its purpose was to "assure the full utilization of the local labor supply in the war effort, using every worker at his highest skill level," and that it would seek to aid in the implementation of the president's order. Going beyond that order, the council added sex to the types of discrimination it would combat, a decision that reflected the presence of women's groups in the organization.[4]

Spurred by black leaders in UAW Local 600, the Reverend Charles A. Hill, a Detroit Baptist minister, formed the largely black Citizens Council for Jobs in War Industry. "A militant protest group," the council resorted to mass meetings and picketing in an effort to promote black employment in Detroit. The withdrawal of the Detroit branch of the National Association for the Advancement of Colored People (NAACP) because of the council's leftist character adversely affected the organization, but during its few months of existence it enjoyed some success in influencing the Ford Motor Company to hire some black women, the most disadvantaged group in the city's labor force.[5]

The MDFEPC proclaimed that it sought to "translate into employment practices at home the democratic principles" for which the nation was "fighting abroad." In an effort to secure financial support so that it could employ a full-time staff, the committee sought to raise funds from private contributors, but it succeeded in doing so "only to a limited extent." It consequently applied for support from the War Chest of Metropolitan Detroit, which, in an action that distinguished Detroit from other cities with fair employment organizations at that time, provided the MDFEPC with the funding that enabled it to employ the needed staff in the summer of 1943.[6]

The two key committees of the MDFEPC were the Case and Clearance Committee and the Legislative Committee. The former handled individual complaints regarding one or another form of employment discrimination, most of them involving race and only "rarely" sex. In dealing with "adamant cases" of discrimination, a group of three or four MDFEPC executive board members would visit the head or personnel manager of a corporation charged with discrimination to persuade him to deal with the matter. Although it lacked any legal enforcement power, the MDFEPC opened "some employment doors previously barred by prejudice" and seems to have persuaded two of the city's largest manufacturing corporations to discontinue the use of discriminatory newspaper advertisements. In August 1943 it agreed to refer all employment discrimination cases to the FEPC, which by then had established a subregional office in Detroit. Limiting itself thereafter to nonreferral cases, the MDFEPC dealt with fifty-seven employment discrimination complaints between August 1943 and August 1945. During its lifetime, the committee handled just under one thousand cases involving more than seven hundred companies and was able to adjust 58 percent of them.[7]

In addition to its educational activities, which it regarded as "indispensably interrelated" with its legislative goals, the MDFEPC sought the enactment of both federal and state fair employment legislation. It lobbied Michigan's senators and congressmen for federal fair employment legislation, and its Legislative Committee helped to draft a fair employment bill that the Detroit Democrat Charles C. Diggs and the Charlotte Republican Murl DeFoe introduced in the Michigan Senate in 1943. Designed "to put teeth" into the fair employment requirement, the measure, which applied only to employers of twenty or more workers, barred sexual as well as racial and religious discrimination and provided for the fining and imprisonment of guilty parties. It passed the Senate unanimously on March 15 but died in the House State Affairs Committee two weeks later. The city's black newspaper, the *Michigan Chronicle*, attributed the defeat to the Michigan Manufacturers' Association. What is puzzling in view of the fate of fair employment bills in the state in the next dozen or so years was the easy approval of the Diggs-DeFoe bill in the Senate, twenty-five of whose thirty-two members were Republicans, as were seventy-five of the one hundred House members.[8]

As it informed the Congress in September 1944, the MDFEPC was especially concerned about the return to Detroit at war's end of two hundred thousand veterans and the effect that this would have on minority-group employment and the "racial harmony" that it believed had been the result of the FEPC, despite the 1943 race riot in the city. "We in Detroit are nervous. We get the jitters. We feel that we are sitting on a powder keg," the MDFEPC executive secretary informed a U.S. Senate subcommittee. The organization, consequently, placed its "primary emphasis" during the state's 1945 legislative session on securing a state fair employment law.

A bill that the MDFEPC had drafted and that applied not only to employers but also to labor unions and employment agencies was introduced on February 18, 1945, by the Harrison Republican, Senator Ben Carpenter. Like the 1943 measure, it included sex among the banned forms of employment discrimination. In hearings on the bill by the Senate Labor Committee, labor, religious, and civic groups pleaded for its passage lest employment discrimination "sow the 'seeds of decay' within democracy and set the stage for Hitlerism in America." Edward M. Swan, the chief FEPC examiner for Michigan, testified that the commission had received 632 complaints from Michigan residents during the preceding year and that he feared the "wholesale discharge" of black workers once the war ended. Unpersuaded by the arguments of the bill's supporters, the Labor Committee failed to report the measure to the Senate floor.[9]

A similar fate befell a House bill, which, like a model Congress of Industrial Organizations (CIO) bill on which it was based, authorized the commission for which it provided to deal not only with complaints of employment discrimination but also with complaints of discrimination related to housing, education, recreation, health, and social welfare. An unusual feature of the bill was its provision for the commission to develop "a comprehensive educational program" for students in the state's public schools designed to "eliminate prejudice based upon race, creed, color, sex, national origin and ancestry." The bill was referred to the House Committee on State Affairs, which, true to its reputation as "a graveyard for progressive legislation," voted not to report the measure to the full House.[10]

There were many reasons for the failure to enact the 1945 state fair employment bills. Sheer racism was not the least among these reasons, one legislator, for example, referring to such a measure as the "Nigger bill." Even though the 1944 state Republican convention had pledged the party's support for fair employment legislation, the heavy Republican majority in the legislature saw the bills as Democratic measures, and Republican Governor Harry Kelly refused to persuade the legislators otherwise. Even though the bill's proponents were prepared to yield on the inclusion of sex among the prohibited forms of discrimination, the ban on sex discrimination proved to be a major obstacle to the measures' passage. "You want to take women out of the home, do you?" exclaimed one legislator. There was, additionally, opposition in the legislature to creating "another commission" and complaints that the bills would "clog" the courts with cases and compel employers to hire unqualified workers. Proponents, finally, thought that the covert opposition of the Michigan Manufacturers' Association was critical to the bills' fate.[11]

By the time another fair employment bill was introduced in the Michigan legislature, the federal government's FEPC had passed from the scene. The FEPC, along with the demand for manpower in a tight wartime labor market, had proved to be a boon to Detroit's nonwhite workers, who, although constituting about 14 percent of the city's civilian labor force at the wartime peak, received 26 percent of the jobs

15

filled through the state's Employment Service Division in 1945. Most of the employment gains occurred in aircraft, ordnance, iron and steel, and nonferrous metals. In the city's auto plants, converted to meet wartime production needs, black employment rose from 4 percent of all workers in 1940 to 15 percent by the end of 1945.

Women also found new jobs in wartime Detroit, but often in sex-typed occupations and at lower pay than male workers received for the same jobs. Black women, the last hired for wartime jobs, did not fare as well in employment as white women did, but the number of black women employed as operatives did increase appreciably during the war. When the war ended, however, Michigan employers, the executive director of the Michigan Unemployment Compensation Commission reported, returned to "the old arbitrary methods of hiring and certain labor locals [returned] to arbitrary practices of opposition to inclusion of all groups in the workforce." As for the FEPC, Congress slashed its budget by half in 1945, and the commission expired the next year.[12]

Despairing that the Michigan legislature would approve a fair employment bill, the Michigan chapter of the Civil Rights Congress, which resulted from the April 1946 merger of three leftist organizations in Detroit, decided in the late summer of 1946 to secure the adoption of such a measure by the initiative route. According to the Michigan constitution, to place an initiated measure on the ballot, the sponsors had to gather signatures by petition equivalent to at least 8 percent of the votes cast for governor in the preceding state election, and they had to present the petitions to the legislature ten days before it convened. The legislature then had forty days to act on the proposed measure. If it failed to do so or if it rejected the proposal, it was to be referred to the voters at the next state election. If the legislature amended the measure, both the amended and initiated proposals were to be referred to the voters.

To carry out its petition drive and to secure the required 133,328 signatures, the Civil Rights Congress in October 1946 formed the Committee for a State FEPC. The MDFEPC joined in sponsoring the initiative effort, and UAW President Walter Reuther, despite his vocal opposition to the far left, was a conspicuous member of the initiating committee that the Civil Rights Congress formed in 1946. Reuther, to be sure, had hesitated to identify the UAW with the Civil Rights Congress, but both his administrative assistant, Leonard Woodcock, and UAW staffer Jack Conway thought that, given the UAW's commitment to fair employment, it would be "somewhat inappropriate" for the UAW president's name not to appear among the sponsors of the petition drive. The fact that the Michigan chapter of the Civil Rights Congress, one of the strongest chapters in the nation, had close ties to organized labor in Detroit, particularly to the large UAW Local 600, a left-wing bastion, no doubt also influenced Reuther. It has been suggested, furthermore, that Reuther, because of his strong support for Jews as a minority group, was influenced by the Jewish presence in the Civil Rights Congress.

The labor movement, and the UAW in particular, proved crucial to the success of the petition drive. Of the 189,650 signatures reportedly gathered, the Wayne County CIO collected 60,387, more than half of these by UAW Local 600. The Communist Party, by contrast, collected only 7,192 signatures, the Civil Rights Congress itself, 16,300.[13]

According to the Committee for a State FEPC, when it submitted its petition for approval in August 1946, before the petition drive began, Secretary of State Herman H. Dignan and Attorney General Foss Eldred advised that the petition was in proper form even though the proposed bill lacked a title. The assistant secretary of state, however, rejected this assertion, claiming that the committee had not inquired as to whether the petition was in proper form. Whatever the truth of this matter, when the signed petitions were submitted to the secretary of state's office in December, Eldred ruled that they were not in "legal form" because the proposed bill lacked a title, and the State Board of Canvassers then rejected the petitions. In January 1947, however, the new attorney general, Eugene Black, ruled the petitions valid, and the Board of Canvassers certified that the petitioners had gathered more than the required number of signatures. The bill was then submitted to the legislature and referred to the Labor Committee in the Senate and the Judiciary Committee in the House.[14]

By the time the initiated bill had been introduced in the Michigan legislature, a new organization, the Michigan Council for Fair Employment Legislation, had been formed "to rally the widest possible . . . liberal progressive support" for fair employment legislation. Although many liberal groups initially had joined in the initiative campaign, they soon had second thoughts about permitting the effort to be led by the Civil Rights Congress, which the liberals regarded as "communist-dominated" and with which they preferred not to be identified. The dominant Reuther wing of the UAW, furthermore, viewed the Civil Rights Congress as "dedicated" to the support of George Addes, whose alliance with the UAW's communist faction Reuther had attacked in gaining the UAW's presidency in 1946 and who was defeated the next year in his bid for reelection as the union's secretary-treasurer.[15]

When the sponsors of the Michigan Council met on January 3, 1947, George Schermer, the director of the Mayor's Interracial Committee of Detroit and the council's chairman, explained that as the petition campaign had neared its close, it became clear to many of the participating organizations that the "narrow sponsorship" of the initiative effort by the Civil Rights Congress would doom its chances of legislative success.

Victory could be achieved, the council believed, only if support for fair employment came from a statewide organization with "the broadest possible representation without undue pressure from special interest groups" and one that would "carry great moral weight with the State Legislature" and would follow normal legislative procedures. The new organization included representatives of the three major religious faiths, the NAACP, the Detroit Urban League (DUL), the Mayor's Interracial Committee, and the Michigan CIO. The honorary chairman was Bishop Francis J. Haas, a former chairman of the federal FEPC.[16]

The initiated bill, which was introduced in the legislature in January 1947, applied to employers of eight or more workers as well as to employment agencies and labor unions, but it did not include sex among the proscribed forms of discrimination. The commission to implement the measure, which was lodged in the Department of Labor, had sub-poena power and could appeal to the courts for the issuance of cease-and-desist orders to those whom the commission found had violated the measure. There was "no great enthusiasm" for the bill either in the Senate, composed at the time of twenty-eight Republicans and five Democrats, or in the House, where there were ninety-five Republicans and four Democrats.[17]

"To condemn a segment of our population forever to underpaid, unskilled work," the Michigan Council declared in a brief submitted to the two committees considering the initiated bill, "is to breed frustration and insecurity incompatible with the national American ideal of equality of opportunity," and, the council warned, would constitute "a social threat to those guilty of discrimination." The council claimed that the experience of the federal government and of the three states (New York, New Jersey, and Massachusetts) which by that time had adopted enforceable fair employment laws proved that the expressed fears of opponents of such legislation were unfounded. The Committee for a State FEPC offered similar arguments in favor of the bill.[18]

Following a state conference to rally the troops, held on January 30 and attended by two hundred delegates, Michigan Council representatives met with individual legislators to push the initiated bill. The council also sought the support of Republican Governor Kim Sigler, who had promised in the 1946 gubernatorial campaign to visit the states with functioning fair employment laws and "to take some action" regarding the matter. Failure of the legislature to act and the consequent submission of the bill to a popular referendum, the head of the UAW's Fair Practices and Anti-Discrimination Department informed the governor, would give "the hate groups in Michigan a new lease on life" and lead to "the most obnoxious appeals to bigotry, prejudice and the fears of narrow self-interest," which is what had occurred when a fair employment measure had been referred to the voters in California in 1946. The Michigan legislature, however, was deaf to the arguments in favor of fair employment, the initiated bill attracting but little support. The Committee for a State FEPC claimed that "industrial and other interests" had created a "slush fund" for "a statewide advertising campaign" and had resorted to "racial and religious prejudice" to defeat the measure.[19]

The legislature's failure to act on the initiated bill required that it be submitted to the voters in the April 7, 1947, election. The effort to secure a favorable referendum vote on the bill was opposed by a newly formed Michigan Committee for Tolerance organized by William H. Leininger, a Detroit industrialist who chaired the Products and Materials Committee of the Detroit Board of Commerce. A member of the right-wing Society of Sentinels, which had ties to the auto companies and was allegedly backed by "a huge slush fund," Leininger had little sympathy for black workers, claiming that they did not take their jobs "seriously" and could not adjust as readily as whites to the "modern high speed industrial system." Claiming that the measure had "the active and open support of the Communist party," the Leininger committee charged that, if enacted, the bill would "play into the hands of Communists and subversive elements," "tend to effectuate and deepen existing prejudices," "incite intolerance and racial discord and strife," and pit "class against class and group against group." It would also, the committee claimed, subject "the motives of all employers to bureaucratic supervision, investigation, and interpretation," be "a severe drain on taxpayers," and even add to the cost of living because of all the litigation that would ensue.[20]

Leininger sought to forestall the scheduled April 7 vote by petitioning the Michigan Supreme Court for a writ of mandamus and prohibition on the ground that the initiated bill was in violation of the state constitution because the measure lacked a title. The court, by a 4–2 vote on March 3, upheld the Leininger argument and ruled the bill off the April 7 ballot. Senator Stanley Nowak, a Detroit Democrat allied with the Committee for a State FEPC, promptly followed the Supreme Court decision by reintroducing the bill in the state Senate. The Michigan Council responded to the Supreme Court decision by arranging for a group of its members to meet with Governor Sigler on March 13 to gain his support for fair employment. The council favored a measure like the New York law, which applied to employers of four or more workers, employment agencies, and labor unions.[21]

In preparation for the Michigan Council's meeting with Sigler, Schermer wrote the governor that the council was "separate and distinct" from the Committee for a State FEPC and had been formed when it became evident that the committee was "dominated by political elements" with which the council's affiliates preferred not to be associated.

19

Schermer informed the governor that the council had no "ulterior, po-litical motive," favored the New York law, which it invited Sigler to sponsor, and wanted to be represented on a committee of legislators and citizens to draft the measure that it urged the governor to appoint.[22]

The council was "encouraged" by its conference with Sigler, but when a delegation from the Committee for a State FEPC met with the governor a few days later, he told them that its bill would not be enacted because of "a widespread belief that its source" was communist—a point, he asserted, that the Michigan Council had confirmed to him. The committee, which had brought two hundred delegates from thirteen Michigan cities to Lansing to lobby for the measure, protested that it was "representative of all sections of the community," that only fifteen thousand of the petition signatures had been gathered by communists, and that the initiated bill was similar to the 1945 measure that had been drafted under the supervision of the MDFEPC by a committee composed of "all interested groups in the community."[23]

Despite Sigler's public statement to the contrary, the Committee for a State FEPC claimed that he had indicated that he would act on a fair employment measure in the existing session of the legislature and would consider both the Nowak bill and a New York–type law. Sigler, however, did not seek a fair employment law in the session, nor did Republican legislators evince any desire to pass such a measure. Quite apart from reiteration by lawmakers that it was communists who favored fair employment legislation, the chairman of the Senate Labor Committee informed the bill's sponsors that most legislators did not believe employment discrimination was a problem in Michigan; and, reflecting a commonly expressed argument, he maintained that em-ployment discrimination, in any event, was "mostly a matter requiring education and time instead of legislation." A senator from East Lansing estimated that 80 percent of the state's workers were not members of any minority group and would themselves be "discriminated against in the scramble" that he presumed a fair employment law would bring. The 1947 regular session of the legislature ended without a fair employment bill being reported to the floor of either house.[24]

Before the legislature convened in special session in March 1948, the Michigan Council for Fair Employment Legislation changed its name and broadened its civil rights agenda. The reason for the change in name was the "tremendous impact" of the report that had just been issued by the President's Committee on Civil Rights appointed by President Harry S. Truman. In its far-reaching report, the committee, quite apart from its recommendations concerning the federal government, called on state governments to establish special units to enforce their civil rights laws and to form permanent civil rights commissions. It urged the states to increase the professionalization of their state and local police units; enact laws providing for fair employment, fair "educational practice" for both public and private educational institutions, and fair health practices; outlaw restrictive housing covenants; guarantee equal access to places of public accommodation; and specify that discrimination in the rendering of public services was contrary to public policy.[25]

The Steering Committee of the Michigan Council on Fair Employment legislation met on November 19, 1947, to consider the report of the Committee on Civil Rights and the reorganization of the council to support "all of the major points" in the document. An organizational meeting followed in Detroit on December 8 at which the participants agreed to establish the Michigan Committee on Civil Rights (MCCR) to replace the council. The co-sponsors of the meeting included religious, labor, civic, and women's organizations, and the more than one thousand persons present pledged their support for the new organization's program to "strengthen democratic rights of all Americans."[26]

The large MCCR organizing committee invited community leaders to another organizational meeting on January 24, 1948, that confirmed the decision to form the MCCR. The conferees agreed that the new organization should be composed of local chapters and cooperating organizations and individuals and that it should "fight in the whole field of civil liberties so dramatically outlined" in the report of the President's Committee.

In a March meeting of community leaders, the MCCR adopted an eight-point program that it would seek to implement. The program called for the passage of a Michigan fair employment law and Michigan support for a federal fair employment statute; cultivating citizen support for the 1885 Michigan civil rights law as amended; combating discrimination in public facilities; "adequate enforcement" of civil rights laws by state and local authorities, and enactment of such additional legislation as needed to end discrimination in public places; elimination of segregation in the Michigan National Guard; examination of the behavior of public school systems and other educational institutions to ascertain if they engaged in practices of segregation and discrimination; investigation and evaluation of the treatment of minority groups by law enforcement agencies in the state; support for proposals in the report of the President's Committee to prevent abridgment in wartime of the civil rights of any group of persons because of race or ancestry, and for "prompt settlement" of the claims of Japanese Americans stemming from their evacuation and relocation in World War II; a study of the status of the civil rights of Native Americans, Mexican Americans, Asian Americans, and migrant agricultural workers; and, finally, an end to discrimination in sports. Among these goals, fair employment legislation was the committee's "top priority."[27]

Seeing fair employment legislation as "a good achievable first goal" of its civil rights program, the MCCR became a "lobbying organization" for the measure. It joined the Civil Rights Congress in seeking to persuade Governor Sigler to make fair employment legislation a part of his program for the 1948 special legislative session. The governor provided contradictory signals regarding his intentions, but in the end he did not include fair employment in his legislative program for the session.[28] As it turned out, it was Sigler's victorious Democratic adversary in the 1948 gubernatorial election, G. Mennen Williams, who would lead the successful fight for the enactment of a Michigan fair employment practices act.

Born in Detroit on February 28, 1911, into a wealthy and devout Episcopalian family, Williams was the heir to part of the Mennen fortune derived from shaving lotions and oil skin preparations, which explains why he was given the nickname "Soapy." He began his schooling in Detroit but transferred to the Salisbury School in Connecticut, from which he graduated. He then went to Princeton University, where he became president of the Young Republicans Club as well as regional president of the National Student Federation of America. After graduating from Princeton in 1933, he enrolled in the University of Michigan Law School. Caught up in the enthusiasm for the New Deal, as were so many college students at that time, Williams joined the law school's Liberal Club and became a Democrat. Interestingly enough, some of the expenses of the club were met by a well-to-do Ann Arbor coal and oil dealer, Neil Staebler, eventually to become a close Williams political ally and the chairman of the Michigan Democratic Party. Williams received his law degree in 1936 and the next year married Nancy Quirk, who became Williams's indispensable partner and was, like him, "a tireless campaigner."

Williams began his long political career in 1938, when he became an attorney with the federal government's Social Security Board in Washington. He returned to Michigan that same year to serve as assistant attorney general in the administration of Michigan's liberal governor, Frank Murphy, who would become an important influence on Williams's subsequent political career. As an assistant attorney general, Williams helped to prepare important milk marketing and housing bills for the state administration. When Murphy in 1939 became the nation's attorney general, he appointed Williams his executive assistant. Williams transferred to the Justice Department's Criminal Division in 1940 when Murphy was appointed to the U.S. Supreme Court.

G. Mennen Williams and Nancy Quirk Williams.
Courtesy Bentley Historical Library.

After resigning his Justice Department position in early 1941, Williams served in the Enforcement Division of the Office of Price Administration (OPA) until he joined the U.S. Navy in August 1942. He served as an intelligence officer on aircraft carriers in the Pacific and was awarded ten battle stars, the Legion of Merit, and the Presidential Unit Citation before leaving the Navy in February 1946 with the rank of lieutenant commander to become OPA director in Michigan. Governor Sigler appointed Williams in 1947 to fill the Democratic slot on the Michigan Liquor Control Commission, a position that enabled Williams to travel about the state and to gain name recognition and political visibility. He became friendly with Hicks Griffiths, who headed the commission's legal section, and subsequently became a member of the law firm of Hicks and his wife, Martha, then a member of the Detroit Ordnance Office's legal staff.[29]

In the 1946 Michigan election, the Republican Party captured not only the governorship but also every state office up for election as well as ninety-five of the one hundred House seats and twenty-eight of the thirty-two Senate seats. The all but moribund and leaderless Democratic Party was controlled at the time by old-guard, conservative elements more concerned about patronage than issues.[30]

It is an oft-told tale that, meeting in the Griffiths home on November 21, 1947, "ardent" New Dealers like Williams and Griffiths joined with liberals like Staebler, Hickman Price, Floyd Stevens, and a few others to consider rebuilding the Democratic Party and moving it in a liberal direction.[31] "An informal group" of liberals had indeed been meeting "for some time" to discuss the rebuilding of the party, but the purpose of the celebrated November 21 meeting, it is now evident, was to block the effort of James R. Hoffa, the head of the Teamsters Union, to gain control of the state Democratic Party. That explains the presence at the meeting of John Gibson, assistant secretary of labor in the Truman administration and a former Michigan labor leader. Having heard rumors about Hoffa's maneuvering, Gibson had come to Michigan to meet with state Democrats about the matter. Hoffa was recruiting Michigan delegates to support his legal counsel, George Fitzgerald, for the position of Democratic national committeeman. Fitzgerald was elected to that position in 1948, and two Hoffa candidates entered the Democratic gubernatorial primary. Following the November 21 meeting, the liberal Democrats began organizing Democratic clubs around the state, and then in March 1948 they formed the Michigan Democratic Club. On May 15, 1948, Williams resigned his Liquor Control Commission position and announced his candidacy for the governorship.[32]

August (Gus) Scholle, the head of the Michigan CIO and the Michigan CIO–Political Action Committee (PAC) and who had met and liked

Williams, became a key ally of the Williams-Griffiths liberals in their effort to take control of the Michigan Democratic Party. Two members of the liberal group spoke for Scholle, and Gibson was a close friend. Angered by the Republican legislature's weakening of the state's labor law in 1947, the CIO-PAC at its March 13, 1948, conference formally linked the CIO with the state Democratic Party so as to make it "*the progressive party of the state.*" "Progressives and liberals within the Democratic Party," the PAC stated, "have often been outnumbered by conservative and reactionary elements. The PAC is unanimous in its opinion that the best way of supporting liberalism within the Democratic Party, to conform to national CIO policy, and to serve the best interests of Michigan labor, is to join the Democratic Party. It is our objective in adopting this policy to remold the Democratic Party into a new liberal and progressive party which can be subscribed to by members of the CIO and other liberals."[33]

The CIO-PAC urged CIO members to become active in the Democratic Party and to seek election as precinct delegates. The CIO was particularly effective in its party organizing activities in Wayne County, where the labor-liberal coalition won control of four of the six congressional districts. The coalition commanded a majority of the delegates to the 1948 state Democratic convention. The delegates permitted the party chairman, John Franco, under attack for "financial irregularities," to complete his two-year term, but it was Hicks Griffiths who managed the party's 1948 campaign and who became the party's chairman the next year.[34]

The UAW, the largest union in the Michigan CIO, joined with other CIO unions in seeking to move the Democratic Party in a liberal direction. In the 1948 campaign the UAW contributed $10,000 to the financially pressed Williams campaign and made every effort to get its members to the polls. Williams also enjoyed the support of the Michigan Federation of Labor.[35]

In a three-way race, Williams narrowly won the Democratic Party primary and then went on to defeat Sigler in the final election. "A big friendly man . . . with a broad smile and a solid jaw," Williams, although not an effective speaker, was a formidable campaigner who inspired audiences with his sincerity and idealism and his "person-to-person" approach. He was committed to liberal reform both out of sincere conviction and because of his deeply held religious beliefs, beliefs of a social gospel sort. "He didn't wear it [religion] on his sleeve," however, an associate recalled. "It was a kind of a piety of action rather than 'words.' "[36]

In the 1948 primary, Williams promised that, if elected, he would seek to implement the report of the President's Committee on Civil

Rights by the "immediate creation" of a state commission that he would assign the responsibility of developing a legislative and educational program "to eliminate discrimination throughout the state," including discrimination in employment. He appealed particularly to labor, liberals, and black and white ethnic groups, before whose meetings he would sometimes appear unannounced to outline his program. Murphy had advised him, "Stick to the minority people, they need your help. They will stick to you." As Williams recalled in an interview some years later, his association with Murphy and the fact that he was viewed as a Murphy protégé evoked "a very warm response" to him among labor and black voters, who had remained devoted to Murphy.[37]

Although Williams defeated Sigler by a vote of 1,228,604 to 964,810, the Republicans retained their solid majority in the legislature, winning twenty-three of thirty-two Senate seats and sixty-one of one hundred House seats. The Democratic Party that had to deal with this legislature was a party in which an "issue-oriented" liberal-labor alliance had gained "dominance" and one that was more concerned with policy than with patronage. It was a party with a large black component and for which civil rights was a critical issue.[38]

As governor-elect, Williams turned to Bishop Haas to serve as chairman of what came to be known as the Governor's Advisory Committee on Civil Rights. Williams looked to the committee "to map out for him a plan of action and specific legislative bills." The creation of the committee followed "rather close consultation" between the governor and George Schermer, whom the governor asked to get the Advisory Committee under way. In addition to Haas and Schermer, the committee included among its nineteen members John Dancy, director of the DUL; Geraldine Bledsoe, chief of Minority Groups Services of the Michigan Employment Service; Walter Reuther, who was represented by William Oliver, the black head of the union's Fair Practices and Anti-Discrimination Department; Episcopalian bishop the Reverend Richard Emrich; and University of Michigan history professor Preston Slosson. In the absence of Haas, Schermer served as the commission's real chairman. Williams had hoped in vain to be able to add some representatives from industry to the group.[39]

In a December 1, 1948, memorandum to the committee, Schermer argued the case for having the governor limit his initial message to the legislature insofar as civil rights were concerned to one or two matters of the "greatest importance" that had already become the subject of much discussion. Although noting that those active in the civil rights field were aware that a number of actions had to be taken "to assure adequate and equal protection of the civil rights of all persons regardless of race, ancestry or religion," Schermer thought it equally evident that even those best informed about the subject knew too little about the civil rights problem in the state to develop "a full and comprehensive legislative program" in the short time before the legislature convened in January. He also thought that the people of the state and the members of the legislature were "too ill informed" about the subject to expect that it would be possible to enact a comprehensive civil rights program at that time.

Since, as Schermer saw it, there already was "general agreement" in the civil rights community that "the most important single issue" was fair employment legislation, he thought "primary attention" should be focused on that subject. As Williams had already suggested, Schermer also advised that a separate commission—or, preferably, given the "status of thinking" in the legislature, the commission established to implement the fair employment law—be authorized to study the entire civil rights field and to undertake an appropriate educational program regarding the subject.[40]

The principal question that the Governor's Advisory Committee sought to resolve in several meetings in the second half of December was whether to recommend to the governor that he urge the legislature to enact a broad civil rights program or to adopt the Schermer position. The chief advocate initially of the comprehensive approach was the UAW's Oliver, but this view attracted little support, the fear being that it would simply increase opposition to any civil rights legislation in the Republican legislature. The recommendation provided the governor on December 23 in preliminary form was that he include in his message "a comprehensive survey of the status of civil rights" in Michigan to demonstrate, as one committee member put it, his "full comprehension of the total problem," but that he request passage of only a fair employment measure. The committee advised further that the agency established to implement such a law be "empowered and instructed" to survey the civil rights field and submit recommendations to the governor for both executive and legislative "remedies." The draft of a fair employment bill that largely conformed to the New York law, as the Advisory Committee preferred, had already been prepared by the MCCR, and it was slightly revised by the Advisory Committee.[41]

Six days after the Advisory Committee submitted its preliminary report to Williams, the MCCR provided the governor's committee with a lengthy memorandum surveying the status of civil rights in Michigan and including a series of recommendations regarding "practical action" that it believed could be taken in "the immediate future."[42] The memorandum noted that the committee, through its chapters and affiliated organizations, had been able "to witness at close range the many violations of civil rights" occurring in Michigan and that it had studied the efforts in other states to deal with such violations. The committee observed that prejudice not only had "a corroding effect" on the individuals involved but was also "dangerous to the American way of life as well as to the economy, health and general welfare of the community."

The MCCR characterized the state of civil rights in Michigan as of 1948 as presenting "an ugly picture," thus indicating the formidable task the Williams administration faced in seeking to address the problem. It noted that minority groups in the state were "constantly humiliated, their livelihood menaced, and their welfare endangered." It thought that "the vicious effects of discrimination" were perhaps most evident in the area of employment, noting that 44.4 percent of all job orders handled by the Michigan State Employment Service in April 1947 contained some sort of discriminatory specification and that three-fifths of the job listings in the spring of 1948 were not open to nonwhites. The DUL files, the committee reported, contained many case histories revealing that jobs in banking, department stores, and in some utilities, as well as most managerial positions, were closed to blacks.

The MCCR noted that Jews were also the victims of employment discrimination. A survey by the Jewish Community Council of Detroit revealed that most banks and trust companies hired only white Christians and that jobs in engineering and some other occupations were closed to Jews. Other surveys, the MCCR reported, indicated that Catholics, the foreign-born, and members of other minority groups were also debarred from some types of employment.

Surveys in various Michigan cities, the MCCR noted, revealed the dismal state of nonwhite employment. A January 1948 survey by the Lansing chapter of the MCCR thus indicated that none of the city's stores, offices, banks, restaurants, or theaters employed nonwhite help. City government agencies employed blacks only as janitors or for maintenance jobs, and there were only two salaried nonwhite employees in the city's factories. Employers candidly admitted that skin color was the reason for this state of affairs.

Blacks were largely excluded from skilled jobs in Saginaw, and as of May 1946 there was not a single black or Mexican American nurse in any of the city's hospitals, nor were the hospitals training any members of these minority groups. The paper and chemical plants in Kalamazoo, according to another 1946 survey, did not hire blacks, the paper manufacturers preferring to recruit and train white workers from Kentucky and Tennessee. Black workers were also discriminated against in Kalamazoo with regard to upgrading and promotions, as employers conceded. In Detroit, many employers at the time of the MCCR report were refusing to hire qualified nonwhite workers even though the city faced "a serious labor shortage."

For the state as a whole, there had been a decline since the end of the war in the job placement of nonwhites by the State Employment Service. Such placements had dropped from 16.5 percent of the total in 1945 to 10.3 percent in 1947 even though the number of black applicants for jobs was increasing and the number of white applicants was declining. The MCCR called attention to the fact that in states such as New York, New Jersey, and Massachusetts, which had enacted fair employment legislation, there had been a lessening of job discrimination and that former opponents of such legislation had come to recognize the desirability of laws of this kind.

"One of the most degrading aspects of discrimination," the MCCR observed, was the "daily humiliation" minority-group members faced as the result of their being denied access to places of public accommodation. Michigan law, as already noted, forbade such discrimination, but the applicable legislation was not being effectively enforced. Detroit and Grand Rapids were thus the only two cities in the state where blacks could secure hotel accommodations other than for some special event. Some hotels in the state openly advertised that they were available only to Gentiles, and Jews had sometimes been evicted from a hotel when their religion became known to the hotel management. Although supported by state funds, the Michigan Tourist Council circulated literature from hotels in the state that discriminated against minority groups. Most restaurants in Saginaw, Lansing, and downtown Detroit would not serve blacks, and a Lansing survey indicated that some stores in the city "deliberately" gave blacks poor service. The MCCR also called attention to "the widespread discrimination" in the area of sports in the state, notably in bowling and baseball.

In the area of education, the MCCR reported that discrimination occurred in the hiring and placement of teachers based on their race, color, creed, and national origin. The committee noted that it was the practice of public schools throughout the state to place black teachers only in schools with large black enrollments. In Saginaw, the public schools did not employ a single black or Mexican American teacher. Minority-group teachers were sometimes employed only as substitutes and were discriminated against in promotions to the positions of assistant principal and principal. Relying on a survey of the Jewish Community Council of Detroit of questions asked on forms for admission to thirty-one colleges and universities in the state, the MCCR concluded that only four did not ask discriminatory questions, and it suggested that quotas existed to limit the enrollment of minority-group members in some of the state's professional schools.

29

The MCCR characterized the record of public housing in Michigan as "an unfortunate chapter" in the state's history, and it deplored the "mass demonstrations" by whites that had occurred in the state to protest black occupancy in a particular neighborhood. Rabble-rousers, it also noted, had sought to encourage violence and to raise funds for themselves by challenging the U.S. Supreme Court decision in 1948 declaring restrictive housing covenants to be legally unenforceable.

The MCCR found it intolerable that the Michigan National Guard was segregated by state law. In its brief treatment of the state's police, the MCCR stressed the importance of harmonious relations between police forces and minority groups. The committee deplored the hate literature derogatory of minority groups and generally of an anonymous nature that was being circulated in some places in the state, such as Dearborn.

Surveys in Saginaw, Kalamazoo, and elsewhere provided the MCCR with evidence of discrimination in the availability of health services. Tax-supported hospitals in the state, the MCCR indicated, "generally" practiced "segregation on the Mississippi pattern or outright exclusion." Very few hospitals made it possible for black doctors to secure the training and experience needed to advance in their profession or for black women to obtain the training they needed to become registered nurses. As the committee observed, state funds were being used to send black women wishing to become nurses for training outside the state. The MCCR thought that discrimination in health services was graphically demonstrated when a black football player injured in a game in Detroit was refused admission by a Detroit hospital to which he had originally been taken in the company of "students of all races and creeds."

Migrant workers, as we shall see, were critical to the harvesting of Michigan crops, but the MCCR appraised the treatment the migrants received in Michigan as "shameful." It recalled that in the Bay City area in August of that year, a group of black migrants from Georgia had been held in "virtual peonage," and it observed that "even a superficial investigation" revealed that commitments regarding wages and housing made to migrants when they were engaged were not lived up to once they arrived in the state. The children of minority-group migrant workers, the MCCR informed the Governor's Advisory Committee, were discouraged from attending public schools in many communities of the state and were often discriminated against when they did attend.

The MCCR report supported its characterization of the state of civil rights in Michigan in 1948 as presenting "an ugly picture." At the same time, the report ignored discrimination against women, the elderly, and the physically handicapped, and it had surprisingly little to say about the critical problem of discrimination with regard to private housing. Its emphasis, reflecting what had occurred in the civil rights area since 1941, was definitely on fair employment, which the MCCR characterized as "the foremost civil rights problem in the state."

Like the Advisory Committee, the MCCR recommended that Michigan enact a fair employment practices law similar to that of New York and that it also make provision for the study of discrimination in "all or specific fields of human relations" by the commission established to enforce the fair employment law. It called for public hearings regarding discrimination in public accommodations, health, education, and housing as "an effective educational device," and it recommended that public funds be withheld from hospitals and other health agencies guilty of discrimination, and from housing developments in the absence of an agreement not to segregate residents.

The MCCR urged that the budgets of colleges and universities in the state contain a requirement that all questions of a discriminatory nature be removed from application forms, that their records be opened to "bona fide representative citizens organizations" to ensure that their admissions policies were free of discrimination, that public hearings be held regarding "the threat to academic freedom" in the state, and that meetings of their supervisory boards be open to the press. The committee also called for legislation to ensure "equality of opportunity in the operation and provision of health and educational institutions and facilities."

The MCCR recommended that the state's attorney general enforce the 1885 civil rights act more vigorously and that legislation be considered to strengthen enforcement. It called upon the Michigan Tourist Council and other state agencies not to distribute advertisements and other promotional materials by hotels and restaurants that discriminated. It urged the immediate desegregation of the Michigan National Guard, an educational program for members of the State Police to increase their understanding of intergroup problems, and provision by the state government of training facilities to increase the professionalization of local police forces. It also recommended the enactment of legislation requiring the identification of the sponsors of literature derogatory of racial, religious, and nationality groups.

The MCCR called for "a thorough investigation" of the treatment of migrant workers by their employers and for action "to the limit of the law" by the appropriate state agencies if the investigation supported reports concerning the mistreatment of the seasonal laborers in the state. It also advised that the state Department of Public Instruction take the necessary "remedial actions" regarding the education of migrant children.[43]

For Williams, committed as he was to the enhancement of the civil rights of all Americans, the MCCR's recommendations were a call to action. During his six terms in office, he sought to implement just about all of the committee's recommendations. The year 1948 not only marked the beginning of "the Williams Era" in Michigan but also, as a distinguished Michigan African American remarked, "the beginning of the new era of political participation of Negroes in Michigan."[44] It also marked the beginning of a new era of civil rights in general in the Wolverine state.

Williams was reelected governor five successive times after his initial victory, but he decided not to seek a seventh term in 1960. He was succeeded as governor by the state's Democratic lieutenant governor, John B. Swainson, who served only one two-year term. He was defeated for reelection in 1962 by Republican George Romney, who remained the state's governor until the close of 1968.

Michigan's population during the years Williams, Swainson, and Romney served as the state's chief executives increased about 28 percent, from 6,332,000 to 8,096,000. The state's nonwhite population grew at a much faster rate, increasing from 442,296 in 1950 to 991,006 in 1970, or about 124 percent. The population of the state's largest city, Detroit, actually fell in these two decades from 1,849,560 to 1,512,893, but the black population of the city rose sharply at the same time, from 16 percent of the total in 1950 to 29.1 percent in 1960 and 43.6 percent in 1970. Michigan's per capita income in 1949 was $1,520 as compared to $1,384 for the United States as a whole. The comparable figures for 1968 were $3,703 and $3,421.[45]

Two major problems facing Michigan's state government between 1949 and 1968 were the parlous condition of the state's budget and the method of apportioning seats for the state's legislature. In the second half of the 1950s in particular, the Michigan economy was severely affected by the decentralization of the automobile manufacturing industry and the consequent loss of auto jobs, as well as by automation, recession, and cutbacks in defense orders. The state lost about 180,000 jobs between 1953 and 1957, and the number of defense jobs fell from 215,000 in 1952 to 46,000 in 1959. The state government budget at the same time was rising from $500 million in 1949 to $1.2 billion in 1961. Expenditures in those years tripled for education, doubled for mental health, and went up 50 percent for welfare.[46]

The Michigan state government did not have the kind of tax system that could readily adjust to the state's economic condition. Michigan had neither a personal income tax nor a corporate income tax. A constitutional amendment approved in a referendum in 1946, moreover, required that two-thirds of the revenue from the state government's three-cent sales tax be returned to local school districts and one-sixth to the state's cities, villages, and townships. The effect of the amendment was to divert 77 percent of the state government's revenues to local government. To complicate matters further, the state was not permitted to contract a debt exceeding $250,000, and a 1954 constitutional amendment limited the sales tax to three cents.[47]

To cope with its fiscal problems, the state government sought to economize, even as the demand grew for the expansion of state services and to impose new taxes. The state government's deficit as of July 1, 1958, was $21.1 million, and it continued to rise the next year, reaching $95.4 million on July 1, 1959. The state government was briefly unable to meet its payroll in early May 1959, the press reporting that Michigan was "going broke." Governor Williams, in response to these conditions, called for a graduated personal and corporate income tax, but the tax bill that the legislature passed in 1959 provided instead for an intangibles tax, an increase in the business receipts tax, and a 1 percent "use tax." The Michigan Supreme Court soon ruled the use tax a violation of the limit imposed on the sales tax by the state constitution. This led the legislature to reconvene in December 1959 and to approve some nuisance taxes and an increase in the corporation franchise tax. With expenditures still exceeding revenues, the legislature the next year authorized the annual appropriation of the interest from the Veterans' Trust Fund for general state government purposes. The legislature also proposed a constitutional amendment permitting a four-cent sales tax that was narrowly approved in a referendum and became effective on February 1, 1961.[48]

Governor Swainson, like Williams, sought to persuade the legislature to adopt a personal and corporate income tax. He was rebuffed by the legislators, who let some nuisance taxes expire on July 1, 1961, but then reimposed some of them the next year as the state continued to run a deficit. Michigan's new constitution, which became effective on January 1, 1964, prohibited the state government from imposing a graduated income tax and required the governor, with the approval of the "appropriating committees" of the legislature, to reduce authorized expenditures whenever it appeared that revenues for the fiscal year would be below the estimates on which the appropriations for the period had been based.

An improving economy while George Romney was governor eased the budgetary crisis in Michigan, but there was a growing understanding in the state that its tax system had to be reformed to provide needed revenue for education and other purposes and that the state's taxes on business, which were above those of neighboring states, had to be reduced. The legislature responded in 1967 by approving a 2.6 percent personal income tax, a 5.6 percent corporation income tax, and a 7 percent tax on the receipts of financial institutions, and by abolishing the business receipts tax and the corporation franchise tax. The legislation also authorized municipalities to impose a 1 percent income tax on residents and a 0.5 percent income tax on nonresidents who worked in the city.[49]

The apportioning of seats in the Michigan legislature became a matter of growing concern as the state became increasingly urbanized. The Michigan Senate as of 1950 consisted of 32 seats, with each county entitled to a seat if its population equaled 0.5 percent of the state's population. The House of Representatives was made up of 100 members chosen from single districts that supposedly represented population. In 1952 the voters approved an amendment to the constitution that increased the size of the Senate to 34 and the House to 110 without significantly changing the method of apportionment. The lawmakers the next year reapportioned the legislature in accordance with the amendment. The population of the Senate districts ranged from 61,000 to 364,026, the population of each House district from 32,913 to 67,110. "The cows outvote the people," the *New Republic* commented.

Because of the overrepresentation of rural areas, the apportionment system clearly favored the Republican Party, particularly in the Senate, the party's "stronghold." Of the 34 Senate seats, the Democrats between 1952 and 1962 never held more than 12, even though, as in 1958, the 12 Democratic winners received forty-six thousand more votes than the 22 Republican winners. The Democrats gradually increased the number of their House seats, from 34 of 100 in 1952, to 51 of 110 in 1954, and to 55 of 110 in 1958, but then slipped a bit to 52 of 110 in 1962.[50] As we shall see, the state's apportionment system was changed by Michigan's 1963 constitution and by U.S. Supreme Court decisions in 1962 and 1964. The consequences of the changing composition of the Michigan legislature for civil rights became evident during the Romney governorship.

2

"A JEWEL IN THE CROWN OF ALL OF US": Michigan Enacts a Fair Employment Practices Act, 1949–1955

"We have fallen short in guaranteeing first class citizenship to all of our people, regardless of creed or color," G. Mennen Williams declared in his inaugural address as governor on January 1, 1949. "We of the Western democracies," he asserted, "live in a civilization built upon the teachings of the Man of Nazareth. It is for this purpose—that men may in fact live together as brothers having a care for one another—that modern democratic states exist."[1]

In an interview in October 1949, Williams made it evident that he regarded both legislation and education as necessary to combat prejudice and discrimination against minority groups. As governor, he sought to educate public opinion regarding civil rights and to create "a favorable climate of opinion for disadvantaged groups," used his authority as governor to take appropriate administrative action, and attempted to persuade the Michigan legislature to enact appropriate civil rights legislation. It was obvious to him that African Americans in particular had long been victims of discrimination in the nation. As one of Williams's influential black trade union supporters recalled in an interview, Williams "identified with the kind of gut issues that affected the blacks' life chances. . . . [T]here was a kind of quality of color-blindness about him that was just unique." Williams's commitment to civil rights was not, however, confined to blacks but rather embraced other disadvantaged groups as well, notably women, Native Americans, migrant workers, and the physically handicapped. The same can be said of John Swainson.[2]

In the press, on the radio, and in speeches and appearances before various civic groups during his governorship, Williams sought to keep the issue of civil rights before the Michigan public and to make clear where he stood on the matter. "There can be no standing still on the question of civil rights," he stated in a 1958 address. "We either go forward to removal of all the arbitrary discriminations imposed by one group on another, or we continue to live in a world of myriad discriminations made tolerable only because we recognize their evil and are seeking to eliminate them as quickly as possible." "Discrimination," he asserted at a civil rights luncheon that same year, "not only violates our political principles, it violates divine law. . . . To eliminate discrimination is to do nothing more than to put our moral principles into practice in our daily lives." Swainson echoed Williams's words. "The state," he declared at a meeting of state agency heads in 1961, "must provide leadership for the rest of the nation in demonstrating so strong a commitment to the democratic ideals of the nation that it may be said of us: they practice what they preach; they have made democracy a living thing."[3]

The Michigan Committee on Civil Rights (MCCR), as noted, had made clear to Williams how wide-ranging were the civil rights problems that confronted Michigan. The governor's Advisory Committee on Civil Rights had recommended that Williams assign top priority in the civil rights field to fair employment, and the governor heeded that advice.

Although, as Thomas R. Dye has noted, the governor of a state "sets the agenda for public decision making," it is the legislators who serve as the "arbiters of public policy."[4] As we have seen, however, the legislators whom Williams and Swainson confronted were predominantly Republicans and were unresponsive to the governors' importunities. Many Republican legislators, moreover, did not have to fear reelection since the seats they held were not particularly competitive, at least before 1954.[5]

Ideologically, the Republican Party with which Williams had to deal was oriented in precisely the opposite policy direction than the liberally oriented Democratic Party. Michigan in the 1950s has been characterized by one scholar as "a primary example of the bipolar interest group politics." The Michigan Manufacturers' Association reputedly exercised "inordinate power" in the state Republican Party, and the state's automobile manufacturers had become a major influence in shaping Republican legislative policy. Many Republican legislators, moreover, were from small towns and rural areas and were not inclined to support legislation strongly backed by the UAW and the CIO and designed to benefit minority groups predominantly residing in the state's larger cities. Whatever their home district, also, Republican legislators tended to vote in a conservative direction with "a high degree of party cohesiveness." They were partial to the business community and favored lower taxes and limited government services rather than the socially activist government preferred by the Williams administration and its labor and liberal allies. The fact that Williams in the second half of the 1950s came to be seen as a possible Democratic presidential candidate added an "explosive issue" to partisanship in the state and helps to explain why, following Williams's big victory in 1954, the Republicans, as one scholar put it, "set out with compulsive determination to get" the governor.[6]

In his study of gubernatorial-legislative relations in Michigan, David William Winder contended that Williams, as governor, worked "closely" with his own party on policy issues but not very effectively with the Republican opposition in the legislature. Given the fact that the legislature was dominated not only by a rival party but by one whose reaction to Williams, as one writer commented in 1959, ranged from "black hatred to merely malevolent suspicion," it is hardly surprising that Williams sought to appeal over the head of the legislature to public opinion. He sought by radio, the press, luncheon club speeches, and contact with civic groups to mobilize support for his program. Also, as will become evident from his efforts to persuade the legislature to enact a fair employment law, his chief civil rights objective during the first half of his governorship, Williams at least sometimes recognized that a governor with a legislature controlled by the opposition party could not be overly partisan in dealing with the lawmakers if he wished to accomplish anything.[7]

In his first message to the legislature, on January 6, 1949, Williams announced that his first priority in providing "first class citizenship" for the state's inhabitants was the enactment of fair employment legislation. "Leaders everywhere," he stated, agreed that this was "the next step to insure the practice of our religious and political beliefs in human brotherhood." As his Advisory Committee had recommended, Williams urged a law modeled on the New York fair employment statute and also advised that the commission provided by the law be authorized "to survey all types of infringement upon civil rights and to report to the Legislature and Governor regarding its findings and recommendations."

To deflect possible criticism, Williams stressed that the legislation he was recommending did not require employers to hire unqualified workers, nor did it call for quotas of workers of particular races or nationalities. Further to reassure the legislators, Williams noted that the New York commission dealing with that state's fair employment law had settled all the discrimination complaints it had received by negotiation and conciliation and without the need for formal hearings or the issuance of commission orders and that "entire industries and businesses" had voluntarily abided by the law. The Williams message inaugurated "a heated six-year legislative struggle between liberal and conservative forces in Michigan" that culminated in the enactment of a state fair employment practices law in 1955.[8]

It is not difficult to understand why it took the Williams administration six years to persuade the Michigan legislature to enact a fair employment law. "Civil rights legislation," a study of state fair employment legislation indicated, "fared better" when Democrats controlled a state legislature than when Republicans did. This, however, was hardly the situation in Michigan. In most states, the initial opposition to fair employment legislation came from business and employer groups, and there was no doubting the strength of such groups in Michigan or their opposition to fair employment legislation. The state's Retail Merchants Association thus opposed fair employment legislation as infringing upon "the right of employers and union members to choose their associates," exposing employers to "uncontrollable harassment and oppressive practices," creating racial and religious discord, and seeking to achieve by law what could "only come from the hearts of man." When UAW President Walter Reuther approached some "big industrialists" in Michigan in 1953, presumably including automobile manufacturers, to seek their support for the fair employment measure then before the legislature, "not a single one of them" was willing to voice approval.[9]

Opponents of fair employment legislation in Michigan and elsewhere were convinced that a majority of the public opposed such laws as favoring "an unpopular minority." That is why legislators who opposed fair employment legislation but who did not wish to appear hostile to the groups that might benefit from such a law regularly suggested that the matter be decided by popular referendum. It is also why proponents of the legislation just as regularly opposed the referendum tactic, claiming, as George Schermer stated at the outset of the Williams administration, that a referendum on fair employment lent itself to "exploitation by subversive and hate groups on both the extreme left and right." He cited not only the aforementioned California referendum as a case in point but also, ignoring the role of other groups, referred to the 1947 initiative-referendum proposal in Michigan as "a Communist inspired deal" that had spawned the right-wing Michigan Committee for Tolerance.[10]

Arrayed against the opponents of fair employment legislation in Michigan in 1949 were the governor, a variety of civic and religious groups, and the UAW. Experience had demonstrated that the governor's support was "almost indispensable to success of a [state] civil rights law," and there was never any question about Governor Williams's wholehearted support for civil rights legislation in general and a fair employment law in particular.[11]

Religious leaders were "significant actors in the drive for civil rights" across the nation, and the leaders of the three major religious faiths in Michigan were conspicuously present in the MCCR, as were the representatives of various civic groups. The role of organized labor in the fair employment struggle was "ambiguous" and depended on whether the unions were industrial or craft unions, particularly unions in the building trades. The industrial unions in the mass production industries, which typically included many black members, generally supported fair employment legislation. Craft unions like those in the building trades, concerned about job security and operating apprenticeship programs that all but excluded blacks, were opposed to such laws or were, at best, neutral. In Michigan, the key union was the UAW, which, at least at the leadership level, was consistently in favor of fair employment legislation, as was the Michigan CIO.[12]

Despite occasional criticism of the Republican opposition in the legislature, Williams in seeking a fair employment law acted on the understanding that such a measure could pass the Michigan legislature only with Republican support. The son of the Republican legislator who played the largest role during the Williams governorship in seeking fair employment legislation testified to the governor's genuine effort to accommodate the opposition party in order to get a bill passed.[13]

Although Williams had called for a fair employment law in his initial message to the legislature, his administration did not immediately submit a bill on the subject. Seeking bipartisan support for fair employment, Schermer and some other MCCR members met on January 28, 1949, with young Republican legislators who appeared inclined to support such legislation and received their assurance that they could enlist Republicans to co-sponsor a bill and then get "a favorable vote" on it if the Democrats held back and did not try to take "special credit" for the bill for their party. Schermer then contacted the governor's office, and the administration agreed to wait for a week before submitting a Democratic bill in the hope of gaining bipartisan support. It turned out, however, that the young Republicans were unsuccessful in negotiating with older Republicans.[14]

On February 8, 1949, Representatives Martha Griffiths and Leo J. Doyle, Democrats from Detroit and Flint, respectively, introduced the administration's fair employment bill in the House. It applied to employers of eight or more workers, employment agencies, and labor organizations, defined what constituted illegal unfair employment practices, and provided for a commission of five appointed by the governor without a requirement for bipartisan membership. It authorized not only aggrieved individuals but the chairman of the Michigan Unemployment Compensation Commission (MUCC), the state's attorney general, and the prosecuting attorney of any county to file employment discrimination complaints with the commission. Before holding public hearings, the commission, which was to enjoy subpoena power, was to seek compliance by "informal methods of persuasion and conciliation," and its findings as to the facts were to be "conclusive." It was empowered to issue cease-and-desist orders to respondents to halt discriminatory practices, and it could specify the affirmative action they were to take. Its orders were to be enforceable in the courts, and violators were subject to imprisonment for not more than one year and to fines of not more than $500.

The commission was authorized by the proposed bill to appoint "local, regional, or state-wide" advisory agencies and conciliation councils that it could empower to study discrimination in "all or specific fields of human relationships, or in specific instances of discrimination because of race, creed, color or national origin." These agencies were to make recommendations to the commission for "policies and procedures" and for "programs of formal and informal education" that the commission could recommend to the appropriate state agency. The commission was also "to make an annual survey of the existence and effect of discrimination because of race, creed, color or national origin in the enjoyment of civil rights" by Michigan's inhabitants and report to the governor with recommendations for "remedial action."[15] The bill represented what the Williams administration considered a proper fair employment measure, but in the end the administration had to settle for a somewhat weaker bill.

Before a public hearing was held on the Griffiths-Doyle bill, the UAW Fair Practices and Anti-Discrimination Department and the MCCR sought to build support for the measure. The Fair Practices Department distributed three thousand pamphlets entitled "CIO Wants FEPC," and the two organizations sponsored a Lincoln Day conference devoted to fair employment. Representatives of the MCCR, the Detroit Council of Churches, and the Mayor's Interracial Committee appeared on February 18 before the Resolutions Committee of the state Republican convention to argue their case. The next day the convention adopted a platform plan endorsing state enactment of a fair employment law. Addressing an AFL-CIO dinner on March 22, Williams hailed fair employment legislation not only as "a moral advance" but also as a way to improve "the national economy and unity."[16]

At a public hearing on March 23 on the Griffiths-Doyle bill by the House State Affairs Committee, "a highly diversified army," to quote a newspaper account, "stormed the legislative ramparts" seeking a fair employment law. Labor leaders, priests, ministers, rabbis, black leaders, representatives of women's groups and civic organizations, and "many an earnest John Doe" appeared to testify. They stressed the widespread existence of employment discrimination in the state and asserted that Michigan "must lead the Middle West in a return to basic principles of democracy." Recognizing that the Republican majority would not accept the administration bill, MCCR representatives met with Republican legislators the next day to set forth the MCCR's minimum requirements for a fair employment bill: an independent commission, a clear definition of what constituted unfair employment practices, mandatory investigation and conciliation before public hearings, and authorization for the commission to issue cease-and-desist orders enforceable by the courts.[17]

There appeared to be a fair amount of Republican support in the legislature for a fair employment bill, but for a weaker measure than the Griffiths-Doyle bill. That support, however, evaporated when the Republicans decisively defeated the Democrats in the 1949 spring election on April 4, capturing the positions of highway commissioner and superintendent of public instruction and the open seats on the State Board of Education, the State Board of Agriculture, and the University of Michigan Board of Regents. The chairman of the Republican Legislative Policy Committee reportedly told Martha Griffiths, "You might as well withdraw the FEPC bill."

As the press had predicted, three Republicans introduced a fair employment bill in the House on April 14, but it fell well short of the minimum MCCR requirements. It applied only to employers of twelve or more workers, did not provide for a separate commission but only for a board in the Department of Labor chaired by the commissioner of labor, and the board was to follow the rules of evidence in its hearings, which the MCCR feared would "hamstring its conduct." Unlike the administration bill, the Republican bill did not include a penalty clause or any provision for "affirmative action" following a board finding of discrimination. The intent of the bill's authors, Schermer thought, was "to sabotage the whole concept of positive action" in dealing with employment discrimination. The Republican Legislative Policy Committee, furthermore, arranged to have even this bill submitted to a referendum.[18]

The MCCR appeared before the House State Affairs Committee, to which the Republican bill had been referred, in an effort to secure amendments to strengthen the measure. They succeeded to a degree, but the provision for a referendum remained intact, which led the MCCR to advise Democratic legislators to oppose the bill. In the end, the State Affairs Committee, composed of six Republicans and three Democrats, voted on April 28 not to refer either the Republican or the Democratic bill. Griffiths moved the next day to discharge the committee from further consideration of the Democratic bill, but this was defeated in a straight party vote, 57 to 39. Although a "substantial number" of Republicans reportedly favored fair employment legislation, they voted in opposition under strict party discipline and in accordance with the legislature's tradition since the adoption of the state's 1908 constitution not to override committee decisions regarding the reporting out of bills.[19]

The defeat of fair employment legislation in the 1949 legislative session led the social gospel–minded Williams to wonder, "Are we meeting the test of what a good Christian community should be doing?" Reporting "quite a bit of unrest among Negroes" as a result of what had occurred, a Detroit Urban League (DUL) official advised Williams to request a special session of the legislature in 1950 to deal with fair employment. The governor received similar advice from the Detroit and Wayne County Federation of Labor, the Anti-Defamation League, and the MCCR. It was apparently the opinion of those favoring a special session that it would be better for the administration to try again and be defeated than to leave the measure's supporters "divided and filled with suspicion" regarding the administration's "true motives and intentions." If the governor did not act, the administration was warned, it would give the opposition "an entering wedge into the racial group vote."[20]

August Scholle, the head of the Michigan CIO, dissented from the advice Williams was receiving to place fair employment on the agenda for the special session. His guess was that the only bill that could emerge from the session would require its submission to the voters for approval, and he feared that would "set back" fair employment legislation for years to come and might even lead to the defeat of the Democratic ticket, including Williams, in the next state election. What Scholle preferred was an Advisory Committee resolution calling on the legislature to establish a bipartisan commission to recommend a fair employment bill to the next regular session of the legislature in 1951.[21]

Williams was initially inclined to agree with Scholle, but he decided on March 9 to "open the session" to consideration of a fair employment bill if he could get bipartisan support for the measure in advance. This, Williams believed, was the only way success could be achieved in the session. He consequently invited the majority and minority leaders of the two parties and representatives of the MCCR to meet with him on March 16 to consider the matter. The conferees agreed to form a committee of six made up of two Senate members, two House members, and two MCCR representatives to look into the subject.[22]

It proved difficult for a time to find a Republican senator willing to serve on the committee, but a full committee was eventually put together. Robert Montgomery of Lansing, the Republican House member on the committee, thereupon proposed the creation by the legislature of a study commission made up of representatives of the two parties and the MCCR to visit the states with fair employment laws, talk to members of their fair employment practices commissions, employers, and other parties affected by the legislation, and report to the 1951 legislature. Bishop Francis Haas refused to serve on the committee, saying that the proposal had come eight years too late, but the MCCR reluctantly agreed to participate. Montgomery then submitted a resolution to the special session calling for the implementation of his proposal, but he withdrew it just before its formal reading by the clerk of the House, allegedly at the request of the Republican Legislative Policy Committee. A few days later Griffiths and thirteen House Democrats, in an action urged by the MCCR, introduced a resolution calling for an interim legislative committee to study the operations of existing state fair employment laws. The resolution was referred to the Rules Committee, where it died, and the session ended without any further action being taken on fair employment. Perhaps understandably abandoning bipartisanship for the moment, Williams blasted the Republican behavior on fair employment as presenting "a record studded with broken promises, political weasel words, the quick brushoff and the double cross."[23]

The 1951 regular session witnessed another effort by some Republicans, led by the seventy-five-year-old Representative Louis C. Cramton of Lapeer, to secure the passage of a fair employment bill. Once again the effort was marked by failure, but Cramton, who had joined with two other Republicans in 1949 to introduce a fair employment bill, doggedly continued to fight until victory was secured in 1955. Cramton had begun his long career of public service in 1903 as a law clerk for the Judiciary Committee of the Michigan Senate. He then served as deputy commissioner of railroads and as secretary of the state's Railroad Commission before winning election to the state legislature in 1909. Elected to Congress in 1912 to represent Michigan's Seventh Congressional District, Cramton remained a member of Congress until 1931. In 1921 he became chairman of the subcommittee in charge of appropriations for the Department of the Interior and gained a reputation as the "stepfather of America's National Parks." A "conservative on most issues," Cramton, a Lincoln-style Republican, was a determined foe of racial discrimination. As a congressman, he was a strong supporter of Howard University, one of whose buildings was named after him and from which he received an honorary degree in 1942. He served as a Michigan circuit court judge from 1933 to 1941 before being elected to the Michigan House in 1948.[24]

On February 8, 1951, Cramton introduced a fair employment bill in the House "with no expectation of success but to keep the record straight as to . . . [his] own views." Contacted shortly thereafter by the MCCR, he satisfied himself as to "their integrity, their good faith and their very substantial influence as a federated organization." Acting, to some degree, on the advice of the MCCR, Cramton began revising his bill. He was joined by seven other Republicans, including Montgomery, who was by then speaker pro tem and chairman of the State Affairs Committee, in introducing the revised bill on March 21. The "law against discrimination," as Cramton titled the bill, applied to employers of twelve or more persons, employment agencies, and labor organizations, established an "equal opportunities employment board" as a division of the Department of Labor, and authorized the board, the attorney general, and organizations seeking to combat discrimination or to promote equal employment opportunities to initiate employment discrimination complaints.[25]

Seeking support for his bill, Cramton turned to Tom Downs, a Democratic member of the MUCC, which became the Michigan Employment Security Commission (MESC) later that year. Explaining to Cramton the "dilemma" the State Employment Service faced, Downs noted that the MUCC had removed the designation of color from the application cards of those seeking jobs and also had been attempting for the preceding eleven years to persuade employers to hire the best-qualified workers regardless of their race, color, religion, or place of birth. If the Employment Service, however, refused to accept discriminatory job orders, Downs observed, employers could turn to private employment agencies or could hire at the plant gate. If, on the other hand, the Employment Service processed discriminatory job orders, it would, in effect, be aiding the discrimination practiced by employers. The solution for this dilemma, Downs concluded, was "a strong and effective" fair employment law.[26]

Downs's letter to Cramton was supplemented by Harry C. Markle, the executive director of the MUCC, who noted the extensive character of employment discrimination at that time. A review of 2,265 job orders at three Employment Service offices, Markle reported, revealed that 55 percent of the orders were closed to nonwhites and that many of the remaining 45 percent were "slanted with 'white preferred.' "[27]

Permitting the Republicans once again to take the lead, Williams supported the effort to push the Cramton bill through the legislature. Not only was the "moral case" for fair employment "overwhelming," the governor told an MCCR rally, but with the nation mobilizing its "military and economic strength" to meet the demands of the Korean War, it was essential that workers be given the opportunity to contribute without regard to their race, color, religion, or ancestry. Representatives of the MCCR, the UAW, the NAACP, and the Michigan Council of Churches all testified before the House State Affairs Committee on April 18 in favor of the Cramton bill, but employer groups were conspicuous by their absence. By that time, three Republican senators had submitted a bill similar to the Cramton bill, with Senator Clarence A. Reed of Detroit declaring, "An FEPC law has been part of the Republican platform for some time, and I think we should take action on it."[28]

Despite Reed's remark, neither the House nor the Senate fair employment bill emerged from committee. Cramton blamed the defeat on "high Republican circles outside of the Legislature," whereas the *Michigan Chronicle* attributed what had occurred to "organized merchant and management groups" that it believed had helped to defeat fair employment legislation in 1949 as well. The MCCR's executive secretary took some solace from the defeat, seeing it as a sign of "progress" that the House State Affairs Committee had failed by only one vote to report the Cramton bill to the full House, whereas "a clear majority" of the committee had bottled up fair employment legislation in 1949.[29]

According to his son, Cramton was "so damned mad and hurt" when his bill was killed that he could not speak to his son for the next twenty-four hours. "As a lifelong Republican," Cramton wrote the chairman of the Republican State Central Committee, "I naturally desire the restoration of that party to state and national leadership and believe the public welfare requires that." But that would not occur, he warned, until the party "ceased to be simply a party of opposition. It must be FOR worthwhile policies," he urged, "policies based on fundamental justice and regard for the public welfare." He thought that the right to earn a living and to support and educate one's family was "that kind of issue," involving, he asserted, "the fundamental issue of human rights upon which our nation is founded." Even though, he wrote, he had tried to make his bill a Republican bill, a point that the MCCR had publicized, and had gotten seven other Republicans to join him in introducing it, the Republican Party had opposed the measure simply because fair employment legislation was something that the state Democratic Party and the Democratic governor had proposed. Noting that at his age he had "no political ambitions to advance," he informed the chairman that he would introduce a slightly revised bill in the next session of the legislature, and he wanted the party to come to his support.[30]

The fight for a fair employment bill was renewed in the 1952 legislative session. Williams, as before, called on the legislature to enact a fair employment law, and Cramton, joined by the House Republican leadership and after discussion with the MCCR, once again introduced a fair employment bill. A similar bill was introduced in the Senate. Relating his bill to the Cold War, Cramton argued that the measure was needed "not only to protect minority rights but to unify citizens against communism." Neither bill emerged from committee, Cramton's bill having been killed by a 4–4 vote in the State Affairs Committee after a fifth Republican supporter failed to appear for the vote. Cramton, however, promptly introduced another bill, and the Detroit Democrat and minority leader in the House, Ed Carey, submitted a bill of his own.[31]

Still hoping for bipartisan support for fair employment legislation, the MCCR negotiated with the chairmen of the two state parties and with the majority and minority leaders in the legislature. It held an Education Conference on the subject in Lansing on February 14 that was attended by representatives of twenty-two organizations, and the next day a " 'citizen's lobby' swarmed through the Capitol" seeking support for fair employment. The MCCR also arranged for a series of regional conferences in the state to "educate" the public regarding the meaning of fair employment practices.[32]

Fair employment supporters were heartened when the second Cramton bill was transferred from the State Affairs Committee—the inveterate opponent of liberal legislation—to the House Judiciary Committee, which the MCCR thought gave the measure "a fighting chance of being reported out." In an action hailed by the MCCR's executive director as "the most significant progress in the history of FEPC legislation in Michigan," the Judiciary Committee reported the bill out on March 3 by a 6–0 vote, the first time a fair employment bill had reached the floor of either house of the legislature since Williams had become the state's governor. This set the stage for "the hottest floor fight" of the session ten days later. Opponents first tried to kill the bill by moving to have it referred to the Ways and Means Committee on the ground that the bill did not contain a specific appropriation for enforcement. The motion was defeated by a 43–43 vote. An effort to make the bill unacceptable as too inclusive by adding the aged and physically handicapped to the groups protected against discrimination also met defeat.

The opposition then resorted to "devious parliamentary tricks" to prevent Cramton from speaking for his bill. When he finally did begin to speak, twenty-five Republican legislators, in what the *Detroit Free Press* characterized as "one of the strangest maneuvers on record," quit the chamber, refusing to listen to the bill's author. While Cramton spoke, there was "a constant rattling of chairs, slamming of steel file drawers, and trooping in and out from the Republican side of the House." "My grandfather and father voted for Abraham Lincoln," Cramton said. "I never thought I would see the time that Republicans would leave their seats rather than hear a Republican discuss the vital question of human rights." How, he asked, could Republicans expect to win votes in Detroit if "they keep slapping minorities in the face?" He charged that the Michigan Manufacturers' Association had "lobbied emphatically" against the bill. According to one press account, Cramton was reduced to tears as he spoke.[33]

In the heated debate that followed Cramton's speech, one Republican opponent of fair employment questioned whether blacks had the ability "to assimilate equal opportunities." Another Republican quoted an unidentified Democrat as having allegedly said that a favorable vote on the bill would "bring all the Polacks to the polls," and he refused to apologize when Democrats demanded that he do so. Supporters of the bill defeated fifteen emasculating amendments, but the measure was in the end defeated by a 45–46 vote, "buried under an avalanche of bitterness, rancor, and broken promises." Thirteen Republicans joined thirty-two Democrats in voting for the measure, with all the no votes being cast by Republicans. An analysis of the Republican vote on the bill revealed no direct connection between the percentage of blacks in a particular legislative district and the vote of the representative from that district.

Representative William S. Broomfield of Royal Oak explained that he had voted in the negative because the existence of employment discrimination had not been "substantiated by an impartial study" and that, in any event, the problem was to be solved by "educational and religious advancement," not by legislation. Responding to Cramton's appraisal of fair employment as an antidote to communism, Republican Representative Harold R. Estes of Birmingham characterized the Cramton bill as moving Michigan into "the realm of a Socialistic state." The debate on the bill, Estes stated, "must make the Socialist and Communist elements in our country laugh with glee because it tends to incite racial hatreds of the most violent kind, a condition which Joe Stalin will approve with delight."[34]

Some progress regarding fair employment was made at the municipal level in November 1952, when Pontiac and River Rouge, the latter by referendum, adopted fair employment ordinances. A petition drive by radical groups in Detroit to place a fair employment ordinance on the city ballot failed to receive the necessary number of signatures, largely because the principal religious and labor groups seeking a state fair employment law feared that the proposed referendum would be defeated and would doom their cause. They had reason to fear, judging from a careful survey of 530 white Detroit citizens conducted between May and August 1951. Of those surveyed, a minimum of 54 percent and perhaps as many as 75 percent (if those who provided "neutral, ambiguous and not classifiable" responses were assumed to "lean one way or the other in about the same proportions as the other respondents") opposed the treatment of blacks as citizens with "full and equal rights." They also indicated that they did "not want colored people moving into white neighborhoods, intermingling with white people."[35]

Stressing the need for state action and also for an investigation by the federal government's Committee on Government Contract Compliance, Walter Reuther informed Williams that he had learned of several instances in which Detroit employers with defense contracts had refused to hire nonwhites. Reuther's allegation was confirmed by DUL visits to twenty-five firms in the city with defense contracts. The UAW president noted that the refusal of employers to hire minority-group members at a time when there was a manpower shortage in Detroit had led employers to recruit workers from outside Michigan, which, he claimed, intensified the city's housing shortage and strained community relations.[36]

No doubt reflecting his concern about the difficulty of securing fair employment legislation from the Michigan legislature, Williams in September 1952 raised with the MESC the possibility of its simply refusing to service discriminatory job orders. This would have followed the practice in Illinois, which, like Michigan, was without a fair employment law but where the governor had issued a directive prohibiting the state's job placement agency from accepting discriminatory job orders. The heads of the MESC and its Employment Service Division thought, however, that such a policy would be counterproductive and "to the detriment of minority groups." Quite apart from the fact that they did not believe that the law under which the Employment Service Division operated permitted it to reject discriminatory job orders, they contended, as they regularly had, that such a policy would simply lead private employers to turn to private employment agencies or to do their own hiring, which, indeed, had happened on a large scale in Illinois. This, they insisted, would make it more difficult for the Employment Service Division to combat employment discrimination through its education program, for which the division claimed a good deal of success in securing "relaxation of discriminatory specifications" by employers who used the service. The solution for the problem, they concluded, as Downs had earlier, was a fair employment law "with teeth in it." The four MESC commissioners appeared to agree with this judgment.[37]

In April 1952 the DUL and the MESC agreed that the DUL would no longer process job orders, leaving that task entirely to the MESC, and would concentrate on "job development." The DUL's intention was to "intensify its work in pioneering the introduction of Negro workers" in industries and businesses from which they had been excluded and to gain "public acceptance of the Negro both as a citizen and as a worker." Following this agreement, the two organizations began to visit employers whose job orders contained discriminatory specifications in an effort to persuade them to submit "unqualified job orders" and also, it was hoped, to secure "a closer relationship between concerned parties." In what appeared to be a major victory, they secured the agreement of the

Big Three automobile manufacturers to abandon their use of "restricted job orders." Job discrimination, however, continued in the automobile manufacturing industry. The Big Three thus refused to agree to UAW requests to include a nondiscrimination clause in union contracts, and blacks continued to be placed in "the most dangerous and undesirable jobs in the industry."[38]

Joined by four other Republicans, Cramton on February 1, 1953, introduced still another fair employment bill in the Michigan House. Stating that he was responding to the concerns of "those who do not want radical action but do want accomplishment," Cramton described the measure as "a much gentler bill" than several states had enacted into law. The new bill did not give the proposed fair employment commission the power to initiate complaints or subpoena power, nor did it prescribe criminal penalties for offenders. It required the commission to rely on "conference, conciliation and persuasion" when it found probable cause for discrimination before it could proceed to a public hearing. It relied on court enforcement and did not provide that commission findings as to the facts were to be regarded as "conclusive" when its orders were appealed by respondents. A few days later Ed Carey introduced a stronger bill that gave the commission for which the measure provided both subpoena power and the power to initiate complaints, did not require it to rely on informal methods of persuasion and conciliation before proceeding to a public hearing, and made commission findings "conclusive as to the facts."[39]

In an effort to marshal support for fair employment legislation, the MCCR, in addition to inaugurating a program of local community fair employment conferences, joined with the Michigan Conference of NAACP Branches, the African Methodist Episcopal Conference, and a number of "likeminded" labor, religious, civic, and fraternal organizations in sponsoring a "mass mobilization" in Lansing on February 19 for a fair employment practices law. Governor Williams, who proclaimed February 19 "Equal Opportunity Day" to coincide with the mobilization, joined Republican Lieutenant Governor Clarence Reed in addressing 785 conferees representing forty-one organizations who came to Lansing for the event. Emissaries from Connecticut and New Jersey provided testimony at the mobilization regarding the success of fair employment laws in their states. Reed, for his part, reminded those present that he had introduced a fair employment bill as a senator and that fair employment was a plank in the Republican national platform. The Democratic governor and the Republican lieutenant governor announced that they had secured pledges that day from a majority of members of their respective parties in the legislature that they would support fair employment legislation. The Republican state convention, which met a few days later, characterized fair employment and civil rights as "moral obligations" but did not endorse any specific bill.[40]

"This year, I am emphasizing the Eisenhower leadership," Cramton explained regarding the tactic he was pursuing to secure support for his fair employment bill. He was referring to President Dwight D. Eisenhower's promised support for state fair employment legislation in a presidential campaign address of October 17, 1952, and in a message to Congress of February 2, 1953. Eisenhower had stated that he expected his administration "to make true and rapid progress in civil rights and equality of employment opportunity" as the result of presidential leadership "exercised through friendly conferences with those in authority in our states and cities." Writing to Eisenhower on February 26, Cramton emphasized that the president's support as "our acknowledged national leader" was necessary to push a fair employment bill through the Michigan legislature. He asked the president for "any expression he might care to make concerning the pending legislation."[41]

Two months later Cramton protested to U.S. Senator Charles E. Potter, a Michigan Republican, that Eisenhower had ignored Cramton's February 26 letter. Since he had served nine terms in Congress, Cramton wrote, he was "not an unknown upstart of uncertain responsibility." "Hurt" by what had occurred, Cramton stated, "I have never had any such brush off as this." He maintained that there was "rapidly spreading support" for his fair employment bill and that should Williams seek in 1954 the U.S. Senate seat then held by Republican Homer Ferguson, as Cramton assumed the governor would, the Republicans would lose the seat and perhaps control of the Senate and the House as well if the electorate questioned Eisenhower's sincerity in making campaign pledges. The Republican Party, Cramton thought, had "to wake up," "show interest in the common man," and "cease to slap in the face important minorities." Cramton sought to enlist the aid of both Potter and Ferguson in securing the president's support, but although Potter indicated that the president was willing to talk to Cramton, all that resulted was Eisenhower's agreeing in August to autograph a picture for Cramton.[42]

Seeking to win over opponents of fair employment legislation, the MCCR arranged a visit to Michigan on March 10 by Roderick Stephens, a "prominent" businessman, a lifelong Republican, and a member of the Advisory Committee to the New York State Committee on Discrimination, which administered the state's fair employment statute. Stephens, in a press conference, reviewed the legislative history of the New York law and countered arguments against the proposed measure in Michigan. He then met at lunch with a number of Michigan businessmen, and his arguments in favor of fair employment legislation appeared to make a favorable impression on them.

At a dinner meeting that same evening attended by Stephens, ten Republican state senators, and an MCCR representative, the raw politics of the fair employment issue came to the fore. Stephens sought to persuade the Republican senators that the party would benefit both locally and nationally from Michigan's enactment of a fair employment law. Rebutting this argument, several senators contended that black and other minority-group members in their districts were committed to the Democratic Party and would remain so even if the Republican legislature followed Stephens's advice. One senator asserted that he found it difficult to understand how minority-group members who, he claimed, voted against Republican candidates in the state could expect Republicans in the legislature to give favorable consideration to minority-group legislative demands. Some senators, according to a summary of this "within the family" discussion, commented that "the American concept of majority rule and the obligation of the majority to safeguard the rights of the minority" were actually "in jeopardy because of the . . . trend toward dictation to the majority and the threats of political reprisal expressed by minorities."[43]

The MCCR, the usual labor, religious, and civic groups, and the assistant director of the New York State Division against Discrimination all testified on March 27 before the House State Affairs Committee in favor of fair employment legislation, and not a single person appeared to testify in opposition. Noting that eleven states and twenty-five cities had adopted fair employment measures of one sort or another by that time, the MCCR called attention to the continuing evidence of employment discrimination in Michigan. It reported that except for government and minority-group agencies, there were no openings for nonwhites in Detroit in professional, managerial, clerical, or sales positions. Cramton paid "high tribute" to the MCCR, asserting that in his long legislative experience he had never "found more enjoyment in association with any other group."[44]

Revealing what was on his mind, Eugene C. Betz of Monroe, the chairman of the State Affairs Committee, asked during the hearings whether blacks migrated in larger numbers to states with fair employment laws than to states without such legislation. Proponents of the bills assured Betz that census reports answered this question in the negative. "Telling employers they must do certain things," a Midland Republican House member charged, "will make them resent it." Opponents claimed that the proposed legislation constituted "a serious infringement upon private business," discriminated against employers, and, judging by the experience of other states, would prove to be "costly and ineffective."

The opposition once again prevailed, the State Affairs Committee voting not to report either the Cramton or the Carey bill. Noting that his bill had fallen but one vote short of being reported to the floor, Cramton wrote Senator Potter, "I counted on Presidential leadership to give me that one more vote," but "the Whitehouse [sic] had no word for me." Williams sought a meeting with the State Affairs Committee in the hope of reviving one of the bills, but he failed in the effort, the same fate that befell a Democratic attempt to have the Cramton bill taken from the State Affairs Committee.[45]

Cramton, for the moment, enjoyed greater success outside the legislature than in that body. Governor Williams proclaimed March 5, 1953, "Judge Cramton Day" in honor of Cramton's fifty years of public service. "You are the most interesting man in the Michigan legislature," Martha Griffiths had told Cramton a few days earlier. In September the Michigan State Bar, in response to Cramton's "tearful pleading," gave its approval to fair employment legislation for the first time. The decision, however, was reversed by a 1,999 to 1,338 vote when member lawyers were polled on the issue in 1955. In February 1954 the American Jewish Congress honored Cramton with its Amity Award in recognition of his support for fair employment.[46]

Preparing for the 1954 legislative session and still another battle over fair employment, Williams, in an "unsuccessful move," addressed a letter to each member of the legislature calling for support for fair employment legislation solely on its merits, not on a partisan basis, and "separate from all the controversial issues" that would be before the legislature in the session. Like Cramton, Williams also appealed to Eisenhower for support. In reply, the special counsel to the president informed the governor that fair employment was "a matter about which he [Eisenhower] feels very strongly" and that he was interested that Michigan was considering a fair employment measure, a response that fell short of what Williams would have liked.[47]

The MCCR, for its part, gained what it claimed was a commitment from John Feikens, chairman of the Republican State Central Committee, that he would "make every effort" to persuade the Republican Legislative Policy Committee to include fair employment legislation as part of the party's program for the 1954 session of the legislature. Feikens, who had advised the MCCR that there was "strong opposition" in the committee to such legislation and whose own position on the subject, judging from the relevant correspondence, may have been less supportive than the MCCR indicated, failed to persuade the committee to endorse a fair employment measure. In the end, Feikens himself joined the opposition, claiming that such legislation would "set up a class with special privileges" and "might infringe too much on the rights of employers."[48]

The Michigan Republican Party as of 1954 was actually "badly split" on the issue of fair employment. Some Republicans, like Cramton, supported fair employment legislation out of sincere conviction. Others believed that the party could not undo Williams's "stranglehold" on the black vote or defeat the governor in the 1954 state election unless Republican legislators voted for fair employment. Republican opponents of fair employment legislation, according to an Associated Press reporter, were heavily influenced by the fear of business groups that such legislation "would lead them into ticklish racial disputes."[49]

Republican ambivalence regarding the fair employment issue was very much in evidence in the 1954 session of the Michigan legislature. Before the legislature convened, the Republicans began considering a tactic that would make it appear that their party favored fair employment and that it was the Democrats who opposed it. The idea was to add a right-to-work provision to a fair employment bill banning discrimination for "any . . . reason" not relating to the ability of the individual to perform the job. "A fair employment law is a right-to-work law," a Republican senator declared. Since the proposed provision would have proscribed compulsory union membership as a condition for employment, Republicans assumed that Democratic legislators, given their party's ties to the unions, would have to vote against a bill containing this provision. Once the session was under way, the Republicans, as we shall see, sought to play the right-to-work card.[50]

Joined by three other Republicans, Cramton on January 13 submitted a fair employment bill that was similar in the main to his 1953 bill and acceptable to the MCCR. By this time, Cramton, at long last, had received word from the Eisenhower administration that the president stood by his earlier statements on fair employment and believed that they should be of "considerable help" to Cramton in his effort to secure enactment of a fair employment bill. Conveying this information to Cramton, the special counsel to the president made it clear at the same time that the president deemed it inadvisable to take a position on "a special legislative proposal" in a state. Cramton was pleased with this word from the White House and hoped that it would "prove sufficient to put through" his bill. His hopes were dashed, however, when the State Affairs Committee voted 6–2 on February 2 not to report the bill to the floor.[51]

The next day Representative Carey moved to discharge the State Affairs Committee from further consideration of the Cramton bill. Seeking to prevent Carey from speaking in support of his motion, the majority floor leader, Harry T. Phillips of Port Huron, moved the previous motion. The Phillips motion was approved 51–37, applying what Cramton described as "an absolute gag rule." Six Republicans voted with thirty-one Democrats against the Phillips motion. Carey and Cramton then took advantage of a constitutional provision "to insert some remarks in the record," Cramton stressing what he characterized as White House support for the bill, the state party's platform plank supporting fair employment, and his strong belief that the bill would pass if sent to the full house. Conforming to tradition, the House defeated the Carey motion, 53–35. What had occurred, Cramton informed the White House, demonstrated "to what extent the Republican controlled legislature" was "under the command of some concealed special interest."[52]

Representative Adrian deBoom of Owosso followed the defeat of the Cramton bill by introducing a fair employment bill with the right-to-work provision included. Carey denounced the provision as a "union-busting device to defeat fair employment," and the MCCR called it "a cheap political trick to defeat FEPC by attempting to create disunity among FEPC supporters." The deBoom bill was referred to the State Affairs Committee along with a bipartisan measure modeled after the key New York law that had been introduced on February 5 by Cramton, one other Republican, and three Democrats, one of them black. "All the time," Cramton explained to the White House as to why he had joined with Democrats in introducing the bill, "the Democrats had wanted a bipartisan bill, and although they have given 100% support in every way to the proposed legislation, I had kept it a Republican bill until now." Because of "suffering from gag law Republican domination," however, he had decided for the first time, he said, to adopt a bipartisan approach to fair employment legislation. Once again, however, neither the deBoom bill nor the bipartisan bill emerged from committee.[53]

On February 4, 1954, three Senate Democrats from Detroit introduced a strong fair employment bill (Senate Bill No. 1163), and, no doubt to the surprise of many, the Senate State Affairs Committee, by a 5–1 vote, reported the bill to the full Senate on March 2 with a recommendation for approval. After the bill had been "watered down" by the removal of subpoena power for the commission that was to administer the measure as well as in other ways, the Senate approved the bill by a 20–11 vote. The opposition consisted entirely of Republicans, most of them coming from small towns or rural areas. The legislative representative of the Michigan Manufacturers' Association denounced the Republican senators who had voted for the bill and looked to the House to "bury" the measure. As reporter Carl Rudow speculated in the *Detroit News* following the Senate vote, if the bill were subsequently to die in the House, the favorable Senate action could be seen as "fakery" on the part of senators who knew the House would kill the measure. This, as it turned out, is precisely what occurred.[54]

Following the Senate approval of Senate Bill No. 1163, a bipartisan House delegation visited Speaker Wade Van Valkenburg, a Kalamazoo Republican, to request that the bill be referred to the Judiciary Committee rather than to the "not so tender mercies" of the State Affairs Committee. Van Valkenburg denied the request but promised, should it prove necessary, to appear before the State Affairs Committee to urge a favorable vote on the bill and, if that failed, to ask the Republican caucus to assist in having the bill reported out of committee. In the event, the State Affairs Committee killed the bill on March 23 by a straight party vote of 6–3 without Van Valkenburg having delivered on his promise to intervene. Unidentified legislators who favored the bill had vainly sought to persuade the six Republicans on the committee to vote otherwise. One Republican justified his opposition because, he claimed, he had observed blacks "driving Cadillacs and taking trips abroad," and another Republican opponent said that he had feared party disapproval if he voted in the affirmative.[55]

Following the State Affairs Committee vote, Cramton moved to have the bill taken from the committee. In the heated debate that followed, Van Valkenburg took the floor to argue against the bill he had promised to support. Disparaging the very concept of fair employment, he said, mockingly, that he had received a large number of letters in favor of the bill and had sent them to the "Committee on Religion and Benevolent Societies." Betz charged that the bill had been "conceived in the halls of the Communist Party" and that it had "take[n] in a lot of innocent people like Judge Cramton." Cramton's motion was defeated by a 54–43 vote, eleven Republicans breaking party ranks to join the Democrats in support of the motion. In a public statement following the defeat of the bill, an angry Williams declared, "By killing a measure already passed in the Senate, the House leadership has treated its own party's pledge as a scrap of paper."[56]

As 1954 drew to a close, the friends of fair employment took heart from the fact that, for the first time in the Williams governorship, one house of the legislature had approved a fair employment bill and also that Ecorse and Hamtramck had been added to the municipalities with fair employment ordinances. The governor summoned MCCR representatives and other supporters of fair employment legislation to his office on December 30 to consider a bill for the 1955 legislative session modeled after Senate Bill No. 1163. The meeting, which proved to be "quite fruitful," resulted in a redraft of No. 1163 for introduction in the 1955 session of the legislature. In his message to the legislature urging enactment of a fair employment law, Williams once again emphasized that the issue was "above partisanship and politics." When an individual suffered discrimination, the governor said, "the whole community suffers along with the immediate victim."[57]

The bill that emerged from the deliberations in the governor's office was introduced in the House on January 25, 1955, by a bipartisan group consisting of Cramton and two Republicans and Carey and one other Democrat. It provided for a four-member commission appointed by the governor, who was also to designate the committee chairman. No more than three commissioners could be from the same party, which meant, in effect, that the governor's party would most likely have a commission majority. The commission's principal office was to be in Detroit, where the state's blacks were concentrated. The commission was to have both subpoena power and the power to initiate discrimination complaints. The commission was directed "to prepare a comprehensive educational program designed for the students of public, private and parochial schools and for all other residents, to emphasize the origin of prejudice against . . . minority groups, its harmful effects, and its incompatibility with American principles of equality and fair play."[58]

The supporters of fair employment legislation mounted a "vigorous campaign" for the bill, their hopes "a great deal higher than in the past" because of the Democratic sweep in the 1954 state election. The UAW Fair Practices and Anti-Discrimination Department sought to arm fair employment supporters with answers to common objections to such measures. Supporters were advised to make it clear that the law would not force employers to hire any particular workers but only not to discriminate in their selection of employees because of their race or religion. Were a charge of discrimination to be made, supporters were advised to point out, the burden of proof would be on the commission administering the act, not on the accused employer. Supporters were to respond to allegations about the allegedly high cost of implementing a fair employment law by noting that the experience of states with such laws had demonstrated that the cost would be "infinitesimal." They were to deal with the question of whether legislation could make people "good" by arguing that laws were "a means of pressure to make people behave in a social fashion rather than in an anti-social one." Prepared to meet employer objections to fair employment legislation, proponents of the measure viewed "with some dismay" the release of the news in May that the Michigan State Bar had reversed its earlier approval of a fair employment law for Michigan. There was also concern among supporters about the effort of the Detroit Civil Service Commission to be exempted from the application of the proposed measure.[59]

The day after the bipartisan fair employment bill was introduced, the Employers' Association of Grand Rapids sent all members of the legislature a list of its objections to a fair employment law. The association contended that such a measure would force employers "to employ or promote members of 'minority' groups at [the] expense of 'majority' groups, without regard to one's right to choose with whom he will work," even though the right to select one's associates was "essential to the free right to earn a livelihood, essential to liberty of contract and the . . . pursuit of happiness." This argument was obviously designed to relate existing employment discrimination to the wishes and prejudices of employees rather than to the hiring and promotion decisions of employers. The employers, however, did make clear their opposition to what they claimed was their being "forced" by such legislation to hire particular job applicants.

Resorting to the argument ad horrendum, the Employers' Association contended that a law barring employment discrimination because of race and religion might serve as a precedent for legislation prohibiting discrimination because of age and height and weight as well as discrimination in areas other than employment. Bills such as Cramton and Carey were proposing, the Employers' Association insisted, would lead to "needless litigation" and would increase rather than reduce "unreasoning discrimination" where it existed. The Cramton bill, the association charged, ignored the rules of evidence and the right of the accused to a jury trial and would create an "unnecessary" state agency that would be staffed by persons "partial to minorities who would seek to perpetuate the agency *at the expense* of the taxpayers." The Employers' Association, finally, complained that supporters of fair employment opposed a right-to-work clause in such a measure because they favored "compulsory union membership."[60]

The debate on fair employment in 1955 was complicated by the question of whether to add sex discrimination to the proposed ban on discrimination because of race, religion, nationality, and ancestry. This was a matter of particular concern to some rank-and-file CIO supporters of the measure. When the Jewish Labor Committee of Detroit, a staunch supporter of fair employment and well aware that sex discrimination was "a major problem" in Michigan, wrote to the American Jewish Congress for advice on this matter, Will Maslow, director of the Commission on Law and Social Action of the congress, responded that discrimination based on sex, age, or physical handicap was an "entirely different problem" from discrimination based on race and religion. If sex discrimination were added to the measure, he feared that the commission administering the law would be "flooded" with so many complaints that it would neglect its primary purpose of combating ethnic prejudice. Mildred Jeffrey, who had served as the first director of the UAW's Women's Bureau, established in 1944, recalled that race was "the dominant problem" when fair employment legislation was first being considered, and sex was "way down in the priority list." The supposition, she remembered, was that the addition of sex discrimination to a fair employment bill would cost the measure the support of the Catholic Church, among others.[61]

The House State Affairs Committee reported the fair employment bill out on April 7 after it had weakened the measure by adopting twenty-six amendments. According to the UAW Fair Practices Department, Robert W. Waldron, a Grosse Pointe Republican whom the department dubbed "the spokesman of the obstructionist bloc," had the members "dizzy" as he allegedly "set a probable record for the introduction and withdrawal of amendments." One amendment called for submission of the bill to a referendum in November 1956, which prompted Cramton to ask, "Do we need a referendum on the question of the Golden Rule?"[62]

Formed at the beginning of 1955 and made up of representatives of the principal Michigan organizations seeking fair employment legislation, the Michigan Coordinating Council for FEPC, which was cooperating with the MCCR and the NAACP, dispatched 125 supporters to Lansing to contact legislators and assist Cramton and Carey in killing "the most crucial amendments" that weakened the fair employment bill. The MCCR saw itself at this point in time as "in the last stages of its superhuman effort" to secure a Michigan fair employment law. The House responded to the Coordinating Council lobbying by defeating the "crippling amendments" by sizable votes, largely restoring the provisions of the original bill. The "biggest fight" on the floor of the House was over the commission-directed "comprehensive educational program." The House approved the bill by an 80–27 vote.[63]

The House-approved bill was considerably weakened in the Senate, even though supporters of the measure succeeded in defeating some of the amendments that most troubled them. The Senate State Affairs Committee, which approved the bill by a 4–3 vote, stripped the commission of subpoena power and the authority to initiate complaints of employment discrimination and, presumably in the interests of home rule, to establish local conciliation councils. The committee increased the size of the commission to a bipartisan six, specified that the commission was to elect its own chairman, moved the commission office from Detroit to Lansing, and eliminated the provision of the bill calling for an educational program in the schools. Whereas the House bill had not applied the ban on employment discrimination to religious corporations, the Senate bill specifically included such corporations. This action almost certainly reflected the view of some legislators that since religious groups had been "so active" in promoting fair employment legislation, they should be among those to whom the law applied.

The Senate approved the amended bill on May 24 by a 20–13 vote, ten Republicans joining ten Democrats in voting for the measure. Republicans cast all the no votes, Senator Lewis Christman of Ann Arbor, for one, explaining that the measure would lead to "breaking down our judicial system." Republican senators who voted in the affirmative may have shared the view of Senator Harry Hittle of East Lansing, who stated that he was voting for the measure because it was the "only bill . . . creating any commission" in the state that did not specify that its findings were to be "final with respect to all the facts" when a commission order was appealed to the courts but provided rather that appeals were to be tried de novo. This, he thought, preserved the rights of Michigan citizens "more completely and comprehensively" than any other state law. The House concurred in the Senate amendments to the bill the very next day by a 96–0 vote. The House, quite properly, ordered that the measure be known as the Cramton bill, although Cramton sought in vain to have the honor shared with Carey.[64]

Williams hailed the bill that emerged from the legislature as "a jewel in the crown of all of us." One hundred persons jammed the executive office on June 29 to witness the governor's signing into law of the Michigan Fair Employment Practices Act, the measure's official name. Williams distributed four of the five pens he used in the signing to Cramton, Carey, an MCCR representative, and an NAACP representative, keeping the fifth for himself. He said that he was "especially pleased" that the fight for the law had been over "a moral issue," and he praised the religious and labor groups for their support of the measure. When the bill went into effect on October 14, 1955, Williams remarked, "We have written the dignity of man into the law of the state."[65]

The Fair Employment Practices Act applied to employers of eight or more persons (about thirty-six thousand employers), employment agencies, labor organizations, and the state government and its political and civil subdivisions. It did not apply to domestic service, but, unlike the laws of some other states, it covered nonprofit organizations of "a fraternal, religious, charitable, social, or educational character." It made it an unfair employment practice for an employer, because of "the race, color, religion, national origin or ancestry of any individual, to refuse to hire or otherwise discriminate against him with respect to hire, tenure, terms, conditions of employment, or any matter, directly or indirectly related to employment except when based on a bona fide occupational qualification." Employment agencies were similarly forbidden to discriminate against individuals in classifying them or referring them for employment, and unions were not to discriminate against any individual or "limit, segregate or qualify" union membership because of race, color, national origin, or ancestry in any manner that would deprive the individual of opportunity for employment, limit that opportunity, or otherwise affect the status of the individual as an employee so as to "affect adversely" his wages, hours, or terms of employment. Unlike the laws of some other states, the Michigan statute also applied to contractors and subcontractors employed by the state government and local governments, and a violation could be considered "a material breach of contract."

Recognizing that asking certain kinds of questions of individuals could lead to discrimination, the statute forbade employers, employment agencies, and unions, except where based on "a bona fide occupational qualification," to elicit information from an individual before employment or admission to membership concerning race, color, religion, or national ancestry, or to keep a record of such distinctions. They could not publish notices or advertisements indicating a discriminatory preference, limit employment or membership by a "quota system or otherwise," or utilize placement services or training schools that themselves discriminated.

The law created a Fair Employment Practices Commission (FEPC) of six members appointed by the governor with the consent of the Senate, no more than three of whom could be from the same political party. In processing complaints of discrimination, which the aggrieved individual had to file within ninety days of the alleged act of discrimination, the commission, as in most states with fair employment laws, was to employ "informal methods of persuasion and conciliation" to secure compliance before resorting to public hearings, and it was not to disclose the names of respondents in doing so. The commission was not given the power to subpoena the production of records by respondents. If, after a public hearing, the commission concluded that discrimination in violation of the law had occurred, it could order the respondent to "cease and desist" and to take such "affirmative action" as would carry out the purposes of the act, including hiring, reinstating, or upgrading the aggrieved employee with or without back pay, requiring the admission or restoration of individuals to union membership, and requiring reports as to "the manner of compliance." The commission could appeal to the state's circuit courts if its orders were disobeyed, making Michigan the tenth state with an enforceable fair employment discrimination law. Any complainant, intervener, or respondent claiming to be aggrieved by a commission order or by the commission's refusal to issue a complaint could appeal to a state circuit court, the appeal, as in some but not all of the states with fair employment laws, to be tried de novo by the court. Employers, employment agencies, and unions that refused to post notices of the commission setting forth provisions of the law and other relevant information were subject to a fine of $100 to $150.

Covered employers, employment agencies, and unions were forbidden to instigate or coerce an action declared to be an unfair labor practice or to discriminate against an employee, union member, or job applicant because the individual had opposed or supported a practice forbidden by the law or made a charge, testified, or assisted in an investigation under the act. Nothing in the act, on the other hand, required an employer to hire any particular individual or a union to admit someone to membership other than on the basis of the individual's qualifications.

The commission was authorized to create local or state advisory agencies to "aid in effectuating the purposes" of the act. The commission could recommend "formal or informal programs of education" and could empower the advisory agencies that it created to "study the problems of discrimination in all or specific fields of human relationships when based on race, color, religion, national origin or ancestry." The advisory agencies could then make recommendations to the commission for "the development of policies and procedure." The provision regarding advisory agencies went beyond the area of employment discrimination, as did the law's requirement that the commission was to survey at least annually "the existence and effect of discrimination . . . on the enjoyment of civil rights" by the state's inhabitants and was to recommend "remedial action, legislative or otherwise," to the legislature and the governor.[66]

Like most state fair employment laws, the Michigan statute had a crucial defect—the commission could not itself initiate complaints, nor was it given specific authority to deal with "discriminatory employment practices" in particular industries. Even most of the states with fair employment laws permitting the initiation of complaints by the state enforcement agency, a particular state official, or a private agency interested in civil rights relied almost entirely on the initiation of complaints by aggrieved individuals. The need, also, to proceed by a case-by-case approach limited the success of the Michigan FEPC, as it did the commissions of most states with fair employment laws.[67]

Why, after so long a struggle, did a fair employment bill finally survive the legislative gauntlet in Michigan in 1955? Given Republican predominance in the state legislature, the bipartisan approach that Williams had espoused from the start was certainly a factor. Cramton's son remarked that the Williams administration and the governor consistently permitted the Republican Cramton to take the lead, "watched [for] their cue," and never sought to "embarrass" him but also "never failed to deliver" when their support was needed. The reapportionment of the legislature in 1953 may also have been a factor, since it contributed to the increase of Democratic representation in the House from 34 of 100 members in 1953 to 51 of 100 members in 1955, and to the far more modest increase in the number of Democratic senators from 8 of 32 to 11 of 34 during the same years. Most important, probably, was Williams's big victory in the 1954 gubernatorial election, his plurality increasing from 8,618 votes in 1952 to 253,008 in 1954, the Democratic sweep of the statewide offices in the 1954 election, and the party's strong showing in the 1955 spring election.[68]

In choosing the Democratic members of the FEPC, Williams recognized the role that labor and religious groups had played in securing the legislation. He thus selected Alex Fuller, a member of the executive board of the Michigan NAACP and executive vice president of the Wayne County CIO Council; the Reverend John M. Finnegan, pastor of St. Patrick's Catholic Church in Detroit; and Sidney M. Shevitz, an attorney who had served three terms as president of the Jewish Community Council of Detroit. The Republican members the governor appointed were Anne P. Cook, a school board member who had supported fair employment legislation; Harry J. Kelly, manager of industrial relations of the American Seating Company of Grand Rapids and director of the Grand Rapids Employers' Association; and Dr. Chester A. McPheeters, minister of the Metropolitan Methodist Church of Detroit and a former president of the Detroit Council of Churches.[69]

During the approximately eight years of its existence, the FEPC sought faithfully to implement the statute that had created it, and it encouraged employers voluntarily to adhere to the principle of merit employment. Its jurisdiction and powers were, however, limited; it lacked strong state legislative support; and it was dealing with a difficult problem. Its success, though real, would prove to be somewhat limited.

3

"A SMALL BEGINNING":
Fair Employment
Practices, 1955–1963

As the Fair Employment Practices Commission (FEPC) was about to assume its duties, a report to the governor by the Michigan Employment Security Commission (MESC) revealed the dimensions of the employment discrimination problem in the key Detroit labor market. Of the job openings for male workers as of June 25, 1955, one-half were for whites only, although 26 percent of the male job applicants were black. Employers specified that many of the jobs available were for males only, even though women were well trained and fully qualified for these jobs. Fifty-eight percent of the jobs available for females were restricted to white women at a time when 24 percent of the women job applicants were black. Most employers also specifically defined "age hiring ranges," and only 10 percent of the employers were willing to hire workers more than forty-five years of age. Although 7 percent of the male applicants for jobs were physically handicapped, only 2.3 percent of the employers using the MESC were prepared to hire such workers.

The problem of race discrimination in employment was less serious in outstate Michigan and in the Upper Peninsula than in the Detroit area because of the much lower concentration of African Americans outside the Detroit labor market. Even in one small labor market in the Lower Peninsula, however, eleven of twelve employers confined their job listings to "whites only," even though only nine nonwhite residents were members of the labor force in that job market. The MESC survey not only revealed the extent of the problem the FEPC faced in dealing with racial discrimination, over which it had jurisdiction, but also indicated the limitations of the law under which it operated since the measure did not prohibit discrimination because of sex, age, or physical handicap.[1]

Before the new FEP Act went into effect on October 14, 1955, the members of the commission whom Williams had appointed selected Sidney Shevitz as their acting chairman. The governor urged the commission to pursue an "aggressive program" and to select a staff from among the state's racial and minority groups to the extent that civil service rules and regulations permitted. Authorized by the FEP Act to appoint a full-time director and a staff, the commission chose Louis Friedlander, a Wayne State University associate professor of public administration, as the agency's temporary director and selected a staff of ten professionals and seven clerks. Responding to the governor's advice and practicing what it preached, the commission appointed a staff that included several blacks, a Protestant, a Catholic, and a Jew.[2]

In December 1955, after a nationwide search, the FEPC appointed John G. Feild as the commission's executive director. Feild had served as executive secretary of the Toledo Board of Community Relations and had then been elected president of the National Association of Intergroup Relations Officials. A native of Detroit, he had once been a field representative of the city's Mayor's Interracial Committee and had been active in Williams's 1948 gubernatorial campaign. As deputy director the commission selected William Seabron, who had been active in the Urban League in Detroit and Minneapolis during the preceding eleven years. An FEPC field representative later recalled that Feild was "a man with an idea a minute" and that Seabron was "a dignified and gregarious man, the elder statesman of the staff."[3]

Harry Kelly succeeded Shevitz as FEPC chairman in March 1958, and Alex Fuller was elected vice chairman. Fuller then succeeded to the commission chairmanship, to be followed by Louis Rosenzweig, who had been serving as a commission member. Feild resigned late in 1958 to become special assistant for legislative affairs to Michigan Senator Philip Hart. Feild later became director of the Community Relations Service of the U.S. Conference of Mayors. He was succeeded as the FEPC's executive director on June 7, 1959, by Frederick B. Routh, a New York University Ph.D. in human relations who had been serving as head of the Southern Regional Council. Feild described Routh, who had been born in Wyandotte, Michigan, in 1924, as "among the half-dozen outstanding persons" in the nation in the area of fair employment. Routh resigned his position on April 11, 1962, to become executive director of the National Association of Intergroup Relations Officials. Although he appraised the FEPC as "the best Commission" of its type in the nation, he informed Governor John B. Swainson that he was resigning because of his "increasing frustration" with the refusal of the state legislature

Fair Employment Practices Commission, 1958.
Left to right, Alex Fuller, Louis Rosenzweig, Harry J. Kelley,
John G. Feild.
Courtesy Michigan State Archives.

"to move ahead in the area of civil rights and civil liberties." He was succeeded by Edward N. Hodges, an African American who had served as the commission's director of conciliation and claims coordinator from the FEPC's beginning. Soon thereafter Seabron was replaced as deputy director by Mitchell Tendler.[4]

The FEPC's professional staff remained at its original size of ten despite a growing caseload and the commission's assumption of increased responsibilities. Asserting that experience had demonstrated "a significant relationship" between the rapidity with which the agency could process a claim and "the quality of the adjustment," the FEPC sought funding after its first year for two additional field representatives. The legislature, however, rejected the request, as it would similar requests during the life of the FEPC. The commission was so strapped for funds that the commissioners themselves had to supplement the FEPC's meager budget from their own pockets. The FEPC lost four staff members in its first year because of its low salaries. All four were eventually to become directors of important government agencies.

Lack of staff and staff turnover slowed the work of the commission and weakened its "enforcement thrust." Routh thus advised Williams in August 1960 that the 120 claims that were then pending were about double the "desirable number at any one time." New York, which probably had the strongest fair employment agency and a black population about twice the size of Michigan's, had a professional staff of eighty and a budget of $980,000 in 1960 for its commission, as compared to Michigan's staff of ten and a budget of $148,000. Yet even the New York budget and staff were "not fully adequate" to deal with employment discrimination in that state.[5]

The FEPC not only suffered from lack of budget and staff, but it also believed that its effectiveness could be increased if certain changes were made in its governing act. It would have liked the FEP Act to cover employers with as few as four rather than eight employees, bringing Michigan more in line with the laws of those states that covered employers with six or fewer employees. It also wanted to have the authority to initiate complaints, subpoena documents and witnesses, and have appeals from its decisions governed by certiorari rather than being tried de novo. If it had initiatory power, as six of the twelve states with fair employment commissions did by 1959, the FEPC believed that it would be able to survey employment practices in particular industries and make appropriate recommendations as a result. The lack of subpoena power, it claimed, "impeded expeditious processing of complaints." The commission wanted the time limit for the filing of complaints extended from ninety days to six months. And finally, the FEPC wanted its jurisdiction expanded to encompass housing, education, and public accommodations, since, as Routh put it, it was "impossible to solve the problems of integration in employment . . . without touching the problems of the other three." Nine of the twelve states with commissions in 1959 had the broader jurisdiction that the FEPC sought in vain for itself.[6]

As soon as the FEP Act became effective, the commission called on public and private employers, labor organizations, employment agencies, and all organizations concerned with employment to become familiar with the act's requirements. It advised them to review their employment practices and policies to ascertain if they conformed to the law, to consult with the commission regarding the act and their existing and proposed employment policies, and to adopt employment policies and practices consistent not only with the letter of the law but also with its spirit.

The commission assured employers that it would not "hit [them] over the head" but would proceed rather by mediation and education. "We are not out to wield a stick," one commissioner declared. The commission opened temporary offices in Detroit and Lansing, and it began to consult with Assistant Attorney General Gerald D. White regarding rules for processing complaints and conducting hearings. It adopted its Official Rules of Procedure early in February 1956 following a public hearing in which seventy union representatives, employers, and attorneys participated. The rules were then approved by the state's attorney general and signed by the governor.[7]

The FEPC saw itself as having three roles: providing education and community services, conducting research, and processing complaints. Its program of education and community service was designed to secure voluntary compliance with the law by influencing public opinion to support merit employment. The commission sought at the same time to make employers, labor organizations, and employment agencies aware of their responsibilities and to make citizens aware of their rights under the statute. The hope was to develop a realization that merit employment was "not only morally right" but was also "economically sound and socially desirable, that restrictive practices tend not only to depress the lives of individuals and their families but are a community blight," and that merit employment could generate "community growth." Like similar agencies in other states, the FEPC saw the "educational process" as "the main support of its program to achieve employment on merit."[8]

The FEPC's education program involved community-wide meetings, neighborhood employment and industry-wide conferences, meetings with a variety of groups, and efforts to spur the vocational training, counseling, and preparation of minority youth for employment. Its surveys of major industries and communities were designed to provide a picture of them insofar as employment opportunities for minority-group members were concerned. After its initial surveys of some communities, the FEPC concluded that a good deal of job discrimination was due to "error without intent—an outgrowth of custom and tradition rather than conscious policy." This state of affairs, it believed, had produced "attitudes of futility" among minority- group members and had led them not to bother to apply for particular jobs. The commission discovered that every community had an "employment system" of which individuals had to become a part if they were to have equal opportunity for employment. The FEPC's education and community service activities sought to deal with aspects of this "system" in an effort to increase employment based on merit.[9]

The first of the FEPC's neighborhood employment conferences was held on Detroit's west side in 1956. Sponsored by the FEPC and eighty-four other organizations, including the Detroit Urban League (DUL), business and industrial organizations, unions, and schools, the conference produced information on employment practices and trends, acquainted neighborhood leaders with programs and facilities enabling minority-group youth and the unemployed to gain "effective skills" through academic and technical training, and encouraged these leaders to disseminate this information to the members of their organizations and the general community. The FEPC staff had met with DUL representatives before the conference to share information in an effort to strengthen relationships between the two organizations.[10]

The industry-wide conferences were designed not only to increase awareness of fair employment practices but also to lead to the adoption of voluntary programs to achieve merit employment. The FEPC held such conferences over the years with private employment agencies, bank and insurance company executives and personnel, hotel and restaurant employers, taxicab companies in the Detroit area, and over-the-road and city trucking firms in Grand Rapids. These conferences were supplemented by informational luncheon meetings in various cities designed to acquaint representatives of business organizations, labor unions, government, religious organizations, and minority groups with the fair employment philosophy and the "partnership approach" of the FEPC, to find solutions for local employment problems, and to offer FEPC services to aid the effort.

The commission met with high school government students and held a press conference with the editors of high school newspapers to explain merit employment and the "processes and services" of state government. It sponsored a conference on training and vocational opportunities in Flint to provide community leaders with information about job trends, employment standards, and training opportunities, and organized a youth motivational conference for high school students in the same city. It met with the vocational education directors and the cooperative education and apprentice coordinators of the Michigan school system. FEPC representatives appeared on television and spoke on the radio, the commission provided "bus cards" for public vehicles in various cities to advertise fair employment, and it issued a variety of publications.[11] There is no doubt about the seriousness with which the FEPC viewed its educational responsibilities.

The FEPC program of research was "action oriented." It was designed to help the commission get to know the communities in which it operated by becoming familiar with the patterns of minority-group employment and ascertaining the effectiveness of the complaint process. The research included community profiles of Grand Rapids, Kalamazoo, Lansing, and Muskegon that dealt with factors relating to manpower particularly as they affected minority-group members. The profiles helped the FEPC to devise appropriate programs and services for the communities involved. An FEPC field investigator referred to the community surveys as "sort of 'quick and dirty' social profiles of the locality, with emphasis on . . . the decision makers and the opinion moulders."

The FEPC research program also included pilot studies of occupational choice and integrated workforces; a seminar on economic and social mobility in an urban community; a high school dropout study; a comparative analysis of the values, attitudes, and school achievement of black and white youths; a pilot study of policies and practices with respect to the integration of blacks by selected employers, unions, and employment agencies; and a study of employer use of nonwhites in the Detroit area. The FEPC's Research and Survey Division also made periodic analyses of the FEPC's claims operation. Frances R. Cousens, the FEPC's director of research, referred to these claims studies, with some justice, as "rather pedestrian" and as suffering from a lack of "any type of evaluation."[12]

Authorized by the FEP Act to set up advisory councils in different communities, the commission selected Grand Rapids, Kalamazoo, Lansing, and Muskegon as the sites for such councils. These cities were chosen because they "differed considerably in their economic base as well as community structure and population characteristics." The commission did not establish an advisory council in Flint, but it did work with local organizations to develop particular projects there. The councils, whose membership varied from twenty-nine to thirty-five, were designed to include a cross section of the community leadership and to serve as a vehicle for examining employment discrimination in the community and to devise plans to deal with it. The chairman of the council was usually "someone from the 'power structure' of the locality." The FEPC provided the councils with staff services, but they were "largely autonomous" in character.

Like the FEPC itself, the advisory councils conducted surveys of various sorts; held employer, trade union, school administration, retailer, training and vocational opportunity, and motivational conferences; and surveyed employment, training, placement, and "aspirational patterns" in the community. The aim was "to bring peer pressure" on those who made employment decisions and to create a climate in which merit employment would become the "community norm" and thereby reduce the need for FEPC regulation. The FEPC deputy director concluded in 1961, however, that the councils "fell far short" of what had been expected of them.[13]

In its role of processing complaints of employment discrimination, the FEPC decided to use the term "claims" rather than "complaints" as a "less pejorative" term for charges of discrimination by employers, employment agencies, and labor organizations. When a claim was filed with the commission, the FEPC chairman assigned it, on a rotating basis, to one of the commissioners, who was assisted by staff personnel in evaluating the claim. If the investigating commissioner decided that there was insufficient evidence to support the claim, he recommended to the full commission that the claim be dismissed. If, on the other hand, the investigating commissioner found "probable cause" to substantiate the claim, he attempted to eliminate the discriminatory employment practice by "conciliation and persuasion."[14]

The purpose of the conciliation conference, which was "a closed, confidential meeting," was to seek to arrive at an agreement with the respondent to correct the discriminatory action. The conference involved the respondent and his representative or representatives, the investigating commissioner, the commission staff member dealing with the case, the FEPC's director of conciliation, and its executive or deputy director. The name of the respondent was kept confidential at this stage of the proceedings. The conciliation conference was based on the premise that problems of employment discrimination could be "settled in candid, straightforward and open-minded discussion across the conference table, in an atmosphere of peaceful negotiation, giving full consideration to the equities of the claimant and the respondent."

Following the conciliation process, the investigating commissioner recommended to the full commission either approval of the agreed-upon adjustment of the claim or its dismissal. This was followed by commission action on the recommendation. The adjustments made provided for continued FEPC contact with the claimant and the respondent to determine if the terms of the settlement were being observed, especially if the settlement called for granting the claimant the next vacancy in the respondent's firm. The FEPC's intention was to conduct a three- to six-month review of all adjusted claims. The commission did conduct some adjustment reviews, but it did not have sufficient staff to follow up most adjustments—a common problem in the states with fair employment agencies.[15]

If conciliation failed and there appeared to be "probable cause" for commission action, the FEPC forwarded the claim for evaluation to the assistant attorney general working with the commission. The claimant and respondent were then notified that a public hearing would be held on the claim, a rare event in the history of the Michigan FEPC and the other state fair employment agencies. The hearing was conducted by a hearing commissioner or a panel of commissioners. After the hearing, the full commission examined the evidence and then issued an order either dismissing the claim or ordering the respondent to "cease and desist" the practice complained of and to take appropriate action regarding the claimant. Depending on the case, employer respondents were ordered to offer the claimant immediate employment with or without back pay (the most common order in Michigan and elsewhere), to consider the claimant for the next vacancy, to correct company application forms, and, for a government agency respondent, to grant the claimant a civil service hearing. Employment agencies were ordered not to accept discriminatory job orders or to adopt a policy of referral based solely on the qualifications of applicants. Unions were ordered to admit the claimant to membership or, more commonly, to base referrals for jobs solely on merit. The ability of Michigan and other state fair employment agencies to issue enforceable orders was, of course, critical to their success.

The FEPC's procedures were unusual in that whereas the other state fair employment agencies, with the exception for a time of New Jersey, issued public findings of probable cause *before* conciliation was undertaken, that finding and the revelation of the respondent's name occurred in Michigan only *after* conciliation had failed. Michigan adopted this procedure in the belief that "early confrontation and loss of privacy" reduced the chances of successfully resolving a claim, whereas confidentiality could be offered as a "reward" to the respondent were the conciliation process to prove successful. One result of the FEPC procedure, one staff member pointed out, was that the Michigan commission had "less to show" for its efforts than if it had followed the more common state agency procedure in dealing with claims.[16]

The FEPC at its outset released a Pre-Employment Inquiry Guide that informed employers that it would henceforth be illegal for them to seek information from job applicants regarding their birthplace, parents, color, religion, and clubs and societies to which they belonged. Applicants for employment could not be asked to submit birth certificates, photographs of themselves, or naturalization papers. The commission thus rejected a request by the Jackson, Michigan, public schools to permit the photographing of job applicants after they had been interviewed but before a decision was made as to their employment, a request by the Michigan Board of Nursing that its application form be permitted to include the banned information, and a request by the Barbers State Board of Examiners that application forms for barbers include a question about color. The commission granted "partial exemption certificates" to employers with defense contracts governed by national security regulations permitting them to ask prospective employees about their citizenship and birth if this was a "bona fide occupational qualification."[17]

71

Lest the keeping of records affect promotions of minority group employees, the FEPC also barred retention of post-employment records that included the kind of information forbidden in pre-employment inquiries. When the commission found it necessary to determine the number of black employees in a particular job category, it initially relied on a head count conducted on a visual basis. Its rule of thumb in doing so, its chairman reported, was "if they are so light you cannot tell by looking, they do not count" as black. At the end of 1962, however, the FEPC ruled that post-employment records including race could be kept by employers so that the commission could determine "progress in fair hiring and promotion practices." Hodges specifically permitted the Michigan Highway Department, the Wayne County Road Commission, and the city of Detroit to follow this practice.[18]

FEPC rules prohibited the use by employers of employment agencies known to represent only one group of workers. This raised questions about the job placement efforts of the DUL. The commission ruled that the DUL could continue its existing program but that it should remove any literature indicating that its services were "exclusively" for one group and also that its staff should henceforth be available to serve all those with employment problems. The FEPC, however, did not object to the DUL's advising employers regarding the use of techniques that could aid in the employment of qualified minority-group workers. DUL representatives and the FEPC professional staff met periodically to ascertain the progress being made in the placement of African Americans in firms that had previously excluded them.[19]

Since several Michigan municipalities had created agencies to deal with fair employment, the question arose regarding their jurisdiction as compared to that of the FEPC. Attorney General Paul Adams resolved the matter on May 22, 1958, ruling that the FEP Act "preempted the field" and superseded local ordinances dealing with employment discrimination. The FEPC, however, advised local agencies that they could continue to play an educational role regarding fair employment and could be of "valuable assistance" to the FEPC in this respect. Quite apart from the issue of jurisdiction, Routh thought the preemption doctrine justified because the local agencies, in his view, had been "completely ineffective."[20]

During its approximately eight years of existence—it was replaced on January 1, 1964, by the Michigan Civil Rights Commission—the FEPC processed 2,048 claims, an average of 256 per year. About half of the claims of discrimination (1,018) involved hiring, and about 27 percent (568), discharge. Other types of discrimination alleged by claimants involved conditions of employment (181), referrals (148), upgrading (101), union membership (23), layoffs (18), and disciplinary action (4).

Race was the issue in about 94 percent (1,924) of the claims, religion in 78 claims, and national ancestry in 46 claims.

About 40 percent (812) of the respondents were commercial firms, and about 36 percent (752) were industrial firms. Government agencies were the respondents in 259 claims (about 12.5 percent of the total), unions in 121 claims, and employment agencies in 99 claims. The percentage of claims involving government agencies was more than double the percentage of workers in the state employed by such agencies. According to an FEPC field representative, this may have been because public officials were simply less cooperative than other types of respondents in reacting to allegations of discrimination processed by the FEPC. It is more likely, however, that blacks in particular had "greater expectations" of receiving fair treatment from public than from private employers and were consequently more likely to file claims against government agencies and more likely to believe that they would succeed in doing so when they thought they had been the victims of discrimination.

The Detroit metropolitan area was the location of about 70 percent of the claims, explained by the fact that about 80 percent of the state's minority-group population was located there, the relatively high number of jobs in the area, "the complexity and magnitude of the [area's] economy," and the allegedly "greater group awareness and community organization" there than elsewhere in the state. About two-thirds (1,322) of the claimants were between the ages of twenty-one and forty, about 83 percent (1,690) had completed high school, and about 20 percent (414) had had some college education. The typical claimant was a black male between the ages of twenty-one and forty who had been born in the South but had lived most of his life in the North and had been educated there, had graduated from high school, and claimed discrimination in applying for a semiskilled job.[21]

Of the 2,048 claims, 37 percent (708) were adjusted, and orders were issued in 13 instances following public hearings. The Michigan FEPC rate of adjustment compared with a 32 percent average rate for the other states with fair employment agencies. Just about half (1,105) of the claims were dismissed for lack of probable cause, 51 because of lack of jurisdiction, and 46 for other reasons. The reasons for a finding of lack of probable cause might have been that the claimant was not qualified to fill the particular job, the job had already been filled by a qualified applicant before the claimant filed his claim, the claimant did not follow required procedures in applying for the job, the claimant's record did not warrant his promotion, or the claimant had been disciplined for violation of rules, not because of race, religion, or ancestry. The commission might have lacked jurisdiction because the respondent firm had fewer than eight employees or the claimant had filed the claim after the ninety-day deadline. Claimants withdrew 57 claims, and 68 claims were pending when the FEPC gave way to the Civil Rights Commission.[22]

The number of claims did not in itself indicate the extent of job discrimination with which the FEPC had to deal. Individuals might not have been aware of discriminatory practices affecting them, might have been unaware of their rights under the law, or might have feared retaliation if they complained about not being promoted or about one or another aspect of their job. Sometimes respondents adjusted claims voluntarily before the commission processed them. Sometimes the FEPC found that a particular claimant had not been the victim of discrimination, but it nevertheless found "patterns of exclusion or other discriminatory practices" involving particular respondents. Hodges consequently concluded that the number of claims filed should be seen "more as a symptom . . . than as a diagnosis of the condition."[23]

Some claims adjusted by the FEPC led to the employment of nonwhites for the first time in a variety of business enterprises. Among the "firsts" were a field investigator in a large national financial concern with thirty-eight offices in Michigan, sales and managerial personnel in a large department store, a salesman in a national chain of shoe stores with sixteen outlets in Michigan, a salesman in a multi-million-dollar sporting goods company, a salesman and managers in a large department store that had previously employed blacks only as janitors or elevator operators, an adjuster in an auto insurance firm, and the first black apprentice accepted by a "highly skilled" craft union. Sometimes an adjusted claim served to secure a position not only for an aggrieved individual but also for others who were "similarly situated." The adjustment of a single claim of a black clerical worker against a large insurance company with two thousand employees in Michigan thus led not only to the employment of the claimant but also to jobs for seven additional black clerical workers. As the result of a claim processed in Michigan, a nationwide business training school not only began referring graduates on a nondiscriminatory basis but also adopted the same merit employment policy across the nation. Sometimes an adjustment not only dealt with the "specific relief" of a claimant but also referred to employment "patterns and practices" in a particular firm or industry.[24]

Among the claims processed by the FEPC during the eight years of its existence, several stand out: Checker Cab, William Ragland, Joan Lesniak, River Rouge Savings Bank, Irene B. Ellison, and Marlene E. White. Discrimination cases involving the Michigan Highway Department and the racetrack industry were also of particular importance. The Checker Cab case originated in the complaint of six blacks that the company had denied them employment as drivers because of their race.

The company did not cooperate with the FEPC in its investigation of the claim and denied the commission access to records that it had requested. The FEPC then scheduled its first public hearing for September 1957, but just before the hearing was completed, the company asked that it be adjourned and agreed to the conciliation of the claim. Checker Cab then agreed to interview the claimants as candidates for employment. It offered positions to the two claimants who had not in the meantime taken other jobs and agreed to subscribe to a policy of merit employment. The company soon hired additional blacks, and by the end of January 1960 about three hundred of the company's more than one thousand drivers were black, whereas there had been no black drivers prior to the conciliation agreement. The company was "startled to discover" that its receipts actually increased after it began hiring black drivers. Michigan employers, the FEPC chairman subsequently declared, had "discovered . . . that their fears and fantasies of financial setback, production disruption, revolution and assorted mayhem" as the result of integrating their workforce had been "wholly unfounded."[25]

William Ragland was an employee of Detroit's Department of Water Supply who alleged in January 1957 that the department maintained racially segregated locker facilities. While the FEPC was examining the claim, the department discharged Ragland, who then filed a second claim alleging that the discharge was in retaliation for his filing the original claim. The department maintained that the dismissal was due to Ragland's excessive absences from work, tardiness, and "work attitude." When it became clear that the matter could not be resolved by conciliation, the claimant having died in the meantime, the commission ordered a public hearing and then ruled that the discharge had been in violation of the FEP Act and that the department should make a back pay settlement with the Ragland estate from the date of his death, should cease all discriminatory practices, and should inform its employees that they could turn to the FEPC without fear of department retaliation.

Continuing to resist, the Department of Water Supply, which had refused to supply the FEPC documents it had requested, appealed to a state circuit court for a jury trial of the case de novo. The state claimed that the department was not entitled to a trial de novo but only to the type of review afforded when there was an appeal from a circuit court to the state supreme court, that is, an appeal "for all practical purposes" by certiorari. The Department of Water Supply's appeal was still pending in May 1962, when the city of Detroit, after the issue raised by the department's appeal had been settled in the FEPC's favor in another case, agreed to pay Ragland's estate $3,250. Mayor Jerome Cavanagh also issued an order forbidding discrimination in city employment, and the Department of Water Supply informed its employees that they could complain to the FEPC without fear of retaliation.[26]

Joan Lesniak filed a claim on September 1, 1959, against the Wayne County Civil Service Commission, her former employer, for failing to reinstate her on an employment eligible list as of July 29, 1959, because of her nationality and ancestry. The respondent claimed that Lesniak had resigned voluntarily and had "a long record of mental illness." It asserted that it would not place her on the eligible list unless she could provide evidence of recovery from her illness. When the FEPC concluded that there was "insufficient grounds" to sustain the Lesniak claim, she appealed the commission decision to the Wayne County Circuit Court. Since her appeal included many allegations not included in her original claim to the FEPC, the court viewed the case as an appeal for a hearing de novo. The state's attorney general moved on behalf of the FEPC to dismiss the appeal, claiming that a hearing de novo would constitute a "usurpation of administrative and legislative functions in violation of the separation of powers doctrine" of the state constitution.

The circuit court denied the FEPC motion, leading the commission to appeal the decision to the Michigan Supreme Court. In a unanimous decision on November 30, 1961, the supreme court, concluding that although part of one section of the FEP Act called for a trial de novo on appeal, the rest of that section and another section of the act pointed in the opposite direction, ruled that the intent of the legislation was "to grant an appeal in the nature of certiorari." As the FEPC noted, the effect of the supreme court decision was that when a claimant appealed a commission finding of no probable cause, the commission was to take testimony on the record, which would then be available to the appropriate court in the event of an appeal. The decision thus resolved a matter that had been in dispute since the passage of the FEP Act. It also led the commission to approve a change in its rules permitting a claimant whose claim had been denied by the commission to file for a reconsideration and to secure a public hearing.[27]

Loy A. Cohen, a young African American with a business administration degree, filed a claim with the FEPC on December 14, 1959, alleging that the River Rouge Savings Bank had denied him a position as a teller because of his race. After denying Cohen a job, the bank hired two white tellers without college degrees. The River Rouge and Ecorse branch of the NAACP had for sometime been picketing the bank, located in a black neighborhood, in an effort to persuade it to hire blacks. In the FEPC's view, however, the NAACP's objective was "something less than employment on the basis of merit." The commission's effort to resolve the claim by conciliation failed, the bank denying that it had discriminated against Cohen and claiming that he had not filed a job application or, if he had, it had been lost. After a public hearing beginning on November 10, 1959, the FEPC ordered the bank to hire Cohen as a teller, cease its discriminatory hiring policies, and post a written policy of nondiscrimination satisfactory to the FEPC. The bank appealed the FEPC order to the Wayne County Circuit Court, seeking a trial de novo. When Judge James Montante denied the appeal, the bank took its case to the Michigan Supreme Court, which denied the application. The case was finally settled at the end of 1963 after the FEPC had found Cohen's allegedly missing job application. Although not admitting discrimination, the bank agreed to adopt a written policy of nondiscrimination, interpret it to employees and recruitment sources, and reimburse Cohen, who by then was self-employed, $500 for the expenses he had incurred in pursuing his claim.[28]

Irene B. Ellison filed a claim on February 23, 1959, alleging that she had been denied a position of admitting clerk at the Highland Park General Hospital because of her race even though she had passed a civil service examination for the position. After she filed the claim, the hospital hired her as a clerk-typist, a higher-paying job than that of admitting clerk. The FEPC nevertheless processed the claim as involving possible discrimination. After failing to resolve the matter by conciliation, the commission found probable cause for the complaint and scheduled a public hearing for December 13, 1959. Joined by the city of Highland Park and the Highland Park Civil Service Board, the hospital thereupon filed an appeal in the Wayne County Circuit Court challenging the constitutionality of the FEP Act. The circuit court upheld the act's constitutionality, as did the Michigan Supreme Court, on appeal, in a decision handed down on November 30, 1961. The FEPC then decided on a public hearing of the claim, but Ellison by then had moved from Highland Park and was no longer eligible for civil service employment there. The FEPC consequently had no choice but to dismiss the complaint.[29]

Marlene E. White, in the FEPC's first case involving an airline, filed a claim against Northwest Airlines in March 1958 alleging that she had been denied a position as stewardess because of her race. The company at the time had been refusing to hire blacks and other minority-group members for the flight cabin, claiming that their employment might adversely affect "turnover points, housing problems and customer relations," especially in the southern states. In this case, Northwest claimed that White's hips were too wide by airlines standards for "walking up and down an airplane aisle." This contention led to much merriment among FEPC employees and the offers of volunteers to measure the claimant's hips. During the course of the investigation of the White claim, the commission investigator did indeed compare White's hip measurement with those of Northwest Airlines stewardesses and found no basis for the company's allegation.

Following a lengthy FEPC investigation and many informal meetings between the company and the commission, Northwest hired White as a statistical clerk and then as a reservations clerk. After a series of conciliation conferences in 1960 had failed to resolve the original complaint, the FEPC held a public hearing on February 21, 1962, and determined that Northwest Airlines had rejected White as a stewardess because of her race. The commission ordered the company to abandon its discriminatory practices and to enroll White in its next training class for stewardesses. The company complied, and White soon began to take her regular turn as a stewardess. Northwest a short time later hired a second black stewardess.[30]

In January 1961, Representative Roger B. Townsend, a Flint Democrat, called for the creation of a House committee to investigate alleged discrimination in hiring and promotions by the Michigan Highway Department. Highway Commissioner John C. Mackie denied the charge point by point and called for an FEPC investigation of the matter. There was discussion within the Swainson administration as to how to proceed in the affair, particularly because of the importance of the politically powerful Highway Department, the state government's largest employer, concern about the NAACP reaction, and because of the lack of respect for the black legislator making the charge against the department. In the end, the administration decided to go ahead with the FEPC probe.[31]

The commission made an extensive six-week investigation of the Highway case that consumed 960 hours of staff time. Routh, assisted by Seabron and Hodges, took personal charge of the investigation, and two racially integrated teams of field representatives devoted full-time to the matter. They interviewed management executives, supervisors, engineers, highway technicians, and department employees, including twenty-six African Americans, examined thousands of documents, and sent questionnaires to more than three thousand contractors and subcontractors. The investigation, the FEPC noted, was "without precedent" in Michigan. It culminated in a sixty-six-page report issued on March 19, 1961.[32]

The investigation revealed that the Highway Department did not have a written policy of nondiscrimination, nor did it appear that it had held staff meetings or staff conferences regarding the matter. The state's civil service merit system and its rules and regulations requiring a policy of nondiscrimination did, however, cover most of the jobs in the department. The investigation, indeed, revealed that a "de facto policy of non-discrimination" had been in effect in the department since 1957. Between 1933 and 1954, the department had hired no more than 2 blacks in any one year, but it had hired 4 in 1955, 8 in 1956 (the first full year that the FEP Act was in effect), 12 in 1957, 15 in 1958, 19 in 1959, and 17 in 1960. As of January 27, 1961, however, only 90 of 4,510 Highway employees (2 percent) were black, and of 253 employees in pay classifications higher than IIIA (about $10,105), none was black. There were a few blacks in supervisory positions in the department, but there was limited opportunity for African Americans to advance to such positions. The investigation, nevertheless, uncovered "no widespread practice of discrimination," and black employees indicated that there had been "a marked improvement" in terms of nondiscrimination since 1957.

Judging from its interviews with black employees, the commission concluded that whatever discrimination there might be in the department was at lower levels of supervision, not at the top. Black interviewees indicated that discrimination in housing and public accommodations in many sections of the state where jobs were available made employment of blacks in the Highway Department less likely than otherwise would have been the case. Although state government contracts had to contain a nondiscrimination clause, the Highway Department, the investigation revealed, had made no effort to enforce the requirement even though it regularly enforced other contract requirements. The FEPC concluded that the relatively small number of blacks in the department was due to that factor, the fact that recruitment of workers occurred in district offices in predominantly white communities in the state, and referral to jobs by largely white department personnel.

The FEPC recommended that the highway commissioner immediately issue "a clear, definitive, written policy of non-discrimination" that was to be communicated and explained to all supervisory personnel and distributed to all employees. The commissioner was also instructed to issue a written policy of nonretaliation against employees who made charges of discrimination to Highway Department management, the Civil Service Commission, or the FEPC. The department was advised to establish a program of orientation and training of supervisors at all levels of the department on the subject of merit employment; establish a section whose responsibility it would be to make "a systematic periodic review" of personnel practices, particularly with regard to merit employment; establish a procedure for the implementation and periodic review of the nondiscrimination clause in Highway Department contracts; review its "promotional potential rating procedures"; instruct district office managers and other relevant personnel to work with the local leadership in communities where housing and public accommodations limited black employment; and make a semiannual review of its nondiscriminatory program and report the results to the FEPC for the next two years.

In its wide-ranging report, the FEPC recommended that all state government agencies largely follow the commission recommendations for the Highway Department, and it urged the legislature to outlaw discrimination in housing, public accommodations, education, and recreational facilities and to appropriate sufficient funds for the FEPC to establish a contract compliance division to enforce the nondiscrimination clause in state government contracts. It recommended that the governor issue a code of fair practices for the executive branch of state government and all state government agencies, a recommendation, as we shall see, that Governor Swainson promptly implemented.[33]

Acting quickly, Mackie by the middle of September had implemented all of the FEPC's recommendations for his department. Swainson praised what had been done as "examples of the best kind of leadership and action in the area of human rights" and "a model for other departments in state government."[34]

After the Trade Union Leadership Council, an organization of trade unionists seeking to combat discrimination and promote civil rights, charged that discrimination had prevented blacks from obtaining other than menial positions in the state's racetrack industry, Swainson on April 21, 1961, asked the FEPC to investigate employment practices in the industry. Commission representatives explored the matter in meetings with representatives of the six racing associations in the state, the principal unions representing the industry's employees, and the major concessionaires in the industry. The racing associations reported that most of their employees were represented by a local of the Building Service Employees Union, which largely controlled hiring practices for most racetrack jobs by its referral system. Similar authority was exercised in their jurisdiction by the Teamsters, the Hotel and Restaurant Workers, and the Bartenders Union. Of the 1,826 employees of the six tracks, only 55 (3 percent) were nonwhite, and of the 587 employees of Sportservice concessionaires, 62 (11 percent) were nonwhite. The referral system had led to much "inbreeding" and the hiring of friends and relatives of existing employees. Although Michigan law required that 85 percent of track employees be residents of the state, the requirement had not been effectively enforced.

The FEPC recommended that the industry issue a formal, public written statement of nondiscrimination that was to be included in all requests to the unions for referral lists and was to be posted in all track hiring locations. The associations were also to accept applications from all job seekers and to fill all vacancies in accordance with the requirements of the FEP Act. Each union in the industry was to issue a public written statement of nondiscrimination regarding membership and referral practices, and the concessionaires were to issue a statement of nondiscrimination for all relevant job categories. All members of the industry were to provide equal opportunity for promotion and transfer for all of their employees and were to provide the Racing Commission annually for five years a list of all those employed during the racing season and to designate their job category, seniority date, and race. The lists were then to be referred to the FEPC. The legislature was asked to strengthen the requirements of the 85 percent rule.[35]

Beginning on March 20, 1962, the FEPC, in cooperation with the Racing Commission, held a series of meetings with the racetrack associations, the unions in the industry, and the concessionaires. The members of the industry then agreed on a declaration of policy that employment in the industry was to be open to all regardless of their race, religion, or nationality and that spelled out the steps to be taken to implement that policy. The opening of the 1962 racing season saw "the beginning of the dropping of the color bars" in those job categories from which blacks had previously been excluded. The FEPC asserted that, to its knowledge, this was "the first instance of an entire industry, anywhere in the United States, joining collectively and subscribing affirmatively to merit employment without regard to race, religion or nationality background."[36]

The issue of worker time off for religious holidays and religious observance "plagued" the FEPC for some time and became "a full-blown problem" in 1960. The commission in January 1961 set forth several criteria to be followed by employers and employees regarding this matter. The employer was to grant an employee's request if it was reasonable and timely, and failure to do so or taking disciplinary action against an employee for absence from work after denial of such a request was to be considered a violation of the FEP Act. If the employee's absence, on the other hand, would cause "serious disruption" of the employer's business, the employer was not required to approve the request. "Mere inconvenience or even serious inconvenience" caused the employer or co-workers by the employee's absence was not, however, deemed as sufficient cause for an employer to deny an employee request for time off for a religious holiday. The FEPC left it to the discretion of the employer whether to pay an employee for time absent from a job for religious reasons.[37]

Many employers complied with the FEP Act voluntarily without waiting for claims of discrimination to be brought against them. Within a few months of the statute's implementation, more than six hundred employers had asked for the FEPC's aid in the revision of their employment application forms. Many employers, without any prompting from the FEPC, drafted statements of employment policy prohibiting discrimination. Feild complimented newspapers for their "almost perfect

81

compliance" with the ban on publication of discriminatory "help wanted" ads. Both the Detroit Tigers baseball team and the Detroit Lions football team committed themselves in 1956 to a policy of merit employment. Governor Williams reported in 1960 that some of the largest corporations in the state had asked the FEPC what they must do to comply with the FEP Act, and one large auto company "completely rewrote its personnel manual" as a result. Sometimes negotiation regarding a single claim against a particular firm led to "a chain reaction resulting in unanticipated and sweeping changes in employee utilization."[38] The record of the Checker Cab Company is a case in point.

Well aware of the limitations of the individual complaint approach, the FEPC encouraged business firms to take affirmative action to increase minority employment. Affirmative action for the FEPC did not mean acceptance of racial quotas or racial preference in hiring. Its stress, the FEPC chairman informed a congressional committee, was on "individual rights," not "group rights." There was no such thing, he stated, as "white rights" or "Negro rights" but only "human rights and constitutional rights." Affirmative action for the FEPC meant such things as visits by job recruiters to black colleges to seek out potential employees and telling placement officers in colleges and universities of the desire of employers to interview qualified blacks.

Chrysler Corporation adopted an Affirmative Action to Implement Merit Employment Policy that an FEPC field representative appraised as "one of the most thorough and conscientious efforts to achieve an integrated work force at all levels of job classifications." The field representative nevertheless noted "the disappointing results" of this effort and the "obvious gaps" in the company's seemingly extensive recruitment procedures. She reported that the company had enjoyed more success in upgrading black employees, six of whom had been upgraded to foremen, than in recruiting new employees. General Motors, the state's largest employer, did not take any initiative to implement the FEP Act, a commission field representative reporting in 1961 that he could not recall a single instance in which the corporation had taken action regarding merit employment without "stimulation" by the FEPC.[39]

The FEPC sought to secure the voluntary adherence of employment agencies, not just of employers, to the requirements of merit employment. When it conferred in May 1957 with representatives of thirty private employment agencies, they "clearly recognized their stake in an 'open system'" and candidly admitted that it meant more fees for them. Those present recognized that "the most significant pool of underutilized skills" in the state was that of "the minority group clerical," but the agencies claimed that the job placement of this group was "the most difficult" for them. They indicated, however, that they had been able to place more minority applicants on the basis of merit since the FEP Act had gone into effect than before that time. The commission reported in 1961 that 82.5 percent of the private employment agencies had received job application forms from nonwhites by then and that 58 percent of the agencies had been able to place at least some of them. For 12 percent of the latter, this constituted their first nonwhite placements.[40]

When an American Jewish Committee survey in 1963 revealed that a large number of employment agencies in the Detroit area discriminated against blacks, Jews, and Catholics, the FEPC decided to use the information as "a useful tool and vehicle" to convince the private employment agency industry to agree to a firm commitment to eliminate bias in its operations. In a closed meeting on June 25, 1963, with eighty-five representatives of forty-five agencies, most of them in the Detroit area, the FEPC encountered some opposition from among those present but also "a greater willingness than in previous meetings to comply with the [FEP] law." Thirty-eight of the agencies signed a Declaration of Equal Employment Opportunity committing them to five actions: the issuance of "a clear, definitive policy of non-discrimination" that was to be disseminated regularly to agency supervisors and interviewers; refusal to accept any job orders based on race, color, religion, national origin, or ancestry rather than solely on "specifications of occupational fitness"; classification and referral of all qualified applicants based solely on occupational fitness; maintenance of applicant records and job orders without any kind of code indicating race, color, religion, national origin, or ancestry; and a "thorough review and re-evaluation" of all agency order-taking, classification, and referral procedures to ensure "complete compliance" with both the letter and the spirit of the FEP Act. The FEPC's executive director, Edward Hodges, hailed the action as "unprecedented in the private employment agency field."

In preparation for the June 25 meeting, the Michigan Private Employment Agency Association established a Human Relations Committee to work with the FEPC to eliminate discrimination in the private employment agency field. Some agencies outside Detroit added their signatures to the Declaration of Equal Employment Opportunity, seventy-six owners of eighty-five employment offices having done so by August 13. That number represented about 60 percent of the Class II agencies in the state, that is, agencies that did not deal exclusively with domestics and baby-sitters.[41]

The FEPC, of course, was concerned not only about the behavior of private employment agencies but also of the MESC and its Employment Service Division, which made about 16 percent of all job placements in the state as of 1955. The MESC had operated a Minority Groups Services Program since 1938. Initially concerned only with blacks, the program was broadened to include all minority groups following the issuance in June 1941 of President Franklin D. Roosevelt's Executive Order No. 8802. The MESC's policy was to treat all applicants seeking jobs, referrals, or other MESC services without discrimination. It carried on a program of training and retraining of staff members, and its Minority Groups Services consultant was authorized to examine any record in an MESC branch office, discuss employment problems with managers, supervisors, and agency employees, assist in the training program, and report the findings to the state administration with recommendations and "follow-up." It appears that no other state had such an arrangement at that time.[42]

Until 1950 an indication of race was kept on applicant cards and other MESC records, and the monthly placement reports included information on the number of applicants by race. The MESC leadership regarded this practice as "an excellent supervisory and training tool." At the request of "concerned community groups," however, the MESC removed race designations from all MESC forms. Tom Downs, whom Williams appointed to the commission in 1953, recalled in an interview, however, that when race could no longer be designated, commission staff would place a circle around a numeral on the cards of blacks as a means of identifying their race. This practice, Downs recalled, continued after the FEP Act went into effect even though the MESC director had forbidden the use of such designations. When Downs pointed out that the practice was a violation of the law, commission employees removed the circle with an ink eradicator, but since what had been done was evident on the cards, Downs insisted that the cards be recopied.[43]

Following enactment of the FEP Act, MESC Director Max Horton informed agency personnel that discriminatory orders were not to be accepted even if the jobs were for employers with fewer than eight employees and hence not covered by the act. If a hiring authority submitted a job order with discriminatory specifications, the order taker was to seek to persuade the employer involved to remove the restriction. If the effort of persuasion failed, the order taker was to report that fact to the Employment Service supervisor, who was to decide what additional steps to take. "Alleged or apparent violations" of the FEP Act were not, however, to be reported to the FEPC, since this at the time violated the non-disclosure-of-information policy required by the Michigan unemployment compensation law and the federal government's Bureau of Employment Security, which met part of the cost of the Employment Service in Michigan and of the similar agencies in other states. If it could not persuade an employer to abandon discriminatory specifications in a job order, MESC policy was to deny the employer the agency services but to take no further action. This was unlike the policy in New York and Wisconsin, where the state government equivalents of the MESC informed the state fair employment agency when they received such orders.[44]

In a policy statement of February 17, 1957, the MESC once again went beyond the requirements of the FEP Act by forbidding discrimination involving one of its own employees not just because of race, color, religion, or national ancestry but also because of sex, "organizational politics, or any other affiliation (except as . . . [might] be required by law), or any other factors not related to ability to do the job." The MESC Minority Groups Services was by then training branch and office staff to apply the provisions of the FEP Act, evaluating branch office services to minority-group workers, cooperating with other agencies and community groups in seeking to encourage the acceptance of workers on the basis of merit alone, and joining in the FEPC education program in the communities of the state.[45]

In July 1959 the FEPC and MESC agreed on a procedure for dealing with discrimination complaints submitted to the FEPC against the MESC as either an employer or a referral agency. The agreement provided that the FEPC was to forward such complaints to the director of the Employment Service Division. The Employment Service consultant assigned to Minority Groups Services was to gather the necessary information about each claim or inquiry and was to report the findings to the MESC director, who was to review the matter and transmit such reports as he deemed necessary to the FEPC. No branch office records, however, were to be made available to the FEPC. If it was dissatisfied with the MESC findings, the FEPC was to ask the MESC director for an additional investigation. The FEPC was to provide the MESC with information about the disposition of claims involving MESC employees or MESC activities.[46]

The arrangement between the FEPC and the MESC was modified in February 1960, the MESC yielding a bit of its independence. Henceforth, when the FEPC received a claim against the MESC in its role as a referral agency, representatives of the two commissions were to conduct an "on-the-spot investigation," and the MESC was to make available to the investigators all requested records to the extent that federal and state laws, regulations, and policies permitted. If probable cause to support the claim was found, personnel of the two agencies were to participate in a conciliation conference to see if they could agree on an adjustment. Any adjustment agreed to was not to constitute an admission of discrimination by the MESC or a finding of same by the FEPC. If an adjustment could not be reached by conciliation, the FEPC, if a majority of the commissioners agreed, was to arrange for a public hearing. The FEPC was then to provide the MESC with information regarding the FEPC's disposition of the claim. When the MESC was the respondent in a claim against it as an employer rather than as a referral agency, the FEPC was to process the claim in accordance with Civil Service Commission policies, which were similar to the procedures obtaining in claims against the MESC as a referral agency.[47]

When an FEPC field representative, in seeming conformity with the agreement between the two commissions, subsequently asked the MESC for a response to an employer's claim that the MESC had failed to refer blacks to him, Horton surprisingly charged that this violated the agreement between the two agencies. "We are not to be a policing arm of the FEPC," he complained to Routh. Since the records of the MESC did not refer to race, he asserted that it would be difficult, if not impossible, to provide the information requested. Horton insisted, moreover, that the information would prove nothing since even the total absence of black employees in a business firm did not in itself prove the existence of discrimination.

The director of Vocational Services of the DUL bluntly charged the MESC with discrimination in its referral policies, and Horace Sheffield, executive vice president of the Trade Union Leadership Council, agreed. There was, to be sure, pressure on the MESC and the similar agencies in other states to fill discriminatory job orders, since the federal government allocated funds to these agencies on the basis of the number of workers placed. Also, promotions within the agencies were often based on the number of placements by agency employees. Since it was easier to place white than nonwhite job applicants, this sometimes led to discrimination against blacks. "I get rated by the number of people I place," an MESC employee declared. "If I don't place enough, I get called upstairs. Therefore, I send people to places where I think they will be employed, and this means I send them by race." The director of one MESC branch told the U.S. Commission on Civil Rights that he discouraged an employer from requesting workers of "any color" by telling him, "You know darn well that you can't find 20 Niggers willing to work." It was undoubtedly the willingness of MESC leaders to fill discriminatory job orders if the agency could not persuade hiring authorities not to discriminate in their choice of workers that caused it to resist for so long the referral of discriminatory job orders to the FEPC.[48]

The FEP Act applied not only to the MESC as an employer but also to the entire state civil service and state government employees. In 1952, before the enactment of the FEP Act, the Civil Service Commission (CSC), allegedly at the request of the Vocational Services Department of the DUL, dropped reference to race and creed from applicant forms for state civil service examinations. Once the FEP Act went into effect, the CSC took steps to ensure that its hiring and contract practices conformed to the law. CSC rules prohibited discrimination not only for partisan reasons, as before, but also because of race, color, creed, national origin, and ancestry, as the FEP Act required. Civil service employees or applicants who believed themselves victims of discrimination could submit their claim to either the CSC or the FEPC, and FEPC decisions in such instances were subject to CSC review in accordance with "established procedures" since the FEPC did not have jurisdiction over the CSC as a constitutional agency.[49]

Pursuant to the FEP Act, the state Administrative Board on October 15, 1956, required that all contracts and subcontracts of the state government and its subdivisions contain a clause requiring contractors not to discriminate against employees or applicants for employment. Any breach of this "covenant" was to be regarded as "a material breach of contract." Detroit instituted its own contract compliance program in 1962. The FEP offered its services to the city government in the screening of city contractors to ensure observance of the FEP Act.[50]

On the recommendation of the FEPC and at the request of Governor Williams, the heads of thirty state boards and commissions met in the state executive office on August 6, 1957, to review state government personnel practices as affected by the FEP Act. Williams informed those present that he wanted the state government, the respondent by then in six complaints, to be "a model" for fair employment and to "keep pace with progressive practices in private industry." He urged state agencies to follow not only the letter of the law but its spirit as well and to take steps to ascertain if qualified minority-group members did not apply for state jobs because they assumed that they would be rejected. The CSC reported that it was making FEPC services available to the twenty-seven thousand state employees and all applicants for state employment. According to Frank Blackford, the executive secretary of the State Employees Retirement Board, there was actually "a great deal of racial discrimination" in the state civil service at that time. Blackford maintained that the CSC was not guarding against this "carefully enough" and was accepting "the merest arbitrary excuses" for the existence of discrimination.[51]

Williams instructed state agency heads in August 1959 to make certain from time to time that the state civil service was "in order" insofar as fair employment was concerned. Testifying at the end of 1960 before the U.S. Commission on Civil Rights, Routh reported that the state government record regarding fair employment was "pretty good."[52]

Enforcement of fair employment requirements in the state civil service was stepped up when John B. Swainson became Michigan's governor. Born in Windsor, Canada, on July 31, 1925, Swainson moved to Michigan two years later. After graduating from high school in Port

Huron, where he was captain of the school football team, Swainson at age eighteen enlisted in the U.S. Army. While serving with the 95th Infantry Division near Metz in France, Swainson lost both of his legs when the jeep in which he was riding struck a land mine. One leg was blown off immediately, and the other had to be amputated in a field hospital shortly thereafter.

After returning to the United States, Swainson received a law degree from the University of North Carolina in 1951. Two years later he was elected to the Michigan Senate, and then in 1956 he was chosen the Democratic Party's minority leader in that body. He was elected lieutenant governor in 1958 and then won the governorship in 1960, becoming the state's second-youngest person to hold that position. Swainson's public policy commitments as governor were largely similar to those of his immediate predecessor. He served only a single two-year term as governor, being defeated by Republican George Romney in the 1962 election.[53]

Soon after Swainson took office, the state administration decided, as the FEPC had recommended, to promulgate a Governor's Code of Fair Practices for state government employees. The code was the product of a draft by the FEPC and ensuing discussion between that agency and the CSC, and it incorporated to some extent practices and policies already in effect. "The existence of a fair employment practices act in our state," the code declared, "imposes a special responsibility on all agencies to keep their own houses in order. . . . State government, as an employer, has a responsibility to serve as a model of business, industry, labor, and private employment agencies." There was to be no discrimination in state employment with respect to recruitment, hiring, upgrading, conditions of employment, referral to training, or dismissal. State employees were to be appointed on the basis of "merit alone," and no state application or personnel form was to make a reference to race, religion, color, or national ancestry. Appointing authorities were to make a "special effort" to ensure that any flexibility they might have in selecting personnel was not used to limit the employment of minority-group persons. State facilities were to be free of segregation, were to be available without discrimination, and were not to be used to further discrimination.

The code required state agencies to "cooperate fully" with the FEPC, and constitutionally created agencies like the CSC were to work out agreements with the FEPC. State agencies like the Employment Service Division that were engaged in employment referral and placement were to fill jobs on a nondiscriminatory basis, to refuse to accept discriminatory job orders, and to refer such orders to the FEPC. This resolved the simmering dispute over this matter between the MESC and the FEPC

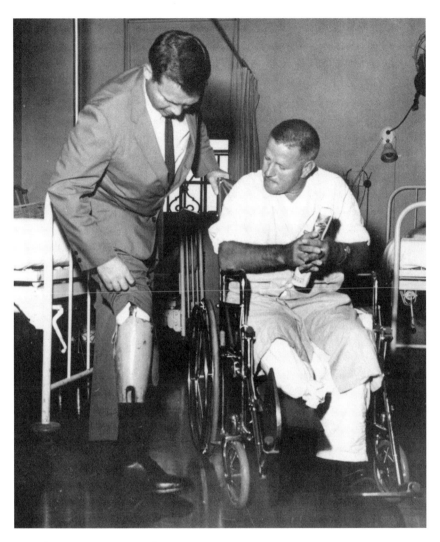

John B. Swainson (standing).
Courtesy Bentley Historical Library.

and followed the Bureau of Employment Security's withdrawal of its objection to the practice.

The code provided that there was to be no discrimination in the awarding of state licenses, and state licensing authorities were to take disciplinary action against licensers found to have discriminated. All state contracts and subcontracts were to include the provisions of the

89

FEP Act prohibiting discrimination in contracting and subcontracting. All state educational, vocational guidance, counseling, apprenticeships, on-the-job training programs, and all similar programs in which the state participated were to be open to all who qualified without discrimination. State financial assistance was to be denied applicants who discriminated and was to be withdrawn from recipients engaged in discrimination insofar as that was consistent with the statute under which the state agency involved operated. All state agencies were regularly to review their personnel practices and policies to ensure that they did not contribute to discrimination, and they were to emphasize the principle of nondiscriminatory employment in their programs of orientation and training. They were required to file annual reports of activities undertaken to effectuate the code and were to place a copy of the code in "prominent locations" in state facilities.[54]

The Governor's Code, as Routh noted, called on agency heads, in effect, to go beyond the mere processing of claims and to engage in "affirmative action." The code was soon reported to be "having a good effect on the thinking of many executives," but Max Horton, resistant to the end, expressed "shock" that the MESC—which, he reiterated, was not an "enforcement arm" of the FEPC—would henceforth have to inform that agency when the MESC received discriminatory job orders. The code, however, left the MESC with no choice in the matter, and it soon reported that it had "fully implemented" the code.[55]

Wayne State University, to which the code applied, sought the advice of the state's attorney general when the FEPC demanded that it provide the commission with a "racial census" of the university's nonacademic employees. The commission made the demand after a black university employee claimed that blacks did not have equal access to all nonacademic positions in the university. Asking "what constituted being a negro," the Wayne State Board of Governors was willing to permit the FEPC in processing the claim to make a visual survey of the employees involved but not a head count. Swainson, however, supported the FEPC decision to conduct the census by an employee questionnaire, which is what was done.[56]

Concerned that some state agencies had done little or nothing to implement the code, Swainson called the heads of state agencies together on November 27, 1961, "to show that he 'meant business'" about code enforcement. Following remarks by the governor and some federal officials who were present, there was a question-and-answer period during which state agency heads were "asked point blank" to discuss the status of their units with regard to employment opportunities and the provision of services. The meeting, the first of its type in any state according to the executive director of the U.S. Commission on Civil

Rights, who was present, made agency heads aware of what they could do "within the framework of the law" to eliminate discrimination in employment in their agency as well as in their provision of services, and it appears to have convinced those present that the governor, indeed, "meant business."[57]

In its first annual report regarding the code for the year 1961, the FEPC indicated that twenty-two claims of discrimination had been filed against eight different state agencies. None of the claims had been dismissed, eleven had been adjusted by the corrective action of the respondent, and two were pending. Swainson informed a subcommittee of the U.S. House of Representatives that the code had "spurred state action" to combat discrimination in state government employment. The state auditor general, in response to the code, went beyond the requirements of the law and the code, as the MESC had already done, by barring sex discrimination in his agency and, as a result, had hired the first woman auditor in the history of the state. The state adjutant general formed a personnel committee to implement the code and was able to report that, as of September 1, 1962, the once all-white Michigan National Guard included 25 black officers and 179 black enlisted men.[58]

The code remained in effect when George Romney succeeded Swainson as governor on January 1, 1963. That it did not command universal support among state agencies became evident when each state agency was asked to provide information on its compliance with the code as of July 1, 1963. Only sixty-six of the ninety-five state agencies even bothered to report, and the statements of many that did reply could only be described as "vague." Surprisingly, only forty-one of the sixty-six that replied indicated any awareness of the requirements of both the law and the code that state contracts were to be awarded on a nondiscriminatory basis. Eight departments provided information indicating that 1,052 of their 10,072 employees were nonwhite, but just about half (505) of these employees were in a single agency, the MESC, 21.2 percent of whose employees were nonwhite. Of the MESC nonwhite employees, 108 (21.3 percent) held professional positions, and the remainder were in clerical positions.[59]

The FEPC remained active in 1963, Romney's first year as governor, and, as we shall see, he was as staunch a supporter of the commission and the FEP Act as Williams and Swainson had been. Reaching beyond the state government, the FEPC in 1963 worked out an agreement with the Detroit Civil Service Commission regarding the processing of claims against city departments and the Detroit commission itself. The respondent in seventeen claims in 1963, the state CSC, for the first time in its history, ordered a complete study of nonwhite employment in the state service to ascertain the possible existence of discrimination, a study that was just getting under way as 1963 came to a close. Also in 1963, the FEPC issued a pictorial report of its accomplishments that attracted the attention of the U.S. Information Administration, which distributed the report internationally.[60]

It is difficult to measure the degree of success the FEPC enjoyed between 1955 and 1963 in lessening employment discrimination in Michigan. It is also difficult, if not impossible, to separate the effects of FEPC actions from other factors affecting employment patterns, such as automation (which had an especially adverse impact on black workers), the ups and downs of the business cycle, the decline in manufacturing jobs in the Detroit metropolitan area, the frequent lack of seniority among blacks with jobs, and the employment efforts of the DUL.

The FEPC was handicapped in what it could accomplish, as we have seen, because it could not initiate complaints, its budget and staff were limited, and it lacked lacked authority to deal with the "vocational development system." It may also be true to some degree, as Herbert Hill contended, that blacks, who were the principal victims of employment discrimination, were reluctant to file complaints with the FEPC since they did not believe that the likely results justified the effort. Although the MESC cooperated with the FEPC, it did not combat employment discrimination as vigorously as it might have. The head of its Civil Rights Section (the name MESC's Minority Groups Services took in December 1963) thus reported at the end of 1963 regarding MESC efforts in combating employment discrimination, "There have been break-throughs here and there in the past, but no concentrated drive, no great thrust, no heavy running against the tide of community patterns and opinions."[61]

The FEPC, to be sure, did achieve some significant employment gains for nonwhites: it was responsible for changes in the employment policies of the Highway Department, the racetrack industry, and the state civil service, and the FEP Act and the commission induced some voluntary compliance by employers. The general impression of FEPC officials and of those who examined its operations was that the commission had achieved a rather modest result, a judgment that the facts tend to support. Hodges thus declared in March 1961, "While we still have a long way to go before total merit employment becomes a reality, you should know that the Commission has noted an improving economic climate across the state." Rosenzweig declared that same year that the FEPC had proved in five years that "government activity in this area [fair employment] is practicable[,] and enforceable legislation, competently drafted and skillfully administered, can bring about and assist desirable changes toward a more democratic society."[62]

Horace Sheffield told the U.S. Commission on Civil Rights in December 1960 that the FEPC had "helped materially" in securing merit employment but that it could have done a better job had it been given initiatory power and provided with more staff and budget. The Michigan State Advisory Committee to the U.S. Commission on Civil Rights told the commission in 1961 that discrimination in Michigan was "lessening very gradually." It reported that "the highly qualified minority group applicant" had "a chance for a fairly good job in competition with a less-qualified white applicant" but that the black worker of "average ability" was at "a distinct disadvantage."[63]

In the FEPC's annual report for 1962, Hodges asserted that the record demonstrated "the changing [employment] policies and practices leading toward a better future." He conceded, however, that what had been accomplished represented "a small beginning" and that in "many areas of employment," the FEPC had "barely scratched the surface of discrimination." He noted in October of that year that "blatant, unashamed discrimination" had become "unfashionable." If discrimination remained the policy of an employer, he asserted, it often assumed "subtleties" that hid it from "the untrained observer" and made it "difficult even for the experienced investigator to detail." The "subtleties" he cited were such things as testing and screening procedures, residence requirements, and "gentlemen's agreements [of employers] with referral agencies." Even if it was the policy of a company not to discriminate, " 'middle' or 'lower' management" personnel might nevertheless do so. When the FEPC conducted adjustment reviews in the spring of 1963 involving twenty-four companies that had been the respondents in claims adjusted by the commission, it discovered that, except for three of the firms, there had been no "appreciable change" in the composition of their workforces.[64]

Whatever success the FEPC may have enjoyed in lessening employment discrimination in production jobs and at the state government level, its record with regard to managerial, administrative, and white-collar positions, as Routh observed in December 1961, did not present "a pretty picture," the employment of nonwhites in such positions being "very, very rare." Not only blacks but Hispanics and Jews also were often excluded from such positions, and Jews were rarely found in "the line positions of management" in major companies.

Walter Reuther observed in late 1960 that although there had been some progress in the employment of blacks in the production departments of auto companies, not one black had a white-collar classification in General Motors, only three had such classifications in the Ford Motor Company, and a few more than that number in Chrysler Corporation.

In Detroit-area plants of Chrysler Corporation, although 24 percent of 41,892 employees were black, there were only 24 nonwhites among the 7,425 skilled workers, only 10 among 3,000 salaried workers, and none among 1,890 engineers. About 40 percent of Ford's 35,650 workers in the area were black, but only 259 of 7,450 skilled trades workers were nonwhite. In GM plants in the Detroit area, 23 percent of 39,723 employees were black, but only 67 of 11,125 skilled workers were of that color.[65]

The opportunity for blacks to qualify for skilled jobs in the automobile manufacturing industry and in construction was severely limited by the blatant discrimination against them in securing apprenticeships. As the director of Vocational Services of the DUL informed the U.S. Commission on Civil Rights at the end of 1960, there were "serious inequities" in Michigan in the apprentice training programs, and, he asserted, both management and labor were at fault. For the state as a whole at the end of 1960, less than 2 percent of the trainees were black, and three-fourths of them were enrolled in the trowel trades. None of 350 Chrysler Corporation apprentices was black, and only 1 of General Motors's 289 apprentices was nonwhite. In the apprenticeship training program conducted jointly by the Automotive Tool and Die Manufacturers' Association and the UAW, all 370 apprentices in 1961 were white, and only 1 black had ever participated in the program.

In Detroit's Apprenticeship Training School, of 1,418 students in July 1963, only 12 were black. Although the Detroit Board of Education operated the school, the selection of the students was left to the joint apprenticeship committees of the various construction trades, and the pattern was for the unionists to select relatives and friends for the training. Also, a high school diploma was required for prospective applicants to qualify for an apprenticeship in the seventeen construction trades, which proved to be an obstacle for at least some potential black applicants. The result was that blacks were almost entirely shut out from training to become plumbers, electricians, and ironworkers. In October 1963, as the FEPC was coming to an end, only 1.4 percent (22) of the 1,623 apprentices were nonwhite.[66]

At a meeting on July 9, 1963, the Joint Construction Activities Committee of the Detroit Metropolitan Area agreed on a program of "affirmative action" by member contractors and local unions to encourage application for apprenticeship openings without regard to race, creed, color, or national origin. Local unions also agreed to adopt a nondiscriminatory policy in accepting qualified applicants for membership. The committee's action was influenced by President John F. Kennedy's extension of the authority of the President's Committee on Equal Employment Opportunity to contracts for construction financed by federal funds. This was a step forward in Detroit's construction industry that was to bear fruit in the future.[67]

A comparison of black employment in various occupations in Michigan in 1950 and 1960, three years before the FEPC came to an end, reveals how limited the progress in black employment had been other than in the occupations of operatives, laborers, and service workers. What stands out, surprisingly, is how much more successful nonwhite women were than nonwhite males in improving their occupational status during the decade. Whereas black males made up 6.5 percent of the Michigan labor force in 1950 and 8 percent in 1960, they held only 1.7 percent of the professional positions in 1950 and 2.5 percent in 1960; 1.6 percent were managers and proprietors in 1950 but only 1.5 percent in 1960; 3.9 percent held clerical positions in 1950, but that figure had fallen to 3.6 percent in 1960; 1.5 percent held sales positions in 1950 and 2.1 percent a decade later; 3.7 percent were craftsmen in 1950, 4.2 percent in 1960. Only the percentage of black males who were service workers, operatives, or laborers exceeded the percentage of black males in the state's labor force. Blacks constituted 14.2 percent of the service workers in 1956 and 15.1 percent in 1960, 9.7 percent of the operatives in 1950 and 11 percent in 1960, and 20.2 percent of the laborers in 1950 and 19 percent in 1960.

Black females made up 7 percent of the Michigan labor force in 1950 and 9 percent in 1960. In the decade they increased their percentage of technical and professional positions from 2.8 to 5, as managers and proprietors from 3.1 to 3.3, as clerical workers from 1.9 to 3.7, as sales employees from 2 to 2.6, as craftsmen from 4.4 to 4.6, as service workers from 13.8 to 15.5, and as laborers from 18.5 to 19.8. The percentage of black women engaged in private housework fell slightly, from 33.7 percent to 31.7 percent. Despite the improvement in their occupational status, 67 percent of the black women employed in 1960 were still laborers, service workers, and domestics. The same pattern of black male and female employment appears to have continued to the end of the FEPC's existence.[68]

In Detroit, the occupational distribution of black males, who made up 10.7 percent of the labor force in 1950 and 11.7 percent in 1960, and black females, who made up 11.1 percent of the labor force in 1950 and 14.5 percent in 1960, conformed pretty largely to the state pattern for the decade. Black male clerical workers, however, increased in the decade from 4 to 6 percent of the total, and black craftsmen from 12 to 13 percent. Female clerical workers constituted 16 percent of the total female employment as compared to 3.7 percent for the state as a whole. Seventy-six percent of the black male workers in 1950 and 73 percent in 1960 and 79 percent of the black females in 1950 and 71 percent in 1960 were concentrated in the operative, laborer, service worker (including household workers for women) category, only a slight improvement for the decade in these low-level occupations.[69]

In Muskegon, there was "very little upgrading" of black employees in the 1950s. In three of six manufacturing groups employing eighty-five hundred workers, according to a study by the Trade Union Leadership Council, there was no evidence of any black employment except for one engineer trainee. In Kalamazoo, on the other hand, although three "significant" manufacturing groups totally excluded blacks, black employment improved in the 1950s in the durable goods and chemical industries, and, for the first time, blacks in "very limited numbers" secured sales, clerical, technical, and professional positions.

In Ann Arbor in 1961, black employees were largely confined to the sanitation department. White firemen, indeed, had threatened to resign if blacks were appointed to their ranks. There was one black police officer in the city and two or three black clerks in the Municipal Court. After the FEP Act went into effect, Michigan Bell Telephone Company changed its employment policy and hired a few blacks, and the Michigan Consolidated Gas Company hired a black bookkeeper and a black custodian. Banks and retail stores were not hiring blacks, but the city's hospitals had "made changes for the better" regarding black employment. As a black leader in the city noted, blacks aged eighteen to twenty-two were "ill-prepared" for skilled labor and generally lacked the college education that would have improved their occupational potential.

In the Lansing area, of six manufacturing firms employing about 20,000 workers in 1957, two employed between 700 and 1,200 workers depending on demand, but as in other Michigan cities, nearly all were unskilled manual workers. The other four firms employed an average of 3,200 workers. Two of these firms had never employed an African American, and the other two employed 60 African Americans, of whom 50 were unskilled, 5 semiskilled, and 5 skilled.[70]

As it was about to give way to the Michigan Civil Rights Commission, the FEPC thought that its successor's number one priority should be racial equality in apprenticeship programs and the "fuller use of Negroes and other minorities in white collar jobs." Although, as Hodges concluded as the FEPC came to an end, much remained to be done to achieve fair employment in Michigan, the FEPC had "laid a good foundation for the work of the Civil Rights Commission."[71]

4

"WRESTLING WITH . . . THE CAUSE OF CIVIL RIGHTS," 1949–1962

"We are wrestling with what [is] best to do to promote the cause of Civil Rights," Governor Williams wrote in March 1950 when it had become evident that the state legislature would not in the near future pass a fair employment practices law, which the governor had made his top civil rights legislative priority. The governor's Advisory Committee on Civil Rights suggested that with a fair employment law "dead," the governor should focus his attention on other civil rights matters, such as employment in the state government, discriminatory advertising by the Michigan Tourist Council, segregation in the Michigan National Guard, discrimination in higher education, police behavior, and failure to enforce the state's public accommodations law. The Michigan Committee on Civil Rights (MCCR) had a roughly similar agenda for the governor, but it also thought that the treatment accorded migrant laborers in the state should be addressed.[1]

While pressing the state legislature to enact the civil rights legislation that they thought necessary, Governors Williams and Swainson took action where they could to promote the cause of civil rights in Michigan. Both governors, for example, began bringing members of minority groups and women, who had been shunned by their predecessors, into state government and the upper ranks of the Democratic Party.

Williams thought it essential for state government to set an example for the private sector by the appointment of qualified persons without regard to their race, religion, or sex. As one woman prominent in Democratic politics at the time recalled, Williams "wanted the voice of these people heard." Blacks, who, a distinguished state African American recalled, had been treated as "colonials" before, now received important state appointments and became "full participants" in Democratic Party councils and party decision-making, including membership on the Democratic State Central Committee. The 1948 election, another black leader noted, "marked the beginning of the new era of political participation of Negroes in Michigan."

Williams appointed blacks to a number of state boards and commissions, in many instances the first time a member of their race had held such a position. In 1950 Williams appointed Charles Jones to fill a vacancy on the Detroit Recorder's Court, the first black to serve as a judge in Michigan. Blacks were "ecstatic" about the appointment even though Jones was subsequently defeated in the election for the judgeship. In October 1954 Williams appointed Wade McCree, Jr., who had been serving on the Workmen's Compensation Commission, to the Wayne County Circuit Court, McCree becoming the first black circuit court judge in Michigan's history. He won election to the position the next year. Williams made the McCree appointment just before the 1954 state election, rejecting advice not to take the action lest it hurt the Democratic Party at the polls.

In November 1956 Williams appointed Assistant Prosecuting Attorney Edwin D. Davenport to the Common Pleas Court of Detroit. Davenport was elected to the judgeship the next year and subsequently to the Recorder's Court. To fill a vacancy, Williams, in September 1959, appointed Otis Smith, who had been serving as chairman of the state's Public Service Commission, to the position of state auditor general, the first time a black had ever served on the state's Administrative Board. Smith won election to the position in 1960, reportedly "the highest elective administrative office" held by an African American in the United States at that time. Swainson appointed Smith in 1961 to fill a vacancy on the Michigan Supreme Court, the first black ever to have served on the state's highest court. Swainson also appointed the first black member of the state's Civil Service Commission.[2]

Williams also brought Jews into state government to an unprecedented extent. His first judicial appointment, to the Common Pleas Court of Detroit, went to Nathan Kaufman. Williams appointed Victor Baum to the first circuit court vacancy the governor had to fill; and he selected Charles Levin to fill a vacancy on the Michigan Supreme Court. Williams also appointed Jews to positions in the state's executive branch, selecting Lawrence Gubow to head the Corporation and Securities Commission and Leon Cohen to serve as deputy attorney general. Williams, a Jewish source indicated, "was the way a lot of Jews got involved in politics" in Michigan.[3]

Women achieved unprecedented prominence in Democratic politics in Michigan during the Williams-Swainson era. In the 1948 election, the Michigan Democrats selected Margaret Price as the party's candidate for auditor general, the first woman candidate of either major party for a position in the state government's executive branch. She was defeated in the election and again for the same position in 1950, but in 1952 the party selected her to be its national committeewoman, a position in which she served for a decade. Adelaide Hart served for most of the Williams governorship as the state party's vice chair and was "a great fighter for the voice of women in the party." Helen Berthelot helped to conduct several of Williams's campaigns for governor as well as John Swainson's 1960 campaign. All in all, women were included as equals in Michigan's Democratic Party once Williams became governor. He was concerned about having their electoral support, and, as Adelaide Hart recalled, "he would come home from anywhere to attend a women's conference."[4]

Acting on the suggestion of a group of prominent Michigan clergymen and laymen, Williams on October 21, 1952, appointed a seven-member nonpartisan, nonsectarian committee to monitor state elections and to call to the attention of party leaders any appeals for votes based on "racial and religious bigotry" in the hope of deterring that kind of campaigning. The state chairmen of both the Republican and Democratic Parties endorsed the idea. The committee, which selected the Episcopalian bishop, the Reverend Richard S. Emrich, as its chairman and Boris Joffe, the financial director of the Jewish Community Council of Detroit, as its secretary, released a Statement of Principles to Guide Conduct of Political Campaigns just before the 1952 election. During the campaign, the committee attacked a black newspaper for an advertisement that it viewed with "abhorrence" and the *Christian Science Monitor* for an editorial that it criticized as "scarcely sane" and as "in every way unfair to our Roman Catholic brethren."[5]

The committee, which eventually took the name Fair Election Practices Committee, continued during the Williams and Swainson governorships to seek "standards of fairness" in election campaigns and to investigate and make public "exhibitions of racial, religious, or nationality discrimination." It exposed an "apparently fictitious white citizens council" statement in the 1956 campaign; "VOTE RIGHT VOTE WHITE" literature in the 1957 Detroit Common Council election; and numerous instances of anti-Catholicism in the 1960 election, including a UAW publication (for which the union later expressed regret) that claimed that only "bigots" opposed the election of John F. Kennedy as president.[6]

How the committee operated is evident from its activity in the 1962 state election. Serving without statutory authority and without a staff, the committee met in early September with the chairmen of the two parties to secure their endorsement of what by then was designated the Code of Fair Campaign Practices. The committee then sent a copy of the code to each of the 340 candidates for office in Michigan that year. About half of the candidates returned the code with their signatures indicating approval. Although "religiously bigoted" campaign material was much less in evidence in the 1962 campaign than it had been in 1960, the committee had to deal with an "anti-Catholic, anti-Jewish and anti-Negro letter" in support of the Republican Party that the leaders of both parties promptly repudiated. The committee, at the same time, criticized the *Illustrated News,* a black periodical, for making "racist appeals" in congressional races in Wayne County. It also condemned campaign appeals to support or oppose one or another candidate because of race or nationality.

The committee in the 1962 campaign investigated a serious charge by a Michigan state senator that "Fascist" elements were attempting to seize control of the Republican organization in Wayne County "to further an extreme political philosophy" and were "playing upon anti-Semitic and anti-Negro sentiments" with this in view. The committee enlisted the assistance of Michigan's secretary of state in an effort to determine the accuracy of the senator's allegation, but it was unable to corroborate the charge. As in earlier campaigns, the committee issued a warning against " 'last minute' appeals to racial and/or religious bigotry," and it concluded that the warning had been effective.[7]

There was a backlash against the Fair Election Practices Committee. In 1959 the Grand Rapids Association of Regular Baptist Churches, which at that time represented eighty-six churches, protested as an infringement of constitutional rights and as "un-American in implication and practice" the committee's sending a telegram to a member church criticizing the listing in the church bulletin of the church affiliation of candidates for office in the city's primary election. In 1961 the same association expressed its considerable displeasure with the rebukes administered by the committee to member churches for injecting religious prejudice in the 1960 Kennedy-Nixon campaign by disseminating a pamphlet entitled "The Pope for President" and also asking church members to sign "a pledge not to vote for a Catholic." The state fellowship of Regular Baptists adopted a resolution condemning what it regarded as improper interference with "Protestant pastors in the free use of their pulpits in faithfully exposing . . . movements which endanger our freedom and sacred heritage." It petitioned the governor not to continue the committee or, if it was continued, to instruct it not to interfere with the freedom of speech and press of the fellowship's churches and their members.[8]

In 1963 the committee was attacked from another direction. In a letter to Governor Romney, the Michigan chapter of the American Civil Liberties Union (ACLU) expressed sympathy with the purpose for which the committee had been established but asserted that the ACLU thought it "improper for a public or quasi-public body to sit in judgment of utterance of expression protected by the First Amendment." The Romney administration pursued the matter with the ACLU, the governor's legal adviser concluding that the ACLU's position was "somewhat extreme" but "not entirely without merit." He thought that an alternative to a committee appointed by the governor might be the formation of an entirely private organization of respected citizens for the same purpose. Romney, under the circumstances, decided not to continue the Fair Election Practices Committee.[9]

Governor Williams in early 1957 expressed the view that the election committee had been "somewhat effective," and a key aide of the governor concluded in 1960 that the committee, by its very existence, had made "a significant contribution to the level and 'climate' of campaigning in Michigan." The committee itself reported at the end of 1960 that although it had not always been able to "dissuade" organizations or individuals from engaging in bigotry in election campaigns, it had at least served as "an inhibiting factor." There is, however, little evidence to conclude that the character of campaigning in Michigan had improved to any significant degree as the result of the committee's presence, and it is impossible to determine whether the committee had deterred a greater resort to bigotry by one source or another than might otherwise have occurred. The *Detroit News,* in an editorial of November 6, 1962, criticized the committee as "a pusillanimous agency," a harsh but perhaps accurate appraisal.[10]

Quite apart from the efforts of Williams and Swainson to bring members of minority groups into state service and to involve them and women in Democratic politics, Williams in February 1950 used his authority as governor to order the state Military Board to amend its regulations so as to prohibit discrimination because of race, color, religion, or nationality in the enlistment, assignment, and promotion of members of the Michigan Military Establishment, the National Guard. "We do not ask a man's color or race or religion when we send him out to face death or injury for the safety of our homes in time of war," Williams declared. "We should follow the same policy in time of peace." When the governor issued his order, there was one all-black battalion in the Michigan Guard but no racial integration.

The Guard put the governor's executive order into effect on April 1. Williams explained that his order was to be carried out gradually as billets opened and that the order, in any event, did not require the breaking up of units or the transfer of personnel. By the time the governor's desegregation order was issued, similar action had been taken by Connecticut, Illinois, and New Jersey. Three years later Williams reported that the order was being "smoothly carried out" despite concern when it had been issued that it would be ineffective. As late as July 1967, however, as we shall see, the Michigan Guard, like the Guard elsewhere in the nation, remained an essentially lily-white organization.[11]

Michigan in 1958 advanced the cause of civil rights in law enforcement in a modest way when the legislature enacted a measure providing for the mandatory return of fingerprints, arrest cards, and descriptions of persons who had been apprehended but had then been released without being charged or who had been charged but not convicted. The principal area of concern regarding civil rights and law enforcement was not, however, the composition of the Michigan National Guard or the treatment of arrest records but rather the behavior of police forces in the cities of the state, and especially in Detroit.

After a survey of civil rights in the state, the Michigan State Advisory Committee to the U.S. Commission on Civil Rights reported in 1959 that there was a "real basis" for the charge that the police often ignored the rights of minority-group members and sometimes treated them with "callousness and perhaps even brutality." The general attitude of police officers regarding blacks, in the judgment of the Detroit Urban League (DUL), appeared to be "one of restraint and suppression," the police viewing themselves as "guardians of white supremacy" and as being "more interested in tyrannizing Negro residents than in the protection of their rights as fellow citizens." Civil rights groups in the state noted that the police often arrested blacks "on suspicion, without evidence and without charges."[12]

The racial divide in Detroit with respect to the police was illustrated in a 1951 survey in which 42 percent of black respondents as compared to 12 percent of white respondents appraised the city's police department as "not good" or "definitely bad." The executive secretary of the Detroit NAACP told the U.S. Commission on Civil Rights that blacks in Detroit were subjected to "unreasonable and illegal arrests, indiscriminate and open searches of their person on the public streets, disrespectful and profane language, derogatory references to their race and color, interference with personal associations . . . and violent, intimidating police reaction to their protests against improper treatment." A retired black police officer recalled that police in one Detroit precinct in the 1950s amused themselves by beating up blacks. A former Detroit police officer also reported that the department had "a definite policy of not enforcing any of the laws that deal[t] with antidiscrimination." The managing editor of the black Detroit newspaper, the *Michigan Chronicle,* and a longtime observer of police behavior asserted at the same time that brutality against blacks by the police was "commonplace" and that he had personally observed police, without apparent cause, beating up blacks under arrest.[13]

In Detroit as of 1958, blacks constituted 23 percent of the city's population but only 3 percent of the city's police force. This was not because blacks had failed to apply for positions in the department at least in proportion to their numbers in the city but rather because subjective screening procedures employed by the department led to its rejection of a much higher proportion of black than of white applicants. Eighty percent of the black police were assigned to the four of the fifteen city precincts that had a large black population, and not a single black officer was assigned to six precincts. Segregation was the rule in the department in walking beats, riding in scout cars, and partner assignments. Black police were permitted to supervise only other blacks and were permitted to patrol only in "certain clearly defined areas." Similar conditions prevailed in cities such as Flint and Muskegon.[14]

The Detroit Police Department adopted a series of procedures between 1946 and 1960 to address some of the complaints regarding its treatment of blacks. In 1946 the department agreed with the Detroit NAACP to process complaints from the association, and in 1957 the department improved the processing system that it had been using. It had received fifty-one complaints of police brutality from the NAACP by late 1960, but the police chief reported that in the majority of the incidents there had been no proof of police use of physical force.

In January 1959 the department, in its chief's view, took "another forward step" by requiring immediate police investigation whenever a police officer had used force or a citizen or a police officer had been injured in connection with a police incident, whether or not a complaint had been submitted to the department. Of 264 such incidents in 1959 involving 149 blacks and 115 whites, the department found the citizen at fault in 260 of the incidents. In 230 additional incidents in the first nine months of 1960, involving 148 whites, 121 blacks, and 1 Native American, the department found the citizen at fault in 223 of the cases. To deal with the understandable allegation that these figures were the result of police investigation of their own conduct, the Wayne County prosecutor in May 1960 established a Civil Rights Board to make an independent investigation of such incidents.[15]

Acting on the advice of the city's Commission on Community Relations, which the Common Council had established in 1953 to succeed the Mayor's Interracial Committee, Mayor Louis C. Miriani, in August

1958, appointed a prestigious thirteen-member Citizens Advisory Committee on Police Procedures that included four blacks. Before the committee reported in March 1960, the Police Department announced in February 1959 that scout cars would be integrated on a temporary basis. When this policy was soon made permanent, white police officers responded by staging a slowdown in the writing of tickets, the number soon dwindling to about 5 percent of the normal total. By the middle of December 1960, 34 of the department's 118 scout cars had been integrated. The police commissioner, however, concluded that the integration policy had been "a terrific flop" since the "work production" of the integrated crews had been "far below normal." Quite apart from scout cars, by the end of 1960 some integration had occurred in the department's various bureaus, and black police were serving in all of the city's police precincts.[16]

In its March 1960 report, the Citizens Advisory Committee stated that the Detroit Police Department was "among the best in the nation." The committee, nevertheless, recommended changes in the department's recruitment procedures and the establishment of a citizens committee to receive complaints of police misconduct. Police Commissioner Herbert Hart rejected the latter recommendation, but he did establish a Community Relations Bureau in the department to investigate complaints of police misbehavior and to represent the department at community relations meetings. He had earlier instructed inspectors in each precinct to hold quarterly meetings with community groups and monthly meetings with supervisory officers to review community relations among other matters.[17]

When Jerome Cavanagh became Detroit's mayor at the beginning of 1962, he appointed a staunch advocate of civil rights, George Edwards, as the city's police commissioner. Edwards informed the Fair Employment Practices Commission (FEPC) that his department would faithfully observe the terms of the mayor's first executive order requiring that city employees be "recruited, appointed, trained, assigned, and promoted without regard to race, color, religion, national origin, or ancestry." Edwards decided to include the phrase "an equal opportunity employer" in all police recruitment literature. He also sought conscientiously to deal with complaints of police misconduct, particularly by blacks. "My job," he recalled, "was to teach the police they didn't have a constitutional right to beat up Negroes on arrest." He told the police that it was "their job . . . to serve the citizens, not to ride herd on them." At night, he sometimes rode along in a scout car to observe the police "deal with the human beings who are the raw material to build a democratic civilization." He insisted that members of the department's traffic division treat blacks courteously.

Edwards initiated a massive police recruitment campaign aimed particularly at blacks, but the results during the two years of his commissionership were meager. Of 457 police hired, only 19 were black. By the end of 1963, 3.28 percent of the force was black, a very slight improvement since Edwards had become police commissioner. Edwards, however, could point to some modest improvement in police assignments and promotions, and there appeared to be real progress during his commissionership in the integration of scout cars. Police departments, however, often prove to be resistant to change, and when Edwards left his position, the executive secretary of the Detroit NAACP complained that the department was still "clearly a segregated institution" with "very little career promise for the Negro officers."[18]

The FEPC, it will be recalled, wished to have its jurisdiction expanded to include public accommodations, education, and housing. Williams and Swainson sought at various times to persuade the legislature to follow this course, but without success. Michigan had a public accommodation statute, the so-called Diggs Act, an upgrading of the 1885 civil rights law, but it had proved to be ineffective, as the MCCR had informed Williams as governor-elect. A black legislator thus remarked in 1956, "I have had to drive hours to find a restaurant that would serve me."[19]

Discriminatory treatment by public accommodation facilities led to national and international embarrassment for Michigan during the Williams and Swainson governorships. In the summer of 1953 the *New York Times* reported that black U.S. Air Force personnel assigned to a radar site and an interceptor squadron to guard the Sault had been refused service in restaurants, taverns, and barbershops in the area. "It's like putting Negro boys in jail to send them up here," declared the director of the United Services Organization. Responding defensively, the secretary of the Sault Ste. Marie Chamber of Commerce commented, "This is a small town. We didn't know how to treat them." Governor Williams appointed a special committee to look into the episode and asked the executive secretary of the Michigan Veterans Trust Fund and the state relations officer of the American Red Cross to discuss the affair with community and military leaders in the area.[20]

In July 1961 four officials from Kenya and Tanganyika who had been refused a second round of drinks by two Lansing-area bars complained that they had been the victims of discrimination. John A. Hannah, president of Michigan State University and chairman of the U.S. Commission on Civil Rights, expressed regret about the incident, and the FEPC's executive director forwarded Swainson's apology to the chief of the Protocol Division of the State Department. The president of the

United States and the State Department urged state governors to take action to prevent discrimination against nonwhite foreign diplomats when they traveled within the United States. In still another embarrassing incident that led to an expression of regret by Governor Swainson, a white professor was not permitted on the golf course in Stony Lake because he was accompanied by a black educator.[21]

Only rarely were violators of the Michigan public accommodations law brought to justice. "It is a criminal statute," the FEPC's executive director declared in 1962, "unpublicized, largely unknown and many times unaccommodating to the person discriminated against." As we have seen, many victims of discrimination were unaware of the law or reluctant to lodge a complaint, prosecutors were often loath to prosecute violations, and juries, "often sympathetic" with the practices that were the subject of complaint, were reluctant to convict. In Cass County, when a justice of the peace handed down some convictions in public accommodation cases, the local prosecutor and the circuit court judge were "quite disturbed" by the action, and the police ceased to take complaints to that justice of the peace.[22]

In February 1949 the executive board of the MCCR formed a subcommittee to investigate discrimination in places of public accommodation. The committee collected data on the reception of mixed racial groups by selected restaurants and conferred with law enforcement agencies about enforcement of the Diggs Act. In Detroit, where the Mayor's Interracial Committee joined in the effort, the mayor and the police commissioner were actually little concerned about the matter at that time, but the Wayne County prosecutor and his Civil Rights Board secured some convictions against restaurants that had discriminated against minority-group members.[23]

The UAW played a key role in inducing the American Bowling Congress, the chief amateur bowling organization, to alter its policy of limiting membership in the congress and its tournament competition to whites. Since many UAW locals had bowling teams, the union's new president, Walter Reuther, instructed the union's Fair Practices and Anti-Discrimination Department at the end of 1946 to deal with the matter. The department then took the lead in the formation in April 1947 of the Committee for Fair Play in Bowling, chaired by Hubert Humphrey, then mayor of Minneapolis, and Betty Hicks, the national women's amateur golf champion. Governor Williams supported the effort, informing the head of the Fair Practices and Anti-Discrimination Department in May 1949 that the American Bowling Congress would not be permitted to use the State Fairgrounds since there was "no justification" for the use of state property for events involving racial discrimination. In 1950 the congress abandoned its policy of racial exclusion.[24]

Since some restaurants near auto plants in Michigan refused to serve blacks, despite the Diggs Act, the UAW mounted a campaign against them beginning in 1949 that enjoyed some success over time. The Jackson, Michigan, Community Relations Board decided at its first meeting in 1949 to deal with discrimination by local restaurants.[25]

The Detroit Commission on Community Relations established an Equal Public Accommodations Committee in 1957 to seek the "racially unrestricted use" of places of public accommodation by both residents of Detroit and visitors to the city. The committee had two subcommittees, one that was to develop an educational program designed to "create a climate of opinion favorable to the concept of equal public accommodations," the other to review procedures for the enforcement of the Diggs Act. Shortly after the committee had been formed, many places of public accommodation in the city, particularly in the downtown area, began to offer service on a nondiscriminatory basis.[26]

An effort by Senator Charles Diggs, Jr., in 1952 to extend the Diggs Act to cover bars met with defeat in the Michigan Senate. The next year the Senate also defeated another Diggs proposal, to remove the property tax exemption from public cemeteries, libraries, charitable institutions, and churches that discriminated.[27] The Diggs Act was, however, extended in 1956 to cover motels. The Jewish Community Council of Detroit and the Anti-Defamation League (ADL) had been seeking since 1944 to persuade the state government to ban the discriminatory advertising and practices of Michigan tourist hotels and resorts, since they were partly subsidized by state funds. In the spring of 1953 the Michigan Regional Advisory Board of the ADL authorized a pilot program to survey a group of resorts that had included discriminatory language in their promotional literature and had appeared to discriminate against potential Jewish guests. The survey was restricted to cabins, motels, and resorts listed by the Automobile Club of Michigan. Two letters seeking reservations were sent to each facility in October 1955, one signed with a "Jewish-sounding name" like Goldberg and the other with a "non-Jewish name" like O'Brien. Eighty-eight of 125 resorts (70.4 percent) returned identical letters to the senders, but 37 (29.6 percent) treated the senders differently, leading the ADL to conclude that these facilities were closed to Jewish guests. Nonwhites also suffered discrimination in seeking accommodations in such establishments, particularly in rural areas and north of the Bay City–Muskegon line.[28]

The 1956 amendment to the Diggs Act not only placed motels in the same category as hotels, inns, and restaurants insofar as discrimination was concerned but also increased the minimum fine for offenders from $25 to $100 and authorized the sentencing judge to revoke the state or city license of the guilty facility. The alternative to a fine, as before, was a fifteen-day jail sentence. The amendment was especially important for motels and other covered facilities holding liquor licenses, establishments that previously had been subject only to the regulations of the Liquor Control Commission.[29]

Shortly after Williams signed the 1956 measure into law, the state attorney general issued an opinion barring the Michigan Tourist Council from accepting any advertising limiting facilities or particular activities to "gentile clientele." In August 1957 the attorney general ruled that the appropriate court, in accordance with the Diggs Act, could revoke the liquor license of a golf club that limited its membership to Caucasians. On the other hand, he ruled in July 1957 that a nursing home operated by a private lessee was not "a place of public accommodation" as defined by the statute. Although the practice did not involve the Diggs Act, the secretary of state's office in 1955 forbade the use of race as a description in driver's license permits.[30]

The 1956 Diggs Act amendment did not, as it turned out, end discrimination by Michigan resorts. As part of a national survey of the resort industry in 1958, the Michigan office of the ADL discovered that 48 percent of cottage rentals in Michigan resorts, as compared to a national average of 26 percent, discriminated against minority-group members. The survey appears to have led the state tourist industry to adopt a voluntary code of ethics that barred discrimination, but the discrimination continued. As a black woman who had found race to be a factor in seeking public accommodations in the summer of 1962 for travel in southern Michigan reported, "Discrimination in public accommodations in Michigan makes ease of traveling for Negro families still very remote."[31]

There was no state agency during the Williams and Swainson administrations to deal with violations of the Diggs Act. The attorney general urged local prosecutors to publicize the act lest violators go unpunished because of lack of awareness of the statute. If complaints of violation were filed with the attorney general rather than a local prosecutor, the attorney general informed the appropriate prosecutor of that fact and recommended prosecution if it appeared warranted. The Williams and Swainson administrations believed that the better way to deal with enforcement of the Diggs Act was to extend the FEPC's jurisdiction to cover public accommodations, but the state legislature disagreed.[32]

The Diggs Act did not apply to medical facilities. In September 1953 a committee of the Michigan State Bar claimed that TB sanatoriums in the state were practicing racial discrimination. This was a matter that Senator Diggs had already called to the attention of the tuberculosis controller of the city of Detroit, alleging that patients were assigned to beds according to their race. When Williams learned of the state bar

108

allegation, he informed Dr. Albert E. Heustis, the state health commissioner, that it was the policy of the Williams administration that there was to be no discrimination based on race, religion, or ancestry in any state facility, and since the county sanatoriums were partially funded by the state, the policy applied to these institutions.

Heustis subsequently informed the governor that he had contacted the medical directors of the institutions named in the bar committee report and had been assured that these facilities did not discriminate on the basis of race but only on the basis of "disease status, personality traits, and the wishes of the patients themselves." The concern of Heustis and the medical directors of the sanatoriums about "congenial relationships" among patients—which, in effect, meant their racial segregation—was denounced by the FEPC's William Seabron as acceptance of a "time-worn cliché." Seabron reminded Heustis that the sanatoriums were dealing with individuals, not groups, and that race, in itself, did not assure "individual compatibility." There was, however, no immediate change in the policy of bed assignments for TB patients in the state facilities.[33]

The problem of medical service and race in Michigan went well beyond bed assignments of patients in TB sanatoriums. The MCCR, it will be recalled, had informed Williams as governor-elect that black patients in tax-supported hospitals in the state were segregated and were sometimes the victims of "outright exclusion," black doctors could not get needed training experience in these hospitals, and black nurses could not become registered nurses in most hospitals. The DUL viewed racial discrimination by private hospitals in Detroit as the "most glaring problem" faced by the city's blacks in the area of health care.[34]

In 1952 the Mayor's Interracial Committee appointed a Medical and Hospital Study Committee of thirty-five "distinguished citizens representing all aspects of Detroit's community life" to review racial factors in hospital policies and practices in the city and to recommend measures to eliminate discrimination. The committee found "some serious problems" in the various aspects of hospital and medical practices that it examined. Only two of the nine hospital-affiliated nurse training schools, for example, regularly enrolled qualified black students. Of the twenty hospitals offering internship training, only four had a record of accepting black interns. Few of the 170 black physicians in the city had staff appointments in the voluntary nonprofit hospitals, and except for government hospitals, patients in the wards and semiprivate rooms were generally segregated. No single hospital or medical institution was mentioned by name in the reports.[35]

The Detroit Commission on Community Relations followed up the Study Committee's report by appointing an Advisory Committee on Hospitals to implement the Study Committee's recommendations. The

Advisory Committee focused its attention on three areas: individual hospitals and medical institutions, hospital planning and funding, and governmental action. Its goal was for Detroit to "lead the nation in achieving a completely nondiscriminatory, equal opportunity system of medical and hospital practice."[36]

Insofar as individual hospitals and medical institutions were concerned, the committee reported that the University of Michigan and Wayne State University medical schools and Wayne State and Mercy College Schools of Nursing were open to all qualified students. Six of the seven hospital-affiliated schools of nursing were apparently nonrestrictive in their admissions. The seventh assured the committee that it would adopt an "inclusive policy of admissions," and following the committee report, it accepted its first black student nurse. The committee as late as November 1961 was still negotiating with "major teaching hospitals" in the Detroit area regarding internship and residential training programs, and it reported in that year that it could not certify a single hospital as being "free of discriminatory practices in all phases of its operation."[37]

Insofar as hospital planning and funding were concerned, the key state agency, the Michigan Office of Hospital Survey and Construction, consistent with the federal government's Hill-Burton Act as amended, required that all hospitals receiving federal funds for construction had to agree beginning in late May 1958 to follow a policy of nondiscrimination in "all phases of their operation." Following discussions with the committee, the executive committee of the greater Detroit Hospital Council, which served as the planning and coordinating body for seventy hospitals in the Detroit area, recommended in early 1961 that its hospital members adopt a model resolution of nondiscrimination that the Advisory Committee had been urging. The Allocations Committee of the Metropolitan Building Fund, a private organization that raised funds for hospital construction and expansion, incorporated the model resolution in its statement of principles and in its contracts with recipients of its funds.[38]

The Advisory Committee also involved itself in the effort to resolve the controversy in Detroit regarding the Medical Center Redevelopment Plan. The plan called for the clearing of about two hundred acres of land in the center of the city and the development there of a center for medical service, education, and research. Not only did the plan involve the displacement of black churches in the area, but there were also allegations by the DUL, the Detroit NAACP, and an organization of black doctors that three of the four hospitals that were to form the nucleus of the center engaged in discrimination against black doctors and in patient room assignments. In early 1961 the four hospitals agreed to follow a policy of nondiscrimination in all phases of their operations, as Hill-Burton required and as the Detroit Common Council insisted. At least one of the four hospitals did so, however, "with such reluctance as to endanger the entire project." In September 1962 the Greater Detroit Association of Hospital Personnel Directors pledged itself to follow the principles of merit employment.[39]

If police departments proved resistant when it came to implementing policies and practices of nondiscrimination, the same can be said for at least some Detroit hospitals. On June 13, 1963, eleven years after the Detroit city government had begun examining racial factors in hospital policies and practices in the city, Richard V. Marks, the secretary-director of the Detroit Commission on Community Relations, reported that the Advisory Committee on Hospitals had certified only two Detroit hospitals, Harper Hospital and Children's Hospital, as "free from bias" in the various areas of medical training and service that the committee had examined. "This," Marks asserted, was "eloquent testimony to the resilience of racial discrimination" in Detroit.[40]

Michigan since 1867 had prohibited segregation in public schools, and the Fair Employment Practices Act applied to public schools as employers. This, however, did not mean that the field of education was free of discrimination in the post–World War II era. The MCCR had alerted Williams to this problem as he was about to take office, and charges of discrimination in education echoed throughout the years of the Williams and Swainson governorships. Blacks, it was alleged, were discriminated against in admission to public and private schools, vocational and trade schools, colleges and universities, and, especially, professional schools, which, some suspected, had quotas to limit black admissions. If black teachers could find positions, they were assigned, it was alleged, to schools with predominantly black enrollments, were sometimes retained only as substitute teachers, and were conspicuously discriminated against when it came to promotions to assistant principal or principal. Application forms for teaching positions in some school districts contained questions regarding race, religion, and ancestry despite FEPC orders to the contrary. Public school boundaries, it was charged, were gerrymandered so as to concentrate black pupils in black schools. Permission granted to college students to select their dormitory roommates, the Michigan State Advisory Committee to the U.S. Commission on Civil Rights pointed out, constituted a form of "permissive segregation." To be sure, at least some of the school segregation that existed was the product of housing segregation, the Governor's Advisory Committee on Civil Rights observing that "segregated housing and segregated schools go hand in hand."[41]

The FEPC substantiated many of the charges leveled at the educational establishment, Edward Hodges asserting in 1962 that there was discrimination "at every level of education" in Michigan. The discrimination not only involved blacks, the FEPC reporting in September 1958 that it had found five instances of religious discrimination in school board hiring. It noted also that school boards, as charged, were still asking prohibited questions and requiring photographs of job applicants. Frederick Routh told the U.S. Commission on Civil Rights in late 1960 that "too many school systems" in the state were assigning black teachers to black schools and that "all sorts of strange and subjective factors" affected the employment of teachers.[42]

The Michigan State Advisory Committee, after surveying sixty-six "representative school districts" in Michigan in 1959, found little if any hiring of nonwhite teachers in white school districts and noted that there was a "reservoir" of unemployed but qualified minority-group teachers in the state. It concluded, however, on the basis of the responses to a questionnaire by nineteen institutions of higher education, that there was "little or no discrimination" in admissions in these institutions. Two years later it reported that it had found little discrimination in higher education, "especially among top level administrators." A resolution approved that same year, however, by the Michigan State Conference of NAACP branches charged that the state-supported universities discriminated in admissions, employment, placement, and dormitory room assignments, accepted scholarships that were discriminatory, and recognized student organizations that discriminated. Another NAACP resolution, however, praised the University of Michigan for its stand against discrimination. Calling Governor Swainson's attention to the NAACP's charge of discrimination in education in Michigan, an aide noted that the recently adopted Governor's Code of Fair Practices had been distributed to the state's colleges and universities and suggested that no action beyond that be taken by the state government for the time being.[43]

A good deal of the concern about discrimination in public education centered on Detroit, where about 45 percent of the schoolchildren by 1960 were nonwhite. In a 1957 survey by the University of Michigan Institute for Social Research, 56 percent of Detroit's white residents responded that black children should be "completely integrated into formerly all-white classes," 9 percent that they should attend the same schools as whites but should be placed in separate classes, and 35 percent that there should be "complete segregation" of the two races. Blacks complained that the Detroit school administration was following racially discriminatory policies that resulted in the segregation of both students and faculties.

At the beginning of 1960, 75 of Detroit's public schools were, indeed, all white, 8 were all black, 31 had at least 90 percent white enrollment, and 70 had at least 90 percent black enrollment. Eighty-nine of the schools, about one-half of the total, had what was considered a mixed enrollment, namely, more than 10 percent of students of each race. White schools had white teachers, whereas black teachers, who constituted 21.6 percent of the city's public school teachers, were concentrated in black schools. The school administration insisted that the segregated student bodies resulted from segregated housing patterns, but the vice president of the Citizens Association for Better Schools asserted in 1960 that "in many instances" it was the actions of the school administration that had resulted in "the promotion and maintenance of a segregated school system."

Samuel H. Brownell, Detroit's superintendent of schools, told the U.S. Commission on Civil Rights in December 1960 that black teachers taught in black schools because the schools were in the neighborhoods where they lived and where they preferred to teach, but he reported that he had instituted a policy "to break that down." He disputed the charge of critics of the school administration that as blacks moved westward in the city in the 1950s, school administrators redrew the boundaries of the school system's nine administration districts so as to maintain a pattern of segregation. Whatever the cause, as of 1961 a majority of the students in four of the nine districts were black, including 95 percent of the students in the central district, and the students in three districts were almost entirely white.[44]

Although the executive secretary of the Detroit NAACP at the time later appraised Brownell as "a very able man" but "one who didn't really want to come to terms with race," the superintendent and the Detroit school board were by no means unresponsive to the issue of racial discrimination in the schools. In December 1955 the board voted to require contractors to include a stipulation not to discriminate in their contracts with the school system. In a successful effort to increase the number of black teachers, the board in 1956 formed biracial recruitment teams and biracial selection review committees. In 1959 it began to eliminate the optional attendance areas in neighborhoods undergoing transition from white to black. The choice available to them had permitted pupils in these areas to attend either one of two high schools and, in effect, had enabled white pupils to escape attending predominantly black high schools.[45]

After committing the school system in a 1959 bylaw not to "discriminate against any person or group because of race, color, creed, or national origin," the school board in December of that year appointed a Citizens Advisory Committee on Equal Educational Opportunities. In 1960 the board adopted an open schools policy that permitted parents, if the school their children normally would have attended was unable to provide them with "schooling essential" to them, to send their children to any school that had space for them, provided that the parents furnished the transportation. When the school board arranged in the fall of 1960 to transfer 311 black elementary school children from two overcrowded inner-city schools to two all-white schools and one almost entirely white school on the city's northwest side, parents' groups in the areas to which the black pupils were to be transferred began to circulate petitions for the recall of the school board members, and white parents kept about 60 percent of their schoolchildren from attending classes for three days.[46]

The status of the Detroit school system regarding segregation and integration was made evident in March 1962 when the Citizens Advisory Committee on Equal Educational Opportunities made its long-awaited report. Despite the aforementioned reforms, the committee found a "clear-cut pattern of racial discrimination in the assignment of teachers and principals to schools throughout the city," and it expressed dissatisfaction with the pace at which the school board was adjusting school attendance boundaries to combat racial and class segregation. It pointed to "grave discrimination in employment and training opportunities" in the apprenticeship program in the schools and recommended that additional resources be devoted to culturally deprived students, that high school textbooks be aimed more at black students, and that school administrators develop "a higher sensitivity to human and intergroup relations."

The Detroit Board of Education, in short order, approved most of the Citizens Committee's recommendations. Since the school board, as noted, had agreed in 1959 to ban discrimination in "all school operations and activities," Dr. Remus Robinson, the board's only black member, charged that the Citizens Committee's report made it evident that there had been "obvious laxity" and even "insubordination" in the implementation of board policies.[47]

For civil rights advocates in Michigan and for the Williams and Swainson administrations, the proper way for state government to have dealt with discrimination in public education, as with discrimination in public accommodations, was the extension of the jurisdiction of the FEPC or a similar commission to cover education. Of even greater concern to the civil rights forces than the discrimination in education and in the use of public accommodations was discrimination with regard to housing. Housing discrimination had proved to be "the most resistent [sic] of all fields to the demands for equality of opportunity."[48]

5

"THE MOST PRESSING PROBLEM" IN CIVIL RIGHTS: Housing Discrimination, 1949–1962

Housing discrimination was a matter of critical importance in Michigan and elsewhere in the nation in the post–World War II era. In Detroit, for example, it was "the crucial area of intergroup conflict." There was, however, widespread and vigorous opposition in Michigan to the enactment of fair housing legislation. As the director of Community Services of the Michigan Civil Rights Commission declared in 1965, although the state's whites "at least" claimed that they favored merit employment, there was "a vocal opposition to equality of housing from many segments of the community, including 'respectable' individuals and organizations."[1]

Housing segregation between 1949 and 1968 was pervasive in Detroit and its suburbs, where 79 percent of the state's 450,000 blacks as of 1950 resided, and in outstate Michigan as well. As Detroit's black population increased from 16 percent of the city's population in 1950 to 29 percent in 1960, the resultant changes in the character of neighborhoods created disturbances that sometimes "reached riot proportions." When asked in a 1951 survey how to improve relations between blacks and whites in Detroit, 56 percent of the white respondents advised, "Segregate Negroes in their place of residence." Housing segregation in the city grew worse in the 1950s as the percentage of nonwhites in census tracts that were 50–100 percent nonwhite increased from 71.2 to 81, partly reflecting the sheer increase in the percentage of blacks in the city. Many census tracts in the western and northeastern parts of Detroit

115

as of 1960 were nearly all white, whereas tracts in the central part of the city were almost all black.

Detroit's blacks, to be sure, improved the quality of their housing in the city in the 1950s as some of them moved to housing in outlying areas vacated by whites who had moved to the suburbs. What was occurring, however, was "a pattern of racial succession rather than integration." Black housing, moreover, remained "substantially inferior" to white housing. Whereas 11 percent of the whites in the city lived in substandard housing in the early 1960s, 27.2 percent of the city's blacks lived in such dwellings and yet paid disproportionately more in rent than whites did. Many blacks "lived in housing that was overcrowded, rat infested, and had leaky roofs, holes in the walls, and defective plumbing." Although about 100,000 homes were built in the Detroit metropolitan area between 1945 and 1955, only an estimated 2,000 of them were constructed in areas for sale to nonwhites. In Detroit's suburbs, the disparity in the quality of housing occupied by whites and blacks in 1960 was even greater than in the city proper, with 33.2 percent of the blacks in the suburbs, as compared to 8.3 percent of the whites, living in substandard dwellings.[2]

Housing segregation and inferior housing for nonwhites in the years 1949 to 1968 were not confined to the Detroit area. After conducting housing hearings in seven Michigan communities, the Michigan Civil Rights Commission concluded in 1967 that about 90 percent of Michigan's nonwhites lived in residentially segregated areas. "Negroes," it stated, "have been forced to live apart in urban ghettoes and, in some cases, in rural ghettoes." Dearborn, with a population of 112,000 in 1960, did not permit blacks to live in the city even though about 15,000 blacks were employed in the city's factories. Owosso, similarly, did not include any blacks among its 17,000 inhabitants. "Segregated housing patterns," moreover, "served to perpetuate and aggravate discriminatory practices and attitudes in all sectors of community life, including schools, churches and public facilities." Housing segregation, civil rights advocates maintained, also led to "increased mortality, morbidity, delinquency, risk of fire, inter-group tension, loss of revenue and other harmful conditions."[3]

Not only blacks but also Jews and members of various immigrant-nationality groups were victims of housing discrimination. A 1958 survey of real estate agents in the Detroit suburbs revealed that 50 percent of them discriminated against Jews in "varying degrees."[4] As the nation learned in 1960 and as we shall see, the affluent Grosse Pointe suburbs of Detroit had since 1945 been using a screening system that discriminated against blacks, Jews, and other ethnic groups seeking to purchase homes in these suburbs.

Until 1948 the Michigan Corporation and Securities Commission, the state agency that licensed real estate brokers and agents, enforced the Code of Ethics of the National Association of Real Estate Boards. The code specified that "a realtor shall never be instrumental in introducing into a neighborhood a character of property or occupancy, members of any race or nationality, or any individual whose presence will clearly be detrimental to property values in the neighborhood." Realtors in Detroit were penalized or actually expelled from the Detroit Real Estate Board (DREB) if they violated the code. Racially restrictive covenants were widely used in Detroit and elsewhere until the U.S. Supreme Court, in *Shelley* v. *Kraemer* in 1948, made such covenants unenforceable. One of the four cases involved in the decision (*Sipes* v. *McGhee*) had originated in Detroit and had been litigated by Minnie and Orsel McGhee with the aid of the NAACP. *Shelley* v. *Kraemer* led the Federal Housing Administration (FHA) to abandon its long-standing practice of using race as a criterion in determining whether to extend loans to purchase housing in particular neighborhoods. In the case of *Phillips* v. *Neff*, in 1952, the Michigan Supreme Court held that the equal protection clause of the Fourteenth Amendment prevented "the maintenance of an action for damages for the breach of a reciprocal racial restriction on the use of property."[5]

Quite apart from the no longer legally enforceable restrictive covenants, mortgage bankers in Michigan refused to make conventional, FHA, or Veterans Administration (VA) loans to blacks seeking to purchase homes in previously all-white neighborhoods or charged them higher interest rates than they charged white purchasers. Lenders similarly were disinclined to make conventional loans to builders seeking funds to construct dwellings in neighborhoods likely to become integrated because of their location. Real estate brokers in Detroit and elsewhere sometimes played on the fears of white homeowners to encourage them to resist the entry of nonwhites and Jews into their neighborhoods. Black real estate brokers in Detroit in 1956 attributed housing segregation in the city to "interlocking business interests such as the Real Estate Association [DREB], Michigan Bankers Association and various building associations" that sought to "landlock non-white families in defined urban residential ghettos." The black realtors complained that the DREB refused to accept black members and claimed that board members kept separate listings for whites and nonwhites and ignored *Shelley* v. *Kraemer*.[6]

The Michigan State Advisory Committee to the U.S. Commission on Civil Rights depicted a pattern of housing segregation in the state that began with a "gentlemen's agreement" to keep nonwhites and Jews out of certain neighborhoods. When the nonwhite proportion of

117

the neighborhood began to approach 50 percent, "the most violently 'anti' citizens" departed, soon to be followed by other whites until the neighborhood became 100 percent nonwhite.[7]

At its September 1962 convention, the Michigan Real Estate Association adopted a new policy statement to replace the 1950 Code of Ethics. Officially adopted by the National Association of Real Estate Boards the next year, the statement declared that realtors had "no right or responsibility" to determine the racial, religious, or ethnic composition of an area or neighborhood. No realtor was to "assume to determine the suitability or eligibility of any prospective mortgagor, tenant, or purchaser," and, unless a client instructed otherwise, was to submit to the client "all offers made by any prospect in connection with the transaction at hand." The property owner represented by the realtor, moreover, was to "have the right to specify in the contract of agency the terms and conditions thereof," and the realtor was to have both "the right and duty to represent such owner by faithfully observing the terms and conditions of such agency free from penalty and sanctions for so doing." This, as we shall see, became the position to which Michigan realtors consistently adhered until state law in 1968 forced them to abandon the policy. The Detroit Urban League (DUL), however, maintained that the contention of realtors that they were, as required, simply carrying out the instructions of sellers who wished to discriminate was "nothing but a dodge" since, the DUL claimed, it had knowledge of real estate transactions in which the broker, not the seller, was responsible for the discrimination.[8]

In the evolution of state government policy regarding housing discrimination, the first step commonly, beginning with New York State in 1939, was to prohibit discrimination in public housing. By the end of 1950, four other states had joined New York in outlawing such discrimination. The next step was to prohibit discrimination in publicly assisted housing, the "first comprehensive statute" in this regard being the 1950 Weeks-Austin law of New York State. Six states had followed New York by 1957. New York also took the lead among the states in enacting legislation in 1954 to prohibit discrimination in housing receiving FHA or VA mortgage insurance. The final step in the evolution of state legislation regarding housing discrimination was the banning of discrimination in some portion of the private housing market. Colorado, Connecticut, Massachusetts, and Oregon, following the lead of New York City and Philadelphia, adopted laws of this sort in 1959, and five additional states did so in 1961.[9]

In a 1950 speech to the Michigan branch of the NAACP, Williams remarked that the housing shortage in Michigan affected the people of the state as a whole but that "the most grievous suffering" was among blacks and others "confined by prejudice to restricted living areas." Despite these remarks, the governor, as we have seen, focused his energies in the civil rights area until 1955 on seeking to secure a state fair employment law, not a fair housing law. On April 11, 1952, however, the Michigan legislature, following the lead of six other states by then, approved a statute providing that all people within the state's jurisdiction were to "be entitled to full and equal accommodations, and advantages, facilities and privileges of . . . government housing."[10]

The issue of public housing in Michigan centered on Detroit, where most of the state's public housing was located. The Detroit Housing Commission (DHC), composed of five members appointed by the mayor and who served without compensation, began operating public housing projects in the city in 1938, when tenants moved into Brewster Homes and Parkside Homes, the former reserved for whites, the latter for blacks. Over the next few years four additional public housing projects were built in the city, three of them occupied by whites, and the fourth, after bitter controversy, by blacks. The DHC also operated the temporary World War II and veterans' housing projects in the city on a segregated basis. In its first policy statement regarding racial occupancy, the commission announced in 1943 that it would "not change the racial pattern of a neighborhood" in determining the occupancy of public housing units. The Mayor's Interracial Committee criticized this policy as "wrong," noting that public housing was "the *one point* at which the government of the City of Detroit . . . [contributed] most to racial discrimination and prejudice."[11]

Shortly after the enactment of the 1952 statute banning discrimination in public housing, the DHC rescinded its 1943 racial occupancy policy statement and adopted a new policy regarding the occupancy of public housing units. "In the selection and removal of tenants of housing projects," the policy now stated, "the commission will be guided by the best interest of all the people of the City for the purposes of protecting their rights and promotion of the harmony amongst them, all in accordance with the Constitutions and laws of the United States and the State of Michigan." The next year the first units of the Edward Jeffries Homes were completed, and they were made available on an integrated basis. The policy of racial discrimination, however, continued in the other permanent projects, blacks charging that the DHC was creating "Uncle Tom's Cabins." One of the temporary projects had been integrated beginning in May 1962, but the DHC had begun to dispose of these projects by that time.[12]

On June 5, 1950, in a case litigated by the Detroit NAACP, ten Detroit black applicants for public housing initiated a suit against the DHC regarding its administration of public housing. At the time, the

119

eligible pool of certified applicants for public housing in Detroit was composed of 383 whites and 7,709 blacks. The case was not decided until June 22, 1954, when federal District Court Judge Arthur Lederle found that the DHC's "strict policy of racial segregation" violated the Constitution and laws of the United States. He enjoined the DHC from maintaining racially segregated projects, leasing public housing units on the basis of race or color, and maintaining separate lists of white and black applicants for public housing. Of the seven permanent projects at that time, four were all white, two were all black, and Jeffries Homes was integrated.

In an action that "appalled" supporters of housing integration in Detroit, the DHC appealed the district court's order. The commission did not call for a reversal of the Lederle decision, but, believing that desegregation had to be achieved "on a gradual basis," it asked for "sufficient time within which to complete orderly and peaceful integration." By the time the U.S. Court of Appeals for the Sixth Circuit ruled on the appeal on October 5, 1955, the Charles Terrace Project in the city had been integrated. The circuit court upheld the lower court's decision, but it noted that as a result of the U.S. Supreme Court decision in *Brown* v. *Board of Education* (*Brown II*) on May 31, 1955, "with all deliberate speed" had become the law "governing segregation and integration in the case of public facilities."[13]

Integration of Detroit's public housing proceeded at a snail's pace following the circuit court decision. In 1957 George A. Isabell, a former DHC member, complained to the Detroit Common Council that the commission was violating both the "letter and spirit" of the Lederle decision and that the circuit court decision was being implemented not by "deliberate speed" but rather "with all deliberate delay and procrastination just short of open defiance." Because of continuing accusations of this sort, Mayor Louis Miriani in 1958 directed the Detroit Commission on Community Relations (DCCR) to investigate the DHC's procedures regarding public housing occupancy. On the basis of a staff audit of housing applications during a three-month period, Richard V. Marks, the secretary-director of the DCCR, reported in August 1959 that the DHC was continuing to separate white and nonwhite housing occupants by race. He noted, for example, that Jeffries Homes, 45 percent of whose occupants had once been white, had by then become an overwhelmingly nonwhite project.[14]

Following the Marks report and at the mayor's suggestion, the DHC and the DCCR formed a Joint Committee to review the occupancy policies and practices of the DHC. The committee's deliberations led to a new policy statement by the DHC on November 12, 1959, that it would thereafter "avoid or refrain from any policy or practice which results directly or indirectly in discrimination or any form of segregation by reason of race, color, religion, national origin or ancestry." The Joint Committee also recommended changes in the procedures and forms used by the DHC and the inauguration of an in-service training program for DHC personnel, recommendations the DHC adopted and implemented.[15]

As the DHC proceeded to integrate the city's public housing projects, homeowner groups petitioned from time to time to have the city dispose of the integrated projects and those scheduled for integration. As of December 1960, there were 3,738 whites and 3,931 blacks in Detroit's seven projects. Two projects were entirely nonwhite, allegedly because the occupants wanted it that way—the same argument that had been used to defend segregated schools. Nonwhites constituted 91.8 percent of the tenants in Jeffries Homes and from 3.1 to 7.7 percent of the occupants of the other four projects. Although the degree of integration of the projects was thus rather modest at best, Marks nevertheless stated at the end of 1960 that "the lingering issue of public housing integration [in Detroit] has finally been resolved." Four years later, at the end of 1964, integration had been achieved in four of the projects, blacks in these projects ranging from 12.2 percent to 37.6 percent of the occupants. Since only 22 percent of the public housing projects in forty-five states at that time were racially integrated, the Michigan record for integration as of the end of 1964 was better than the average for the nation.[16]

Addressing one of his aides, Williams on February 13, 1957, expressed the need for his administration to "develop some civil rights program" to supplement the Fair Employment Practices Act. "Some of our friends in this area," the governor asserted, "are restive that there is nothing being done." Fearing they would "come up with an unwise program," he thought his administration should sponsor "an affirmative program to channel their energies into a more productive line." There was also concern in the Williams administration that if it did not expand its civil rights efforts to include the critical area of housing, there might be racial trouble in Detroit and possibly elsewhere in the state.[17]

Responding to these concerns, Williams asked the FEPC to make a study of housing and "other attendant questions" and to see what could be done to "alleviate friction" and improve community relations. His aim, Williams told the Democratic State Central Committee, was to broaden the jurisdiction of the FEPC to cover discrimination in areas other than employment. He asserted that it had taken six years to secure fair employment legislation and that he had not thought it "prudent" while the FEPC was getting under way and then gaining public confidence to attempt to expand its role. Since the FEPC, as he saw it, had by then been "thoroughly accepted," he believed that the time had come "to take some forward steps" regarding civil rights.[18]

At an augmented staff meeting on September 30, 1957, all of those present agreed that Michigan should be brought in line with some other states in the civil rights area by expanding the FEPC's jurisdiction. By that time, the administrative commissions corresponding to the FEPC in eight other states exercised jurisdiction over public accommodations and education, and the commissions in five states exercised jurisdiction over housing. The day before the staff meeting, Williams, seeking bipartisan support, had expressed an intention to limit the extension of the FEPC's authority to public accommodations and public education. The administration's caution was largely explained by its awareness of the opposition that inclusion of housing in the FEPC's jurisdiction would encounter in the legislature. By the end of 1957, however, the Williams administration had decided to include publicly assisted housing within the jurisdiction of a proposed civil rights commission that would replace the FEPC.[19]

Beginning in 1958, Williams and then Swainson and their supporters in the legislature annually supported bills to bring public accommodations, education, and housing within the jurisdiction of a state civil rights commission. The commission for which these bills provided was to exercise its authority essentially as the FEPC did, except that most of the bills granted the proposed commission initiatory power in filing complaints and specifically provided that appeals from its orders were to be by certiorari rather than being tried de novo. The debate in the legislature regarding these proposed measures focused almost entirely on their housing provisions, the sections on public accommodations and education proving to be far less controversial and sometimes being almost ignored.[20]

In his message to the legislature of January 9, 1958, Williams proposed that the lawmakers forbid discrimination in the sale or rental of housing of four or more "contiguously located units" financed by or dependent on public aid, including loan guarantees. In a more sweeping proposal, he also called for legislation to prohibit state-licensed real estate bankers or agents from accepting discriminatory property listings and from discriminating in transactions involving the sale or rental of any housing.[21]

Meeting with Williams a few days after the delivery of his message, representatives of the Michigan Coordinating Council on Civil Rights, which the civil rights organizations that had campaigned for a fair employment law had formed in 1957, pressed the governor to seek a ban on discrimination in privately financed housing, not just publicly assisted housing. "We try to take the realistic point of view on legislation,"

Williams responded. "We recognize we are getting into the tender area where the problem is most acute," he said, and he did not want to "give enemies the chance to raise a lot of hubbub." He correctly noted, moreover, that his recommendation regarding real estate brokers would "effectively meet the problem" of private housing.[22]

In response to the governor's recommendation, two bills—one sponsored by Democrats, one by Republicans—were introduced in the Michigan House, composed at the time of forty-nine Democrats and sixty-one Republicans. The bills defined publicly assisted housing as housing that the state or one of its political subdivisions had exempted from taxes in whole or in part, constructed on land sold below cost by any of these units of government pursuant to the Federal Housing Act of 1949, "acquired or assembled" by any of them for such construction, or "for the acquisition, construction, repair or maintenance of which" any of them had provided financial assistance. The owners of such property were forbidden to discriminate in its sale, rental, or lease on the basis of race, color, religion, national origin, or ancestry. One of the bills applied to all publicly assisted housing, the other was limited to residences in which one of four or more units on contiguous land was owned by or whose sale was controlled by the same person. Neither bill emerged from committee, the fate that was to befall all housing, public accommodations, and education discrimination bills during the remainder of the Williams administration and the successor Swainson administration. As to why the House State Affairs Committee had killed the two 1958 bills, the committee's chair, the die-hard Portland Republican Lloyd Gibbs, bluntly declared, "We killed them because we wanted to."[23]

In his 1959 message to the legislature, Williams renewed his request for the expansion of the FEP Act into "a basic civil rights code" that would include "the remaining areas of racial friction": housing, public accommodations, and education. Insofar as housing was concerned, Democrats in the House and Senate responded with bills limited to publicly assisted housing of three or more units, whereas Louis Cramton introduced a bill that applied not only to all publicly assisted housing but also to private housing. This corresponded with the position regarding housing discrimination by the state Democratic Party's Subcommittee on Discrimination and the Coordinating Council on Civil Rights, which thought that the governor should go for the "maximum" because it was "right" even if he did not believe that there was "a lot of support" for such a bill. Representatives of the state's major religious faiths, as well as labor, civic, and community groups, supported the legislation, claiming that it reflected "not just the climate of opinion in the state, but also throughout the nation." An aide complained to Williams that the Coordinating Council had gotten "involved in capitol corridor [sic] politics" in supporting the Cramton bill and by so doing had "damaged the chances of any kind of all-out fight by our people" to support the more modest Democratic measures.[24]

Homeowners, builders, realtors, and taxpayers registered their opposition to the 1959 civil rights bills, particularly their housing provisions. "We don't like this pushing, shoving, and needling to force home owners to do things," declared a representative of the Greater Lansing Board of Realtors. The Michigan Real Estate Association complained that the measures deprived the owner of property of the constitutional right of "freedom of choice in the sale or rental of his own residential property." It insisted that rather than alleviating discrimination, the bills, if passed, would lead to a decline in investment in new housing and would exacerbate "tensions" between the races. The association maintained that advocates of the measures did not seem to realize that the "inevitable result" if the bills became law would be "the scrapping of property rights and the adoption of Communist Ideology through the ownership of property by the state."

Quite apart from the criticism by realtors, Republican Speaker of the House Don R. Pears of Buchanan remarked that a "frequent question" asked about open occupancy was whether it would lead to a black influx in white neighborhoods. A representative of the Detroit Taxpayers Union warned that "every apartment building in Detroit . . . [would] be emptied of white people" were any of the bills to pass. The Michigan Council of Churches found itself "under fire" from some of its constituents because of its association with the Coordinating Council and its support for legislation banning housing discrimination. Veteran lawmakers said that the opposition to the civil rights bills was "more outspoken than any within their memory" regarding social legislation. Even though Pears, who had promised Williams that one of the bills would be reported out of committee, in the end joined the governor in supporting the civil rights bills, they died in committee in both houses of the legislature. The Coordinating Council complained that both parties had been "remiss" in delivering their promised support for civil rights legislation.[25]

Having failed to persuade the legislature to act on housing discrimination, Williams appealed directly to the realtors themselves. In an address of February 18, 1960, to the Northwestern Realty Association and the Wayne County Board of Realtors, the governor asked his audience to anticipate Brotherhood Week, the week that followed, by helping to fulfill the American "promise of equal opportunity for all." Recognizing that "cracking the color line in housing" was "much tougher than in employment," the governor appealed to the realtors' "sense of religion," their "sense of humanity," and their "sense of American destiny." He rejected what he labeled the myth that "the darker the hue of the tenant, the lower the value of the property," asserting that studies indicated that "minority group occupancy in and of itself did not affect property values one way or another." What did result from housing discrimination and the confinement of minority groups to "already overcrowded areas," he said, was "slums, juvenile delinquency, health and fire hazards, and a host of similar social blights." The speech, as Williams reported, created "some stir." "Flabbergasted," with some exceptions, that the governor had spoken to them as he had, the realtors accused Williams of "dropping 'a bomb.'"[26]

Following the governor's lead, Democrats in the House, who had established a special committee on civil rights, introduced a measure in the 1960 session of the legislature that they characterized as a "Bill of Rights" and that applied to discrimination with respect to public accommodations, education, and housing. The bill's definition of housing discrimination included the refusal of licensed real estate agents and their brokers or representatives "to rent, lease, sell, or to vary the terms of rental, leasing or sale of a housing accommodation" because of race, color, religion, or national origin, and to refuse "to receive or transmit any bona fide offer to sell, purchase, rent or lease any housing accommodation." Broader in its definition of housing discrimination than previous Democratic bills, the measure applied to private as well as publicly assisted housing. Those persons selling or renting their own homes or housing of not more than four units, one of which the seller occupied as a residence, were exempted from the measure. As in the preceding two years, the housing section of the bill proved to be its "most controversial portion."[27]

Four hundred African Americans from all over Michigan converged on Lansing on March 9 to support the Democratic bill and to demonstrate against what they characterized as "a 'do nothing' Legislature." Unsurprisingly, the House State Affairs Committee refused to report the bill. Chairman Gibbs, engaging in what proponents of the measure called an "infamous 'walkout,'" deliberately absented himself on the final day for reporting out bills so that the measure could not be considered because of the absence of the committee's chair. The Democrats then filed a motion to have the bill discharged from the committee, but they abandoned their motion in favor of a proposal by some Republicans that members of the two parties join in an effort to secure the discharge of a weaker Republican civil rights bill. In a House evenly divided between the two parties, the bipartisan motion failed by a 53–51 vote, 60 votes being required to secure the discharge.[28]

What happened regarding housing in the Michigan legislature in 1960 attracted far less public attention than the public revelation for the first time of the infamous Grosse Pointe screening system involving the disposition of property in the five Grosse Pointes in suburban Detroit. As the system worked beginning in 1945, when it was adopted by the Grosse Pointe Brokers Association (GPBA), a private detective investigated prospective home purchasers at a cost of ten dollars per report. The detective customarily told interviewees that he was investigating a prospective employee. If interviewees provided different views of a prospect, the detective took "the average." The investigation was divided into two parts. Section A, for 50 points, was concerned with whether the prospect's "way of living" was "American." The questions dealt with such matters as the prospect's country of origin, his occupation, whether his friends were "predominantly American," his appearance (very or slightly "swarthy"), and his accent. Section B, for the remaining 50 points, was concerned with a prospect's "General Standing," including such matters as the reputation of his employer, whether the prospect's "dealings" were considered "reputable," how neighbors viewed his family, his dress, his education, and the appearance of his home. There were separate questions concerning religion, grammar, and military service.

The minimum passing grade for a prospect was 50 points. Although the passing grade for different nationality groups varied over time, at the time the system was revealed Polish Americans needed 55 points; southern Europeans (Italian Americans, Greek Americans), 75 points; and Jews, 85 points, later raised to 90. Because Jews were viewed as "different from those in other categories," they received fewer points than other prospects for the same answers. African Americans and persons of Oriental descent were entirely eliminated from consideration.

The detective sent three copies of his report to the Grosse Pointe Property Owners Association (GPPOA) and three to the members of a rotating committee of three brokers, each of whom graded the report. If the prospect received a passing grade from two committee members, the broker who had initiated the inquiry was so informed. If the prospect failed, members of the GPBA and other brokers who used the system were notified. An "Explanatory Leaflet" sent to GPPOA members stated that the only purpose of the screening system was to maintain property values by keeping out "undesirables." The leaflet pointed out that since U.S. Supreme Court decisions had made restrictive covenants "virtually unenforceable," "gaps in the screening process" could be "closed to the extent that there . . . [was] behind the plan a large and active group of property owners determined to close them."

Of 1,597 prospects investigated from 1945 to 1960, 939 passed and 658 failed. Others qualified without investigation. If a broker sold property to an ineligible prospect, the broker was to forfeit to the GPBA the commission for the sale, including the share of the salesman. If this was not done, the offending broker was expelled from the association. The fund that paid for the system was derived from a thirty-dollar assessment on members of the GPBA, 10 percent of the gross commissions of the brokers and any money they paid in fines, and dues paid by the approximately one thousand members of the GPPOA, which had been formed in 1950 and whose members were assessed "in proportion to the value of the property protected." In 1950, the phrase "screening process" was changed to the less pejorative "reference report system."[29]

After being "secretly used" for fifteen years, the Grosse Pointe system came to public attention as the result of a suit brought in the St. Clair County Circuit Court by John A. Maxwell. Unable to complete a "mansion" he was building, Maxwell had borrowed $50,000 from Grosse Pointe Properties, Inc., which had been formed "specifically to assist in the completion of the house" and which took a mortgage on the property and reserved the right to approve or disapprove any prospective purchaser thereof. When Maxwell sought to pay off the mortgage, Grosse Pointe Properties ruled him "undesirable," presumably because the U.S. government was prosecuting him for fraud. Maxwell, however, charged that the GPBA and the GPPOA had formed Grosse Pointe Properties specifically to prevent him from selling his property to a black. During the course of the trial, Maxwell's attorney, in questioning the executive secretary of the GPPOA, "uncovered" the existence of the screening system.[30]

The Maxwell trial was ignored by the press, just as some earlier references to the system in the black press had failed to attract attention. The Michigan Regional Office of the Anti-Defamation League of B'nai B'rith, which had heard rumors about the Grosse Pointe system, did, however, become aware of the trial. It secured a copy of the form used to rate prospective Grosse Pointe property buyers and then held a press conference on the subject. It supplied information regarding the system to Michigan's attorney general, Paul Adams, and its Corporation and Securities commissioner, Lawrence Gubow, as well as to local television stations, the local office of *Time* magazine, and the *New York Times*. The screening system became international news, not just national news, receiving front-page treatment in Switzerland, Australia, Japan, and Hong Kong.[31]

Adams on April 18, 1960, denounced the Grosse Pointe system as "morally corrupt" and revealed that his office was investigating it. Governor Williams characterized the system as "odious" and "strange and unhealthy." In a joint statement, the GPBA and GPPOA responded that "the system would seem to be the most careful and considerate method possible for making the best of a difficult fact—of prejudices which affect real estate values."[32]

127

Adams and Gubow, both dedicated civil rights advocates, arranged for public hearings concerning the point system. The hearings began in Detroit on May 2, 1960, and attracted a national and international press. Speaking for the Grosse Pointe realtors, Paul Maxon claimed that the same plan was followed in "fine residential communities" elsewhere in the nation but in a "more informal manner." The plan reflected "a sincere attempt to maintain values and maintain neighborhoods," declared the president of the GPBA, conceding that prejudice was "undemocratic." An audience of forty, mostly women, cheered Maxon when he finished reading his statement and occasionally "hooted" the state's solicitor general, who questioned Maxon. So many ethnic minorities were affected by the Grosse Pointe system that the Williams administration recognized that the hearings provided it with an "effective public relations sounding board." When the hearings resumed on May 11, the public learned that the mayor of Grosse Pointe Woods had himself been expelled from the GPBA for selling homes to two purchasers of Italian descent, one of whom had emigrated from Italy forty years earlier and the other of whom had been born in the United States.[33]

"Any system that rates American people on a point system," Adams had said at the beginning of the hearings, "is un-American, and I will do everything in my power to strike it down." It is hardly surprising that when the hearings concluded on May 13, Gubow and Adams announced that a rule was needed to govern "the unlawful activities by brokers under a screening system based upon discriminations in regard to race, color, or creed." In a letter to the attorneys for the GPBA and GPPOA, Gubow and Adams informed them that "there must be a complete and absolute abandonment of the screening and reporting system" within thirty days or the state would impose all sanctions permitted under the law. Responding with defiance, the two associations criticized the hearings as a "cheap political circus to further the personal political ambitions of the attorney general."[34]

On May 27 the Corporation and Securities Commission announced a proposed rule—it became Rule 9—to govern the discriminatory acts of licensed real estate brokers and salesmen. "A broker or salesman," the rule stated, "acting individually or jointly with others, shall not refuse to sell or offer for sale, or to buy, or offer to buy, or to appraise or to list, or to negotiate the purchase, sale, exchange or mortgage of real estate, or to negotiate for the construction of buildings thereon, or to lease or offer for lease, or to rent or offer for rent, any real estate or improvements thereon, or any other service performed as broker or salesman, because of the race, color, religion, national origin or ancestry of any person or persons." Under existing law, the Corporation and Securities Commission could revoke the license of a real estate broker or salesman for "unfair dealing," and the commission was now proposing to construe racial, ethnic, and religious discrimination as "unfair dealing."[35]

Although official adoption of the new rule did not require preceding public hearings, the commission nevertheless held such hearings in Detroit on June 21 and in Grand Rapids on June 28. In an opening statement at the Detroit hearings, attorneys for the GPBA, the GPPOA, and Grosse Pointe Properties, with questionable accuracy, insisted that the screening system was "a purely advisory plan of informing sellers to whom they are selling" and that the only person who could veto a sale was the owner of the property. Ninety-two Grosse Pointe residents submitted a letter to Gubow at the beginning of the Detroit hearings condemning the screening system. Of twenty-six witnesses at the Detroit hearings, sixteen favored the proposed rule, and ten opposed it; in Grand Rapids, the comparable numbers were twenty-nine and seven. The principal opposition to the rule came from real estate associations, real estate brokers, and homeowner groups. "The overwhelming preponderance of testimony," Gubow concluded, "confirmed the need for State action" and not just applying to the Grosse Pointes. The Corporation and Securities Commission consequently formally adopted Rule 9 on June 30. It was to go into effect on August 14, 1960.[36]

The reaction to Rule 9 of most realtors, who conducted "a massive campaign to panic home-owners" concerning the rule, was summed up by William R. Luedders, president of the DREB. Realtors, he asserted, were not "free agents" but were "merely the representatives of the owners," who could legally dispose of their property as they saw fit. "For a state official," Luedders said, "to prohibit an agent from carrying out the instructions of his employer seems to me a precedent which places all businessmen in danger of government by bureaus." There was also strong opposition to the rule in the state legislature. The Joint House-Senate Committee on Administrative Rules voted 4–1 in early August to petition the 1961 legislature to overturn the rule. When the legislature convened, both houses, indeed, voted to abolish Rule 9, the Senate by a 19–12 vote, the House by a 64–35 vote, but the legislators could not override the veto of Governor Swainson. A coalition of Democrats and moderate Republicans killed a similar effort in the 1962 legislature. The same fate befell repeal efforts in the Michigan Constitutional Convention, which was in session from October 3, 1961, to August 1, 1962.[37]

In the event, Rule 9 never went into effect, although the GPBA officially terminated the screening system on August 24, 1960, and the GPPOA, in effect, followed suit. On August 13, the day before the rule was to go into effect, three Lansing real estate firms, acting on behalf of the 1,975 members of the Michigan Real Estate Association and contending that the rule unconstitutionally deprived property owners of their right to sell their property to whomever they wished and would do "great" harm to brokers, secured a restraining order from Ingham County Circuit Court Judge Samuel Street Hughes to prevent the rule from going into effect. The case was eventually appealed to the Michigan Supreme Court, with amicus briefs in support of the rule being filed by the American Civil Liberties Union, the NAACP, the Anti-Defamation League, the American Jewish Congress, and the American Jewish Committee. In an opinion handed down on February 6, 1963, by the court's "most liberal justice" and from which there was no dissent, the court concluded that the practice proscribed by the rule was not "commonly understood" to be included in the term "unfair dealing." The court also ruled that the action of the licensees forbidden by the rule could not be construed as state action and hence forbidden by the equal protection clause of the Fourteenth Amendment.[38]

Successful in preventing the legislature from abolishing Rule 9, Swainson in his one term as governor was no less determined than Williams had been in seeking to persuade the legislature to agree to the creation of a civil rights commission to deal with discrimination in housing, public accommodations, and education as well as employment. He contended that there was a "profound" and "fundamental" relationship among these aspects of civil rights and that the state had to deal with all of them. When he learned late in 1961 that an assistant general counsel of the United Automobile Workers who had just arrived in Detroit had been unable to lease an apartment because of his race, the governor remarked, "The question of open housing may well be central to our entire efforts in the field of human relations."[39]

The FEPC prepared drafts of a civil rights bill for the Swainson administration to submit to the legislature in its 1961 session. Indicating that not only principle was involved, Frederick Routh wrote the governor, "Many political observers feel that the big city, minority group vote was a decisive factor in the Democratic victory in the November [1960] election. This, I believe, adds a strategic urgency to the moral imperative to move ahead on civil rights now." The administration was, indeed, prepared "to move ahead," but the legislature was not. The civil rights bills introduced in 1961 in a legislature made up of fifty-six Republicans and fifty-four Democrats in the House and twenty-two Republicans and twelve Democrats in the Senate failed once again to emerge from committee. A House Democratic leader charged that "bitter ignorance" had once again "prevailed," whereas a spokesman for a homeowners association complained that a "minority group" kept "agitating the civil rights issue." The Coordinating Council correctly attributed the "lack of movement" regarding civil rights measures that it favored to the fact that housing was "a more emotional issue" than employment and that it was consequently more difficult to put together a bipartisan coalition that could achieve legislative success.[40]

In a message to the legislature in 1962, Swainson noted that the U.S. Commission on Civil Rights regarded housing discrimination as the nation's "most pressing problem" in civil rights. He characterized the Grosse Pointe screening system as "only the most flagrant example" of housing discrimination in the state and called for legislation to ban discrimination not only in public housing but in "all publicly supported, guaranteed, and underwritten housing" as well as in multiple dwellings of four or more units, and also to prohibit discriminatory practices by licensed realtors. When the House State Affairs Committee failed to take action on two civil rights bills following a clash in the hearings on the bills between the civil rights forces and the Michigan Real Estate Association and homeowner organizations, Swainson reminded the committee that both parties had pledged their support for fair housing. The ineffable Gibbs, who accused the civil rights advocates of "harassing the public constantly," responded that the governor had "entertained" the State Affairs Committee and that, in any event, the tax issue before the legislature was more important than civil rights.

The Senate State Affairs Committee not only refused to heed the governor's wishes but moved in the opposite direction. It reported out a bill giving property owners the right to sell or rent their property to whomever they wished and voided any act to the contrary. It also reported a second bill authorizing the revocation of the license of a real estate agent for "screening prospective purchasers" without authorization by the seller to do so. An irate Swainson rebuked the Republican-dominated committee for seeking to make it "public policy" for one state inhabitant to discriminate against another. Both measures in the end failed of enactment. Michigan at the close of the Swainson governorship not only lagged behind other states regarding open occupancy in publicly assisted housing, but eight states by that time had enacted legislation also banning discrimination in private housing to one degree or another.[41]

Despite the lack of progress in dealing with housing discrimination at the state level, the Michigan State Advisory Committee to the U.S. Commission on Civil Rights reported in 1961 that it had found some "signs of increasing citizen concern" about the matter at the local level. In Ann Arbor, where realtors and managers of large rental units refused "to sell, lease, or rent" to blacks "outside certain predetermined areas," a University of Michigan committee on discrimination in off-campus housing adopted a policy on May 9, 1961, of denying university services to owners and landlords who discriminated in the sale or rental of housing except for those who provided rooms in their own homes for not more than two students. Also, the Ann Arbor Area Fair Housing Association staged a successful campaign to desegregate the 422 rental apartments in nearby Pittsfield Village. Aided by thirteen Ann Arbor and Detroit organizations, it picketed the Ann Arbor office of the Detroit firm that managed the apartments as well as a downtown Detroit building that it also managed, and it staged "silent protest marches" through the village on eighteen consecutive Sundays and also an "Equality Vigil" in the village over a weekend. The demonstrations ceased on August 14, 1962, after the Pittsfield management adopted a policy of nondiscrimination in the rental of the village apartments.[42]

In Kalamazoo, the City Commission officially declared its opposition to segregated housing in 1955. At the suggestion of the city's Council on Community Relations, more than a thousand of the city's inhabitants signed a newspaper advertisement supporting the right of individuals regardless of their race or religion to buy or rent homes in the neighborhood of their choice. In Pontiac, the city's Public Housing Commission adopted a nondiscriminatory occupancy policy on November 19, 1961.

Nonwhites in both Kalamazoo and Ann Arbor were reportedly able to secure mortgage credit for homes in new locations on the same terms as whites, and in Lansing and Ann Arbor, blacks in increasing numbers had succeeded by 1961 in obtaining FHA-insured home loans. An African American had been added to the local real estate board in Flint by then, and two had joined the Detroit board. In Ypsilanti, a nonprofit corporation had constructed rental housing on an open occupancy basis.[43]

Frustrated by the state legislature's failure to provide for fair housing, members of religious groups in Detroit, the DCCR, and other organizations and individuals interested in the promotion of civil rights decided that it was necessary to organize to combat housing discrimination in the metropolitan area. A "loose fellowship" of professional and lay persons in the area, united by the belief that housing discrimination was "a keystone in all discrimination," came together in May 1960 to form the "predominantly white" Greater Detroit Committee for Fair Housing Practices. The committee quickly attracted about eight hundred members, many of them affiliated with one organization or another but not officially representing their organization on the committee.[44]

In 1962 the Greater Detroit Committee initiated three activities to promote fair housing in the Detroit metropolitan area. For one thing, it adopted a Fair Practice Code for Real Estate Brokers and Agents. Signers of the code stated their agreement that "every person has a right to sell or buy a home anywhere without restrictions based on race, religion, or national ancestry." Committee members pledged themselves to list and sell property in any neighborhood to "any responsible person" without discrimination, to "promote stable neighborhoods with regard to true and proper real estate values," to "refrain from unscrupulous selling methods causing panic and discord in neighborhoods" (i.e., blockbusting), and not only to aid minority groups in finding housing of their own choice in areas where that right had been denied but also to aid majority-group families to return to integrated neighborhoods if they so desired. Just how many real estate brokers actually signed the code is uncertain.

In an effort to demonstrate that there was "no 'safe' place for a bigot" in the area, the Greater Detroit Committee beginning in 1962 also sought to persuade residents of Detroit and its suburbs to sign "Covenant Cards" indicating that they would "welcome" persons in their neighborhood without regard to their race, religion, or national origin. As of April 24, 1965, 3,352 Detroiters and 994 suburban residents had signed the cards.[45]

The most important of the three activities of the Greater Detroit Committee launched in 1962 was its Fair Housing Listing Service. This was a register of property in the metropolitan area available for sale or rental on an open occupancy basis as well as a listing of minority-group families who might be interested in buying or renting such property. The committee used the register to introduce prospective buyers and renters to owners, and it provided housing aides to assist those willing to "pioneer" in new areas. Although the committee indicated in September 1965 that the listing service was opening up "many new areas" for integrated housing, the chair of the service reported in March 1967 that it had actually attracted "very limited support" because it had not been able to provide enough choices of housing in any one area to make it "economically feasible for an open housing broker to really operate profitably in that area." Prospective minority purchasers and renters also feared the reaction of the white community to "integrated housing" and the possibility that violence might occur if they purchased or rented homes in white neighborhoods. "Pioneers in housing are few and far between," the chair of the service declared. The Greater Detroit Committee continued, however, to operate its listing service, and as of June 1968 it was listing homes available for occupancy in many Detroit suburbs, including Grosse Pointe Shores.[46]

A second organizational result of the concern of community groups and individuals in the Detroit area to combat housing discrimination was the decision of the city's three major religious faiths to hold a Tri-Faith Conference on Open Occupancy in January 1963. The idea for such a conference developed out of a series of meetings beginning in 1960 organized by the Neighborhoods Housing Committee of the Jewish

Community Council of Detroit. At a June 5, 1962, meeting of about 150 clergy and members of different congregations and community groups sponsored by the three faiths to consider the problem of open occupancy and the stabilization of neighborhoods in the Detroit metropolitan area, the sponsors were asked to establish a committee to plan a metropolitan conference on open occupancy. An executive committee, formed after the meeting and consisting of a representative of each of the three faiths and two DCCR representatives, decided to hold such a conference in January 1963. "It will be a powerful stroke for a greater degree of justice in housing to have Catholics, Jews, and Protestants stand together with a common purpose," declared the executive director of the Michigan Council of Churches. The conference was designed "to present an image to the metropolitan community and to the state of status, respect and power groups taking a definite stand" on open occupancy.[47]

The delegates who gathered for what was designated the Metropolitan Conference on Open Occupancy recommended that "every church and synagogue become a generating center of the forces of intergroup understanding and welcome in its neighborhood and community." They urged that a committee be created in each state legislative district to seek a state open occupancy law and that the three faiths support the "comprehensive civil rights legislation" that Williams and Swainson had proposed. They also proposed that the churches, parishes, and Jewish congregations establish committees on public affairs or social action whose concern would be "the equality of all citizens, the destruction of every vestige of discrimination against all groups and the reduction of attitudes of prejudice to a minimum." The executive committee formed after the conference held a series of religiously oriented conferences on housing in the Detroit metropolitan area. It sought to help middle-class blacks "move into the larger community" and to persuade whites that it was their "moral duty" to support these efforts.[48]

Supporters of fair housing in Detroit were fiercely opposed by a variety of neighborhood associations and homeowner groups. At least 192 such organizations were formed between 1943 and 1965, constituting "one of the largest grassroots movements" in Detroit's history. For these organizations, composed of middle-class and working-class whites, including union members, "the issues of race and housing were inseparable." Unwilling under the circumstances to enact a fair housing ordinance, the Detroit Common Council in 1962 adopted a Fair Neighborhood Practice Ordinance that was to be enforced by the DCCR. Designed particularly to deal with blockbusting, the ordinance restricted the number of realty signs, their location, and the length of time they could be displayed, and made it unlawful to refer to race in seeking property listings or in realty advertising. Although the ordinance was "loosely enforced," the DCCR had found 855 violations by July 1966 and had recommended 12 prosecutions resulting in 7 convictions.[49]

Stalled at the state level, the cause of open housing in Michigan received a small boost when President John F. Kennedy issued an executive order on Thanksgiving Day in 1962 forbidding the FHA, the VA, and the Farmers Home Administration from providing loans to builders who refused to sell to minority-group members. The Corporation and Securities Commission promptly called for a meeting of federal, state, and Detroit officials to discuss the implementation of the order in Michigan.[50] As we shall see, however, far more important for the cause of open occupancy than the president's executive order and the efforts of organizations in cities like Detroit to deal with housing discrimination were the provisions regarding civil rights in the constitution drawn up by the Michigan Constitutional Convention of 1961–62 and then approved by the state's voters.

6

THE DISADVANTAGED, 1949–1962:
The Aged, Women,
Native Americans,
and the Physically Handicapped

The civil rights program of the Williams and Swainson administrations was by no means limited to African Americans among the disadvantaged groups in the state. There was also a growing concern after World War II in Michigan and in many other states about the discrimination suffered by the aged, women, Native Americans, and the physically handicapped. The Williams and Swainson administrations believed that the state government had an obligation to deal with the problems these groups faced. As Williams put it, "We are all children of one God who looks upon us equally regardless of what color we may be and without regard to other differences which may have come by chance."[1] Williams and Swainson were undecided for a time as to how the state government could best meet its obligations to the disadvantaged, and, as noted, they faced a state legislature far less committed to civil rights than they were.

THE AGED

In Michigan and elsewhere in the nation, the aged, rapidly increasing in numbers after World War II and becoming a larger and larger voting bloc, understandably attracted the attention of public policy makers. There was a growing concern about the health, housing, and income of the aged as well as their social adjustment and preparation for retirement. Insofar as the civil rights of the aged were concerned, the focus initially was on the job discrimination they experienced.

According to a Census Bureau study of March 1952, 58 percent of men aged sixty-five to sixty-nine but only 13 percent of women of that age range remained in the labor force. Employers tended to retain older workers already on their payroll but were apt to apply "strict age limits" in hiring new older workers. A November 1954 survey of state Employment Security offices across the nation by the Department of Labor's Bureau of Employment Security (BES) revealed that workers over age forty-five constituted about one-third of all job applicants but received only 18 percent of nongovernmental job placements. In Michigan and elsewhere, job opportunities "progressively decreased" for workers beginning at age forty.[2]

Research in the 1950s indicated that older workers were "highly reliable and useful," had low absentee rates, and could be counted on for "steady output." A study of the production records of 137 workers aged sixty to sixty-five in three Chicago plants revealed no difference between their work records and those of workers aged forty to forty-five.[3]

The delegates who gathered for the National Conference on Aging in Washington in 1950 mounted a "wholesale attack" on the tendency to retire older workers from the labor force. Since the delegates believed that "a role in the productive life of the community" was "the most important status-giving activity" that could be provided most older people, they thought the elderly should be permitted to work as long as they were "able and willing" to do so. The conferees recognized that this might necessitate a shift of the elderly workers to jobs for which they were suited. Research, however, indicated that "continued inactivity" was all too often the lot of retirees, contributing to their "physical and mental deterioration."[4]

Most employers saw matters rather differently than aging experts did. Older workers, employers contended, were less efficient and phys- ically fit than younger workers, could not meet production standards, were "set in their ways," more costly to train, and more susceptible to injury and occupational diseases than their younger counterparts. Employers complained that older workers added to the employer cost of workmen's compensation insurance, group insurance, and indus- trial pension plans, and employers claimed that insurance companies "surreptitiously" urged the employment of younger workers. The pub- lic, employers insisted, preferred to see younger workers employed as receptionists, service workers, and even as typists and stenographers. As the director of the Employment Service Division of the Michigan Employment Security Commission (MESC) testified in 1959, a study of Detroit in 1956 indicated that "most of the reasons" employers gave for not hiring older workers did "not stand up under the light of any scientific appraisal."[5]

Age discrimination in employment was "rampant" in the post– World War II years. The MESC reported in September 1955 that most

Michigan employers specified "age hiring ranges," that only 10 percent of male job applicants were hired after age forty-five, and that some employers considered applicants aged thirty-five as too old. A U.S. Department of Labor official reported in 1958 that 67 percent of the jobs available in Detroit carried age restrictions. More than 35 percent of the restrictions applied to job applicants aged forty-five and older, and more than one-half set the age limit at fifty-five.[6]

The obvious way for Michigan to have dealt with the problem of age discrimination in employment was to pass a law to ban such discrimination, as some states had done. Michigan's executive branch, however, was slow to come to this conclusion, and the state legislature was slower still to take the necessary action.

The MESC, as Wilma Donahue, the state's leading gerontologist, put it, occupied "the hottest seat of all" when it came to employment of the elderly. It sought to aid them in finding jobs, but when Williams became governor, it lacked the commitment to the aged to perform that job effectively. A study by the BES in 1950 of the various state employment service agencies concluded that twice as many job applicants over age forty-five could have been placed if more time had been devoted by these agencies to counseling and seeking to place such workers. This became the path the MESC followed in the absence of a state ban on age discrimination in employment.[7]

In its report of January 1953, the Governor's Commission to Study the Problems of Aging, which Williams had appointed in the spring of 1951, recommended that the MESC implement a program of service to older workers and that it train counselors for the task. In its report for the fiscal year ending June 30, 1953, the MESC noted that it had "accelerated" its services to older workers and that the 30,463 workers over age forty-five whom it had placed in the fiscal year represented a 62.3 percent increase over the previous year despite a tight labor market.[8]

In the 1955 session of the legislature, the lawmakers enacted a measure specifically assigning the MESC the responsibility of placing workers aged sixty-five and older and stipulating that a special unit to deal with this matter be established in each MESC branch office. Since employment discrimination against the aged, however, occurred as early as age forty-five, the Legislative Advisory Council on Problems of the Aging, which the legislature had created that year, was "not happy" about limiting services for the aged to those sixty-five and older. The U.S. Department of Labor, which had initiated a study of services for the aged by Employment Security Commissions in eight cities, including Detroit, had set age forty-five as the beginning age for which special employment services were needed.[9]

In November 1955 the MESC submitted a series of recommendations to the governor's office regarding employment services for the aged. It noted that studies of the aged had indicated that for many older workers—and especially those under sixty-five and still able to work—employment was "the only real answer" to their economic problems and that the same was true for those aged sixty-five and over not covered by old age and survivors insurance or private pensions. If employment opportunities were to be recognized as "a right," the MESC recommended, arbitrary age restrictions for hiring should be removed; compulsory retirement at "a fixed chronological age" should be abandoned; the state should expand its rehabilitation program to include those with employment handicaps due to age; the adult education program should seek to improve the competitive position of the aged in the labor market; community workshops (sheltered workshops) should be developed to provide part-time employment for the aged; the recently enacted state law requiring the MESC to provide special services for those aged sixty-five and over should be amended to include all those whose employment problems were caused by their age; and a program of public education should be developed to deal with the problems resulting from aging and the degree to which individuals, the state's communities, and the state government had to "accept responsibility for prevention, alleviation and solution" of these problems.[10]

Appraising the problem of employment of older workers as "a pressing one of national concern," the BES instructed the state-funded Employment Security Commissions to develop "a total office program" for services to older workers. Each state agency was to designate a specialist on services to older workers in the state agency's administrative office, and a similar official was to be designated in the branch offices. The state commissions were instructed to seek to persuade employers to consider the employment of older workers on the basis of their qualifications and to remove arbitrary age limits for hiring. The commissions were to seek to develop suitable job openings for older workers, publicize their qualifications and abilities, and develop cooperative arrangements with local community agencies and organizations to ensure that older workers who required services of one kind or another to prepare for employment were referred to the proper agency.[11]

In response to the BES order, Max Horton, the MESC's head, designated B. H. McGinn as the state's older worker specialist. It was McGinn's responsibility to give "leadership, direction and functional supervision" to the statewide program of services for older workers. The MESC's Detroit office assigned a full-time older worker specialist to provide services to older workers, and the MESC's long-term plan called for a full-time specialist in its major branch offices and a part-time specialist in the remainder of its sixty-five branch offices. The MESC instructed all the branch offices to increase immediately the services they provided older workers and to ensure that these services were "adequate." Within a few years, the MESC branch offices had either a specific "Older Worker Specialist" or "a designated person" to assist older workers having difficulty finding a job.[12]

The gains derived from intensive placement efforts for older workers became evident when the BES's Older Worker Study in the Detroit metropolitan area and elsewhere, conducted between January and May 1956, was released early in 1957. The study indicated that prejudice against workers aged forty and over was "a very real thing" and was "deeply imbedded in the thinking of all segments of the community—including the workers themselves." Only one-third of the job listings in Detroit were open to qualified workers regardless of age, and when age was listed for job openings, 52 percent of the jobs were closed to those over age forty-five. The study indicated that the provision of employment services for older workers required "substantially more time" of placement officials than the services for younger workers. "Intensive job development" and placement efforts for older workers, however, resulted in a 569 percent increase in "call-ins," a 650 percent increase in job offers or referrals, and a 555 percent increase in placements for the "experimental group" receiving "unlimited services" as compared to the "control group," which received only the regular services. As a consequence of the study, the federal government allocated additional funds to the states for job services to older workers.[13]

The Detroit study spurred the development of the MESC's older worker program. The program provided that all applicants for employment, regardless of age, were to be handled by regular staff members for registration, selection, counseling, and referral, but if it became apparent that an older worker was having special employment problems because of age, the older worker specialist in the branch was called in for consultation or the worker might be referred for one or another of the special services available in the branch, such as counseling, testing, or job development. The state administrative office provided the branch specialists with relevant training on how to assist older workers, including some of the techniques developed as the result of the BES study, such as group guidance and staff clinics. The MESC also sought to educate employers and the public about the "favorable attributes" of older workers.[14]

The MESC's intensive efforts to place older workers produced positive results. In 1957 the commission placed 19.8 percent of the 27.5 percent of the job seekers aged forty-five and over, as compared to its placement of 15 percent of the 35 percent of the job seekers of this age in 1950. Although placement of older workers did not improve in fiscal year 1958, it increased to 21.2 percent in the next two fiscal years. In a demonstration project in Lansing funded by the BES that began in 1959 and continued for a second year, the MESC Lansing branch was able to increase the placement of workers aged forty-five and over by 13 percent by 1962. The project provided "specialized but integrated services for older workers in counseling, job development and placement," as well as promotional advertising in the community in behalf of older workers.[15]

The governor's office decided early in 1957 to consider seeking an amendment to the Fair Employment Practices (FEP) Act to outlaw employment discrimination based on age. The matter was referred to the Interdepartmental Committee on Problems of the Aging that Williams had appointed in 1950. When the committee met on January 14, 1957, John Feild, the FEPC's executive director, reported that Massachusetts and Pennsylvania already had such laws and that in Pennsylvania more complaints had been initiated in the first five months that the law had been in effect than the complaints based on race, religion, or ancestry over a twelve-month period. He thought that a ban on age discrimination would require "a different type of regulation and investigating staff" than the state FEP Act did, largely because there might be "real economic considerations" for the employer in hiring elderly workers, such as increased insurance and pension costs and the consequent need to permit exemptions from the law. Believing that the "exact nature of the problem" of age discrimination in employment was "not known," the Interdepartmental Committee recommended that the governor appoint a representative group to explore the matter.[16]

After being turned down by a number of businessmen, including George Romney, to whom he offered the chairmanship of what became the Study Committee on the Employment of the Older Worker, Williams appointed Edwin J. Forsythe, assistant director of the University of Michigan–Wayne State University Institute of Labor and Industrial Relations, to the position. The remaining members of the twenty-one-member commission were drawn principally from business and labor in the state and the state government. Williams asked the commission to "study and define" the nature of the problem of the older worker and to recommend what the state and local governments, employers, and unions should do so that "this vast pool of skill" would not be lost to the state and nation.

The Study Committee operated through three subcommittees, one to review existing legislation relating to aging and to make recommendations for legislative and administrative action to limit age discrimination in employment, a second to develop programs to increase the employability of individuals in the middle and upper years of age, and a third to recommend a program to promote public understanding of the positive benefits to be derived from the employment of middle-aged and older men and women. The first committee included among its members both John Feild and Wilbur J. Cohen, who had left his position as director of the Division of Research and Statistics of the Social Security Administration in 1956 to accept a position as professor of public welfare at the University of Michigan.[17]

The committee, Forsythe told the governor, found that "one highly significant factor" affecting the employability of older workers was the obsolescence of skills once essential to industry. Their health and the downturn in the state's economy, he reported, had also impaired the opportunity of older workers for employment. The chairman noted that labor force forecasts indicated that the numbers of those aged twenty-five to forty-four, who then made up "the 'prime' labor supply," were likely to decline as a proportion of the labor force in coming years and that the growth in the labor force would be among those younger than twenty-five and older than forty-four. This, he said, made it essential to increase the employability of the older workers.[18]

In its final report, submitted on May 28, 1959, the Study Committee called for the enactment of legislation to prohibit age discrimination in the employment of workers aged forty to sixty-five unless the employer could justify the presence of "bona fide occupational qualifications" relating to age. The committee did not specifically recommend that the FEPC administer the proposed law but only that "an appropriate state agency" be authorized to do so. It recommended further that the civil service of the state and local governments follow the practice adopted by the federal government on July 1, 1955, and remove age limitations for civil service positions. Subject to the approval of the BES, the Study Committee also advised that the MESC act be amended to make the commission's services for older workers available not just to those over age sixty-five but also to persons encountering problems in securing employment because of their age, whatever that age might be.

The Forsythe committee urged that the governor and legislature establish a planning body at the state level to "coordinate a program of training, retraining and rehabilitation" for older workers and to determine the occupations and industries for which these workers might be trained. It also recommended that a commission on aging be created to survey the resources and services available for older workers and to publish a directory of those resources and services, to take steps to educate and stimulate local groups to meet their responsibilities to the aged, and to stimulate institutions of higher education to initiate courses of study to enable unemployed older workers to develop new skills that would enable them to find employment. Finally, the committee proposed that the MESC, in cooperation with other agencies, develop "simple, under-standable public information documents" concerning older workers.[19]

By the time the Study Committee reported, the state legislature was beginning to grapple with the problem of age discrimination in employment. A bill to ban such discrimination was introduced in the House in January 1958, and the Senate in July of that year created a special committee to investigate discrimination in employment for those over forty years of age. Six states had approved age discrimination laws by the middle of September 1958, and the Eagles, who were pushing the issue nationally, were drafting a bill for Michigan. In January 1959 three Republican legislators sponsored a bill to amend the FEP Act to include age discrimination, and the Legislative Advisory Council, which had earlier expressed doubts about the wisdom of such legislation, endorsed the measure. The Williams administration, for its part, sought to secure the legislative adoption of some of the measures recommended by the Forsythe committee, but it left office without seeking the enactment of a law barring discrimination in employment because of age. It remained for the Swainson administration to follow that course.[20]

Both Swainson aides and the FEPC thought that a legislative ban on age discrimination, like the laws of the states that had dealt with the issue, should be limited to those aged sixty-five and over. It was for this group, they believed, that "the real hardship" existed. If the ban on employment discrimination were extended to those less than sixty-five years of age, one aide predicted, the agency administering the measure would be "swamped with cases" that it "would ultimately have to reject." In his recommendation to the legislature to enact an age discrimination law, however, Swainson did not set any specific age limit. Including the recommendation among others relating to the aging, Swainson declared, "Our generation will be judged by historians by our attitude toward the aging and the aged." U.S. Secretary of Labor James P. Mitchell, a Republican, applauded Swainson's effort to deal with age discrimination.[21]

Bills introduced in the 1961 session of the Michigan legislature, one of which set the age limit at sixty and another with no specified age limit, failed to emerge from committee. In calling for the 1962 session of the legislature to deal with the problem, Swainson asserted that employment discrimination against men began at age forty-five and against women at age thirty-five. The problem of employment for older workers, he pointed out, had been intensified as the result of automation, the relocation of plants, and business mergers. He noted that the laws of the fifteen states that had such legislation by that time had had "a marked and salutary effect on job opportunities for older workers." The legislature, however, was unpersuaded by the governor's argument. It would be three years before another Michigan legislature would be able to muster the votes to pass a bill banning discrimination in employment because of age. In the meantime, the MESC continued to offer its expanded services to older workers.[22]

WOMEN

Although Williams, to a greater extent than his predecessors as governor, appointed women to office and involved them in Democratic politics, little was done during his years as the state's governor to deal with discrimination suffered by women. Women, like the aged, were the victims of employment discrimination, but the FEP Act did not apply to them. Although 815,000 women held jobs in the state in 1943, that number fell to 595,000 after V-J Day and declined by an additional 20,000 by June 1952. The MESC was placing fewer women in jobs than the corresponding agencies in other states were during the early years of the Williams administration, allegedly because of the greater proportion of jobs in Michigan in the "heavy, durable goods category." In fiscal year 1952, for example, the MESC placed 27 percent of the women job applicants, whereas the average for the nation was 32 percent. "Ladies and foundries don't mix too well," the MESC declared in its annual report for that year.[23]

As the MESC informed the governor in September 1955, employers designated many jobs as for males only even though women were fully qualified for the positions. The UAW complained that the MESC itself was guilty of discrimination against women job seekers, particularly black women. Quite apart from discrimination against women in hiring, Michigan, other than in manufacturing industries, did not have a law requiring women workers to receive equal pay with men for equal or similar work, nor did it have a minimum wage law to cover the many occupations in which women were employed that were not covered by the federal Fair Labor Standards Act.[24]

Governor Williams recommended in 1951 that the state legislature give "careful attention" to the need for a minimum wage law to cover occupations not protected by the federal law, but the legislature refused to enact such a law while Williams was the state's governor. The Michigan State Employees Association, which had a membership of 12,000 from among the state's 29,000 employees as of 1956 and its first woman president that year, committed itself to follow the example of Colorado and Nebraska and to seek an equal pay law for Michigan, but the legislature was unresponsive for the time being. The legislature, however, opened up one job category to women in 1955 by repealing the law confining the licensing of bartenders in the state's larger cities to males.[25]

Soon after the passage of the FEP Act, the MESC thought it necessary for the governor to designate an agency to study "the employment situation" of women in Michigan and to develop a proper program as a result. Such a program, the MESC believed, should include the requirement of equal pay for equal work and should also make provision for working mothers. In a policy statement addressed to its own employees, the MESC early in 1951 announced that it would not discriminate for or against any of them because of their sex.[26] In fiscal year 1960 the MESC's Kalamazoo branch office sponsored a ten-week stenography refresher course for mature women. The success of the course led the commission to provide the same kind of course in Grand Rapids and Muskegon. The MESC cooperated with other agencies and civic groups in encouraging employers to accept women workers on the basis of their qualifications. In 1961 various professional and civic groups in the state sponsored a number of clinics dealing with "Job Opportunities for Mature Women."[27]

In an effort to combat sex discrimination in the workforce, the Women's Department of the UAW mounted an attack on the state's protective labor legislation that had theoretically been designed to protect the health and safety of women workers. At the UAW's 1957 convention, Caroline Davis, the department's head, complained that employers were taking advantage of this legislation "to prevent women from being upgraded, hired, or retained on their jobs." The UAW women also sought to have the ban on discrimination in government contracts apply to sex as well as racial and religious discrimination. When President Kennedy's 1961 Executive Order 10925 forbidding federal contractors to discriminate against employees or applicants for employment failed to include sex discrimination, Davis, who was a member of the Government Contracts Committee of the President's Commission on the Status of Women, issued a minority report criticizing the omission.[28]

When Swainson became Michigan's governor, the state government began paying increasing attention to the civil rights of women workers. On September 30, 1961, the Michigan Department of Labor, the Women's Bureau of the U.S. Department of Labor, and Michigan State University's Labor and Industrial Relations Center and Continuing Education Service sponsored the Michigan Conference on Employment Problems of Working Women. The conference was designed, among other things, to "review and assess the . . . status of women workers as reflected in legislation and practices of minimum wage, equal pay, hours, and working conditions" and to "analyze woman's dual roles as homemaker and wage earner."[29]

The conferees at the September 30 conference agreed to give priority to seeking the enactment of an equal-pay-for-equal-work law and a state minimum wage and maximum hour law, establishing a Women's Division and a Children's Division in the Michigan Department of Labor, developing training and retraining opportunities for women, providing day care for the children of working mothers, and addressing migrant labor problems. Discussion following the conference also led a few weeks later to the establishment of the State Council to Mitigate the Employment Problems of Working Women in Michigan.[30]

On February 5, 1962, four buses carrying three hundred women from the Detroit area who were members of the Oakland Community chapter of the Michigan Federation of Business and Professional Women's Clubs arrived in Lansing to support equal-pay-for-equal-work legislation. Twenty-one states had such laws by that time. The legislature responded, enacting a measure the next month that made it a misdemeanor for an employer to discriminate in the payment of wages "as between sexes who are similarly employed." Surrounded by women when he signed the bill into law, Swainson characterized the measure as "a great step forward in employment legislation in Michigan." The governor also called for the enactment of a state minimum wage law, something thirty-five other states had done by then. Five separate minimum wage bills were introduced in the legislature that year, and, unlike the federal law, they covered retail clerks, laundry workers, waitresses, chambermaids, and agricultural workers. The bills did not emerge from committee, the State Council attributing the failure to its belief that most people were "unaware of the large gap" in the minimum wage provision of the Fair Labor Standards Act. The council made the enactment of a minimum wage law its "number one priority" for the next twelve months and mounted an educational campaign with that goal in view.[31]

The State Council's concern about day care for the children of working mothers was in the meantime being addressed by the Day Care Committee of the Michigan Youth Commission, a thirty-member group that the Youth Commission established in May 1961. The committee assessed existing day care facilities in the state as "inadequate," precariously financed, and "frequently inappropriate and sometimes dangerous." It initiated an investigation of day care problems in the state that the State Council characterized as "one of the most thorough and important investigations into day care needs undertaken in any state." One of the Day Care Committee's initial proposals was that each school district in the state should establish a nursery school–day care facility that would integrate the services provided by the two.[32]

On August 20, 1962, Swainson, making good on a promise of some months earlier, appointed a state Commission on the Status of Women to parallel the President's Commission on the Status of Women that President Kennedy had appointed in December 1961. Michigan was the first state in the nation to establish such a commission. Swainson asserted that he wanted the commission to develop recommendations designed to end sex discrimination in both public and private employment and to indicate the services needed to enable women "to continue their traditional activities within the home while making a maximum contribution to their communities, the state and the nation." He wanted the commission to investigate the differences in the legal treatment of men and women with regard to "their political and civil rights, property rights and family relations" and to determine what services women required as wives, mothers, and workers in such areas as education, counseling, training, home services, and day care.[33]

Swainson noted that women working full time the year round had average yearly earnings of $4,300 in 1960, which was only about three-fifths as much as men earned. Black women had averaged only $2,280 for the year. The governor observed that even working women with adequate incomes had "special problems" if they were also mothers and that "prevailing prejudices and outmoded customs" served to prevent the full realization of their potential. The problem of discrimination against women, he said, had to be dealt with on "a comprehensive basis" so that Michigan could "erase every trace of discrimination against women who work, wherever it may be found."[34]

Swainson appointed Dorothy McAllister, a member of the State Board of Libraries, to serve as chair of the twenty-member Commission on the Status of Women. An aide to the governor noted that there was only one African American on the committee. "The problem," as the aide saw it, "was to get more [blacks] on without making it obvious." He advised the governor to appoint six new members to the commission, among whom he could include two blacks "without raising too many eyebrows." This is precisely what Swainson did, adding Rosa L. Gragg, president of the National Council of Negro Women, and Esther LaMarr, executive secretary of the Detroit Commission on Children and Youth.[35]

To carry out its mission, the commission established six committees: Employment Policies and Practices in State and Local Government; Private Employment Policies and Practices; Labor and Social Legislation; Politics and Civil Rights; Education; and New Services. The full commission quickly endorsed a state minimum wage law covering both men and women, estimating that of 881,000 women in the state labor force, about 50 percent were not covered by the federal law and were not in occupations represented by labor unions. Twenty-three states had enacted minimum wage laws by the end of 1962.[36]

Insofar as state government employment was concerned, Franklin K. DeWald, the state's personnel director and a member of the commission, provided the group with a state Civil Service Commission report of

148

August 2, 1961, indicating that of 31,472 state employees at the time, 13,116, or 41.6 percent, were women. On the higher levels of the classified civil service, however, only 327 of 3,340 positions, about 10 percent, were held by women. DeWald offered various explanations for this disparity, noting also that, on the average, more women had risen through the ranks in the classified civil service than their counterparts had in private industry.[37]

The committees of the Commission on the Status of Women reported as the Swainson administration was giving way to the Romney administration. The Private Employment Policies and Practices Committee reported that there had been a 20 percent increase in the 1950s in the percentage of women fourteen years of age and over in the Michigan labor force and that women by the end of the decade made up about 30 percent of the state labor force. The Labor and Social Legislation Committee thought that an appraisal of how protective labor legislation affected women workers was required. The Political and Civil Rights Committee decided to consider the desirability of amending the FEP Act to cover sex discrimination and also the enactment of a statute creating "a civil right for women to equal opportunity in employment" to be enforced by a women's division of the Department of Labor. The Education Committee decided to consider methods of educating women for the "multiple roles" demanded of them and the inclusion of women on the governing boards and policy-making bodies in state institutions of higher education. The New Services Committee decided to study "threshold training to make women employable," including part-time work in the home. The committee indicated that in conducting its studies, it would be aware of women's "emotions" such as "*guilt* because of leaving the family [to work]; *loneliness* as a stimulant for their desire to work; and fear of inadequacy in meeting working conditions." The fruits of the commission's labors were to become evident during the governorship of George Romney and later.[38]

NATIVE AMERICANS

Native Americans in Michigan, the executive secretary of the Governor's Study Commission on Indian Problems declared in September 1957, received the "same second-class citizen treatment" that African Americans did. Governor Williams brought the conditions of the state's Native Americans to public attention as part of his general concern for the disadvantaged groups in Michigan, but the state government did little between 1949 and 1962 to alter the status quo insofar as Native Americans were concerned.[39]

In 1934 the federal government transferred the Native American boarding school in Mt. Pleasant, Michigan, to state ownership on the condition that Native Americans residing in Michigan would be "accepted in State Institutions in entire equality with persons of other races, and without cost to the Federal Government." Once the transfer was effected, the state government provided "all normal public services" to resident Native Americans.[40]

Four Native American reservation communities were created in Michigan under the Indian Reorganization Act of 1934, three in the Upper Peninsula, one in the Lower. The largest was the Keweenau Reservation in L'Anse in Baraga County, composed of Chippewa and with an estimated population in 1950 of 1,322 on the tribal roll. The Bay Mills Reservation, also made up of Chippewa, was located in Chippewa County and had an estimated population of 84 in 1950. Some Native Americans who made up part of the Bay Mills group were located on Sugar Island, east of Sault Ste. Marie. The Hannahville Reservation, located in Menominee County in the southern part of the Upper Peninsula, was composed primarily of Potawatomi and had a population of 161. The Hannahville Indians were the only Native American group in the state with a substantial number of full-blooded Native Americans. The Isabella Reservation, the only reservation in the Lower Peninsula, was located on the outskirts of Mt. Pleasant in Isabella County. It was a Chippewa community with an estimated population of 414.

There was an unincorporated group of Native Americans known as the Northern Michigan Ottawa Association living along the eastern shore of Lake Michigan and with a reported population of about 4,000. There were also about 4,000 Native Americans living off the reservations, particularly in the Lower Peninsula, who were "assimilated" in the urban areas in which they resided. There was actually a great deal of uncertainty as to the actual size of the Native American population in Michigan. According to the 1950 census, there were 17,000 Native Americans living in Michigan, but this is almost certainly an inaccurate figure since there was no agreed-upon definition at the time of who was a Native American.[41]

The four reservations were under the jurisdiction of the Great Lakes Consolidated Agency of the Bureau of Indian Affairs (BIA), located in Ashland, Wisconsin. Just about all the agency did with regard to Michigan's Native Americans was to protect the 7,818 acres of tribal land held in trust for the Native Americans by the federal government. The federal government also owned 4,022 acres in Michigan resettlement land (land acquired by the federal government and turned over to the BIA), and there were 14,079 acres in allotted land ("Indian-owned land in restricted allotment status"). There was no BIA contact with Native Americans not living on restricted land. The Native Americans could not sell restricted land without BIA approval, and the sale of forest products from such land could only be done under the authority and supervision of the BIA. The federal government made two part-time contract doctors available to Keweenau and Hannahville reservations and contributed $2,500 annually to provide medical and hospital services for "borderline cases." Just about all the government services Michigan Native Americans received, however, were provided not by the federal government but by the state and local governments, the superintendent of the Great Lakes Agency optimistically reporting in 1956 that Michigan had treated its Native American citizens "very well."[42]

The principal problem faced by Michigan Native Americans was their lack of a decent income. Many lived on land that could not support them, particularly the cut-over forestlands of the state. They were principally employed as woodworkers or wage workers in nearby communities. Their opportunity to earn a decent wage was limited by their location in "poor economic regions" of the state and their lack of skills. Their economic status was "probably the lowest of all the minority groups" in the state.

Michigan's Native Americans suffered from "a marked lack of medical care" and had a high incidence of tuberculosis and cardiac problems. Native American children received only a limited amount of public education, their parents unable to purchase needed books and supplies and often even clothing for their children and requiring their labor to supplement the family income. As of 1950, Native American adults in Michigan had attended school for an average of only six years, and only 6 percent were high school graduates. Native Americans were "victims of the same racial discrimination" experienced by other minority groups in the state. The Hannahville Indians thus reported that they were discouraged from patronizing certain restaurants and that their children had been subjected to discrimination as public school students. There was also job discrimination against Native Americans in some of the "upstate communities" where they were concentrated. A Williams aide attributed the discrimination suffered by Michigan's Native Americans to their "inferior economic position."[43]

Several issues led Williams to establish the Governor's Study Commission on Indian Problems. One of these issues concerned the small Burt Lake Band of Ottawa Indians, who had taken their name from a village and lake in Cheboygan County. Between 1846 and 1849 the Burt Lake Indians had purchased 375 acres of land from the federal government, President James K. Polk patenting the land to the governor of Michigan to be held in trust for the Indians. Near the end of the nineteenth century the township supervisor placed the land on the tax rolls without the knowledge or consent of the Burt Lake Band. Since the Indians had never paid taxes on the land and did not do so after the land had been placed on the tax rolls, their taxes were declared delinquent, and their land was sold to John W. McGinn for sixty-five dollars. In October 1900, McGinn, accompanied by the local sheriff and his deputy, dispossessed the Indians living on the land, and McGinn set fire to all the buildings on the property except the church, which was later used as a barn.[44]

When Williams called a conference on Native American problems on March 12, 1956, twenty Native Americans in headdresses and led by John Shawanesse of Harbor Springs, a historian of the Burt Lake Band, protested McGinn's "shameful deed" and what the group called the "legalized arson" of fifty-six years earlier and demanded compensation. Williams, who was himself an honorary chief of the Ottawa tribe, promised to have the state's attorney general examine the question. The next month the deputy attorney general advised the governor's office that the Native Americans should address their complaint to the federal government since it had exclusive jurisdiction over the matter. The Burt Lake Band problem attracted a good deal of support in the state, much of it coming from non-Indians, and it helped to persuade Williams, who continued to seek legal advice on the subject, to create the Indian Study Commission.[45]

The Eisenhower administration's termination policy was designed to turn over to the states the federal government's responsibilities for the Native Americans and to authorize them to acquire their tribal lands for individual ownership. This led to a bill in Congress in 1954 applying the termination policy to Michigan's Indian tribes. The position of the BIA was that it could not "efficiently" provide services to Michigan's Native Americans and that its responsibility to do so should therefore be turned over to the state. The concern that the federal government would be "closing shop" in Michigan was a key factor leading Williams to appoint his Indian Study Commission. The cost of termination would actually have added little to Michigan expenditures, but the state government was concerned that the Native American lands were not taxable and wondered how termination would affect claims being pursued by Michigan's Native Americans at the federal level. The Williams administration decided in the end neither to oppose nor to endorse the 1954 termination bill, which, in the event, did not pass, the fate that befell similar bills in 1956 and 1957. A majority of the state's Native Americans appear to have opposed termination, fearing that the state government would not protect their rights and privileges.[46]

Another concern of the Williams administration regarding the state's Native Americans was the lack of reliable information concerning their status. Williams was also motivated to act by his sympathy for the plight of the Native Americans. "The difficulties that from time to time confront the Indians of Michigan," he wrote at the end of 1956, "have long been of concern to me." There was thus ample reason for Williams to establish a commission to study the state's Native American problem. "Michigan's Indians, who have taken their troubles to Washington for 150 years," the *Lansing State Journal* remarked in May 1956, "are going to get some attention from a new group of Great White Fathers in the state capitol."[47]

On July 25, 1956, Williams announced the appointment of the Governor's Study Commission on Michigan Indian Problems. He selected Chief Moses Gibson of Harbor Springs to chair the eighteen-member commission, six of whom were Native Americans, and R. G. Mulcahey, director of social services at the Coldwater Home and Training School, to serve as executive secretary. In poor health, Gibson died just as the commission got under way. Williams replaced him with Francis Wakefield, a "highly cultivated Ottawa" who had worked among the state's Native Americans. The governor suggested that the commission gather the facts about Michigan's Native Americans and "their way of life," study their claims against Michigan and their education and health problems, and outline their "social service needs." He indicated that he did not intend that the Native Americans be given "preferential treatment" or made "wards" of the state, but, he asserted, they had "a right to receive equal treatment and an equal opportunity to share in social and economic rewards and opportunities for advancement."[48]

The Study Commission, which lacked funds and a staff, met only four times in 1956 and 1957. At its first meeting, the commission appointed committees to deal with Native American economic security, education, and claims. At subsequent meetings, the commission gave consideration to the development of industries in "indigent areas," asking the federal government to authorize additional cutting by Native Americans of timber on tribal and allotted lands, encouraging employers to pay Native Americans higher wages, aiding Native American crafts, providing scholarships and paying the tuition of Native American children living on nontaxable lands to attend public schools in certain areas so as to relieve local communities of the burden, educating whites about Native Americans, establishing a statutory commission on Native American problems, the likely consequences of termination, and the Burt Lake Band claims. The three committees agreed that "more accurate information" was needed about almost every aspect of Native American life in Michigan. The commission was "distracted" from the start by efforts of Native Americans to have the state government press their claims against the federal government for the nonfulfillment of treaty obligations.[49]

The Study Commission did not meet after July 20, 1957, although individual members continued to play a role in Native American affairs. Three members thus met in November 1957 with the North American Indian Club of Detroit, a session attended by about fifty persons, half of them representing various Native American tribes. Those present agreed that "the most pressing need" of Michigan's Native Americans was education at all levels, and the group favored the payment of a small amount of state money to supplement local taxes for public school education for Native Americans. It was noted at the meeting that although about a half dozen scholarships were available for Native Americans at the University of Michigan, they were not being used because relatively few Native Americans had finished high school and the scholarships covered only tuition. The group agreed that the second most important Native American need was medical care.[50]

Wakefield did not submit a final report for the commission until December 23, 1960. The report recommended that the federal government permit Native Americans living on tribal or resettlement land to buy the land and to cut and sell more of the timber than was then permitted. The commission favored the establishment of a state small business administration to assist Native Americans to establish their own businesses, especially in lumbering and fishing; the use of state funds to assist Native Americans who completed grade school to enroll in high school; grants to Native American high school graduates to learn a trade; state scholarships to qualified Native Americans to attend not just the University of Michigan but also other state-supported institutions of higher education; state loans to Native Americans to relocate in the state to seek work and to aid them in adjusting to their new location; and the encouragement of Native American arts and crafts for sale to tourists.

The commission noted that there was discrimination against Native Americans in employment and education and in their "general acceptance" by non-Indians. It thought that the Michigan Council of Churches might be able to help with this matter, noting that only the Roman Catholic Church at that time was doing "a great deal" in this regard. The commission urged its own continuation and that it be provided with sufficient funds so that its chairman and executive secretary could travel to various Native American groups in the state to assist them in carrying out the commission's recommendations.[51]

Although the Indian Study Commission accomplished little, a student of the organization maintained that it was "an important first step in the development of services to Indians by the state of Michigan." It served at the very least to "educate its members," and it was the first time that Native American leaders had been called together by the state government to discuss their problems. The commission lapsed with the end of the Williams governorship. Swainson did not renew it, but Governor Romney, as we shall see, was to appoint another commission.[52]

Graphic evidence of the discrimination Native Americans faced in Michigan was provided in August 1960 when the body of George Vincent Nash, a World War II veteran, was removed from the White Chapel Memorial Cemetery in Troy just after the graveside service because he was a Native American, a full-blooded Winnebago. He was to have been buried in the White Chapel Cemetery alongside his wife, who was a Caucasian. Williams declared what had occurred "a shock to him" and "an insult to the dignity of American citizens," and Attorney General Paul Adams characterized the incident as "practically the ultimate in discrimination." Defending the action, the head of White Chapel asserted that if an exception had been made in this instance, forty thousand plot owners would have taken action against the cemetery since they had "paid for the restriction" as to who could be buried there. Nash was reburied in Pontiac the next day with "full military honors and tribal ceremonies." Williams asked the attorney general to see if legislation was needed to deal with discrimination of this sort, and Adams, with the help of the North American Indian Club of Detroit, drafted a bill forbidding cemeteries in the state to discriminate in burials on the basis of race. The bill, however, failed to pass the legislature in 1961, as did a similar bill the next year.[53]

THE PHYSICALLY HANDICAPPED

The effort to expand the frontier of civil rights in Michigan between 1949 and 1962 embraced the physically handicapped as well as African Americans, the aged, women, and Native Americans. That this was a problem in Michigan was indicated in a 1955 MESC report revealing that only 10 percent of employers in the Detroit labor market were willing to employ the handicapped. The Williams and Swainson administrations sought to achieve "equality of treatment for handicapped workers" and to persuade employers to consider the "abilities" of the handicapped, not their "disabilities."[54]

The view developed after World War I that it was possible to rehabilitate persons with severe handicaps and to move them from dependence to independence. In 1920 the federal government inaugurated a program of federal grants to the states to encourage them to establish vocational rehabilitation programs for civilians "disabled in industry or otherwise." State agencies of vocational rehabilitation were established to administer the state programs, which had to be approved by the federal government, and the states had to match the federal grants. Michigan began its vocational rehabilitation program with its 1921 Acceptance Act and the establishment of the Office of Vocational Rehabilitation. "Permanent and substantial support for vocational rehabilitation" was provided beginning in 1935 with the enactment of the Social Security Act.[55]

The vocational rehabilitation programs as they developed in the various states were commonly administered by state departments of education, the pattern followed in Michigan. This led to "an overemphasis on education and training and an underemphasis on physical restoration." In an effort to strengthen the federally supported state programs of vocational rehabilitation, the federal government in 1954 substantially increased its grants to the states and pledged itself to provide increasing funding in future years.

It was realized by 1943 that many persons were handicapped because of a physical condition that medical science could remove or ameliorate. This led state offices of vocational rehabilitation to initiate programs of "physical restoration," not just vocational education, with each state developing a program that the federal Office of Vocational Rehabilitation had to approve. In Michigan, the state Office (later Division) of Vocational Rehabilitation, the Department of Public Instruction, and the Michigan State Medical Society cooperated in developing the "Michigan Plan," whose objective was to restore the handicapped to their "maximum physical function."[56]

The process of rehabilitation in Michigan began with a complete medical examination of the handicapped individual if he or she was of employable age, a report of which was sent for evaluation to a medical consultant in one of the state's eight district offices of the state Office of Vocational Rehabilitation (OVR). The consultant was then to recommend appropriate physical restoration services, if justified. If the physical defect interfered with the economic activity of the handicapped individual, the consultant could approve a training program for a new occupation appropriate for someone with that individual's physical limitations. In the meantime, a field agent for the district office was to evaluate the handicapped individual's record, perhaps administer "intelligence, aptitude and interests tests," and counsel the individual regarding a suitable occupation. A "plan" would then be formulated for the individual, subject to the approval of the state OVR, involving needed physical restorative services and training for an occupation.[57]

The final stage in the rehabilitation process for those considered able to work was placement and then follow-up and job adjustment. This was the responsibility of the OVR. In 1950 the office placed 5,500 handicapped persons, but the number fell to 3,255 in fiscal year 1956–57 and 2,964 the next year.[58]

The OVR was also concerned about individuals with severe disabilities who were "homebound." Beginning in 1955, it sponsored a federally subsidized "special craft program" in the Upper Peninsula for seventy-five homebound disabled that it subsequently extended on a statewide basis. The homebound were taught to make different craft products that were sold at a sales outlet during the Michigan tourist season. By 1961 the program was serving 9,300 persons.[59]

The rehabilitation of the disabled was, in a real sense, a paying proposition. The 3,100 disabled who had been rehabilitated and placed in 1953 increased their average weekly earnings from $5.34 before rehabilitation to $47.48 afterwards, and their purchasing power had increased by $6 million at a cost to the state of $1,358,000. In fiscal year 1959–60, 529 welfare clients were rehabilitated at a cost to the state of $169,000 but at a saving in welfare costs of $565,000. In their first year on the job, the 529 earned $1,278,000 and paid an estimated $150,000 in state taxes.[60]

Michigan increased its appropriation for vocational rehabilitation in 1954 to match the increased federal allotment that began that year. The legislature, however, despite prodding by Williams and Swainson, failed after that time to take full advantage of the increased federal funds available to the state. The state appropriation for vocational rehabilitation increased from $500,000 in fiscal year 1954–55 to $864,308 in 1960–61, but that cost Michigan $4,161,230 in lapsed federal funds that would have been available to the state had the legislature been more forthcoming.[61]

Because of its failure to take full advantage of available federal funding, Michigan lost ground in its rehabilitation of the handicapped as compared to other states, and it was unable to serve many of the handicapped needing assistance if they were to find work. In 1951 Michigan's expenditure for vocational rehabilitation of seven cents per capita exceeded the national average of six cents, but by 1958, when the national average per capita was eleven cents, the Michigan per capita expenditure was only eight cents, placing it forty-fourth among the states. By 1961 Michigan had fallen to forty-seventh place. The Michigan OVR estimated in 1957 that 90,000 persons in the state were in immediate need of vocational rehabilitation, but only 13,000 received some kind of rehabilitation service that year, and the situation did not improve during the next several years. Each year about 11,700 individuals were added to the ranks of the disabled, but Michigan was able to rehabilitate less than one-third of them.[62]

Michigan's vocational rehabilitation program "made history" in 1958 when the OVR and the UAW-Kaiser-Frazer Social Security Fund inaugurated a special project in behalf of disabled former employees of Kaiser-Frazer. What was involved was the selection and the reemployment of physically handicapped workers displaced by the company's shutdown. The project became a model for other states to follow. A similar program was initiated the same year when Williams instructed the MESC and the Department of Public Instruction to develop a project to retrain handicapped workers displaced by automobile company mergers so that they could obtain skilled jobs not then being filled by instate workers.[63]

The MESC had the responsibility of placing the "moderately disabled," those with job skills who did not require medical or restorative service. The commission eventually had one person in each of its branch offices and a special unit in Detroit to serve this group. It sought to develop job openings for them at "equal wages in competition with other workers" and encouraged employers to remove the "artificial barriers" to the employment of these workers and to make "ability to do the job" the criterion for hiring the moderately disabled.

The annual number of MESC placements of the moderately disabled ranged between 1949 and 1962 from a high of 15,000 to a low of 7,780. The placements were as high as 84 percent of the applicants one year but were generally closer to 50 percent. Between 35 and 45 percent of the placements were of veterans, who received preference over non-veterans. In 1956 the MESC arranged with the Workmen's Compensation Department to accelerate the return to work of individuals disabled by work injuries.[64]

In accordance with action by Congress in 1945, the secretary of labor in 1947 established the National Employ the Physically Handicapped Week. Congress then provided that the first week in October was to be the week the program was implemented. In 1962, in order to include the mentally handicapped, the committee operating the program was renamed President's Committee on Employment of the Handicapped. State agencies in Michigan and elsewhere cooperated with the federal committee in observing the week.[65]

Governor Williams contended that the employment of the handicapped that might result from the efforts of the President's Committee and the states in a single week in October could be increased if "educational and promotional" work for the placement of the handicapped were "continuous throughout the year." With that purpose in mind and believing that the state "should set a good example in the employment of the physically handicapped," Williams in May 1949 formed the Governor's Commission on the Employment of the Physically Handicapped "to stimulate a public awareness" of the employability of such workers. The commission, which served as a "statewide policy making body," eventually had twenty-three members drawn from labor, management, veterans, civic groups, and state agencies.[66]

The commission suffered from poor leadership until 1958, its chair lacking experience in dealing with the handicapped. Organizations of the handicapped complained that the commission had too many state government members and insufficient representation of the handicapped themselves. "The whole damned thing is so bureaucratic-minded that it will bog down any affirmative action worth anything," declared an official of the American Federation of the Physically Handicapped.[67]

The commission was reorganized in January 1958, and Judson Perkins, the public relations director of the General Telephone Company of Muskegon, became the new chairman. In accordance with the pattern of similar commissions in other states, nine of the twenty-three commission members were drawn from private business, seven of them being personnel officials in their firms. "Here," a Williams aide declared, "is where the big selling job must be done if the physically handicapped are not only to be hired on an equal basis, but also if they are to be retained on the jobs they now hold." Williams thought that "one of the important frontiers in our continuing struggle to break down artificial barriers against the hiring of qualified handicapped workers" was to educate business and industrial personnel officials by involving them in the effort. He was especially concerned during what was then a time of economic recession that the handicapped not be the victims of discrimination in layoffs, and he understood that the attitude of management was critical to decision-making in the matter.

Although the Williams administration did not meet the demands of some of the organizations of the handicapped to increase their representation on the Governor's Commission, the commission did establish a Citizen's Advisory Committee for Handicapped and Community Organizations to "act in an advisory and liaison capacity" to both the commission and the governor. In 1962, at Swainson's behest, the commission dropped "physically" from its name to bring it into line with the renaming of the President's Committee that year.[68]

One of the principal activities of the Governor's Commission was publicizing the importance of employing the handicapped on the basis of their abilities. This involved radio and television messages, a statewide essay contest on employment of the handicapped, a kinescope on "Hiring the Handicapped," providing speakers to address the subject, publication of a newsletter, and the distribution of literature, films, and posters. A great deal of the publicity occurred during National Employ the Physically Handicapped Week, the commission coordinating a wide range of public and private activities across the state in support of the national employment effort. In 1950 the commission claimed that 1,625 handicapped individuals, including 739 veterans, had been placed in jobs as the result of its activities during the week. During the week in 1958, Williams declared that each Michigander, whether an employer or not, had an opportunity to aid the handicapped by filling a bag of "discards" for Goodwill Industries, the state's largest employer of the physically handicapped, which trained the handicapped for jobs in its eight sheltered workshops in the state.

It does not appear that the commission was all that successful in educating the public about the employability of the handicapped. In 1961, Governor Swainson, whose own physical handicap made him particularly sensitive to the plight of the handicapped, thus remarked that "the chief obstacle" to the commission's success was a "lack of public understanding of the potential of the rehabilitated handicapped person to contribute to society." This, of course, was precisely the message the commission had tried so hard to deliver.[69]

Believing that the best way to secure the employment of the handicapped was on a local community basis, the Governor's Commission sought to establish "a permanent Mayor's Committee in each sizable community in the state" to deal with the matter. Many of the local committees that were organized—forty-six, for example, by 1954—were active only during National Employ the Handicapped Week. Williams told commission members in March 1958 that the commission had not "reached its full impact" in terms of forming strong local organizations, noting that only one-third of the local committees were active throughout the year. Detroit did not even establish a local committee until 1958.[70]

A major concern of the Governor's Commission beginning in the late 1950s was the long-term compensation costs that an employer incurred as the result of the aggravation of a pre-existing injury of a physically handicapped employee. If these costs were not somehow limited, and Michigan was one of twenty-two states with the "greatest number of second injury restrictions," the commission was afraid that it could not persuade employers to hire a handicapped person with a disability that might be aggravated on the job. The way to deal with this problem was to amend the state's compensation law to limit the employer's liability for second injuries. New York, for example, had done that in 1945 by adding a provision to the state's workmen's compensation law that limited the employer's liability to 104 weeks for the payment of a compensation claim resulting from a second injury. The Michigan commission pressed for an amendment to the Michigan workmen's compensation law limiting the employer's liability to 52 weeks for a second injury so as to "make employment of [the] handicapped a more attractive policy for employers." A second-injury measure was enacted by the legislature and signed by the governor in April 1960, but it failed to resolve the second-injury problem.[71]

The Michigan House of Representatives created a special committee in 1955 to study problems relating to the physically handicapped and to serve as an interim committee between legislative sessions. The committee complained about the lack of coordination among the state agencies dealing with the problem and thought that the responsible agencies should first find jobs for the handicapped and then prepare them for the jobs rather than first rehabilitating them and then seeking to place them. The committee concluded, partly as the result of its hearings, that the Governor's Commission had "bogged down to practically nothing." The committee's criticism did not, however, serve as a spur to needed legislative action, the legislature, for example, refusing to appropriate the funds for vocational rehabilitation requested by the governor and failing to meet the demands of the Governor's Commission regarding the second-injury fund. A Republican House member conceded that the handicapped were "a kind of 'orphan' from the legislative standpoint" despite the legislature's having "comprehensive knowledge" about the subject.[72]

Not until early 1961 did the Governor's Commission address itself to the problem of access to public buildings by the physically handicapped. The impetus for the action was the submission to the governor by the President's Committee on Employment of the Handicapped of a set of standards designed to make public buildings "accessible to the ambulatory handicapped." The "American Standards," as they were named, had been drafted by the President's Committee and the National Society of Crippled Children and Adults in cooperation with numerous government and private organizations and then approved by the American Standards Association.[73]

Michigan did not have a state building code at the time, which meant that there was no state government mechanism to enforce regulations designed to eliminate architectural barriers to the handicapped in public buildings. Swainson, however, as an aide noted, took "vigorous steps to launch a statewide program" to eliminate such barriers on a voluntary rather than a mandatory basis. He instructed the Governor's Commission to contact planning authorities for public buildings throughout the state to implement the American Standards and to develop a program to inform the public of the importance of such action.[74]

On October 2, 1962, Swainson helped to initiate a survey of public buildings in the state capital. Conducted by the Community Services Council for the greater Lansing Area, this was the first citywide survey of its kind in the state. Its aim was to provide access to the buildings and to eliminate rest rooms in the buildings that had no facilities for the handicapped, telephone booths that were too small for them, and telephones that did not have devices for the hard of hearing. If you could not enter a building, you could not work there, the governor's office noted, thus relating the access problem to the mission of the Governor's

Commission on Employment of the Handicapped.[75] This was, to be sure, a very small beginning of what was to become a major nationwide effort to make buildings accessible to and usable by the handicapped.

Among the disadvantaged groups in Michigan, none was more disadvantaged or enjoyed fewer rights than the migrant workers who flocked to the state to care for many of its crops. It is hardly surprising that the Williams administration began to focus the state's attention on their plight.

7

"THE EXCLUDED":
Migrant Farm
Labor, 1949–1962

"These migrant workers," a Michigan Roman Catholic source observed in 1950 regarding Michigan's migrant workers, "have no rights or privileges as citizens in the community." They were "the excluded," not covered by most of the legislation that benefited others in the state. According to the Michigan State Advisory Committee to the U.S. Commission on Civil Rights, the migrants were "tantamount to third-class citizens." They had "less legal, sanitary and economic protection than medieval serfs," a *Detroit Free Press* reporter commented in 1954.[1]

Although viewed as the home of the automobile manufacturing industry, Michigan was also an important agricultural state when G. Mennen Williams became the state's governor in 1949. The cultivation and harvesting of many of Michigan's crops depended on hand labor, and local sources could not supply a sufficient number of workers to meet the demand during peak periods of production. It was consequently necessary for Michigan growers to secure agricultural workers from other states and from outside the United States. The recruitment, transportation, housing, health, and movement from crop to crop of these workers constituted Michigan's migratory agricultural labor problem.[2]

In 1948 Michigan ranked first in the nation in the production of cucumbers, sour cherries, and celery, second in peaches, onions, and cantaloupes, and third in strawberries, cabbage, snap beans, cauliflower, market tomatoes, and carrots. Sugar beets and cherries required the largest number of workers among Michigan's agricultural crops as of 1948, but mechanization was beginning to reduce the need for sugar beet workers. The decline in the number of these workers, however, was offset by the greater need of labor for other crops, notably pickling cucumbers and tomatoes.[3]

In the years just before Williams became governor, the number of out-of-state workers coming to Michigan annually to work on its crops ranged between 30,000 and 40,000. That number rose to 50,000 in 1957 and 66,000 in 1960. About 40 percent of the migrants in peak employment years in the 1950s were Mexican Americans from Texas, about 35 percent were from states like Arkansas and Missouri, and about 25 percent were black. Along with California and Florida, Michigan was one of the three leading states in the use of out-of-state migratory laborers. The migrant workers in Michigan were supplemented in the early 1950s by about 40,000 seasonal workers resident in the state itself.[4]

In addition to employing workers from other states, as well as a small number from Puerto Rico and the British West Indies, agriculture also made use of workers from Mexico, the braceros. In 1942 the United States arranged with Mexico for 60,000 Mexican nationals to enter the United States to work in agriculture and on the railroads. This arrangement became a matter of law the next year, when Congress enacted Public Law 45. In 1944 about 2,000 braceros were helping to harvest Michigan sugar beets and cherries. In 1951 Congress enacted Public Law 78, authorizing the U.S. government to negotiate with Mexico for the admission of Mexican nationals as farmworkers in those portions of the United States that the secretary of labor certified as having a shortage of agricultural labor despite employer efforts to meet the demand from the local labor supply. The agreement with Mexico required that the braceros receive the local prevailing wage, "adequate and sanitary free housing," "decent meals at reasonable prices," insurance to cover injuries and occupational diseases, and return transportation to Mexico. These conditions of employment did not apply to migrant workers from inside the United States, and they were conditions that some employers "continuously and repeatedly violated."

The bracero program continued until the end of 1964. In Michigan between 1949 and 1962, the number of braceros ranged from 2,230 in 1951 to 14,500 in 1961 and generally exceeded 10,000. Most of the braceros were involved in the production of sugar beets and cucumbers.[5]

Migrant workers started arriving in Michigan in May. Their number peaked in July and then began to decline, most of them having left the state by late November. To remain employed while in the state, the migrants generally had to move from crop to crop depending on the seasonal character of the different crops. Some migrants were recruited by the sugar companies and grower associations like Michigan Field Crops, Inc., but the responsibility for securing needed workers was increasingly assumed by the Farm Placement Section (FPS) of the Michigan Employment Security Commission (MESC), and the FPS also played a crucial role in distributing workers from crop to crop.[6]

Some migrant workers were brought to Michigan by crew leaders, but more were so-called "free wheelers" who came in family groups on their own. Crew leaders recruited workers, transported them to Michigan by truck, and served as intermediaries between the growers and workers and as subcontractors, sometimes supervising the work of their crew and paying them their wages. The common method of employment was "the family contract system," the work involved being treated as "a family job" that included the labor of the wife and children of the male family head.[7]

Responding to the concern of some state officials as well as private citizens, Governor Harry F. Kelly in 1945 appointed an interagency committee that initially took the name Governor's Committee on the Education, Health and Welfare of Migrant Workers. On the basis of information it had gathered, the committee submitted a report early in 1947 describing the deplorable conditions under which the migrants were transported to Michigan and then lived and worked there. Unable itself to conduct a comprehensive examination of the employment of migratory labor in Michigan and the importance of such labor to the state's economy, the Governor's Committee recommended that the governor appoint a study commission on the subject, a step already taken by several other states.[8]

The Governor's Committee's brief description of the conditions of migrant labor in Michigan was supported by evidence that subsequently became available. In transporting migrants to Michigan, crew leaders, who were criticized by the committee, used "old and dilapidated" vehicles not "fit to haul cattle." They sometimes packed as many as thirty migrants in a single truck for a journey of sixteen hundred miles, with perhaps an occasional ten-minute rest period. They sometimes misrepresented the nature of the work available to the migrants whom they transported, occasionally charged them excessive fees for crew leader services, and sometimes improperly collected a percentage of their wages from both the migrant and his employer.[9]

The family contract system involved the use of children of very tender ages. The federal government's Sugar Act of 1937 proscribed government benefits to sugar growers who employed children under fourteen years of age, and a January 1950 amendment to the Fair Labor Standards Act (FLSA) prohibited children under sixteen from working while school was in session on farms whose products entered interstate commerce. Both statutes, however, were regularly violated in Michigan and other states using migrant labor. The U.S. Department of Labor

165

reported that there had been 3,465 violations of the FLSA amendment in 1951 and that of the illegally employed children, 15 percent ranged in age from five to nine and 51 percent from ten to thirteen. Interviews with fifty-eight Spanish-speaking migrant families between 1943 and 1947 revealed that children under fourteen years of age were working in the sugar beet fields despite the Sugar Act.[10]

Migrant children had "the lowest educational attainments of any group in the Nation." Their school attendance was "sporadic," and their educational achievement "meager." The migrants generally arrived in Michigan a month or two before the public schools closed for the summer and then left the state after school had been in session for two to three months in the fall. As many as two-thirds of the migrant children did not attend school at all while in Michigan. Some migrant parents were unfamiliar with Michigan's compulsory school attendance law, and a shortage of attendance officers meant that the law, in any event, was not consistently enforced. Lack of funds for textbooks and supplies and even for suitable clothing often deterred migrant children from attending school, as did the desire of parents, because of their inadequate income, for the labor of their children.[11]

The seriousness of the education problem was revealed in studies of Bay and Van Buren Counties in 1954. Of 413 migrant children of school age in Bay County in May, only 65 were reported to be enrolled in school, even though school authorities encouraged attendance in that month since the annual state grant for primary schools was based on attendance in May. About three-fourths of the school-age migrant children in the county were retarded from one to six grades. Of 1,542 school-age migrant children in Van Buren County, only 22 were reported as enrolled in public school, and of 318 children studied, about one-third were retarded from one to three grades. Because of their educational retardation, migrant children who did attend school were placed in classes with resident children younger than themselves, which created "a problem of social adjustment" for the migrant students. Migrant children often had problems with the English language, and since they were in school for such a brief period, they received a minimum of instructional assistance. Teachers were not always in sympathy with the migrant children in their classes or trained to deal with them, and the instructional materials available were not necessarily suitable for these children.[12]

The quality of housing for the migrants, generally provided to them free of charge, was very much affected by the fact that farm owners did not regard the expenditure to provide proper housing warranted for workers who were rarely resident on their farms for more than a few weeks. Migrants were housed in every conceivable type of dwelling, "cabin houses, house trailers, wagon houses, vacant farmhouses, army pyramidal tents, barracks, tool sheds, granaries, chicken houses, brooder houses, barns and garages." As the *Detroit Free Press* observed in August 1955, "Everything with a roof" was "being used as a shelter." The better housing was generally located in crop areas requiring the labor of migrants for four or more months, on farms of larger growers, and where braceros made up the workforce.[13]

In Isabella County in 1945, seventeen migrants were found living in a one-room dwelling, and a survey two years later in the same county revealed that fourteen of twenty wells serving twenty-five migrant dwellings were contaminated to some degree. Black migrants in the late 1940s were "jammed into pig sties and hen houses." In 1956 the chair of the Social Action Council of the Detroit Archdiocesan Council of Catholic Women reported that migrants were living in barns too run-down to house farm equipment, with terrible or nonexistent washing and cooking facilities, and with so little sleeping space that mothers had to suspend their babies from "sack-like devices from the ceiling." Other migrant dwellings, she noted, lacked windows, screens, and garbage receptacles. The only toilet facilities available to some migrants were uncovered pits. When the MESC chair reported at a commission meeting that migrants were living in "chicken coops, literally," a commission member remarked, "And damn small chicken coops, too."[14]

On the basis of information gathered in sixteen farm counties in 1961, it appeared that migrant housing conditions had improved ever so slightly. The Michigan State Advisory Committee reported to the U.S. Commission on Civil Rights that year that some migrant housing in Michigan was "excellent," "far more" was "bad," and "very little" met "minimum standards." The housing provided in the early 1960s by the Monitor Sugar Company and the Michigan Sugar Company on the one hand and the Lake Odessa Canning Company on the other illustrated the contrast in the housing available to migrants. The two sugar companies, employing braceros in the main, had constructed permanent cement block housing and had provided a bed, mattress, and blanket for each worker, sleeping space of thirty-two square feet per worker, a safe supply of water, cooking and heating facilities, electric lights, and needed utensils. On the other hand, when a Michigan Department of Health inspector examined the housing provided at two sites by the Lake Odessa Canning Company, he discovered that one was "a dilapidated brick farm house" whose brick was falling apart and whose sink was stopped up. The house lacked screens and was "alive with flies," the sanitation was "terrible," and the privies were unsatisfactory. He characterized the housing at this site as "not inhabitable." He described the quality of the three buildings at the second site as "terrible" and advised that the buildings be condemned. There were no screens on the buildings, no running water, and no indoor toilet facilities.[15]

The Michigan Department of Health reported in December 1951 that the health of the state's migrant workers had been "long neglected." Their health was adversely affected by dietary deficiencies, unsanitary and congested living conditions, lack of knowledge of "simple health measures," and their inability to receive "early and adequate medical care." Most migrants, indeed, received medical care only in the event of "severe emergencies." Ten of the state's counties with a substantial number of migrants did not even have county health departments. The migrants suffered particularly from respiratory infections, dysentery, diphtheria, smallpox, and venereal disease. In Saginaw County in 1948, the rate of tuberculosis for Spanish-speaking migrants was twenty-seven per thousand as compared to one per thousand for the county's population as a whole. In the same county, three times as many migrant as non-migrant infants died within one year of birth. When migrant parents in Bay County were asked about the size of their family, they were apt to reply, "so many children born and so many living."[16]

In the 1957 and 1958 crop years, Michigan and Texas joined with the U.S. Public Health Service in a joint study of 141 migrants who had trucked to Michigan and then returned to Texas. One in five of these migrants reported having had health episodes requiring medical care while in Michigan. Medical care was often delayed for migrants until an emergency developed, or care was interrupted because the migrant had to move to a new location. Only two migrants had failed to pay at least something for their medical care, but they generally found it difficult to pay hospital bills of more than $100.[17]

There was "a significant number of complaints" from both domestic and foreign migrants about their low earnings. Most were paid by the piece, the rate varying by the crop, and the difference in pay among a group of migrants working in the same field sometimes ran as high as six dollars a day. One of Michigan's leading authorities on the subject of migrant labor told a U.S. Senate subcommittee in 1952 that there was "general agreement" that the income of Michigan's migrant workers was below what was required to maintain "a minimum standard of health and comfort." This was partly because migrants earned nothing at all during part of the year.[18]

The communities to which migrants came for part of the year tended to deny any responsibility for them. "Well, we don't look at them as trash, which of course they really are," declared one woman in summarizing the attitude of at least one community. A key migrant defender remarked of the migrants, "They can't fight the community that won't give up its stupid prejudices." The community view of migrants was illustrated in 1952 when the Reverend Shirley E. Greene, the research project director of the National Council on Agricultural Life and Labor, decided to locate one of the council's study projects on the education of migrant children in Berrien County. The Governor's Study Commission on Migratory Labor, about which there will be more later, met with Greene and invited him to proceed. Greene, however, felt compelled to abandon the study because of opposition from the County Board of Education and the Berrien County Farm Bureau. The Farm Bureau president informed Greene that most bureau members did not believe that there was a migrant education problem in the county and that the bureau was "very much aware of the many National Organizations of Socialistic Trend" that were "worming their way into our local governments and organizations." The bureau, indeed, requested that the FBI investigate the organization sponsoring the proposed study. Greene entitled his report to the Governor's Commission regarding what had occurred, "The Iron Curtain in Berrien County."[19]

When Williams became Michigan's governor, there were few laws and regulations in effect that would have enabled the state government to cope in any serious way with the many problems of the state's migrant laborers. It lacked the authority to regulate crew leaders, to set a minimum wage for migrant workers, to limit the labor of migrant children, and to deal with wage discrimination. Migrant workers were not covered by the state's workmen's compensation law, and they were ineligible for old age and unemployment insurance. They could qualify for public relief only if they had lived continuously in one county of the state for at least one year with the intention of making Michigan their home, and they could receive Aid to Dependent Children only if the child or its mother had been physically present in Michigan for at least one year. These were hardly conditions that migrants could meet. The state government could set housing standards only for communities with populations of more than ten thousand, which excluded most communities with large numbers of migrants.[20]

The MESC aided migrant job seekers in finding work and aided employers in finding suitable migrant workers. The Department of Labor accepted claims of migrant workers for wages due them, but the state's wage recovery law lacked teeth. There was a single overnight stopover camp for migrants, operated by the city of Benton Harbor, which charged seventy-five cents per person per day for use of the facility. County welfare departments could provide temporary emergency relief for indigent migrants and could return them to their home states if they were stranded in Michigan. The welfare departments could also approve emergency hospitalization for indigent migrants, and the county health departments were responsible for hospitalization of indigent migrants with TB or other "dangerous communicable diseases." The compulsory school attendance law covered migrant children under sixteen years of age.[21]

The growers in Michigan, on the whole, were very much opposed to state and federal legislation to deal with migrant problems. They claimed that the living and working conditions of migrant laborers were better than the press reported, that the growers' "good 'side'" was largely ignored, and that they were being unfairly presented in "a very unfavorable light." The growers were also inclined to blame the migrants themselves for at least some of the conditions about which they complained. Speaking for a group of Berrien Springs growers, one farm operator, in opposing migrant housing legislation, claimed that the migrants "abuse[d]" the good housing facilities provided them. "I know from personal experience," he remarked, "that many of these people are the type you can't legislate into changing their habits."[22]

Legislation, the growers insisted, was not the answer to migrant problems. If minimum wage legislation were enacted to cover migrants, the associate general counsel of the Michigan Farm Bureau contended, it would lead to migrant unemployment. Child labor legislation applying to migrants, he claimed, would create an economic problem for migrant families and increase juvenile delinquency. A representative of the Great Lakes Cherry Producers denied that there was any real child labor in cherry picking in Michigan since the picking occurred while the schools were not in session, the children were under the supervision of their parents, and the children could work at their own pace since they were paid by the piece. Another grower declared that child labor taught the children involved to be "useful citizens."

The registration of crew leaders, the executive secretary of the Michigan Cooperative Growers Association insisted, would constitute "discrimination in its rankest form," and he opposed any migrant wage legislation because of differences in the nature of work from crop to crop. Housing legislation was also unnecessary, he claimed, because competition among growers would force them to improve the quality of migrant housing. A representative of the Michigan Association of Cherry Producers told a U.S. Senate subcommittee in 1961 that growers were improving housing "as fast as migrants" could "absorb" the improvements and that the growers would continue to make improvements if not "saddled with Government regulations."

The director of the Michigan Department of Agriculture informed Governor Swainson in August 1962 that the growers feared any legislation to aid migrants, even if it were "worthwhile," lest it prove to be a "foot-in-the-door for unneeded and damaging restrictions in the future." One grower asserted, "I don't think that the Government should have anything to do about our Migrant Labor as Farming is to[o] uncertain to have a given rule to go by for our help."[23]

Catholic and Protestant organizations in Michigan sought to meet some of the migrant needs not being met by the growers or by the government. The Mexican Apostolate of Guadalupe, under the auspices of the Bishop of Saginaw, provided Spanish-speaking priests and seminarians to minister to migrants' spiritual and secular needs. The Apostolate provided recreation for migrants, maintained a clinic in Saginaw, and provided prenatal and postnatal care for migrant mothers. The National Council of Catholic Women sponsored a series of summer schools for migrant children in different communities, furnished clothing to the needy, and provided them with medical aid. The Beet Workers Defense Committee in Detroit, led by Father Clement Kern, rector of Most Holy Trinity Parish, was particularly concerned about the economic welfare of the migrants and their lack of bargaining power, and so it sought to organize them and to improve their wage contracts.[24]

Protestant denominations in Michigan sought to serve the migrants through the Michigan Migrant Ministry. Established in 1940, the Ministry was an interdenominational and interracial organization under the supervision of the Division of Home Missions of the National Council of Churches. Much of its funding was provided by the Michigan United Church Women. Its projects in the agricultural counties were administered by local migrant committees under the direction of the State Migrant Ministry Committee. The projects lasted anywhere from three to fourteen weeks, and the number of counties involved varied from year to year.[25]

The Migrant Ministry described its program as "centered in the Christian faith" and as seeking "to share that faith with the migrant, to develop in him a sense of his personal worth, belonging and responsibility." It sought also "to awaken the community" to its obligation of "sharing," to challenge local churches to welcome the migrants, and to persuade the state government "to apply Christian principles to the economy in which migrants live and work."[26]

The most common Migrant Ministry project was the Bible School, and there were also projects to teach youngsters to read and for adult education. The Ministry provided nursing services to some migrant camps and worked with county health departments to provide migrants with free chest X rays, vaccinations for their children, and other health services. Family night was a common Ministry activity, as were a variety of recreational events, particularly for migrant youngsters. The Ministry operated several day care centers, visited the camps to provide "Christian counseling and friendliness," visited migrants in the hospital or in jail, and distributed clothing to needy migrants. In 1958 it began to operate centers in various communities that migrants in the area could visit for rest and recreation.[27]

The religious organizations in Michigan certainly offered migrants a variety of services, but the aid they provided helped only at the margins. Only the federal and state governments could adopt the "systematic and comprehensive approach" that the problems of the migrants required. The federal government was quicker to respond than Michigan was. As we have seen, it sought to deal with the labor of migrant children as early as 1937. In 1954 the Bureau of Employment Security adopted the Annual Worker Plan, a plan already in use in some East Coast states. The implementation of the plan was entrusted to FPS personnel in the various states, who were to work with migrants in their home states to plan a series of seasonal jobs for them for the year. Michigan, which had already been seeking year-round placement for dairy and general farm migrants, implemented the Annual Worker Plan in 1957 and was able as a result to shift about one-third of the migrants from job to job.[28]

A 1950 amendment to the Social Security Act provided old age and survivors insurance coverage for migrants who earned $100 from a single employer in one year. Legislation in 1956 authorized the Interstate Commerce Commission to issue "reasonable requirements" for the comfort and safety of migrants transported across state lines for more than seventy-five miles. Regulations effective in 1957 provided that the vehicles used to transport migrants henceforth had to have seats and safety equipment, and drivers had to secure a doctor's certification that they had the "minimum physical requirements" for the job. There had to be a stop for rest every eight hours and every six hundred miles, with stops in between for personal needs.[29]

In December 1959 the Department of Labor issued a series of regulations setting forth minimum standards regarding housing and wage rates that migrant employers had to meet before a state farm placement agency could extend job orders to workers for interstate clearance. Employers, also, could not obtain foreign workers if they failed to meet the domestic labor standards. The standards were very "general in nature," leaving it to the state governments to determine their actual application. In Michigan the MESC had to apply the standards, but it did not receive any additional funds to do so and found the task to be "quite a chore." It did, however, work with the Department of Health and local health officials to determine the appropriate health and safety standards for the migrant camps. In the first year, 1960, the MESC's FPS found 42 of the 479 camps it inspected to be "doubtful and subject to review by health officials." State and county health officials reported "deficiencies" in 43 of the 351 camps they inspected.[30] Of 2,943 camps inspected in 1961, 1,967 had deficiencies on first inspection, but reinspection reduced the number to 375, of which 80 were denied FPS services. In 1962, of 3,229 camps inspected, 1,298 had deficiencies, 74 percent of which were quickly corrected.[31]

The federal government's 1961 Housing Act provided for loans to farm owners to improve the housing of seasonal laborers. The next year the Migrant Health Act made federal grants available to state and local governments and nonprofit agencies for clinics and a variety of health services for migrants. The effect of these two statutes in Michigan became evident while George Romney was the state's governor.[32]

An aide advised Williams soon after he became Michigan's governor to keep in mind that Michigan needed migrant laborers and to seek to ensure that they did not "spread any contagious diseases" to Michigan citizens. "These workers," the aide also noted, "are human beings and deserve the rightful protection of the State." A few months later the Committee on Education, Health and Welfare of Migrant Workers, commonly referred to as the Inter-Agency Committee, recommended to Williams, as it had to Governor Kim Sigler, that he appoint a committee to study the problems of migrant workers.[33] Williams, however, did not act on the committee's recommendation until March 1952. He may have been deferring to the legislature, which had appointed an Interim Committee in 1949 to examine the problems of migrant labor and which did not complete its work until 1951—but, as it turned out, without issuing a report. Williams may also have been awaiting the report of the President's Commission on Migratory Labor, which President Harry S. Truman had appointed in 1950, to ascertain its relevance for Michigan. The committee's 1951 report, which focused public attention on the migrant labor issue, proved indeed to be a spur to state action.[34]

On March 6, 1952, Williams announced the appointment of a twenty-five-member Governor's Study Commission on Migratory Labor. The committee was co-chaired by Professors Edgar Johnston of Wayne University and John F. Thaden of Michigan State College, both of whom had developed an interest in migrant labor, and included representatives of the producers and processors of agricultural crops, the three major religious faiths, and the relevant state government agencies. The governor instructed the commission to study the problems of migrant labor and to recommend "corrective measures." Williams acted on the assumption that the problems of the migrants could not be solved by "techniques designed for the resident population."[35]

The Study Commission, which investigated a myriad of matters affecting migrants, operated through four subcommittees dealing with economic problems, education, health and welfare, and community relationships.[36] The Study Commission made its recommendations to Williams in final form and without dissent on January 25, 1955. The

173

recommendations covered almost every aspect of migrant life and labor and provided the state government with a comprehensive agenda for action. With regard to economic problems, the commission recommended legislation to regulate crew leaders and labor contractors who brought agricultural workers into the state and transported them within the state. It advised that reception centers (like the Benton Harbor facility) be established for migrants; the MESC's Farm Labor Advisory Council include not only representatives of agricultural and food processing organizations, as was then the case, but also representatives of the migrants and the public; state agencies dealing with employers of migratory labor urge them to use written agreements or contracts with their workers; the state highway laws be amended to provide for the safe transportation of migrants; the federal Inter-Departmental Committee on Migrant Labor be urged to advise standards for the "safety and convenience" of migratory workers; a study be made of the average earnings of migrants working on different crops; a study be conducted as to how migrants could receive unemployment insurance coverage; the Study Committee on Workmen's Compensation that Williams had just appointed develop a plan to cover migrant workers under the Michigan compensation law; and a handbook in Spanish and English be published to provide migrants with necessary information about the state.

Regarding education and child labor, the commission recommended that assistance be provided local school districts so that they could absorb migrant children and develop a program for their needs; conferences and workshops be organized in areas with large numbers of migrants to acquaint teachers with "the most effective materials and methods" to teach migrant children; teacher education institutions include the teaching of migrants in their pre-service training and provide instructional and teachers' guides for teachers of migrant children; and the Department of Public Instruction (DPI) set up one or more " 'pilot' summer schools" for migrants and make provision also for migrant children of nursery school age.

The commission also recommended that the DPI arrange to issue work permits to migrant children in accordance with provisions of the FLSA as amended in 1950 to forbid children under sixteen years of age from working while schools were in session; the DPI arrange conferences in selected areas of the state with large migrant populations to consider the education of migrant children; attention be devoted to securing more effective enforcement of school attendance laws; the Michigan Child Labor Act be amended to conform to the Michigan School Code and the minimum requirements of the FLSA for child labor; the federal government be asked to provide sufficient funds for the Wage and Hour Public Contracts Division of the U.S. Department of Labor to make regular checks of the FLSA provisions applying to the work of children during school hours; the DPI consider modifications in the state aid formula for local schools to encourage the school districts to provide summer schools for migrant children; the DPI continue its efforts to secure the cooperation of the federal and state governments with regard to migrant education; and the education of migrant children receive special attention at the 1955 White House Conference on Children and Youth.

In the health and welfare area, the commission recommended that the limitation of the authority of the state government to set minimum housing standards to communities of at least ten thousand population be removed and that there be a "continued emphasis on the improvement of migrant housing through the cooperation of the Michigan Department of Health, the Michigan State College Extension Service and voluntary organizations"; consideration be given to legislation to increase the state subsidy to local health departments so that they could add to their staffs when migrants were in their counties and could offer the migrants better medical service; health departments be established in the counties that did not then have them; the Department of Health furnish additional services to migrants; consideration be given to migrant labor in planning health and medical care facilities; Michigan Hospital Service and Michigan Medical Service be commended for their efforts to provide prepaid medical care for migrants and be encouraged to continue these efforts; the law be revised so that needy migrants could secure temporary relief, with the state and possibly the federal government supplementing local funds for this purpose; consideration be given to formulating a plan to provide medical and hospital care for migrant "hardship cases"; and the Michigan Health Council be asked to urge local health councils to devote special attention to migrant problems.

With respect to community relations and adult education, the commission recommended that the legislative appropriation for adult education make county boards of education eligible for reimbursement from adult education funds that the DPI distributed; the Michigan State College Cooperative Extension Service receive additional funds for its services to migrant families and migrant employers; the Agricultural Extension Service undertake a program of farmer education in an effort to provide a better relationship between farm employers and migrant laborers; the Michigan State Library provide a librarian and bookmobile to demonstrate to county and local libraries the use of suitable reading material and audiovisual equipment for migrants; the DPI provide consultant services to local public schools and county boards of education to aid them in providing programs for migrant adults and children; migrant councils be organized in areas of migrant concentration; and county forums and the media be used to promote community under-standing of migrant problems. Finally, the commission recommended the continuation of the Inter-Agency Committee on Migratory Labor and urged the governor to appoint a Citizens Committee on Migratory Labor that would include representatives of the growers, processors, organized labor, and the public.[37]

The commission's recommendations, although somewhat diffuse, touched on just about every aspect of Michigan's migrant labor problem. U.S. Secretary of Labor James P. Mitchell praised the commission's work and its recommendations, informing Williams that the commission had taken "an important step forward not only in Michigan but in all of the States which are bound to Michigan by this interstate movement of workers."[38] The problem for Michigan regarding the commission's report was that its key recommendations required legislative action, and that proved to be an insuperable obstacle during the Williams and Swainson administrations, as it had been in so many areas involving civil rights and state aid for the disadvantaged. As we shall see, however, the Romney administration was able to secure the adoption of many of the commission's recommendations.

The Study Commission's recommendation that Michigan Hospital Service and Michigan Medical Service be encouraged to continue their efforts in behalf of migrants did not in the end yield the results for which the commission had obviously hoped. The two services had met with the commission in the late spring of 1953 and proposed to make Blue Cross and Blue Shield available to interested growers for their migrant workers. The two services offered the growers at the regular group service rate their $2,500 ward medical surgical contract. The proposal attracted scant support among the growers, and in 1953 and 1954 Blue Cross and Blue Shield enrolled only six groups in three different small fruit areas. The two services decided to abandon the effort early in 1955 just after the Study Commission had reported. The growers, for the most part, lacked both the time and the desire to enroll their migrant workers.[39]

That the legislature would be unreceptive to migrant aid legislation was probably predictable given the power of the growers in the state, the lack of power and even of voting rights on the part of the migrants, and the conservative Republican domination of the legislature. When the MESC chairman in 1951 had proposed some migrant measures to the legislature, Republican Elwood G. Bonine of Vandalia responded that if the legislature proved favorable to what the MESC was propos-ing, it would encourage the "in-migration" of additional migrants and cause many migrants already in the state to remain there rather than to return home.[40]

After the Study Commission made its report, Republican State Senator Bert J. Storey of Belding, chairman of the legislature's interim committee to study migrant labor, guessed that no legislation would result from the Study Commission's efforts. Interested himself in an orchard, he asserted, "As an employer, I feel we're doing everything possible and some besides for these workers." He claimed that his study of migrant conditions in two counties indicated that the migrants did not have any grievances. Republican Don Pears of Buchanan agreed, claiming that in the one-day hearing the interim committee had held, most complaints came not from the migrants but from "the guy on the outside." To the consternation of the Study Commission, the state health commissioner and two MESC officials presented "a fairly rosy picture" of migrant conditions in the hearings. Actually, as Edgar Johnston pointed out, the interim committee had not made "any very extensive exploration" of the migrant problem and had even confused domestic migrants with braceros. A Williams aide characterized the interim committee's report as "a complete whitewash." Unsurprisingly, however, the Michigan Farm Bureau praised the report.[41]

Bills were introduced in the legislature in 1955 providing for the licensing of labor contractors and agents, modifying Michigan's child labor law to cover migrants, regulating migrant housing, and making the Study Commission "a permanent statutory agency." Despite the efforts of the Williams administration, none of the measures was enacted. The Study Commission came to an end soon after it made its 1955 report, but the Inter-Agency Committee, which had ceased its activities, was reappointed by Williams in 1956.[42]

Democrats in the legislature introduced migrant bills similar to the 1955 bills in both houses in the 1956 legislative session. Enacting these measures, Williams declared, was "primarily a matter of protecting the dignity" of individuals who came to Michigan to earn a living. Seeking to enlarge support for the bills, Williams contended that they were designed not just to aid migrants but also for "the protection" of Michigan citizens, since if "disease, squalor and injustice" were permitted among migrant workers, the "evil effects" would "not be limited to them but felt in . . . [the] entire community." Democratic House leaders, responding to the usual arguments advanced against aiding migrants, remarked, "We are dealing with human beings, not cattle. We must see they are treated like humans, instead of animals." As in 1955, however, the migrant bills failed to pass in either house.[43]

Exercising his administrative authority, Williams at the end of 1957 instructed the Public Service Commission to examine Interstate Commerce Commission regulations regarding the interstate travel of migrants and then to issue state regulations extending the same protection to migrants traveling within Michigan.[44] During the remainder of the Williams governorship, however, the administration's efforts to push migrant aid legislation came to naught, even though such legislation was endorsed by the Governors' Conference on Civil Rights, the Council of State Governments, the President's Commission on Migratory Labor, and the 1959 Mid-American Conference on Migratory Labor. Even a 1958 Williams request for a $10,000 appropriation for an experimental summer school program for migrant children and a similar request for $15,000 the next year failed to win legislative support. When the *Reporter* magazine in a 1959 article asserted that little could be expected from state legislatures in dealing with migrant labor problems, Williams understandably wrote the periodical, "How well we in Michigan know this to be true." The Inter-Agency Committee informed the governor in November 1960 that it had been "difficult . . . to sustain interest and continuity" even among committee members in view of the legislature's "continued rejection" of administration proposals.[45]

Michigan, the Michigan Migrant Ministry lamented in its 1960 annual report, had been "very slow in following the example of many states" in adopting migrant labor reform legislation. As Johnston noted, Michigan had "fallen far behind several states with fewer migrants in dealing with major problems concerning them." By the spring of 1961 nine states had set a minimum age for the employment of children in agriculture outside of school hours. Seventeen states had extended their workmen's compensation laws to cover agricultural workers to one degree or another. Three states had adopted wage payment laws applying to migrants, nine had laws or regulations applying to labor contractors, seven had laws or regulations establishing safety standards for vehicles used to transport farmworkers, and twenty-four had laws or regulations applying to migrant labor camps. Hawaii provided unemployment insurance coverage for agricultural laborers, and four states provided them with temporary disability benefits.[46]

The migrant reform situation did not improve during the Swainson administration. The Michigan House passed a "watered down bill" in 1961 providing for the registration of crew leaders, but it died in the Senate even though it had the support of the Michigan Farm Bureau. In the 1962 session of the legislature, five House bills and two Senate bills dealing with migrant issues failed of enactment. "How long," the Michigan Migrant Ministry asked, "is the legislature of Michigan, the third largest user of migratory labor in the nation, going to ignore the needs of these people so necessary to our economy?" The Inter-Agency Committee became "inoperative," causing Frederick Routh to comment that this left "a chink in the armor of protecting disadvantaged groups from discrimination and exploitation."[47]

The repeated failure of the state legislature to enact legislation to deal with migrant labor problems did not mean that the state and local governments were stopped from aiding the migrants at least to some extent. The MESC and the FPS continued to play an important role in the recruitment and placement of migrants and in enforcing federal government regulations applying to braceros as well as domestic migrants. MESC staff members served as labor consultants and mediators in responding to employer requests for assistance in approving employer-employee relations and migrant requests to resolve a particular labor problem or a misunderstanding. The MESC also met with community representatives in an effort to improve community acceptance of the migrants.[48]

The Department of Labor continued to collect wages past due to migrants, the Department of Social Welfare licensed day care centers for migrant children, and local welfare departments distributed surplus commodities to needy migrants. Many communities provided recreational programs for migrants, of which the largest was Hart's annual fiesta that began in the late 1940s. The Department of Agriculture's Extension Service designed "economical housing units" as a guide for growers who employed migrants.[49]

Migrant health was a subject of particular concern for the state and county health departments partly because of the fear, as Williams had stressed, that contagious diseases among the migrants might spread to the larger community. The Department of Health, as noted earlier, inspected the sanitary conditions and water supplies of the migrant camps. Depending on the funds available, county health departments continued to provide chest X rays for migrants to determine if they were suffering from tuberculosis, administered blood tests, and provided for emergency medical care. State and county public health nurses arranged for the immunization of migrant children, counseled migrants on health matters, and sometimes arranged for their medical care. The Michigan Department of Health cooperated with the U.S. Department of Health, Education and Welfare in a clinical study of the effect on migrant health of transportation, the type of work of migrants, and changes in work locations.[50]

In Van Buren County, to which ten to thirteen thousand migrants came annually, health and sanitation problems and an increased rate of enteric diseases among migrant workers caused the county's health department and its Board of Supervisors to develop a migrant health program in 1955. Meetings were held with both growers and migrants, and then a Migrant Health Committee was appointed on which grower representatives predominated. The committee enlisted the aid of Western Michigan College as well as a committee of doctors and hospital administrators. In addition to the usual chest X rays, the committee developed a health education program. The growers voluntarily adopted a set of housing standards and installed showers in migrant dwellings that the migrants often destroyed. The county nursing staff, as part of the health program, worked closely with the county day care program.[51]

The chief innovative project in the area of education for migrant children took place in Bay County in 1956 and 1957. The stimulus for the project was the 1954 survey of the county that had revealed the extent of educational retardation among migrant children. The Governor's Study Commission and the Inter-Agency Committee had both recommended a summer school program as the best way to deal with migrant education, since these were largely the months that the migrants actually spent in the state. The Michigan Youth Commission secured a $4,000 grant from the National Child Labor Committee for the Bay City summer school, and plans for the school were developed by the county school superintendent, the DPI, the MESC, the Michigan Youth Commission, and the Governor's Study Commission.[52]

The summer school, the first of its kind in Michigan, ran for seven weeks, from July 9 to August 24. The pupils, who came from Spanish-speaking families, were assigned to two classes, one for twenty-six children aged four to seven, the other for twenty-three children aged eight to thirteen. One of the two teachers had a Mexican background. The objective of the school program was to make the students "feel secure" and bring them up to grade level. The program was explained to the parents so as to overcome their "distrust and fear" and to influence them to enroll their children. Family nights were held regularly during the course of the program to acquaint the parents with what their children were doing in the school, to provide them with advice on housekeeping, sanitation, and the preparation of nutritional meals, and to inform them about available community resources. This made the project "a learning center for the entire family."

The summer school students were provided free transportation and were served milk in the morning and a hot lunch. County health department nurses and doctors examined the children, treated their illnesses, and provided the parents with health education. The curriculum consisted of reading, writing, arithmetic, and language in the morning and social studies and special projects in the afternoon. A Spanish class was also included to help the pupils "feel proud of their heritage." Special assistance was provided students with "severe vocabulary and accent handicaps." Substantial use was made of movies, filmstrips, and other visual aids, which were provided by Central Michigan College, and the

Michigan State Library supplied books. An individual "progress sheet" was kept for each pupil. Although only twenty-eight of the sixty children whose parents were contacted appeared for class the first day, attendance for the summer session averaged 76.8 percent, about equal that for public schools in the county during the regular school year.[53]

When a DPI official visited the school, he thought that the teachers were "functioning splendidly," and it looked to him that the school was having "a most successful beginning." The chairman of the Michigan Youth Commission thought that the school marked "a milestone in Michigan" and demonstrated what could be done for the education of migrant children with "help and leadership."[54]

The Bay City School Program was continued for a second year in 1957, financed once again by the National Child Labor Committee and with the state government providing funds for the school lunches. About 52 percent of the students who enrolled in 1957 had attended the school the previous year, and average attendance for the summer rose to 83.6 percent. Field trips were added to the program in 1957, and parents met one evening every week to receive instruction in spoken English, home hygiene, and child care. A survey of the parents revealed that they "deeply appreciate[d]" the program, and they even offered to pay "something" so that the program could be continued. The Michigan Congress of Parents and Teachers, the Michigan Farm Bureau, the Michigan Migrant Ministry, the Council of Catholic Women, and the Inter-Agency Committee all urged the continuation of the program, but all to no avail.[55]

The Hartford and Keeler school districts provided a school for migrant children in 1959 that ran from April 1 to June 1 and September 7 to November 1, dates corresponding to the time migrants were in the two districts. The students, as in Bay County, were assigned to two classes, one for grades one to three, one for grades four to six. The classes were taught by retired teachers, and the stress was on reading, writing, and arithmetic. Hartford charged the parents two dollars per month for the rental of books and supplies. The two schools were repeated in 1960 and 1961, and Ionia County in the latter year also introduced a special school for migrant children.[56]

The public revelation of the miserable condition of Michigan's migrants and the efforts of the Williams administration and Democratic legislators to secure migrant reform legislation appear to have convinced many growers that some corrective action on their part was essential to forestall the kind of migrant legislation that they feared might impair their operations. The Michigan Farm Bureau at the end of 1954 asked the Michigan State College Cooperative Extension Service to conduct a program of education for growers so that they could improve employer-employee relations. Growers spent $2,750,000 between 1948 and 1954 for new, permanent housing for migrants and $500,000 for the repair and improvement of existing housing. A large group of Berrien fruit farmers voluntarily agreed in 1956 to adopt a set of housing standards for their farms. In the cherry-producing sections of the state, permanent structures began to replace pyramidal tents. Some growers began to carry liability insurance to cover on-the-job accidents of their workers, provide migrants with aid in times of need, help them to find additional employment, and pay their hospital bills.[57]

The Williams administration, at the very least, helped to focus public attention on Michigan's migrant problems and to provide the information on which a program of migrant reform could be based. It appears to have influenced at least some growers to improve the lot of the migrants on their farms and to persuade the Michigan Farm Bureau that it could not categorically reject all proposals for migrant reform. The major results of the Williams administration efforts on behalf of migrants were not, however, to become evident until George Romney became the state's governor.

As Williams looked back on his years as governor in his January 11, 1961, "exaugural address" to the Michigan legislature, he stated, "We elevated human dignity by expanding the frontiers of civil rights."[58] His administration had certainly helped to make civil rights a major issue in Michigan, and it could point to some positive accomplishments in this area, such as the Fair Employment Practices Act. The civil rights frontier, however, would have to be expanded a great deal further before Michigan could justly claim leadership among the states in the civil rights protection it accorded its inhabitants and its migrant farmworkers.

8

"THE DEMOCRATS MUST STAND UP AND BE COUNTED"

Mennen Williams not only endeavored to make the Democratic Party of Michigan a force for civil rights and equal opportunity for the disadvantaged; he also attempted to move the national Democratic Party in the same direction. At the national governors' conference in July 1952, he sought support for an "all-out civil rights plank" in the 1952 Democratic platform. At the Democratic national convention that year, he consequently supported the presidential candidacy of Estes Kevaufer, who had taken the "strongest position on civil rights" among the party's presidential candidates. Although the platform the convention adopted was not what Williams would have preferred, he wrote Paul Douglas that the two of them had "gained" in the fight for a more liberal party. "We may have lost the battle," Williams asserted, "but I am inclined to believe that we are going to win the war."[1]

Williams was to have been the principal speaker at a Jefferson-Jackson Day dinner in Birmingham, Alabama, in 1955, but he withdrew when he became aware of a city ordinance requiring that his audience was to be racially segregated. "I cannot take part in a public gathering from which members of any race are barred by law," he declared. Earlier in the year, Paul Butler, the chairman of the Democratic National Committee, had appointed Williams chairman of the party's Nationalities Committee, which was designed to attract ethnic groups to the Democratic Party. Speaking at a Nationalities Group program in Los Angeles in January 1956, Williams asserted, "The denial of opportunity to racial, nationality and religious groups plays directly into the hands of those who would destroy us." He criticized President Dwight D. Eisenhower for failing to support the kind of civil rights program Democrats like himself were advocating.[2]

Before the 1956 national Democratic convention, the Michigan Democratic Party called for the national Democratic Party to adopt a strong civil rights plank and to "lead the way to the complete elimination of segregation." The Michigan party favored a platform plank calling for a federal fair employment practices law, abolition of the poll tax, an anti-lynching law, establishment of a federal commission to make appraisals of the civil rights field and to recommend appropriate action, elevation of the Civil Liberties Unit in the Department of Justice to division status, refusal of Congress to seat anyone elected to either house by the unconstitutional and illegal denial of the right to vote, and refusal to provide federal funds to support segregation in housing and education. As in 1952, however, the civil rights platform plank the convention adopted fell short of what Williams and the Michigan Democratic Party favored.[3]

At the beginning of 1957, Williams and Governor Averell Harriman of New York were appointed to the Democratic National Advisory Committee that the executive committee of the Democratic National Committee had established. In the fall of 1957 Williams and Harriman agreed to hold a governors' conference on civil rights to be made up entirely of governors whose states had adopted fair employment practices laws. The purpose of the conference was for the governors to discuss their experience in administering their fair employment laws, see if they could promote interstate cooperation regarding fair employment, and determine how they could accelerate fulfillment of the legislation's objectives.[4]

At Williams's suggestion, staffs of the two governors met in Detroit on November 8 to plan an agenda for the conference, which was to be held in New York on December 12, 1957. Twelve states were invited to participate, all but one of them headed by a Democratic governor. The draft statement prepared for the conference took note of the twenty-five states that protected the civil rights of their citizens by constitutional or legislative measures dealing with such matters as employment discrimination and discrimination in education, public accommodations, and housing. The statement pledged the states attending the conference "to work toward broader coverage" of civil rights and to enlarge the attendance at a second conference of governors by including not only states with fair employment laws but also states that had enacted civil rights legislation dealing with other matters. The draft statement also called for federal-state cooperation in dealing with Native Americans

G. Mennen Williams and Averell Harriman,
Governors Conference on Civil Rights, 1957.
Courtesy Bentley Historical Library.

and migrant workers and the elimination of discrimination by federal contractors and wherever federal tax funds were involved.[5]

Harriman opened the Governors' Conference in New York and then turned the chair over to Williams. "Our leadership in the free world," Williams stated, "is being judged by the uncommitted people of Asia, Africa and India as much by the progress we make in the field of human rights as by our prowess in the field of space and missiles." The conference, the first time the governors of some of the states had come together "to take constructive action on civil rights," agreed to establish a continuing organization to be called the Committee of Governors on Civil Rights, and Williams was named chairman. The focus of the meeting was on fair employment at both the federal and state levels. The "politically sophisticated" correctly saw the purpose of the governors present as seeking to commit the Democratic Party to a strong civil rights position and, perhaps, to counter the Southern Governors Conference. There was also some speculation that the conference was related to a possible Williams presidential candidacy in 1960, a subject that was, indeed, under intense consideration by the governor and his staff. A report of the conference dealing mainly with the experience of states having fair employment acts was published by the American Jewish Congress.[6]

The governors present at the New York conference agreed to establish an Interim Sub-Committee to develop plans for the operation of the Governors' Committee. Chaired by John Feild, the executive director of the Michigan Fair Employment Practices Commission, the subcommittee held the first of its three meetings in Detroit on April 11, 1958. In accordance with the draft statement preceding the first Governors' Conference, the subcommittee recommended that the governors expand the membership of the Governors' Committee to include the governors of states with public programs to broaden civil rights guaranties in their states but not necessarily having a fair employment law. Following the subcommittee's recommendation, the Governors' Committee decided to invite to the second conference the governors of all states having "any form of publicly financed civil rights or human relations program." Before the second conference convened, members of the Governors' Committee provided "consultative assistance" to two states contemplating the enactment of fair employment laws, decided to add federal-state relations regarding civil rights to the agenda of the second conference, and met informally with the executive director and executive secretary of the new U.S. Commission on Civil Rights.[7]

Eighteen states were represented in Detroit in January 1959 for the second Governors' Conference. Williams presided, and the keynote address was delivered by John A. Hannah, chairman of the U.S. Commission on Civil Rights. The conferees called attention to the fact that more than two-thirds of the nation's population by then enjoyed the protection of state "statutory civil rights safeguards." They called on the federal government to match the record of the states and urged the president "to use his prestige and power to give guidance and leadership" to the civil rights cause so as to "create a positive climate of public opinion." They urged Congress to enact legislation to protect voting rights, "facilitate the orderly desegregation of the schools," enact a federal fair employment practices law, and "curb violence and intimidation."[8]

At the third and, as it turned out, last meeting of the Committee of Governors on Civil Rights, in St. Paul, Minnesota, in March 1960, fifteen states were represented but only five by their governors. Speaking to a Brotherhood Week banquet during the conference, Williams was critical of the federal government and especially the president for having "done too little" to advance the cause of civil rights in the nation. Praising the "passive resistance" by blacks to segregation in the South, Williams observed, "we have [civil rights] frontiers of our own to tame."

Acting on the recommendation of the Interim Sub-Committee, the conferees in St. Paul adopted a statement recognizing the responsibility of "all levels of government" for "continued and intensified progress in the field of human rights." The statement placed special responsibility on the governors to take the lead in this regard in their states, called for federal government action to deal with voting rights, fair employment, and housing ("a field of urgent importance"), and both federal and state action in dealing with the migrant labor problem.[9]

Williams continued his efforts to identify the Democratic Party with a strong civil rights position following the St. Paul conference. He thus enlisted support for civil rights by the governors attending the Democratic Midwest Governors Conference in Detroit in March 1960. Since this was to be "the last significant Democratic gathering" before the party's national convention, Williams was especially anxious that the conference be "a vehicle for liberalism." The governors present, with Williams playing a prominent role, pledged themselves "to use every influence, moral, educational and political to eliminate under law all barriers to the individual enjoyment of all civil rights so that the dignity of citizenship shall become a reality in fact as well as in law." The Michigan Democratic Party, for its part, urged the national party to adopt a platform asserting that the protection of civil rights was "the crucial domestic issue of our time" and required "dynamic Presidential leadership."[10]

Prominent Michigan blacks in the Democratic Party were concerned as to whether John F. Kennedy, the potential Democratic nominee for the presidency in 1960, would provide the "dynamic" leadership for civil rights for which the Michigan party had called. They were aware that Kennedy had enjoyed the support of southerners in his bid for the vice presidential nomination in 1956 and that at a Democratic Party Relations Conference in the summer of 1959, he had been the only Democratic presidential candidate to support a compromise on civil rights measures then before the Congress. When Williams decided to support Kennedy's nomination after a meeting of the two on Mackinac Island in late March 1960, there was a "mixed reaction" among Michigan's Democrats.[11]

To satisfy the Williams voters, especially blacks, Kennedy, an aide advised the governor, "must give you something to work with." A delegation that included Williams, Michigan civil rights leaders, and prominent blacks such as Damon Keith, head of the Michigan NAACP, visited Kennedy in Washington on June 20, 1960, to seek clarification of his civil rights views. Kennedy, who was "sharply questioned" by the black leaders, responded that the civil rights issue was of "overwhelming moral significance" and promised, if elected, to use the prestige of his office "to completely eliminate second class citizenship in America for all Americans." He stated that he was "strongly" opposed to discrimination in housing, public and private, and would, as president, provide "effective guaranties of the right to vote" and support "complete desegregation" of all publicly supported federal activities.

Kennedy was obviously saying what he undoubtedly assumed the blacks present wanted to hear. When, however, he then said that despite his opposition to discrimination in housing and public schools, he would put his "primary emphasis" on securing a federal fair employment practices law, the general response of the Michigan civil rights group was that "he didn't understand the name of the game." It was their position that the civil rights issue facing the nation at that time could not be separated in that way. According to John Feild, one of those present, Kennedy was "quite visibly affected by that response." He then amended his position to say that, "politically," he believed that a fair employment law was the only civil rights measure he could obtain at the outset of his administration. The Michigan group reportedly found that contention acceptable, possibly because Williams himself had come to the same conclusion when he first became the state's governor. On the other hand, the civil rights forces in Michigan and elsewhere were pressing by 1960 for more than just the enactment of fair employment legislation. In any event, a confidential memorandum of the Michigan group's visit with Kennedy, perhaps written by Williams himself, indicated that the black visitors had been "favorably impressed" by Kennedy and "came away sold."[12]

If Kennedy were to become the 1960 Democratic presidential nominee, an aide advised Williams after the June 20 meeting, the party platform would be seen as Kennedy's. This, the aide continued, meant that the platform had to include "clear and precise language" regarding civil rights, presumably identifying the national Democratic Party with the civil rights position of the Michigan party. Testifying at the Resolutions and Platform Committee hearings on July 8, 1960, Williams emphasized the critical importance of the civil rights issue. "I cannot stress too greatly," he declared, "my feeling that the times demand that the Democrats must stand up and be counted on this central question of contemporary civilization. It is my deep belief that discrimination is immoral, in the deepest sense un-American, and wherever the government is involved, it is unconstitutional."[13]

At their 1960 national convention, the Democrats adopted "the boldest civil rights plank in their history." As Williams and the Michigan

Democratic Party, the Governors' Committee on Civil Rights, and the Midwest Democratic governors had been urging, the party committed itself to enforce the voting laws vigorously, enact a federal fair employment law, and bring an end to discrimination in education and housing. The platform praised "the peaceful demonstrations for first-class citizenship" that had been occurring in the South and called for "strong, active, persuasive leadership" by the president with respect to civil rights. Pleased with the platform, the Michigan delegation to the convention was unanimously opposed to Kennedy's choice of Lyndon B. Johnson as his running mate. When the chairman of the convention moved to make the Johnson nomination unanimous, Williams jumped to his feet and voted no. Having decided not to seek another term as governor, Williams was later recognized for his pre-convention support of Kennedy and his identification with the civil rights cause by being appointed assistant secretary of state for African Affairs.[14]

John Swainson never attained the national stature that Williams had, but there is no question that he shared Williams's views regarding civil rights. At the 1962 annual conference of the nation's governors, Swainson opposed a civil rights resolution submitted by the resolutions committee as doing "little to bolster previous such resolutions." It was the duty of the governor, Swainson said, "to lead the way in assuring every citizen of our free society equal opportunity." If "even one man, woman or child of any race, creed, color or national origin remains shackled by bonds of inequality in our country," he declared, "we are not performing as our forefathers intended." He submitted a resolution calling for equal access to the ballot and public office, equal opportunity with regard to employment, education, and housing, equality of access to public facilities and public accommodations, and "equality of justice and protection under law." Nineteen governors supported the Swainson resolution, the conference hardly speaking with one voice on the subject.[15]

As president, Kennedy did not fulfill the high hopes Michigan's civil rights advocates had for him. Ironically, it was the administration of Lyndon B. Johnson, whose vice presidential nomination Michigan Democrats had opposed, that secured from the Congress the kind of civil rights legislation that the Williams and Swainson administrations had been seeking at the national level. By that time, however, the governorship of Michigan was no longer held by a Democrat.

9

CIVIL RIGHTS AND THE MICHIGAN CONSTITUTION OF 1963

"Of all the Constitutions in the fifty states, the new proposed Constitution of Michigan does more in the field of civil rights than has been done in any state Constitution." These words were spoken by the chairman of the U.S. Commission on Civil Rights, John A. Hannah, after the delegates to the Michigan Constitutional Convention of 1961–62 had completed their deliberations.[1] He was referring to the Declaration of Rights in the new constitution and, even more so, to the fact that the Civil Rights Commission for which the document provided was the only such body in the fifty states to be accorded constitutional status.

The guaranties of civil rights in the Michigan constitution as of the time the constitutional convention began its proceedings in 1961 were, as we have seen, "fragmentary and incomplete." The Declaration of Rights in the existing constitution did not include an equal protection clause, nor did it prohibit discrimination based on race, color, religion, or national origin.[2] It was not, however, civil rights concerns that provided the impetus for the drafting of a new constitution for Michigan to replace the 1908 constitution but rather the state's fiscal problems and its legislative apportionment system.[3] An "aggressive political campaign" to place the issue of a constitutional convention before the voters was mounted by the League of Women Voters, the Junior Chamber of Commerce, and the Citizens for Michigan, founded in 1959 by George Romney, president of the American Motors Company. The voters on April 3, 1961, narrowly approved a referendum calling for revision of the state constitution. A

191

primary election to select delegates for the convention was held on July 25, followed by a general election on September 12.

Of the 144 delegates the voters elected, 99 were Republicans and 45 were Democrats. All but 4 of the Democrats were elected from districts in the Detroit metropolitan area, whereas only 15 of the Republican delegates were chosen from that region. Thirteen of the Democratic delegates were black, constituting, according to Detroit's future mayor, delegate Coleman A. Young, "the largest number of Negroes to be part of the writing or rewriting of any state constitution" to that time. Of the 11 women delegates, 6 were Republicans and 5 were Democrats. The Democratic delegates were a "much more homogeneous group" than their Republican counterparts, composed of conservatives from "rural, outstate districts" and a much larger group of moderates and liberals from suburban Detroit and "second-line urban areas in outstate Michigan." Although the delegates did not always divide along party lines, partisanship was thrust to the fore when Republican Romney, who had been saying since early 1961 that he might become a candidate for Michigan's governorship, officially announced his candidacy on February 10, 1962. The convention began its deliberations on October 3, 1961, and essentially completed its work on the new constitution on May 11, 1962, although the final convention session was held on August 1 of that year.[4]

The convention occurred at a time of considerably heightened national concern about civil rights. It followed the sit-ins that began on February 1, 1960, in Greensboro, North Carolina, the Freedom Rides that started in May 1961, the civil rights protests in Albany, Georgia, that began in the fall of 1961 and the arrest there of Martin Luther King, Jr., in December, and the initiation of the Kennedy administration's Voter Education Project in May 1962.[5]

Romney had wanted to be named president of the convention, but the position went to Steven Nisbet, a member of the State Board of Education. "Very angry" at being passed over, Romney was selected one of the convention's three vice presidents, all of them of equal status, although Romney, according to fellow vice president Democrat Tom Downs, wanted to be made the first among the three. The distinguished University of Michigan political scientist Professor James K. Pollock, chairman of the convention's Committee on Declaration of Rights, Suffrage and Elections and himself a Republican, privately viewed Romney as "quite a prima donna." In a convention note of January 13, 1962, Pollock referred to "the obvious motions that George Romney was going through to get himself in position to become a candidate" for governor. Whatever his political ambitions, Romney played a key role in the convention and proved to be a staunch defender of civil rights.[6]

Legislative apportionment became "the hottest issue" in the deliberations of the Michigan Constitutional Convention of 1961–62. The new constitution provided for a Senate of 38 members chosen from districts in which the population was "weighted" 80 percent and area 20 percent. The House was to consist of 110 members, with each county that had a population of not less than 0.7 percent of the state's population to constitute a separate representative area and each county with a smaller population than that to be combined with another county or counties to form a representative area of not less than the 0.7 percent figure. The remaining House seats were to be "apportioned among the representative areas on the basis of population by the method of equal proportions."[7]

While Michigan's constitutional convention was in session, the U.S. Supreme Court ruled in *Baker v. Carr* in 1962 that the districts for the election of members of the lower house of a state legislature were to be equal in population. In *Reynolds v. Sims* in 1964, the Court extended the principle of equality of population for electoral districts to both houses of a state legislature. In 1964, for the first time, the members of the Michigan legislature were elected from districts that were approximately equal in population. The state Democratic Party was the immediate beneficiary of the new system of apportionment, its membership in the Senate increasing from 11 of 34 seats in 1962 to 23 of 38 seats in 1964 and its membership in the House in the same years from 52 to 73 of the 110 seats. The Republicans, however, made an electoral comeback in the next few years, winning 21 of the 38 Senate seats and one-half of the House seats in 1964 and 26 of 38 Senate seats and 53 of 110 House seats in 1968.[8] Legislative reapportionment, generally speaking, produced a legislature somewhat more sympathetic to civil rights than the legislatures with which Williams and Swainson had had to deal.

As it turned out, civil rights became "one of the most discussed" and most contentious issues at the constitutional convention.[9] Until late in the convention, the Committee on Declaration of Rights, Suffrage and Elections grappled with the problem. It drew up a new section for the constitution's Declaration of Rights dealing with equal protection and discrimination, but it decided against acting on the question of whether to establish a civil rights commission to enforce the civil rights provisions of the constitution and the relevant state laws. That matter, as it turned out, was addressed by the Committee on the Executive Branch.

The Committee on Declaration of Rights, Suffrage and Elections was composed of ten Republicans and five Democrats. Chairman Pollock described his committee as having among its members "everything from McKinley Republicans over to pretty close to pinks." Among the former, he appears to have included fellow Republicans Detroiter J. Harold Stevens, the committee's first vice chairman, and Edward K. Stranahan

193

Michigan Constitutional Convention, 1961–62.
Courtesy Bentley Historical Library.

from Charlevoix. Pollock did not indicate which of the Democrats he thought were "close to pinks," but he was presumably referring to Democrats who were to his ideological left and were liberals rather than "pinks." Pollock actually thought that Democrat Harold Norris, a Detroit College of Law professor and the committee's second vice-chairman, was actually "a very wise man" although "too talkative," and the committee's chairman had a favorable opinion of Robert Hodges, a law school graduate from a trade union family. As for the other three Democrats, Norris described the Reverend Malcolm Dade, a black, as "a kindly man committed to civil rights"; Lillian Hatcher, also a black, as "a dedicated trade unionist"; and Peter Buback, as experienced in local government. The head of research for the committee was Professor Alfred H. Kelly, chairman of Wayne State University's history department.[10]

The questions that concerned the Pollock committee regarding the drafting of a civil rights section for the new constitution were whether to include an equal protection clause; whether to ban discrimination not only because of race, color, religion, and national origin but also because of sex and age; whether to prohibit discrimination not only by public authorities but also by private parties; whether to specify the particular areas to which the ban on discrimination should apply; and whether to exempt private housing from any ban on housing discrimination. After some committee members and Kelly made presentations to the committee regarding "problem areas" in the civil rights field, the committee turned its attention to the drafting of a rights section to submit to the convention. Pollock's assumption at this stage of the proceedings that what the committee would agree to would not be "very much different" from the Declaration of Rights in the 1908 constitution proved to be erroneous.[11]

Seeking support for a strong civil rights provision, Norris, Hatcher, and Dade turned on October 31 to the Michigan Coordinating Council on Civil Rights. Hatcher indicated to the council "the need for a strong Civil Rights lobby," and Norris expressed the desire of his group to work with the council. The council promptly drafted a proposal calling for the addition of a section on equal protection and nondiscrimination to the state constitution's Declaration of Rights that Norris on November 13 converted into Proposal No. 1216. "No person," the proposal stated, "shall be denied the equal protection of the laws of the state or any subdivision thereof. No person because of race, color, creed, religion, national origin, age or sex shall be subject to any discrimination in any civil rights by any person or by any firm, corporation, institution, or labor organization, or by the state or any agency or subdivision thereof. Each person shall have the right to equal opportunity to secure employment, education, housing, and public accommodations." In its inclusion of private parties, sex, and age and in its specific reference to employment, education, housing, and public accommodations, the Norris proposal staked out a position from which the Pollock committee and the convention would retreat. By November 26 the Coordinating Council itself had dropped sex and age from its proposal, and age discrimination, unlike sex discrimination, never became an issue of importance in the Rights Committee or in the convention.[12]

On November 30 John Hannah, who was a Republican delegate to the convention, made a more modest proposal than Proposal No. 1621 to the Rights Committee. Because of the federal and state constitutions and pertinent civil rights legislation, Hannah contended, there was no need to refer to such matters as education and employment in a new Declaration of Rights. Nor, apparently, did he think it necessary to refer to sex or age discrimination or to ban discrimination by private parties. After consulting with the staff of the U.S. Commission on Civil Rights, Hannah offered the following as the proper language for the new constitution's Declaration of Rights:

> Section 1. *Inherent Rights*. This constitution is dedicated to the principles that all persons have a natural right to life, liberty, the pursuit of happiness, and the enjoyment of the rewards of their own industry; that all persons are entitled to equal rights, opportunities, and protection under the law; and that all persons have corresponding obligations to the people and to the state.
>
> Section 2. *Civil Rights*. No person is to be denied the enjoyment of any civil or political right because of race, color, religion, or national origin. The legislature shall implement this section.

In supporting this proposal, Hannah, Pollock later told the convention, gave the Rights Committee "impressive and moving advice" about the need for what he was proposing to protect African Americans and other minorities against discrimination.[13] In view of Hannah's position in the nation and in Michigan, it is not difficult to surmise that his recommendation to the Rights Committee caused at least some among the majority Republicans to conclude that a civil rights addition to the 1908 constitution was required.

The Hannah proposal did not deter Democratic members of the Pollock committee from seeking a stronger civil rights section for the new constitution than Hannah had recommended. On December 8 seven Democratic delegates, including Hatcher and Norris, the principal draftsman, submitted Proposal No. 1621 to the Rights Committee. It was little different from Proposal No. 1216 except that discrimination on the basis of sex and age had been dropped from the earlier proposal, probably in an effort to attract support among committee members who favored a less inclusive proposal than No. 1216.[14]

On December 13 former president Dwight D. Eisenhower addressed the convention, stressing the states' important role in the American system of government. In the question-and-answer session that followed the address, Norris, attempting to gain support for Proposal No. 1621, asked Eisenhower a question not specifically based on his talk but rather on a statement in the report of the Commission on National Goals that Eisenhower had appointed, namely, that the "goals" of "equal rights before the law and an equal opportunity to vote, to be educated, to get a job, to buy a house" were to be "achieved by action at all levels." "Do you believe," Norris asked, "that 'action at all levels' to secure equal opportunity for employment, housing and education includes appropriate expression in a state constitution, and would not a clear cut expression at the level of state government on behalf of such equal opportunity, be helpful in strengthening America's moral position in the world?" To this question Eisenhower replied, "Well, I think it is essential. . . . I would be very much in favor of it."[15]

Hoping to gain added support for Proposal No. 1621, the civil rights forces in the convention pressed for public hearings on the rights issue. "Responding," in Pollock's view, "largely to Negro delegates" but also, and not incidentally, to the unanimous request of Pollock's own committee, the convention agreed to hold rights hearings in Detroit, Flint, and Saginaw on December 18 and 19. "I think the reasons for the hearings are largely public relations," a disgruntled Pollock commented. Citing the hearings in Detroit in December 1960 by the U.S. Commission on Civil Rights and also the 1961 report of the Michigan Advisory Committee to the U.S. Commission on Civil Rights, the Coordinating Council called attention in the Detroit hearings to the extensive discrimination against nonwhites in housing, employment, education, and law enforcement as justifying the need for Proposal No. 1621. Strong support for the proposal was also voiced by the secretary-director of the Detroit Commission on Community Relations, Richard V. Marks. As 1961 drew to a close, there was "great pressure" on the Rights Committee, as Pollock noted, to add a section to the constitution's Declaration of Rights calling for "equal protection and no discrimination." "I have hundreds of letters in favor of this," Pollock wrote, "and apparently there is no serious objection to it."[16]

On January 11, 1962, Pollock presented a rights proposal to his committee that he characterized as a combination of Hannah's proposal and a civil rights provision of the new Hawaiian constitution. "No person," what became Proposal No. 26 stated, "shall be denied the equal protection of the laws, nor be denied the enjoyment of his civil or political rights or be discriminated against in the exercise thereof because of race, religion, sex or national origin. The legislature shall have the power to enforce this section by appropriate legislation." As Norris quickly pointed out, the proposal did not apply to private parties, as Proposal No. 1621 did. Pollock responded that he did not think that this was his committee's responsibility. Unlike Proposal No. 1621, also, the Pollock proposal did not include reference to education, employment, housing, and public accommodations, but it did ban sex discrimination.[17]

Women's rights advocates were divided on the question of banning sex discrimination in the Michigan constitution, just as they were divided on the addition of the Equal Rights Amendment to the U.S. Constitution. Some women, to be sure, favored a state constitutional ban on discrimination against women, but they feared that this would invalidate the protective legislation for women that reform-minded social feminists had sought to secure over the years and would remove the obligation of husbands to support their wives and divorced women's ability to obtain alimony. When Patricia Barrymore, Status of Women chair of the Michigan Division of the American Association of University Women, wrote convention delegate Dorothy Siegel Judd on December 11, 1961, that a guarantee of equal employment regardless of sex or marital status should be included in the Declaration of Rights, the Grand Rapids Republican Judd, a League of Women Voters activist, responded, "I have spent my forty years in the League fighting for the equal rights amendment . . . and I am too old now to start off in the opposite direction." To put a reference to sex in the constitution, she said, would be "an anachronism." When the Rights Committee met on January 12, 1962, it discussed the sex discrimination issue "at length," particularly whether the inclusion of the word "sex" would have a negative effect on dower rights, property rights for women, and labor legislation designed to protect women workers.[18]

The principal debate in the Rights Committee was between supporters of the Pollock proposal and supporters of Proposal No. 1621, to which had been added the sentence, "The courts of the state shall afford every person a remedy, both legal and equitable, against such discrimination." An informal vote on January 16 revealed a division in the committee along party lines, the Republicans favoring the Pollock proposal, the Democrats, Proposal No. 1621. The minority, however, agreed that they would present their proposal to the convention as "a minority of preference and not opposition." The committee then unanimously adopted Pollock's Proposal No. 26.[19]

Pollock presented Proposal No. 26 to the convention on January 19, and on February 1 it came up for debate in the Committee of the Whole, to which it had been referred. Pollock now described the proposal as "a modification and synthesis" of the civil rights provision of the Hawaiian constitution "incorporated" in the Hannah proposal and a proposal (No. 1014) by Norris that also essentially repeated the key civil rights provision in the Hawaiian constitution. Although Proposal No. 26 did not refer to the specific civil rights areas to be protected against discrimination, Pollock nevertheless told the convention, "The principal but not exclusive areas of concern [with regard to civil rights] are equal opportunities in employment, education, housing and public accommodations." Observing that the proposal was not "directly enforceable . . . in regard to private persons," Pollock explained that, "as a general proposition," the committee majority thought that "constitutional limitations should restrain government action and not . . . define private duties." It was for the legislature, he said, to decide just what private discrimination should be forbidden and what sanctions should apply.

Further explaining Proposal No. 26, Pollock told the convention that "in recognition of the modern doctrine of the equality of women," the proposal included "a guarantee against discrimination by sex." Commenting on this point, Harold Stevens remarked, "We did not feel so much it was necessary, but the ladies wanted it in. They feel they must be designated as a minority group." The committee, he said, had concluded that the proposed language would not "interfere with the statutory or constitutional rights provided for women."

The minority gained an important supporter when Romney rose to say that although Proposal No. 1621 was "to some extent statutory in character" and "subject to some abuse," he favored its specificity because of "the urgency of dealing with the problem promptly and thus taking steps" that were "important to harmony within our state, and to the understanding of our true attitude and position in the world." Former Republican congressman Alvin M. Bentley of Owosso also expressed support for the minority proposal but offered an amendment to limit its housing reference to public housing. After Hannah opposed the Bentley amendment as divisive, the delegates rejected it by an 8–80 vote. The last, however, had not been heard in the convention regarding the matter of private housing.

Delegate Lewis Hubbs of Gladwin thought that the minority went "too far in its attempt to preserve individual freedom." Republican Ruth G. Butler of Houghton "urge[d] the dames to vote against" Proposal No. 1621 "because there's no sex in it," a comment that produced laughter. The minority proposal was subsequently defeated by a 50–80 vote. Malcolm Dade, a supporter of the minority proposal, nevertheless thought Proposal No. 26 "a great step forward" and asked on February 2 for its unanimous approval, stating, "I think we have written into the law of the state of Michigan a concept of democracy that is very fundamental and very gratifying." Assembled in Committee of the Whole, the delegates responded by approving the proposal by a 126–0 vote.[20]

The vote of February 2 did not put to rest the question of whether there should be some reference to private housing and sex discrimination in the proposed civil rights section for the new constitution. The effort to include language that would permit private property owners to dispose of their property as they saw fit began in the Pollock committee in December 1961, when Republican Weldon O. Yeager of Detroit sought to persuade the committee to reject Rule 9, which, it will be recalled, prohibited real estate licensees from discriminating on the basis of race, religion, or national origin. Yeager proposed that the Declaration of Rights include the right of real property owners "to sell, lease or rent their private real property . . . to any person whatsoever." The Yeager proposal led to a committee hearing in Lansing on December 6, which, according to Pollock, "brought up quite a bevy of people from Detroit" who provided the committee with "very impressive . . . testimony" in favor of Rule 9. Representatives of the Michigan Coordinating Council on Civil Rights testified that the Yeager proposal "would make bigotry and prejudice a part of the Constitution." The proposal attracted scant support in the committee and was defeated by a 3–11 vote. Stevens then sought "to get at the right of the home owner to dispose of his property as he wishes" by what became Proposal No. 45: "The right of the owner of real property to convey, grant, devise or control said property shall be limited only by general law. The legislature shall not delegate this power." The committee approved the Stevens proposal on January 24 by a 9–5 vote. Pollock, who thought the proposal "merely a statement of law as it has existed for years" and hence "meaningless," joined four Democrats in opposition. Pollock then presented Proposal No. 45 to the convention and recommended its approval as an amendment to Proposal No. 26.[21]

When Proposal No. 45 was first debated on the convention floor on April 10, Pollock defended it as creating "a specific constitutional guarantee" of a "long established principle of the common law" and as "not at odds" with the civil rights section the delegates had already approved. Opponents claimed that the proposal was "unnecessary," had been "very cleverly drawn" to "cover" its "intent" to abrogate Rule 9, and would give "constitutional sanctity" to the right to discriminate against blacks. The proposal was defeated by a 59–63 vote.[22]

Proposal No. 45 came before the convention a second time on April 26. Supporting the proposal, Republican Richard Kuhn of Pontiac declared, "I think we've done a lot for civil rights. I think we've done a lot for a lot of people and now I think we should take care of the property owners of the state of Michigan, and give them some protection which they so rightly deserve." Such prominent Republicans as Hannah and John B. Martin, chairman of the Committee on the Executive Branch, attacked the proposal, Martin declaring that its "sole purpose" was to sanction "segregated communities." The measure was defeated for a second time by a 47–73 vote, Romney and Pollock joining the opponents, and then for a third time on May 7 by a 54–70 vote.

The advocates of Proposal No. 45 did win something of a victory when they secured approval of a proposal stating, "The legislature may by concurrent resolution empower a joint committee of the legislature, acting between sessions, to suspend any rule or regulation promulgated by an administrative agency subsequent to the adjournment of the last preceding regular legislative session. Such suspension shall continue no longer than the end of the next regular legislative session." It was understood by those favoring a ban on housing discrimination that the proposal was directed at Rule 9. They were very much aware that the proposal made it possible for a group of legislators to suspend an administrative rule like Rule 9 without a roll call vote, and if the legislature took no action when it returned in session, the joint committee could renew its suspension of the rule.[23]

The question of whether to ban sex discrimination in the Declaration of Rights proved to be a troublesome matter for convention delegates. In their debate on the subject, they reflected some of the same difference of opinion that has continued to be associated with the matter. Speaking for at least some of the women in the convention, the Dearborn Democrat and League of Women Voters activist Katherine Cushman declared on the convention floor on April 18, "We are not completely sure at the present time whether the mention of sex is a good idea or a poor idea in the constitution." When Proposal No. 26 came back to the delegates from the Committee on Style and Drafting on April 26 for a second reading, Pollock announced that two amendments would be offered dealing with sex, "as interesting a subject," he said, "as that always is," a remark that produced laughter. Judd, Cushman, and two other delegates then offered an amendment to drop the word "sex" from the place it then occupied in the proposal and to add, instead, "No woman shall be discriminated against because of sex or marital status in the securing of employment or in promotion therein." Judd and her colleagues singled out employment discrimination because they regarded it as "the particular discrimination" that was most difficult for women to deal with at that time. They added "marital status" because employers, when having to lay off workers, generally dismissed married women before unmarried women since employers assumed that married men were obligated to support their wives. When the presiding officer then said that the question was open for amendment, "all male delegates rose," and once again there was laughter. Menominee Republican Charles E. Perras remarked, "In case there was any doubt over what this was for, it was in honor of 'sex,'" which once again produced laughter. Understandably annoyed at the repeated display of male chauvinism on the convention floor, Cushman interjected to say that she hoped the subject could be discussed without laughter.

The fear of women like Cushman was that the outright constitutional ban on sex discrimination that was being proposed would make "reasonable classification" based on sex unconstitutional. "Being women," Judd, apparently retreating from her earlier position, declared, "we want equality with men, but we also want our special privileges too." Norris opposed the amendment, contending that the inclusion of the word "sex" in the ban on discrimination did not preclude "reasonable classification." When the delegates voted 68–44 not to omit "sex" from Proposal No. 26, Judd, disturbed that the men "took it all as a joke," withdrew the fair employment amendment.

In an effort to resolve the classification issue, delegate Ann E. Donnelly, a Highland Park Republican, offered as an amendment to the nondiscrimination section of Proposal No. 26, "This shall not be construed to prevent reasonable classification for the protection of women." The amendment was initially defeated by a voice vote, but it was approved the next day, as was the retention of the word "sex." The delegates then approved Proposal No. 26 once again, this time by a 116–3 vote, Judd voting in the negative.[24]

Despite the April 27 vote, all reference to sex was soon to be dropped from Proposal No. 26. Alerted by the convention's co-directors of research, Alfred Kelly and University of Michigan law professor Charles Joiner, the Grosse Pointe Shores Republican William B. Cudlip, chairman of the convention's Committee on Style and Drafting and himself "a distinguished attorney," sought advice on the sex issue from Professor Paul C. Kauper, a Michigan law school professor and considered the state's "foremost constitutional expert." "We are bothered," Cudlip wrote Kauper regarding Proposal No. 26 in the form in which it had just been approved, "because of possible future inability of the legislature to enact discriminatory laws beneficial to women over and above any laws passed pursuant to the police power." Kauper responded that the inclusion of the word "sex" in the proposal would "create difficulties" for the legislature and the courts since, as legislative measures and court decisions had indicated, "classification by sex," unlike classification by race or religion, "might be reasonable depending on the purpose to which it is directed." Even if the Donnelly amendment were added to the proposal, Kauper doubted that the inclusion of the word "sex" would be "of sufficient advantage to women in the enjoyment of political or civil rights to outweigh the legislative classification problem it introduced."[25]

When Proposal No. 26 came back to the convention for a third and final reading on May 7, Cudlip not only read portions of Kauper's letter but also noted that Kelly, Joiner, and many lawyer delegates were "very much disturbed" at the action the convention had taken regarding the sex issue. "Women," he said, "need to be discriminated against for their own benefit many, many times." He feared, however, that the language the convention had adopted did "not go far enough to protect them." Lillian Hatcher was outraged by what had occurred. Kauper and the men, she asserted, simply did not see the matter as women did. She was not surprised, she said, that some women—she meant women like Judd and Cushman—also wanted to omit any reference to sex, since, she remarked, some slaves had not wanted to be free from their bondage either. Donnelly also objected to what Cudlip had proposed, charging that "the underlying motive behind this" was "not to protect women."

Observing that women suffered "unfair discrimination on account of sex" but also had "certain protections" for the same reason, Cushman thought it best under the circumstances to leave the matter to be dealt with by the legislature rather than by constitutional language that might "lead to unfortunate results." Judd agreed, and the two of them, along with Romney, were among the eighty-two delegates who accepted the Cudlip recommendation. Hannah, Pollock, and Norris joined Hatcher and Donnelly among the forty-eight delegates who voted to retain the word "sex" as well as the reasonable classification provision. Proposal No. 26, minus the reference to sex discrimination, thus remained in the form in which Pollock had first presented it to the convention. This meant that, subject to the approval of the voters, the new Michigan constitution would contain a section dealing with equal protection and nondiscrimination that supporters claimed was "the best in any state constitution."[26]

Women did secure a "vital change" in the new constitution regarding the property rights of married women, although it was not part of the Declaration of Rights. What became Article X, Section 1 of the new constitution provided, unlike the old constitution, that the real and personal property a woman acquired before marriage as well as any property she acquired while married were for her to dispose of as though she were unmarried.[27]

In addition to housing and sex discrimination, another issue that divided the delegates regarding the new constitution's Declaration of Rights was that of search and seizure. The 1908 constitution contained a section that, although providing a guarantee against "unreasonable searches and seizures," specified that this should "not be construed to bar from evidence in any court of criminal jurisdiction, or in any criminal proceeding held before any magistrate or justice of the peace, any narcotic drug or drugs" or any of a long list of "dangerous weapon[s] . . . seized by any peace officer outside the curtilage of any dwelling house in the state." The U.S. Supreme Court, however, in the 1961 case of *Mapp v. Ohio*, appeared to have invalidated this provision by ruling that state courts, just like the federal courts, had to exclude evidence resulting from an unreasonable search or seizure. The Pollock committee, consequently, dropped the 1908 provision in favor of a statement that "evidence obtained in violation of this section shall not be used except as authorized by law."

When the Pollock committee reported its decision regarding search and seizure to the convention, some delegates protested that the language on the subject in the existing constitution was needed to combat "gang-sterism and traffic in narcotics" and that the decision as to whether the proviso was constitutional should be left to the Michigan Supreme Court. Coleman Young responded that the issue posed was one of "human rights" as far as blacks in the state were concerned. Sidney Barthwell, another black Detroit delegate, stated that the police had searched him many times and, indeed, had done so that very afternoon as he was walking down the street. The friends of civil liberties and civil rights did not, however, prevail, the delegates voting 74–62 to retain the proviso in the existing constitution with a minimal change in the language.[28]

"More deep-rooted emotion was roused in Con Con on the creation of a civil rights commission than over any other issue," a veteran *Detroit News* reporter commented.[29] The individual most responsible for placing the issue of a civil rights commission before the convention was a non-delegate, Albert Wheeler, an associate professor of bacteriology at the University of Michigan and a leader in the Ann Arbor–Ypsilanti NAACP. Perhaps acting on the advice of Professor Robert Harris of the University of Michigan Law School, Wheeler informed the deputy director of the Michigan Fair Employment Practices Commission (FEPC) that he would bring to the October 31 meeting of the Coordinating Council on Civil Rights Steering Committee not only a nondiscrimination proposal for the new state constitution but also a proposal calling for the establish-ment of a civil rights commission in the executive branch of the state government that would be vested with the authority to enforce the constitution's civil rights provisions. Wheeler said that he was consid-ering sending the proposal to the Committee on the Executive Branch rather than the Rights Committee because of "the possible reactions of Professor Pollock," whom Wheeler obviously knew. The Committee on the Executive Branch was composed of fourteen Republicans and seven Democrats and was chaired, as already noted, by John B. Martin, a Republican national committeeman and a former state senator and state auditor general.[30]

The Wheeler proposal for a state civil rights commission attracted surprisingly little support at the Steering Committee meeting on October 31. Although Lillian Hatcher saw "merit" in the idea, the prevailing view was that the proposal was "statutory" or "legislative" rather than "constitutional," was not "politically feasible," and, if presented and defeated, might "hinder" attempts to secure desired civil rights legislation. In the end, the committee approved a motion that council members could support the proposal individually but that it was not to go forward as the Coordinating Council's recommendation.[31]

Wheeler, in the end, submitted his proposal to both Pollock and Martin as the proposal of the Ann Arbor–Ypsilanti branch of the NAACP and asked the two to discuss the matter with one another. Writing to Hatcher, Wheeler asserted that the proposed commission would be "the instrument for giving reality and strength to any general [civil rights] provision" in the constitution. In an enclosed document, he offered the two principal reasons that would consistently be employed to justify inclusion of the commission in the constitution. Responding to what he categorized as "the most common and justifiable argument" against according a civil rights commission constitutional status, namely, that the proposal was "legislative," Wheeler noted that the existing constitution included a civil service commission, against which a similar charge could be made. Secondly, he called attention to the fact that since the 1955 enactment of the Fair Employment Practices Act, the state legislature had again and again failed to follow the recommendation of Williams and Swainson to broaden the FEPC's jurisdiction to include education, public accommodations, and housing. Under the circumstances, Wheeler concluded, a constitutional provision to accomplish that purpose was "the only proper recourse."[32]

Wheeler sought to win support for a civil rights commission by writing to delegates, polling NAACP branches, and contacting individuals and groups that might endorse the idea. He continued, however, to meet opposition within the civil rights community because of the supposed legislative character of his proposal and because of the fear, as Michigan Supreme Court Justice Otis M. Smith informed Wheeler, that the proposal would "bring out the bigots" while having "almost no chance of adoption."[33]

On December 5 Hatcher, Daisy Elliott, a Detroit Democrat and Committee on the Executive Branch member, Coleman Young, and others submitted proposals Nos. 1522 and 1523 to the Committee on the Executive Branch. No. 1522 provided for a civil rights commission with "enforcement powers to eliminate discrimination and segregation based on race, religion, color, national origin or ancestry in employment, housing, education, public accommodations and such other rights, privileges and immunities as are guaranteed under this Constitution." No. 1523 specified how the commission, which was to replace the FEPC, should be constituted and the procedures that it was to follow in exercising its authority.[34]

Not having heard from Pollock or Martin, Wheeler wrote Martin on December 26 to express his fear that the civil rights commission proposal would be "bypassed." When Wheeler then inquired of Pollock whether the Rights Committee would hold hearings on Proposals Nos. 1522 and

1523 so that Wheeler and others could testify, Pollock, who thought the commission proposal was not the responsibility of his committee and was, in any event, "a statutory matter," replied that convention hearings had already been completed. Pollock was indignant when Martin, who, Pollock thought, left "something to be desired as chairman," agreed to hold hearings on the proposals. Pollock later testily complained that even though he had "worked very hard to get through a real strong . . . civil rights section, . . . this Dr. Wheeler, . . . one of the more aggressive Negroes, kept telephoning me and sending me stuff" about establishing "this damn commission."[35]

Testifying on January 4, 1962, before the Committee on the Executive Branch on Proposals Nos. 1522 and 1523, Hatcher predicted that the establishment of a civil rights commission would be "a step in the right direction to once and for all eradicate discrimination in Michigan in all areas." Wheeler received his opportunity to testify on January 31. After asserting that blacks suffered from poor health, "substandard housing, poor economics, inadequate education and the frustrations and despairs generated by discrimination and segregation," he contended that if minority groups were to be accorded equality of opportunity, it was not only necessary to enact "adequate laws" but to provide "realistic machinery for their enforcement." He noted that twenty states had already created civil rights commissions, although none had been given constitutional status, and that Michigan had to go the constitutional route because of the Michigan legislature's failure to convert the FEPC into a civil rights commission with expanded jurisdiction. Following Wheeler's testimony, the Executive Branch Committee referred Proposals Nos. 1522, 1523, and 1569, which also called for a civil rights commission but did not spell out the areas over which it would have jurisdiction, to its subcommittee on executive reorganization, chaired by Alvin Bentley.[36]

Daisy Elliott essentially repeated Wheeler's arguments in seeking to persuade the Bentley subcommittee to report to the full committee in favor of a civil rights commission. The subcommittee agreed to support the following as an amendment to the Committee on the Executive Branch's Proposal No. 71: "Within 2 years after the adoption of this constitution, the legislature shall establish a civil rights commission within the executive branch to secure the protection of the civil rights guaranteed by this constitution. In the event the legislature does not so act, the governor shall by executive order establish such a commission." The amendment, drawn up by Bentley and Elliott, was an obvious compromise between the position of committee members who viewed the establishment of a civil rights commission as a legislative matter and those who were willing to give the commission automatic constitutional status.[37]

The full Committee on the Executive Branch unanimously accepted the subcommittee recommendation on March 5. Wheeler thought that the proposal was "the very minimum that could be written" in view of what could be expected from the legislature. Indeed, the legislature that very month rejected all the civil rights bills submitted to it, and Wheeler was now prepared to take the issue to the black electorate if black convention delegates, "to advance their own political ambitions," settled for what the Committee on the Executive Branch was proposing.[38]

On March 28 Martin brought the civil rights commission proposal before the convention assembled as Committee of the Whole. That initiated a prolonged and heated debate focusing on the questions of whether to leave the initiative for establishing the commission to the legislature, as proposed, or to make the decision self-executing, whether to spell out the civil rights areas over which the committee would have jurisdiction, what the composition of the commission should be, and how broad its administrative authority should be. Supporting the proposal, Martin reported that his committee had concluded that it was "not sufficient to make general statements in the matter of civil rights but that some action" was "needed to secure the protection of these rights other than the general statement that such rights exist." The members of the committee, he said, agreed that "under ordinary circumstances" the establishment of the commission was a statutory matter, but he reminded the delegates that the lawmakers had not considered the issue "in plenary session in any form." Also, he asserted, his committee was "impressed with the vital character of the rights involved" and the necessity of protecting them "if we are going to live in peace and harmony with our fellow men here in the state of Michigan and elsewhere."[39]

Proposal No. 71 drew strong support from both Hannah and Romney. In an "impassioned plea" that brought "a rare burst of applause from the delegates and the gallery," Hannah asserted that "the most important single problem" facing the nation was "the problem of decent treatment for minority groups," particularly for blacks. He saw "nothing but good" coming from the proposal not just in terms of its domestic impact but also in terms of the Cold War, whose outcome, he maintained, was "going to be determined to a large degree by how we treat minority groups at home."

"I speak," the Mormon Romney declared, "as a member of a minority group that knows the long time harmful effect of persecution and discrimination." He justified giving the commission constitutional status because "extraordinary circumstances require extraordinary action," and, he declared, "we have an extraordinary case of human injustice that we are dealing with." He wanted Michigan to be "a leader in eliminating racial discrimination."[40]

Proposal No. 71 was criticized on the convention floor from both the right and the left. Speaking for delegates opposed to a commission with any real power, Weldon Yeager complained that the proposal would create "an administrative monster" that would "take on the aspect of 'thought police'" and "could put any citizen in criminal jeopardy." Those who shared Yeager's concerns sought to strip the commission of the normal powers of administrative bodies and to limit its role essentially to that of "study and education." They could not, however, persuade a majority of the delegates to support their position.

Those who favored a strong commission were concerned that the rights the proposed commission was to protect were not spelled out in the Martin proposal, but they were even more concerned that the establishment of the commission was not to be self-executing. Partially to meet the latter concern, Norris and Melvin Nord, a Detroit attorney and law professor, offered an amendment providing for the creation of a commission whose members would be appointed by the governor "to secure the protection of the civil rights guaranteed by the law and by the constitution." The legislature was to prescribe the composition of the commission as well as its duties and powers.[41]

When debate on Proposal No. 71 was to resume on the morning of March 29, Martin asked for more time so that differences could be worked out between majority and minority members of his committee. Once deliberations resumed later in the day, Norris and Nord withdrew their amendment in favor of a much stronger amendment, in which they joined, offered by Richard Austin, Don Binkowski, Elliott, and Young, all of them Detroit Democrats. In addition to providing for the creation of a civil rights commission by the constitution itself, the Austin amendment stated, "It shall be the duty of the commission, in a manner which may be prescribed by law, to investigate violations of, and to secure the protection of the civil right[s] to employment, education, housing, public accommodations, and to such other civil rights as provided by law and the constitution." Austin explained that the sponsors had withheld their amendment until the convention had decided that it wanted to adopt "the concept of a civil rights commission," which it now seemed prepared to do. "We have gone part of the way," he said, "let's go all the way." Romney praised the Austin amendment, and Hannah urged its support. The proposal, Hannah stated, was an effort to recognize that persons who were not born white should have the same opportunity as other citizens to develop their potential through education and the jobs they held, the right to live in a decent home, and "the right to be recognized as an individual." Whether one was an African American, a Jew, or an Asian American, he said, "the damning characteristic of the civil rights problem in this country and in all others is the fact that we brand people as a group." The issue of group rights as compared to individual rights that Hannah posed was to divide the civil rights movement in the years to come.

Defending the designation of the civil rights areas over which the proposed commission would have jurisdiction, Nord noted that these were the "exact civil rights" mentioned as being covered in the report of the Pollock committee, but, it should be added, not in Proposal No. 26 itself. Martin, by this time, had changed his mind about leaving the establishment of the commission to the legislature, telling the delegates now that since the legislature had had the civil rights matter in its "lap" for so long, he did not "want it to continue to lie in the same lap for another 15 to 20 years while the problem gets worse and worse." He stated that his committee was not prepared to embrace the Austin amendment, but he nevertheless conceded that the amendment appeared to have been "drawn in a judicious . . . and . . . careful manner."[42]

After numerous amendments had been offered, the delegates, in a "strong display of bipartisanship," approved the Austin amendment by a 74–43 vote, moderate Republicans joining Democrats to constitute the majority and "the bloc of out-state Republicans" making up the minority. The debate, which had "raged" hour after hour, did not conclude until 11:20 P.M., and the parliamentary situation at the time of the vote was confused. There were "plenty of hot tempers" among Republicans, as well as rumblings about reversing the vote. Two weeks earlier, Republican moderates, led by Romney, and conservative farm-bloc Republicans, led by former state treasurer D. Hale Brake of Stanton, had reached a compromise on such crucial convention issues as legislative apportionment and taxation. Civil rights, which had not been a part of the compromise agreement, now endangered the accord, the farm bloc threatening "to bolt the compromise." The Republicans held a special caucus early in the morning of March 30, a Friday, and when the convention reassembled, Brake moved that the report of the Committee of the Whole on Proposal No. 71 be postponed until Tuesday, "because," he said, "we have some studying we wanted to do on it." Democrats objected "rather sharply," Robert Hodges calling the motion "the most shocking thing to date in this convention," but the delegates approved the Brake motion by a 82–46 vote.[43]

Following the vote on the Brake motion, the Republican caucus appointed a ten-person group to deal with the Austin amendment. At stake for the Republicans, as the *Detroit Free Press* saw it, were the votes of blacks and other minority-group members that, it was assumed, gubernatorial candidate Romney would not want to lose. The caucus, in the end, hammered out a compromise acceptable to both wings of the Republican Party that was brought to the floor of the convention on April 5 by Richard C. Van Dusen of Birmingham and six other Republicans, including Martin, Hannah, and Bentley.[44]

Like the Austin amendment, the Van Dusen proposal provided for a self-executing civil rights commission "to investigate alleged discrimination against any person because of race, religion, color or national origin in the enjoyment of the civil rights guaranteed by law and by this constitution and to secure the equal protection of such civil rights without discrimination." The proposal, however, omitted the "specific civil rights" enumerated in the Austin amendment, Van Dusen asserting that it would be "redundant" to include them in view of the report of the Pollock committee. It is likely, however, that it was the concern about private housing that led the caucus to drop the inclusion of the enumerated rights lest the specific mention of housing be interpreted as restricting the right of property owners to dispose of their property as they saw fit.

The Van Dusen proposal provided for an increase in the membership of the proposed civil rights commission from a bipartisan four, the number previously approved by the delegates, to a bipartisan eight serving staggered four-year terms. Hannah explained that with the membership limited to four, each party would want to appoint one black and "possibly" also a member of another minority group, but that a membership of eight made possible the "full representation of the minority groups and at the same time the maintenance of equal or majority membership by folks that are not generally discriminated against."

The Van Dusen proposal also sought to respond to the concerns of many Republicans about a commission with too much power. It provided that the exercise of the commission's authority had to be "in accordance with the constitution and of general laws governing administrative agencies"; it denied the commission subpoena power; and it specified that "nothing" in the section defining the commission's powers was to "be construed to diminish the right of any party to direct and immediate equitable relief in the courts" of the state.[45]

Democrats favoring the Austin amendment attacked the Republicans for abandoning bipartisanship in dealing with civil rights and, as Coleman Young put it, making "all basic decisions" by "deals" within the party. "Civil rights," he said, had "been thrown into the deal," and victims of discrimination in the convention most affected by civil rights provisions, like himself, had been "excluded from any consideration." The Austin amendment supporters sought to restore "the major fields of discrimination" omitted from the Van Dusen proposal. This was not necessary, Pollock stated, since no one intended to exclude the rights in question, and he thought that it would not be "good constitutional language" to insert the words. "It seems to me," he added, "that we have gone much farther than my committee had imagined. We thought that everyone would be so satisfied with the civil rights amendment that to carry it on to set up a commission and to put the commission in the constitution, and now to add this very specific language, seems to me to be going so far it isn't very good constitution making." Although Hannah and Romney voted with them, the Austin amendment supporters failed to command a majority on the issue.

Unable to add the language they desired to the Van Dusen proposal, supporters of the Austin amendment also failed to persuade the delegates to strengthen the powers of the proposed civil rights commission. On April 6 the Committee of the Whole approved the Van Dusen proposal by a 101–9 vote. Austin characterized the proposal as "a halting step in the right direction," but Daisy Elliott thought it "a giant step forward in the area of civil rights."[46]

When the Van Dusen proposal came back for a second reading on April 24, all efforts to amend it failed. On May 8, however, on the third reading, the delegates, reversing an earlier decision, approved by a voice vote an amendment providing that "appeals from the final orders of the commission, including cease and desist orders and refusals to issue complaints, shall be tried de novo before the circuit court . . . having jurisdiction provided by law." This meant that the reviewing court could simply disregard the record of fact on which the commission had made its decision. This completed the convention's deliberations on the civil rights commission issue, and the resultant Article V, Section 29, of the Michigan constitution distinguished Michigan as the only state in the nation with a civil rights commission in its constitution. In the form in which it was adopted, it was, as Hale Brake correctly observed, "not as much as many of the members wanted" but "more than many of them expected to get."[47]

In addition to including an equal rights and nondiscrimination section in the constitution's Declaration of Rights and establishing a civil rights commission in the executive branch, the delegates also added a civil rights section to the constitution's education article and strengthened the protection against discrimination of employees in the state government's classified service. "Every school district," the new constitution stated, "shall provide for the education of its pupils without discrimination as to religion, creed, race, color, or national origin." In presenting this language to the convention, Alvin Bentley, chairman of the convention's Education Committee, indicated that his committee was aware that some would say that the proposed addition to the constitution was unnecessary in view of U.S. Supreme Court decisions. His committee, however, Bentley told the delegates, believed that "this concept" was "so important to the preservation of our democracy" that the members wanted "to leave no doubt as to where Michigan stands on this question." The existing constitution protected personnel in the classified service from discrimination because of race, religion, or partisan considerations in demotions or removals. The new constitution extended the ban on discrimination to appointments and promotions as well.[48]

The convention also agreed to increase the term of the governor to four years beginning with the 1966 election and to consolidate the numerous state administrative agencies into not more than twenty departments. Candidates for governor and lieutenant governor, also, were henceforth to run as a team. The constitution no longer provided for the popular election of highway commissioner, auditor general, and superintendent of public instruction and removed the governor's authority to fill judicial vacancies. As we have already seen, there were also changes in the new constitution regarding fiscal matters and legislative apportionment.[49]

Convention delegates approved the new constitution in its final form on August 1, 1962, by a vote of 98–43. The majority was made up of ninety-three Republicans and five Democrats; forty Democrats and three Republicans were in the minority. The Democrats were joined in their opposition to the new constitution by the Michigan NAACP and the Michigan AFL-CIO. Quite apart from their opposition to the constitution's legislative apportionment system and its ban on a graduated income tax, the Democrats and their allies were not entirely happy with the civil rights provisions of the new constitution even though they were considerably stronger than the corresponding provisions of the old constitution.[50]

Voters narrowly approved the new constitution on April 1, 1963, by a 810,310 to 803,436 vote, and it went into effect on January 1, 1964. Whatever doubts staunch civil libertarians might have had regarding the document's shortcomings were largely dispelled when Attorney General Frank J. Kelley, a Democrat, issued a lengthy formal opinion on July 22, 1963, regarding the authority of the new Civil Rights Commission. The commission, Kelley ruled, had "plenary power in its sphere of authority to protect civil rights in the fields of employment, education, housing and public accommodations" and had "authority to enforce civil rights to purchase, mortgage, lease or rent private housing." The legislature, he maintained, was "without authority to abrogate or limit" the commission's power in the fields specified. Kelley also ruled that the provision of the constitution authorizing a joint legislative committee to suspend the rules of administrative agencies did not apply to agencies with constitutional status, such as the Civil Rights Commission. The expansive Kelley opinion was based on the attorney general's reading of the convention debates, court decisions, and the federal Civil Rights Act of 1866 as it applied to housing.[51]

The Kelley opinion was at variance with the views of such legal scholars as Professors Kauper and Roger Cramton of the University of Michigan Law School. Cudlip informed Dorothy Judd that he had not spoken to a single convention delegate who agreed with Kelley's opinion regarding the civil rights protected by the constitution. One can guess that Cudlip was referring particularly to private housing. "I would be less than honest," Hannah told Judd, "if I did not say that I was surprised by the sweeping authority conferred on . . . the Civil Rights Commission" by the Kelley opinion. Hannah, however, was not inclined to argue about the matter since he liked the outcome.[52]

Richard Van Dusen, who became the legal adviser to Michigan's new governor, George Romney, thought that Kelley had "stretched a good bit in several . . . areas" and that it was "a little difficult to find support for some of his broader claims." Romney, however, viewed the opinion as vindicating his own role in the convention and as refuting the charge by some Democrats that the new constitution was just "a piece of paper." "Michigan's new constitution," the governor publicly stated, "contains the most complete, the most direct and clearest expression of state policy guaranteeing human rights of any state constitution in the country, and the civil rights commission established . . . provides an unequaled opportunity for Michigan to blaze new trails for other states to follow."[53] Beginning on January 1, 1964, the Civil Rights Commission began to "blaze" those "trails".

10

THE YEAR OF
TRANSITION:
1963

In the 1962 Michigan gubernatorial election, Republican George Romney defeated incumbent Democrat John B. Swainson by 80,573 votes. Romney was reelected by a 382,913 vote plurality in 1964 despite the Democratic landslide in the presidential election, and he then won reelection in 1966 for a four-year term by a margin of 527,047 votes. In November 1967 Romney announced his candidacy for the 1968 Republican nomination for the presidency but then withdrew the candidacy early in 1968. He resigned the governorship in January 1969 to accept the secretaryship of the Department of Housing and Urban Development in the cabinet of President Richard Nixon.[1]

Born on July 8, 1907, in Mexico, to which his polygamous Mormon grandfather and grandmother had fled, Romney returned to the United States with his parents in 1912. After serving from 1926 to 1928 as a messenger for the Church of Jesus Christ of Latter-Day Saints, Romney in 1929, while a student at George Washington University in the nation's capital, joined the staff of Senator David I. Walsh of Massachusetts, a Democrat. Romney took a job with the Aluminum Company of America in 1929 and then came to Michigan in 1939 to serve as manager of the Detroit office of the Automobile Manufacturers Association. In 1948 he accepted a position with the Nash-Kelvinator Corporation and as its executive vice president in 1954 helped to arrange its merger with the Hudson Motor Car Company to form the American Motors Corporation. Later in that same year Romney became the new corporation's chief officer.

Romney served as chairman of the Citizens Advisory Committee on School Needs in Detroit in 1957 and 1958. In 1959 he helped to form and served as chairman of the nonpartisan Citizens for Michigan, which, as we have seen, helped to prepare the ground for the Michigan Constitutional Convention of 1961–62. He did not identify himself as a Republican until he sought election as a delegate to the convention, and in the 1962 gubernatorial campaign he was critical of both major parties.[2]

A moderate Republican, Romney could point to an excellent civil rights record when he became governor. As managing director of the Automotive Council for War Production in World War II, he had been critical of segregation in defense housing. In a 1950 appearance before the Detroit Common Council as a member of the Citizens Housing and Planning Council, he protested the segregation in Detroit's housing program. While serving as the head of American Motors, he was one of the few corporation executives in Michigan to support the enactment and implementation of the Fair Employment Practices Act. In 1959 the Anti-Defamation League of B'nai Brith awarded Romney its Americanism citation. He further enhanced his civil rights credentials in 1961–62 as a delegate to Michigan's constitutional convention.[3]

"A deeply religious" Mormon who was reportedly characterized by his associates as "a self-righteous, fiercely ambitious man with a bad temper and a messianic sense of destiny," Romney was a highly successful governor. He was able to fashion "a kind of bipartisan coalition of moderates" in the legislature that enabled him to reach most of his legislative goals. Many Republican lawmakers who had helped block the enactment of the Williams and Swainson legislative proposals agreed to similar proposals advanced by Romney. "He sounds like Williams," Democrats were saying by the end of Romney's first term. A booming state economy that developed soon after Romney took office contributed to his popularity and his legislative success.[4] At the same time, the growing influence of the civil rights movement in the nation as the result of the racial demonstrations in Birmingham, Alabama, beginning in April 1963, President Kennedy's effort to secure major civil rights legislation, the March on Washington on April 28, 1963, and the enactment of the Civil Rights Act of 1964 and the Voting Rights Act of 1965 facilitated Romney's efforts to gain support for civil rights action in Michigan.[5]

Since the state's new constitution did not take effect until January 1, 1964, the Fair Employment Practices Commission (FEPC) continued to function during Romney's first year as governor, and the civil rights provisions of the 1908 constitution, as amended, remained in effect. Romney had left no doubt where he stood on civil rights in his addresses in the 1962 gubernatorial campaign. In his first State of the State message

George Romney and Lyndon Baines Johnson.
Courtesy Bentley Historical Library.

on January 10, 1963, he declared that "Michigan's most urgent human rights problem" was "racial discrimination—in housing, public accommodations, education, administration of justice, and employment." He called for increased funding for the FEPC's education program and to enable it to add to its staff and to open new branch offices, legislation to prohibit discrimination by labor organizations and apprenticeship programs, and increased funding for the vocational training of the physically handicapped. He appointed Joseph Bell, Jr., to serve as vice chairman of the state Republican Party, the highest party position in either state party attained by an African American to that time. In March 1963 he appointed Leo Greene, a black Flint mortician, as the governor's special adviser on minority relations.[6]

At the outset of his governorship, Romney considered "the most crucial and pressing problem" regarding civil rights to be housing discrimination, which he appraised as "a massive problem" in Michigan. Addressing the Metropolitan Conference on Open Occupancy at the beginning of his term, he asserted that "a fair and open housing market" was "a public responsibility and a public goal" that one's sense of justice demanded. He defended Rule 9 but thought that the owner of private property was "free to be bigoted" and that open occupancy was primarily "a challenge to the conscience and hearts of men and women" rather than to the conscience of the state.[7]

When the Michigan Supreme Court on February 6, 1963, in *McKibbin v. Corporation and Securities Commission,* declared Rule 9 unconstitutional, Romney asked the state legislature to embody the principle of the rule in legislation and also to enact a measure embodying the chief features of Detroit's Fair Neighborhood Practice Ordinance. He also recommended legislation to prohibit brokers and real estate salesmen from "encouraging, suggesting or recommending discrimination" based on race, color, religion, or national ancestry, agreeing among themselves to discriminate, or inducing "panic selling based on prejudice." A weaker measure than Romney had recommended passed the Senate but died in the House State Affairs Committee, Republican Chairman Lloyd Gibbs declaring, "I didn't care anything about it and there didn't seem to be anyone else who wanted it either." Soon thereafter Attorney General Kelley issued his opinion that the new Civil Rights Commission had the authority to deal with discrimination regarding private housing. Romney apparently anticipated the Kelley ruling, stating at the beginning of July that since the new constitution prohibited discrimination in any form, no new state civil rights legislation was any longer required.[8]

In 1963 two city governments proved themselves readier than the state legislature to accept the principle of fair housing. Ann Arbor in September 1963 became the first community in the state and the sixteenth in the nation to adopt a fair housing ordinance, and Grand Rapids followed suit in December.[9] In Detroit the Common Council asked the city's Commission on Community Relations to draft an open housing ordinance. When the resulting proposal was introduced in the Common Council on July 1, 1963, the Greater Detroit Homeowners Council, which claimed to represent forty homeowners' organizations, responded by circulating petitions to prohibit any restriction by public authorities on the sale or rental of homes. In a few days, the Homeowners' Council gathered the number of signatures required to submit the proposed ordinance to a referendum should the Common Council fail to act on it.

Before the Common Council decided what to do about the proposed fair housing ordinance, Kelley ruled on October 3, 1963, that were Detroit to adopt either the fair housing ordinance or the Property Owners' Rights Ordinance, it would be superseded by the new state constitution, which, the attorney general asserted, gave the Civil Rights Commission (CRC) the sole authority to enforce civil rights in housing. Kelley, however, ruled that the enactment of a city ordinance whose primary purpose was not enforcement but "education, counseling, conciliation, [and] mediation" was within a local government's authority. Six days after the Kelley opinion and probably influenced by it, the Common Council rejected the fair housing ordinance by a 7–2 vote. Since, as Duane Lockard indicated, "the major focus of the [housing discrimination] problem" was "inevitably at the city level," the preemption doctrine that Kelley announced, in Lockard's view, had "little to be said" for it and "much to be said against it."[10]

In the several months before the new state constitution went into effect, Romney sought to enlist the leadership of the two political parties and of the state's various local governments in support of civil rights. At a time when the state's Republican Party appeared to be insensitive to civil rights as a result of the behavior of party leaders in the legislature, Romney was probably "seeking to disengage" the civil rights issue from a "partisan context" and to give the Republican Party "a New Image." Taking the position that civil rights was "a moral issue" that transcended "partisan political considerations," the governor met with the chairmen of the two parties at the beginning of July to draft a bipartisan civil rights program. He secured their agreement to support the creation of community human relations commissions where they did not already exist—only twelve communities actually had such councils at the time. This was reportedly the first time in Michigan's modern political history that the two parties had agreed "to forge a partnership on a vital issue."[11]

Following the July meeting, the two party chairmen each appointed a Human Relations Coordinator, John B. Martin for the Republicans and

Norman Crandall for the Democrats. Their responsibility was to do all they could to secure the "active support" of their respective parties in "achieving full recognition" of the civil rights guaranteed by the state constitution to all the state's inhabitants. To meet this obligation, the two coordinators urged their party members to support the CRC and to do what they could to see that it was provided with an adequate budget so that it could develop "an effective program in the areas of education, housing, employment, and public accommodations." They also encouraged party members to participate in the conferences of various groups that the governor had urged the CRC to arrange to implement the new constitution's civil rights provisions; work with community leaders to organize human relations commissions where they did not already exist; persuade employers and employer organizations to implement a policy of merit employment; encourage boards of education in the state to hire teachers without discrimination, assure equal opportunity for all students, and develop programs that emphasized "tolerance and sensitivity to the rights of all citizens"; aid in developing programs of adult education and vocational education to provide workers and students with needed skills; aid in community efforts to combat discrimination in housing and public accommodations; urge unions to make their apprenticeship programs available to minority-group members; and make Michigan a state where all of its citizens were free to travel without discrimination. To achieve these goals, Martin and Crandall advised the county chairmen of the two parties to appoint local human relations coordinators to develop plans to improve human relations in their respective jurisdictions.[12]

When Romney met with the chairmen of the two parties early in July, they agreed that the governor should arrange to meet with the mayors and council presidents of communities in the state with large black populations to stimulate civil rights action in their communities. On July 17, accordingly, the governor invited 125 local governments in the state and the FEPC to a conference on July 26 to formulate plans for local action to promote human rights.

"The Civil Rights movement sweeping over the nation today," Romney remarked in addressing what was called the Mayors' Conference on Civil Rights, "completely overshadows every other domestic issue, and the cause of human rights is finally receiving the top-PRIORITY attention it has deserved for a long time." He stressed that this was "not only a Negro movement" but "a thoroughly American movement." He distinguished between "two dimensions" of the civil rights struggle. One was the effort to eliminate discrimination in public policies relating to education, housing, employment, and public accommodations. This "dimension," he noted, had been effectively addressed in Michigan's new constitution. The second and, as Romney saw it, more difficult "dimension" of the issue was "the campaign to eliminate racial prejudice in the hearts and minds of individuals—the wellspring of discrimination." The promotion of civil rights, he asserted, consequently involved not just law enforcement but "the much more complex task of education and moral persuasion."

Every county in the state, Romney advised, had to take whatever civil rights action was required by local conditions. He noted in this connection that blacks seeking public accommodations in the state were "sometimes subjected to embarrassment and humiliation." He also called attention to suburban areas that prevented blacks from obtaining housing by restrictions of one sort or another. Once again, he urged local communities to deal with civil rights without regard to partisan political considerations. "We must have leadership at the local level," he asserted, "which has the courage to break the ugly circle [sic] of intolerance which threatens to make a mockery of our freedoms." He expressed his agreement, finally, with the Kelley interpretation of the powers of the CRC, promised that the commission would work closely with local communities, and warned that it would seek "uniform enforcement" if local officials did not themselves deal with housing discrimination. An aide to the governor thought that the conference had gone "over well in every respect" and had set the stage for "a continued balanced and non-partisan treatment of the whole area of civil rights."[13] Certainly the governor had left no doubt where he stood on the matter.

Romney's commitment to the civil rights cause and his efforts to prepare the ground for the implementation after January 1, 1964, of the civil rights provisions of the 1963 constitution were supplemented by Attorney General Kelley. In December 1962 Kelley created a Civil Rights and Civil Liberties Task Force in his office composed of the deputy attorney general, the assistant attorney general, and the solicitor general. The task force, apparently the first of its kind in the nation, was to analyze civil rights questions as they arose in the state, coordinate the activities of the attorney general's office in dealing with the matter, and recommend a proper course of action. It was also to serve as a liaison between the attorney general's office and federal, state, and local agencies and to exchange information with "interested private groups" as a possible basis for legislation.[14]

After President Kennedy in June 1963 called for action "at all levels [of government] to meet the massive civil rights crisis facing our nation," Kelley on June 13 took a series of actions in response. He invited black community leaders and other community leaders to meet with him to advise him on how law enforcement officers could aid in the promotion of civil rights. He announced that task force members would meet with prosecuting attorneys and other law enforcement officials in various parts of the state to urge "stricter and more prompt enforcement" of the state's public accommodations law, the so-called Diggs Act, and to instruct them how that was to be done. If local officials did not take the necessary action to enforce the law, he announced, the attorney general's office would do so itself.

Kelley announced that he would meet with the superintendent of public instruction and interested citizens to consider problems stemming from the de facto segregation of the public schools and that he would take legal action where there was *"real evidence of intentional segregation."* His office, he stated, would maintain contact with the U.S. Department of Justice to ensure that state action regarding civil rights was coordinated with federal action. Finally, he characterized the opinion he was about to issue regarding the civil rights provisions of the new constitution as "one of the most important ever issued because it spelled out a public policy which recognized a civil right to equal opportunity in education, housing and public accommodations."[15]

After initiating public hearings regarding the enforcement of the state's public accommodations law, Kelley informed Romney that public accommodations were "generally available" on a nondiscriminatory basis in major metropolitan areas in the state but that discrimination in some rural areas was "reported to be fairly widespread." Kelley also concluded that provisions of the law were not well understood by owners and managers of public facilities or by minority groups. Romney informed Senator Warren G. Magnuson of Washington, who had inquired about the matter, that the mere existence of the law was insufficient "to close the gap between the principle and practice of non-discrimination" and that local prosecutors had to enforce the law. He reported that he had taken steps to inform owners of public accommodations, local officials, and minority groups regarding the law and had instructed the attorney general to ensure that local enforcement was "thorough" and in accordance with the law's "spirit." Actually, Kelley's action in this regard appears to have been taken on his own initiative.[16]

As far as public education was concerned, Superintendent of Public Instruction Lynn Bartlett called in 1963 for "more accurate treatment of minority groups in school books." A Committee for Better Human Relations of the Michigan Curriculum Program developed a policy in that regard that was sent off to textbook publishers as a guide. In June, Bartlett and other state school superintendents who had "problems of racial imbalance" in their state school enrollments met with President Kennedy at his request to consider how to deal with that problem. The next month Bartlett and a group of educators, clergymen, and civil rights leaders took some exploratory steps to halt de facto school segregation.

They agreed that housing was the basic problem in this regard and took note of the assignment of black students to black schools, but they disagreed on the use of busing as a remedy. A state Senate study committee dealing with the implications of the new constitution for the state concluded in August that de facto school segregation should be dealt with by local school boards, not by the yet-to-be-functioning CRC. There the matter rested for the time being.[17]

Romney gave the FEPC his strong support during its final year. Employment discrimination, he asserted, had "no place in the State of Michigan. Our Judaic-Christian precepts, man's responsibility to his fellow man, and State policy," he declared, all prohibit employment discrimination, and the government had to take the lead in securing employment on the basis of merit alone. "I shall not be satisfied," he announced, "until all workers and job applicants are considered for employment on the basis of their skill without regard to race, religion, or nationality." He insisted that merit employment actually increased both efficiency and productivity.

In coordination with the FEPC, Romney on September 5, 1963, held a Governor's Conference on Equal Employment Opportunity in Michigan. His hope was to stimulate the conferees to "renewed concern, action and leadership in establishing merit employment throughout Michigan" and to do so on "a massive scale." Employers were asked at the conference to pledge themselves to undertake a program of "affirmative action" to achieve merit employment. The pledge involved their promulgating "a clear, definitive policy of non-discrimination" and distributing it to all their employees, particularly to supervisors and personnel officials; notifying all recruitment sources that the employer's company was an equal opportunity employer; reviewing and reevaluating all company personnel procedures; taking a personnel survey to determine the distribution of employees in all branches of the company and reporting the results to the FEPC; emphasizing merit employment in all supervisory training sessions; including the phrase "An equal opportunity employer" in all newspaper hiring advertisements; and seeking FEPC "technical and consultative assistance" in promoting merit employment.[18] It would soon fall to the CRC to ascertain the effect on employment of the Governor's Conference, but Romney had once again made his own position clear.

The bill to replace the FEPC with the CRC and to provide the CRC with the jurisdiction accorded it in the 1963 constitution was not enacted by the legislature and signed into law by the governor until December 1963. The House had sought to include a ban on sex discrimination in the measure, but the Senate rejected the idea. The bill made the rule-making authority of the commission subject to the state's administrative procedures law, which would have permitted the legislature to veto CRC rulings. Kelley, however, ruled that the legislature lacked authority to exercise this power since the CRC was a constitutionally created agency. Although not included in the language of the constitution, the measure approved by the legislature, in accordance with the decision of the constitutional convention, denied the CRC subpoena power and provided that appeals from its orders were to be decided de novo in the appropriate state court. Despite the limitations on the commission's authority, some lawmakers feared that the CRC would have too much power. "It looks to me," declared Republican Gail Handy of Eau Claire before the bill was approved, that "if you're a white man you're going to be in jeopardy from now on."[19]

In late August 1963 Romney informally appointed the eight members of the CRC, but they were not officially appointed until January 1964. The co-chairmen were John Feikens, a Detroit attorney and former federal judge, and Damon Keith, chairman of the Detroit Bar Association's civil rights committee, member of the Detroit Housing Commission, and former head of the Michigan NAACP. The other six members were Sidney M. Shevitz, president of the Jewish Community Council of Metropolitan Detroit and a former acting chairman of the FEPC; the Reverend A. A. Banks, Jr., pastor of the Second Baptist Church in Detroit and vice president of the Detroit Council of Churches; Richard E. Cross, the board chairman of American Motors; William T. Gossett, an attorney and a former Ford Motor Company vice president; the Reverend Theodore E. La Marre, pastor of St. Joseph's Catholic Church of Saginaw; and Kenneth W. Robinson, a UAW regional official. The Michigan NAACP praised the appointments.[20]

Romney met with Keith and "civil rights groups" in December 1963 preparatory to the CRC's assumption of its duties. Although the conferees recognized that laws and regulations could not in themselves "correct the injustices that constituted the racial problem," they thought it equally evident that without laws and regulations, progress to achieve civil rights would be slow. They consequently agreed that one of the first actions of the commission should be the issuance of "a direct, unequivocal policy statement" that would make it clear to the people of the state that the commission regarded its objective to be "the earliest possible total elimination of all unjust discrimination or segregation" based on race, religion, color, creed, national ancestry, and, interestingly enough, sex. They further agreed on the critical importance of the CRC's executive director in the fulfillment of the agency's responsibilities, and they did not want him to be "a *moralist* or *gradualist*."

Romney remarked to the group that many citizens had "voiced the opinion or the fear" that the commission would devote almost all of its

Damon Keith.
Courtesy Bentley Historical Library.

attention to Detroit and other large cities in the state. The governor did not disagree that the larger communities, given their racial composition, should receive more attention than the smaller cities, but he maintained that however small the black population of a city, it should receive "adequate Commission interest and assistance." "The civil rights of 3000 Negroes in Ann Arbor," he said, "are as vital as those of the half-million in Detroit." Noting that the human relations commissions in the smaller cities were "more conservative" than those in the larger cities, he suggested that the CRC, to combat this, appoint in each county a

John Feikens.
Courtesy Michigan State Archives.

citizens advisory committee made up of individuals active in the pursuit of interracial justice who could assist the commission in its work.

In contrast to the almost exclusive focus of the constitutional convention in dealing with civil rights on employment, education, housing, and public accommodations, Romney called the attention of the civil rights group to "other major problems of injustice" that he believed had been overlooked. He specified in this regard unequal law enforcement; poor legal representation by lawyers hired by blacks; discrimination in providing services by some state agencies; services to and the placement of orphans, mentally retarded, and other handicapped minority children; use by state agencies of in-state and out-of-state firms that discriminated; the possible unavailability of health care on a nondiscriminatory basis; and discriminatory practices in manpower retraining programs. He also suggested that the CRC might wish to ask the legislature to extend the coverage of the fair employment requirement to employers with less than eight employees.[21]

When the CRC replaced the FEPC on January 1, 1964, fourteen complaints were in some phase of the conciliation process, and forty-eight complaints were under investigation. The CRC absorbed the FEPC staff of seventeen and had been authorized by the legislature to increase the number to twenty-seven. Civil rights achieved departmental status in October 1965, but the role of the CRC remained unchanged.[22]

As the CRC began to function, Richard V. Marks, the secretary-director of the Detroit Commission on Community Relations, observed that the CRC had "an unparalleled opportunity to affect the human rights condition throughout the state of Michigan."[23] The years to come would determine the extent to which the CRC would take advantage of that opportunity.

11

THE CIVIL RIGHTS COMMISSION AND EMPLOYMENT DISCRIMINATION

The Civil Rights Commission (CRC) held its first meeting on January 3, 1964, at which time the commissioners formally elected John Feikens and Damon Keith as co-chairmen and Sidney Shevitz as secretary. Burton I. Gordin was selected as the commission's executive director the next month. A graduate of Temple University and the recipient of a master's degree in social work from Bryn Mawr, Gordin had been on the staff of the Philadelphia Fair Employment Practices Commission and was serving at the time of his Michigan appointment as executive director of the Philadelphia Commission on Human Relations.

While a private in the U.S. Army in World War II, Gordin had attended a propaganda class in which a captain said in one of his lectures that Hitler had probably been "right" in his treatment of the Jews. Gordin complained about this remark and received a public apology. "I've always felt outraged over the plight of people who can't defend themselves," Gordin said at a later time. "I hate to see a minority group abused, just as I hate to see a child abused."[1]

Arthur Johnson, executive director of the Detroit branch of the NAACP since 1950, was appointed the CRC's deputy director in May. In the next few months the CRC appointed directors of its various divisions—Compliance, Community Services, Education, Housing, Research, and Public Information. The Compliance Division was responsible for receiving and investigating complaints of discrimination, assuring compliance with the nondiscrimination clause in state contracts, and conducting inspections and surveys of industries and firms within the

Burton Gordin.
Courtesy Michigan State Archives.

commission's jurisdiction. The Community Services Division was to work with local governments and citizen groups to assist in the development of programs to deal with local civil rights problems. The Education Division was responsible for developing and conducting voluntary "affirmative action programs" by different groups to combat discrimination. The Housing Division was to encourage voluntary actions to end housing discrimination. The Research Division was to collect data and conduct research to assist the CRC in its program planning. The Public Information Division sought "to alert Michigan citizens to their rights and responsibilities" and to inform them of CRC activities.[2]

As he assumed his new duties, Gordin let it be known that he did not "subscribe to the narrow view that we just sit back and wait for complaints to come to us. Our job is to go into the community, work with community groups to identify problems and solve them." He characterized "breaking down bias barriers" as "only half" of the commission's job. "The other half," he declared, was "assuring that there are minority applicants who are ready, willing and able to walk through the doors of opportunity." He viewed employment and education as "the most important" civil rights issues at the time and regarded housing as "the next frontier of the civil rights movement."[3]

The CRC pledged itself to follow "fair but firm policies." The co-chairmen made it clear that the commission was dealing with "the rights of people as individuals" since, in their view, civil rights accrued to individuals, not to "a group." Asked if the CRC would resort to conciliation and education in processing complaints or would use the "big stick," Feikens responded that the commission would employ all three methods. "We mean business in ending discrimination," he said. Like the Fair Employment Practices Commission (FEPC), the CRC from the start decided to keep confidential the names of persons alleged to have engaged in discrimination unless a formal complaint had been issued against them following the failure of the conciliation process. Unlike the FEPC, however, the CRC believed that its constitutional status gave it the power to initiate complaints.[4]

It was the belief of the CRC from the start that "mere enforcement of Constitutional and legal prohibitions against discrimination" was insufficient to assure equal opportunity for all of Michigan's citizens and that "affirmative actions" by "all the institutions" of the state government and all the state's communities were required. The CRC pledged itself to give "leadership, encouragement and know how to these voluntary affirmative efforts." It believed that the "civil rights struggle" involved not only "protection against discrimination" but also the resolution of "basic social and economic problems in the fields of education, employment, housing, law enforcement and social services." Since the commission understood that it would never have the budget or staff to provide every community in the state with the programs it needed, it decided to encourage and cooperate with local human relations agencies and programs.[5]

The CRC in its first year established offices in Lansing, Detroit, Flint, and Grand Rapids, and it had established six additional offices by early 1968. The commission's budget increased from $174,135 in fiscal year 1963–64 to $1,391,576 in fiscal year 1967–68, and the staff by the latter fiscal year had grown from the 17 the CRC had inherited from the FEPC to 123, more than half of whom were nonwhite. About

231

one-half of the staff were engaged in the commission's law enforcement activities, the other half in its "affirmative action programs." The commission's rising caseload and the resulting backlog of cases as well as its "preventive, educational and community relations programs" stretched the commission's budget to the limit and caused it, beginning in 1967, to seek federal financial aid for one program or another.[6]

Once Gordin joined the commission, it adopted rules for the processing of complaints and the required posting of commission notices. The first CRC rule stated that the commission's jurisdiction was not limited to the processing of complaints and defined the areas within its jurisdiction. Other rules set forth the procedure for filing complaints and the steps that the CRC would take in investigating and resolving them. The CRC made one change in the procedure that the FEPC had followed in dealing with complaints by authorizing the appointment of referees to conduct hearings when a complainant appealed a commission dismissal order or was dissatisfied with the terms of a conciliation agreement.[7]

The CRC made its services available to the local human relations commissions, twenty-seven of which had been established by early 1966 but only six of which had a professional staff. Most of the local commissions were actually "ineffective," and, as Gordin saw it, often served as "a buffer against those who want[ed] to do something about local problems." Despite Attorney General Kelley's ruling that the CRC had "plenary authority" in the areas of its jurisdiction, the CRC assured the local commissions that although they lacked enforcement powers, the Kelley ruling did not mean that they lacked authority. It urged the local groups to investigate and conciliate complaints, engage in "programs of information, education and community relations," and undertake affirmative action programs. The CRC, for its part, stood ready to assist in these endeavors.[8]

In 1966 the CRC held workshop conferences with representatives of government, business, labor, social agencies, citizen groups, educators, and foundations to consider aspects of the civil rights problem. On April 26 and 27, 1966, the commission sponsored a conference on "The Unfinished Business of Civil Rights" that involved workshops on law enforcement, education, employment, and housing. Feikens and Keith explained that the conference was needed because racial inequality in Michigan not only "persisted" despite the efforts of the preceding twenty years but in some areas had actually "increased."[9]

During the Romney governorship, the fair employment practices requirement was finally extended to cover both age and sex. The Michigan Employment Security Commission (MESC), which had been influenced by the Lansing Older Worker Demonstration Project to reorganize its Older Worker Program, advised Governor Romney in the summer of

George Romney and senior citizens.
Courtesy Michigan State Archives.

1963 that it had concluded from its experience that legislation was necessary to "eliminate the age barrier" to employment. Twenty states and Puerto Rico had taken such action by that time. Romney did not immediately act on that advice, but he joined with Michigan Commission on Aging Chairman John B. Martin in appointing ten task forces on aging, one of which was a Task Force on Employment. When the latter task force reported the next year, only one of its twelve members called for legislation to ban age discrimination in employment. On Romney's recommendation, however, the legislature in July 1965 took that step by amending the Fair Employment Practices (FEP) Act to include discrimination because of their age of persons aged thirty-five to sixty unless this was a requirement in a federal or state employment training program or was a "bona fide occupational requirement."[10]

The new statute, the CRC explained, meant that employers could not discriminate against older workers covered by the law in hiring, tenure, or terms and conditions of employment; employment agencies could not discriminate because of age in classifying or referring workers; labor unions could not discriminate against or segregate older workers or qualify union membership so as to deprive older workers of employment or adversely affect their employment conditions; and state and local government contractors had to observe the law's terms. The statute did not prohibit retirement systems or policies that did not use age as a "subterfuge to evade the act." The CRC held conferences with many groups regarding the statute and sought the cooperation of the Michigan Classified Advertising Managers Association in advising clients against the use of discriminatory advertising, which the commission regarded as "a major point of control" in enforcing the act. The CRC had processed 102 age discrimination claims by the end of 1968.[11]

In a feeble and puzzling reaction to the age discrimination law, the Michigan Civil Service Commission (CSC) initially raised the age limit for a few classified positions to sixty, but it raised the limit to only fifty for a far larger number of positions that had had an even lower age limit. It excepted the State Police and hospital and conservation officials from even these age limitations. After being criticized for age discrimination by some Republican senators, the CSC announced in January 1966 that it would soon "fully comply with the spirit of the law."[12]

The MESC, which had eighteen older worker specialists by the time the age discrimination law was passed, made an even "greater effort" after that date to secure the placement of older workers, and it informed the CRC whenever it could not persuade an employer to conform to the age discrimination law. It also initiated a project in Jackson and Grand Rapids to acquaint older workers with techniques known to be helpful in finding jobs. The agency's State Supervisor of Services to Older Workers assigned older worker specialists who had been trained in the placement of such workers to twelve MESC branch offices.[13]

The MESC reported after a couple of years that the age discrimination law had "abruptly reversed" the decline in its placement of older workers by ending employer resistance to the placement of the qualified elderly. Although workers aged forty-five and over constituted 12 percent of MESC placements in 1965, the percentage rose to 23 in 1966, 27 in 1967, and 28 in 1968, and the absolute number placed increased from 35,823 in 1965 to 60,770 in 1968. How many of these workers were over sixty years of age the MESC did not say, although we can safely assume that they were the hardest among the older workers to place since they were not covered by the age discrimination law.[14]

In 1968 the federal government banned discrimination against workers aged forty to sixty-five by firms affecting interstate commerce that employed twenty-five or more employees. The statute, which set a higher age limit than the corresponding Michigan law, supplemented Michigan's efforts to combat age discrimination in employment.[15]

The Michigan legislature did not approve a ban on sex discrimination in employment until the end of 1966. In May 1964 the Social and Labor Committee of the Governor's Commission on the Status of Women approved by a 9–2 vote a motion supporting the principle of equal opportunities for women in hiring, promotion, and training in both public and private employment and calling for a committee of representatives of the appropriate state agencies to study how to implement the motion. Inexplicably, however, the committee reversed a decision the commission had taken in January 1963 and defeated by a tie vote a motion to recommend adding a ban on sex discrimination to the FEP Act.[16]

As the MESC indicated in its report for the fiscal year ending June 30, 1966, the nondiscriminatory employment of women remained a "major" problem in the state, particularly in the Detroit metropolitan area. Women found it difficult to secure jobs other than in the service occupations and in clerical positions, and there was "blatant" discrimination against them in manufacturing industries. Because of this state of affairs, the MESC added service to women job applicants to the responsibilities of the State Supervisor of Services to Older Workers.[17]

Following the precedent of the federal Civil Rights Act of 1964, the Michigan legislature added a ban on sex discrimination to the FEP Act that Romney signed into law on December 21, 1966. The state CSC responded by reducing the number of job classification restrictions applying to women from 300 to 135. By July 1968 women had increased their percentage of jobs in the classified state service from 41 to 46, and the number of women in the top seven job classifications had risen from twenty-nine to sixty-two.[18]

By September 30, 1969, the CRC had received 508 complaints from women alleging violation of the sex discrimination law. Two men had also filed sex discrimination claims, complaining that their employer permitted women but not men to wear Bermuda shorts to work. The respondent in this case promptly agreed to abandon the regulation. The CRC reported in 1969 that it had enjoyed "considerable success" in persuading employers to revise employment policies and practices that discriminated against women. The adjustment of sex discrimination complaints with respect to hiring, upgrading, and recalls to work also led to numerous retroactive wage payments. One such case involved a nationwide oil company that had refused to hire a woman as a gas station attendant, claiming that this was a job suitable only for males. The CRC investigation of the complaint led the company to change its policy throughout the nation and to offer the Michigan complainant a job and to reimburse her for lost wages.[19]

Despite the sex discrimination law, many employers were reluctant to abandon traditional views about gender and continued to define jobs as "male" or "female." Sometimes employers defended themselves against charges of sex discrimination by claiming that they were simply complying with protective labor laws. The CRC, however, refused to accept exceptions from the law based on what were alleged to be gender qualifications, such as the lifting of heavy weights. The "most obvious gap" in the effort of women to achieve employment opportunities equal to those of men was in "higher level" managerial and professional positions.[20]

From its inception to the end of 1968, the CRC processed 5,640 claims, the number rising steadily from 478 in the commission's first year to 2,041 in 1968. Among the claims, 86.7 percent involved allegations of discrimination because of race; 3.9 percent, national ancestry; 1.8 percent, religion; 1.8 percent, age; and 5.4 percent, sex. Approximately 66 percent of the claims involved allegations of employment discrimination; 13.3 percent, law enforcement; 9.5 percent, housing; 8.5 percent, public accommodations; and 1.95 percent, education. Just under 65 percent of the claims were filed in the Detroit tri-county area. Of the claims disposed of between 1964 and 1968, about 31 percent were adjusted, about 60 percent were dismissed because of insufficient evidence, 6 percent were withdrawn by the claimant, and 0.9 percent were dismissed for lack of jurisdiction. Among the claimants, 82.67 percent were black and 14.57 were white. In 1968, at least, 2.8 percent of the claimants were listed as Latin American (Hispanic).[21]

Among the numerous employment discrimination claims, about one-third involved allegations of improper discharge; 21 percent, discrimination in hiring; 11.5 percent, discrimination in upgrading; and 12.7 percent, discrimination regarding terms and conditions of employment.[22] Expressing the CRC view, Gordin asserted that "no problem of racial equality" was "more basic than employment." He noted in the spring of 1966 that whereas the median wage of white workers in Detroit in 1964 was $9,800, that of nonwhite workers was $5,400. Although the nonwhite unemployment rate was double that of whites, Gordin maintained that the underemployment of blacks was "an even bigger problem," the CRC concluding that about 50 percent of the nonwhite population was both "under-employed and under-trained." The commission also found that blacks were not hired to fill the junior positions that could have led to better jobs for them through promotion. The nonwhites, the CRC observed, were "an undeveloped resource" that was "operating at an estimated 60 percent of its economic and educational potential."

Blacks, estimating their chances of success, were more likely to file claims of employment discrimination against firms with a large number of blacks in their employ than against firms that excluded blacks. As for employers, a few firms by the end of 1965 were "actively seeking" to recruit qualified blacks, a majority were *passively* complying with the law, [and] some were deliberately disobeying it."[23]

The CRC finally resolved a troublesome employment discrimination complaint that had been filed in 1959 by two Taylor Township schoolteachers who claimed that they had been suspended because of their race. When the FEPC ordered their reinstatement, the respondent appealed to the relevant circuit court, which ruled that the school board was entitled to a trial de novo in the case. The FEPC appealed the decision to the state supreme court, which decided that the commission order was to be heard on the record only. In August 1966 the school board agreed to hire the two teachers and to pay them $17,500 in back pay, the largest monetary settlement in any case handled by the FEPC or the CRC to that time.[24]

The CRC recognized from the start that the individual complaint approach was an ineffective means to achieve "full and equal opportunity" to participate in the life of the state by all of its inhabitants. It consequently favored the use of its initiatory power in the "regulatory and educational field." It saw this power as "a preventive measure to anticipate problems, tensions and conflicts" and, it was hoped, as a means of dealing with racial problems before they led to "demonstrations in the streets." As it turned out, however, the CRC used its initiatory power sparingly, allegedly because of limited resources.[25]

Quite apart from its processing of complaints, the CRC worked with employers to assist them in adopting voluntary affirmative action programs and to achieve racial and religious equality of opportunity in their workforce. As part of an affirmative action program, the commission wanted employers to publicize their merit employment programs, make a head count of their employees, advertise job openings in minority communities, ensure that job selection standards were related to job requirements, eliminate subjective factors in oral examinations, assign workers on "a first qualified basis," follow an equal employment policy in promotions, make benefits available without discrimination, and encourage equal employment opportunities in negotiating contracts and in the use of public funds.

The CRC officially announced its affirmative action program late in December 1964 just after it had reached such an agreement with the Fred Sanders Company, a confectionary concern that employed two thousand workers in more than one hundred outlets in the state. The company, which had cooperated with the CRC in "an intensive personnel study," committed itself to make public a policy of equal employment covering recruitment, hiring, training, assignments, and employment benefits, to eliminate "any possible . . . restrictions of minority groups," and to place employees in the company stores without regard to their location.[26]

237

In May 1967 Sears Roebuck and Company agreed to adopt an affirmative action program for its Detroit Group stores. The company committed itself to review all of its minority-group employees and to determine if their potential exceeded the requirements for their existing positions; intensify its recruiting in the Detroit area; encourage supervisory employees to participate in programs in their area to improve racial understanding and to take an active part in local civic affairs; explain to all unit managers and staff personnel the need to recruit, hire, and train blacks; make certain that every eligible employee had the opportunity to sign up for the Sears Extension Institute training course; examine promotion policies to ensure that promotions were available to all employees on the basis of merit and without discrimination; meet with CRC personnel whenever the commission thought that necessary; and indicate that it was an "equal opportunity employer" in its help-wanted advertisements and place such advertisements in the *Michigan Chronicle*, an African American weekly.

In late June Sears Roebuck agreed to submit to the CRC every ninety days a statistical employment report for each of its Detroit Group stores. The report was to include a head count of employees in each store by job classification and race as well as a list of "significant personnel transactions" affecting minority-group employees. Also, beginning June 29, CRC personnel were to conduct a personnel survey of each Sears store in the Detroit metropolitan area, and the survey was to be reviewed by the commission and A. D. Swift, the Detroit Group stores manager.[27]

The visits of CRC field representatives to the Sears stores in the late summer of 1967 and their examination of the company's centralized credit system and its warehouse central service department revealed that about 11.5 percent of the eight thousand Sears employees in the area were black. Only 3.2 percent of the black employees, however, were classified as managers and officials, and only 2.3 percent of the male sales force was black. One-third of the company's black male workers were employed as porters and janitors. Black women made up 10.4 percent of the company's female sales force, but they were concentrated in inner-city stores and "the less lucrative sales departments," and many worked only part time.[28]

When CRC officials met with Swift to discuss the commission's findings, they commended him for the progress the company had made in nonwhite employment in inner-city stores. They emphasized, however, the company's failure to have improved nonwhite employment in its five suburban stores and in its credit system and warehouse operations. The CRC made recommendations to Swift as to how to deal with this problem that he largely accepted. By September 1968 Sears was clearly making progress in the implementation of its affirmative action program.

The percentage of its black employees had risen from 11.5 to 16.2 percent, there had been an increase of black employees in eight job classifications in the Sears suburban stores, and an African American had been appointed director of urban affairs on the staff of Group managers for the company's Detroit stores.[29]

The CRC was much less successful in dealing with the Big Three automobile manufacturers than in dealing with Sears Roebuck. In the commission's first three years, the 253 claims against the Big Three accounted for 20 percent of all the claims filed with the commission. Most of the claims were dismissed, since the companies sought to avoid findings of probable cause as well as public hearings involving claims in which they were the respondents. In the CRC's view, the auto companies were more concerned about avoiding legal problems than in creating employment opportunities for minority-group members.[30]

Toward the end of 1966 the CRC sought funding from the federal government's Equal Employment Opportunity Commission (EEOC) for a two-year affirmative action program for the state's automobile manufacturing industry in cooperation with the Big Three and the United Automobile Workers (UAW). The EEOC approved a grant of $20,000 for the program during its first year. An element of the program was to be a "clear communication" from the top management of each company to all of its personnel making hiring and upgrading decisions that the objective of the program was the substantial increase in the number of nonwhite employees in "all job classifications."[31]

The Big Three rejected the proposal that the EEOC had approved because of the inclusion of the UAW and because they preferred "a distinct company-oriented affirmative operation" to the "industry-wide cooperative approach" that had been proposed. The CRC consequently submitted a new proposal to the EEOC that called for a separate program for one year for each of the Big Three that was estimated to cost $100,000. The EEOC agreed in July 1967 to provide $20,000 for the program. The CRC hope was that of an anticipated increase of eighty thousand automobile industry jobs by 1970, fifteen to twenty thousand would go to blacks. For a second time, however, the needed support for the program from the Big Three was not forthcoming—a major defeat for the CRC in its voluntary affirmative action efforts.[32]

When it became apparent to the CRC that its voluntary affirmative action approach, as with the Big Three, had failed to produce the hoped-for results since there was no "legal backup" for its efforts, the commission secured funding from the EEOC to initiate complaints against twenty-two large companies whose workforces reflected a "possible pattern of racial and ethnic exclusion." General Motors, William Beaumont Hospital, Michigan Mutual Life Insurance Company, and the Whitehead-Kales Company, all of them among the twenty-two companies, contended that the FEP Act gave the CRC no such authority, whereas counsel for the CRC argued that the 1963 state constitution authorized the action. William Beaumont subsequently agreed to cooperate with the CRC, but only if the commission's complaint against the hospital was first withdrawn, which the CRC refused to do. As the Romney administration drew to a close at the end of 1968, the CRC was encountering increasing resistance from employers in its efforts to promote affirmative action programs and merit employment.[33]

The FEPC, as we have seen, had advised the incoming CRC to make racial equality in apprenticeship programs its top priority. In an elaborate study entitled "Equal Opportunity in Job Training and Placement for Minority Youth in Michigan," the first draft of which was completed on December 1, 1964, the Michigan State Advisory Committee to the U.S. Commission on Civil Rights characterized apprenticeship as the "last stronghold of tradition," a stronghold that black youth found it difficult to penetrate. Their representation in apprenticeship programs had not improved since the FEPC had first looked into the matter. Of 1,008 students in manufacturing and engineering in the Detroit Apprenticeship Training School as of June 1964, only 40 were nonwhite, and only 28 of the 1,581 students in the building trades were nonwhite. In the Grand Rapids area as of April 1, 1964, there were only 2 nonwhites among 700 apprentices in registered programs.

Beginning in January 1964, the Bureau of Apprenticeship Training (BAT) of the U.S. Department of Labor, which registered apprenticeship programs conducted by Joint Apprenticeship Committees made up of employer and union representatives, required that apprentices be selected for these programs without discrimination. The CRC's director of Education and Community Services thought that the best way to cope with discrimination regarding apprenticeships was to insist on the enforcement of the nondiscriminatory clause in state contracts, especially as applying to training facilities in the skilled crafts. Gordin saw the problem as of "tremendous importance" to the CRC, since, he explained, many of the employment problems of minority youth resulted from "historical patterns of exclusion and discrimination in training opportunity."

In an effort to improve communication between the administrators of apprenticeship programs and black youths who might apply for the programs, the MESC and the Detroit office of the BAT agreed in early 1964 to open an Apprenticeship Information Center in Detroit. Along with the Trade Union Leadership Council, the center tried to recruit blacks for apprenticeship training, but it had difficulty initially finding black youths with sufficient preparation for the training. By February 1968 there had been some increase in the number of minority apprentices in the manufacturing trades, especially among the Big Three automobile manufacturers, but very little in the building trades despite the efforts of the Information Center, the CRC, and the Detroit Board of Education. As Gordin reported, the center was operating not only with "limited staff" but also with "limited effectiveness."[34]

In addition to initiating and processing individual complaints and encouraging voluntary affirmative action by employers, the CRC sought to promote merit employment by implementing contract compliance procedures. The commission initiated its contract compliance program in July 1965 and made it part of a new State Code of Fair Practices. Contractors for goods or services in excess of $500 and employing at least three workers had to agree not to discriminate against their employees or applicants for employment because of race, religion, color, national origin, age, or, eventually, sex. The nondiscrimination commitment, which was also binding on subcontractors, applied to employment, upgrading, compensation, demotion or transfer, layoffs, termination, recruitment, advertising, and selection for training, including apprenticeships. The contracting companies, moreover, were encouraged to set "specific goals" for hiring blacks, and they had to file compliance reports with the CRC at times it specified. If the commission, after a hearing, found that a contractor had not complied with the agreed-upon contractual obligations, it could certify the finding to the State Administrative Board, which could order the contract's cancellation and could declare the contractor ineligible for future contracts with the state government and its political subdivisions.[35]

Most companies subject to the contract compliance procedures agreed to hire nonwhites at double the percentage of nonwhites resident in the communities from which the contractors normally hired workers. Some agreed to employ a specific number of nonwhites by a particular date, and dates were usually set for follow-up CRC reviews.

The CRC's deputy director, the head of its Compliance Division, and some of its field representatives concluded eventually that the contract compliance program would be more effective if pre-contract award procedures were adopted requiring the implementation of nondiscriminatory employment policies by an employer as a condition of receiving a state contract. If a prospective contractor was not already implementing such a program to "a sufficient degree," the CRC, it was proposed, was to devise a specific plan of affirmative action as a condition for awarding the contract. After the Administrative Board gave the pre-award program its required approval in April 1968, the CRC phased in the new program and by November 1968 was conducting pre-award reviews of all state contracts in excess of $50,000. The results in terms of nonwhite employment proved to be impressive, as we shall see.[36]

The CRC regarded the construction industry as "one of the toughest targets in the whole civil rights field." Not until it applied its pre-contract award procedures was it able to improve the status of nonwhites in the industry to any appreciable degree. At the end of 1965 Michigan became one of eleven states to receive federal government funds for a study of white and nonwhite participation in the building trades. The CRC contracted with Wayne State University for its Institute of Labor and Industrial Relations to conduct the study, which was completed in July 1966. On the basis primarily of an examination of the pattern of employment in the Lansing and Grand Rapids metropolitan areas, the study staff found that the number of blacks in the construction industry workforce approximated the proportion of blacks in the population of the two areas, but whereas 70 percent of all the workers in the industry were in managerial and skilled trades jobs or were foremen, about 70 percent of black workers were in semiskilled or unskilled jobs. About 27 percent of the black workers were in the trowel trades. In the five apprentice schools that trained young men for skilled trades jobs, blacks made up only 1.7 percent of the 12,466 students enrolled.

The Institute study confirmed that training opportunities in the construction industry were almost always awarded from within the industry itself and that most candidates for apprenticeships were referred by relatives, friends, or contractors. At the journeyman level, the industry also relied mainly on "informal or internal" methods of recruitment. For jobs for which union contracts stipulated union referral procedures, the union referrals received preferential treatment for journeyman positions. In some of the larger building trades unions, at least half of the workers qualified for journeyman status without any apprenticeship training but rather by "supervised on-the-job experience." Although blacks held about half of the semiskilled and unskilled construction jobs in the Detroit area, the study did not find that they were achieving journeyman status either by work experience or on-the-job training.

The construction study revealed that despite increased governmental and private efforts, there had been no significant increase in the degree of black participation in the industry. Not a single Detroit building trades union was seeking to increase the number of blacks for apprenticeship training or journeyman status, and most union officials whom the study staff contacted had not paid any attention to applicable federal and state laws regarding fair employment. The study concluded that construction industry officials did not view the limited participation of blacks in the industry as a problem, nor did they evidence any desire to initiate affirmative action programs to increase job applications or jobs for minority-group members. Because of the shortage of skilled labor in the Lansing and Grand Rapids areas, however, employers there did begin to work with the Urban League to recruit black workers.[37]

Once the construction study had been completed, the CRC began to put together a Committee on Affirmative Action consisting of representatives from contractor groups, building trades unions, the black community, the education profession, and government agencies. The committee's assignment was to prepare recommendations to the construction industry that would enable it to increase nonwhite employment in the skilled trades and to "change a pattern of exclusion" that the construction study indicated characterized the industry.

In meetings with the Committee on Affirmative Action, contractor groups, the unions, and the relevant government agencies agreed to work with the CRC to develop programs of affirmative action designed to increase the opportunity for minority-group workers to gain high-paying skilled jobs in the industry. The CRC also convened a meeting of contract review personnel of the federal and state governments and the city schools in the Detroit metropolitan area to improve cooperation among them, the first intergovernmental approach to contract compliance in Michigan. When the CRC in August and September 1967 conducted thirty-six reviews of state government contractors, it discovered that each of them was implementing an affirmative action program and had increased the participation of blacks in their workforces since 1965–66.[38]

The results of the efforts of the CRC and its Committee on Affirmative Action proved, on the whole, to be "disappointing," as were the various efforts to increase black apprenticeships. The MESC did place a few black applicants in skilled construction jobs, but there was no indication of employer upgrading of black workers or of efforts to contact black laborers' locals for possible job applicants. Blacks as of December 1968 comprised only 2.2 percent of the 32,900 journeymen and 4.7 percent of the 3,195 apprentices in sixteen of the most poorly integrated building trades unions in the Detroit area. In the trowel trades, by contrast, blacks constituted 26 percent of the 4,963 journeymen and 5.5 percent of 164 apprentices, and the Laborers Union local had a membership that was 70 percent black. In eight racially exclusive skilled trades in the Detroit Board of Education's skilled apprenticeship program, however, some progress had been made, the enrollment of blacks increasing from 0.9 percent of the total in October 1965 to 3.8 percent in December 1968. Other than in the trowel trades, less than 2.2 percent of the members of building trades unions were nonwhite. The outstate building trades unions were almost completely white or, at most, had a token number of black members.[39]

Since its affirmative action approach to the construction industry had produced only meager results, the CRC sought to deal with the matter by its pre-contract award procedures. Starting in November 1968, it began to require prospective state contractors in the construction industry to employ a representative number of minority-group apprentices and journeymen as a condition for securing a state contract. The CRC had finally hit upon a procedure that would yield results. By February 10, 1971, the number of nonwhites among the skilled building trades and road construction workers in the state had increased 90 percent since the pre-award contract program had been initiated.[40]

In 1966, in response to complaints by African Americans that hospitals in the state discriminated in the employment of black physicians and health professionals, the CRC conducted a series of field reviews of Detroit-area hospitals, some of the reviews being made in conjunction with the U.S. Office of Equal Health Opportunity. The CRC reported in February 1967 that it had found "little confirmed discrimination" in hospital employment, but at the same time it documented a shortage of blacks at the higher skill levels in these hospitals and the continued exclusion of blacks from some hospital departments. A "very few hospitals" employed only a token number of blacks, which led the CRC to work out agreements with them to undertake "specific affirmative steps" designed to increase black hiring.

The CRC thought that "the most significant finding" of its hospital reviews was the extent of improvement in black hospital employment in the preceding few years. Fifteen Detroit-area hospitals that in 1965–66 had 87 blacks with medical staff appointments had increased that number to 121 by early 1967. Blacks, however, were conspicuously absent from hospital boards of trustees, whose influence extended to all phases of a hospital's operation, and quite a few hospitals did not have a single black intern or resident on their staff. Many of these hospitals, however, had begun to take "positive steps" to recruit blacks for these positions.[41]

As part of its health care investigation, the CRC in early 1967 conducted a statewide survey of nonwhite enrollment in nursing, X-ray technology, and medical technology training programs. It found that in the five hospital-run registered nursing schools in Detroit and in the School of Nursing associated with three religious hospitals, only 26 (2.1 percent) of 1,213 students were black. There were actually many black applicants for admission to the various nursing schools, but nearly all were screened out because of inadequate preparation. The CRC, consequently, began to work with the Michigan League of Nursing to develop programs initiated by the league to meet this problem. Blacks were better represented in hospital-run schools of medical technology and X-ray technology than in the nursing schools. Fourteen (11 percent) of the 113 medical technology students and 19 (21.5 percent) of the 88 X-ray students were black.[42]

One area in which nonwhites made appreciable gains in employment while Romney was governor was in the state civil service. Toward the end of 1963, as already noted, the CSC began to conduct a racial count of all state government employees, and in May 1964 it made the first of a series of reports on nonwhite employment in the state civil service. As of March 1964, the initial report indicated, 8.6 percent (2,711 persons) of the 31,505 in the classified civil service were nonwhite, which was below the 9.4 percent of the state's nonwhite population as of 1960. Almost 60 percent of the nonwhite civil servants were employed in Wayne County, where they made up 33.7 percent of the total number of state civil service employees. Nonwhites were found in only 306 of the 2,000 classified positions in the state civil service, and their classifications were generally below those of white employees. The CRC attributed this racial disparity to the fact that nonwhite civil servants averaged two and one-half years of education less than their white counterparts. The median salary of nonwhites was $4,714, as compared to $5,513 for whites. Whereas 39.1 percent of the whites had been promoted to their position, this was true of only 29.1 percent of the black employees.[43]

Meeting with the CSC in May 1965, the CRC, concerned about the racial disparity in state civil service employment, stressed the need for the CSC to review its hiring procedures. A follow-up CSC racial study released the next month revealed that nonwhite employment in the classified service had increased to 9.5 percent of the total, a 15.2 percent increase since the 1964 study. Nonwhites had also experienced a "slight upward mobility" in the service since the previous report and had also narrowed the black-white salary differential ever so slightly. Franklin De Wald, the state personnel director, pointed to these gains in responding to criticism by some legislators that the CSC was guilty of employment discrimination.[44]

In an effort to assure blacks that the state government was a model employer, the CSC in late 1965 issued a new Code of Fair Practices for state employees that Romney approved. In January 1966 the CSC temporarily suspended its rules regarding citizenship and residence requirements for civil service employment so as to facilitate nonwhite recruitment. In an effort to determine if "a greater recruiting effort" would positively affect nonwhite employment in the civil service, the CSC advertised in the black press, and CSC officials made recruitment visits to black organizations and high schools in the state with a large black enrollment. The chief of the CSC's Recruiting Service visited four black colleges in Tennessee and established liaison with them for the future.[45]

In February 1966 the CSC and the CRC agreed to undertake a joint Affirmative Action Research Program. The program involved the racial designation of all civil service employees from the application process to the hiring process; a study of "availability patterns" of whites and nonwhites and the effect on appointments of the "rule of three"; an analysis of promotional patterns, job specifications, and civil service examinations; an expansion of recruitment efforts among minority groups; and a study of employment patterns in the civil service. There was to be a report sheet on race for each civil service applicant that was to be kept separate from the job application form. Authorities were to contact each of the three applicants who scored highest on the examination for a particular position, and if the individual who scored highest on the examination did not receive the appointment, the agency involved had to explain why.[46]

The CSC created a special Employment Service in May 1967 to deal with problems relating to recruitment and placement of the "disadvantaged," such as nonwhites, the mentally retarded, and refugees, and to coordinate the CSC Equal Employment Opportunity Program. In August the CSC authorized state government departments to hire and train individuals among the hard-core unemployed. The commission also reviewed entry-level jobs so as to eliminate "artificial barriers" to employment, and it expanded its recruitment efforts.[47]

The new CSC procedures had a positive effect on nonwhite employment. By early 1969 nonwhite civil service employees comprised 11.9 percent of the state government total as compared to the 8.6 percent in March 1964. They served in 22 percent of the classified positions as compared to 15 percent in 1964, and they had increased their median classification level from 03 to 04 during the same time. Although the total number of state employees had increased about 36 percent since 1967, the number of nonwhites had increased by 94.5 percent. Somewhat more than 80 percent of the nonwhite civil service employees, however, were concentrated in four departments—mental health, labor, social services, and civil rights—and 75 percent of the nonwhites as compared to 56 percent of the whites were in the six lowest pay grades.[48]

The process of integration appears to have proceeded more slowly at the local government than the state government level. Rita A. Scott, the CRC's director of education, asserted early in 1967 that she had visited many local government facilities during her three years as a CRC official and had been disappointed at the lack of "a visible" minority-group presence in their workforces. "Government," she declared, "has a special responsibility to set an example for the entire community." When the CRC's Contract Compliance Division surveyed the Wayne County government in 1968 to assist it in achieving merit employment, it found that there had been little progress in reaching that goal. Of the thirty-seven departments it surveyed, some were making no progress, some were actually losing ground, and some were making "only token efforts" to provide equal employment opportunities. The CRC recommended specific steps that the county government could take to improve the racial status quo. It also offered assistance to "a limited degree" to other local governments in the development of programs to rectify or eliminate practices that appeared to lessen employment opportunities for minority-group members.[49]

As the Romney administration came to a close, the CRC was rather discouraged about the degree of progress that had been made since 1964 in achieving employment opportunities in the state free of discrimination. Possessed of greater authority than the FEPC, the CRC, to be sure, had been responsible for gains in employment by minority-group members in several areas of the economy. The state Department of Civil Rights nevertheless informed Governor William Milliken in May 1969 that efforts since the enactment of the FEP Act in 1955 had failed to produce equal employment opportunities in the state. Blacks, Hispanics, and other minority groups, it noted, continued to be heavily overrepresented among the underemployed and the unemployed and continued to have difficulty securing skilled jobs, and there had been scant improvement with regard to age and sex discrimination. The commission also reported that many unions had done precious little to assist employers who had undertaken equal opportunity programs and that some unions had "engaged in subtle practices and nonfeasance" resulting in discrimination against nonwhites.[50]

To achieve better results in the future, the CRC proposed an increase in its investigatory staff to speed up the processing of complaints; increased use of its initiatory power to deal with the discriminatory practices of large employers and unions; increased assistance to state and local governments to increase the employment of minority-group members and women; expansion of the contract compliance program to include all contracts let or administered by the state government and its civil and political subdivisions; securing regular reports from employers who had entered into agreements with the commission and initiating reviews of their employment practices where necessary; encouraging contractor associations not to sign agreements with unions or other referral sources unless they had a representative number of minority-group members in their ranks or had a program to achieve that result; and bringing employers committed to the hiring of minority-group members and the underemployed and unemployed into contact with one another.[51]

What the CRC was suggesting on the basis of five years of experience was essentially to combat employment discrimination by more of the same. It had failed to achieve better results in lessening employment discrimination not because of lack of commitment or effort but because of the immense difficulty of the problem that it confronted. Employment discrimination, moreover, was only one of the types of discrimination with which the CRC had to deal. It also had to address itself to discrimination in education, public accommodations, housing, and law enforcement.

12

THE CIVIL RIGHTS COMMISSION AND DISCRIMINATION IN EDUCATION, PUBLIC ACCOMMODATIONS, AND HOUSING

EDUCATION

As already noted, the Michigan constitution of 1963, supplementary state laws, and federal and state court decisions required every school district in Michigan to "provide for the education of its pupils without discrimination as to religion, creed, race, color or national origin." The Civil Rights Commission (CRC) established by the same constitution was committed to the elimination of racial discrimination in public education in Michigan. It made some headway in pursuing this objective between 1964 and 1968 but much less than it would have liked.

When the CRC assumed its duties, there was an awareness in Michigan that, despite legislation and court decisions, a great deal of de facto school segregation existed with respect to both pupils and their teachers. This was to some extent, as we have seen, the product of housing patterns, the manner in which the boundary lines of school attendance areas had been drawn, and the manner in which white and black teachers were assigned to the schools where they taught. Minority-group schoolchildren were likely to attend schools inferior to the schools white children attended both in their physical facilities and in the quality of their teaching. There was also a "high correlation" between the degree of segregation of a school and the level of educational achievement of the students in that school. Because of the autonomy of local school districts, it was difficult for the CRC to deal with segregation and racial discrimination in the state's school system.[1]

249

A school racial census conducted by the state Department of Education early in 1967 revealed that the "predominant pattern" of enrollment in the state was for white students to be enrolled in predominantly white schools and blacks in predominantly black schools. Of the 1.83 million pupils at that time, 84.8 percent (1.5 million) were white, 13.7 percent (250,109) were black, 0.2 percent (2,968) were Native Americans, and 0.1 percent (2,581) were Asian American. About 90 percent of the teachers were white, and about 8 percent were black; among the school principals, 97.3 percent were white. Just about 60 percent of the white pupils attended schools without a single black pupil, and less than half of the schools had any black pupils. There also continued to be "a striking relationship" between the race of pupils and the race of their teachers. Also, the larger the proportion of black pupils in a school, the lower was the teachers' appraisal of the academic ability of their pupils.[2]

A CRC study in the fall of 1966 indicated that among those in the state aged eighteen to twenty, 9 percent of the whites but only 4 percent of the blacks were enrolled in institutions of higher education. The black dropout rate was double that of white students, partly because black students were more likely to have to support themselves while in college. Black college students tended to prepare themselves for careers in such fields as teaching and social work rather than in higher-paying fields like science or engineering. The CRC stressed the need for academic help for blacks to assist them in overcoming problems stemming from the kind of elementary and secondary education they had received. The commission also called for the allocation of funds for scholarships for minority students, and it urged college and university representatives to meet to consider how they could relate equality of opportunity to admission procedures, minority-group participation in all curricular areas, development of curricular programs on intergroup relations and civil rights, and minority-group faculty recruitment and retention.[3]

Education complaints to the CRC between 1964 and 1968 constituted only about 2 percent of the claims the commission processed, less than the claims in any other civil rights area within the commission's jurisdiction. About 68 percent of the claims involved public schools, about 11.7 percent, private schools. Racial discrimination was the basis for nearly all the education claims.[4]

The CRC, with "little publicity," assisted individual school boards in operating the schools within their jurisdiction in a nondiscriminatory manner. In the 1965 school year, commission staff aided Wayne County school officials in implementing the federally funded Wayne County Desegregation Project that was designed to "improve understanding of racial integration problems" by a program of racial education for school administrators, boards of education, and selected classroom teachers in the forty-three school districts in the county. At the time, only fifteen of these school districts had black pupils, and only ten had black teachers. The staff also helped the Detroit public schools to initiate a contract compliance program requiring school contractors to observe the state constitution's equal employment guarantee.[5]

In September 1966 the CRC gave the Lansing School Board commission approval to bus 177 high school students in an effort to achieve "greater racial balance" in the city's public high schools. When an organization calling itself the People's Action Committee on Education secured an injunction to block the implementation of the busing plan, the CRC secured permission to intervene as a friend of the court to challenge the restraining order. The state Court of Appeals eventually authorized the Lansing board to proceed with the busing, ruling that a school board in the state could consider race in this way in seeking to desegregate schools.[6]

In April 1966 the CRC and the State Board of Education adopted a joint policy statement in which they agreed to use their powers to secure "the complete elimination of existing racial segregation and discrimination in Michigan's public schools." Recognizing the relationship between "racial imbalance" in the schools and segregated residential patterns, they urged school districts to be "creative" in seeking to reduce or eliminate school segregation. They thus advised school boards to consider racial balance in selecting sites for new schools, the expansion of school facilities, the transfer of pupils from overcrowded schools, and the reorganization of school attendance areas. They stressed the importance of "democratic personnel policies" and called for "affirmative efforts" to integrate school staffs and to attract minority-group personnel. They advised school districts to select instructional material that encouraged respect for "diversity" and reflected minority-group contributions to American history and American culture. These suggestions would be followed in many school districts in Michigan and around the nation in the years to come.

The State Board of Education assigned staff to work with the CRC and local school districts to implement the joint statement and to achieve integration. The CRC, for its part, reiterated its readiness to assist local school boards in "defining problems and moving affirmatively to achieve quality integrated education of ethnic and racial groups" in the state. The superintendent of public instruction later asked the school systems to report on steps they had taken to implement the statement and to indicate what actions had been particularly effective.[7]

The state legislature quickly acted to implement one of the policy statement's recommendations by enacting a measure in June 1966 requiring school textbooks to recognize "the achievements and accomplishments of the ethnic and racial groups" in the state. The measure required the superintendent of public instruction to make an annual random check of school textbooks and to report on the progress made in attaining the statute's objective. The Michigan law was reportedly the first of its kind in the nation.[8]

In fiscal year 1966–67 the CRC staff initiated actions in school districts in nine cities to encourage pupil desegregation. The commission also responded to the requests of schools, organizations, and individuals in school districts in thirteen cities to deal with problems of integration, curricular development, and intergroup tension. When a CRC survey of teacher education programs in the state revealed that they paid scant attention to cultural diversity and intergroup relations, the commission recommended changes in the programs to deal with such matters. It also assisted school boards and administrators, teacher organizations, the Michigan Federation of Teachers, and the Michigan Education Association in developing in-service training programs, designing relevant survey research projects, and analyzing segregation problems.[9]

No city in the state devoted more attention to the issue of race in its public schools than Detroit, more than half of whose public school students were black by 1960. The March 1962 report of the city's Citizens Advisory Committee on Equal Educational Opportunities had revealed the substantial extent to which the city's school system was affected by racial discrimination. The school board was prodded to act to combat discrimination not only by this report but also by a federal lawsuit initiated in 1962 by black parents against one of the city's elementary schools, the demands of both mainstream and militant black organizations, and the quiet pressure exerted through the city's Commission on Community Relations by Mayor Jerome Cavanagh, who took office on January 1, 1963.

From 1963 to 1968 the Detroit school system moved in the direction of greater integration of pupils, faculty, and supervisory staff and also sought to adjust instructional materials to the changing racial composition of the city's schools. Partly because of the rapidly increasing number of black students and the decreasing number of white students, however, integration at the student level proceeded at a very slow pace. To be sure, the number of city schools without any black pupils decreased from seventy-three in 1961 to twenty-two in October 1966, but the number of all-black schools increased from eight to fourteen at the same time. According to the calculations of a committee of the National Education Association, 67 percent of the Detroit schools were segregated in 1961 and 65 percent in 1965, hardly a significant change.[10]

In 1964 the Detroit school administration redrew district lines in an effort to further school integration, but without conspicuous success. Detroit had been busing schoolchildren for many years, but in 1966 the school board decided to use busing only for purposes of school integration. In the same year the school board decided to permit students to transfer from one school to another as part of the board's "open schools policy" only if the transfer contributed to school integration.[11]

Following the Advisory Committee's report, the school board and school administration began to shift teaching personnel to achieve more racially balanced faculties. In a further effort to increase faculty integration, the school board decided to assign new teachers to the first teacher vacancy rather than permitting them any longer to choose from a list of three schools. In 1965 the board decided to follow faculty assignment procedures that would result in students' being exposed to teachers and administrators of different races, and service in an integrated school became a criterion for faculty promotion. The number of black teachers in the school system increased from 21.6 percent of the total in February 1961 to 31.7 percent in February 1966, a figure that corresponded closely with the percentage of blacks in the city's population. Whereas forty-one schools had been without a single black teacher in October 1963, there was only one such school in October 1966. Black teachers, however, continued to be assigned to schools that were predominantly black. In the 1965–66 school year, for example, two-thirds of the black elementary school teachers were teaching in schools that were 90–100 percent black.[12]

The Detroit school system was particularly concerned about the special needs of culturally deprived students, and it led the nation in seeing to it that minorities, particularly blacks, were fairly and accurately portrayed in textbooks and visual materials used in the schools. It thus joined thirteen other cities at the end of the 1950s in creating the Great Cities School Improvement Project to provide what was characterized as the "total education of . . . culturally deprived children." The program received Ford Foundation funding in 1960 and federal funding beginning in 1964, which extended the program to twenty-six schools and 24,000 schoolchildren. A roughly similar program, the Great Cities Extended School Project, also received federal funding, and it was made available to 15,000 to 20,000 additional Detroit students and their parents in fifty-one schools in culturally deprived neighborhoods. The Shared Experiences Project that the school system devised in 1965 enabled 23,000 children attending schools of different racial composition in the 1966–67 school year to join together in a variety of extracurricular activities.

In 1962 the Detroit school system began work on what came to be known as the Detroit City Schools Reader Series, the first primers in the nation depicting white and black youngsters and their families engaged in common activities. The school board informed publishers in 1963 that the school system would not purchase textbooks that did not provide fair treatment of minorities and their contributions to the nation. The school system also established a committee to preview visual aids to be used in the city schools to ensure that they depicted blacks in a nondiscriminatory manner, and in May 1967 the school board decided to provide publishers of schoolbooks with illustrations reflecting the pluralistic nature of American society.[13]

The limited effect of Detroit's school reforms was highlighted by a high school boycott in 1966 and a report on the city's high schools two years later. The dissatisfaction of many black students with the quality of their education was demonstrated when the students of Northern High, more than 98 percent of whom were black and most of whom did not appear to be making much academic progress, initiated a boycott of their classes on April 8, 1966, the day before the Easter break, and did not return until April 18. The poor quality of education at Northern High, moreover, was by no means unique, as demonstrated by the final report in June 1968 of the High School Study Commission, which included the chairmen of twenty-two high school study groups. Although some schools were excepted from the criticism, the report drew a devastating picture of the city's high schools in almost every respect. Bad as the schools were in general, the black schools were even worse, and black schoolchildren were more dissatisfied with their schools than white students were with theirs.[14] It would not prove easy in the years ahead for school authorities and others to cope with the problems presented by inner-city schools.

PUBLIC ACCOMMODATIONS

The CRC enjoyed more success in the area of public accommodations than in the field of education. The most numerous complaints addressed to the commission regarding public accommodations were for the withholding of service or providing "unequal service" by restaurants, bars, and other retail trade establishments. The commission satisfactorily adjusted more than half of the public accommodation complaints, well above the average rate of adjustment for other civil rights issues.[15]

In a meeting with tourist industry representatives on June 2, 1964, the CRC informed those present that it would strictly enforce the public accommodations law and would use its legal powers if necessary to do so. It warned the industry against advertising of any kind that specified or even intimated discrimination by using such words as "restricted" or "selected" clientele. It indicated, furthermore, that it would make "spot check" visits to enforce the law. In the next few weeks a team of twelve specially recruited and trained CRC representatives, seven of whom were black, visited about thirty-three hundred hotels, motels, eating and drinking establishments, and recreational facilities in seventy-seven of the state's eighty-three counties. Fifty-seven of the facilities required a second visit because the owners refused to display the required poster containing an abstract of the state's public accommodations law or wished first to discuss the posting with an attorney. In the end, only one establishment refused to obey the commission, which pronounced the visits "a resounding success."[16]

Some members of the state legislature's Senate Business Committee complained the next year that the CRC had sent biracial teams to lodgings and resorts the previous year to test compliance with the law by seeking to register as guests. "You are creating racial unrest, not harmony," one senator charged. The CRC responded that race was not a consideration for those whom it employed and that no testing had been involved in the visits. Romney defended the commission, saying that its efforts were designed to end discrimination and "human injustice" and that under Michigan law, racially mixed couples were not to "be treated any differently than anyone else." Damon Keith accused the senators who had criticized the CRC visits as using "McCarthy-like tactics" and as appealing to "Michigan's racists and bigots."[17]

In the summer of 1965 a biracial team of six CRC representatives toured Michigan resort areas around the Great Lakes shoreline to ascertain if the required posters were being displayed, answer questions, and make sure that public accommodations were free of discrimination. Their purpose, the CRC insisted, was not "to test compliance" but rather "to educate and persuade." The CRC also held meetings in 1965 and later with the Michigan Tourist Council and tourist industry representatives in an effort to encourage self-policing by the industry. One result of these efforts was a decline in the number of all-black resorts.[18]

The CRC also sought to ensure that barbers in the state conformed to the public accommodations law. It conferred with the State Board of Barber Examiners with this in view and mailed public accommodation posters to all the barbershops in the state. Although the American Bowling Congress had given up its policy of racial exclusion in 1950, the Pontiac Community Bowling League, made up of eighteen black bowling teams, complained to the CRC in 1965 that its teams were not permitted to bowl at favorable times in the city because of their race. The CRC thereupon ordered Pontiac's Orchard Lane bowling alley to make "prime or favorable bowling time" available to the black teams on an equal basis with white teams, and the facility complied.[19]

Following other public accommodation complaints, the CRC gained blacks admission to the sectional tournament of a contract bridge association and to a golf club in Novi, persuaded a skating rink not to charge blacks more than whites for the rental of skates, and secured blacks admission to a health clinic that had discouraged black applicants by one tactic or another. After a Detroit finance company, in accordance with its regular policy, refused a loan to a black male married to a white woman, the CRC persuaded the firm to extend loans to "all credit worthy consumers" without regard to race, religion, and national ancestry. The commission also secured the agreement of two Detroit cemeteries not to discriminate by race in arranging for burials, which led to complaints by two white burial plot owners.[20]

The CRC even dealt with the segregation of prisoners in the state, reaching a tentative agreement in February 1967 with Oakland County to end racial segregation in the county jail. A survey of state correctional institutions that the CRC conducted in conjunction with the Michigan Department of Corrections resulted in improvement in job assignments for black personnel and the addition of black employees in the jails.[21]

The absurd lengths to which racial discrimination was sometimes carried in Michigan was illustrated by the so-called "White French Poodle Affair." When a black woman sought to purchase a white poodle at an animal protection agency in March 1965, an agency employee refused to make the sale, claiming that the dog "did not like Negroes." During the conciliation process, the salesman admitted the charge, and the agency agreed to follow a policy of nondiscrimination in the sale of animals in the future. Since the white poodle had become ill by then and had been put to sleep, it was agreed that the claimant would be free to purchase the next "white" dog.[22]

The CRC sought to ensure that health care would be available to the state's inhabitants on a nondiscriminatory basis. It thus arranged for the Michigan insurance commissioner to issue an order in the summer of 1966 requiring Michigan Hospital Service (Blue Cross) to include a nondiscrimination clause in its contracts with participating hospitals. Governor Romney then issued an executive order entrusting the CRC with the enforcement of the order.[23]

The CRC also dealt with civil rights issues regarding referral to nursing homes in Wayne County and bulletin boards in Dearborn that were at least tangentially related to the public accommodations area. As part of its "multi-faceted program to assure equal opportunity and services in the health care area," the CRC instituted a study of patient referrals to Wayne County nursing homes. The data the commission compiled indicated that the four principal referral sources contributed directly to "the extreme racial imbalance" of patients in many of the county homes. The four had referred 64 percent of white patients to predominantly white homes (less than 10 percent black patients), 35 percent to integrated homes (not more than 90 percent of one race), and less than 1 percent to predominantly black homes (less than 10 percent white patients). Twenty-nine percent of black patients, by contrast, had been referred to predominantly black homes, 71 percent to integrated homes, and none to predominantly white homes. The study led the CRC to meet with officials of the referral agencies to seek the elimination of race as a factor in making patient referrals.[24]

The first cease-and-desist order issued by the CRC, in January 1965, involved the city government of Dearborn. In December 1964 the Dearborn Community Council complained to the CRC that items "defamatory to the Negro race" were being posted on public bulletin boards in city buildings. When conciliation failed, the commission held a public hearing on the complaint. This led to a CRC order forbidding the municipal government from posting material on city bulletin boards that tended "to degrade or humiliate or defame or hold up to public ridicule the Negro race." The irrepressible mayor of Dearborn, Orville L. Hubbard, attacked the Dearborn Community Council as "a collection of oddballs if there ever was one," denounced the hearing as "a kangaroo court," and criticized John Feikens, who along with Damon Keith presided over the hearing, as a "loud and mealy- mouthed type of guy" who was "nasty" and "mean" and "a sort of shriveled up thing anyway." When the Dearborn city administration ignored the CRC order, contending that the commission lacked jurisdiction over the city, the CRC filed a petition in Wayne County Circuit Court to secure enforcement of the order. The commission withdrew its petition after Hubbard agreed to a legal stipulation requiring the city government to abide by the CRC order.[25]

HOUSING

Since Attorney General Frank Kelley, as we have seen, had ruled that the CRC had "plenary power" to protect civil rights in housing, including private housing, the Romney administration apparently saw no need to press for fair housing legislation once the commission began to operate on January 1, 1964. In line with the Kelley ruling, the CRC let it be known that it would accept, investigate, and seek to resolve all complaints regarding housing that were brought to its attention, including complaints not only against real estate brokers but against private property owners as well. It anticipated legal challenges to its assertion of jurisdiction over private housing, regarding that matter indeed as the "most pressing" question concerning its jurisdiction.[26]

The pervasiveness of housing discrimination in Michigan was all too apparent to the CRC. "I do not know of one white community or white section of a city," declared the CRC's director of Community Services in 1965, "where a Negro citizen visiting a realtor chosen at random or

257

a home advertised for sale will get the fair and equitable treatment that is theoretically required by the law and this Commission." The CRC official characterized housing as "the most apparent and frustrating problem in Michigan for the Negro middle class and for the working class attempting to get out of the ghetto." The first black who moved into a white neighborhood, he observed, had "to undergo a vigorous ordeal" that sometimes involved violence.

At the beginning of 1965 the CRC declared that housing would be its "prime target" that year, and it announced "a stepped-up campaign" against discrimination in the sale and rental of housing at the beginning of the next year. "Regardless of what else is done," the CRC's executive director declared in April 1966, "if the basic patterns of housing segregation and discrimination are not broken, we are destined to live generation after generation in a divided society with all of its threats to freedom and the social order."[27]

In September 1965 the CRC signed an agreement with the six different federal housing agencies that pledged the signers to "mutual assistance and cooperation" in the housing field. The agreement provided for cooperation in the investigation of complaints in areas of shared jurisdiction, the exchange of information regarding housing activities and programs, and for builders and lenders who participated in federal housing insurance programs to comply with the civil rights provisions of the Michigan constitution. At the time the agreement was concluded, the CRC was not all that happy with the vigor with which federal housing agencies were dealing with housing discrimination, but the commission was to turn to the federal government for help on several occasions in the next few years, notably in Jackson and Detroit.[28]

The CRC, as we have seen, believed that affirmative action was required to assure progress in protecting the civil rights of the state's inhabitants. Insofar as housing was concerned, this meant that the commission would seek to persuade members of the housing industry to agree voluntarily to follow a policy of open occupancy. Beginning with the Detroit Real Estate Board in October 1964, CRC commissioners or staff members met with local boards of realtors, brokers, and developers as well as with the Michigan Real Estate Association to encourage housing industry members to assume leadership in the drive for open housing. The CRC made it clear at these meetings that its jurisdiction extended to "all housing."[29]

When the CRC met with the Michigan Real Estate Association on March 16, 1965, the association declared that it believed that property owners should be free to dispose of their property as they wished without government involvement and that real estate brokers should similarly be free to carry out the instructions of their clients even if they wanted the brokers to discriminate. At the same time, the association asked the commission to provide the housing industry with "guidelines" so that brokers would know whether they were complying with the law. Not yet prepared to take that step, the CRC responded that it would continue to proceed by the case-by-case method it had been following from the start. Although there was "little concord" at the meeting, the commissioners chose to believe that "a great change had taken place in the thinking of . . . members" of the industry during the preceding two years and that the realtors agreed that "they had a responsibility and a role to play in removing the ancient housing barriers facing minority groups."[30]

Although it continued to insist that brokers were bound by the wishes of the property owners who engaged them, the Michigan Real Estate Association nevertheless repeatedly claimed that it supported the principle of fair housing. Despite those protestations, however, Michigan real estate dealers contributed twice as much as the realtors of any other state to the successful lobbying effort to defeat the inclusion of a fair housing provision in a federal civil rights bill in 1966. To the dismay of the CRC, the Real Estate Association advised Congress that blacks should be given " 'equivalent' housing so that they . . . [would] learn to live in new surroundings," thereby becoming "vastly more acceptable to the white majority in the years that lie ahead." In a letter that they did not send, the CRC co-chairmen informed the association that its statement to Congress was "morally indefensible" and an "insult" to every black in the nation.[31]

The CRC in March 1966 changed its mind about issuing guidelines to the housing industry. It now advised real estate boards and associations to agree among themselves to operate on a nondiscriminatory basis, incorporate the "State Legal Guarantees in Housing" in their Code of Ethics, display an "Equal Opportunity in Housing" sign in their places of business, instruct their personnel on "how to deal impartially with the public," conduct a program of education and information about nondiscriminatory housing, especially for new members, and employ "qualified minority group personnel" in their organizations. Local real estate boards were specifically advised to grant membership to brokers who normally served the minority community, a rarity at the time. Apartment owners and managers were advised to advertise that their units were open to all on a nondiscriminatory basis and to maintain the same level of rents, service, and personnel after integration as before integration.[32]

Governor Romney sought to abet the efforts of the CRC by appealing to the housing industry to act voluntarily "to bring about 'a completely free and open housing market.' " Speaking to the Michigan real estate convention in September 1965, he told his audience "not to downgrade their profession by 'saying you are puppets in an impersonal transaction where vital human interests are at stake.' "[33]

To "expose the anatomy of segregation and discrimination in housing," to inform the public and itself about the matter, and to "mobilize support" for the commission effort to create an open housing market, the CRC agreed in August 1965 to hold a series of public hearings on the subject in different communities in the state. The CRC hoped that the hearings would aid in the development of "a unified code of conduct throughout the state pertaining to housing rights."[34]

The commission held housing hearings in Saginaw in June 1966, in Jackson in September 1966, in Flint in November 1966, and in Muskegon in April 1967, and more general hearings on the state of race relations, including housing, in Pontiac in June 1968. The hearings, the commission concluded, demonstrated that "a discriminatory housing market, coupled with sub-standard housing in negro sections, effectively prevented negro families from upgrading their living conditions." Saginaw, the CRC found, was "a severely segregated city"; Jackson exhibited "a clearly segregated pattern of housing typical of northern industrial cities"; Flint was 94 percent segregated; and Pontiac was "clearly segregated with non-whites confined to a slowly expanding ghetto in the southern part of the city." The problem of segregation was intensified, the commission reported, by urban renewal projects and highway construction, which displaced nonwhites in particular, forcing them to relocate in a constricted housing market that denied them freedom of choice. This was partly because there was a shortage of housing open to blacks that they could afford to rent or buy. The CRC did not hold housing hearings in Detroit, but the effect of urban renewal projects and highway construction on housing segregation was painfully apparent in that city also, lending support to the assertion that "slum removal equals Negro removal."

The "housing patterns" in the communities it studied, as the CRC indicated in its report on Jackson, seemed to be "controlled by members of the real estate profession." Realtors claimed that they were simply following the discriminatory instructions of their clients, but the commission noted that they also refused on their own initiative to show property to blacks in white neighborhoods and declined to service open occupancy listings. Minorities also appeared to be the victims of poor code enforcement. Partly because of the discrimination they suffered, nonwhites, the commission found, occupied a "disproportionate amount" of housing "unfit for human habitation."

The CRC's recommendations to the various communities in which it conducted hearings were roughly similar. The communities were urged to enact "comprehensive" fair housing ordinances; staff housing information centers to aid minority groups in securing housing without discrimination; create citizen advisory committees on housing to advise their respective cities regarding equal housing opportunities, relocation, and the supply of housing; increase the supply of "standard low cost housing" by one means or another; and seek ways to help families with low incomes and poor credit ratings to secure funding for housing.[35]

The Federal Housing Administration (FHA), at the CRC's request, conducted a survey of housing in the Jackson metropolitan area, presumably to reveal the need for low-income housing. The FHA informed the CRC that it was doing what it could to persuade private developers to erect low-income housing but that they claimed there was insufficient demand to justify the effort. Housing and Urban Development (HUD) officials demanded that Jackson promise to adopt a new housing code as a condition of receiving future federal loans and grants, and the agency threatened to withhold housing funds from the city unless it made its code enforcement procedures "more effective."[36]

Despite the realtors' general obduracy regarding open housing, the CRC's hearings, as the commission's executive director indicated, increased public awareness of the problem of housing segregation and "stimulated developments" that provided some "affirmative steps toward open housing." Muskegon adopted a fair housing ordinance in the same month that the CRC hearing was held in the city, and the same was true of Jackson. Denounced by the Jackson Board of Realtors and white citizen groups, the Jackson ordinance was submitted to a referendum of the voters on April 11, 1967, and was defeated by a vote of better than two to one. Jackson took some steps to adopt other CRC housing recommendations, but the results were minimal. The CRC, indeed, was so displeased with the behavior of Jackson's real estate brokers that it requested federal and state agencies to adopt "get tough" policies with the brokers.[37]

What appeared to stand in the way of local action regarding housing discrimination in Michigan was the Kelley preemption ruling of September 1963. The Ann Arbor housing ordinance of September 1963 went into effect on January 1, 1964, the city's attorney having persuaded the city council that Ann Arbor was not bound by the Kelley opinion. In May 1964, however, a city judge ruled the ordinance unconstitutional, in part because, in the judge's opinion, it improperly invaded the state's jurisdiction. On appeal, a state circuit court on June 18, 1965, upheld the ordinance's constitutionality insofar as any challenge to state authority was concerned, although the court found the procedures for handling complaints under the measure to be unconstitutional. Ann Arbor thereupon amended the ordinance at the end of 1965, replacing the invalid procedures.[38]

The circuit court's upholding of the Ann Arbor ordinance led Michigan's attorney general and his staff to review the preemption doctrine as it applied to housing. At the same time, several local units of government asked the state legislature to overrule the doctrine. A bill to do so was introduced in the House, but it did not pass. On August 21, 1967, however, the attorney general ruled that the state constitution did "not inhibit municipalities from enacting fair housing ordinances or imposing criminal penalties for violations thereof" even though such ordinances could not provide for civil enforcement, for which, he held, the CRC had sole authority. The CRC, indeed, had taken it upon itself in December 1966 to notify cities that they could adopt fair housing ordinances providing for criminal sanctions. By the time of the Detroit riot of July 1967, eight Michigan cities had adopted fair housing ordinances.[39]

The color line was also broken in the Grosse Pointes, which, as we have seen, had brought housing discrimination in Michigan to both national and international attention. Prodded by the Grosse Pointe Human Relations Council, which had been formed in 1964, the Grosse Pointe Real Estate Brokers Association agreed early in 1966 that its members would not refuse to show homes to blacks, and it accepted the fact that blacks would be living in the Pointes, but it would not sign a statement to that effect. On July 19, 1966, the first black family moved into Grosse Pointe Woods, the CRC having cooperated with the Grosse Pointe Human Relations Council to prepare the community for the move. The family initially "met hostility as well as welcome," but resistance soon subsided and "friendliness prevailed." The Grosse Pointe Committee for Open Housing, formed in April 1966 and composed of representatives from each of the five Grosse Pointes, let it be known that it would assist minority-group members to obtain housing in the Pointes.[40]

Detroit was not among the cities that adopted fair housing ordinances before the Detroit riot of July 1967. The city, indeed, seemed for a time to be moving in the opposite direction. In September 1964 the voters approved an ordinance prepared by the Detroit Homeowners Council that its opponents characterized as the "Ghetto Ordinance." The Michigan Supreme Court had ruled that the ordinance must go on the ballot after the Wayne County Circuit Court, in response to a legal challenge by the NAACP, had held the proposed ordinance unconstitutional, stating that its "real purpose" was "to advance the cause of racial bigotry in the field of housing." In the end, the ordinance did not go into effect since the Wayne County Circuit Court ruled it unconstitutional in a second lawsuit.[41]

In July 1966 the Detroit Common Council approved an "equal service annex" to the 1962 Fair Neighborhood Practice Ordinance that made it a misdemeanor for a real estate broker to refuse to show a property listed for sale, rental, or lease or to refuse to forward an offer to the owner of a listed property because of the race, color, or national origin of the prospective buyer. In fourteen months of enforcing the annex, the city's Commission on Community Relations was unable in dealing with housing complaints to make it possible for a single black to purchase a home of his choice.[42]

The Greater Detroit Committee for Fair Housing Practices continued its efforts to bring open housing to the Detroit metropolitan area. In early 1965, with the cooperation of the Detroit Urban League, it launched Operation Open Door. The program was designed to encourage blacks to seek housing in white neighborhoods, convince whites in the city who were planning to flee to the suburbs that there was "no place to run or hide," and persuade real estate brokers that open occupancy was "coming." The operation involved two teams, a shoppers team and an escort team. The former was composed of minority-group members seeking to rent or buy in a white neighborhood; the latter was made up of white volunteers who accompanied the shoppers and acted as though they were interested in renting or buying property. Initially, it seems, the idea was for blacks described as "lookers" to be followed by white "lookers" so as to ascertain whether the property owner who was approached provided the same information to both whites and blacks. The Greater Detroit Committee, as a matter of fact, had in 1962 approved a Congress of Racial Equality plan to have black and white couples visit the sellers of white-owned homes to ascertain their availability for open occupancy. As in Detroit, escort services were provided for black housing shoppers in two of the city's white suburbs. It does not, however, appear that Operation Open Door attained any significant success, particularly in the Detroit suburbs.[43]

Its concern for the availability of housing on a nondiscriminatory basis led the CRC to deal with the relocation of those displaced by urban renewal projects and highway construction, public housing, the use of public funds for housing, and the protection against violence of blacks who moved into white neighborhoods. The CRC's objective with regard to the displacement of families and individuals by urban renewal and highway construction was to ensure that blacks received equal treatment with whites in the appraisal of their property that was to be destroyed and that the housing available to the displaced did not "perpetuate or extend" discrimination and segregation. The commission viewed the relocation process, actually, as "a unique opportunity to alter . . . restrictive housing patterns."

On October 24, 1966, the CRC provided local officials with a set of relocation policies and guidelines that it wished them to follow. It recommended that the communities involved develop a "relocation plan" for their projects that specified the housing needs of those who were to be displaced and what housing would be available in the community to meet those needs. The commission advised that projects should be "timed" so that suitable housing was available at the time the displacement occurred. The relocation agency in the community was to inform those being displaced of their right to obtain housing without discrimination as regards their race, color, religion, or national origin. To ensure that minority-group members being displaced received fair treatment, the CRC advised that arrangements be made for them to participate in "the programming and execution of relocation projects." CRC regional officials sought to have the cities concerned apply the guidelines, and commission members and staff met with local officials to discuss such relocation matters as the availability of suitable housing for displaced minority-group members.[44]

The Lansing NAACP branch complained in October 1965 that the state Highway Department was appraising white homes at a higher figure than comparable black homes that were to be demolished in an integrated neighborhood to make way for Highway I-496. The CRC responded by securing Highway Department approval for the commission to appoint "qualified appraisers" to check the charges against the department, and the department agreed to delay demolition while the study was under way. The appraisers in the end did not find any evidence of "direct discrimination" by the Highway Department, but even though the blacks involved received fair compensation for their property, they still found it difficult to secure suitable new housing because of the shortage of housing available in general and to them in particular.[45]

Toward the end of 1966 the Michigan legislature enacted a measure providing that residential dwellings were not to be demolished to make way for highway construction until the residents displaced by the action were provided with suitable housing elsewhere. The statute required the Highway Department to cooperate with local government officials in preparing a plan for relocation that had to be submitted to the State Administrative Board for approval. Following a meeting with the CRC in late April 1968, the Highway Department agreed to involve "citizen advisory councils" in the development and execution of highway relocation plans before they were submitted to the State Administrative Board.

The state legislature sought to ease the relocation problem by a 1966 law establishing a State Housing Development Authority whose "main thrust" was to provide low-cost housing for families displaced by highway construction and urban renewal projects. The legislature did not initially provide the authority with the "tools" needed to do the job, but the lawmakers largely remedied the problem by legislation enacted in 1968 and in the early years of the governorship of William Milliken, who succeeded Romney. In November 1969 the Housing Development Authority announced that it was aiming in the next twelve months to finance and subsidize the construction of twenty-five hundred units of housing for low- and moderate-income families at a cost of $50 million.[46]

The CRC intervened when it believed that public housing construction plans of one city or another appeared likely to "perpetuate or extend" segregation. Working with HUD, the CRC in 1965 persuaded Ypsilanti to abandon two public housing sites that the commission believed would increase segregation in the city. The commission had less success initially in dealing with Flint regarding a public housing site to which the CRC objected but that the federal government had approved. In the end, however, HUD followed the commission's recommendation regarding the matter. In January 1967 the CRC sent local government officials a set of public housing guidelines and policies that it had devised in consultation with the U.S. Public Housing Assistance Administration as well as a list of suggested measures to implement the guidelines. The commission recommended that local governments and public housing authorities select public housing sites that would contribute to the desegregation of homes and schools. It noted that "the concept of 'scattered sites' " and the "imaginative" use of federal housing programs, such as rent supplements, could help to achieve that purpose. It advised that communities assign applicants for public housing so as to achieve integration in each project and that the applicants consequently "should not be asked their preference for assignment as between different housing projects."[47]

The chief public housing issue with which the CRC dealt after it issued its public housing guidelines concerned the city of Detroit. When the director of the Detroit Housing Commission asked the CRC early in 1966 to review proposed sites in Detroit for one thousand public housing units, the CRC's Housing Division concluded that the units were to be located in predominantly black areas and would further housing segregation in the city. The Housing Commission, in response, proposed sites outside predominantly black sections of the city, but the Common Council rejected some of the sites and failed to act on some of the others. The CRC turned to HUD Secretary Robert Weaver in June 1968 to review the site selection in Detroit to determine if public funds were being used to contribute to segregation. In 1969, finally, the Housing Assistance Administration granted Detroit approval for one hundred homes in scattered sites, as the CRC desired. Whether public housing, publicly assisted housing, or urban renewal was involved, the CRC consistently maintained that public funds should not be used to "further or perpetuate racial discrimination and segregation in housing."[48]

Working with state and local officials, the CRC sought to protect blacks who moved into white neighborhoods against violence. When an interracial couple moved into Warren in June 1967, "a violent mob" of more than one hundred persons shouted threats at the couple, threw smoke bombs into their house, and broke some windows. The CRC responded by asking the governor to instruct the State Police to deal with such situations in the future whenever local police were "unable or unwilling" to do so. Letting it be known that it would seek "appropriate action" if the civil rights of the individuals involved were not protected, the commission discussed the matter with officials in the U.S. attorney's office and decided to contact local prosecuting attorneys regarding the prosecution of those committing acts of violence or property damage in such instances and to seek peace bonds from those making such threats. It sought the advice of the state's attorney general regarding the possibility of securing a court order against those threatening damage or violence. Following a meeting between the CRC and local officials and community leaders, the city of Warren appointed a special committee to coordinate efforts to reduce tensions in the subdivision where the violence had occurred.[49]

A good deal of the CRC's time regarding housing was taken up with the investigation and disposition of the complaints of individuals that their civil rights in this area had been violated. By the end of 1968 the CRC had received 535 housing complaints, which constituted about 9.5 percent of all the complaints it had received. The number rose from 60 in 1964 to 131 in 1967. Slightly less than three-fourths of the complaints involved the withholding of accommodations for allegedly discriminatory reasons. Of the other complaints, 13.3 percent involved discrimination in housing terms or conditions, 1.8 percent involved "unlawful inquiry," and about 10 percent concerned such matters as withholding loans or aiding and abetting discrimination. About 63 percent of the complaints related to discrimination in renting, and 34 percent involved the purchase of a home. Racial discrimination was the basis for about 90 percent of the housing complaints, as compared to 6 percent for national origin and about 3 percent for religion.

Housing complainants had the highest occupational status among the complainants in the various areas of the CRC's jurisdiction. Among the housing complainants, 47.6 percent were employed in white-collar jobs and 15.6 percent in blue-collar jobs. The housing complainants, about one-half of whom had attended college and one-third of whom were college graduates, had the highest level of education among those who brought complaints to the CRC. Reflecting the existence of housing discrimination and segregation throughout the state, housing was the only civil rights area in the CRC's jurisdiction in which there was an almost equal distribution of complaints in the Detroit metropolitan area and in outstate Michigan.

Of the housing complaints to the end of 1967, 42.1 percent were dismissed for lack of sufficient evidence, 8.1 percent were withdrawn by the complainant, and 48.4 percent were satisfactorily adjusted. The remedies in the satisfactorily adjusted complaints involved such matters as the sale or rental of the dwelling to the complainant if it was still available at the time of the adjustment, the sale or rental of a similar accommodation if available, or the sale or rental of the next vacancy in a similar accommodation.[50]

The first CRC-ordered public hearing resulting from a civil rights complaint involved housing, and three of the first six civil rights complaints that had led to court appeals as of April 1966 also were concerned with housing. The initial CRC order involving a public hearing, an action one of the CRC co-chairs characterized as a "monumental thing," was directed at the Cutler-Hubble Company of Detroit, the real estate manager for two Ann Arbor apartment complexes. Two Ann Arbor blacks charged that the company had refused "to show or rent" them an apartment, and two white apartment residents, who had picketed Cutler-Hubble in support of the black complainants, charged that the firm had refused to renew their leases because of "their sympathies with civil rights causes." After a three-day hearing in June 1965, the CRC found the company manager guilty of discrimination and ordered Cutler-Hubble to make a "suitable apartment" available to the principal petitioners and to cease unlawful discrimination in the renewal of the leases of the two white complainants. By then, the Ann Arbor fair housing ordinance, which Cutler-Hubble had successfully challenged in municipal court, had been upheld on appeal in a state circuit court, as already noted.[51]

The second of the housing cases that was appealed to the courts originated in a complaint by a Michigan State University student that the East Lansing real estate broker Richard C. Claugherty had denied the student the rental of an apartment because he was black. The CRC in late September 1965 ordered Claugherty to cease discriminating in the rental of apartments, ruling that the real estate office as well as the home of a licensed broker used as a place of business were places of public accommodation within the meaning of the state's public accommodations law, a contention of the commission in the Ann Arbor case also. Claugherty appealed the ruling to the Ingham County Circuit Court, which decided in late June 1967 in Claugherty's favor. The court held that a realtor's place of business was not a place of public accommodation under the law even though the agency had been licensed by the state. It also held that the student claimant had not been denied a civil right guaranteed by the 1963 Michigan constitution, challenging the Kelley opinion on this point.[52]

The third of the housing cases resulting in a CRC order and a court appeal ended up in the Michigan Supreme Court. Freeman Moore, the black assistant principal of Ecorse Junior High, made a deposit to reserve a building site for a home in the North Georgetown Green subdivision of Oakland County. The money was returned to Moore by William J. Pulte, president of William J. Pulte, Inc., and the Beech Grove Investment Company, the subdivision land developer, because Moore was black and, Pulte said, this "wouldn't be advantageous to the subdivision." "I told Mr. Moore," Pulte said, "that he had a cross to bear in life and it was the color of his skin."

Pulte turned to the Oakland County Circuit Court for an injunction to prevent the CRC from investigating the case, claiming that the state was without authority to prevent discrimination in the sale of private property. The court dismissed the Pulte suit in September 1965, ruling that the CRC could not be prevented from seeking "to eliminate discrimination by conciliation, persuasion and adjustment as directed by the Michigan constitution." The court, however, agreed with Pulte that "in absence of a statute or other prohibition, it . . . [was] not illegal for the owner to select a purchaser of real property based on religious, racial, or ethnic considerations." This once again challenged the Kelley ruling regarding the powers of the CRC under the Michigan constitution.[53]

Following the court's ruling, the CRC held a public hearing on the Pulte case and in February 1966 ordered the respondent to cease violating the civil right of individuals to buy homes regardless of race as guaranteed by the Michigan constitution. Pulte responded by filing a complaint in the Oakland County Circuit Court against the CRC, seeking "a trial de novo and quashing the cease and desist order." At the request of Governor Romney, the Michigan Supreme Court authorized the Oakland County Circuit Court to certify to the supreme court the "controlling questions of public law involved in the case." On April 1, 1968, in Beech Grove Investment Company v. Civil Rights Commission, the state supreme court, by a 5–3 vote, concluded that there was "a civil right to private property both at common law and under the 1963 Michigan Constitution where . . . that housing has been publicly offered for sale by one who is in the business of selling housing to the public." The court, however, stated that it was not deciding whether that civil right also existed when housing was "offered for sale by one not in the business of selling housing to the public, or by his representative." The decision, for the first time, placed the Michigan Supreme Court imprimatur on the Kelley-CRC view that the civil rights provisions of the 1963 Michigan constitution applied to the disposition

268

of private property, at least under certain circumstances. The court also accepted the CRC view that a realtor's office was a place of public accommodation. It is noteworthy that the court opinion was written by Paul Adams, who had played so prominent a role in the adoption of Rule 9.[54]

The state government of Michigan did not join some of the state's cities in enacting a fair housing measure before the Detroit riot. Three different housing bills failed of passage in the legislature in 1965, and although a 1966 anti-blockbusting bill that penalized real estate brokers and salesmen for inducing panic selling passed the Democrat-controlled House, it died in the Democrat-controlled Senate.[55] It was rioting in Detroit and in other Michigan cities in July 1967 and racial turbulence elsewhere in the state that in the end persuaded the legislature to take the step that it had so long avoided and to pass a fair housing bill.

In dealing with discrimination in employment, education, public accommodations, and housing, the CRC's focus was primarily on African Americans. It was, to be sure, mindful of discrimination against women, Native Americans, the physically handicapped, and migrant workers, but its role regarding these disadvantaged groups was rather marginal before 1969. It fell to other state government agencies to make equality of opportunity for these groups their primary concern.

13

WOMEN, NATIVE AMERICANS, AND THE PHYSICALLY HANDICAPPED, 1964–1968

WOMEN

When George Romney took office in January 1963, the Governor's Commission on the Status of Women that Governor Swainson had appointed had been functioning for only a few months. Its committees were seeking to discover what had been done and what needed to be done "to meet the changing and multiple roles of women," and they were beginning to submit reports regarding their particular concerns. The commission's only specific recommendation for legislation, as we have seen, was the enactment of a state minimum wage law applying to both female and male workers.[1]

The Swainson commission continued to meet while the incoming Romney administration decided whether the commission was to have a future and, if so, what its composition should be. The new state administration soon decided that the work of the commission should "go forward," but with some change in its membership. In June 1963 Romney reorganized the commission, reappointing thirteen of its members and appointing thirteen new members. He instructed the commission to "secure appropriate recognition of women's civic and political accomplishments . . . strengthen home life by directing attention to critical problems confronting women as wives, mothers, homemakers and workers . . . recommend methods of overcoming remaining discrimination against women in employment and in civil, political and property rights," and "promote more effective methods for enabling women to

271

develop their skills and for the State to utilize them for its pressing problems."[2]

By the time the Governor's Commission submitted its first report to Romney at the end of October 1964, the legislature had enacted a minimum wage law. The commission, however, was displeased that the wage levels the law set were below the federal minimum wage and did not require time-and-a-half pay for hours above forty per week. The commission was also concerned that the Equal Pay–Equal Work Law was not being effectively enforced by the state government and that women in the state service were suffering discrimination as a result.[3]

The October 1964 commission report contained the reports of its aforementioned six committees. The reports presented a nice overview of the kinds of issues being addressed at the time regarding women's role in society. Issues that were to become important at a later time, such as sexual harassment, were notably absent from the committee reports.

The Committee on Education recommended that counseling and guidance programs in elementary and secondary schools be "stepped up" so as better to prepare non-college-bound females for their role in the home, the community, and the workforce. It urged the Michigan Employment Security Commission (MESC) to publicize the occupational training and retraining available to women under the federal government's Manpower Development and Training Act and Area Redevelopment Act, the creation of additional community colleges in the state beyond the existing eighteen, and the inclusion of technical training for women in these colleges. The University of Michigan had established a Center for Continuing Education for Women that year, and the Education Committee recommended that all state-supported colleges and universities do likewise. It also recommended that female students, beginning at the elementary school level, should receive the kind of education essential for their entering into particular professions, and it pointed to the existing shortage in the state of teachers and nurses.[4]

The Committee on State and Local Employment Policies and Practices urged state and local governments to adopt "the best personnel policies" and by so doing to serve as a model for private employers with regard to employment and promotion procedures, salaries, and fringe benefits. The committee observed that although the fifteen thousand women in Michigan employed by governmental units constituted 39 percent of the governmental workforce, they occupied less than 10 percent of the executive positions. The committee noted that there were twice as many women as men teachers in the state but that the percentage of women holding positions at upper administrative levels in the public schools was declining. About 47 percent of employees in the state universities and colleges were women, mostly in secretarial positions. Although relatively few women employed by the institutions of higher education held executive positions, the percentage of women so employed was nevertheless well above the percentage of women occupying such positions in other branches of state and local government.[5]

The Committee on Private Employment Policies and Practices urged adoption of a bill pending in the legislature providing that the 1909 law limiting female employment to a maximum of fifty-four hours per week and, since 1959, ten hours per day be amended to provide protection for women workers such as required rest and meal periods in the working day. The committee was troubled that too many "occupational boundaries" were determined by gender.[6]

The Committee on Civil and Political Rights recommended that a study be made of the common-law practice followed by Michigan that a married woman's residence was to be that of her husband. It also recommended study of the law regarding alimony and property settlements in divorce proceedings and the development of counseling and retraining programs for women who had undergone "the trauma of divorce." It joined the National Commission on the Status of Women in recommending publication of the "Know Your Rights" pamphlet for women. The committee expressed disappointment at the small number of women serving as policy makers in government and offered a variety of suggestions designed to encourage women to register and vote in larger numbers than they were then doing. It was concerned that as of the beginning of 1964 only 1 Michigan woman was serving in the U.S. Congress, none in the state Senate, 5 in the Michigan House, and only 84 among the 725 members of the various state and local government commissions. It noted, however, that Governor Romney as of October 1964 had appointed 125 women to state boards and commissions and 31 women to judgeships.[7]

The Committee on Social and Labor Legislation called for granting the commissioner of labor rule-making authority in the administration of labor standards legislation and the appointment to the Department of Labor of a woman charged with responsibility for women's affairs. Differing with the Committee on Private Employment Policies and Practices, the Committee on Social and Labor Legislation recommended not only the lowering of the legal limit of working hours but also the application of such legislation equally to men and women workers. It urged a study by an advisory committee of the feasibility of granting women workers mandatory maternity leave without loss of reemployment and seniority rights. It called attention to the fact that more than half of the women workers in the state were married and that whereas women workers were earning an average of $2,438 for the year, men were earning an average of $5,211.[8]

The Committee on New and Expanding Services paid particular attention to the subject of child care. Michigan at that time was one of forty-one states approved by the federal government's Children's Bureau to receive federal funds for child care made available by the Public Welfare Amendments of 1962. The committee recommended that the funds be used to improve "standards and practices" of licensed day care facilities and to study additional day care needs.

Of 337 nursery schools and day care centers licensed at the time by the State Department of Social Welfare, none served children under two and a half years of age, and there was no licensed baby-sitting program in the state. The committee recommended that day care service be extended to include children younger than two and a half and also that training and certification procedures be developed for baby-sitting under the direction of either a public or private community agency. It also urged the establishment of an after-hours program in public schools for elementary schoolchildren. Responding to the growing concern about child care, the Department of Social Services created a state Child Care Committee in 1968.[9]

The Committee on New and Expanding Services called for a study of the Aid to Dependent Children (ADC) program so as to permit "a more realistic budget" for the families involved and also to permit the working ADC mother to keep more than the first fifteen dollars of her pay without reducing the size of her monthly grant, as was then the rule. The committee recommended the establishment where they did not already exist of "professionally supervised homemaker services" to meet emergency family needs and to forestall "family breakdowns." In an effort to encourage volunteering by women, it recommended "pin money" payments for those qualified for the role.[10]

The Governor's Commission appraised Michigan as "a leader in recognizing women's rights." It noted in this regard that the 1963–64 legislature had not only adopted the minimum wage law but also a record budget for education; a mandatory teacher tenure act; a high school district consolidation measure designed to provide a high school in every school district; a community college act to improve the quality of these colleges and to include training classes for adults and high school dropouts; authorization for circuit courts to establish marriage counseling services to reduce divorce rates; a measure requiring doctors to report cases of child abuse to the proper authorities; and a law calling for vocational retraining programs for young people to combat delinquency. The commission nevertheless conceded that its report "only scratched the surface of the needs of women" and that much remained to be done.[11]

The Governor's Commission urged that statewide meetings be held to present its report to the public and to encourage local action to implement the report's recommendations. Four such regional meetings were held between June 30 and November 5, 1965, in Traverse City, Grand Rapids, Jackson, and Detroit. Many of the commission's recommendations were endorsed at these meetings, but the 150 attendees at the Grand Rapids meeting, clearly revealing some of the differences among women regarding gender roles, were concerned that the role of women as wives and mothers should not be "under-stressed" in seeking an end to sex discrimination. The Grand Rapids audience recommended that programs be implemented to emphasize the "importance of home, of being a good wife and mother, and of being an educated wife and mother."[12]

With its 1964 report, the Governor's Commission, limited to a two-year life by a state constitutional provision applying to special commissions, came to an end. On November 22, 1967, however, Romney appointed a twenty-eight-member Second Special State Commission on the Status of Women. He instructed the new commission to concern itself with cases of discrimination against women workers; cooperate with the Department of Labor and the Civil Service Commission (CSC) regarding illegal employment practices and violations of labor laws; develop ways of strengthening home life; develop a program that would permit women to make greater contributions to society as the result of continuing education and retraining and by volunteer service; make recommendations for actions regarding women by the state's schools and colleges; serve as "a clearing house and coordinating body" for both government and private activities regarding the status of women; maintain contact with governmental agencies concerned with the status of women; and recommend legislation and administrative actions designed to secure equal treatment of, and opportunities for, women.[13]

By the time Romney appointed the second commission, the state government had taken a variety of actions regarding the status of women deriving, to some degree, from the recommendations of the first commission. Legislation had been adopted making provision for the establishment of day care centers in the public schools and also providing for a careful review of support arrangements for children involved in divorce settlements. As already noted, the Fair Employment Practices Act had been amended by then to cover sex discrimination. The inspection staff of the Bureau of Safety and Regulation, which was responsible for enforcing statutes of particular interest to women, had been doubled since the 1964 report of the Governor's Commission.[14]

Most important of the legislative actions stemming from the report of the Governor's Commission was the repeal in July 1967 of the law limiting the hours of women workers to fifty-four per week.[15] The repeal brought into sharp focus the dispute among women themselves as to whether protective labor legislation benefited or harmed working women. Caroline Davis, the director of the United Automobile Workers (UAW) Women's Department, was dead set against legislation singling out women workers for protection, however much such legislation might have been justified at the beginning of the century to protect women against exploitation by employers. She maintained that state labor laws applying to women that dealt with such matters as maximum hours of work, the maximum weight a woman worker should be permitted to lift, night work, working around ovens and on belts and wheels, hazardous occupations, rest and meal periods, and employment preceding and following childbirth discriminated against women by limiting both their occupational opportunities and their earnings. The fifty-four-hour law in particular, Davis contended, affected job opportunities for women in the automobile industry.[16]

The repeal of the fifty-four-hour law was to have taken effect on November 1, 1967. Business and professional women and the UAW's Women's Department supported the repeal, claiming for one thing that Title VII of the federal Civil Rights Act of 1964, which banned employment discrimination on the basis of sex, required the states to conform. Myra Wolfgang, however, the head of Local 705 of the Hotel and Restaurant Workers, led a delegation of women to Lansing to protest the repeal. Most of the women were from Detroit, and they were joined by YWCA women from fourteen communities; by women from religious groups, neighborhood organizations, and the Women's International League for Peace and Freedom; and by Mort Furay, head of the Hospitality and Constituent Allied Trades of the AFL-CIO. For two hours the delegation hectored Lieutenant Governor William Milliken, who was substituting for the absent Romney. They complained that the repeal had passed both houses of the legislature "quietly" and without a preceding public hearing and maintained that since most women workers were not union members, they could be forced because of the repeal to work as long as their employers wished and would be unable to fulfill their role as wives and mothers. One result, opponents of the repeal claimed, would be an increase in family problems and juvenile delinquency. They called on Michigan women to declare November 1, 1967, "a day of 'ignominy and mourning.'"[17]

As it turned out, the fifty-four-hour repeal statute did not go into effect on November 1, 1967. Before that date the legislature enacted a measure creating an Occupational Safety Standards Commission with the authority to establish standards, codes, and regulations to protect the health and safety of Michigan workers. The act stipulated that protective legislation then on the books, which included the fifty-four-hour law, was to remain in force until the new commission devised the relevant standards. Most employers assumed that the hours repeal had become effective on November 1, 1967, and as a result the Big Three automobile manufacturers and some other employers began to have women employees work more than fifty-four hours a week. Attorney General Frank Kelley, however, ruled on March 18, 1968, that the old hours law was still in effect, causing General Motors, for example, to conclude that it must observe the fifty-four-hour limit lest it otherwise face criminal prosecution.[18]

When the Occupational Safety Standards Commission held hearings on the hours repeal issue on August 19, 1968, Betty Finegan, representing the Status of Women Commission, testified against repeal. She contended that the protection of women who could not or did not wish to work more than fifty-four hours a week was "a very real need." Ideally, she asserted, protective labor legislation should apply equally to both sexes, but the commission, she reported, did not believe that protective labor legislation for women should be repealed until that result could be achieved. She also expressed doubt that Title VII superseded legislation like the fifty-four-hour law.

UAW women who favored repeal agreed with the Status of Women Commission that laws limiting the hours of labor should apply to both sexes, whereas UAW women opposing repeal maintained that the women "hardest hit" by repeal would be "the poorest and most exploited" among them. Writing to Walter Reuther, a female UAW staff member noted that while repeal was briefly thought to be in effect, Chrysler Corporation had worked some of its women employees up to sixty-nine hours a week; and a member of the Amalgamated Meat Cutters' Union testified that she had been compelled to work thirteen hours a day, seven days a week. Even the UAW's Mildred Jeffrey, an opponent of protective labor legislation, conceded in a later interview that the repeal of the hours legislation "hurt a lot of women."[19]

The hours repeal issue was resolved when the federal government's Equal Employment Opportunity Commission took the position that federal law, in effect, outlawed the Michigan law as of the end of 1969. Kelley accordingly ruled on December 30, 1969, that the Civil Rights Act of 1964 superseded the fifty-four-hour law but that employers of fewer than twenty-five workers, who were excepted by the federal law, were still subject to the Michigan law.[20]

The Status of Women Commission recommended soon after its formation that it be given statutory status. The legislature complied, and Romney signed the bill into law on February 19, 1968. The new commission, titled Michigan's Women's Commission, as its predecessor had recommended and effective as of November 15, 1968, was placed in the Executive Office, again as its predecessor had urged.[21]

The Women's Commission was immediately concerned with improving the status of women in the state civil service. The CSC in 1965 had begun moving in this direction by reducing the number of job classifications with gender limitations from 300 to 135. Although the percentage of women in the classified civil service had increased from 41 percent in 1961 to 46 percent in 1968, the percentage of women in the top seven classification levels had increased from 29 to 62. In a key action, Romney in 1965 appointed the first woman member of the Michigan Civil Rights Commission (CRC). The Women's Commission began collecting the names of women it believed qualified for other gubernatorial appointments. A review ordered by Governor Milliken that was completed in fiscal year 1970–71 nevertheless revealed that the status of women in the state service remained "far below" that of white males.[22]

The Status of Women Commission assembled material for a publication dealing with the laws of special interest to women. Issued at the end of 1968, the pamphlet dealt with such subjects as marriage and divorce, the married woman and her property, social security, laws pertaining to working women, and political matters. Women were informed where they might seek help when needed.[23]

The CRC, beginning at the end of 1966, processed claims charging discrimination in employment because of sex. It had processed 444 such claims by the end of 1968, sex claims constituting 8.2 percent of the total claims and 11.7 percent of the employment claims in 1968.

In a study published in 1968, the CRC reported that women were "not on an equal footing with men" in their participation in higher education. They were more likely than men, the CRC noted, to withdraw from college for marriage, had more "limited career goals," and were apt to major in such two-year programs as nursing and home economics. The CRC recommended that female students be counseled in high school to prepare themselves in the physical and social sciences and to enter such fields as engineering. Vocational guidance of junior and senior high school female students became a special concern of the Status of Women Commission in 1968, and it developed plans for pilot counseling projects in Pontiac, Kalamazoo, Flint, and Mt. Clemens. Its emphasis, however, was less on the college-bound student than on the non-college-bound so that she could find suitable employment.[24]

The Status of Women Commission and the Women's Commission that succeeded it also concerned themselves with the controversial questions of sex education in the schools, family planning, and abortion. In May 1968 the Status of Women Commission endorsed a sex education bill enacted that year that permitted school districts to establish "wholesome and comprehensive sex and family planning programs." The commission believed that "every woman has the right to determine how many children she shall bear and how they shall be spaced" in accordance with her "personal beliefs and convictions." It was a matter of the "very first priority" in the commission's view to expand community resources to reach women who had been denied this right because of lack of information. The commission made it evident in 1969 that its belief that a woman had "a right to choice in determining her reproductive life" included the right to an abortion and "the right to personal privacy." The commission, consequently, called for the repeal of Michigan's anti-abortion law. It did not, however, accept the position that an abortion should be performed on demand as a means of birth control or for an unwanted pregnancy.[25]

The debate among women on the Status of Women Commission regarding the stance the commission should take on the proposed Equal Rights Amendment (ERA) to the U.S. Constitution illustrated once again the reluctance of commission members to push for the elimination of protective labor legislation for women. A special committee the commission had appointed to study the matter recommended at a May 24, 1968, commission meeting that it go on record as opposing the amendment. The special committee contended that the adoption of the ERA would "nullify" state labor laws designed to protect women just when such legislation had become more necessary because of the increasing number of women in the workforce. Moreover, the committee maintained, adoption of the ERA would create "endless and useless confusion" regarding laws dealing with "property, personal status and marriage."

After much debate, the commission adopted a motion expressing its opposition to the ERA. Citing the Fifth and Fourteenth Amendments to the U.S. Constitution as its justification, the commission called for "equal opportunities and equal status for women." It declared, however, that in "certain areas real equality [could] be obtained only through a difference in treatment rather than identity in treatment." The way to eliminate discrimination against women in legislation regarding employment, property, personal status, and marriage, the motion stated, was by "specific bills for specific ills."[26]

Women in Michigan became "increasingly militant" in the 1960s and improved their status somewhat, but, as the CRC reported in the spring of 1969, they remained the victims of a great deal of discrimination. Restaurants, bars, financial institutions, insurance companies, credit departments, retail shops, and landlords continued to discriminate against them. Financial institutions insisted on male co-signers when women sought loans, and the same was true when women sought to open charge accounts. Women complained that they were charged more than men for insurance and received smaller benefits. They contributed the same amount to retirement funds as their male counterparts but often received smaller benefits when they retired. Many landlords would not rent to single women. Women were "legally" excluded from the apprenticeship trades and "illegally" shut out from some professions, and they continued to suffer discrimination in employment. They complained that female students in the public schools were channeled in the direction of "women's work."[27] Women activists obviously had a full agenda to occupy them as the 1960s came to a close.

NATIVE AMERICANS

In February 1968 a member of the Michigan CRC described the state's Native Americans as "aliens in their own land," with "less education, a higher death rate, less longevity, a lower standard of living, [and] the lowest of the jobs of any ethnic group residing in the continental United States." Governor Williams, it will be recalled, had appointed a Governor's Study Commission on Indian Problems that had begun to address the deplorable conditions of the state's Native Americans, but it had accomplished little beyond bringing the matter to public attention and initiating a few modest attempts to alleviate Native American distress. The commission had lapsed at the end of 1960, and the Swainson administration had not appointed a successor.[28]

Native Americans who had served on the Williams commission, among others, urged Governor Romney to appoint another Indian commission. Romney was also motivated to take that step because the state House of Representatives was in the process of organizing a Special House Committee on Indians, and the governor wished to have an agency in the executive branch to deal with the committee. On June 3, 1964, Romney established the Governor's Commission on Indian Affairs, a fifteen-member body chaired by Herbert E. Cameron, president of the Bay Mills Community. The governor instructed the commission to deal with the social, economic, and cultural problems facing the state's Native Americans. He looked to the commission to bring Native Americans into "the mainstream of society" and to enjoy rights equal to those of other members of society.[29]

Following a recommendation of the Indian Affairs Commission, the legislature in 1965 established the statutory Michigan Commission on Indian Affairs in the Department of Social Welfare. It was authorized to investigate "alleged problems" affecting Native Americans, assist their economic development, and aid them in realizing the educational benefits promised them by treaty and state laws and in improving their health and general welfare. Romney saw the primary responsibility of the commission as focusing on Indian problems and attempting to coordinate the efforts of the relevant state agencies in dealing with these problems. Six of the members Romney appointed to the commission had served on the Williams commission, and five were themselves Native Americans. The legislature did not approve a deficiency appropriation to support the commission until April 1966, and the commission did not hold its first meeting until June of that year.[30]

The Governor's Commission did not view the problems of Native Americans as different from those of other racial, ethnic, and religious minorities in the state. It did, however, assume that Native Americans had rights not enjoyed by other minorities because of the various treaties Native Americans had concluded with the federal government. The commission held hearings at each of the four Michigan reservations and also in nonreservation areas with a substantial concentration of Native Americans. It gathered a good deal of information in the process about the poor conditions under which most Michigan Native Americans lived. The commission did not in itself initiate programs to deal with these conditions but rather tried to assist state and federal agencies in seeking to improve the lot of Native Americans. Its principal concerns were the "image" of Native Americans, their education, health, and housing, the implementation in Michigan of federal programs for Native Americans, and, to a lesser extent, discrimination against Native Americans in the state.[31]

The Indian Affairs Commission construed the problem of the Native American image as twofold: the need of Native Americans for increased pride in their heritage and achievements and the need for non–Native Americans to develop "a realistic view" of Native American history, culture, and contributions to society. The commission suggested a variety of ways to address these matters, such as the collection of examples of Native American arts and crafts, Native American pageants and exhibits, collection of Native American memorabilia and documents pertaining to Native American history, preservation of Native American languages and dialects, and segregated education of Native American schoolchildren. The commission established a committee on the preservation of Native American culture, and the statutory commission sought to restore "the arts and crafts talents" among Native Americans. Less and less, however, was heard about the Native American image in the state government's deliberations after early 1965.[32]

It is understandable that the two Indian commissions devoted a good deal of attention to Native American education. The average educational level of the state's Native Americans in the early 1960s was 8.1 years, the school dropout rate was 60 percent, and Native American children were absent from school an average of five to eight weeks during the school year. When the Indian Affairs Commission began to function in 1964, it discovered that the state's superintendent of public instruction was unaware of the Native American school dropout problem and that nonreservation Native Americans needed help in securing an education for their children. The federal government's Bureau of Indian Affairs provided college scholarships for Native Americans, fifteen of which were made available to Michigan in 1964 and twenty-three in 1968. Michigan Native American youths, however, were generally unaware of the availability of these scholarships. Public authorities had done little to publicize them, and, unlike such states as Minnesota, Wisconsin, and Iowa, Michigan did not provide the needed matching funds for the scholarships. The statutory commission urged the state government to provide the needed matching funds and advised the legislature to create a committee to deal specifically with Native American education. The commission succeeded in securing scholarships and other forms of educational assistance for academically promising Native American young people. As of early 1968, 145 Native Americans were enrolled in Michigan colleges and universities.

When the Indian Affairs Commission discussed Native American education at its March 6, 1965, meeting, it distinguished Native Americans from other minorities and went on record as favoring all–Native American boarding schools rather than integrated schools. Its fear was that if Native American children coming from impoverished homes had to compete in school with Caucasian children, the Native American children would develop an inferiority complex that would cause them to lose pride in their heritage. The commission believed that a Native American school, by contrast, would serve to "perpetuate Indian heritage and culture."[33]

In 1965 the Indian Affairs Commission aided in the development of an experimental Job Training Center in Mt. Pleasant to provide training for Native Americans in such basics as reading and arithmetic as well as vocational skills. Funds later made available under Title V of the Economic Opportunity Act made it possible to train Native Americans on two reservations in various trades, particularly carpentry.[34]

Housing conditions on the Indian reservations were "almost universally substandard. Dirt floors, crowded rooms, and general squalor" were "commonplace." Tribal councils were eligible to apply for federal funds for low-income rental housing, and this made possible a housing project for Native Americans in Mt. Pleasant in early 1967 and the development of other projects later. Michigan, beginning in 1966, took advantage of another Title V program that made it possible for family heads to learn a building trade by participating in the remodeling and reconstruction of homes belonging to persons receiving either Old Age Assistance or ADC.[35]

The health condition of Michigan's Native Americans was deplorable. Their infant mortality rate was double that of the population at large, and the average age of Native Americans at death was forty-two, as compared to sixty-five for non–Native Americans. In the summer of 1968 two third-year University of Michigan Medical School students, sponsored by the Michigan Commission, conducted a health and nutrition study of thirty-nine Native American adults and seventy-four Native American children. Among the adults, 17.9 percent had a history of tuberculosis, and 20.5 percent had diabetes. The children had been hospitalized at about three times the national rate, mostly for respiratory infections, digestive disturbances, and surgery. Later studies supported the survey results.[36]

In the summer of 1968 the Michigan Commission and the Michigan Department of Public Health, supported by a variety of voluntary organizations and individual physicians and dentists, began conducting a multiphasic Native American screening program that was completed early in 1969. Seventeen screening tests were conducted in four areas with substantial Native American population. Of 308 Native Americans screened, 196 had health abnormalities, particularly high blood pressure. A separate screening study was conducted at two reservations to test for tuberculosis. On one of the reservations, one-third of 238 Native Americans tested positive; on the other, 99 percent of the 50 screened tested positive, and 1 eventually died. The project helped persuade the federal government to quadruple its expenditure for similar projects.[37]

The Michigan Commission participated in 1967 in a $2 million Northern Michigan Rural Employment Project supported by the federal government's Office of Economic Opportunity. Combining training, placement, and social services, the project was designed to increase economic opportunity and "stability" in a ten-county region in the northwestern part of the state in the Lower Peninsula and the eastern portion of the Upper Peninsula. In the summer of 1967 the commission began looking into the possibility of developing a Native American community action program (CAP) under the Economic Opportunity Act of 1964. In March 1969 the federal government provided $50,000 for a Native American CAP in Michigan to be administered by the Inter-Tribal Council that had been formed in June 1968 and that included representatives of each of the four Michigan reservations, to which the program was limited. It was a small CAP with a staff of only three. The CAP's first program was the development of a cooperative to produce tepees for sale. Michigan also benefited from the assignment to the state of VISTA volunteers who provided reservation and non-reservation

283

Native Americans as well as other low-income groups with a variety of services. In an action especially important for Michigan's Chippewa and Ottawa tribes, the federal government's Indian Claims Commission at the end of 1968 awarded members of the two tribes $10.8 million as the result of land claims arising under an 1836 treaty.[38]

Both the Michigan Commission and the CRC were concerned about the discrimination suffered by Michigan's Native Americans. Father Theodore E. LaMarre characterized Native Americans as "the unchampioned minority" in the state since there was less information about their plight than about that of other groups suffering from poverty. A Protestant minister who was a member of the Indian Affairs Commission and who had worked with the Hannahville Indian Community in Menominee County informed the commission in October 1964 that "anti-Indian feeling" was strong in nearby communities, especially among whites at the same economic level as the Native Americans. He thought that the poor condition of the roads in the Native American community resulted from discrimination against Native Americans by county officials. Another commissioner reported that Native Americans believed that blacks fared better than Native Americans when it came to workmen's compensation and welfare assistance. The CRC's education director met with the Indian Affairs Commission in October 1964 to offer CRC assistance in dealing with discrimination against Michigan's Native Americans.[39]

In the fall of 1965 and spring of 1966, Richard Anderson, director of the CRC's Grand Rapids regional office, toured the Native American areas in the state, particularly in the Upper Peninsula, to familiarize himself with the condition of the resident Native Americans and to offer them the CRC's services. Although he found it difficult "to pin down allegations of racial discrimination" that would have been subject to the CRC's jurisdiction, Anderson nevertheless concluded that it was "quite possible, even probable" that discrimination had occurred and was occurring. The CRC, to be sure, received only one official complaint from a Native American source while Romney was governor, a complaint involving public accommodations, but Anderson was undoubtedly correct in believing that Native Americans simply did not file claims with the CRC even when justified.

Anderson saw "a number of parallels" between the situation of Native Americans, particularly in the northern part of Michigan, and the situation of blacks in urban ghettos. He concluded therefore that some programs developed for the urban ghetto might be adopted by the state government in seeking to cope with Native American problems, especially poverty. He advised the CRC to include Native Americans in CRC programs dealing with education, affirmative employment practices, housing, law enforcement, and the like and also to develop cooperative relationships with agencies and organizations that could help to improve Native American conditions in the state.

The CRC began to pay "increasing attention" to Native Americans by early 1967, and it was planning to establish an office in Mt. Pleasant to serve them. It failed to take that action, although it apparently did inform Native Americans of the civil rights legislation that was supposed to protect them against discrimination. There was talk in 1969 of adding a Native American to the CRC, but the discussions along this line proved fruitless, and the step was not taken until 1979. In the end, the CRC's interest in Native Americans proved to be marginal to its interest in other minorities experiencing discrimination.[40]

During the Romney governorship, as during the Williams governorship, the Michigan state government probably helped to increase public awareness of the plight of the state's Native Americans. It made little progress, however, in improving their condition and status. Reflecting their dissatisfaction that so little had been accomplished, Native American leaders began disrupting meetings of the Michigan Commission and demanded the resignation of the commission's chairman and staff director. The Native Americans urged that more Native Americans be added to the commission and that its power to deal with other state agencies be strengthened. Governor Milliken appointed a special committee to consider changes in the statute that had created the commission, and legislation in 1972 providing for a new commission did require that at least seven of its members be Native Americans. It also placed the commission in the Executive Office rather than in the Department of Social Services, where it had been lodged. As for the CRC, it continued to be concerned about discrimination against Native Americans, but its main concern in later years appears to have been its efforts to protect Native American fishery treaty rights against "harassment and threats of violence."[41]

THE PHYSICALLY HANDICAPPED

Some progress was made during the Romney governorship regarding the employment of the physically handicapped without discrimination and on the basis of their ability to perform the job. Romney in May 1963 reactivated the Governor's Commission on the Employment of the Physically Handicapped, reappointed Judson Perkins as its chairman, and asked it to "accelerate its program wherever possible." The governor soon added five new members to the commission and reappointed fourteen others. Essentially only an advisory body, the commission operated without a professional staff of its own and with a budget so meager that it could not even provide for "necessities." Not until 1965 did the commission have a full-time secretary, provided by the MESC and the Division of Vocational Rehabilitation (DVR). Romney later recommended that the commission be given statutory status, and the legislature responded with a measure that became effective on March 8, 1968.[42]

The commission sought to promote the employment of the physically handicapped by participation in the national essay contest for high school students dealing with topics such as "How Handicapped Workers in My Community Are Proving That Ability Counts" as well as in the National Employ the Handicapped Week. It presented citations to individuals and organizations for achievements in this area and made a Handicapped Citizen of the Year award. The commission's principal activity, however, was to encourage the formation of citizens committees at the local level to aid the handicapped. Made up of personnel from business, labor, religious, educational, medical, and government organizations, the local committees sought to create a climate of acceptance of the handicapped as workers and tax-paying members of the community. The Governor's Commission sought to assist and guide the local committees in spurring the retraining and employment of the physically handicapped. The basic staff work for the local committees was performed by MESC and DVR personnel.

The Romney administration in 1968 pointed to the success of the local committees in places like Flint and Battle Creek, where handicapped individuals drawn from the welfare and unemployment rolls were aided in finding employment. The efforts of the various local communities also helped to reduce somewhat the prejudice that existed with respect to the employment of the handicapped.[43]

The principal responsibility for training the handicapped for remunerative employment rested with the DVR. As Romney noted in his first State of the State address in January 1963, the vocational training program for the handicapped was "woefully inadequate," and it remained that way throughout the Romney governorship. The federal government provided $60 for every $40 the state expended for vocational rehabilitation until 1965, when the federal share was increased to $75 for every $25 in state expenditure. From fiscal year 1963–64 to fiscal year 1968–69, a grand total of $58,422,824 in federal money would have been available to Michigan had it provided $28,783,054 in matching funds, but Michigan, despite a 119 percent increase in state revenue while Romney was governor, appropriated only $9,272,903 during those years, costing the state almost $34 million in federal matching funds.[44]

The shortfall in funds obviously limited the number of the physically handicapped the DVR could serve. The increased funding available as compared to earlier years, however, made it possible to increase the number of new cases the DVR accepted from 6,247 in 1963–64 to

16,500 in 1967–68, and its caseload rose from 12,223 to 28,863 during these years. The DVR at the same time developed relationships with a variety of organizations that enhanced its ability to serve the handicapped. It jointly sponsored a rehabilitation program with the Department of Mental Health and cooperated with the MESC in developing a test of the aptitude of the handicapped for vocational rehabilitation for particular jobs. Vocational rehabilitation counselors from the DVR's thirty district offices visited the MESC offices to identify employment opportunities for the DVR's rehabilitation clients. The DVR entered into cooperative arrangements with high school districts to provide rehabilitation services for physically handicapped pupils. It conducted rehabilitation programs with carriers of workmen's compensation insurance that were designed to restore the injured to employment, and it assigned DVR state office personnel to work with the Governor's Commission.[45]

The MESC sought as part of its responsibilities to find employment for the moderately disabled. It also referred a small number of the handicapped for training by the federal government's Manpower Development Training Administration and the Area Redevelopment Administration. Seeking to enhance the employability of the handicapped, many of whom lacked the needed motivation, the MESC devised a Human Resources Development Program that involved "intensive [employment] services" for the handicapped ranging from outreach to placement. The number of the handicapped actually placed by the MESC ranged from a high of 12,033 of the 16,098 provided employment services in the fiscal year ending June 30, 1964, to a low of 9,020 of 16,692 serviced in the fiscal year ending June 30, 1968. In May 1967 the Civil Service Department established a Special Employment Program that sought to plan for the recruitment and placement in the state service of various disadvantaged groups, including the physically handicapped and the mentally retarded.[46]

As a survey of employers revealed, the lack of a provision for a second-injury fund in the state's workmen's compensation law that would have encouraged employers to hire handicapped persons with disabilities subject to "deterioration" or "aggravation" continued to be an obstacle to the placement of some of the handicapped. A June 1965 revision of the state's compensation act limited the compensation for injured employees to fifty-two weeks, with the possibility of an additional fifty-two weeks following a hearing, but without actually establishing a second-injury fund. A proper second-injury fund was not established until 1969.[47]

There was some progress in Michigan during the Romney governorship with respect to the accessibility of public buildings to handicapped persons. When Romney took office, Michigan was without any legislation regarding this matter, but the State Building Division did stress the importance of accessibility in the design of new state buildings. In 1966, Michigan, joining more than twenty other states, required that all future buildings funded by state or local funds, as well as all public school buildings, meet "specifications permitting easy access and use to the physically handicapped."[48]

The CRC was minimally involved in state efforts before 1969 to deal with the handicapped. It did, however, agree in March 1968 to support the effort by the Michigan Council on Blindness to secure an amendment to the Fair Employment Practices Act prohibiting employment discrimination because of physical disability. It was not, however, until 1976 that Michigan enacted legislation prohibiting discrimination against the handicapped not just in employment but in other matters as well.[49]

14

"DISTURBING CONDITIONS AND UNMET NEEDS": The Migrant Labor Problem, 1964–1968

The Williams administration had provided a good deal of information regarding the sad plight of migrant labor in Michigan, but the state legislature, it will be recalled, had refused to enact the reform measures recommended by the governor. As in some other areas of state affairs, George Romney was able to persuade a majority of the legislature to adopt migrant reform proposals that were largely similar to measures that lawmakers had rejected during the preceding few years. The state government was also able during the Romney years to use available federal funds to deal with a variety of migrant matters. Toward the end of the Romney governorship, the Michigan Civil Rights Commission (CRC) began to address itself to the state's migrant labor problem. The effect on the quality of migrant life in Michigan was, however, rather limited.

Like Michigan and some other states, the federal government in the 1960s paid increasing attention to migrant labor matters. This coincided with the effort of Cesar Chavez beginning in 1962 to organize California's farmworkers, an effort that attracted national attention and enjoyed the strong support of United Automobile Workers president Walter Reuther.[1] The first important measure enacted by Congress was the already noted Migrant Health Act of 1962. The Farm Labor Contractor Registration Act of 1962 was designed to "weed out" crew leaders operating in interstate commerce who exploited seasonal farmworkers. Beginning in 1964, the Manpower Development and Training Act made funds available for the training of migrants seeking to leave the migrant stream. The Housing Acts of 1964 and 1965 provided funds for the building of farm homes designed to attract "a more stable labor supply" and authorized the Farmers Home Administration to make grants covering two-thirds of the cost of "decent, safe and sanitary low-rent housing."

Of special importance to states like Michigan, the Economic Opportunity Act of 1964 made federal funds available for up to 90 percent of the cost of a variety of programs to aid migrants, such as day care, education, housing, and sanitation. The Elementary and Secondary Education Act of 1965, as amended in 1967, authorized $40 million for the special education of migrant children to be distributed to the states on the basis of the number of migrant children of school age in the state. Amendments in 1966 to the Fair Labor Standards Act applied the minimum wage requirement for the first time to farm operators using five hundred man-days of labor in any quarter of the preceding calendar year, a man-day being defined as any day in which an employee performed farm labor for at least one hour. The total man-day requirement plus the exclusion from the act's coverage of migrant workers paid by the piece eliminated about 70 percent of the migrant workers from the act's minimum wage guarantee.[2]

The major change in the supply of migrant labor in Michigan in the 1960s was the termination of the bracero program by the federal government as of December 31, 1964. Although this action displeased many Michigan farm operators, the mechanization of Michigan agriculture at the same time reduced somewhat the state's need for out-of-state farmworkers. The number of such workers fell from 49,692 in 1965 to 40,356 in 1969. A majority of these workers continued to be Spanish-speaking Mexican Americans from Texas. The remainder of the migrants coming to Michigan were non-Hispanic whites from various states and blacks coming predominantly from Tennessee and Arkansas.[3]

There was no real change in the 1960s as compared to the 1950s in the "general attitude" regarding the migrants of the Michigan communities to which they came. Most residents viewed the Mexican Americans as "dirty Mexicans" and treated them as such. Seldom, indeed, were they even "addressed as persons." The head of the Rural Manpower Center of Michigan State University informed a U.S. Senate subcommittee that the center had "encountered very serious community discrimination" against migrants. A Democratic state senator thought that the migrants were "not even second-class citizens" in Michigan. As one militant migrant put it near the end of the decade, the migrants were "voiceless, powerless—the forgotten people."[4]

The quality of migrant housing, despite some improvements in the 1950s and the early 1960s, continued to be a major problem while

George Romney was Michigan's governor. A child welfare worker assigned to the migrant camps in the summer of 1964 by the Department of Social Welfare appraised the condition of the camps as "horrid." The housing was overcrowded and the sanitation miserable. "Stale water," she reported, "stands in low places and the smell of urine and feces pervade[s] the ground as well as the children. I can't speak for India," she remarked, "but *never* I thought in America! And, why in Michigan!" After touring migrant areas in July 1965 along with other state legislators, Senator Sander M. Levin concluded that more migrant housing was "miserable and unfit for human habitation" than was acceptable. The typical migrant dwelling, the legislators discovered, was a twelve-by-twelve unit with a two-burner stove, a pit latrine, and one outdoor water faucet. Most of the housing lacked running water, washbasins, refrigerators, and flush toilets. Fire safety regulations applying to the camps were "woefully deficient," as evidenced when six migrant children were incinerated in a tenant shack in a migrant camp in March 1967. A few months later five migrant children died as the result of a fire in their one-room cabin on a fruit farm in Bainbridge Township.[5]

The migrants' earnings were, of course, limited by the seasonal character of their work. In 1965, for example, Michigan migrant workers averaged 122 days of farm employment as compared to 243 days of work for the average worker in the state. Migrants' average hourly earnings were well below those of other nonskilled laborers in the state. A Michigan Migrant Ministry official, moreover, claimed that migrants were "consistently cheated" by employers regarding the payment of wages due them.[6]

The problem of low pay for migrant workers in Michigan as well as the exploitative behavior of some crew leaders attracted nationwide attention as the result of a 1969 story by the Chicago newspaper columnist Mike Royko. Referring to a 1968 episode, Royko wrote, "Chicago Skid Row bums are being plucked from Madison St. to work for almost nothing as farm laborers in Michigan." The crew leader involved, Wadell Williams, was recruiting workers to serve as tomato pickers near Blissfield. The workers, it turned out, did not receive even the very small wages promised them and had also been mistreated. Once the news broke, the Michigan state government contacted the U.S. Department of Labor to ensure that the license Williams had received under the federal government's Farm Labor Contractor Registration Act would not be renewed.[7]

Under the sponsorship of the Michigan State Horticultural Society, growers in Michigan responded to the migrant labor problem by forming the Farm Labor Management Committee of Michigan (FLMC) in 1960.

291

The objective of the FLMC, made up of representatives from various regional grower groups and with state government officials serving as consultants, was to study the problems of migrant labor and to educate and encourage growers to adopt "improved management techniques" that would, hopefully, benefit employer, employee, and the general public. In cooperation with the Department of Public Instruction, the FLMC developed a twenty-hour training program for farm operators and their foremen in eleven different locations in the state. It assisted the Michigan Farm Labor Service in the preparation of a handbook on farm labor management and worked with the Department of Agricultural Engineering of Michigan State University in developing plans for the construction and remodeling of housing for migrant workers.[8]

The FLMC's chairman conceded that one of the organization's purposes was to forestall government intervention in migrant matters by having the growers "take the lead in the area of human relations" by improving farm labor practices. Although, he asserted, there was no assurance that legislation being proposed to aid the migrants would make their lives "any more pleasant and profitable," it would "most surely . . . make the life of the grower much more frustrating and his costs decidedly higher." He feared that social reformers had "goaded" legislators into a "war on farm labor." Many growers, he claimed, were "hanging on by living on their depreciation," and he was concerned about what increased labor costs would do to them.[9]

Whereas the FLMC sought to improve the quality of farm labor management, other private organizations sought to improve the lot of the migrants themselves. The Michigan Migrant Ministry, "the largest Protestant interdenominational service project of its kind" in the nation, continued as in the 1950s to sponsor a variety of local secular and religious projects for the benefit of the migrants. As of 1964, thirty local Migrant Ministry committees administered the agency's programs with the aid of sixty-five staff persons and twenty-three hundred community volunteers and with funds provided by churches and a variety of interested organizations and individuals. As part of its summer program, it enlisted "worker friends"—young volunteers who joined migrant crews for the summer. It also began engaging "community workers" who served throughout the year in various parts of the state to provide "community education" on migrant problems and assisted migrants seeking to settle in the state. In 1968 the Migrant Ministry began to concern itself with legislation dealing with migrant life. In July of that year it gave its support to the table grape boycott instituted in California by Cesar Chavez and the United Farm Workers Organizing Committee, viewing the "issue at stake" to be the right of farmworkers to organize and bargain collectively with their employers.[10]

The Migrant Apostolate Centers in the four Catholic dioceses in the Lower Peninsula continued in the 1960s as in the 1950s to deal with the spiritual and physical needs of migrants and ex-migrants. Their secular program included camp visits, day care centers, welfare services, vocational upgrading, medical assistance, assistance in employment and housing, instruction in English, and adult education. In the 1960s the Apostolate Centers placed special emphasis on seeking to gain community acceptance of the migrants. Aided by a federal grant, the Michigan Catholic Conference, which coordinated the apostolate programs, assisted in setting up a job training center in Lansing to train 150 hard-core unemployed, half of whom were ex-migrants. Centers were also established in some inner-city neighborhoods where migrants had settled.[11]

To take advantage of Title III-B of the Economic Opportunity Act, the Michigan Council of Churches and the Michigan Catholic Conference joined forces in March 1965 to form Michigan Migrant Opportunity, Inc. (MMOI). Its objective was to "plan, conduct, coordinate, and supervise health, education, and welfare activities which promote human and material well-being of migrants and ex-migrants and their families." It was managed by a board of directors of twenty-four members, eight selected by the Michigan Council of Churches, eight by the Michigan Catholic Conference, and eight migrants and nonmigrants selected by the "client population" in four regions of the state, each of which had a regional board to supervise program activities. Slightly more than a third of MMOI staff members were migrants. The Office of Economic Opportunity (OEO) provided the new organization with a grant of $1,338,926 for a period of twelve and one-half months for day care, youth programs, adult education, work experience, housing improvement, emergency medical and dental care, and emergency food and clothing. The federal poverty grant for the program, which serviced about ten thousand persons, was reportedly the first in the nation to be administered jointly on a statewide basis by Catholic and Protestant organizations. The relevant state agencies provided MMOI with consultative services.[12]

MMOI received additional grants after the initial 1965 one, and its program expanded accordingly. In 1967 it set up twelve "community assistance centers" to aid migrant families attempting to settle in Michigan. It was succeeded on April 1, 1968, by United Migrants for Opportunity, Inc. (UMOI), which, like its predecessor, was funded under the Economic Opportunity Act. It provided services for migrants essentially similar to those MMOI had provided. It also sponsored three new programs involving college and university students: a summer program in which forty-eight college students provided information to migrants about their rights and the services available to them, which the students helped the migrants to obtain; a college scholarship program that made grants to fifteen migrant youths to cover their college expenses; and a program in which fifteen law school students provided migrants with needed legal assistance.[13]

In 1963 the Michigan Citizens' Council on Agricultural Labor was formed to bring together organizations and individuals interested in the problems of agricultural labor. The council's major objective was to disseminate information about the subject of farm labor, which led to its publication of *Perspectives on Michigan Farm Labor Problems*, a survey of state government services and health services available to migrants. The council became inactive, however, after about three years of operation.[14]

Toward the end of the 1960s the migrants themselves and organizations supporting them sought to put pressure on the state government to enact legislation to deal with migrant conditions. On Easter Sunday in March 1967, Ruben Alfaro, a Lansing barber who had once been a migrant and was serving as director of the newly organized Concerned Citizens for Migrant Workers, led a seventy-mile march from Saginaw to Lansing to demonstrate concern for the migrants' plight and to present a "Declaration of Grievances" to Governor Romney. They marched, the demonstrators declared, because migrants were "the forgotten men of the nation." Actually, only about a dozen members of the Concerned Citizens marched the entire distance, but about eight hundred sympathizers gathered at the state capitol as part of the demonstration. "Help us [governor]. Help us be treated as human beings," pleaded the marchers, who enjoyed the support of the Michigan AFL-CIO and the Michigan Catholic Conference. Romney was not present at the capitol building since he did not deal with office business on Sundays. Lieutenant Governor William Milliken accepted the petition from the demonstrators and promised that they would receive "full and fair consideration." Romney met with a group of the demonstrators a few days later to hear their demands, and he subsequently assigned a staff aide to work with the group.[15]

On April 10 there was another march to Lansing by the same group to complain that the governor had failed to act on two bills of concern to the migrants. Two days later, Cesar Chavez, who had originally intended to participate in the Easter march and was then involved in the Delano grape strike, appeared in Michigan to lend his support to the Michigan migrant cause. "I think something important is beginning here," he said, but he thought that his own organization did not have sufficient resources to aid the Michigan migrants. While Chavez was in the state, the effort to organize what came to be known as the Michigan Committee to Aid Farm Workers (MCAFW) was announced by Brendon Sexton, director of the UAW's Leadership Center. Along with Sexton, the members of the Steering Committee of the new organization were Monsignor Clement Kern, William G. Bennalack of the Migrant Ministry, and Jack Carper of the Jewish Labor Committee, who served as the MCAFW's coordinator.

The goals of the MCAFW were to secure the passage of legislation to aid the migrants and also to promote their unionization. The organizers believed that the migrants' civil rights were being violated, as was their "personal dignity." They hoped that the UAW, which had aided Chavez's efforts to unionize California farmworkers, would raise funds to promote the unionization of Michigan farmworkers. The MCAFW's plan was to work through committees devoted to specific issues such as civil rights, with a coalition of groups supporting the effort. The UAW formed a committee of local union presidents and representatives of its regional districts to aid the MCAFW. Carper reported in January 1968 that "starting from very nearly ground zero," the MCAFW had assembled "a coalition to support farm worker interests and needs." Included in the "coalition" were the Concerned Citizens for Migrant Workers, the Migrant Ministry, the state NAACP, the Michigan Catholic Conference, the Jewish Labor Committee, the Bishop's Committee of the Spanish Speaking, and Latin Americans United for Political Action.[16]

Claiming that migrant workers in Michigan were "being frozen out of every social program offering protection and benefits to working people," the MCAFW lobbied the legislature in 1968 for migrant legislation that the committee favored. It brought Dolores Huerta, the vice president of the United Farm Workers Organizing Committee, to Michigan to aid the cause. The effort met with the usual opposition in the legislature, one lawmaker claiming that he had seen migrants drive to work in "big white Cadillacs" and that some of them earned more than he did.[17]

Like the Concerned Citizens for Migrant Workers in 1967, the MCAFW decided to stage a demonstration at the state capitol on Easter Sunday, April 14, 1968, to publicize the organization's legislative demands. Carper wrote Romney in advance that it was useless for the MCAFW to meet with him since the governor and his office were "an integral part of the process whereby farm workers" were "locked in poverty" by actions of the legislature that Romney had approved. About six hundred demonstrators appeared for the rally in front of the capitol, and some of them even got into the building thanks to two Detroit legislators. As in 1967, Romney remained at his East Lansing home during the demonstration.

"Our problems, grievances and our demands will not go away," Alfaro declared to the demonstrators. "We are tired, frustrated people at this point. Help us before our people turn to other means. Help us before we have to have another report of the National Advisory Commission on Civil Disorders,[18] only this time on the rural subghettos of America." A Romney aide phoned Carper the next day to seek a meeting of the MCAFW with Romney, but Carper, Alfaro, and Bennalack ruled this out, Carper insisting on "a significant gesture of good will," such as extending the minimum wage act to cover agricultural workers, as a precondition for a meeting. As it turned out, the legislature turned down the migrant labor bills before it that year. The MCAFW soon faded from the scene, but it was not without some modest effect since it apparently helped persuade the CRC to investigate the condition and treatment of Michigan's migrants, and some of the measures it had sought were later enacted into law or implemented administratively.[19]

A new organization, La Raza Unida, appeared in Michigan as the MCAFW passed out of existence. It had been organized in El Paso, Texas, in 1967 as "a loose coalition of Spanish speaking organizations." A Michigan branch was established in Lansing the next year made up of representatives of Spanish-speaking groups in the state. Its concern was Michigan's Hispanics, whether they were residents or migrants. It sought to secure employment for Hispanics, the creation of a scholarship fund for them, and the teaching of Mexican American history in Catholic schools. La Raza looked to the Catholic Church for support.[20]

The state administration was hardly as opposed to aiding the migrants as the MCAFW and other organizations contended. On June 4, 1964, Romney appointed a twenty-person Governor's Commission on Migrant Labor to examine the problems of migrant workers and their employers and to recommend "voluntary, administrative, and legislative action" to deal with migrant problems. The commission included growers, church and labor representatives drawn from the Michigan Citizens' Council on Agricultural Labor, and three Mexican Americans. The chairperson was Rebecca Tompkins, a member of the Michigan Cherry Producers Association.[21]

In its annual reports in 1965 and 1966, the Governor's Commission provided factual data concerning the health, education, welfare, and employment of the migrants and made numerous recommendations regarding one or another migrant problem. The commission noted that crops requiring seasonal labor in Michigan in 1964 were valued at almost $175 million, with cherries and strawberries requiring the largest number of workers during peak periods of employment. About 90 percent of the migrants, it reported, worked no more than three to six weeks on any one farm.[22]

Although tactfully commending employers of migrant labor for what they had done to improve the condition of their workers, Romney observed that the special problems the migrants faced required government intervention for their amelioration. He consequently recommended the enactment into law—or at least the study—of the commission's recommendations. He also established an Inter-Agency Council of Migrant Labor to be responsible for "over-all planning and coordination to assist migrants."

Unlike the lawmakers during the Williams and Swainson governorships, the Michigan legislature between 1964 and 1969 enacted measures dealing with such migrant problems as housing, health, crew leaders, the transportation of migrants, rest stops, child labor, and wages. In 1968 the legislature provided for the establishment of an Agricultural Labor Commission in the Department of Labor and authorized it to cooperate with governmental agencies and private groups in dealing with the problems of agricultural labor and in seeking to improve the working and living conditions of these workers.[23]

Michigan received a federal grant of $25,000 in 1963 to help provide services for poor children while their parents worked. Proper care for their children was an especially serious problem for migrant parents. Some mothers took their children with them to the fields and kept them in locked cars during working hours. Babies were sometimes placed on the grass near where their mothers worked, which explains why some children were found playing in irrigation ditches. School-age children sometimes remained at home during school hours to look after younger children. The federal funding enabled Michigan to establish eight day care centers for migrant children. The centers were operated by private agencies such as the Migrant Ministry. All were licensed by the Department of Social Welfare, and all had to meet its standards and were subject to its rules. Fifty day care centers were operating in the state in the summer of 1965, some federally supported and others supported entirely by local community organizations. Beginning in January 1966, the state had to match the federal funds for day care centers.[24]

In 1966 MMOI received an OEO grant for migrant day care that enabled it to provide day care service for 910 families for eighteen weeks during the year. The Michigan State Department of Education received a $2 million federal grant that led to its operation of fifty-nine day care centers to accommodate an average daily number of five thousand children aged four to twelve. The centers were operated by individual school districts under the direction of the Department of Education. In a program closely coordinated with that of the department, UMOI at the same time operated a day care service for 1,030 children aged three and four.[25]

One of the migrants' greatest needs was the proper education of their children. Given the time the migrants were in the state, this generally meant summer school education. In 1965 the Michigan legislature appropriated $15,000 for the operation by school districts, on an experimental basis, of elementary school classes for migrant children from June to August 1965. Since the measure, however, was not signed into law until July 22, too late for the Department of Education to develop a program for that year, the money was never used. Several community organizations had operated summer school classes in earlier years, but only in 1965 did a full summer school program become available to at least some migrant children thanks to an OEO grant of $800,000 to MMOI to operate summer schools at four migrant centers. MMOI used the funds to serve an estimated six thousand children.[26]

Amendments to the federal government's Elementary and Secondary Education Act in 1966 and 1968 increased the federal contribution to the states for migrant education based on the number of migrant children of school age in the state. The 1968 amendment extended the grant to "five year" migrants, that is, those "settling out" for five years after ceasing to be migrants. Michigan received $524,000 for migrant education in 1967, $2,084,085 in 1968, and more than $3 million in 1969.[27]

Michigan initiated its program under the Elementary and Secondary Education Act in 1967, and by the next year 10,795 migrant children were attending summer school for an average of six weeks and an instructional day of seven hours. An additional 5,395 children attended regular schools during the school year. The total cost of the program was met by the federal government. The staff of the Compensatory Education Section of the Department of Education, which was in overall charge of the program, consisted of a coordinator and three consultants, of whom two were Mexican American and one, black. As it developed in the next few years, the program sought to employ teachers experienced in teaching disadvantaged youth. Michigan attempted to secure some of the teachers from Texas and Florida, the home states of so many Michigan migrants. Fourteen Mexican American teachers were thus recruited for the summer of 1968. Each classroom teacher was assisted by three teacher aides, a social worker, a social worker aide, and a guidance counselor, all of them drawn, if possible, from the ethnic group served by the school. A project director served as principal. The social worker aide worked with the families of migrant children who had "emotional and social needs" and also sought to gain community acceptance of the migrants. The subjects taught were reading, writing, arithmetic, social science, art, and music. English was taught as a second language. The teachers received in-service training and were provided with a *Handbook for Teachers of Migrant Children*. The program included the transportation of the children to the schools from the camps in which they lived, field trips, medical and dental service, three meals a day, and emergency clothing if needed. Day care and Head Start were sometimes associated with the summer schools. The 1968 summer school program was considered "perhaps the largest summer migrant education program" in the nation.[28]

During 1969 and 1970 thirteen year-round migrant education programs were operating in Michigan. Of the 2,109 children enrolled, 77 percent were Mexican Americans, and 14 percent were black. These programs took place in the public schools, most migrant children attending the regular classes. They also received special assistance for about two hours a day and benefited from some of the same auxiliary services provided the migrant summer school children.[29] The Michigan migrant education program also included two bookmobiles and a mobile unit that brought audiovisual and library material to concentrations of migrants who had dropped out of the migrant stream. The overall program in 1968 involved two hundred teachers and teacher aides.[30]

Those involved in the migrant education program thought it had resulted in "definite gains . . . both in academic achievement and pupil growth in self-confidence." The migrants themselves, however, testified before the CRC in 1968 that the program was not achieving its goals. They complained that it was both poorly administered and ineffectively implemented at both the regional and local levels, that teachers and administrators lacked interest in the program, that there were not enough Spanish-speaking administrators, and that the program did not provide a "meaningful education" for the children. A University of Michigan graduate student active in the 1968 summer school program characterized it as a "super-duper baby-sitting job."[31]

The generally low level of education of adult migrants—farmworkers over age forty-five averaged only 6.2 years of schooling according to a 1960 nationwide survey—was an obstacle to keeping them informed about their legal rights and responsibilities and the community services available to them, since some could not read the necessary informational material. The Catholic Apostolate, the Migrant Ministry, MMOI, and UMOI all addressed this matter to some degree. The Adult Education Division of the Michigan Department of Education and many local school districts aided UMOI in particular in planning an adult education program. The goal of the program was to enhance the employability of migrants who wished to leave the migrant stream and find more stable employment. UMOI and the Michigan Employment Security Commission (MESC) both took advantage of Manpower Development and Training Act funds to provide adult migrants with "basic education" in Kalamazoo and Muskegon in 1969.[32]

Like education, the poor health of migrants became a subject of public and private action in the 1960s. The migrants continued to suffer from "poor nutrition, diarrheal diseases, skin infections, and respiratory infections," and their infant mortality rate was double that of the resident population. Migrants received practically no prenatal care, 65 percent of them had not received any medical care, and 77 percent had never seen a dentist. Migrants, generally speaking, lacked the education, experience, and self-confidence either to recognize or sometimes to admit the need for medical attention, and the communities to which the migrants came were commonly unaware of their health problems.[33]

Relatively little had been done to address the migrant health problem until the enactment of the federal Migrant Health Act of 1962, which was extended for three years in 1965 and two years in 1968. The statute authorized the distribution of federal funds to public and nonprofit organizations to establish health service clinics for migrants and their families, to train persons to serve in these clinics, and also for hospitalization and special projects to improve health services for the migrants. Michigan supplemented the Migrant Health Act with project grants to local health departments and community agencies, a 1965 law requiring agricultural employers of one or more workers employed for five or more consecutive weeks to provide them with medical and hospital coverage, and a 1966 law providing for state reimbursement in full of county expenditures for hospital services to migrant workers.[34]

Michigan was actually "slow" to take advantage of the Migrant Health Act, partly because of "local opposition" by medical associations. As of January 2, 1964, only one migrant health project financed by federal funds had been established in the state, but as the result of "educational and promotional activities," six additional projects were developed that year, two by the state Department of Health, three by local health departments, and one by Michigan State University. Altogether, the clinics served about eighteen thousand persons. The Department of Health also established a Migrant Health Unit in 1964 to provide liaison among state, local government, and private agencies dealing with migrant health and also "to stimulate and improve" the use by migrants of the county health departments in the sixty-eight counties that had such departments.[35]

The eight migrant health projects in existence by 1968 served fifteen counties employing two-thirds of the migrant workers in the state. Local health departments, aided by the state, sponsored seven of these projects, and a nonprofit corporation in Benzie County sponsored the other. The projects provided diagnosis and treatment of minor illnesses in a clinic or a physician's office, drugs, immunization, medical and

300

consultant services, outpatient services like X rays, hospital care, dental care, nursing service, health education, and sanitation services. Of the total cost of $1,363,911, the federal government provided 52 percent ($708,001), the state and local governments, 48 percent ($655,910). The effect of the projects varied widely from county to county depending on the degree of local support and local attitudes.[36]

Intimately related to the migrants' health problems was the quality of their housing. As we have seen, in conformity with U.S. Department of Labor regulations, the MESC inspected camps in which workers from outside the state who had been recruited by that agency were employed. A majority of the migrants coming to Michigan were not, however, recruited by the MESC, which in 1965, for example, inspected only about 30 percent of the migrant camps. Although growers continued to build new living units and service buildings that provided showers, toilets, and laundry facilities, legislators who visited some of the camps in 1965 found the facilities "horrendous." As one of them said, the housing was "not *all* bad," but "it was mostly all bad," and most of it was "unfit for human habitation." Most migrants in the 1960s, as in the preceding decade, were housed in one-room dwellings, with a two-burner stove, a pit latrine, and one outdoor water faucet. Most of the housing lacked flush toilets, washbasins, running water, and refrigerators.[37]

Seeking to improve the quality of migrant housing, the legislature enacted a measure in 1965 requiring employers of five or more migrant agricultural laborers, beginning on January 1, 1966, to obtain an annual license from the state health commissioner in order to operate. The department was to grant the license if the camp conformed to the minimum regulations specified by the department regarding such matters as sewage, water supply, plumbing, and rubbish and garbage disposal. If the camp did not meet the minimum standards, the camp operator could receive a provisional license if he agreed to a "definite improvement program." A camp operator could receive a temporary license pending the results of an inspection or the correction of specified items, but he could not receive more than two consecutive temporary licenses; and as of January 1969, no further temporary licenses were to be issued. Violations of the act and the attendant regulations were deemed misdemeanors punishable by a fine of $200 or ninety days in jail. The measure provided for the establishment of an Agricultural Labor Camp Unit in the Division of Engineering of the Department of Public Health to implement the licensing program. The federal government's Department of Health, Education and Welfare funded the program until the 1968 fiscal year, when the program was jointly funded by the federal and state governments. The statute applied to 2,574 of the 3,500 camps as of 1966.[38]

To assist it in preparing the rules for camp licensing, the Department of Public Health appointed an Ad Hoc Advisory Committee of thirteen members representing growers, agricultural processors, migrant workers, local health departments, religious and fraternal organizations, and the general public. The rules went into effect on February 14, 1966. The Michigan standards were basically equivalent to the federal standards for the camps in the state coming within its jurisdiction, except that the Michigan standards did not originally require showers and hand-washing facilities. Growers spent an estimated $750,000 in improving their camp facilities during the first year the new program was in effect. Since many growers, however, found it difficult financially to make the necessary improvements, the legislature enacted a measure that became effective in August 1970 providing $500,000 for grants to the growers on a matching basis to build or repair migrant housing.[39]

The University of Michigan School of Public Health evaluated the 1965 licensing act after it had been in effect for two years and concluded that living conditions in the camps were better than they would have been without the statute. When the CRC interviewed migrant workers in 1968, however, many rated their housing as only "fair" and complained about leaky roofs and poor maintenance. The Agricultural Labor Camp Unit found an average of 3.5 violations (a total of 8,589) per camp in 1966 and 3.3 per camp (6,188) in 1967. The most frequent violations involved fire safety, toilet facilities, garbage and refuse disposal, lighting, and ventilation. The CRC staff, after talking to migrant workers and visiting the camps, concluded that they largely remained "far below decent living standards and even the most minimal standards of human dignity." The inspection legislation was "gutted," according to one source, when the penalty for violations was reduced from a "high misdemeanor" to a "normal misdemeanor." This removed violation cases from the state courts to local courts, which allegedly put "cronyism in the picture." Only six camp operators were taken to court in 1968 for camp violations, and they mostly received fines of not more than fifteen dollars.[40]

The Agricultural Labor Camp Unit received many complaints from growers about worker destruction of property such as newly installed screen doors and interior furnishings. Despite improvements made by all but a small minority of growers, however, 92 percent of the inspected camps as late as the summer of 1969 had no running water in their housing, 42 percent had leaky roofs, none had flush toilets, and 40 percent lacked bathing facilities. Legislation effective in January 1971 required showers and hand-washing facilities in migrant housing for the first time. Bad as the housing was, UMOI, which deplored the condition of the camps, concluded in the summer of 1968 that the Michigan camps were of better quality than those in other states.[41]

Although agriculture was the third most hazardous industry in the United States, Michigan did not until 1965 join the sixteen states that made at least some workmen's compensation available to migrants. The bill the governor signed into law that year, which became effective on May 1, 1966, provided that agricultural employers of three or more employees paid *hourly wages* for at least thirteen weeks in a fifty-two-week period were to be covered by the state's Workmen's Compensation Act. Not only did the statute exclude migrant workers paid by the piece, as most were, but it was also made even more restrictive in 1967, when it was amended to require that the agricultural workers covered by the law had to work thirteen consecutive weeks. Agricultural employers of one or more workers employed at least thirty hours per week for five consecutive weeks, however they were paid, were to provide their workers—who, of course, did not receive workmen's compensation—with medical and hospital coverage for personal injuries suffered in the course of their employment.[42]

The difficulty of applying workmen's compensation to migrant agricultural workers and the "exceedingly high rates" initially set by the insurance companies led the legislature to defer the effective date of the statute for one year. When the act did become effective on May 1, 1967, the Michigan Insurance Bureau found it difficult to decide on the rate or rates to recommend because of the lack of experience in the state in dealing with this type of insurance, the different rates seemingly needed for different types of farms, and the apparent inapplicability of the rates set in other states. The bureau set a rate for comprehensive coverage on December 1, 1967, but some companies offered coverage at different rates. Michigan was still struggling with this problem when the 1960s came to a close.[43]

Michigan adopted a minimum wage law in 1964, amended in 1966, that covered agricultural employers of four or more workers between the ages of eighteen and sixty-five who were employed at any time during the calendar year. The statute applied to workers engaged in harvesting activities whether they were paid by the hour or the piece. The minimum hourly wage was set at $1.00 beginning January 1, 1965, $1.15 beginning January 1, 1966, and $1.25 beginning January 1, 1967. The pay for piece-rate workers was to be the equivalent of the hourly rate and was to be set by a Wage Deviation Board appointed by the governor and made up of three employers, three employees, and three members of the general public. The board was to report by July 31, 1966, later extended to May 1, 1967, and was to set a piece rate that would be the equivalent of the minimal hourly wage when applied to a worker of average ability and diligence in harvesting a particular crop. Growers could deduct up to 16 percent for housing (if the housing had been licensed under the 1965 act), board, clothes, and other goods and services customarily provided their piece-rate workers, but only with the consent of the Wage Deviation Board. Hourly workers were to receive a statement of their wages, the number of hours worked, and the deductions from their wages, and employers subject to the act had to post a copy of the regulations in "a conspicuous place."[44]

The 1965 Michigan minimum hourly wage was slightly below the average hourly rate of $1.013 for farm labor in 1964; and the 1967 rate, although above the federal minimum wage of $1.00 for that year, was below the $1.30 average hourly wage for farm labor in Michigan. The Wage Deviation Board rates for particular crops were approved by the governor on June 14, 1967, and became effective on July 1, 1968. The CRC concluded in 1969 that the piece rates paid migrant workers were "consistently" below the hourly minimum rate, the difference varying from crop to crop. Another study indicated that the minimum wage law was "full of fish hooks for the worker and escape hatches for the employer." Growers sometimes made illegal deductions from worker wages and sometimes ignored the law altogether. The law was poorly enforced, partly because the legislature did not appropriate enough funds for that purpose. Employees who believed they were not receiving the proper minimum wage could seek the amount due them through the courts within a three-year period, but this was hardly a recourse of which migrant workers could avail themselves.[45]

In an effort to deal with employer violations of the minimum wage law, the legislature in 1969 adopted an amendment to the 1925 Payment of Wages Act that removed the act's exemption of agricultural labor. The amendment required employers to pay their migrant workers at least once every two weeks and to provide them with an itemized statement of their earnings and the employer deductions.[46]

As of the mid-1960s the old age insurance provision of the Social Security Act covered farmworkers who were paid at least $150 a year by an employer or who had worked twenty or more days for an employer for cash pay. The terms of the act excluded many migrants, and even when the law seemed to apply, it was indifferently observed. Growers told touring legislators that if a worker did not want his social security tax withheld, the employer did not do so. Some growers and crew leaders kept proper records, some did not. Agricultural employees were covered by the unemployment insurance provision of the Social Security Act if they worked for an employer who employed twenty or more workers for twenty weeks in the calendar year, which excluded most migrant workers.[47]

Because of residence requirements, migrants were excluded from the welfare assistance legally available to residents. As a result, migrants in need often had to turn to the Migrant Ministry or the Michigan Apostolate Center for emergency aid. In April 1968 the U.S. Supreme Court invalidated state residency requirements for welfare assistance. The state government thereafter met 40 percent of the county welfare costs. Food stamps also were made available to needy migrants.[48]

Child labor remained prevalent in Michigan agriculture in the 1960s despite the federal government's Sugar Act and the Fair Labor Standards Act. The CRC thus reported in 1968 that more than half of the migrant labor force in Michigan consisted of youngsters aged twelve to eighteen. As of 1965, ten states had laws limiting the employment of children in agriculture outside of school hours, but Michigan was not among them. Agricultural employers continued to defend the use of child labor. The secretary of the Michigan Association of Cherry Producers thus wrote the U.S. Senate Subcommittee on Migratory Labor in 1963 that migrants worked as a family and would be discouraged from seeking employment if restrictions were placed on the employment of their children. "There are valuable lessons of responsibility to be gained" from the employment of children, he added, "as well as the importance of keeping them occupied."[49]

Michigan followed the lead of other states in 1966 by supplementing the federal government's Farm Labor Contractor Registration Act with legislation providing for the licensing and regulation of emigrant agents operating within the state. The agents had to pay an annual license fee, submit a $2,000 performance bond, and file weekly reports listing the members of their crew, their wages and terms of employment, the transportation arrangements, and the type and place of work of the crew. As with the federal law, the hope was to remove crew leaders who exploited the workers in their charge.[50]

Federal law provided for the regulation of the interstate transportation of migrants by certain kinds of motor vehicle carriers. Michigan in 1965 enacted legislation requiring the State Department of Agriculture to adopt rules and regulations by July 1, 1966, to protect the health and safety of migrant agricultural workers on their way to and from their employment in groups of three or more in a motor vehicle carrier. The authority to establish the rules and regulations governing the motor vehicles covered by the law was transferred by another 1966 law from the Department of Agriculture to the Public Service Division of the Department of Commerce.[51]

In 1966 the Michigan legislature recognized the need for temporary rest stops for migrants while they were en route to their place of employment. The legislation authorized two such stops, one in the southeastern part of the state, one in the southwestern part, but the legislature failed to appropriate the necessary funds to set up the facilities. The Benton

Harbor rest camp that had been available to migrants gave way at the same time to real estate expansion.[52]

Acting on a recommendation of the Governor's Commission on Migrant Labor, the legislature appropriated funds in 1965 for the establishment of a Rural Manpower Center at Michigan State University. The center was charged with developing a program of research and education regarding "the human factor in agriculture." In fulfilling its obligations, the center created a number of task forces to deal with housing, farm labor management, grower education, the training of migrant workers, and the education of migrant children. It included a Knowledge Center that accumulated data concerning farm labor and issued reports on the subject. In 1966 a special task force of the center developed a set of criteria for the evaluation of rural housing, including housing for farm labor, and it encouraged growers to improve their housing. At the request of the Wage Deviation Board, the center gathered the productivity data required for the board to set the minimum piece rates for migrant workers. In 1967 the center conducted a series of workshops and meetings designed, among other things, to acquaint growers with the labor regulations affecting them. It also undertook a study of farm accidents in Michigan so as to facilitate the application of the state's Workmen's Compensation Act to farm labor.[53]

The governor and the Governor's Commission, in an effort to encourage local action to improve the lot of the migrants, recommended in 1965 that counties in which migrant laborers were employed in large numbers should establish county migrant labor councils. Eight such councils had been established by the end of 1968, serving as "a kind of 'responsible conscience' " for the well-being of migrant laborers and as a forum where interested parties could develop plans for migrant improvement. Made up of growers, businessmen, teachers, and church people, among others, the councils generally provided migrants and their families with health and recreational services. On the whole, however, they appear to have been of little effect, at least in the short run.[54]

Since the bulk of the migrants were members of minority groups and were commonly the victims of discrimination, it is surprising that the CRC did not address itself to the migrant problem until 1968. On March 1, 1968, Roy O. Fuentes, director of the Northern Michigan Region of the CRC and the commission's liaison with Hispanics in the migrant stream, submitted a report to the commission on the problems of the state's migrant workers. Although focusing on the out-of-state migrants, about two-thirds of whom were Hispanic, Fuentes noted that there was "a great deal of unrest" in the state's resident Hispanic community that was "hidden all too often under the shadow of the great Negro revolution." He described the sad lot of the migrants and noted, correctly, that the federal and state legislation to improve migrant conditions was being weakly enforced, "with the leniency weighted toward the employer." He deplored the attitude toward the migrants in the communities where they lived and worked, asserting that the prevailing view was that the migrant was a "foreigner" who was "supposed to come, do his work, and leave quickly and quietly" without receiving the benefits reserved for residents. Fuentes urged the CRC to make the public aware of "the gross pattern of discrimination [against migrants] because of national origin and race" and to survey major migrant campsites in the state, hold a public hearing to receive migrant testimony, and recommend appropriate "protective legislation."[55]

One Romney aide thought that the Fuentes assessment was "a remarkably unbalanced and unfair presentation of the issues," largely because he had ignored the employer point of view. Another Romney aide, however, maintained that the assessment, although "somewhat overdrawn in spots," was "basically accurate." This aide thought that the growers had been successful over the years in protecting their interests vis-à-vis the migrants and that, therefore, a focus on the migrant problem from the migrant point of view was "not necessarily out of order."[56]

The CRC, perhaps also responding to the MCAFW and the urging of the governor, followed Fuentes's advice and held a public hearing on migrant farm labor on August 25 and 26, 1968. As the commission noted, this was its "first close look at the conditions associated with seasonal farm labor." Preceding the hearing, 1,114 migrants and 194 growers responded to a CRC informational survey dealing with housing, education, social services, medical care, wages, and migrant aspirations. The commission employed five Spanish speakers to conduct interviews with migrants in thirteen counties.

In their responses to the CRC survey, the growers stressed the improvements they had made in camp housing in the preceding three years and claimed that they abided by legislation and regulations pertaining to their migrant workers. Although 91 percent of the growers maintained that their workers received a "fair wage," 39 percent of them conceded that they did not provide their employees with the required rate sheets indicating the minimum piece rates that had been set, and 10 percent admitted that they did not provide their workers with the required statements about their hourly pay and employer deductions. The project staff encountered growers who described Mexican Americans as "happy simple people who had not yet advanced to the mechanical aptitude of an Anglo."

Migrants in their responses complained about the quality of their housing. Only 29 percent of the migrants agreed with the growers that they were receiving a fair wage, and 4 percent claimed that they had not been paid wages due them. Black migrants reported that they were paid less than white migrants. Although staff interviewers thought that the migrants feared to be honest about their treatment, migrants nevertheless expressed their dissatisfaction with the migrant way of life. Only 5 percent of the migrants indicated that they wanted their children to become migrant laborers.[57]

Growers, migrants, state officials, and representatives of private organizations—about three dozen persons in all—testified at the CRC public hearings. Approximately two hundred migrants attended the hearings. As in the written responses, some witnesses presented "a grim picture" of migrant conditions.[58] The CRC concluded from the hearings that "very serious problems" had been raised that needed to be addressed. In the CRC's view, migrant laborers had been "systematically excluded from civil and legal rights, opportunities, and privileges" in three general ways. For one thing, they were not covered by either the National Labor Relations Act or the Michigan Labor Mediation Act, and the laws that did apply to them were inadequate if not "meaningless." Second, the CRC reported, the relevant laws were weakly enforced by an insufficient number of staff persons, who, in any event, were indifferent or insensitive to migrants and their problems. Not enough of those dealing with migrants spoke Spanish, and the agencies involved did not inform migrants of their rights and failed to contact them when necessary. Finally, the CRC maintained, there was a lack of coordination among the state agencies involved with migrants and "gaps" in the services available to them.

Quite apart from its specific recommendations regarding employment, housing, education, health and social services, community attitudes, and federal government responsibilities for migrants, the CRC recommended that Michigan extend to migrants the same protections provided workers in other occupational groups. It urged that agencies working with migrants employ Spanish-speaking personnel, develop informational material for migrants written in understandable Spanish, and design services to reach the migrant population. It recommended that task forces at both the federal and state levels develop ways to coordinate the work of the agencies dealing with migrants, eliminate gaps in the services for them, and enforce the laws applying to them. It also urged that residency laws barring migrants from receiving social service benefits be repealed.[59]

The CRC met with state and local officials to discuss its report and recommendations, which it published in both Spanish and English, and it was pleased with the reaction to the report throughout the nation. It continued to press for the migrant legislation it thought needed and

conducted "wage and agency effectiveness studies." CRC field representatives informed migrants of their rights under the law with regard to
their wages and told them whom to contact if they wanted legal aid, if
they needed assistance in obtaining social services, or if they experienced
discrimination because of their national origin, color, race, religion, age,
or sex. The commission worked with Lake Michigan College to develop
educational programs to assist migrants and ex-migrants seeking a "new
living and working environment." In 1970 it assigned three Spanish-
speaking staff members to recently established migrant centers in the
state to counsel migrants who were having problems with growers, accept their complaints, and provide them with needed referral services.[60]

The CRC was concerned not only with migrants but also with
Hispanics, many of them former migrants who had settled in Michigan.
Indeed, by the end of 1969 the commission was beginning to shift
its concern from migrant laborers to the special problems of former
migrants and the resident Hispanic population. In 1968 it held meetings
with Hispanics in eight cities to inform them of their legal rights, secure
their cooperation in effecting community change, increase Hispanic
employment both in the private and public spheres, and encourage
eligible Hispanic families to avail themselves of OEO aid. The CRC
also served as a consultant to La Raza Unida. The head of the CRC
Compliance Division met with Mexican American groups in Saginaw in
May 1968 to discuss the civil rights problems they had encountered and
accepted six complaints from them alleging denial of equal employment.
In the summer of 1968 the CRC added two Mexican Americans to its
staff, and it made "a diligent effort" to add more. In August 1969
Governor Milliken appointed a Hispanic who was the grandson of
a migrant farmworker to the CRC itself. In 1970 the CRC initiated
an Urban Pilot Project that involved the assignment of bilingual field
representatives to Battle Creek and Lansing to determine the extent of
discrimination and disenfranchisement experienced by former migrants
making the transition to urban residence.[61]

Responding to a CRC recommendation, Governor Milliken in May
1969 appointed a Governor's Task Force on Migrant Labor to develop
recommendations on how to improve the services to migrant laborers
in the state and also to consider the program needs of resident Mexican
Americans who were no longer part of the migrant labor force. In
its final report in October, the task force concluded that Michigan
had done "much more" for migrants than was commonly believed but
that "more" remained to be done. The CRC thought the report "non-
coordinated and non-specific" and "diluted" by the coupling of migrant
programs with those for the rural poor in general. The CRC's "most
serious disagreement" with the task force was its refusal to accept the

CRC recommendation that migrants be accorded the right to bargain collectively through their chosen representatives despite the seasonal character of their employment.[62]

Many task force recommendations were rather quickly implemented either by legislation or executive orders. The actions taken included the establishment of a Michigan Council of Rural Affairs; designation by each appropriate state agency of an individual responsible for its activities in dealing with ex-migrants; providing for better enforcement of existing legislation; appointment of more Spanish-speaking staff; provision of funds to improve migrant housing and for the Department of Education to develop a program of bilingual education; increase of the minimum wage for farm labor to $1.45 on July 1, 1970, and $1.60 on July 1, 1971; the establishment in each county where migrants were employed of an area council consisting of representatives of agricultural employers, migrants, and representatives of state agencies dealing with migrants; and the creation of a new Interagency Committee on Migrant Affairs. Some actions were also taken to improve the condition of migrants who had left the migrant stream to settle in Michigan. Milliken, who had added two Mexican Americans to his own staff, proclaimed in July 1970, with some reason, that more had been done for migrants in Michigan in the preceding twelve months than in any comparable period. He conceded, however, that despite "the good beginning," the state still had "a long way to go."[63]

There is no question that Michigan in the 1960s and early 1970s sought by both legislation and executive action, as well as by the actions of private organizations, to ameliorate the terrible conditions under which migrant laborers lived and worked. Unfortunately, actions taken were not always effectively implemented, and what remained to be done loomed larger than what had been done. When CRC staffers toured migrant facilities in the Benton Harbor area in the summer of 1971 and interviewed migrants, growers, and government officials to ascertain what if any progress regarding migrants had been made since the CRC's 1968 hearings and its 1969 report and recommendations, they were "encouraged by many of the developments." They were "particularly impressed" by Department of Education efforts to provide "innovative and complete services" for migrant youngsters even though the head of the Rural Manpower Center had dismissed the migrant education program as "only a drop in the bucket." They also thought that there was more "dialogue" between growers and their workers than there had been two or three years earlier.

Despite such improvements, the CRC staffers concluded that "the overall picture [was] clearly . . . one of disturbing conditions and unmet needs." They reported that housing conditions were mostly "deplorable"

310

and that migrants paid by the piece, as most of them were, were still not receiving the minimum pay due them. Staff members pointed out that state agency coordination in dealing with migrants remained "a major problem" and that government officials were not "fully sensitive" to migrant needs.[64]

As the 1960s gave way to the 1970s, migrants continued to be victims of discrimination "just below the surface in most communities." They were stereotyped as "lazy," "dirty," and "different." African Americans received the worst treatment among the migrants, but the reception accorded Mexican Americans was "only slightly less devastating."[65]

What is distressing is how little the condition of the migrants improved in Michigan after the 1960s. Reports as late as 1996 indicated that Michigan schools were still failing to educate migrant children, who continued to receive little formal schooling and had a high dropout rate. Migrant pay continued to be low, their work exhausting, and their prospects for improvement just about nil.[66] Resistance to change typified most problems to which the CRC and other Michigan organizations at that time addressed themselves, but none proved as unyielding as Michigan's migrant labor problem.

15

THE CIVIL RIGHTS COMMISSION, LAW ENFORCEMENT, AND THE DETROIT RIOT OF 1967

Because of growing racial turbulence during the years of the Romney governorship and the close association between racial disorders and police practices, the CRC's efforts to influence police behavior and to mitigate racial tensions lest they lead to rioting became an increasingly important commission responsibility and concern. As Burton Gordin, the CRC's executive director, observed, the relationship between police and African Americans became "the flash point" of race-related violence in Michigan and the nation in the 1960s.[1]

Law enforcement complaints were second only to employment complaints among the complaints processed by the CRC, the number increasing from 77 in 1964 to 267 in 1968. Law enforcement complaints constituted 9.8 percent of the complaints received by the CRC in 1964 and 13.1 percent in 1968. The most frequent complaints were for physical abuse, harassment, illegal arrest, and denial of service. The overwhelming percentage of the law enforcement complaints were directed at the actions of police officers. Just under half the complainants were under twenty-nine years of age, and the level of education of law enforcement complainants was lower than for any other civil rights area within the CRC's jurisdiction.[2]

In an opinion issued on December 14, 1964, Samuel H. Olsen, the Wayne County prosecutor, contended that the CRC lacked authority to review the actions of local police officers or the decisions of prosecuting attorneys regarding criminal prosecutions and law enforcement. He advised law enforcement personnel in the county that they were not required to respond to CRC inquiries or to submit to investigation by CRC representatives seeking information about alleged civil rights violations. Attorney General Frank Kelley promptly repudiated the Olsen interpretation of the law and ruled that all state and local law enforcement agencies and personnel were subject to the CRC's jurisdiction in civil rights matters.[3]

The CRC's "first major program" in the area of law enforcement compliance resulted from complaints of discrimination against the Detroit Police Department (DPD), a department that remained at the center of the CRC's concern about law enforcement and civil rights throughout the Romney governorship. Almost three-quarters of the law enforcement complaints processed by the CRC originated in the Detroit metropolitan area, a higher percentage than for any other civil rights area subject to the commission's jurisdiction. Blacks complained about illegal arrests, open searching of their person in public places, physical abuse, and derogatory references to their race and color. In a memorandum to the CRC in early August 1964, CRC staff personnel advised the commission that relations between the police and Detroit's black community were "not good" and were attended by "persistent conflict and tension." One reason for this, the staff believed, was that of 4,600 Detroit police, only 140, or 3 percent, were black in a city whose population was more than 30 percent black. The staff believed that Police Commissioner George Edwards, Jr., and Police Chief Ray Girardin, who succeeded Edwards as commissioner at the end of 1963, "related well" to the black community and that the problem of "community confidence" regarding the police was at the department level below the two. The staff recommended a series of corrective measures to deal with the problem, and although it did not regard "a racial explosion" in Detroit as probable, it thought that prompt "preventive action" was the best guarantee that such an explosion would not occur in the city, as it already had in New York's Bedford-Stuyvesant area, Rochester, Jersey City, and in Michigan on a smaller scale in Jackson and Lansing.[4]

Officials representing the CRC and the DPD agreed in September 1964 that after each agency had independently investigated complaints against the Detroit department, the two would jointly consider the findings and attempt to devise an adjustment. If a civil rights violation had occurred, they were to arrange "corrective, remedial, or disciplinary action" against the offending officer, appropriate relief or remedy for the claimant, and action to prevent recurrence of the offense. If the two could not agree on an adjustment, the CRC, as with other claims, was to hold a public hearing, and, if necessary, issue an order for corrective action. Although the CRC soon announced "significant progress" in closing four cases against the Detroit department, agreeing with the claimant in two of them and with the police in the other two, Burton Gordin was complaining by the end of November that the CRC was "continuing to have difficulty" in conducting investigations of complaints against the DPD. Chief Girardin, to be sure, was cooperating with the commission, but its field representatives were experiencing delays in securing records and information from department subordinates. The police, for their part, were complaining about "harassing" interrogation by CRC personnel.[5]

The CRC and Girardin reached a second agreement in April 1965, slightly amended the next year, that set forth the procedures to be followed in investigating complaints against the department and that seemingly resolved the differences that had affected previous investigations. The two were henceforth to investigate civil rights complaints jointly where practicable, but each could conduct its separate investigation. The DPD agreed to make all relevant records available to the CRC during the course of an investigation of a complaint, except that police personnel could remove documents that were "strictly personal" and had no bearing on the case. Records that the police turned over to the CRC and, beginning in April 1966, any oral or written statements that the CRC obtained from police personnel were to be kept confidential by the commission other than with the permission of the police commissioner, as the result of court process, or at the time of a public hearing. If the CRC found probable cause to issue a complaint, representatives of the two agencies were to meet to seek an adjustment, which was to be subject to the approval of the CRC and the police commissioner. The presidents of the Detroit Police Officers Association and the Detroit Detectives Union criticized the agreement for involving an outside agency in police affairs.[6]

From January 1964 through March 30, 1966, the CRC received a total of 114 complaints against the DPD relating to 78 separate incidents. Sixty-two of the complaints involved allegations of physical abuse; 48, harassment; and 29, verbal abuse. Ten of the claimants were white, the remainder, black. Of the 61 cases resolved as of March 30, the CRC found probable cause for a civil rights violation in 32, which were terminated by adjustment. The CRC believed, however, that the disciplinary actions taken by the DPD for civil rights violations were all too often not commensurate with the seriousness of the offense, going beyond a written reprimand in only two instances. The commission made this point to the DPD on several occasions and did so publicly on April 27, 1965.

The CRC noted that many police officers had met the commission's investigations with "hostility and suspicion," the DPD, like other local police departments in the state, viewing the CRC as "a Negro front organization." The commission did not believe that the education program for police officers that the CRC and the DPD had planned would in itself dispel this kind of reaction. In the commission's view, the "most effective way" to produce a commitment by the police to the principle of equal law enforcement was "statements and actions" by higher officers in the department. Since it also believed that the very small number of black police officers was "a major factor" in causing black suspicion of the DPD, the commission urged the department to make special efforts to hire and promote black police.[7]

The CRC did not itself escape criticism for its handling of complaints against the DPD. A citizens' panel in Detroit complained that the commission investigated claims against the department interminably and that when it did find probable cause for a civil rights violation, it accepted adjustments that did not provide adequate punishment for the offenses committed. The panel urged the CRC to "get tough" with police officers guilty of misconduct and with department officials who failed to take appropriate action against police offenders.[8]

Quite apart from its agreement with the CRC on the procedure for investigating complaints, the DPD took a series of steps designed to eliminate departmental practices that had offended blacks, among others. In December 1964 the DPD discontinued arrests for disorderly conduct, which had been exceeding eight to nine hundred per month and were often an "arrest on suspicion only." In the next few months the department decided to abandon "tipover raids," arrests made without a warrant against "blind pigs," that is, after-hours drinking establishments and gambling facilities. Police officers were ordered to address citizens by their appropriate titles and surnames. The department added to the amount of instruction in human relations in the Police Academy training course, placed an African American on the academy staff, and appointed an African American to serve as administrative assistant to the police commissioner. It reorganized its Citizen Complaint Bureau, which the police commissioner had instituted in 1961 to investigate complaints of police misconduct. The bureau office was now moved out of police headquarters, where it had initially been lodged, and it was authorized not only to investigate citizen complaints but also, for the first time, to initiate investigations on its own.[9]

The CRC's concern about police behavior was not, of course, limited to the DPD. Following some interracial violence in Jackson in the late summer and early fall of 1964, Burton Levy, the CRC's director of community services, met with the Jackson Human Relations Commission, city officials, and the head of the local NAACP to discuss the matter. Characterizing the city as "ghettoized" and as offering blacks only limited job opportunities, Levy advised the Human Relations Commission to meet with local businessmen in an effort to end "bars" to equality of opportunity in downtown stores and shops, and he urged city officials to develop a community educational program dealing with civil rights and human relations. The police chief agreed to work with CRC staff to provide an in-service training program for the city's police force.[10]

Toward the end of 1964, after the Jackson disturbance, the Michigan Association of Chiefs of Police (MACP), at the CRC's suggestion, created a Human Relations Commission to work with the CRC in planning and implementing a program for police officers dealing with civil rights and police-community relations. Early in 1965 the MACP formed a Community Relations Committee to serve as a "liaison and planning group" to work with the CRC in dealing with civil rights matters. In June and July 1965 the CRC, in conjunction with the MACP and Michigan State University's School of Police, conducted civil rights seminars in various regions of the state that were attended by five hundred chiefs of police, sheriffs, State Police officers, and private citizens.

At its annual meeting in 1966, the MACP issued a public statement announcing its intention to work to end discrimination not just in law enforcement but also in housing, education, and employment. The MACP was the first professional police organization in the nation to take such a position. It was also the only state police association to have its own "internal Civil Rights Committee."[11]

The Michigan Law Enforcement Training Act, which became effective on January 1, 1966, provided training standards for police officers and for the establishment of regional training centers to implement the program. Michigan State University had a police training program in effect by then, and Oakland Community College was planning its own program. CRC police-community relations specialists met with directors of the two college programs to plan for the inclusion of civil rights issues in their curricula. By the middle of April 1966, also, ten police departments in the state were including some human relations instruction in their training programs.[12]

The MACP cooperated with the CRC in the development and implementation of the Police Recruitment Project. The project was developed in the summer of 1966 by Burton Levy and Glenford Leonard, the MACP chairman, and was officially launched in March 1967. The chairman of the project was Edward N. Hodges, the former FEPC official who had become general employment supervisor of Michigan Bell. The Office of Law Enforcement Assistance of the U.S. Department of Justice awarded the project a grant of $15,000 in May 1967. The goal of the project was the recruitment of one thousand police officers, half of them black, in the twelve months beginning June 1, 1967.[13]

In addition to issuing promotional materials, the project organized local Police Recruitment Councils in various cities in the state made up of local police officers and community people. The project also established a Project Referral Office in Detroit to accept and follow up on inquiries, applications, and police department referrals. The Chrysler Corporation, Michigan Bell, and the U.S. Community Relations Service aided the recruitment effort. The project was handicapped from the start, however, by the unwillingness of most police chiefs to provide any meaningful support for their particular Recruitment Council and also by the great Detroit riot of July 1967 and the riots in other cities that ensued.[14]

The CRC sought to increase the number of blacks not only in the city police departments but also in the Michigan National Guard. At the request of Governor Romney, Gordin met in January 1965 with a group of black Guardsmen to discuss this matter. There had been about four hundred blacks in the Guard a few years earlier, but that number had dwindled to about one hundred at the time of the meeting. Those present agreed that the Guard, as Governor Williams had ordered, did not discriminate against blacks, but the Guardsmen indicated that members of their race did not "feel welcome" in some Guard units and that blacks were not being "actively encouraged" to join the Guard. Gordin recommended that the governor and the Guard attempt to stimulate black recruitment and that the commanding officers of the Guard receive training in human relations.[15]

On May 5, 1965, Romney issued an executive order declaring that it was "the continuing policy" of the Guard to conduct all of its activities, namely, "enlistment, appointment, assignment, advancement, professional improvement, promotion and retention," without discrimination. National Guard commanders were directed to make this clear in recruitment literature and recruitment efforts and to advise personnel in their units accordingly. The governor instructed the state's adjutant general to issue any directives necessary to implement the order and to review "immediately" any evidence of unequal treatment or "interracial difficulties" in any unit of the Guard and to take whatever corrective action was necessary. The order did not lead, at least in the short run, to any significant increase in the number of black Guardsmen. As of the time of the Detroit riot, the Guard was still being viewed as "all white," although that was not literally true.[16]

The State Police was literally "all white" when the riot began. The organization had made some effort in 1965 to recruit blacks, especially between the ages of eighteen and twenty-nine, but the results were disappointing, to say the least. Toward the end of June 1967, Senator Coleman Young of Detroit asked the CRC to work with the Civil Service

Commission (CSC) to review State Police recruitment procedures, and the CSC promptly complied. CRC officials met with the head of the CSC, the director of the State Police, and Young on July 21, and they agreed on "a number of affirmative actions" by the State Police to recruit nonwhites. Two days later Detroit became the scene of a major race-related riot.[17]

Because of racial conflicts in various parts of the state, the CRC in its first year developed a tension-control program. The commission, indeed, recognized tension control as providing "a creative opportunity" to promote its goals. In August 1964 the CRC provided city officials and police chiefs with some background information on the "Negro Revolution in America" and suggested "preventive steps" they could take to forestall "a racial explosion" in their communities. Mayors and police chiefs were advised to issue an "unequivocal public statement" recognizing the right of all citizens to equal protection and treatment under the law. Communities were asked to consider the establishment of a "Police Review Board" that would include reputable citizens to deal with allegations of police misconduct or brutality, since police investigations of their own misdeeds generally failed to "satisfy . . . the test of impartial and objective determination." The CRC advised police departments to recruit minority members aggressively, make sure that departmental hiring, promotion, and placement policies were free of discrimination, adopt in-service training programs that emphasized "good human relations," and establish "maximum communications and cooperation" with their community and especially with the black leadership in the community.[18]

When there were racial disorders in Benton Harbor, Jackson, and Lansing in 1966, CRC staff members engaged in "prolonged and intensive" work in these communities. The commission's most effective effort in this regard, in its judgment, occurred in Benton Harbor in August. After a night of some violence, CRC officials and State Police arrived on the scene. The next day the CRC staffers secured the cooperation of young persons in the community in helping to keep people off the streets that night, aided adults in forming a "police patrol," worked with the mayors and township officials in the Benton Harbor–St. Joseph area in preparing statements to calm the population and promising to deal with the causes of the disorder, and cooperated with the state and local police.[19]

"The issue facing the cities of our state," John Feikens noted to Gordin in September 1966, "is whether they want an abrasive Michigan Civil Rights Commission to point out these [race relations] difficulties and to sit down and help the cities get into these programs with the Negro groups or whether they wish to remain apathetic until there is violence." Gordin suggested a conference of mayors, city managers, police chiefs, and human relations commissions of about twenty cities with large numbers of minority-group members to discuss preventive action. The CRC followed this suggestion, holding a conference of municipal officials in Lansing in January 1967 that included a workshop on law enforcement. Levy advised those present that if they followed the CRC's suggestions, there was no guarantee that they could prevent a civil disorder in their community, but at least the police department could say that it had not been the cause of the trouble. He recommended that the communities essentially follow the guidelines for tension control that the CRC had set forth in August 1964.[20]

In March 1967 the CRC concluded that there were "potentially explosive community tensions" in eighteen of the state's cities. In May the CRC advised city officials that, in view of the racial disturbances of the previous summer, they must act to improve race relations in their communities, especially in communities with a substantial minority population. The commission advised the strengthening of communication with black leaders in the community, a program of summer employment for minority youth, a recreational program that involved "a broad age group," using the local news media to deal with rumors, convincing victims of segregation and discrimination that the city government was sensitive to their problems and was seeking to correct them, and having the police department "reemphasize the equal application of its rules and regulations regarding courtesy, conduct, and language." City officials were advised that the CRC regional director in their area was available to assist them, and the commission offered its own "cooperation and resources." Regional CRC directors then met with city officials to discuss the commission's advice. "Our thrust," the CRC's director of compliance asserted, "is to see that issues are faced and dealt with so social change can take place in the community, and hopefully eliminate the need for civil disorder."[21]

Preparing for possible racial trouble in the summer of 1967, the CRC organized four teams of regional directors and compliance personnel to respond to "tension situations." The plan was for each team to be headed by a director of operations and to include a command post assistant, a black community contact, and a white community contact. In the event of a disorder in a community, a peace patrol was to be organized that would ask persons in the area of the disorder to leave the scene and would attempt to persuade youths in the community to stay away from the disorder area. The CRC prepared an informational packet for each city with a potential for civil disorder that included the names of key individuals, a community profile, and relevant statistical information.[22]

320

In the end, the CRC's efforts, however well advised, did not prevent the outbreak of race-related rioting in fifteen Michigan cities in July 1967, most notably in Detroit. The Detroit riot, "the worst civil disorder" experienced by any American city in the twentieth century up to that time, resulted in 43 deaths, 657 injuries, 7,231 arrests, 682 riot-connected fires, and the looting of about 1,700 stores. It required the combined force of the DPD, the Michigan State Police, the Michigan National Guard, and the U.S. Army—a total of about seventeen thousand men—to quell the disorder. The other Michigan riots of the same time did not result in any deaths other than in Pontiac, where two blacks were killed.[23]

In the early stages of the Detroit riot, the CRC assisted city officials in the planning of strategy. Staff members kept the governor informed, and Damon Keith and an aide remained at the Detroit command post during the first night of the riot to observe developments and to act in an advisory capacity. As the riot developed, the CRC helped to establish communication between community leaders and city, state, and federal officials, and Keith presided at the key meeting that led to the decision to seek a commitment of federal troops to the city. Commission staff kept in touch with "grass roots community people" in the riot areas, talked with citizens in these areas, and collected information. CRC representatives also met with city officials and community leaders in Pontiac, Flint, Grand Rapids, and Saginaw in an effort to bring the disorders in these cities under control.[24]

On July 28 the CRC began to focus its attention on the constitutional rights of the numerous riot arrestees in Detroit. Commission observers were stationed in thirteen Detroit police precincts, the Detroit Receiving Hospital, the Wayne County Juvenile Home, and the sheriffs' offices in communities in the Detroit metropolitan area. The personnel assigned to serve as observers at the various places of detention were recruited from the CRC staff and the Michigan Department of Social Services. The commission sent telegrams to President Lyndon B. Johnson, Governor Romney, Mayor Jerome Cavanagh, and other government officials requesting that constitutional guaranties be accorded priority in the riot. Sometimes police cooperated with the observers, but at other times they were "hostile." A white police officer in one precinct made "highly derogatory remarks" about a black CRC staff member, commenting that all people like him should be killed. The CRC believed, probably correctly, that the presence of the observers had led to the "civil treatment" of arrestees at the places where the observers had been stationed. The commission concluded that it should have had observers at the places of detention from the very beginning of the disorder.[25]

When Governor Romney soon after the riot asked the various state departments to submit suggestions for appropriate legislation in view of what had occurred, Gordin urged the enactment of the model civil rights bill that had been introduced in the Michigan House in the most recent legislative session. An adaptation for Michigan of the Model Anti-Discrimination Act approved in 1966 by the National Conference of Commissioners on Uniform State Laws, the measure was designed "to codify, clarify and explain civil rights guaranties and establish procedures for their implementation." It covered employment, education, public accommodations, and real property transactions. Gordin also recommended legislation to provide for the revocation of the licenses of real estate brokers and salesmen who discriminated on the basis of race or religion, as well as the imposition of criminal sanctions on violators. As before the riot, he urged that the National Guard and State Police, the color of whose members' skin had become all too evident in the Detroit riot, make a determined effort to recruit blacks. The Michigan NAACP also recommended the enactment of the Model Anti-Discrimination Act as well as a state open occupancy law, and it joined Romney in calling for a substantial increase in the CRC budget. Elected co-chairmen of the CRC in early November 1967, Sidney M. Shevitz and the Reverend A. A. Banks, Jr., called for the elimination of the conditions that had produced the summer's violence. "The constitutional guaranty of equality of opportunity," they declared, "has not been sufficiently realized."[26]

After the Detroit riot, the Civil Service Commission reported that "substantial efforts" had been made by the State Police, aided by the CRC, to recruit nonwhites. On August 18, 1967, the State Police swore in the first black trooper in the fifty-year history of the organization. Thirty blacks sought to join the State Police between July 21, 1967, and January 5, 1968, but only seven of them passed the required written test, three then failed the required background investigation, three were awaiting their background investigation, and one had been placed on the State Police register and offered a position. This altogether dismal result of the State Police's recruiting efforts could hardly have been encouraging to prospective black troopers. As of April 1, 1968, less than 1 percent of the troopers were black. Efforts, however, were under way by then to aid blacks in passing the written examination and to improve the screening process. In December 1968 the State Police and the CRC agreed on the cooperative action the two would take in the event of racial tension or civil disorder in the state.[27]

In the federal government's view, the Detroit riot experience provided strong evidence that the National Guard must recruit more nonwhites. Responding to this contention, the director of the Michigan State

Military Department informed Romney that the Guard had not been seeking to recruit blacks because of the freeze on Guard enlistments and U.S. Army policy requiring the Guard to enlist non–prior service personnel on its waiting list in the order in which they had appeared for enlistment. He noted, however, that the Guard had secured a list of about twenty-five hundred Detroit blacks with prior military experience whom it would invite to Guard social functions so that they could become acquainted with Guardsmen and the Guard. This effort was coordinated with the CRC.[28]

The CRC advised Romney in April 1968 that the police departments in the state were in need of a "drastic, general overhaul." It was becoming obvious by the time the CRC made this judgment that the Police Recruitment Project would not even come close to reaching its goal of five hundred new black police by June 1, 1968. As of the end of December 1967, only ninety blacks and four Hispanics had been recruited by the state's police departments, and the project, if anything, appeared to be losing its momentum. Gordin reported to Romney in May 1968 that the project had demonstrated that "most police people [in Michigan] were unwilling to really go out in the community and actively seek Negro recruits" in the way that industrial firms and the police in Chicago and Philadelphia were doing. He noted, furthermore, that a survey of police departments in the state had revealed that few black police officers had been upgraded to supervisory positions and that this had served to "reinforce the feeling [among blacks] that the police department is the repressive tool of the white majority."[29]

At the request of the governor's office, the CRC in May 1968 prepared an analysis of the state of police-community relations in Michigan. In making the request, Romney was probably responding not just to the CRC but also to the belief of the Michigan State Advisory Committee to the U.S. Commission on Civil Rights that police-community relations constituted "the greatest threat to racial peace in Michigan." In introducing the requested survey, the CRC presented statistics showing the "gross underrepresentation" of blacks in the municipal police departments of the state by comparing the percentage of blacks in a city's police force with the estimated percentage of blacks in its population as of 1967. For Detroit, the comparative figures were 6 (289 officers) and 36; for Grand Rapids, 3.3 (9 officers) and 8.5; for Flint, 1.5 (5 officers) and 21.4; for Jackson, 1 (1 officer) and 11; for Kalamazoo, 2.2 (3 officers) and 7.1; for Pontiac, 3.8 (5 officers) and 19.8; for Saginaw, 7 (11 officers) and 19.4; and for Battle Creek, 4.2 (3 officers) and 7.6. Lansing and Monroe had not a single black police officer.

The CRC attributed the lack of black representation in the police forces of the state to long-standing discrimination, the desire of departments to hire only "extra well-qualified" black applicants, and, in many cities, the lack of black applicants. The CRC had recommended just before it provided this analysis that police departments should represent the proportion of African Americans and Hispanics who resided in the community and that capable black officers should be promoted to positions of leadership. It also believed that police departments should devise some form of citizen complaint procedure.[30]

The black community in Ann Arbor, the CRC reported in its survey, viewed police-community relations as "deplorable, and, at times, bordering on chaos." The commission reported that tension had been heightened in the city when police, a short time earlier, had sprayed Mace on nine blacks. After that episode, the Ann Arbor department suspended the use of Mace and formed a Police-Community Relations Council. The CRC found evidence of "growing mistrust" between young people and the police in Battle Creek, Kalamazoo, and Jackson. It reported that even though conditions had improved in Benton Harbor, there was "a general feeling of distrust" of the police among blacks, especially young blacks. In Flint, many blacks, according to the CRC, complained that the police were guilty of racist behavior in dealing with nonwhites. The Police-Community Relations Division of the Flint department, the CRC thought, had not addressed itself realistically to resolving the tension between the department and the black community.

Although the black community of Grand Rapids had "a negative view" of the city's police, the CRC believed that the situation was improving in that city. The commission gave part of the credit for this to police-community relations and in-service training programs that had been initiated that year. In Pontiac, by contrast, the CRC concluded that tension between blacks and the police was increasing, possibly because of the shooting by the police of two black youths. Tension had also increased in Saginaw, the CRC reported, following a racial disorder in which the police shot eight black youths. The commission judged the Saginaw department's Police-Community Relations Division to be ineffective.

The CRC, unsurprisingly, devoted most of its attention in the May 1968 survey to appraising police-community relations in Detroit. It believed that resentment of the DPD by the Detroit black community had been increasing since the riot and that the police and the black community appeared to be "on a direct collision course." It noted that the commission had been "severely hampered" in investigating complaints against the police because the Detroit Police Officers Association had instructed its members not to answer questions asked by CRC field representatives in conducting investigations. The commission also reported that the city's black community did not believe that the department was making an honest effort to recruit blacks and that blacks resented the manner in which white police treated black police officers, sometimes refusing even to speak to them or placing derogatory remarks about them on precinct bulletin boards.[31]

Detroit had actually begun to step up its efforts to recruit black police just before the CRC made its survey of police-community relations in the state. Mayor Cavanagh in May 1968 appointed a Special Task Force on Police Recruitment and Hiring and also arranged for the DPD to put together a team of sixteen black and four white police officers to devote full time for six weeks to an extensive recruitment campaign. Thirty-five percent of the police hired by Detroit in 1968 were black, as were 23 percent of those hired in 1969. By July 1972 blacks made up 14 percent of the Detroit police, more than double their percentage in 1967.[32]

As it reported to Governor William Milliken in May 1969, the CRC thought that many of the "conflict situations" involving blacks and the police could be reduced or even eliminated by the "professional upgrading of law enforcement." The commission did not believe that police received enough training to deal satisfactorily with the "complex social problems" that faced them. Progress in the CRC's efforts to enlist the cooperation of local police departments in developing suitable human relations programs had been slow, the commission concluded, because of the "less than enthusiastic response" of the various police departments. The CRC, consequently, recommended to the governor that the problem be attacked at the state level and indicated just how that might be done.[33] The CRC had probably done all that it could have in dealing with one of the most unyielding problems in the civil rights area, the relationship between the police and the black community. Progress in this regard would prove to be painfully slow in the years to come.

The Detroit riot and the racial turbulence it helped to ignite in Flint, Pontiac, and elsewhere had a dramatic effect not only on the number of black police hired in Detroit but also on the general employment of nonwhites in the Detroit metropolitan area and elsewhere in Michigan and on housing discrimination both at the local and state levels. There had already been a fair amount of progress regarding nonwhite access to places of public accommodation, but education remained a troubled area after the riot, as it had been before the disturbance.

In its role of ensuring that city contractors pursued a nondiscriminatory employment policy, the Detroit Commission on Community Relations succeeded in opening up a fair number of jobs for blacks. This was especially evident in the construction trades, where the number of black journeymen in the Detroit area rose from 4 percent of the total in 1967 to 16 percent in 1969 (from 11,314 to 66,881). In August 1967 the Manpower Development Committee of the Greater Detroit Board of Commerce (GDBC) launched a campaign to find jobs for ten thousand "previously unemployable" persons, a preponderant number of whom were black. The New Detroit Committee, formed by leading business firms in the Detroit area following the riot, joined in this effort. As part of the campaign, employers agreed to reexamine their job application forms and their hiring standards for entry-level jobs and to initiate or expand training opportunities for marginal workers. In cooperation with the NAACP, the Congress of Racial Equality, and the Franklin-Wright Settlement, the GDBC and New Detroit helped to organize job-recruitment centers in the inner city.[34]

By October 12, 1967, Detroit firms had reportedly hired about five thousand blacks since the beginning of the jobs campaign, and that figure may have been an underestimate. The Big Three automobile manufacturers joined in the effort to provide jobs for the unskilled and the hard-core unemployed. The Ford Motor Company had hired about five thousand of the hard core, many of them obviously black, by the end of October; General Motors claimed that it had employed fifty-three hundred by the middle of November; and Chrysler Corporation reported that by that same time it had hired thirteen thousand workers, 60–70 percent of them black. The J. L. Hudson Company and the National Bank of Detroit also developed programs to hire and train the hard-core unemployed.[35]

One important employment gain stemming from the Detroit riot was the change in employer hiring standards for entry-level jobs. Responding to the urging of the GDBC and New Detroit, employers simplified job application forms, abandoned testing for entry-level unskilled jobs, adopted more liberal policies regarding the dress and deportment of workers, and paid less attention than had been their practice in hiring to previous work experience of prospective employees, references, and police records for minor offenses. "Equal employment opportunity for entry-level jobs has become a reality in Detroit," New Detroit proclaimed in September 1968. "For over 75 years," a Michigan Bell employment supervisor declared, "business tried to screen people out. Now we are trying to find reasons to screen them in." Discrimination against blacks had not, to be sure, suddenly come to an end in Detroit, but the riot did lead to some improvement in employment for them and others, at least at the job-entry level. In a *Detroit Free Press* survey of residents in the 1967 riot areas in the late summer of 1968, 39 percent of the respondents thought that employers had become "more fair" since the riot, as compared to 14 percent who thought that they had become "less fair," and 47 percent who saw no change.[36]

Following the Detroit riot, the state government used its reviews of contracts let by the state and its political and civil subdivisions to secure an increase in state nonwhite employment. In August 1967 the State Administrative Board entrusted the CRC with the administration of the equal employment clause in state and local government contracts. If a CRC review of a particular contract indicated that the contractor's workforce did not "reflect reasonably representative integration in all job categories and in all trades," the commission recommended that the contract be awarded only if the employer took "the actions suggested to correct any inequities" the review had detected. After a contract had been awarded, the commission made periodic reviews to ensure that "opportunities for employment and promotion" remained open to all those who qualified. The results of the contract reviews were impressive. Between August 1967 and the end of fiscal year 1969–70, the CRC made 2,086 contract reviews of 1,213 employers. The total workforce of these employers rose during this period by 2.5 percent (from 1,047,453 to 1,073,811), but the minority-group employment increased by 21.1 percent (from 85,951 to 104,070).[37]

The July riots in Michigan, quite apart from their effect on the employment of nonwhites, helped to increase the number of Michigan cities with fair housing ordinances from eight to fifteen by November 1967, the largest number in any state at that time. The number had increased to thirty-five by October 1968, including some Detroit suburbs that had previously been almost entirely white. In November 1967 the Detroit Common Council adopted a fair housing ordinance that exempted rental units in which rooms were rented to no more than three persons. It was to have gone into effect on December 31, 1967, but before that date petitions with fifty thousand more signatures than were required to refer the ordinance to the voters were filed with the city clerk. In August 1968, however, U.S. District Court Judge Talbot Smith ruled that the matter at issue was no longer one for Detroit voters to decide in view of federal and, by then, state law as well as court decisions. "The status quo cannot be restored," Smith wrote. "Too much has happened."[38]

Flint's city commission agreed to a fair housing ordinance in October 1967 that was to go into effect the next month, but a Committee to Repeal Forced Housing—"a pseudonym," according to a CRC regional official, "for the [John] Birch Society"—forced the measure to a referendum. In balloting on February 20, 1968, Flint became the first city in the nation in which the voters—by a thirty-one-vote margin in this instance—sustained a fair housing ordinance submitted to them for approval or disapproval. Pontiac followed suit by also approving a fair housing ordinance. Grosse Pointe Farms, the largest of the Grosse

Pointes, moved in the opposite direction, however, its residents rejecting a fair housing measure by a vote of 2,271 to 1,596 in an April 1969 referendum.[39]

When Governor Romney called the state legislature into special session following the Detroit riot, the New Detroit Committee sought to persuade him to place a state fair housing law on the legislative agenda. Romney had promised legislators that he would not do so, but after returning from a national speaking tour in which he had stressed the need to deal with racial problems, he felt himself "boxed in and could not say no" to New Detroit. He consequently delivered a special message to the legislature on October 13, while it was in session, calling for a "statewide open occupancy law." He wanted the law to cover commercial and private property owners, mortgage lenders, and real estate brokers and their agents, with exceptions for "so-called 'tight living situations.'" He also called for code enforcement legislation as well as a tenants' rights law designed to create "a covenant of fitness, good repair and compliance with applicable health and safety laws and ordinances for every rental arrangement" in the state. He appraised the housing measures he had recommended as "the most important ever to be considered by the Michigan legislature."

The Romney fair housing proposal caused three hundred Detroit homeowners to parade in front of the state capitol shouting "No forced housing" and "Recall Romney." In an effort to persuade the special session to follow the governor's fair housing recommendation, a large delegation of New Detroit members, other influential Detroit citizens, and Mayor Jerome Cavanagh, in an unprecedented action, flew to Lansing to indicate by their presence their "personal conviction and willingness" to support an open housing law. The measure, however, was defeated in the House toward the end of December by a 47–55 vote, 33 Republicans and 22 Democrats opposing the bill and 21 Republicans and 26 Democrats supporting it. "I think what happened here is a disgrace," declared Acting Governor William Milliken.[40]

In his message on January 11, 1968, to the regular session of the legislature, Romney once again urged the enactment of fair housing and tenants' rights legislation, declaring that these measures had become "the testing ground" since the Detroit riot. "If such legislation is passed," he asserted, "it will strengthen those who seek peaceful, orderly changes. If it is not," he warned, "it will accelerate the recruitment of revolutionary insurrectionists." As the legislature debated a fair housing bill, Romney, who exerted far more leadership in the matter than he had in the 1967 special session, characterized "meaningful fair housing legislation" as "the single most important step the legislature can take to avert disorder in our cities."[41]

The housing bill met the usual opposition from realtors and those who did not believe the state had "the constitutional right to bargain away the inherent and traditional right of the American home owner to a complete freedom of choice as to how and to whom he may sell his home." The measure was strongly supported by, among others, religious groups, New Detroit, the GDBC, the Michigan Federation of Teachers, the American Association of University Women, and the Democratic State Central Committee. The bill, "stronger" than the 1967 measure, passed the Senate on April 4 by a 22–14 vote after what was described as "the bitterest struggle in years" on the Senate floor. The affirmative vote, which, not incidentally, followed the *Beech Grove* decision, was evenly divided between Democrats and Republicans. The measure passed the House more than a month later by a 76–31 vote, 36 Democrats and 40 Republicans voting in the affirmative and 18 Democrats and 13 Republicans casting negative votes. After differences between the bills passed by the two houses had been reconciled, Romney signed the measure into law on June 11, 1968, calling the action "one of the truly significant moments in the social development" of the state.[42]

The Michigan Fair Housing Act forbade owners, real estate brokers, and real estate salesmen to refuse to negotiate a real estate transaction or refuse to discuss "the terms, conditions or privileges of a real estate transaction" with any person because of the individual's race, color, religion, or national origin. It was made an unfair housing practice for a financial institution to discriminate for the same reasons against any person applying for financial assistance in connection with a real estate transaction. Blockbusting was also made an unfair housing practice. If a licensed real estate broker, salesman, or builder was found by the CRC to have engaged in an unfair housing practice, the commission was to certify this fact to the licensing agency, which was bound by the decision and was authorized to revoke or suspend the licenses of the guilty parties. The measure was to be enforced by the CRC, the state attorney general, or the aggrieved party, with the respondent having the right of appeal to a state circuit court within fifteen days of receiving notice of a CRC hearing. The CRC could petition a state circuit court to award a complainant not more than $500 for economic damages suffered as the result of housing discrimination. The court could also fine a respondent not more than $1,000 for an unfair housing practice and not more than $2,000 for violating a CRC housing order. Local governments were authorized to adopt fair housing ordinances not in conflict with the state law.

There were four exceptions to the applicability of the housing law: the rental of housing in a building containing housing accommodations for not more than two parties living independently of each other if the owner, lessor, or a member of the owner's or lessor's family resided in one of the units; the rental of a room or rooms in a single-family dwelling if the owner or lessor or a family member resided there; the sale or rental by the owner or lessor of housing accommodations in a building that contained housing for not more than two families living independently of each other that was not publicly listed or advertised for sale or lease; and rental housing for not more than twelve months by the owner or lessor when it had been occupied by him and maintained as his home for at least three months immediately preceding its occupation by the tenant and temporarily vacated while the owner or lessor maintained legal residence.[43]

Despite the exceptions, the Michigan Fair Housing Act, which took effect on November 15, 1968, was stronger than the federal fair housing law passed that same year and stronger than just about all of the existing state fair housing acts. It is probably more than a coincidence that the state that had experienced the most severe racial disorder of the 1960s adopted so strong a fair housing statute. The CRC made every effort to publicize the law, meeting with members of the real estate industry and sponsoring a statewide conference to consider the legislation. It called on members of the housing industry to take affirmative action "beyond the requirements of the law" so as to "break down racial barriers" in housing. Reacting to the June 17, 1968, U.S. Supreme Court decision in the *Jones* v. *Mayer* case that the Civil Rights Act of 1866 permitted no exceptions on the basis of race insofar as housing discrimination was concerned, the CRC, which had filed an amicus brief in the case, pressed to have the Michigan law conform to the new federal standard. Nothing was done along these lines, however, until 1976, when the new Michigan Civil Rights Act omitted from the 1968 exceptions to the fair housing requirements of the law the sale or rental by the owner or lessor of housing accommodations in a building that contained housing for not more than two families living independently of each other that was not publicly listed or advertised for sale.[44]

Although housing segregation remained very high in Michigan, it may be that the state, Detroit, and Detroit suburban housing measures contributed for a time to decreasing residential segregation in Detroit proper and in Detroit's suburbs. In any event, from 1960 to 1980 the index of dissimilarity, which would have been 100 had there been total segregation, fell from 80.4 to 67.4 in the central city and, very modestly, from 89.8 to 83.9 in the Detroit suburbs.[45]

The same 1968 legislative session that produced the Fair Housing Act also resulted in the enactment of important relocation, tenants' rights, and code enforcement legislation. The relocation statute provided that district areas were to be designated for all "development areas," and citizens district councils of ten to twenty-five members who, to "the maximum extent possible," were to be "representative of the residents of the area and of other persons with a demonstrable or substantial interest in the area" were to be appointed for each. The local officials responsible for preparing the development plan were to seek the advice of the relevant citizens district council regarding "all aspects of the plan, including the development of new housing for relocation purposes." This met a CRC objective regarding the displacement and relocation of minority persons.[46]

The several tenants' rights and code enforcement measures provided that the lessor or licensee of residential premises had to agree formally that the premises were "fit for use" and had to keep them in "reasonable repair." A board of tenant affairs was to be established in each unit of local government with a housing commission that operated one or more housing projects, one-half of the board to be elected from among tenants occupying the projects. The board was to advise the housing commission, review its rules and, if necessary, veto them by a two-thirds vote, and serve as a board of review for tenants or applicants for the housing units. These were "the strongest set" of such measures in the nation at that time.[47]

In the spring of 1967 the National Committee against Discrimination in Housing "commended" the CRC as "having a national impact not only in the public housing field but also in governmentally financed housing renewal and development programs."[48] The enactment the next year of fair housing, tenants' rights, code enforcement, and relocation legislation placed Michigan, which had once lagged in the field, in the forefront of the states seeking to combat housing discrimination.

The civil rights commitment of the post-1948 Michigan Democratic Party, the persistent efforts of the CRC, the pressure of religious and liberal groups, racial trouble in Detroit and elsewhere in Michigan, and a moderate Republican governor able to secure bipartisan support for civil rights measures that he favored all helped to make fair housing and related housing legislation the law of the state of Michigan. At the same time, the long struggle in the state to secure fair housing legislation in particular revealed the strength of the opposition to housing reforms not just by realtors but also by many middle-class and working-class citizens, including union members.[49]

The educational scene remained a troubled one in Michigan following the Detroit riot. Racial turbulence in several schools and conflicts between students and faculties beginning in November 1967 and continuing until February 1968 raised questions about existing school policies regarding the disciplining and suspension of students and how these policies were applied. The CRC, which had involved itself in several of these school incidents, concluded that existing procedures leading to the suspension or expulsion of students—procedures that "most acutely" affected black and poor children—did not conform to the requirements of due process of law. It consequently recommended that "all the safeguards of due process of law," such as the right to counsel, to call witnesses, and to appeal, should be "mandatory" whenever a school district sought to expel a student permanently. The commission asked school districts to review their discipline and suspension practices, provide system-wide notice of existing practices, provide prior notice wherever possible to students and their parents regarding a pending disciplinary action or a suspension, and inform parents that they could seek a hearing in such cases by the State Board of Education or in the courts.

The CRC distributed copies of its discipline and suspension document to educators, parent organizations, civic organizations, and student groups. Commission staff conferred with school officials in twenty school districts to interpret its guidelines, review school practices, and recommend appropriate action. Nine school districts, including that of Detroit, incorporated the CRC's recommendations in their discipline and suspension policies.[50]

There were intergroup conflicts and school disruptions involving allegations of racial discrimination in eighteen Michigan school districts in fiscal year 1968–69. CRC staff members, who became involved in these incidents at the request of school officials, students, or parents, attempted to identify the cause of the trouble and made recommendations designed to alleviate the tension. The CRC urged the school districts involved to establish grievance procedures that would enable students to receive fair consideration and prompt action regarding their complaints. The CRC also aided five school districts in implementing desegregation plans. It developed an interservice program for school administrators and teachers in Adrian and participated in a staff training program in Pontiac.[51]

Despite the overwhelming desire of Detroit blacks for integrated education, the city's schools after the riot became increasingly segregated, as the city itself became increasingly black. The percentage of blacks in the Detroit public schools increased from 56.7 to 63.8 from 1967 to 1970, and the percentage of blacks attending predominantly white schools decreased from 9 to 5.8. In 1968 an effort that had begun in 1965 to preserve racial integration in three Detroit high school constellations by using state funding to enrich the curriculum and provide additional educational services for fifty thousand students collapsed, as population shifts in the school neighborhoods involved reduced white student enrollment.[52]

As in the years just before the 1967 riot, the number of blacks in teaching and administrative positions in the Detroit schools continued to increase after the disturbance. The percentage of black faculty in the public schools rose from 31.7 in October 1966 to 38 in October 1968, and 50 percent of the new hires by the latter date were black. In an effort to place more blacks in administrative positions at a time when so many black teachers lacked the necessary seniority, the school administration reduced the amount of experience required for promotion to such positions. This contributed to an increase in the number of black school principals from 6 percent of the total in February 1967 to 12 percent in October 1968, and an increase in the number of positions above the rank of teacher held by blacks from 192 in October 1966 to 271 in February 1968.[53]

Faced with increasing budgetary problems and the high cost of educating children from disadvantaged backgrounds and unable to secure needed state funds, the Detroit School Board in January 1968 joined three black children and their parents and three white children and their parents in filing a lawsuit against the state of Michigan for failing "to discharge its constitutional obligation to provide equal educational opportunity for all children" attending public schools in the state. The school system failed, however, to win its case.[54]

The CRC's concern about education and civil rights extended to institutions of higher education. The commission conferred with Teacher Corps administrators at Wayne State University and members of the Education Department at Michigan State University in an effort to persuade them to provide more training in their education programs for teaching in the central city. It cooperated with the State Department of Education in December 1968 in sponsoring a seminar for officials of the state's colleges and universities designed to stimulate greater involvement by these institutions in programs to meet the educational needs of minority-group students. It also assisted Eastern Michigan University's Bureau of School Services in developing a civil rights seminar for the directors of Elementary and Secondary Education Act programs in the state.[55]

Although the CRC could point to some civil rights gains in the field of education, it was far from satisfied with the status quo in this area when the Romney administration came to an end. It informed Governor Milliken in May 1969 that the schools were not helping to overcome "the effects of discrimination and deprivation on minority groups." It was concerned about the degree of de facto school segregation, the racial "tensions and misunderstandings" in many school districts, the lack of systematic enforcement of the 1966 state law requiring proper attention in the curriculum to the contributions of minority groups, and the "level of participation" of both minority-group students and employees in institutions of higher education.[56] The CRC, to be sure, was inclined as the Romney administration came to an end to stress Michigan's obvious shortcomings in the civil rights area rather than to point to what had been achieved with regard to fair employment, education, public accommodations, housing, and law enforcement since the establishment of the commission in 1964.[57]

16

SINCE 1968

When Mennen Williams was elected Michigan's governor in November 1948, Michigan lagged behind many other states in the protection it accorded the civil rights of its inhabitants. Thanks to the efforts of Williams, his two successors as governor, John B. Swainson and George Romney, the Fair Employment Practices Commission, and the Civil Rights Commission, Michigan by the end of 1968 ranked among the states most active in the civil rights field.

By the end of the Romney governorship, there had been significant civil rights gains in Michigan with regard to access to public accommodations, government contracting, and the membership of the state civil service, and lesser gains in the areas of private employment, housing, education, law enforcement, and sex and age discrimination. Despite the enactment of both state and federal legislation during the Romney governorship to deal with the many problems of Michigan's migrant farm laborers, their sad condition remained largely unchanged. The same can be said for the efforts of the state government to improve the status and livelihood of Michigan's Native Americans. Many of the civil rights gains between 1949 and 1968 were registered during the Romney governorship. This was the result of a number of factors: the civil rights provisions of Michigan's 1963 constitution and the consequent establishment of the Michigan Civil Rights Commission, the only such body in the nation to enjoy constitutional status; Attorney General Frank Kelley's ruling that the commission enjoyed "plenary power" in the areas of its jurisdiction; the likely influence of the civil rights movement

335

across the nation; and Romney's ability to muster a bipartisan legislative majority for civil rights legislation.

After 1968 Michigan substantially expanded its definition of civil rights that were to be accorded protection and its efforts to promote equality of opportunity for all of its citizens. In fiscal year 1969–70 the CRC initiated a five-year pilot project to help develop an open housing market in the Detroit metropolitan area, and its staff worked with the Michigan State Housing Development Authority in seeking to achieve "a bi-racial occupancy pattern" in the low- and moderate-income housing projects in Detroit. In 1975 the 1968 Housing Act was amended to prohibit housing discrimination based on sex, age, marital status, or physical handicap. It was also made an unfair housing practice for the same reasons to deny a person financial assistance for a housing transaction.[1]

The Fair Employment Practices Act, a key accomplishment of the Williams administration, was amended in 1976 to make it an unfair employment practice to elicit or preserve information about the arrest record of an employee or an applicant for employment unless the arrest resulted in a conviction. The act was further amended the same year to prohibit employment discrimination because of marital status, height, or weight.[2]

In the first half of the 1970s the CRC's Latin American Affairs Program sought to eliminate discrimination against Hispanics resident in the state's urban communities as well as those working as seasonal farm laborers. The commission also attempted to promote bilingual and bicultural programs in both public and private schools and to sensitize the people of the state to the discrimination Hispanics experienced. In June 1974 Governor William Milliken issued an executive order establishing the Michigan Advisory Council for the Spanish-speaking.[3]

The Handicappers' Civil Rights Act of July 1976 culminated a long effort in the state to extend civil rights protection to the handicapped. "The opportunity," the measure stated, "to obtain employment, housing and other real estate and full and equal utilization of public accommodations, public services and educational facilities without discrimination because of a handicap is guaranteed by this act and is a civil right." "Handicap" was defined in the statute as "a determinable physical or mental characteristic."[4]

On July 31, 1977, Governor Milliken signed the Michigan Civil Rights Act, better known as the Elliott-Larsen Act, which the CRC viewed at the time as "the most comprehensive civil rights legislation in the nation." It is noteworthy that the "Elliott" in the act refers to Daisy Elliott, who had played an important role in the Constitutional Convention of 1961–62 in securing support for the decision to establish the Michigan Civil Rights Commission. The statute codified existing civil rights legislation pertaining to employment, housing, public accommodations, public service, and education. Employers, in addition, were forbidden to segregate or classify employees on the basis of sex for purposes of an employee personal benefit plan or any employee welfare benefit plan. The ban on educational discrimination was extended by the statute to include the disciplining and suspension of students.[5]

A 1978 amendment to the Elliott-Larsen Act extended the ban on sex discrimination to include pregnancy, childbirth, and marital conditions related to them but not to "therapeutic abortions not intended to save the life of the mother." A 1980 amendment further expanded the definition of sex discrimination to include sexual harassment, defined as "unwelcome sexual advances, requests for sexual favors, and other verbal or physical conduct or communication of a sexual nature." The Elliott-Larsen Act was amended once again in 1992 to prohibit discrimination by private establishments such as country clubs, golf clubs, sports clubs, and dining clubs.[6]

Michigan in the years after the enactment of the Elliott-Larsen Act continued to strengthen its protection of civil rights. In 1980 the ban on employment discrimination, which at that time covered employers of four or more employees, was applied to employers of a single worker. In the 1980s the Handicappers' Civil Rights Act was amended to expand the definition of mental handicap to include "a mentally ill restored condition," to require the accommodation of the handicapped in all the areas subject to the CRC's jurisdiction, and to define AIDS as a handicap. A 1990 amendment required the accommodation of the handicapped whether their condition was "related or unrelated to ability" and provided full civil rights coverage for all mental handicaps, whereas such coverage had previously been applicable only to housing. The federal government's Americans with Disabilities Act of 1991 included provisions similar to the Michigan legislation, the CRC viewing the federal and state laws as complementary.[7]

At a 1980 public hearing on "Hate Groups That Foment Racial and Religious Violence" held by the Michigan Advisory Committee on Civil Rights to the U.S. Commission on Civil Rights, the CRC reported that it had dealt with "numerous incidents of racial and religious harassment" and that it would continue to monitor such incidents "within the context of its constitutional and statutory authority." Legislation enacted in 1989 made "ethnic intimidation" a felony punishable by two years in prison, a fine of up to $5,000, or both. A person was to be deemed guilty of such intimidation if he or she "maliciously, and with specific intent to intimidate or harass" another individual because of his or her race, color, religion, sex, or national origin, caused physical contact with the

337

individual, damaged, destroyed, or defaced his property, or made threats that there was "reasonable cause to believe" would be carried out.[8]

In 1979, for the first time, a Native American, Beverly Clark, was appointed to the CRC. Seeking to improve the condition of the state's migrant agricultural workers, the legislature in 1989 approved field sanitation rules requiring that toilets, drinking water, and hand-washing water be provided these workers.[9]

Governor Milliken had issued an executive order in 1971 requiring each state agency "to establish and maintain an affirmative action plan of equal employment opportunity" to be overseen by the State Department of Civil Service. As of December 1984, fourteen of twenty-one state departments had a higher percentage of minority-group employees than the 14.8 percent of minority-group members in the state's population as a whole.[10] In an effort to assist minority- and female-owned businesses, the state government adopted legislation in 1981 requiring that minority-owned firms receive 7 percent of the state government's expenditures for the purchase of goods, services, and construction by fiscal year 1984–85 and that female-owned firms receive 5 percent of such purchases by then. This legislative goal had still not been reached when the U.S. Supreme Court in 1989 ruled against the state's set-aside law.[11]

The CRC after 1968 continued to pursue its affirmative action policy with private employers. As the commission interpreted court rulings, its chairman declared in 1979, "If a statistical survey shows that minorities and females are not participating in the workforce at all levels, in a reasonable relation to their presence in the population and the labor force, the burden of proof is on the employer to show that this is not the result of discrimination, no matter how inadvertent."[12]

The expanding jurisdiction of the CRC and the increased types of individuals whose civil rights it protected were reflected in the statistics of the claims that the commission processed. Although race had been the basis for 77.5 percent of the claims in 1971–72, that percentage had fallen to 35.6 by 1995–96. Physical and mental handicaps, which had not constituted a basis for claims in 1971–72, accounted for 11.1 percent of the claims in 1995–96, second only to race as a basis for claims. Pregnancy, gender discrimination, and sexual harassment combined were the basis for 13.6 percent of the claims in 1995–96. Employment discrimination was the principal allegation of complainants both before and after 1968.[13]

The CRC, with reason, claimed in 1992 that Michigan's civil rights legislation was "the most comprehensive in the nation."[14] The "frontiers of civil rights" in Michigan had expanded considerably after 1968, but the solid foundation for that advance had been laid during the preceding two decades.

NOTES

Abbreviations

ALUA	Archives of Labor and Urban Affairs, Detroit, Michigan
BG Papers	University of Michigan Bureau of Government Library Papers
BHL	Bentley Historical Library, Ann Arbor, Michigan
DFP	*Detroit Free Press*
DN	*Detroit News*
DNSB	Detroit News Scrapbook
GMW Papers	G. Mennen Williams Papers
GR Papers	George Romney Papers
JBS Papers	John B. Swainson Papers
LSJ	*Lansing State Journal*
RG	Record Group

Chapter 1

1. Milton R. Konvitz, *Expanding Liberties: Freedom's Gains in Postwar America* (New York: Viking Press, 1966), pp. 255–58.

2. Roger C. Cramton, "The Powers of the Michigan Civil Rights Commission: A Problem in Constitutional Interpretation" [July 1964], pp. 18–19, Box 6, Tom Downs Papers, BHL; Memorandum in Support of Proposal 1621 . . . , December 18, 1961, Box 1, Don Binkowski Papers, BHL; "The Right to Equal Treatment: Administrative Enforcement of Antidiscrimination Legislation," *Harvard Law Review* 74 (January 1961): 526. There is a copy of the 1908 constitution as of 1948 in *Michigan Official Directory and Legislative Manual, 1947–1948*, pp. 42–76.

3. Paul H. Norgren and Samuel E. Hill, *Toward Fair Employment* (New York: Columbia University Press, 1964), p. 4; Harry Ashmore, *Civil Rights and Wrongs: A Memoir of Race and Politics, 1944–1994* (New York: Pantheon Books, 1994), p. 86.

4. Gilbert Osofsky, *The Burden of Race: A Documentary History of Negro-White Relations in America* (New York: Harper and Row, 1987), pp. 400–401; Statement of Clarence W. Anderson before the Sub-Committee of the U.S. Senate Committee on Education and Labor, September 6, 1944, Box 8, League of Women Voters of Michigan (hereafter LWVM) Papers, BHL; Clarence W. Anderson, "Metropolitan Detroit FEPC" (M.A. thesis, Wayne State University, 1947), pp. 23–44; August Meier and Elliott Rudwick, *Black Detroit and the Rise of the UAW* (New York: Oxford University Press, 1979), pp. 114, 213; Memorandum on the Creation of Local Councils, January 21, 1942, Box 6, United Automobile Workers War Policy Division Papers, ALUA; William Hardin to Brother, October 21, 1942, Box 12, UAW Local 51 Papers, ALUA; Constitution of Metropolitan Detroit Council on Fair Employment Practice [April 8, 1942], Box 4, Detroit Urban League (hereafter DUL) Papers, BHL; E. W. McFarland to Detroit Urban League, April 3, 1942, UAW-CIO Release, October 13, 1944, ibid.; In Support of Fair Employment: A History of Four Years of Activities of the Metropolitan Detroit Fair Employment Practice Council (hereafter MDFEPC), January 1942–December 1945, Box 18, Association of Catholic Trade Unionists of Detroit (hereafter ACTU) Papers, ALUA; MDFEPC (Speaker's Material), February 20, 1946, ibid.; Angelina Denise Dillard, "From the Reverend Charles A. Hill to the Reverend Albert B. Cleage, Jr.: Change and Continuity in the Patterns of Civil Rights Mobilizations in Michigan, 1935–1967" (Ph.D. diss., University of Michigan, 1995), pp. 138–39.

5. Dillard, "From Hill to Cleage," pp. 141–44; Meier and Rudwick, *Black Detroit*, pp. 115–17, 151–52, 153–54.

6. MDFEPC, February 20, 1946, Box 18, ACTU Papers; Anderson Statement, Box 18, LWVM Papers.

7. Anderson, "Metropolitan Detroit FEPC," pp. 86–98; Anderson, "A Nine-Month History of the Metropolitan Detroit Council on Fair Employment Practice," pp. 7–9, Box 5, Donald Marsh Papers, ALUA; Michigan Council for Fair Employment Legislation, Meeting of Sponsors, January 3, 1947, UAW Fair Practices and Anti-Discrimination Department (hereafter UAW Fair Practices) Papers, ALUA; Anderson Statement, Box 8, LWVM Papers; MDFEPC, February 20, 1946, In Support of Fair Employment, Box 18, ACTU Papers; Marshall Field Stevenson, Jr., "Points of Departure, Acts of Resolve: Black-Jewish Relations in Detroit, 1937–1962" (Ph.D. diss., University of Michigan, 1988), p. 406. For the effort to secure fair employment in Detroit during World War II, see Andrew E. Kersten, "Jobs and Justice: Detroit, Fair Employment, and Federal Activism during the Second World War," *Michigan Historical Review* 25 (Spring 1999): 77–101.

8. Anderson, "Metropolitan Detroit FEPC," pp. 43–45, 99, 116; Anderson Statement, Box 8, LWVM Papers; MDFEPC, February 18, 1946, In Support of Fair Employment, Box 18, ACTU Papers; Joseph La Palombara, *Guide to Michigan Politics* (East Lansing: Michigan State University Press, 1960), p. 23; Senate Bill No. 226, Michigan Sixty-Second Legislature, 1943 (there are copies of Michigan Senate and House bills in the University of Michigan Law Library, Ann Arbor, Michigan); *Michigan Chronicle*, March 13, 20, 27, April 3, 1943.

9. Anderson Statement, Box 8, LWVM Papers; In Support of Fair Employment, Box 18, ACTU Papers; Report of the 1945 Program Committee . . . , January 9,

1945, Box 45, Civil Rights Congress of Michigan (hereafter CRCM) Papers, ALUA; Dont Repeatitt [*sic*], "History of the FEPC in Michigan" [July 11, 1947], pp. 2–3, 5, Box 8, UAW Fair Practices Papers; Senate Bill No. 134, Michigan Sixty-Third Legislature, 1945; *DN,* March 16, 1945.

10. Anderson, "Metropolitan Detroit FEPC," pp. 118–19, 130; Repeatitt, "History," pp. 6–11, Box 8, UAW Fair Practices Papers; House Bill No. 132, Michigan Sixty-Third Legislature, 1945; Draft Memorandum for Campaign for Michigan State FEPC [1946], Box 12, UAW Local 51 Papers.

11. Anderson, "Metropolitan Detroit FEPC," pp. 131–44; *DN,* August 2, 1944, February 8, 1945; Repeatitt, "History," pp. 1, 13–21, Box 8, UAW Fair Practices Papers; Draft Memorandum [1946], Box 12, UAW Local 51 Papers. The Senate in 1945 was composed of twenty-four Republicans and eight Democrats, the House of sixty-six Republicans and thirty-four Democrats.

12. Duane Lockard, *Toward Equal Employment Opportunity: A Study of State and Local Antidiscrimination Laws* (Princeton: Princeton University Press, 1968), p. 19; Fair Employment Practice Committee, *Final Report, June 28, 1946* (Washington, D.C.: Government Printing Office, 1947), pp. 60–63; Thomas J. Sugrue, *The Origins of the Urban Crisis: Race and Inequality in Postwar Detroit* (Princeton: Princeton University Press, 1996), pp. 25–28, 95; George Schermer, "Effectiveness of Equal Opportunity Legislation," in *The Negro and Employment Opportunity,* ed. Herbert R. Northrup and Richard L. Rowan (Ann Arbor: University of Michigan Press, 1965), p. 72; Anderson, "Metropolitan Detroit FEPC," pp. 110–15; Harry C. Markle to Robert Montgomery, April 18, 1951, Box 175, Michigan AFL-CIO Papers, ALUA.

13. Gerald Horne, *Communist Front? The Civil Rights Congress, 1946–1956* (Rutherford, N.J.: Farleigh Dickinson University Press, 1986), pp. 29–30, 71, 90, 289; Dillard, "From Hill to Cleage," pp. 171, 187–88; William H. Oliver to Reuther, September 10, 19, 1946, [October 30, 1946], Box 89, Walter Reuther Papers, ALUA; Stevenson, "Points of Departure," p. 410; *Michigan Official Directory and Legislative Manual, 1945–46,* pp. 44–45; Jack Raskin to William Cole, August 7, 1946, Box 50, CRCM Papers; Raskin to Board Member, September 13, 1946, Ann Shore to ——, September 23, 1946, Dean A. Robb to Ben Carpenter, October 19, 1946, Box 48, ibid.; Raskin to Malcolm Ross, October 11, 1946, Shore to Sigler, October 15, 1946, Shore to George Addes, December 4, 1946, Box 49, ibid.; Paul Endicott and Shore to Gentlemen, October 15, 1946, Oliver to International Officers et al., November 8, 1946, Oliver et al. to All Local Presidents, November 13, 1946, August Scholle and Barney Hopkins to Presidents, November 2, 1946, Draft Memorandum [1946], Box 12, UAW Local 51 Papers; Michigan Council for Fair Employment Legislation, Meeting of Sponsors, January 3, 1947, Oliver to Sir and Brother, October 28, 1946, Box 8, UAW Fair Practices Papers; *DN,* August 28, October 12, 21, 1946, January 7, 1947; Martin Halpern, *UAW Politics in the Cold War Era* (Albany: State University of New York Press, 1988), p. 226; Stevenson, "Points of Departure," pp. 408–12.

14. Michigan Council for Fair Employment Legislation News Bulletin [January 1947], Box 8, UAW Fair Practices Papers; Statement on FEPC, March 4, 1947, Box 49, CRCM Papers.

15. Schermer to Friend, December 27, 1946, Michigan Council for Fair Employment Legislation, Meeting of Sponsors, January 3, 1947, Box 8, UAW Fair Practices Papers; Oliver to Larry Gettlinger, December 12, 1950, Scholle to Reuther, January 23, 1952, Oliver to Helen Graham, April 1, 1952, Box 25, ibid.; Schermer to Sigler,

March 13, 1947, Box 77, Records of the Executive Office: Kim Sigler, RG 43, State Archives, Lansing, Michigan; John Barnard, *Walter Reuther and the Rise of the Auto Workers* (Boston: Little, Brown, 1983), pp. 111, 116.

16. Michigan Council for Fair Employment Legislation, Meeting of Sponsors, January 3, 1947, Schermer to Friend, December 27, 1946, Box 8, UAW Fair Practices Papers.

17. Submission to Labor Committee . . . , January 29, 1947, Michigan Council for Fair Employment Legislation News Bulletin [January 1947], ibid.; *Michigan Official Directory and Legislative Manual, 1955–1956*, p. 90.

18. Submission to Labor Committee . . . , January 29, 1947, Michigan Council for Fair Employment Legislation News Bulletin [January 1947], Box 8, UAW Fair Practices Papers; Schermer to Sigler, February 6, 1947, Box 77, RG 43; *DN*, January 30, 1947; Norgren and Hill, *Toward Fair Employment*, p. 93 n.

19. State Conference, January 30, 1947, Michigan Council for Fair Employment Legislation, February 3, 1947, Oliver to Sigler, February 10, 1947, Box 8, UAW Fair Practices Papers; Stanley Nowak to Committee for a State FEPC, February 18, 1947, Box 49, CRCM Papers; *DN*, October 27, 1946, February 20, 1947.

20. Schermer to Sponsor, February 20, 1947, Box 8, UAW Fair Practices Papers; Statement on FEPC, March 4, 1947, Box 49, CRCM Papers; Michigan Committee for Tolerance, "The So-Called Fair Employment Practices Measure," n.d., Box 77, RG 43; C. Patt Quinn to Local Unions . . . , March 13, 1946, Box 18, ACTU Papers; Halpern, *UAW Politics*, p. 71; *DN*, January 10, 1945, February 2, March 2, 1947.

21. Shore to Connie Childress, March 2, 1947, Box 48, CRCM Papers; *Leininger v. Secretary of State*, 316 Mich. 644 (1947); *DN*, March 2, 4, 5, 1947; UAW Release, March 4, 1947, Schermer and Olive R. Beasley to Friend, March 6, 1947, Box 8, UAW Fair Practices Papers; Schermer to Sigler, March 13, April 7, 1947, Box 77, RG 43. For the New York law, see Morroe Berger, *Equality by Statute: The Revolution in Civil Rights*, rev. ed. (Garden City, N.Y.: Doubleday, 1967), pp. 162–67, and Paul D. Moreno, *From Direct Action to Affirmative Action: Fair Employment Law and Policy in America, 1933–1972* (Baton Rouge: Louisiana State University Press, 1997), pp. 107–11. See also Jay Anders Higbee, *Development and Administration of the New York State Law against Discrimination* (University: University of Alabama Press, 1966).

22. Schermer to Sigler, February 6, March 7, 13, 1947, Box 77, RG 43.

23. Schermer to Sigler, March 28, 1947, ibid.; Charles H. Hill and O. Walter Wagner to Friend, April 4, 1947, Committee for a State FEPC Release, March 24, 1947, Box 49, CRCM Papers; *DN*, March 9, 15, 20, 1947; *DN*, March 13, 1947, DNSB 8, BHL.

24. *DN*, March 15, 1947; Committee for a State FEPC Release, March 24, 1947, Box 49, CRCM Papers; Sigler to Haas, April 15, 1947, Box 72, Detroit Commission on Community Relations (hereafter DCCR) Papers, ALUA.

25. Oliver to James Carey, November 21, 1947, Box 8, UAW Fair Practices Papers; *To Secure These Rights: The Report of the President's Committee on Civil Rights* (New York: Simon and Schuster, 1947), pp. 151–78.

26. Schermer to Sponsor, November 20, 1947, Schermer to Friend, December 3, 1947, Box 107, United Community Services Central File Papers, ALUA; Schermer, "Proposals for Action," November 24, 1947, "To Secure These Rights," n.d., Box 8, UAW Fair Practices Papers.

27. MCCR Bulletin, January 24, 1948, Emil Mazey to All Local Unions' Recording Secretaries, January 30, 1948, Schermer to Oliver, February 12, 1948, [Oliver] to Friend, February 13, 1948, Schermer to Friend, February 21, 1948, Box 8, UAW Fair Practices Papers; Summary of MCCR Activities, 1948–1950, Box 6, Adelaide Hart Papers, BHL; *DN*, December 9, 1947.

28. Katherine Shannon interview with George Schermer, November 14, 1967, pp. 58–59, transcript in Moorland-Spingarn Research Center, Howard University, Washington, D.C.; Haas to Sigler, July 31, 1947, Beasley to Members, August 8, 1947, Schermer to Bert Storey, April 26, 1949, Box 8, UAW Fair Practices Papers; Administrative Assistant to A. Padover, April 1, 1948, Raskin to Sigler, April 9, 1948, Box 77, RG 43; *DN*, February 25, March 16, 31, 1948.

29. For biographical information on Williams, see Frank McNaughton, *Mennen Williams of Michigan* (New York: Oceana, 1960), pp. 3–93; George Weeks, *Stewards of the State: The Governors of Michigan* (Detroit and Ann Arbor: Detroit News and Historical Society of Michigan, 1991), pp. 110–15; Williams to James Hare, July 27, 1948, Box 5, GMW Non-Gubernatorial Papers, BHL; and Sidney Fine, *Frank Murphy: The New Deal Years* (Chicago: University of Chicago Press, 1979), pp. 447–48.

30. Stephen Sarasohn and Vera Sarasohn, *Political Party Patterns in Michigan* (Detroit: Wayne State University Press, 1957), pp. 54–55.

31. See, for example, ibid., 55; and Dudley W. Buffa, *Union Power and American Democracy: The UAW and the Democratic Party, 1935–1972* (Ann Arbor: University of Michigan Press, 1984), pp. 13–14.

32. Neil Staebler, *Out of the Smoke-Filled Room: A Story of Michigan Politics* (Ann Arbor: George Wahr Publishing Co., 1991), pp. 30–32; Sarasohn and Sarasohn, *Party Patterns,* pp. 4–5; Williams to Staebler, March 17, 1952, Staebler to Williams, March 30, 1954, Box 191, Neil Staebler Papers, BHL; Lawrence L. Farrell to Williams, April 15, 1948, Williams to ——, May 29, 1948, Williams to Farrell, May 29, 1948, Box 5, GMW Non-Gubernatorial Papers; Helen Washburn Berthelot, *Win Some, Lose Some: G. Mennen Williams and the New Democrats* (Detroit: Wayne State University Press, 1995), p. 36.

33. McNaughton, *Mennen Williams,* pp. 104–5; John H. Fenton, *Midwest Politics* (New York: Holt, Rinehart and Winston, 1966), pp. 16–17; Sarasohn and Sarasohn, *Party Patterns,* pp. 54–55; Buffa, *Union Power,* p. 15.

34. Tom Downs to Williams, July 29, 1948, and enclosure, Box 5, GMW Non-Gubernatorial Papers; Sarasohn and Sarasohn, *Party Patterns,* p. 55; Fenton, *Midwest Politics,* p. 19; Buffa, *Union Power,* pp. 15–17, 19, 27; Robert Lee Sawyer, *The Democratic State Central Committee in Michigan, 1949–1959: The Rise of the New Politics and the New Political Leadership* (Ann Arbor: Institute of Public Administration, University of Michigan, 1960), p. 77; Sidney Fine interview with Tom Downs, March 30, 1995, pp. 3–5, transcript in BHL.

35. Buffa, *Union Power,* 9; Sarasohn and Sarasohn, *Party Patterns,* pp. 50–51; Kevin Boyle, *The UAW and the Heyday of American Liberalism, 1945–1968* (Ithaca: Cornell University Press, 1995), pp. 53, 57; McNaughton, *Mennen Williams,* pp. 109–10.

36. McNaughton, *Mennen Williams,* p. 3; Staebler, *Smoke- Filled Room,* p. 33; Interview with Otis Smith by Ruth Wasem and Ruth Bordin, April 18, 1980, p. 11, G. Mennen Williams and Nancy Quirk Williams Oral History Project, 1980–1982, BHL.

37. Williams to Fellow Candidates, August 15, 1948, Box 5, GMW Non-Gubernatorial Papers; Staebler, *Smoke-Filled Room,* pp. 32–33; McNaughton, *Mennen Williams,* p. 235; Fine, *Frank Murphy: The New Deal Years,* pp. 280–81; Sidney Fine interview with Williams, December 1964, pp. 2, 3–5, transcript in BHL.

38. *Michigan Official Directory and Legislative Manual, 1955–1956,* p. 96; Buffa, *Union Power,* pp. 26–27; Fenton, *Midwest Politics,* p. 12; Sarasohn and Sarasohn, *Party Patterns,* pp. 67–68.

39. Schermer to Haas, December 1, 1948, Schermer Memorandum to Members of the Governor's Advisory Committee, December 16, 1948, Box 6, GMW Non-Gubernatorial Papers; Memorandum to Members of the Advisory Committee on Civil Rights, December 1, 1948, Box 73, DCCR Papers.

40. Schermer Memorandum to Members of Advisory Committee on Civil Rights, December 1, 1948, Box 73, DCCR Papers; Schermer to Haas, December 1, 1948, Box 6, GMW Non-Gubernatorial Papers.

41. Advisory Legislative Commission Meeting, December 16, 1948, Schermer Memorandum to Members of Governor's Committee on Civil Rights, December 17, 1948, and enclosed Preliminary Report to Governor, Schermer Memorandum to Governor's Advisory Committee on Civil Rights, December 23, 1948, Schermer to Williams, December 28, 1948, Box 6, GMW Non-Gubernatorial Papers; Governor's Advisory Committee on Civil Rights Minutes, January 12, 1949, Box 73, DCCR Papers.

42. MCCR Memorandum to Committee on Civil Rights, December 29, 1948, Box 73, DCCR Papers.

43. Ibid.

44. Wade H. McCree, Jr., "The Negro Renaissance in Michigan Politics," *Negro History Bulletin* 26 (October 1962): 8.

45. *Michigan Statistical Abstract,* 8th ed., 1970 (East Lansing: Graduate School of Business Administration, Michigan State University [1970]), pp. 110–11; *Michigan Statistical Abstract,* 9th ed., 1972 (East Lansing: Graduate School of Business Administration, Michigan State University [1972]), pp. 5, 11, 47, 48; Sidney Fine, *Violence in the Model City: The Cavanagh Administration, Race Relations, and the Detroit Riot of 1967* (Ann Arbor: University of Michigan Press, 1989), p. 3.

46. Judith Laikin, "What Made the Mess in Michigan," *Reporter,* March 31, 1960, pp. 33–35; James J. Reichley, *States in Crisis: Politics in American States, 1950–1962* (Chapel Hill: University of North Carolina Press, 1964), p. 25; Carolyn Stieber, *The Politics of Change in Michigan* (East Lansing: Michigan State University Press, 1970), pp. 10–11; Willis F. Dunbar, *Michigan: A History of the Wolverine State,* 3rd rev. ed. by George S. May (Grand Rapids, Mich.: William B. Eerdmans, 1995), pp. 52–54.

47. Dunbar and May, *Michigan,* pp. 551–52; Article X, Section 23, Constitution of the State of Michigan of 1908.

48. Dunbar and May, *Michigan,* pp. 551, 560–61; Reichley, *States in Crisis,* p. 34; Stieber, *Politics of Change,* pp. 10–13; "Welfare State in Trouble," *US News and World Report,* February 13, 1959, pp. 49–51.

49. Dunbar and May, *Michigan,* pp. 561, 577–78; Article V, Section 20, Constitution of the State of Michigan of 1963.

50. Article V, Sections 2, 3, Constitution of the State of Michigan of 1908; La Palombara, *Guide to Michigan Politics,* pp. 16, 20; *New Republic,* November 16,

1959, p. 2; *Michigan Statistical Abstract*, 8th ed., 1970, p. 544; Dunbar and May, *Michigan*, pp. 548–50.

Chapter 2

1. Inaugural Address by Williams, January 1, 1949, Box 430, GMW Papers, BHL.

2. Herbert Hackett interview with Williams, October 2, 1949, Box 451, ibid.; Third Annual Conference, Committee of Governors on Civil Rights, March 3–4, 1960, Box 300, ibid.; Memorandum from Williams, March 23, 1960, Goals for America . . . , March 26, 1960, Box 503, ibid.; Interview with Horace Sheffield, January 14, 1980, Ruth Wasem and Ruth Bordin, 7–8, G. Mennen Williams and Nancy Quirk Williams Oral History Project, 1980–1982, BHL.

3. Staebler, *Smoke-Filled Room*, p. 36; Excerpts from Remarks, March 4, 1958, Remarks by Williams, April 27, 1958, Box 428, GMW Papers; Address by Swainson, November 27, 1961, Box 15, JBS Papers.

4. Thomas R. Dye, *Politics in States and Communities* (Englewood Cliffs, N.J.: Prentice Hall, 1969), pp. 142, 145.

5. Stieber, *Politics of Change*, p. 133; La Polambara, *Guide to Michigan Politics*, pp. 16–20; Robert W. Becker et al., "Correlates of Legislative Voting: Michigan's House of Representatives, 1954–1961," *Midwest Journal of Political Science 6* (November 1962): 386–90.

6. Dye, *Politics*, p. 90; Fenton, *Midwest Politics*, pp. 39–40; Sarasohn and Sarasohn, *Party Patterns*, pp. 35–36, 45, 68–69; Neal R. Peirce, *The Megastates of America: People, Politics, and Power in Ten Great States* (New York: W. W. Norton and Co., 1972), pp. 420–21; Stieber, *Politics of Change*, p. 8; Becker et al., "Correlates of Legislative Voting," pp. 393, 396; La Polambara, *Guide to Michigan Politics*, p. 25; David William Winder, "Gubernatorial-Legislative Interaction in Michigan" (Ph.D. diss., Michigan State University, 1982), p. 143; Reichley, *States in Crisis*, p. 32; William Barry Furlong, "A Boy Wonder Begins to Wander," *New York Times Magazine*, November 22, 1959, p. 107.

7. Winder, "Gubernatorial-Legislative Interaction," pp. 142, 146; Malcolm E. Jewell, "The Governor as Legislative Leader," in *The American Governor in Behavioral Perspective*, ed. Thad Beyle and J. Oliver Williams (New York: Harper and Row, 1972), pp. 128, 140; Staebler, *Smoke-Filled Room*, p. 36.

8. Summary of . . . Activities, 1948–1950, Box 7, Mildred Jeffrey Papers, ALUA; Release, January 6, 1949, Box 430, GMW Papers; Howard A. Hamilton, "Michigan's Fair Employment Law," June 20, 1955, p. 19, copy in Box 3, Louis C. Cramton Papers, BHL.

9. Lockard, *Toward Equal Opportunity*, pp. 28, 40–49, 61–62; Becker et al., "Correlates of Legislative Voting," pp. 386–90, 393; La Palombara, *Guide to Michigan Politics*, p. 20; Stieber, *Politics of Change*, p. 133; Peirce, *Megastates*, pp. 420–21; Reuther to Charles C. Diggs, Jr., May 26, 1953, Box 27, Charles C. Diggs, Jr., Papers, Moorland-Spingarn Research Center, Howard University, Washington, D.C.; Michigan Committee on Civil Rights document, n.d., citing Retail Merchants Association Legislative Bulletin, No. 1, January 28, 1952, ibid.

10. Lockard, *Toward Equal Opportunity*, pp. 28, 68–72; Schermer to Williams, January 6, 1949, Box 73, Detroit Commission on Community Relations Human Rights Department (hereafter DCCR) Papers, ALUA.

11. Lockard, *Toward Equal Opportunity*, p. 58.

12. Ibid., pp. 29, 37, 40–42, 58; Stieber, *Politics of Change*, pp. 7–8; Dye, *Politics*, p. 90.

13. Louis C. Cramton, Jr., MS [n.d.], Box 5, Cramton Papers.

14. Schermer to Oscar Baker, February 4, 1949, Box 73, DCCR Papers; Summary of . . . Activities, 1948–1950, Box 7, Jeffrey Papers.

15. House Bill No. 148, Michigan Sixty-Fifth Legislature, 1949 (there are copies of the Michigan bills in the University of Michigan Law Library, Ann Arbor, Michigan).

16. "Fair Practices and Civil Rights," n.d., Williams to Duane Roberts, May 15, 1949, Box 186, Michigan AFL-CIO Papers, ALUA; Michigan Committee on Civil Rights, An FEP Bill for Michigan, March 2, 1949, Schermer Memorandum to Advisory Committee, May 12, 1949, Box 451, GMW Papers; Summary of . . . Activities, 1948–1950, Box 7, Jeffrey Papers; *DN*, March 23, 1949, DNSB 9, BHL; cf. Minutes, Industrial Relations Committee, Detroit Urban League Vocational Services Department, April 21, 1950, Box 6, Francis A. DeWald Papers, BHL.

17. *DN*, March 23, 24, 1949; unidentified clipping [March 24, 1949], in Box 451, GMW Papers; Schermer Memorandum to Advisory Committee, May 12, 1949, ibid.; Olive R. Beasley to Clinton M. Fair, April 8, 1949, Box 3, ibid.; Schermer to Bert Storey, April 26, 1949, Box 8, UAW Fair Practices and Anti-Discrimination Department Papers (hereafter UAW Fair Practices Papers), ALUA.

18. *Michigan Official Directory and Legislative Manual, 1949–1950*, pp. 611–19; House Bill No. 497, Michigan Sixty- Fifth Legislature, 1949; *DN*, March 24, 27, April 10, 30, 1949; Schermer Memorandum to Advisory Committee, May 12, 1949, Box 451, GMW Papers; Schermer to Storey, April 26, 1949, Box 8, UAW Fair Practices Papers.

19. Beasley Memorandum to Fair, April 26, 1949, Fair to T. G. Trumbull, June 22, 1949, Box 3, GMW Papers; *Grand Rapids Herald*, December 19, 1949, clipping in Box 451, ibid.; Schermer Memorandum to Advisory Committee, May 12, 1949, ibid.; Summary of . . . Activities, 1948–1950, Box 7, Jeffrey Papers.

20. *Battle Creek Enquirer News* [October 18, 1949], clipping in Box 451, GMW Papers; Beasley to Williams, December 7, 1949, unsigned and undated Memorandum on FEPC, Box 3, ibid.; R. L. Bradby to Williams, November 21, 1949, Haskell L. Lazere to Williams, December 28, 1949, Drafting and Liaison Committee to Williams, December 30, 1949, Frank X. Martel to Williams, February 7, 1950, Box 328, ibid.; DeWald to Williams, December 9, 1949, Williams to DeWald, December 28, 1949, January 2, 1950, Bradby to Williams, December 23, 1949, Box 228, ibid.

21. Scholle to Williams, December 6, 12, 1949, Box 3, GMW Papers; MCCR State Executive Board to Members, January 5, 1950, Box 8, Jewish Labor Committee (hereafter JLC) Papers, ALUA.

22. Williams to John W. Connolly, March 9, 1950, Box 228, GMW Papers; Summary of . . . Activities, 1948–1950, Box 7, Jeffrey Papers; *LSJ*, March 16, 1950, Nancy C. Williams Scrapbook 4, GMW Papers.

23. Williams to Haas, April 13, 1950, Beasley to Williams, May 18, June 20, 1950, Williams to Leon Soffin, January 5, 1950, Box 228, GMW Papers; CJA [Adams] to Harry Frank, April 11, 1950, CJA to Clarence Lewis, April 14, 1950, Box 328, ibid.; Excerpts from Address of Williams . . . , May 26 [1950], Box 423, ibid.; "Civil Rights" [July 15, 1950], Box 451, ibid.; Summary of . . . Activities, 1948–1950, Box 7, Jeffrey Papers.

24. *Michigan Official Directory and Legislative Manual, 1953–1954*, pp. 252–53; *Flint Journal*, March 4, 1953, clipping in Box 6, Cramton Papers; *DN*, May 26, 1955; House Bill No. 497, Michigan Sixty-Fifth Legislature, 1949; Robert J. Greene, Selections from "What Did You Do Dad before We Knew You? A Memoir . . . ," November 1991, p. 107, Robert J. Greene Papers, BHL.

25. House Bills Nos. 122, 318, Michigan Sixty-Sixth Legislature, 1951; Cramton to Owen J. Cleary, August 16, 1951, Box 3, Cramton Papers; Schermer to Cramton, March 1, 1951, Box 20, DCCR Papers; CJA to William Oliver, January 24, 1951, Box 48, GMW Papers; *Michigan Official Directory and Legislative Manual, 1951–1952*, pp. 112, 255; *DN*, February 8, 1951; [*Detroit Times*, January 10, 1951], N. Williams Scrapbook 6, GMW Papers.

26. Downs to Cramton, March 30, 1951, Downs to All Commissioners, April 13, 1951, Tom Downs Papers, BHL.

27. Statement of Harry C. Markle to Robert Montgomery, April 18, 1951, Box 175, Michigan AFL-CIO Collection; *Michigan Official Directory and Legislative Manual, 1951–1952*, p. 34.

28. Williams to Beasley, March 23, 1951, Box 48, GMW Papers; Testimony on House Bill No. 318, April 18, 1951, Box 6, UAW Fair Practices Papers; *DN*, April 6, 19, 23, 1951; DUL, Vocational Services Department, Monthly Report, April 1951, Box 6, DeWald Papers.

29. Beasley to Williams, April 8, 1951, Box 48, GMW Papers; Beasley to Ed Carey, April 8, 1951, Box 25, UAW Fair Practices Papers; *DN*, April 28, 1951; *Michigan Chronicle*, May 5, 1951.

30. L. Cramton, Jr., to Charles Wortman, May 17, 1951, Box 5, Cramton Papers; Cramton to Cleary, August 16, 1951, Box 3, ibid.

31. Frank Blackford to Hattie M. Phipps, June 23, 1952, Box 71, GMW Papers; B. M. Joffe to CIO Council, January 18, 1952, Box 175, Michigan AFL-CIO Papers; *DN*, January 31, February 7, 11, 1952; House Bill No. 385, Michigan Sixty-Seventh Legislature, 1952.

32. Summary of Action Taken . . . Re: FEPC . . . , March 27, 1952, Box 169, Michigan AFL-CIO Papers; *DN*, February 15, 1952.

33. Beasley to Co-Worker, February 28, 1952, Alex Fuller Papers, ALUA; Beasley to Co-Worker, March 14, 1952, Box 175, Michigan AFL-CIO Papers; *DN*, March 4, 14, 1952; *DFP*, March 14, 1952; *Flint Journal*, March 13, 14, 1952, *LSJ*, March 19, 1952, clippings in Box 9, BG Papers, BHL; unidentified clipping in N. Williams Scrapbook 9, GMW Papers; Beasley Extra, March 4, 1952, Box 8, League of Women Voters of Michigan Papers, BHL.

34. Beasley to Co-Worker, March 14, 1952, Box 175, Michigan AFL-CIO Papers; *Port Huron Times Herald*, March 26, 1951, clipping in Box 451, GMW Papers; Arthur L. Johnson to Friend, enclosing Samuel J. Simmons, "The Defeat of FEPC," ibid.; *Journal of the House of Representatives of the State of Michigan, 1952 Regular Session*, pp. 991–99; *DN*, March 20, 1952; [*Detroit Times*, March 20, 1952], N. Williams Scrapbook 9, GMW Papers.

35. Beasley to MCCR Executive Board, November 10, 1952, Box 175, Michigan AFL-CIO Papers; UAW Release, November 20, 1952, Box 169, ibid.; Joffe to Roy Reuther, March 29, 1951, Emanuel Muravchik to Eleanor Wolf, June 8, 1951, J. Russell Bright to Dear Pastor, May 14, 1953, Box 13, UAW Political Action Department Papers, ALUA; Sugrue, *Urban Crisis*, pp. 171–73; Arthur Kornhauser, *Detroit as the People See It* (Detroit: Wayne State University Press, 1952), pp. 84,

104; Seth Mark Wigderson, "The UAW in the 1950s" (Ph.D. diss., Wayne State University, 1989), pp. 333–34.

36. Reuther to Williams, November 21, 1952, Box 71, GMW Papers; *Ann Arbor News*, November 5, 1952; DUL, Industrial Relations Committee Minutes, April 24, 1951, Box 6, DeWald Papers.

37. O. K. Fjetland to Max M. Horton, January 23, 1953, Minutes, MESC Meeting, February 9, 1953, Box 107, GMW Papers.

38. DUL, Industrial Relations Committee Minutes, April 24, 1951, DUL, Vocational Services Department, Monthly Reports, April, June, September, October 1952, Box 6, DeWald Papers; Sugrue, *Urban Crisis*, pp. 131–33.

39. House Bills Nos. 134, 168, Michigan Sixty-Seventh Legislature, 1953; Statement by . . . Cramton, February 12, 1953, Box 5, Cramton Papers; *DN*, February 12, 13, 1953.

40. Beasley to Cooperating Organizations, January 15, 1953, Beasley to Mrs. Robert McCandliss, February 18, 1953, Box 2, Olive R. Beasley Papers, ALUA; Beasley to MCCR Executive Board, January 16, 1953, Box 25, UAW Fair Practices Papers; Beasley, Attention MCCR Members, February 11, 1953, Box 175, Michigan AFL-CIO Papers; *DN*, February 4, 17, 20, 22, 1953; *LSJ*, February 19, 1953, clipping in Box 9, BG Papers; Louise Caine to Local Presidents, March 21, 1953, Box 8, League of Women Voters of Michigan Papers.

41. Cramton to Eisenhower, February 26, 1953, Cramton to Potter, March 24, 1953, Cramton to Ferguson, May 15, 1953, Bernard W. Shanley to Williams, January 14, 1954, Box 3, Cramton Papers.

42. Cramton to Potter, April 13, 1953, Cramton to Ferguson, May 15, 1953, Shanley to Cramton, August 4, 1953, Potter to Cramton, August 5, 1953, Cramton to Shanley, August 11, 1953, ibid.; Cramton, Jr., to Potter, May 12, June 25, 1953, Box 5, ibid.

43. Beasley to Members State Executive Board, March 17, 1953, Box 8, League of Women Voters of Michigan Papers.

44. Beasley, Call to Action, March 24, 1953, Box 175, Michigan AFL-CIO Papers; Beasley, Summary of Testimony . . ., March 31, 1953, Box 74, DCCR Papers; Beasley to Friend, March 26, 1953, Box 2, Beasley Papers; Haas to State Affairs Committee, March 27, 1953, and enclosure, Box 25, UAW Fair Practices Papers; Beasley to Co-Workers, June 1, 1953, Box 93, GMW Papers; *DN*, April 1, 1953.

45. Beasley, Summary of Testimony on H.B. 134 . . ., March 31, April 19, 1953, Box 74, DCCR Papers; Legislative Report 1953 Session, Box 3, Rollo G. Conlin Papers, BHL; *DN*, April 6, 11, 18, 1953; *LSJ*, April 13, 1953, clipping in Box 9, BG Papers; Cramton to Potter, April 13, 1953, Box 3, Cramton Papers.

46. Griffiths to Cramton, March 2, 1953, Beulah T. Whitby to Cramton, March 4, 1953, Box 3, Cramton Papers; *DN*, September 25, 1953, February 18, September 24, 1954, January 31, February 15, 1955.

47. Williams to Members of Senate and House . . ., December 29, 1953, Box 451, GMW Papers; Williams to Eisenhower, January 5, 1954, Box 118, ibid.; Shanley to Williams, January 14, 1954, Box 3, Cramton Papers.

48. MCCR Release, February 22, 1954, Beasley, "Summary Report 1954 Legislative Campaign . . ., April 15, 1954," April 16, 1954, Williams to Eisenhower, January 5, 1954, Box 451, GMW Papers; Beasley to Feikens, December 30, 1953,

January 11, February 22, 1954, Feikens to Beasley, January 27, 1954, Box 16, Diggs Papers; *DN*, November 26, 1953, February 7, 1954; [*Detroit Times*, December 30, 1953], N. Williams Scrapbook 12, GMW Papers.

49. [*LSJ*, January 3, 1954], clipping in Box 9, BG Papers; *Journal of House of Representatives*, No. 1, January 13, 1954, copy in Box 5, Cramton Papers.

50. Beasley, "Summary Report," April 16, 1954, Box 451, GMW Papers; *DN*, January 10, 17, 1954.

51. House Bill No. 35, Michigan Sixty-Seventh Legislature, 1954; Beasley, "Summary Report," April 16, 1954, Box 451, GMW Papers; Shanley to Cramton, January 14, 1954, Cramton to Shanley, January 20, 1954, Box 3, Cramton Papers; *DN*, February 4, 1954.

52. MCCR Report and Summary of Debate . . . , April 2, 1954, Box 451, GMW Papers; *Journal of the House of Representatives*, No. 15, February 3, 1954, pp. 206–10, copy in ibid.; *DN*, February 4, 1954; Cramton to Shanley, February 5, 1954, Box 3, Cramton Papers.

53. House Bills Nos. 230, 285, Michigan Sixty-Seventh Legislature; Beasley, "Summary Report," April 16, 1954, MCCR Memorandum, February 16, 1954, Williams to Lazere, February 24, 1954, Box 451, GMW Papers; *DN*, February 3, March 3, 1954; unidentified clipping [February 2, 1954], in N. Williams Scrapbook 12, GMW Papers.

54. Senate Bill No. 1163, Michigan Sixty-Seventh Legislature, 1954; Beasley, "Summary Report," April 16, 1954, Box 451, GMW Papers; MCCR Bulletin, March 8, 1954, Box 16, Diggs Papers; *Journal of the Senate of the State of Michigan, 1954 Regular Session*, pp. 182, 487, 535, 543; *Ann Arbor News*, March 5, 1954; *DN*, March 5, 14, 1954.

55. MCCR Bulletin, March 8, 1954, Box 16, Diggs Papers; *Journal of the House of Representatives of the State of Michigan, 1954 Regular Session*, p. 688; Beasley, "Summary Report," April 16, 1954, Box 451, GMW Papers.

56. *Journal of the House of Representatives of the State of Michigan, 1954 Regular Session*, pp. 987–88, 1059–60; Beasley, "Summary Report," April 16, 1954, MCCR Report and Summary of Debate, . . . April 2, 1954, Release, March 30, 1954, Box 451, GMW Papers; *DN*, March 24, 30, 31, 1954.

57. MCCR Special Bulletin, November 26, 1954, Williams Message . . . , January 19, 1955, Box 451, GMW Papers; ABF [Fitt], December 23, 1954, Box 118, ibid.; *DN*, December 16, 1954, clipping in Box 9, BG Papers; *DN*, January 12, 1955.

58. House Bill No. 24, Michigan Sixty-Eighth Legislature, 1955.

59. Oliver to Regional Directors . . . and Staff, January 5, 1955, Box 20, Roy Reuther Files, UAW Political Action Department Papers; "How to Answer Criticism of FEPC," n.d., Box 22, ibid.; Oliver to R. Reuther, March 2, 1955, Box 20, ibid.; Steering Committee Minutes, Michigan Coordinating Council for FEPC, February 15, 1955, Marvin Meltzer to Oscar Baker, February 18, 1955, Box 8, JLC Papers; *DN*, February 15, 1955.

60. Stanley Benford to Members of the Michigan Legislature, January 26, 1955, Box 9, JLC Papers.

61. Meltzer to Maslow, February 2, 1955, Maslow to Meltzer, February 8, 1955, Box 8, JLC Papers; Oral History interview with Mildred Jeffrey, December 30, 1977, p. 75, Institute of Industrial Relations of the University of Michigan and Wayne

State University, Women and Work Program, The 20th Century Trade Union Woman: Vehicle for Social Change, Oral History Program, 1978–1979, BHL; Nancy F. Gabin, *Feminism in the Labor Movement: Women in the United Automobile Workers, 1935–1975* (Ithaca: Cornell University Press, 1990), p. 93.

62. *Journal of the House of Representatives of the State of Michigan, 1955 Regular Session,* pp. 123, 791–92, 870–77; UAW Fair Practice Fact Sheet 9 (April–May 1955), Box 9, JLC Papers; Steering Committee, Michigan Coordinating Council for FEPC Minutes, March 16, April 7, 1955, Box 8, ibid.; *DN,* April 8, 12–14, 1955; *Ann Arbor News,* April 13, 14, 1955.

63. Meltzer to Finlay C. Allen, January 31, 1955, Sheldon Rahn to Jacob Potofsky, April 20, 1955, Box 8, JLC Papers; Michigan Coordinating Council for FEPC pamphlet, Box 147, GMW Papers; Meltzer to Steering Committee Members, April 15, 1955, Box 175, Michigan AFL-CIO Papers.

64. *Journal of the Senate of the State of Michigan, 1955 Regular Session,* pp. 414, 851, 1311–12, 1405–8; *Journal of the House of Representatives of the State of Michigan, 1955 Regular Session,* pp. 876–77, 1618–19, 1664–65; Betz to MCCR, March 31, 1954, Box 16, Diggs Papers; Michigan Coordinating Council for FEPC, Release, May 17, 1955, Box 23, UAW Fair Practices Papers; Beasley to Detroit Civil Service Commission, June 8, 1953, Box 93, GMW Papers; Frederick E. Tripp to Rahn, May 23, 1955, Box 147, ibid.; Oliver to W. Reuther, May 27, 1955, Box 20, R. Reuther Files, UAW Political Action Department Papers; UAW-CIO Fair Practice Fact Sheet 9 (June–July 1955), Box 9, JLC Papers; unidentified clippings, April 14, 25, 1955 in Box 451, GMW Papers; *DN,* March 31, May 20, 25, 26, 1955.

65. Williams to Leon Fram, June 2, 1955, Box 147, GMW Papers; Releases, June 29, October 14, 1955, Box 462, ibid.; *DN,* June 30, 1955.

66. "Public Act No. 251," *Public and Local Acts of the State Legislature of the State of Michigan Passed at the Regular Session of 1955,* pp. 411–17; Betty Lou LeBreton and Preston P. LeBreton, *The Michigan State Fair Employment Practices Act,* University of Detroit Institute for Business Services Research Bulletin No. 103 (Detroit: University of Detroit, 1956). For the laws of other states, see Lockard, *Toward Equal Opportunity,* pp. 77–102 passim; Norgren and Hill, *Toward Fair Employment,* pp. 103–13; and "Right to Equal Treatment: Administrative Enforcement of Antidiscrimination Legislation," *Harvard Law Review* 74 (1961): 528–29, 540, 545, 547.

67. John G. Feild, "Hindsight and Foresight about FEPC," *Buffalo Law Review* 14 (February 1964): 18; Herbert Hill, "Twenty Years of State Fair Employment Practices Commissions: A Critical Analysis with Recommendations," *Buffalo Law Review* 14 (February 1964): 40; Norgren and Hill, *Toward Fair Employment,* pp. 98–99, 230–31, 251; Lockard, *Toward Equal Opportunity,* pp. 77–79, 98.

68. Cramton, Jr., MS, n.d., Box 5, Cramton Papers; Hamilton, "Fair Employment," Box 3, ibid.; *Michigan Official Directory and Legislative Manual, 1955–1956,* pp. 413–27, 547–48, 550–56; Release, October 14, 1955, Box 462, GMW Papers; *Michigan Chronicle,* October 22, 1955; Stieber, *Politics of Change,* p. 122. In the 1955 spring election, Democrats captured the open seats on the State Board of Agriculture and the University of Michigan Board of Regents and came close to electing their candidates for superintendent of public instruction and the open seat on the State Board of Education.

69. Release, August 22, 1955, Box 462, GMW Papers; *DN,* August 22, 1955.

Chapter 3

1. MESC, A Report to . . . Williams, September 1, 1955, Box 163, GMW Papers, BHL; Release, October 14, 1955, Box 462, ibid.; *DN,* September 28, 1955, DNSB 13, BHL.

2. Release, October 14, 1955, *DFP,* October 14, 1956, clipping in Box 462, GMW Papers; Robert J. Greene, "Selections from . . . A Memoir for My Three Sons . . . ," November 1991, p. 109, Robert J. Greene Papers, BHL; *Hearings before the United States Commission on Civil Rights: Hearings Held in Detroit, Michigan, December 14, 15, 1960* (Washington, D.C.: Government Printing Office, 1961), pp. 102, 105; McNaughton, *Mennen Williams,* p. 224.

3. *DN,* December 17, 1955, DNSB 13; *LSJ,* December 17, 1955, clipping in Box 9, BG Papers, BHL; FEPC, *On the Job in Michigan,* November–December 1958, Box 50, Detroit Urban League (hereafter DUL) Papers, BHL; Greene, "Selections," p. 120, Greene Papers; Seabron to Simeon Booker, December 12, 1955, Box 4, William M. Seabron Papers, ALUA.

4. FEPC, *On the Job in Michigan,* January–February, March–April, November–December 1958, Box 50, DUL Papers; *Michigan FEPC,* January 23, 1960, Box 300, GMW Papers; Feild to Williams, March 31, 1959, Williams to B. M. Joffe, April 13, 1959, Harry J. Kelly to Arthur F. Rasch, April 19, 1959, Box 289, ibid.; Routh to Swainson, April 11, 1962, Michigan FEPC Release, June 3, 1962, Louis Rosenzweig to Swainson, August 14, 1962, Box 29, JBS Papers, BHL; *Detroit Times,* July 25, 1957, clipping in Box 462, GMW Papers; *DN,* December 18, 1958, May 29, 1959, DNSB 13; FEPC Release, September 9, 1963, Box 58, GR Papers, BHL.

5. FEPC, *On the Job in Michigan,* November 1956–June 1957, Box 50, DUL Papers; FEPC Release, April 25, 1957, Box 462, GMW Papers; FEPC Memorandum to Budget Director, September 6, 1957, Box 236, ibid.; Seabron to Williams, May 7, 1959, Box 289, ibid.; Routh to Williams, August 15, 1960, Box 318, ibid.; Alex Fuller to Swainson, December 6, 1960, Box 8, Tom Downs Papers, BHL; Feild, "Hindsight and Foresight," 18–19; Norgren and Hill, *Toward Fair Employment,* pp. 100–101.

6. *DN,* October 11, 1959, DNSB 15; Questions and Answers— Lansing Conference, January 23, 1960, Box 2, Records of The Michigan Civil Rights Commission, Information Division, General Administrative Records of the Fair Employment Practices Commission, RG 66-82-A, State Archives, Lansing, Michigan; Hodges Memorandum to Swainson, October 15, 1962, Box 4, ibid.; Rosenzweig to Romney, February 8, 1963, enclosing Michigan FEPC, 1962 Annual Report, Box 12, GR Papers; *Fair Employment Practices at Work in Twelve States: A Report Prepared for the Conference of Governors of Civil Rights States* [1958], pp. 6–8, copy in Box 289, GMW Papers; Special Subcommittee on Labor, House Committee on Education and Labor, *Equal Employment Opportunity,* 87 Cong., 1 sess., 1961, 210.

7. FEPC Statement of Policy, October 14, 1955, Box 462, GMW Papers; Michigan FEPC Anniversary Summary, October 14, 1956, Box 194, ibid.; FEPC, *Information,* April 1956, Box 50, DUL Papers; *DN,* September 28, October 8, 15, November 9, 1955, January 17, 18, 1956, DNSB 13.

8. *Commission on Civil Rights Hearings,* p. 106; FEPC, *Information,* September 1956, Box 5, Louis C. Cramton Papers, BHL; *Fair Employment Practices at Work,* p. 10; Feild to Swainson, February 6, 1961, Box 10, JBS Papers; *Equal Employment Opportunity,* 205.

9. FEPC, *Information,* May–June 1956, Box 8, League of Women Voters of

Michigan Papers, BHL; FEPC, *Information,* September 1956, Box 5, Cramton Papers; Feild Memorandum to Department of Administration, October 11, 1957, Feild Memorandum to Williams, November 7, 1957, Box 226, GMW Papers; Michigan FEPC Anniversary Summary, October 14, 1956, Box 134, ibid.; *Michigan FEPC,* January 23, 1960, Box 300, ibid.

10. FEPC, *Information,* August 1956, Report on Westside Employment Conference . . . , Detroit, December 15, 1956, FEPC, *On the Job in Michigan,* November 1956–January 1957, Feild to William Brown, November 28, 1956, Box 50, DUL Papers; DUL, Vocational Services Department, Monthly Report, November 1956, Box 45, ibid.; *Michigan FEPC,* January 23, 1960, Box 300, GMW Papers; *DN,* December 9, 1956, DNSB 14.

11. *Michigan FEPC,* January 23, 1960, Box 300, GMW Papers; Feild Memorandum to Williams, November 7, 1957, Box 226, ibid.; Seabron to Williams, May 7, 1959, Box 289, ibid.; Michigan State Advisory Committee to the National Civil Rights Commission . . . Report [1959], Box 270, ibid.; Michigan FEPC Anniversary Summary, October 14, 1956, Box 134, ibid.; FEPC, *On the Job in Michigan,* February–March, June–August 1957, March–April, May–June 1958, Box 50, DUL Papers; Greene, "Selections," p. 111, Greene Papers; Questions and Answers— Lansing Conference, Box 2, RG 66-82-A; Michigan FEPC, 1962 Annual Report, Box 12, GR Papers; Katherine Shannon interview with John Feild, December 28, 1967, pp. 22–23, 46–47, Civil Rights Documentation Project, Moorland-Spingarn Research Center, Howard University, Washington, D.C.

12. *Equal Employment Opportunity,* p. 205; Michigan FEPC Anniversary Summary, October 14, 1956, Box 134, GMW Papers; Frances R. Cousens Memorandum to Feild, January 17, 1958, Box 258, ibid.; *Michigan FEPC,* January 23, 1960, Box 300, ibid.; Greene, "Selections," p. 111, Greene Papers; Cousens, "The Need for Direction of the Commission's Research Program," June 1–3, 1961, Box 36, Records of the Michigan Civil Rights Commission: Administrative, RG 74-90, State Archives; Report of the Research Division . . . , September 1956–December 1961, Box 212, Michigan AFL-CIO Papers, ALUA.

13. Proposal for Organizing FEP Councils, n.d., FEPC, *Information,* April 1956, FEPC, *On the Job in Michigan,* February–March, April–May, September– October, November–December 1957, March–April, September–October, 1958, Box 50, DUL Papers; FEPC, *Information,* May–July 1956, Box 8, League of Women Voters of Michigan Papers; FEPC, *Information,* September 1956, Box 5, Cramton Papers; Feild Memorandum to Williams, August 6, 1957, Feild Memorandum to Department of Administration, October 11, 1957, and enclosure, Box 226, GMW Papers; *Michigan FEPC,* January 23, 1960, Box 300, ibid.; Questions and Answers— Lansing Conference, January 23, 1960, Box 2, RG 66-82-A; Greene, "Selections," pp. 110–11, Greene Papers; *Commission on Civil Rights Hearings,* p. 106; Seabron, "Is There a Need to Restructure FEPC Staff Organization . . . ?" [1961], Box 36, RG 74-90; Roscoe B. Ballard to Seabron, December 17, 1959, Thomas J. Peloso to Seabron, December 18, 1959, Box 2, RG 66-82-A; *Equal Employment Opportunity,* p. 205.

14. Greene, "Selections," p. 122, Greene Papers; *Equal Employment Opportunity,* p. 205; Questions and Answers—Lansing Conference, January 23, 1960, Box 2, RG 66-82-A; *Michigan FEPC,* January 23, 1960, Box 300, GMW Papers.

15. Hodges to Walter R. Greene, February 13, 1958, Box 258, GMW Papers; FEPC Memorandum to Budget Director, September 6, 1957, Box 236, ibid.; *Michigan*

FEPC, January 23, 1960, Box 300, ibid.; FEPC, *On the Job in Michigan,* June–August, 1957, Box 50, DUL Papers; Greene, "Selections," p. 118, Greene Papers; FEPC Minutes, March 6, 1961, Hodges Memorandum to Routh, March 6, 1961, Box 1, Records of the Civil Rights Commission: Executive, RG 81-89, State Archives; FEPC Adjustment Reviews [1963], Box 10, RG 66-82-A; Norgren and Hill, *Toward Fair Employment,* p. 111; Lockard, *Toward Equal Opportunity,* p. 80.

16. *Michigan FEPC,* January 23, 1960, Box 300, GMW Papers; FEPC Release, December 19, 1962, Box 9, RG 66-82-A; Greene, "Selections," pp. 112–13, Greene Papers; "Right to Equal Treatment," pp. 540, 548; Norgren and Hill, *Toward Fair Employment,* pp. 108; Lockard, *Toward Equal Opportunity,* pp. 77–79. For New Jersey's "validation conference," see Alfred W. Blumrosen, "Antidiscrimination Laws in Action: A Law-Sociology Study," *Rutgers Law Review* 19 (Winter 1965): 223–24, 250.

17. *DN,* February 19, 1956, DNSB 12; Pre-Employment Inquiry Guide [1956], Box 462, GMW Papers; FEPC Minutes, November 25, 1957, Box 226, ibid.; FEPC, *Information,* April 1956, Box 50, DUL Papers; Seabron to Levi Yerkes, September 26, 1961, Routh to Alice Dorcan, September 28, 1961, Box 7, JBS Papers; Paul Adams, "Michigan's Human Relations Needs," October 28, 1961, Box 15, ibid.

18. *Equal Employment Opportunity,* p. 203; *DN,* December 18, 22, 1962, DNSB 17.

19. Seabron to Ernest L. Brown, February 15, 1956, Box 50, DUL Papers; DUL, Vocational Services Department, Monthly Report, June 1959, Box 45, ibid.

20. Adams Opinion No. 2880, May 22, 1958, Box 3, RG 66-82-A; *Michigan FEPC,* January 23, 1960, Box 300, GMW Papers; FEPC, *On the Job in Michigan,* May–June 1958, Box 50, DUL Papers; *Equal Employment Opportunity,* p. 211.

21. Claims Processed by Michigan FEPC, January 1, 1956, to December 31, 1963, Box 58, GR Papers; Cousens, A Summary Analysis of Six Years of Claims . . . [1962], Box 74, Detroit Commission on Community Relations, Human Relations Department (hereafter DCCR) Papers, ALUA; Michigan FEPC Anniversary Summary, October 14, 1956, Box 134, GMW Papers; FEPC Minutes, January 24, 1958, Box 258, ibid.; Seabron to Williams, May 7, 1959, Box 280, ibid.; Lockard, *Toward Equal Opportunity,* p. 91.

22. Claims Processed . . . January 1, 1956, to December 31, 1963, Box 58, GR Papers; *Michigan FEPC,* January 23, 1960, Box 300, GMW Papers; FEPC, *On the Job in Michigan,* June–August 1957, Box 236, ibid.; Michigan FEPC, 1962 Annual Report, Box 12, GR Papers; *DN,* January 1, 1964.

23. FEPC, *Information,* September 1956, Box 5, Cramton Papers; Hodges to Feild, July 24, 1959, Box 226, GMW Papers; *Michigan FEPC,* January 23, 1960, Box 300, ibid.; Statement of Louis Rosenzweig . . . , November 12, 1959, Box 9, Jewish Labor Committee (hereafter JLC) Papers, ALUA; Hill, "Twenty Years," pp. 25–26.

24. Michigan FEPC Anniversary Summary, October 14, 1956, Box 134, GMW Papers; Feild Memorandum to Department of Administration, October 11, 1957, and enclosures, FEPC Minutes, November 25, 1957, enclosing Executive Director Memorandum to Chief, Claims Division, November 15, 1957, FEPC Minutes, December 18, 1957, Box 226, ibid.; Seabron to Williams, May 7, 1959, Box 289, ibid.; FEPC, *On the Job in Michigan,* February–March 1957, March–April 1958, Box 50, DUL Papers; Hodges Memorandum to Routh, January 10, 1961, FEPC Minutes, January 24, 1962, Box 1, RG 81-89; *Ann Arbor News,* December 19, 1957, clipping

in Box 9, BG Papers; *Equal Employment Opportunity,* p. 205; *Commission on Civil Rights Hearings,* p. 97; Hodges, "Elimination of Discrimination in Employment," March 30, 1961, Box 3, Albert and Emma Wheeler Papers, BHL.

25. FEPC, *On the Job in Michigan,* June–August, November–December 1957, Box 50, DUL Papers; FEPC Minutes, December 18, 1957, Box 226, GMW Papers; *Michigan FEPC,* January 23, 1960, Box 300, ibid.; FEPC Release, October 14, 1962, Box 9, RG 66-82-A; *DN,* December 19, 1957, DNSB 14; *Equal Employment Opportunity,* p. 205.

26. *DN,* March 12, 13, 1957, DNSB 14; *DN,* May 30, 1962, clipping in Box 9, BG Papers; FEPC, *On the Job in Michigan,* February–March 1957, Box 50, DUL Papers; FEPC Minutes, January 23, 1960, Box 300, GMW Papers; Hodges Memorandum to Members of CCAD, May 29, 1962, Box 15, Detroit NAACP Papers, ALUA; Fuller to Swainson, January 4, 1961, State of Michigan in the Circuit Court for Wayne, Estate of William R. Ragland . . . , FEPC Claim No. 287 [1961], Box 10, JBS Papers.

27. Michigan FEPC, 1962 Annual Report, Box 12, GR Papers; *Lesniak* v. *Fair Employment Practices Commission,* 364 Mich. 495 (1961).

28. Lasker Smith to Williams, August 4, 1960, Routh to Williams, August 15, 1960, Box 318, GMW Papers; In Re: Loy A. Cohen v. River Rouge Savings Bank, April 26 1961, Smith to James Hocker, An Open Letter . . . , May 1, 1962, Routh to Lattie Coor, May 10, 1962, Box 29, JBS Papers; FEPC Release, July 13, 1962, Box 9, RG 66-82-A; Michigan FEPC, 1962 Annual Report, Box 12, GR Papers; *DN,* December 14, 1963.

29. *DN,* May 5, 1960; Michigan FEPC, 1962 Annual Report, Box 12, GR Papers; *City of Highland Park* v. *Fair Employment Practices Commission,* 364 Mich. 508 (1961); "Right to Equal Treatment," p. 558.

30. Michigan FEPC, 1962 Annual Report, Box 12, GR Papers; Greene, "Selections," pp. 115–16, Greene Papers; "Right to Equal Treatment," p. 539; FEPC Release, June 19, 1962, Box 9, RG 66-82-A; George E. Bushnell to Hodges, May 10, 1963, Box 4, ibid.

31. Mackie to Fuller, January 19, 1961, Mitchell Tendler to Swainson, January 18, 1961, Mildred Jeffrey to John Murray, February 1, 1961, Dick Miller Memorandum to Swainson, January 24, 1961, Clarence Taylor to Frederick E. Tripp, February 21, 1961, Box 11, JBS Papers; *LSJ,* January 17, 26, 1961, clippings in Box 9, BG Papers.

32. Regulatory Activities [1961], Box 7, RG 66-82-A; Hodges Memorandum to Routh, February 7, 1961, Box 1, RG-81–89; Special Report, An Investigation of the Personnel Policies and Practices of the Michigan Highway Department, March 1961, Routh to Swainson, February 7, 1961, Box 11, JBS Papers; *LSJ,* March 19, 1961, clipping in Box 9, BG Papers; Michigan FEPC, 1962 Annual Report, Box 12, GR Papers.

33. Special Report . . . State Highway Department, March 1961, Box 11, JBS Papers.

34. Mackie to All Employees, March 20, 1961, Mackie Memorandum to All Division Heads, July 12, 1961, Mackie to Routh, September 8, 1961, Coor to Ira Polley, December 4, 1961, Box 15, JBS Papers; Mackie to Swainson, June 15, 1961, Routh to Mackie, October 3, 1961, Swainson to Mackie, October 18, 1961, Box 11, ibid.; *DN,* September 4, 1961, DNSB 16; *DN,* May 16, 1962, DNSB 17; *Ann Arbor News,* September 19, 1961, clipping in Box 9, BG Papers.

35. Michigan FEPC, 1962 Annual Report, Box 12, GR Papers; FEPC Special Report: The Race Track Industry in Michigan, September 1961, Executive Office Release, October 10, 1961, Box 10, JBS Papers; *LSJ,* April 21, 1961, clipping in Box 9, BG Papers; *DN,* October 11, 1961, DNSB 16.

36. Executive Office Release, October 10, 1961, Box 10, JBS Papers; Edgar Hayes to Swainson, December 27, 1961, Box 29, ibid.; Michigan FEPC, 1962 Annual Report, Box 12, GR Papers.

37. Regulatory Activities [1961], Box 7, RG 66-82-A; Hodges Memorandum to Routh, January 10, 1961, Box 1, RG 81-89; FEPC, *On the Job in Michigan, 1960–1961 Special Year End Issue,* Box 74, DCCR Papers.

38. FEPC, *Information,* May–June 1956, Box 8, League of Women Voters of Michigan Papers; Michigan FEPC Anniversary Summary, October 14, 1956, Box 134, GMW Papers; FEPC, *On the Job in Michigan,* November 1956–January 1957, Box 50, DUL Papers; Walter R. Greene Memorandum to All Staff and Commission Members [1961], Box 7, RG 66-82-A; *Commission on Civil Rights Hearings,* p. 7; Hodges, "Eliminating Discrimination," Box 3, Wheeler Papers; *DN,* February 11, April 27, May 27, August 1, 1956, DNSB 13; *DN,* October 11, 1959, DNSB 15.

39. Shannon interview with Feild, pp. 22–23; Edward N. Hodges, "The Negro's Future through Fair Employment Practices," *Negro History Bulletin* 26 (October 1962): 16; Olive R. Beasley Memorandum to Hodges [1962], and enclosure, Greene Memorandum to All Staff and Commission Members [1961], Recruiting Contacts made by Components . . . , June 29, 1962, Box 7, RG 66-82-A; *Equal Employment Opportunity,* p. 200.

40. FEPC, *On the Job in Michigan,* April–May 1957, Box 50, DUL Papers; idem, *1960–1961 Special Year End Issue,* Box 74, DCCR Papers.

41. Hodges to Harold Durbin, June 28, 1963, FEPC Releases, June 26, August 13, 1963, unidentified clipping in Box 9, RG 66-82-A.

42. Minutes, Vocational Services Advisory Committee Meeting, December 2, 1955, Box 6, Francis A. Kornegay Papers, BHL; MESC, *Annual Report for the Fiscal Year Ending June 30, 1956,* p. 28; MESC, Annual Report to . . . Swainson . . . [December 1961], Box 29, JBS Papers; MESC in Its Relationship to Fair Employment Practices [1961], Box 33, ibid.; MESC Minutes, February 9, 1962, Downs Papers.

43. Sidney Fine interview with Tom Downs, March 30, 1995, pp. 9–10, 18, transcript in BHL; MESC Minutes, February 9, 1962, Box 9, Downs Papers.

44. Horton to State Office Administrative Staff . . . , September 26, 1955, Box 163, GMW Papers; MESC in Its Relationship to FEPC [1961], Box 33, JBS Papers; MESC Annual Report to . . . Swainson . . . [December 1961], Box 29, ibid.; MESC Minutes, February 9, 1962, Box 9, Downs Papers; Norgren and Hill, *Toward Fair Employment,* pp. 19, 36–37, 133.

45. Horton to All Employees, April 16, 1957, Box 5, RG 66-82-A; MESC Minutes, February 9, 1962, Box 9, Downs Papers; *MESC Annual Report for the Fiscal Year Ending Nineteen Hundred Fifty Seven,* pp. 3, 29–30.

46. Horton to State Office Administrative Staff . . . , July 8, 1959, Box 4, RG 66-82-A.

47. Statement of Mutual Understanding between the MESC and the Michigan FEPC, February 12, 1960, Box 33, JBS Papers.

48. Horton to Routh, May 24, 1960, Box 4, RG 66-82-A; *Commission on Civil Rights Hearings,* pp. 81–82, 125; *Employment: 1961 Commission on Civil Rights Report* (Washington, D.C.: Government Printing Office, n.d.), pp. 114–16, 118–20,

125; MESC Minutes, September 14, 1961, February 9, 1962, Box 9, Downs Papers; Norgren and Hill, *Toward Fair Employment,* pp. 38–39, 132; Lockard, *Toward Equal Opportunity,* pp. 84–88.

49. DUL, Vocational Services Department, Monthly Report, April 1952, Box 6, Kornegay Papers; Rasch to All Appointing Authorities . . . , April 2, 1957, Box 4, RG 66-82-A; CSC Statement, March 13, 1957, Seabron to Jessie M. Harvey, May 6, 1960, Box 318, GMW Papers; *DN,* February 17, 1956, DNSB 13.

50. Undated Release [1956?], Box 452, GMW Papers; Cavanagh to Commission on Community Relations, October 11, 1962, Box 9, Kornegay Papers; *DN,* December 18, 1962, DNSB 17.

51. Feild Memorandum to Williams, August 6, 1957, Box 226, GMW Papers; Augmented Staff Meeting Minutes, September 30 [1957], Box 407, ibid.; FEPC, *On the Job in Michigan,* June–August 1957, Box 50, DUL Papers; *DN,* August 8, 1957, clipping in Box 9, BG Papers.

52. GM Memorandum to Harry Kelly, August 14, 1959, Box 269, GMW Papers; Routh to Williams, September 24, 1959, Box 289, ibid.; General Departmental Communication No. 17, December 21, 1959, Box 7, JBS Papers; *Commission on Civil Rights Hearings,* p. 99.

53. Weeks, *Stewards of the State,* pp. 116–17.

54. Jeffrey to Swainson, February 17, 1961, Release, March 26, 1961, Jordan Popkin Memorandum to Swainson, March 27, 1961, Box 7, JBS Papers; State of Michigan Governor's Code of Fair Practices, May 1961, Box 10, ibid.; *Ann Arbor News,* May 27, 1961, clipping in Box 9, BG Papers.

55. Routh to Swainson, October 6, 1961, Box 7, JBS Papers; Coor Memorandum to Zolton Ferency, January 8, 1962, Annual Report to . . . Swainson under the Governor's Code . . . , n.d., Box 29, ibid.; MESC in Its Relationship to Fair Employment Practices, n.d., Box 33, ibid.; Frederick B. Routh, "Supplementary Activities for State Governments Seeking to Prevent Discrimination," *Buffalo Law Review* 14 (Fall 1964): 148; MESC Minutes, June 15, August 11, September 14, 19, November 21, 1961, Box 8, Downs Papers; MESC Minutes, February 9, March 19, 1962, Box 9, ibid.; Statement of Mutual Understanding . . . , March 14, 1962, Box 3, ibid.; MESC, *Annual Report of the Fiscal Year Ending June 30, 1962,* p. 60; idem, *Annual Report . . . 1963,* pp. 63–64; Hodges to Romney, August 8, 1963, Box 58, GR Papers; "Right to Equal Treatment," p. 59.

56. Routh note, May 31, 1961, Routh to Swainson, June 23, 1961, Thelma Zwerdling to Zolton Ferency, June 30, 1961, Ferency Memorandum to Routh, July 10, 1961, Box 7, JBS Papers; Routh Memorandum to Adams, June 23, 1961, Box 10, ibid.; *DFP,* June 18, 1961, clipping in Box 7, ibid.

57. Popkin Memorandum to Swainson, October 13, November 7, 1961, Coor Memorandum to Swainson, November 26, 1961, Swainson to State Agency Directors . . . , November 27, 1961, and enclosure, Address by Swainson, November 27, 1961, Coor to Swainson, November 29, 1961, Berl I. Bernhard to Swainson, December 4, 1961, Seabron to Seth R. Phillips, December 21, 1961, Box 15, JBS Papers; Routh, "Supplementary Activities," p. 149.

58. Michigan FEPC Governor's Code of Fair Practices—Annual Report 1961, F. K. DeWald to Swainson, December 13, 1961, Gerald E. Eddy to Swainson, December 18, 1961, Billie S. Farnum to Swainson, February 12, 1962, Ronald McDonald to Swainson, September 26, 1962, Statement by . . . Swainson, January 19, 1962, Box 29, JBS Papers. The MESC was the respondent in the single most

involved case of a complaint directed against a state agency by an aggrieved employee, the case of Carroll D. Little. There is a voluminous record on the Little case in the Downs Papers and the JBS Papers.

59. Hodges to Galen Martin, March 7, 1963, Eugene Busha to Hodges, April 1, 1963, Tendler to Romney, October 23, 1963, Box 58, GR Papers; MESC 1963 Annual Report to Romney of Activities under the Governor's Code . . . , DeWald to Romney, December 20, 1963, Box 419, ibid.; MESC, *Interim Report of Employment Patterns*, March 1, 1963, Box 58, ibid.

60. Statement of Mutual Understanding between Detroit Civil Service Commission and the Michigan FEPC [1963], Box 1, RG 66-82-A; FEPC, *On the Job . . . Merit Employment in Michigan: A Pictorial Report* (1963), Box 409, GR Papers; Romney to Elizabeth A. Wilson, July 10, 1963, Box 12, ibid.; DeWald to Romney, December 20, 1963, Box 419, ibid.

61. Feild, "Hindsight and Foresight," pp. 18–20; Hill, "Twenty Years," pp. 25–26, 40; Sugrue, *Urban Crisis*, p. 144; Geraldine Bledsoe to James R. Sagel, December 11, 1963, Box 10, GR Papers.

62. Hodges, "Eliminating Discrimination in Employment," Box 3, Wheeler Papers; *Commission on Civil Rights Hearings*, p. 97; *Equal Employment Opportunity*, p. 198.

63. *Commission on Civil Rights Hearings*, pp. 36, 80; *Equal Employment Opportunity*, pp. 223–24; *Michigan: 1961 Report to the Commission on Civil Rights from the State Advisory Committee*, pp. 287–88, Box 15, JBS Papers.

64. Michigan FEPC, 1962 Annual Report, Box 12, GR Papers; FEPC Release, October 14, 1962, Box 9, RG 66-82-A; Michigan FEPC, *Adjustment Reviews* [1963], Box 10, ibid.

65. *Commission on Civil Rights Hearings*, pp. 40–46, 63–66, 99–100; Statement of . . . Rosenzweig before Senate Sub-Committee on Unemployment, November 19, 1959, Box 19, JLC Papers.

66. *Commission on Civil Rights Hearings*, pp. 124, 128–30; *Employment: 1961*, p. 107; *DFP*, July 7, 1963; Sugrue, *Urban Crisis*, pp. 116–17.

67. Joint Construction Activities Committee, Resolution on Equal Opportunity of Employment [July 9, 1963], Box 2, Ernest C. and Jessie M. Dillard Papers, ALUA.

68. Research Division, Michigan Civil Rights Commission, A Report on the Characteristics of Michigan's Non-White Population, n.d., Box 19, Detroit NAACP Papers.

69. A Profile of the Detroit Negro, 1959–1967, Box 65, DUL Papers; Sugrue, *Urban Crisis*, pp. 276–77.

70. *Commission on Civil Rights Hearings*, pp. 84–89; Wheeler to Seabron, October 12, 1961, Box 3, Wheeler Papers.

71. *DN*, January 1, 1964.

Chapter 4

1. Williams to Mrs. Sherman Stetson, March 6, 1950, Box 228, GMW Papers, BHL; George Schermer to Williams, May 13, 1949, Draft of Civil Rights Plank . . . , September 25, 1950, Box 451, ibid.

2. Ruth Wasem and Ruth Bordin interview with Otis Smith, April 16, 1980, pp. 19–20, 39, 59–60, with Adelaide Hart, May 20, 1980, pp. 16–17, 26, with

Horace Sheffield, April 14, 1980, pp. 7–8, with Wade McCree, December 17, 1981, pp. 40, 44, 49, with Jane Hart, December 10, 1980, pp. 11–12, and with Alfred B. Fitt, January 19, 1982, pp. 11–12, G. Mennen Williams and Nancy Quirk Williams Oral History Project, 1980–1982, BHL; Democratic Program Service, Democratic State Central Committee, June 1, 1956, Box 451, GMW Papers; McCree, "Negro Renaissance," pp. 7–9; Staebler, *Smoke-Filled Room,* pp. 34, 64–66; *DN,* October 27, 1953, DNSB 12, BHL; *DN,* October 9, 1954, DNSB 13; *DN,* December 28, 1958, DNSB 14; *DN,* November 9, 1960, March 23, October 9, 1961, DNSB 16; Oral History Interview with G. Mennen Williams for the John F. Kennedy Library, April 27, 1960, p. 12, Box 103, GMW Non-Gubernatorial Papers, BHL.

3. *Jewish News,* March 25, 1968, clipping in Box 34, Helen Berthelot Papers, BHL.

4. Staebler, *Smoke-Filled Room,* p. 34; Berthelot, *Win Some, Lose Some,* pp. 28, 94–95, 127–32; A. Hart interview, p. 30; J. Hart interview, pp. 8–10, 12; Wasem and Bordin interview with Nancy Quirk Williams, December 19, 1981, pp. 13–14, Williams Oral History Project.

5. B. M. Joffe to Staebler, October 1, 1952, Citizens Committee to Editor, *Detroit Tribune,* October 28, 1952, Citizens Committee to Christian Science Committee, October 28, 1952, Box 74, GMW Papers; Release, October 21, 1952, Box 451, ibid.; A Statement of Principles to Guide Conduct of Political Campaigns, Box 1, Olive R. Beasley Papers, ALUA; Fair Election Practices Committee, A Summary of Its Activities, enclosed with Jordan Popkin to Williams, August 3, 1960, Box 301, GMW Papers.

6. FEPC Release, October 13, 1954, Box 462, GMW Papers; Staebler to Williams, February 7, 1955, Box 145, ibid.; Joffe to Williams, March 22, 1956, Release, June 6, 1956, Williams to Edward S. Piggins and Gerald K. O'Brien, November 4, 1956, Box 176, ibid.; Popkin to Williams, August 31, 1960, and enclosure, Box 301, ibid.; Emrich to Williams, December 20, 1960, and enclosure, Box 418, ibid.; Joffe to Members, July 28, 1958, Box 27, Mildred Jeffrey Papers, ALUA; Frank M. Thatcher and Wayne K. Anderson to Swainson, March 16, 1961, Walter F. Klein to Swainson, October 27, 1961, Robert Derengoski to Swainson, December 12, 1961, Box 55, JBS Papers, BHL; *DN,* October 16, 17, 20, 21, 31, 1960, DNSB 16.

7. John H. Stahlin to Malcolm Reed, May 10, 1962, Swainson to James M. Hare, June 14, 1962, Fair Campaign Practices Commission, Complaint of . . . Stahlin, August 1, 1962, Swainson to Klein, November 8, 1962, Box 55, JBS Papers; Klein to Swainson, December 24, 1962, and enclosure, Box 68, ibid.; *DN,* August 4, 1962, DNSB 17.

8. Maurice Horn to Williams, March 17, 1959, Box 270, GMW Papers; Thatcher and Anderson to Swainson, March 16, 1961, Box 55, JBS Papers.

9. Ernest Mazey to Romney, June 18, 1963, Romney to Mazey, June 25, 1963, Mazey to Richard Van Dusen, August 30, 1963, Van Dusen to Romney, December 2, 1963, Box 347, GR Papers, BHL.

10. Williams to Lawrence Lindeman, February 27, 1957, Box 208, GMW Papers; Popkin to Williams, August 31, 1960, Williams to Henry Jackson, September 14, 1960, Box 301, ibid.; Emrich to Williams, December 20, 1960, Box 418, ibid.; Klein to Swainson, December 24, 1962, and enclosure, Box 68, JBS Papers; *Commission on Civil Rights Hearings,* p. 8; [*DN,* November 6, 1962], clipping in Box 68, JBS Papers.

11. Williams to Ralph A. Loveland, February 18, 1950, Michigan Military Establishment General Order No. 4, April 10, 1950, Box 374, GMW Papers; Release, February 17, 1950, Excerpts from Williams Address, February 19, 1950, Williams WJR Monthly Broadcast, November 25, 1953, Box 451, ibid.; Fine, *Violence,* p. 194.

12. "Public Act No. 92," *Public and Local Acts of the Legislature of the State of Michigan Passed at the Regular Session of 1958,* pp. 98–99; Michigan State Advisory Committee to the National Civil Rights Commission interim report [1959], Box 270, GMW Papers; [William L. Price], "Profile of . . . Problems Facing Negro People in the Detroit Community," April 1, 1959, Box 46, Detroit Urban League (hereafter DUL) Papers, BHL; Fine, *Violence,* p. 11.

13. Kornhauser, *Detroit as the People See It,* pp. 120–21; *Commission on Civil Rights Hearings,* pp. 304, 323–24, 330–34, 369–71, 374, 497–98; Fine, *Violence,* p. 13. See also Heather Ann Thompson, "The Politics of Labor, Race, and Liberalism in the Auto Plants and the Motor City, 1940–1980" (Ph.D. diss., Princeton University, 1995), pp. 66–68, 92–98.

14. Fine, *Violence,* pp. 11–12; Brown to Williams [January 1959], Box 410, GMW Papers.

15. *Commission on Civil Rights Hearings,* pp. 338–92, 405–6, 408–9; Fine, *Violence,* pp. 13–15.

16. "Conscience of the Community" [1959], Box 8, DUL Papers; *Commission on Civil Rights Hearings,* pp. 345–49, 395–96, 410; Fine, *Violence,* pp. 13–14.

17. Fine, *Violence,* pp. 13–15; *Commission on Civil Rights Hearings,* pp. 395–96, 397–98.

18. FEPC Release, August 22, 1962, Box 6, Records of the Michigan Civil Rights Commission, Information Division, General Administrative Records of the Fair Employment Practices Commission, 1955–1963, RG 66-82-A, State Archives, Lansing, Michigan; Fine, *Violence,* pp. 19, 103–5. For a detailed treatment of the Edwards police commissionership, see Mary M. Stolberg, *Bridging the River of Hatred: The Pioneering Efforts of Detroit Police Commissioner George Edwards* (Detroit: Wayne State University Press, 1998), pp. 125–258.

19. MCCR Memorandum to Committee on Civil Rights . . . , December 29, 1948, Box 73, Detroit Commission on Community Relations (hereafter DCCR) Papers, ALUA; *LSJ,* March 28, 1956, clipping in Box 4, BG Papers, BHL.

20. *New York Times,* August 30, 1953; Release, September 22, 1953, Box 451, GMW Papers.

21. *DFP* clipping, July 20, 1961, Frederick Routh to Angier Biddle Duke, July 24, 1961, Johnson to Swainson, October 2, 1961, Swainson to Johnson, October 13, 1961, Box 7, JBS Papers; Swainson Message to the Legislature, February 2, 1962, Box 33, ibid.

22. Hodges Memorandum to Swainson, October 15, 1962, Box 4, RG 66-82-A; "Civil Rights Commission" [1962], Box 33, JBS Papers; Charles S. Brown to Williams [January 1957], Box 410, GMW Papers.

23. Summary of MCCR Activities, 1948–1950, Box 6, Adelaide Hart Papers, BHL.

24. Wigderson, "UAW in the 1950s," pp. 347–48; Paul Weber to William Oliver, May 23, 1949, Box 451, GMW Papers; Williams to Horatio F. Moran, May 20, 1949, Box 7, ibid.; MCCR, May 5, 1950, Box 20, DCCR Papers.

25. Wigderson, "UAW in the 1950s," pp. 349–50; Analysis of Problems Relating to Restaurant Discrimination around the UAW-CIO Plants . . . [June 6, 1954], folder, Box 20, UAW Political Action Department Papers, ALUA; City of Jackson, Report of Community Relations Board [1949], Box 584, GMW Papers.

26. Dillard, "From Hill to Cleage," pp. 239–42; "The Detroit Commission on Community Relations," March 10, 1958, "Conscience of the Community" [1959], Box 8, DUL Papers; *Civil Rights Commission Hearings*, pp. 191–92.

27. Unidentified clipping, March 8, 1952, in Box 451, GMW Papers; [*DN*, March 8, 1952], Nancy Williams Scrapbook 9, ibid.; [*LSJ*, April 9, 1953], clipping in Box 4, BG Papers.

28. "Public Act No. 182," *Public and Local Acts of the Legislature of the State of Michigan Passed at the Regular Session of 1956*, pp. 337–38; ADL and Jewish Community Council of Detroit Memorandum to Williams, August 1, 1949, Box 7, GMW Papers; ADL, Survey of Practices and Policies of AAA Approved Resorts [1955], Julius Reznik to Williams, April 6, 1956, Box 174, ibid.; ADL Release, March 24, 1958, Box 428, ibid.; "Civil Rights Commission" [1962], Box 33, JBS Papers.

29. "Public Act No. 182," pp. 337–38; Release, April 17, 1956, Box 451, GMW Papers; *DN*, April 18, 1956, DNSB 13.

30. Attorney General Opinions No. 2524, June 4, 1956, No. 3013, July 17, 1957, No. 3041, August 16, 1957, Data Sheet, Michigan, Box 100, John A. Hannah Papers, Michigan State University Archives, Historical Collections, East Lansing, Michigan; Diggs to James Hart, March 24, 1955, Box 16, Charles C. Diggs, Jr., Papers, Moorland-Spingarn Research Center, Howard University, Washington, D.C.; From Sol Rabkin and Theodore Leskes, February 8, 1958, Box 15, DCCR Papers; *DN*, October 9, 1961, DNSB 16.

31. Michigan Advisory Committee . . . Minutes, August 2, 1958, Box 100, Hannah Papers; FEPC Release, March 24, 1958, Box 428, GMW Papers; Morton J. Sobel to Williams, September 26, 1958, Williams to Sobel, September 30, 1958, Box 244, ibid.; Sol I. Littman to James R. Hall, July 7, 1961, Box 67, JBS Papers; *Commission on Civil Rights Hearings*, p. 12; Patricia L. Pilling, "Segregation: Cottage Rental in Michigan," *Phylon* 25 (Summer 1964): 197–201. Cf. Michigan State Advisory Committee interim report [1959], Box 270, GMW Papers.

32. Gerald White to Paul Adams, January 6, 1959, Box 411, GMW Papers; Adams to Charles E. Wilson, February 2, 1959, Box 270, ibid.; Adams to White, February 15, 1960, Box 313, ibid.; Adams, "Michigan's Human Relations Needs," October 28, 1961, Box 15, JBS Papers.

33. [*LSJ*, September 14, 1953], clipping in Box 4, BG Papers; Diggs to Paul Chapman, June 12, 1953, Chapman to Diggs, July 14, 1953, Williams to Heustis, September 22, October 5, December 22, 1953, Heustis to Williams, December 1953, Diggs to Williams, September 23, 1953, William Seabron to Heustis, September 29, 1953, Box 113, GMW Papers; Michigan Tuberculosis Sanatorium Committee Minutes, December 11, 1953, Box 141, ibid.

34. MCCR Memorandum, December 29, 1948, Box 73, DCCR Papers; "Profile of Critical Social Welfare and Economic Problems Facing Negro People in the Detroit Community," April 1, 1959, Box 46, DUL Papers; DUL, "A Review of Equal Opportunity in Eleven Detroit Area Voluntary Hospitals," December 1962, Box 47, ibid.; Richard V. Marks, "The Catalytic Role of Governmental Human Relations Agencies," *American Journal of Public Health* 55 (April 1963): 615.

35. Hospital Study Committee Report No. 1, Second Draft, May 2, 1953, Box 84, DCCR Papers; Activities of the Advisory Committee on Hospitals, 1957 to 1961, Box 83, ibid.; Richard S. Emrich, "Activities of the Citizens Advisory Committee on Hospitals of the Detroit Commission on Community Relations," *American Journal of Public Health* 53 (April 1963): 618–19.

36. Activities of Advisory Committee, Box 83, DCCR Papers; Emrich, "Activities," p. 619.

37. Activities of Advisory Committee, Box 83, DCCR Papers; Emrich, "Activities," p. 619; "The Detroit Commission on Community Relations," March 10, 1958, "Conscience of the Community" [1959], Box 8, DUL Papers.

38. Popkin Memorandum to Administrators . . . , May 28, 1958, Office of Hospital Survey and Construction Press Release, May 28, 1958, Box 29, JBS Papers; "Conscience of the Community" [1959], Box 8, DUL Papers; Activities of Advisory Committee, Box 83, DCCR Papers; Emrich, "Activities," pp. 619–20.

39. *DN,* November 17, 1961, DNSB 16; FEPC Release, August 22, 1962, Declaration of Policy of Greater Detroit Association of Hospital Personnel Directors, September 26, 1962, Box 6, RG 66-82-A; Hodges to Lattie Coor, March 1, 1962, Box 29, JBS Papers; Emrich, "Activities," pp. 619–20.

40. Marks, "Catalytic Role," p. 617; Marks Memorandum for Commission on Community Relations, June 13, 1963, Box 83, DCCR Papers. Cf. DUL, "A Review of Equal Opportunity in Eleven Detroit Area Hospitals," December 1962, Box 47, DUL Papers.

41. MCCR Memorandum, December 29, 1948, Box 73, DCCR Papers; Michigan State Advisory Committee Minutes, July 2, 1958, Box 100, Hannah Papers; Michigan State Advisory Committee Release [1959], Box 270, GMW Papers; Next Steps in Michigan for Civil Rights in 1959, Box 269, ibid.; White to Adams, January 6, 1959, Box 411, ibid.; "Conscience of the Community" [1959], Box 8, DUL Papers; *Michigan: 1961 Report to the Commission on Civil Rights from the State Advisory Committee,* pp. 285–87, Popkin to Swainson, June 21, 1961, Box 15, JBS Papers; "Civil Rights Commission" [1962], Box 33, ibid.; Hodges Memorandum to Swainson, October 15, 1962, Box 4, RG 66-82-A; *DN,* April 27, 1958, DNSB 13; unidentified clipping [December 24, 1958], in Box 462, GMW Papers.

42. *LSJ,* September 24, 1958, clipping in Box 9, BG Papers; *DN,* March 18, 1960; Hodges Memorandum to Williams, October 15, 1962, Box 4, RG 66-82-A; *Commission on Civil Rights Hearings,* pp. 47, 100, 102.

43. Michigan State Advisory Committee Release [1959], Box 270, GMW Papers; *Michigan: 1961 Report . . . from the State Advisory Committee,* p. 288, Popkin Memorandum to Swainson, June 21, 1961, Box 15, JBS Papers.

44. *New York Times,* October 8, 1957; *DN,* October 8, 1957; Fine, *Violence,* pp. 8, 11, 43; *Commission on Civil Rights Hearings,* pp. 132–34, 159–60; Research Department, DUL, *A Profile of the Detroit Negro, 1959–1967,* p. 289, Box 65, DUL Papers.

45. Fine, *Violence,* pp. 8–9.

46. Ibid., p. 9.

47. Ibid., pp. 43–44.

48. [William L. Price], "Profile of Critical Social Welfare and Economic Problems Facing Negro People in Detroit," April 1, 1959, Box 46, DUL Papers.

Chapter 5

1. *Ann Arbor News,* May 8, 1959, clipping in Box 9, BG Papers, BHL; Burton Levy to Burton Gordin, August 31, 1965, Box 28, Records of the Michigan Civil Rights Commission: Administrative, RG 74-90, State Archives, Lansing, Michigan; *Commission on Civil Rights Hearings,* p. 192.

2. Kornhauser, *Detroit as the People See It,* pp. 84, 100; Fine, *Violence,* pp. 11, 57; Richard V. Marks, Population Movement: Housing in a Changing Community, March 19, 1959, in Michigan State Advisory Committee to the National Civil Rights Commission interim report [1959], Box 270, GMW Papers, BHL; Michigan Coordinating Council on Civil Rights, Next Steps for Michigan in Civil Rights in 1959, Box 269, ibid.; Gerald David White to Paul Adams, January 6, 1959, Box 411, ibid.; John J. Musial, Residential Segregation Trends in the Detroit Metropolitan Area, n.d., Box 34, Detroit Commission on Community Relations (hereafter DCCR) Papers, ALUA; Research Department, Detroit Urban League (hereafter DUL), *A Profile of the Detroit Negro, 1959–1967,* pp. 4–5, Box 65, DUL Papers, BHL; "Housing Segregation in Detroit," n.d., Box 70, ibid.; *Commission on Civil Rights Hearings,* pp. 193, 225, 254; Sugrue, *Urban Crisis,* pp. 43, 182–83.

3. [Civil Rights Commission] Suggested Points to be Made re Proposed Housing Legislation [1967], Box 5, RG 74-90; *Michigan: 1961 Report to the Commission on Civil Rights from the State Advisory Committee,* pp. 266–67, Box 15, JBS Papers, BHL; Remarks by Levy, November 5, 1965, Box 19, Detroit NAACP Papers, ALUA; Michigan Coordinating Council on Civil Rights, Next Steps, 1959, Box 269, GMW Papers; Fair Housing Legislation in Michigan, n.d., Box 254, ibid.; Gordin, "An Overview of the Problems in Michigan," April 26, 1966, Box 67, DUL Papers; *Commission on Civil Rights Hearings,* pp. 193–94, 225, 254.

4. Anti-Defamation League Release, March 24, 1958, Box 428, GMW Papers. For housing discrimination against Jews in the Detroit area and for Jewish-black tension regarding housing, see Stevenson, Jr., "Points of Departure," pp. 385–87.

5. Housing Division Memorandum to DCCR, October 7, 1971, Box 36, DCCR Papers; *Phillips v. Neff,* 332 Mich. 389 (1952); Sugrue, *Urban Crisis,* pp. 181–83; Lockard, *Toward Equal Opportunity,* pp. 111–12.

6. Detroit Real Estate Brokers Association to Attorney General . . . , August 1956, Box 17, Jewish Labor Committee (hereafter JLC) Papers, ALUA; [William L. Price], "Profile of Critical Social Welfare and Economic Problems Facing Negro People in Detroit," April 1, 1959, Box 46, DUL Papers; Michigan State Advisory Committee interim report [1959], Box 270, GMW Papers; *Commission on Civil Rights Hearings,* pp. 253–57, 477–78; Sugrue, *Urban Crisis,* pp. 195–96.

7. Michigan State Advisory Committee interim report [1959], Box 270, GMW Papers.

8. A. R. Saunders to Board President and enclosed Statement of Policy, September 19, 1962, Box 29, GR Papers, BHL; DUL, An evaluation of Senate Bill No. 942 . . . , March 28, 1966, Box 53, DUL Papers, Lockard, *Toward Equal Opportunity,* p. 112.

9. Development of Stabilized Living, Housing Task Force Report, 1962, National Conference of Urban League, Box 46, DUL Papers; Lockard, *Toward Equal Opportunity,* pp. 117–18.

10. Excerpts from Governor's Address . . . , February 13, 1950, Box 451, GMW Papers; "Public Act No. 101," *Public and Local Acts of the Legislature of the State*

of Michigan Passed at the Regular Session of 1952, pp. 112–13; Lockard, *Toward Equal Opportunity*, pp. 108, 117 n.

11. George Schermer to Harry Durbin, March 25, 1962, and enclosure, Box 27, DCCR Papers; "The History, Organization, and Function of the Detroit Housing Commission," Box 42, DUL Papers.

12. Durbin to John H. Laub, March 15, 1955, Box 36, DCCR Papers; *Commission on Civil Rights Hearings*, pp. 229, 234–35; Tyrone Tillery, "The Conscience of a City: A Commemorative History of the Detroit Human Rights Commission and Department, 1943–1983" (Detroit Human Rights Department [1983]), p. 14.

13. *Detroit Housing Commission v. Lewis et al.* 226 F. 2d 180 (1955); Durbin to Laub, April 15, May 20, 1955, Durbin to All Staff Members, November 21, 1955, Box 36, DCCR Papers; William T. Patrick to Louis Miriani, August 25, 1959, Box 7, JLC Papers; DHC Monthly Report to the Commissioners, February–March, March–April, September–October 1955, Box 42, DUL Papers; *Commission on Civil Rights Hearings*, p. 236.

14. Isabell and Edward M. Turner to Common Council [1957], Box 43, DUL Papers; Bill Goode to Miriani, September 3, 1959, Box 7, JLC Papers; DCCR Minutes, October 17, 1960, Box 25, ibid.; *Commission on Civil Rights Hearings*, pp. 192, 236. See also *Michigan: 1961 Report to the Commission on Civil Rights*, pp. 260–61, Box 15, JBS Papers. For a rebuttal of the DCCR charges, see DHC Comments . . . , August 7, 1959, Box 7, JLC Papers.

15. *Commission on Civil Rights Hearings*, pp. 192–93, 236–37; "Conscience of the Community" [1959], Box 8, DUL Papers; Tillery, "Conscience of a City," pp. 14–15.

16. *Commission on Civil Rights Hearings*, pp. 192–93; Breakdown of Public Housing Tenants by Race . . . as of December 31, 1964, Box 2, Rose Kleinman Papers, ALUA; Lockard, *Toward Equal Opportunity*, p. 108.

17. Don Slaiman to Don Stevens, December 26, 1958, Box 2, JLC Papers; Williams Memoranda to L. L. Farrell, February 13, March 9, 1957, Neil Staebler to Williams, March 5, 1957, [Charles] Adrian to Williams, March 7, 1957, Richard Henry to Williams, March 7, 1957, Box 207, GMW Papers.

18. Release, April 11, 1957, Box 6, Adelaide Hart Papers, BHL; Release, September 29, 1957, Box 452, GMW Papers; John Feild Memorandum to Williams, August 6, 1957, and enclosures, Box 226, ibid.; Release, September 29, 1957, Box 452, ibid.

19. Augmented Staff Meeting Minutes, September 30, 1957, Personnel-Legislative Conference, December 28 [1957], GMW Papers; Turner to Williams, October 24, 1957, Williams to Turner, November 18, 1957, Box 212, ibid.; Alfred Fitt to John Abernethy, December 12, 1957, Box 207, ibid.; Civil Rights folder in Legislative Program 1957–58, Box 412, ibid.; Lockard, *Toward Equal Opportunity*, pp. 117–18.

20. For the sections of the bills dealing with public accommodations and education, see House Bills Nos. 247, 558, Michigan Sixty-Ninth Legislature, Regular Session of 1958; House Bills Nos. 213, 474 . . . 1959; House Bill No. 373 . . . 1960; Senate Bill No. 1153 . . . 1959; Senate Bill No. 275 . . . 1961; and House Bill No. 254 . . . 1962. There are copies of Michigan bills in the University of Michigan Law Library, Ann Arbor, Michigan.

21. Williams Message to the Sixty-Ninth Legislature, January 9, 1958, Box 431, GMW Papers.

22. Memorandum to Support Proposal No. 1621, December 18, 1961, Box 1, Don Binkowski Papers, BHL; *Detroit Times,* January 15, 1958, clipping in Box 452, GMW Papers; Turner to Williams, January 30, 1958, Williams to Turner, February 5, 1958, Box 238, ibid.; Williams to Johnetta Webb, January 31, 1958, Box 244, ibid.; *DN,* January 15, 1958.

23. House Bills Nos. 247, 558, Michigan Sixty-Ninth Legislature, Regular Session of 1958; *Journal of the House of Representatives of the State of Michigan, 1958 Regular Session,* 1:380, 481, 642, 646; Slaiman to Friend, April 12, 1958, Box 23, UAW Fair Practices and Anti-Discrimination Department Papers, ALUA; *Michigan AFL-CIO News,* March 13, 1958, Box 3, Louis C. Cramton Papers, BHL; *LSJ,* February 27, March 7, 1958, clippings in Box 9, BG Papers; *DN,* March 6, 7, 1958, DNSB 13, BHL; Release, March 6, 1958, Box 452, GMW Papers.

24. Williams Message to the Seventieth Michigan Legislature, January 15, 1959, Box 431, GMW Papers; House Bills Nos. 213, 474, Senate Bill No. 1153, Michigan Seventieth Legislature, Regular Session of 1959; Executive Office Release, March 10, 1959, Box 3, JBS Papers; John Murray Memorandum to Abernethy, September 8, 1958, Report of Subcommittee on Discrimination, November 19, 1958, Box 417, GMW Papers; Charles S. Brown Memorandum to Governor, November 17, 1959, Box 269, ibid.; Minutes of Steering Committee, Coordinating Council on Civil Rights, December 22, 1958, March 18, 1959, Box 21, JLC Papers; Goode, "Present Status of Civil Rights in Michigan" [1959], Box 2, ibid.; Coordinating Council on Civil Rights Releases, May 27 [1959], June 10, 1959, Goode to Members of Legislature, April 28, 1959, Goode to Republican Legislators, May 11, 1959, Box 56, UAW Fair Practices and Anti-Discrimination Department Papers, ALUA; *DN,* March 11, April 1, 16, 28, 30, May 28, July 6, 1959; [*LSJ,* April 26, 1959], clipping in Box 4, BG Papers.

25. Saunders, "High Points of Our Opposition to HB-213 and SB-1153," April 13, 1959, Minutes of Steering Committee, Coordinating Council on Civil Rights, June 10, 1959, Arthur F. Binkowski et al. to Republican and Democratic Leaders, April 13, 1959, Box 21, JLC Papers; Turner and Goode to Pears, June 29, 1959, Goode, "Present Status," Box 2, ibid.; Brown Memorandum to Williams, November 17, 1959, Box 269, GMW Papers.

26. Excerpts from Address by Williams . . . , February 18, 1960, Williams to Clark Shanahan, February 29, 1960, Box 300, GMW Papers; Goode to Friend, April 28, 1960, Box 56, UAW Fair Practices and Anti-Discrimination Department Papers.

27. House Bills Nos. 373, 374, Michigan Seventieth Legislature, Regular Session of 1960; George H. Edwards Memorandum, February 22, 1960, Box 410, GMW Papers.

28. Edwards Memorandum, April 22, 1960, Box 400, GMW Papers; "How to Use This Voting Record Book," n.d., Box 416, ibid.; Minutes of Steering Committee of Coordinating Council on Civil Rights, December 28, 1960, Box 2, JLC Papers; *DN,* March 9–12, 15, 1960.

29. Regulations Governing the Screening Process of Grosse Pointe Broker's [*sic*] Association, October 17, 1945, Box 410, GMW Papers; *Rights* 3 (September 1960): 71–72, Box 314, ibid.; Sol I. Littman to Harold Braverman, May 26, 1960, Part 3, Box 36, DCCR Papers; *DFP,* May 3, 1960; *DN,* May 3, 4, 1960, May 12, 1961; *Commission on Civil Rights Hearings,* pp. 476–77, 478–80, 492–93; Jack Walker, "Fair Housing in Michigan," in *The Politics of Fair Housing Legislation: State and*

Local Case Studies, by Lynn W. Eley and Thomas W. Casstevens (San Francisco: Chandler, 1968), pp. 358–59.

30. Norman C. Thomas, *Rule 9: Politics, Administration, and Civil Rights* (New York: Random House, 1966), pp. pp. 30–31; *Rights* 3 (September 1960): 71, Box 314, GMW Papers. In an earlier case, William E. Bufalino, president of a Teamsters local, filed a $1 million suit against the GPBA and the GPPOA charging discrimination against him because he was of Italian extraction, was characterized as "medium swarthy," and was associated with the jukebox business. He eventually lost his suit. *DN,* May 12, 15, 1960, December 26, 1961, October 2, 1962; *Ann Arbor News,* February 16, 1961, clipping in Box 9, BG Papers.

31. Littman to Braverman, May 26, 1960, Part 3, Box 36, DCCR Papers; Michigan Corporation and Securities Commission Re: The public hearing on . . . No. 9, June 21, 1960, p. 62, Box 6, Records of the Michigan Civil Rights Commission: Information Division, General Administrative Records of the Fair Employment Practices Commission, 1955–1963, RG 66-82-A, State Archives; Kathy Cosseboom, *Grosse Pointe, Michigan: Race against Race* (East Lansing: Michigan State University Press, 1972), p. 6.

32. Thomas, *Rule 9,* pp. 34–35; *DFP,* April 20, 21, 1960.

33. *DN,* May 3,5, 12–14, 1960; *DFP,* May 2, 13, 1960; Brown Memorandum to Governor, May 5, 1960, Box 313, GMW Papers.

34. Adams and Gubow to H. Gordon Wood and George E. Bushnell, May 16, 1960, and enclosed Statement, Box 313, GMW Papers; *DN,* May 14, 1960; *LSJ,* May 18, 1960, clipping in Box 9, BG Papers.

35. Gubow Memorandum to Williams, June 30, 1960, and enclosed statement and rule, Box 314, GMW Papers; *DN,* May 28, 1960; *McKibbin* v. *Corporation and Securities Commission,* 369 Mich. 69, 73 (1963).

36. Gubow Memorandum to Williams, June 30, 1960, and enclosed statement, Opening Statement [June 21, 1960], Michigan Corporation and Securities Commission Re: The Public Hearing, Box 6, RG 66-82-A; *DN,* May 30, June 21, 29, 1960; *DFP,* June 30, 1960; *Commission on Civil Rights Hearings,* p. 78; Thomas, *Rule 9,* pp. 54–57; *Ann Arbor News,* July 2, 1960, clipping in Box 9, BG Papers.

37. *Personally Yours,* Fall 1960, copy in Box 9, JBS Papers; *Michigan: 1961 Report,* pp. 263–64, Box 15, ibid.; *Commission on Civil Rights Hearings,* pp. 242–43, 247, 250–51; *DN,* June 9, July 2, 20, August 5, 13, 31, September 8, 1960, February 13, April 12, 21, 22, 28, May 3, 10, 11, June 3, 1961; *LSJ,* April 13, 1961, clipping in Box 9, BG Papers; *Journal of the Senate of the State of Michigan, March 1961 Regular Session,* 2:1326; Walker, "Fair Housing," p. 361; Thomas, *Rule 9,* p. 59; James K. Pollock, Notes on Con Con Meetings, December 9, 1961, Box 8, University of Michigan Institute of Public Administration Papers, BHL; Committee on Declaration of Rights, Suffrage and Elections, Action Journal No. 36, January 18, 1962, Box 46, Alvin M. Bentley Papers, BHL; State of Michigan Constitutional Convention, 1961, *Official Record,* 1:2272, 2278–85.

38. Thomas, *Rule 9,* pp. 60–61, 62–72; *DN,* August 13, 19, 31, 1960, April 6, June 4, 5, 1962, February 7, 1963; *LSJ,* September 7, 15, 1961, clippings in Box 9, BG Papers; unidentified clipping [April 13, 1962], DNSB 17; Releases, August 15, 30, 1960, Box 19, Executive Message, April 5, 1962, Executive Office Release, June 4, 1962, Swainson to Luanne Hilborn, October 17, 1962, Box 28, JBS Papers; *McKibbin* v. *Corporation and Securities Commission,* 369 Mich. 69 (1963).

39. Swainson Address, November 27, 1961, Box 15, JBS Papers; William B. Gould to Swainson, September 29, 1961, Swainson to Gould, October 26, 1961, Box 17, ibid.

40. Dick Miller Memorandum to Swainson, December 21, 1960, Box 15, ibid.; Routh to Swainson, January 12, 1961, Box 65, ibid.; House Bill No. 465, Senate Bills Nos. 1275, 1341, Michigan Seventy-First Legislature, Regular Session of 1961; Joe Schore to Coordinating Council Steering Committee, March 7, 1961, Box 56, UAW Fair Practices and Anti-Discrimination Department Papers; Report of the Steering Committee Meeting, June 21, 1961, Box 6, RG 66-82-A; *DN,* January 11, March 15, 16, 1961.

41. Swainson Message to the Legislature, February 2, 1962, Box 29, JBS Papers; Executive Office Release, March 13, 1962, Box 67, ibid.; House Bills Nos. 254, 255, Michigan Seventy-First Legislature, Regular Session of 1962; *DN,* March 1, 3, 9, 11, 14, 21, August 21, 22, 1962; *LSJ,* February 21, 28, 1962 [March 14, 1962], clippings in Box 4, BG Papers; Swainson Address, September 24, 1962, Box 67, JBS Papers; Lockard, *Toward Equal Opportunity,* pp. 24, 118–20.

42. *Michigan: 1961 Report,* p. 265, Box 15, JBS Papers; Anna Holden to Swainson, June 3, 1962, Malcolm R. Lovell to Holden, June 26, 1962, Release, August 14, 1962, Box 34, ibid.; Albert Wheeler to Seabron, October 27, 1961, Box 3, Albert and Emma Wheeler Papers, BHL.

43. Non-Discrimination Clauses in Regard to Public Housing in Urban Redevelopment Undertakings, January 25, 1962, Box 41, DUL Papers; *Michigan: 1961 Report,* pp. 265–67 et passim, Box 15, JBS Papers.

44. Statement of Greater Detroit Committee for Fair Housing Practices, n.d., Box 54, DUL Papers; Abraham F. Citron to Gene Wesley Marshall, November 27, 1962, Box 8, Metropolitan Detroit Council of Churches Papers, ALUA; Joe T. Darden et al., *Detroit: Race and Uneven Development* (Philadelphia: Temple University Press, 1987), p. 136.

45. Rose Kleinman to Board Members, May 17, 1962, and enclosed Fair Practice Code, Greater Detroit Committee for Fair Housing Practices Minutes, June 21, 1962, James H. Laird to Friend, March 15, 1962, Box 42, DUL Papers; Greater Detroit Committee for Fair Housing Practices Program, n.d., idem, The Covenant Card Campaign, Covenant Card Breakdown, April 24, 1965, Box 1, Kleinman Papers.

46. Laird to Friend, March 15, 1962, Greater Detroit Committee for Fair Housing Practices Minutes, February 5, June 21, 1962, Box 42, DUL Papers; DUL Department of Housing, Quarterly Report, October–December 1965, Box 63, ibid.; Kleinman to Members of the Interdepartmental Ministerial Alliance, April 30, 1965, Box 2, Kleinman Papers; Kleinman to Gordin, June 14, 1967, Kleinman to Jack Cassidy, June 14, 1967, Box 1, ibid.; Kleinman to Rules Committee, Michigan Civil Rights Commission, February 25, 1966, Box 4, ibid.; Remarks by Kleinman, March 23, 1967, Box 40, JLC Papers; Fair Housing Listing Service . . . , June 6, 1968, Box 36, DCCR Papers; Darden et al., *Detroit,* pp. 137–38.

47. Metropolitan Conference on Fair Housing Practices, "Toward Open Occupancy and Neighborhood Stability" [June 1962], Metropolitan Conference on Open Occupancy Minutes, July 5, 1962, Shore to William Oliver, October 29, 1962, G. Merrill Lenox to George Romney, November 14, 1962, Box 29, JLC Papers; Citron to Marshall, November 27, 1962, Box 8, Metropolitan Detroit Council of Churches Papers.

48. *"Challenge to Conscience"*: *Report of the Metropolitan Conference on Open Occupancy*, January 2–3, 1963, Box 43, DUL Papers; Darden et al., *Detroit*, pp. 132–34; Sugrue, *Urban Crisis*, p. 193; Buffa, *Union Power*, p. 140.

49. Sugrue, *Urban Crisis*, pp. 211–16; Fine, *Violence*, pp. 58–59.

50. Carl M. Brauer, *John F. Kennedy and the Second Reconstruction* (New York: Columbia University Press, 1977), pp. 207–8; *DN*, November 22, 1962, DNSB 17.

Chapter 6

1. Williams to Carolyn Bolton, February 19, 1959, Box 275, GMW Papers, BHL.

2. Pertinent Facts on "Earning Opportunities for Mature Workers . . . ," July 8–10, 1953, Box 586, ibid.; U.S. Department of Labor, Bureau of Employment Security, Employment Service Program Letter No. 698, July 20, 1956, Box 173, ibid.; Anthony Lenzer with Adele S. Pond and John Scott, *Michigan's Older People* (Ann Arbor, 1958), pp. 24–26, copy in Box 235, ibid.; *Report of the Governor's Commission to Study the Problems of Aging*, January 1953, p. 40, copy in Box 173, ibid.

3. W. Andrew Achenbaum, *Shades of Gray: Old Age, American Values, and Federal Policies since 1920* (Boston: Little, Brown, 1983), pp. 61–62; Lenzer et al., *Michigan's Older People*, p. 34; *DN*, April 18, 1957.

4. Clark Tibbitts, National Conference on Aging: A Review of the Main Conclusions. Prepared for delivery, May 28, 1951, Box 5, Clark Tibbitts Papers, BHL; Wilma Donahue Memorandum to the President's Commission on the Health Needs of the Nation, September 23, 1952, Box 67, GMW Papers.

5. *Report of the Governor's Commission to Study the Problems of Aging*, pp. 40–41; Interdepartmental Committee on Problems of the Aging, July 25, 1950, Box 43, GMW Papers; Frederick M. Mitchell testimony, Senate Subcommittee on Problems of the Aged and Aging of the Committee on Labor and Public Welfare, *The Aged and Aging in the United States*, 86 Cong., 1 sess., 1959, 1384–85; Lenzer et al., *Michigan's Older People*, p. 34.

6. MESC Report to Williams on Characteristics of the Unemployed, September 1, 1955, Box 163, GMW Papers; *DN*, October 23, 1958, DNSB 15, BHL.

7. Interdepartmental Committee on Aging, August 8, 1950, Box 412, GMW Papers; O. K. Fjetland to Thomas C. Desmond, April 3, 1950, Box 25, ibid.; John L. Thurston, "Michigan Opportunities and Responsibilities in Aging," May 12, 1952, Box 67, ibid.

8. *Report of Governor's Commission to Study the Problems of Aging*, pp. 43–44; MESC, *Annual Report for the Fiscal Year Ending June 30, 1953*, pp. 17–18.

9. *DN*, February 1, 1955, DNSB 13; MESC, *Annual Report for the Fiscal Year Ending June 30, 1955*, p. 15; Notes for Commission on Aging, July 27, 1955, Box 4, Wilma E. Donahue Papers, BHL; Draft Memorandum on the Subject of Employment Security, November 8, 1955, Box 163, GMW Papers.

10. Max M. Horton to John Sweeney, November 4, 1955, Box 443, GMW Papers.

11. BES, Employment Service Letter No. 698, July 20, 1956, Box 173, ibid.

12. Horton to State Administrative Staff et al., August 21, 1956, Summary of Information from State Departments [December 1956], Box 16, Donahue Papers; Roderick H. McGinn, State Older Worker Program, Box 2, John B. Martin Papers, BHL; MESC, *Annual Report for the Fiscal Year Ending June 30, 1961*, p. 41.

13. Employment Service Division, "Integrated Report. Older Worker Study, Detroit Metropolitan Area, 1957," Box 1, Records of the Department of Social Services: Aging, RG 70-131, State Archives, Lansing, Michigan.

14. MESC, *Annual Report for the Fiscal Year Ending June 30, 1956*, pp. 32–33; *Aged and Aging*, pp. 1383–85.

15. McGinn, State Older Worker Program, December 6, 1957, Box 2, Martin Papers; John Abernethy Memorandum to Governor, January 3, 1958, Charge to the Commission . . . by . . . Williams, January 13, 1958, Box 236, GMW Papers; Jordan Popkin to Samuel Feinberg, January 20, 1958, McGinn to Popkin, September 16, 1958, Horton to Williams, January 29, 1959, Box 413, ibid.; Charles S. Brown to Goodenow L. Thompson, February 19, 1959, Box 267, ibid.; Roscoe A. Walters to Swainson, September 1, 1961, Box 65, JBS Papers, BHL; MESC, *Annual Report for the Fiscal Year Ending June 30, 1958*, p. 42; idem, *Annual Report . . . 1959*, p. 24; idem, *Annual Report . . . 1960*, p. 40; idem, *Annual Report . . . 1962*, p. 54; *Aged and Aging*, pp. 1383, 1388, 1392.

16. Popkin Memorandum to Charles Adrian, January 28, 1957, Popkin to Williams, February 8, 1957, Interdepartmental Committee Minutes, January 14, 22, 1957, Box 204, GMW Papers.

17. William R. Monat to Williams, August 6, 1957, Executive Office Release, December 9, 1957, ibid.; Charge to Commission, January 13, 1958, Box 236, ibid.; Popkin to Feinberg, January 20, 1958, Box 413, ibid.

18. Forsythe to All Committee Members, May 15, 1958, Box 236, ibid.; Forsythe to Williams, May 28, 1959, Executive Office Release, June 2, 1959, Box 267, ibid.

19. Governor's Commission on Employment of the Older Worker, May 28, 1959, Executive Office Release, June 2, 1959, Box 267, ibid.

20. *DN*, January 24, 1958, DNSB 14; Lenzer to Haskell L. Nichols, July 17, 1958, Lenzer to Martin, September 19, 1958, Box 1, Martin Papers; Williams to Monat and Sidney Woolner, June 4, 1959, Box 267, GMW Papers.

21. Popkin Memorandum to Dick Miller, January 9, 1961, Edward Hodges to Popkin, January 21, 1961, Mitchell to Swainson, January 17, 1961, Box 65, JBS Papers; Swainson Message to the Seventy-First Michigan Legislature, January 12, 1961, Box 23, ibid.

22. Frederick Routh and Hodges Memorandum to Executive Office, March 30, 1961, Box 7, ibid.; Miller Memorandum to Swainson, September 12, 1961, Box 65, ibid.; Swainson Message, February 1, 1962, Box 43, ibid.

23. MESC, *Annual Report for the Fiscal Year Ending June 30, 1952*, pp. 33, 37.

24. MESC, A Report to Williams on the Unemployed . . . , September 1, 1955, Box 163, GMW Papers; William Oliver to Caroline Davis, May 8, 1953, Davis to Oliver, May 13, 1953, Box 1, Tom Downs Papers, BHL; "Working Women" [February 1962], Box 56, JBS Papers.

25. Williams Message to the Sixty-Ninth Michigan Legislature, January 4, 1951, Box 430, GMW Papers; *DN*, October 9, 1955, April 6, 1956, DNSB 13.

26. Draft of Memorandum on the Subject of Employment Security, November 8, 1955, Box 163, GMW Papers; MESC Policy Statement, February 17, 1957, Horton to All Employees, April 16, 1957, Box 5, Records of the Michigan Civil Rights Commission, Information Division, General Records of the Fair Employment Practices Commission, 1955–1963, RG 66-82-A, State Archives.

27. MESC, *Annual Report for the Fiscal Year Ending June 30, 1960,* p. 39; idem, *Annual Report . . . 1961,* p. 41.

28. Gabin, *Feminism in the Labor Movement,* pp. 158–59; Oral History Interview with Caroline Davis, July 23, 1976, pp. 138–39, Institute of Labor and Industrial Relations, University of Michigan and Wayne State University, Women and Work Program. The 20th Century Trade Union Woman: Vehicle for Social Change, Oral History Program, 1978–1979, BHL.

29. Program, Michigan Conference on Employment Problems of Working Women, September 30, 1961, Box 56, JBS Papers.

30. State Council to Mitigate the Employment Problems of Working Women Minutes, n.d., ibid.; Michigan Council on Employment Problems of Working Women, January 8, 1962, ibid.

31. *DN,* February 6, 1962, DNSB 17; *DN,* March 2, 1962, *LSJ,* March 9, 1962, *Ann Arbor News,* April 12, 1962, clippings in Box 9, BG Papers, BHL; "Public Act No. 37," *Public and Local Acts of the Legislature of the State of Michigan Passed at the Regular Session of 1962,* p. 33; Excerpts from Address by Swainson, September 25, 1962, Box 56, JBS Papers; Michigan Council on Employment Problems of Working Women, May 1962, Box 7, UAW Women's Department—Dorothy Haener Papers, ALUA.

32. Background of the Day Care Committee, Michigan Youth Commission [1962], Day Care Committee . . . Revised Recommendations of the Sub-Committee on Objectives, November 2, 1962, Michigan Youth Commission Minutes, December 13, 1962, Box 38, GR Papers; Clarice Freed to Swainson, November 23, 1962, and enclosure, Box 68, JBS Papers.

33. Draft for Swainson Address, March 23, 1962, Executive Office Release, August 20, 1962, Box 56, JBS Papers; *DN,* March 24, 1962, DNSB 17.

34. Excerpts from Swainson Address, September 25, 1962, Box 56, JBS Papers.

35. Executive Office Releases, August 20, October 15, 1962, Lattie Coor to Zeli, August 21 [1962], Box 56, JBS Papers.

36. Governor's Commission on the Status of Women Progress Report [1962], ibid.

37. DeWald to Davis, September 28, 1962, Box 17, UAW Women's Department Papers, ALUA.

38. Governor's Commission Progress Report [1962], Box 56, JBS Papers; idem, Minutes, January 23, 1963, Box 1, Records of Management and Budget: Women's Commission, RG 77-78, State Archives.

39. [*LSJ,* September 27, 1957], clipping in Box 4, BG Papers.

40. Department of the Interior, Bureau of Indian Affairs, Division of Programs, *Report of a Socio-Economic Survey of Michigan Indian Reservation Groups,* Report No. 2, December 1951, p. 3 and appendix documents, copy in Box 396, GMW Papers.

41. Ibid., pp. 4–6; "Indian Reservations," Michigan Historical Commission, Information Series, No. 2, January 26, 1956, Robert J. Dominic to Adrian, March 19, 1956, and enclosure, Adrian to Williams, March 12, 1956, Box 399, GMW Papers; John Sweeney to Williams, July 2, 1954, Box 396, ibid.; John N. Seaman to Williams, March 9, 1959, enclosing Report of the Indian Commission, Box 404, ibid.; E. J. Riley to Francis J. Wakefield [November 14, 1956], Wakefield to Williams, November 8, December 23, 1960, in James R. Hillman, *The Minutes of the Governor's Study Commission on Indian Affairs, 1956–1977* (Canal Fulton,

Ohio: Hillman Publishing Co., ca. 1990), BHL; Lewis Beeson to Patrick Dennett, August 20, 1958, Box 1, Records of the Governor's Commission on Indian Problems, RG 65-47-A, State Archives; Frances Densmore, *A Study of Some Michigan Indians* (Ann Arbor: University of Michigan Press, 1949), pp. 2–4, 20–33. I have cited the population figures in Report of the Indian Commission, enclosed with Seaman to Williams, March 9, 1959, Box 404, GMW Papers.

42. *Report of Socio-Economic Survey,* p. 19, Box 396, GMW Papers; Riley to Wakefield [November 14, 1956], Wakefield to Williams, December 23, 1960, in Hillman, *Minutes;* Sweeney to Williams, July 2, 1954, Box 396, GMW Papers; Sweeney to Williams, March 9, 1959, and enclosed Report of the Indian Commission, Box 404, ibid.

43. *Report of Socio-Economic Survey,* pp. 7–8, 10, 15–17, 21–25, Box 396, GMW Papers; Sweeney to Williams, July 2, 1954, Box 396, ibid.; Adrian to Williams, March 21, 1956, Box 399, ibid.; Seaman to Williams, March 9, 1959, and enclosed Report of Indian Commission, Box 404, ibid.; Riley to Wakefield [November 14, 1956], in Hillman, *Minutes;* Beeson to Mrs. Eldred Mathes, March 21, 1956, Box 1, RG 65-47-A; *DN,* September 8, 1956, DNSB 13; [*LSJ,* October 9, 1957], clipping in Box 9, BG Papers; "The Red Man's Appalachia," n.d., Box 329, GMW Papers.

44. "The Sad Story of the Burt Lake Band," *Totem Pole,* March 5, 1956, 1–6; James R. Hillman, *A History of the Michigan Commission on Indian Affairs, 1956–1977* (Clinton, Ohio: Hillman Publishing Co., 1984), pp. 18–19, copy in BHL.

45. Governor's Commission on Indian Problems, March 12, 1956, Beeson to Mathes, April 3, 1956, Horace W. Gilmore Memorandum to Adrian, April 18, 1956, Box 399, GMW Papers; Adrian to Arthur Neef, March 8, April 16, 1957, Box 401, ibid.; Hillman, *History,* pp. 19–20, 27; *DN,* March 13, 1956, DNSB 13.

46. E. Morgan Pryse to Williams, April 15, July 1, December 21, 1954, Sweeney to Williams, July 7, 1954, Sweeney to Pryse, December 13, 1954, Box 396, GMW Papers; Williams to Moses Gibson, July 17, 1956, Box 399, ibid.; Wakefield to Williams, November 8, December 23, 1956, in Hillman, *Minutes; DN,* May 8, 9, 1956, DNSB 13; *Report of Socio-Economic Survey,* pp. 26–36, Box 396, GMW Papers; Hillman, *History,* pp. 22–25.

47. Hillman, *History,* pp. 18, 25; Williams to Nathaniel Smith, February 27, 1956, Box 399, GMW Papers; Williams to Donald Wichman, July 23, 1954, Box 396, ibid.; *LSJ,* May 15, 1956, clipping in Box 405, ibid.

48. Adrian to Dominic, March 13, 1956, Williams to Gibson, July 17, August 10, 1956, Release, July 25, 1956, [Adrian] to Lawrence L. Farrell, May 24, 1956, Adrian to Williams, April 25, August 14, 1956, Gertrude Kurath to Williams, September 3, 1956, Box 399, GMW Papers; *DN,* May 9, 1956, DNSB 13; Hillman, *History,* pp. 15, 27–30.

49. Governor's Study Commission on Indian Problems Minutes, September 7, October 20 [1956], March 30, July 20, 1958, Philip Mason to R. G. Mulcahey, November 19, 1956, Box 1, RG 65-47-A; Seaman to Carlisle Carver, October 23, 1956, in Hillman, *Minutes;* Mulcahey to Adrian, February 18, 1957, Box 401, ibid.; Seaman to Williams, March 9, 1959, and enclosed Report of Governor's Commission, Box 404, ibid.; Beeson to Charles Orlebeke, May 5, 1964, Box 349, GR Papers; Hillman, *History,* pp. 31–36.

50. Mulcahey to Wakefield, July 30, 1957, Seaman to Williams, November 27, 1957, Box 401, GMW Papers; Seaman to Williams, March 9, 1959, Box 404, ibid.;

Wakefield to Williams, December 23, 1960, in Hillman, *Minutes;* Hillman, *History,* pp. 36–37.

51. Williams to Wakefield, October 17, 1960, Box 405, GMW Papers; Riley to Wakefield [November 14, 1956], Wakefield to Williams, November 8, December 23, 1960, in Hillman, *Minutes;* Hillman, *History,* pp. 41–42.

52. Hillman, *History,* pp. 45–46; Seaman to Williams, March 9, 1959, Box 404, GMW Papers; Adrian to Swainson, December 12, 1960, Popkin to Richard E. Dougherty, May 4, 1961, Box 55, JBS Papers.

53. *DN,* August 13, 14, 16, 18, 1960, March 31, 1961, DNSB 16; Williams to J. B. Ancliff, August 18, 1960, unidentified clipping, August 18, 1960, in Box 305, GMW Papers; Robert Deregonski to Paul Adams, August 12, 1960, Box 313, ibid.; *LSJ,* February 12, March 6, 1962, clippings in Box 21, BG Papers.

54. MESC Report to Williams on the Characteristics of the Unemployed, September 1, 1955, Box 163, GMW Papers; Williams to Neil Staebler, March 4, 1958, Williams to Ruth E. Loyster, May 13, 1958, Box 244, GMW Papers; Swainson to Ralph H. Estes, April 25, 1961, Box 55, JBS Papers.

55. Edward F. Sladek, "Vocational Rehabilitation in Michigan," *Journal of the Michigan State Medical Society* 54 (August 1955): 952; C. Esco Obermann, *A History of Vocational Rehabilitation in America,* 5th ed. (Minneapolis: T. S. Dennison, 1968), pp. 217, 225–26, 270; Governor's Commission on Employment of the Physically Handicapped Minutes, March 29, 1958, Box 244, GMW Papers; U.S. Department of Health, Education and Welfare, Office of Vocational Rehabilitation, Michigan: A Five Year Plan [1958], Box 266, ibid.; Michigan Survey of Aging, March 1959, Box 414, ibid.

56. Obermann, *Vocational Rehabilitation,* pp. 273–74, 287, 365; Sladek, "Vocational Rehabilitation," p. 952; Data Sheet, Division of Vocational Rehabilitation [1960], Box 324, GMW Papers.

57. Vocational Rehabilitation Minutes, November 8, 1951, Box 407, GMW Papers; Michigan Survey of Aging, March 1959, Box 414, ibid.; Lee M. Thurston et al. to Governor, November 1, 1951, Box 97, ibid.; *Back to Work through Vocational Rehabilitation, Bulletin VR 600,* n.d., Box 234, ibid.; Sladek, "Vocational Rehabilitation," pp. 952, 958.

58. Clarence V. Smazel to Alfred L. Pond, April 19, 1950, Box 30, GMW Papers; Thurston et al. to Governor, November 1, 1951, Box 97, ibid.; Vocational Rehabilitation Minutes, November 8, 1951, Box 407, ibid.; Governor's Commission Minutes, March 29, 1958, Box 244, ibid.; Horton to Mary Hardenburg, March 29, 1957, Box 226, ibid.; Michigan Survey of Aging, March 1959, Box 414, ibid.; Fjetland, in Interim Committee of the Legislature, Hearings, 1955–1958, Box 3, JBS Papers; Ralf A. Peckham to Coor, July 26, 1962, Box 31, ibid.; *DN,* January 13, 1955, clipping in Box 14, BG Papers.

59. Peckham to Swainson, August 23, 1956, Box 3, JBS Papers; Progress in Michigan Education during Tenure of Lynn M. Bartlett [1961?], Box 1, Lynn M. Bartlett Papers, BHL; Inter-Agency meeting . . . , February 13, 1958, Box 244, GMW Papers; Michigan Survey of Aging, March 1959, Box 414, ibid.

60. Thurston et al. to Governor, November 1, 1951, Extract of Remarks . . . , October 1953, Box 97, GMW Papers; Five Year Plan [1958], Box 266, ibid.; Progress . . . during Tenure of Bartlett [1961], Box 1, Bartlett Papers; *Battle Creek Enquirer and Evening News,* October 6, 1953, clipping in Box 424, GMW Papers;

LSJ, February 21, 1962, clipping in Box 4, BG Papers; Division of Vocational Rehabilitation Program Problems [1961], Box 55, JBS Papers.

61. Data Sheet, Division of Vocational Rehabilitation [1960], Box 324, GMW Papers; Williams Message to Sixty-Ninth Michigan Legislature, March 19, 1958, Box 430, ibid.; Perkins to Loyster, February 6, 1961, Swainson Address, April 27, 1961, Coor Memorandum to Swainson, April 27, 1961, Box 55, JBS Papers; *DN*, January 16, 1957, *LSJ*, February 21, 1962, clippings in Box 14, BG Papers.

62. Building Michigan's Health: A Report of the Michigan Public Health Study Commission, November 21, 1957, Box 227, GMW Papers; Five Year Plan [1958], Box 266, ibid.; Progress Report of the Rehabilitation Project of the Michigan Welfare League . . . , November 13, 1958, Box 593, ibid.; Governor's Commission Minutes, March 29, 1958, Box 244, ibid.; Division of Vocational Rehabilitation Program Problems [1961], Box 55, JBS Papers; *DN*, January 15, 1958, clipping in Box 14, BG Papers.

63. Monat to Farrell, September 18, 1957, Box 211, GMW Papers; Progress in Michigan Education [1961], Box 1, Bartlett Papers.

64. Vocational Rehabilitation Minutes, November 8, 1951, Box 407, GMW Papers; Report of Morris Samsky, n.d., Box 121, ibid.; Extracts of Remarks by Williams, October 5, 1953, Box 424, ibid.; Annual Report by Governor's Commission . . . , 1956–1957 Activities, Appendix I, Box 51, Detroit Urban League (hereafter DUL) Papers, BHL; MESC, *Annual Report for the Fiscal Year Ending June 30, 1951*, p. 111; idem, *Annual Report . . . 1952*, p. 33; idem, *Annual Report . . . 1953*, pp. 16–17; idem, *Annual Report . . . 1954*, pp. 29–30; idem, *Annual Report . . . 1955*, p. 15; idem, *Annual Report . . . 1956*, p. 26; idem, *Annual Report . . . 1957*, p. 29; idem, *Annual Report . . . 1958*, p. 43; idem, *Annual Report . . . 1959*, p. 24; idem, *Annual Report . . . 1960*, pp. 40–41; idem, *Annual Report . . . 1961*, p. 39; idem, *Annual Report . . . 1962*, p. 58; MESC Minutes, April 27, 1960, Box 8, Downs Papers.

65. Obermann, *Vocational Rehabilitation*, pp. 348–50; Paul P. Kimball to Employers, September 20, 1949, Box 6, GMW Papers; Horton to Administrative Staff et al., July 31, 1953, Box 97, ibid.; *LSJ*, October 1, 1950, clipping in Box 14, BG Papers.

66. Williams to Arthur Rasch, September 16, 1949, Box 6, GMW Papers; Plan of Action for Governor's Commission [1949], Mildred E. Anderson to Governor, January 17, 1951, Box 51, ibid.; Governor's Commission By-Laws, December 1957, Box 244, ibid.; Governor's Commission on Employment of the Handicapped, n.d., Box 68, JBS Papers.

67. Anderson to Williams, September 29, October 25, 1951, Paul Strachan to Williams, November 1, 1951, April 20, 1953, Loyster to Williams, January 17, 1952, Marvin Tableman to Loyster, January 2, 1953, Charles Rae Jeffrey to Paul Weber, July 27, 1953, Box 97, GMW Papers; Strachan to Williams, October 4, 1954, Box 121, ibid.; Adrian to Williams, March 29, 1957, Monat to Farrell, July 23, 1957, Monat to Williams [1957], Box 211, ibid.

68. Monat to Williams [July 1957], Monat Memorandum to Farrell, September 18, 1957, Monat to Jeffrey, August 16, 1957, Perkins to Williams, August 27, 1957, Box 211, ibid.; Monat to Williams, January 29, 1958, Williams to Staebler, March 4, 1958, Governor's Commission on Employment of the Handicapped Minutes, March 29, 1958, Governor's Commission on Employment of the Handicapped, April 1958, Monat to Swainson, April 8, 1958, Monat to Staebler, April 18, 1958, Williams to

Loyster, May 13, 1958, Williams to Jeffrey, May 13, 1958, Monat to Perkins, June 9, 1958, Box 244, ibid.; Staebler to Perkins, January 15, 1962, Box 55, JBS Papers.

69. Anderson to Williams, January 17, 1951, Box 51, GMW Papers; Thurston et al. to Williams, November 1, 1951, Box 97, ibid.; Report of Samsky, n.d., Box 121, ibid.; Governor's Commission Minutes, November 21, 1955, Box 180, ibid.; Annual Report by the Governor's Commission, 1956–1957 Activities, Box 51, DUL Papers; Governor's Commission Final Report, November 1960, Box 416, GMW Papers; *DN*, December 1, 1955, *LSJ*, April 27, 1961, clippings in Box 14, BG Papers.

70. Report of Samsky, n.d., Box 121, GMW Papers; Frederick E. Tripp to Edgar J. Burns, March 13, 1950, Box 186, ibid.; Governor's Commission Final Report, November 1960, Box 416, ibid.; Perkins to Williams, January 20, 1958, Governor's Commission Minutes, March 29, July 19, 1958, Box 244, ibid.; Anderson to Williams, January 11, 1951, Governor's Commission . . . 1956–1957 Activities, Box 51, DUL Papers; Governor's Commission Minutes, December 15, 1954, Organizational Structure for Local . . . Committees, enclosed with John Lee to Barney Hopkins, August 12, 1955, Box 209, Michigan AFL-CIO Papers, ALUA; *LSJ*, December 17, 1954, clipping in Box 14, BG Papers.

71. Speech by Benjamin Marcus . . . , December 1, 1959, Brown to Perkins, December 8, 1959, Box 296, GMW Papers; Governor's Commission Minutes, September 26, 1958, Box 221, Michigan AFL-CIO Papers; Governor's Commission Minutes, March 29, May 14, 1958, Box 244, GMW Papers; Governor's Commission Minutes, April 17, 1959, Box 411, ibid.; Governor's Commission Minutes, September 9, 1960, Box 416, ibid.; Governor's Commission Minutes, March 11, 1960, Box 305, ibid.; Governor's Commission Final Report, November 1960, Box 416, ibid.; Perkins to Williams, July 2, 1958, and enclosed Governor's Commission, Limited Liability for a Second Injury, Box 244, ibid.; Proposal submitted by Fred Warner and John Miron, n.d., Box 411, ibid.; Brown Memorandum to Williams, September 24, 1959, Box 296, ibid.; Governor's Commission on Employment of the Physically Handicapped, n.d., Box 68, JBS Papers; Perkins to Thomas Lamb, November 21, 1961, Box 55, ibid.; "Public Act No. 74," *Public and Local Acts of the Legislature of the State of Michigan Passed at the Regular Session of 1960*, pp. 63–64.

72. House Concurrent Resolutions Nos. 27, 61, n.d., Interim Committee of the Legislature, Hearings, 1955–1958, Box 3, JBS Papers; Hugh A. Peters to Williams, March 10, 1958, Box 244, GMW Papers; Adrian Memorandum to Farrell, March 6, 1956, Box 466, ibid.; Burns to Commissioners, February 29, 1956, Box 209, Michigan AFL-CIO Papers; *LSJ*, December 13, 23, 1956, clippings in Box 14, BG Papers.

73. Melvin J. Maas to Swainson, November 16, 1961, Perkins to Swainson, November 22, 1961, Box 55, JBS Papers.

74. Perkins to Russell G. Albrecht, April 17, 1962, Coor to Billy Cairns, April 18, 1962, ibid.; Coor to Loyster, January 10, 1962, Box 31, ibid.

75. Coor to Perkins, September 13, 1962, Executive Office Release, October 2, 1962, Box 55, ibid.

Chapter 7

1. Detroit Archdiocesan Council of Catholic Women, December 1950, Clement Kern Papers, ALUA; *Michigan: 1961 Report to the Commission on Civil Rights from the State Advisory Committee*, p. 285, Box 15, JBS Papers, BHL; *DFP*, August 25,

1954, clipping in Box 471, GMW Papers, BHL; Subcommittee on Migratory Labor of the Senate Committee on Labor and Public Welfare, *The Migratory Farm Labor Problem in the United States*, 87 Cong., 1 sess., 1961, S. Rept. 1098, ix.

2. J. F. Thaden, "Migratory Agricultural Workers in Michigan: The Origins of the Problem," August 15, 1949, Box 73, GMW Papers.

3. Ibid.; Michigan State Employment Service, Employment Service Division, Occupational Guide, Seasonal Farm Jobs in Michigan, March 1951, Box 285, GMW Papers; Dennis Nodín Valdés, *Al Norte: Agricultural Workers in the Great Lakes Region, 1917–1970* (Austin: University of Texas Press, 1991), pp. 97, 134–37; Noel W. Stuckman, "Some Economic Aspects of Increasing Cucumber Yields in Michigan" (MS, Department of Agricultural Economics, Michigan State University, 1959).

4. Valdés, *Al Norte*, pp. 99, 105–6, 138–39; Governor's Study Commission, Handbook on Migratory, Seasonal, Agricultural Workers in Michigan, September 29, 1953, Box 97, GMW Papers; Michigan Migrant Ministry, Annual Report, 1960, and Report of Projects, Box 2, Michigan Migrant Ministry (hereafter MMM) Papers, BHL.

5. Richard B. Craig, *The Bracero Program* (Austin: University of Texas Press, 1971), pp. 3–5, 53–56, 89, 178; Anne B. Effland, "The Emergence of Federal Assistance Programs for Migrant and Seasonal Farm Workers in Post–World War II America" (Ph.D. diss., Iowa State University, 1991), pp. 16–17, 29–31, 36; Valdés, *Al Norte*, pp. 94, 100–104, 140, 150–51; Statement by Edgar G. Johnston, October 7, 1952, Box 1, Edgar Johnston Papers, ALUA; L. Craig to Williams, May 18, 1959, Box 274, GMW Papers; MMM, Annual Report, 1961, Box 2, MMM Papers; *DFP*, May 31, 1954.

6. Michigan State Employment Service, Employment Service Division, Occupational Guide, March 1951, Box 585, GMW Papers; Thaden, "Migrant Agricultural Workers," Johnston Statement on Migratory Labor in Michigan [March 11, 1952], Box 73, ibid.; Edgar Grant Johnston, "Migrant Workers in the State of Michigan," MASCD Issue Paper [1970], p. 2; Valdés, *Al Norte*, pp. 91–92, 138.

7. Handbook, Box 97, GMW Papers; Johnston Statement [March 11, 1952], Box 73, ibid.; Johnston, "Migrant Workers"; Valdés, *Al Norte*, pp. 55, 58–59.

8. Valdés, *Al Norte*, p. 113; Lee M. Thurston Memorandum to Dr. Elliott, February 26, 1947, Box 14, Records of the Executive Office: Kim Sigler, RG 43, State Archives, Lansing, Michigan; Thaden, "Migrant Agricultural Labor in Michigan" [1947], Box 225, John F. Thaden Papers, ibid.

9. Interdepartmental Committee Recommends . . . [June 1947], Box 14, RG 43; *DFP*, March 30, 1948; *DN*, March 14, 1962; Farm Placement Section (FPS), *Post-Season Farm Labor Report, 1956*, p. 8; Governor's Study Commission on Migratory Labor, Economic Sub-Committee, Report of Meeting, December 11, 1953, Box 223, Thaden Papers.

10. Handbook, Box 97, GMW Papers; Johnston Statement [March 11, 1952], Box 73, ibid.; Valdés, *Al Norte*, pp. 43–44.

11. Thaden, "Migratory Agricultural Workers," Johnston Statement [March 11, 1952], Box 73, GMW Papers; Handbook, Box 97, ibid.; MMM, Annual Report, 1962, Box 2, MMM Papers; Mrs. John R. Golden, "The Migrant Problem in Michigan," *American Child* 39 (January 1957): 7; Jerome G. Manis, *A Study of Migrant Education: Survey Findings in Van Buren County, 1957* (Kalamazoo: Western Michigan University Press, 1958), pp. 16–17, 22.

12. Henry J. Ponitz, "These, Too, Are Our Children," *Michigan Education Journal*, December 1, 1955, pp. 92–94, copy in Box 34, JBS Papers; Joint Meeting of Governor's Study Commission and Interagency Committee, October 20, 1954, Box 277, Thaden Papers.

13. MESC Minutes, October 12, 1960, Box 8, Tom Downs Papers, BHL; Handbook, Box 97, GMW Papers; Golden, "Migrant Problem in Michigan," p. 7; *DFP*, August 25, 1954, August 28, 1955.

14. MESC Minutes, October 12, 1960, Box 8, Downs Papers; Johnston Statement [March 11, 1952], Box 73, GMW Papers; unidentified clipping [June 1950], in Kern Papers; *LSJ*, February 22, 1956, clipping in Box 20, BG Papers, BHL.

15. *Michigan: 1961 Report*, pp. 280–85, Box 15, JBS Papers; Albert E. Heustis Memorandum to Zolton Ferency, August 24, 1962, and enclosure, Max M. Horton to Ferency, September 24, 1962, Box 34, JBS Papers; *The 50 States Report: Submitted to the Commission on Civil Rights by the State Advisory Committees, 1961* (Washington, D.C.: Government Printing Office, n.d.), pp. 280–85.

16. Michigan Department of Health Program Statement, December 1951, Box 61, GMW Papers; Statement of E. F. Sladek ..., November 20, 1952, Box 97, ibid.; Johnston Statement [March 11, 1952], Box 73, ibid.; Handbook, Box 97, ibid.; Sladek to Members of the Subcommittee ..., November 24, 1952, Michigan Welfare Conference, November 12, 1952, Box 223, Thaden Papers; *DFP*, October 15, 1956.

17. Public Health News, June 5, 1958, Box 471, GMW Papers; Subcommittee on Migratory Labor of the Senate Committee on Labor and Public Welfare, *Migratory Labor Bills*, 88 Cong., 1 sess., 1963, 89; *Journal of the Michigan State Medical Society* 57 (June 1958): 892; Helen L. Johnston, *Health for the Nation's Harvesters: A History of the Migrant Health Program in Its Economic and Social Setting* (Farmington Hills, Mich.: National Migrant Worker Council, 1985), p. 96.

18. FPS, *Post Season Farm Labor Report, 1953*, p. 22; Sladek to Members of the Subcommittee ..., November 24, 1952, Box 223, Thaden Papers; Johnston Statement [March 11, 1952], Box 73, GMW Papers; Handbook, Box 97, ibid.

19. Study Commission Sub-Committee—Education and Child Labor Minutes, July 29, 1952, Michigan Welfare Conference, November 12, 1952, Box 223, Thaden Papers; Greene to Michigan Governor's Study Commission, February 18, 1953, Box 226, ibid.; Project Lacota, Migrant Ministry, August 31, 1956, Box 1, MMM Papers; *Ann Arbor News*, September 27, 1959, clipping in Box 20, BG Papers.

20. Michigan State Employment Service, Regulatory Controls and Activities Affecting Welfare of Migrant Workers in Michigan, November 1951, Box 585, GMW Papers; Handbook, Box 97, ibid.; FPS, *Post Season Farm Labor Report, 1949*, p. 29; idem, *Post Season Farm Labor Report, 1950*, p. 33; idem, *Post Season Farm Labor Report, 1951*, p. 16.

21. Michigan State Employment Service, Regulatory Controls, November 1951, Box 585, GMW Papers; Handbook, Box 97, ibid.; Report of First Meeting, Governor's Commission ..., March 24, 1952, Box 1, Johnston Papers; Governor's Study Commission Minutes, December 12, 1952, Box 223, Thaden Papers.

22. Joint Meeting, Governor's Study Commission and Interagency Committee, October 20, 1954, Box 277, Thaden Papers; G. S. McIntyre to Swainson, August 14, 1962, Box 34, JBS Papers; *Migratory Labor*, p. 151; *LSJ*, February 22, 1956, clipping in Box 20, BG Papers.

23. Subcommittee on Migratory Labor of Senate Committee on Labor and Public Welfare, *Migratory Labor,* 86 Cong., 1 sess., 1959, 149–51, 156, 163–65, 171–76, 203–10; idem, 87 Cong., 1 sess., 1961, 180–81; Joint Meeting Governor's Study Commission and Interagency Committee, October 20, 1954, Box 277, Thaden Papers; Governor's Study Commission Minutes, March 24, September 12, December 12, 1952, ibid.; Waldo E. Dick to Patrick V. McNamara, February 20, 1962, Box 534, Patrick V. McNamara Papers, ALUA; McIntyre to Swainson, August 14, 1962, Box 34, JBS Papers; *LSJ,* September 24, 1955, clipping in Box 20, BG Papers.

24. Report of First Meeting of Governor's Study Commission, March 24, 1952, Box 1, Johnston Papers; Johnston Statement [March 11, 1952], Governor's Study Commission Minutes, May 27, 1952, Box 73, GMW Papers; *Migratory Labor,* 1959, pp. 219–20; FPS, *Post Season Farm Labor Report, 1950,* p. 35; idem, *Post Season Farm Labor Report, 1951,* p. 16; idem, *Post Season Farm Labor Report, 1955,* p. 18; idem, *Post Season Farm Labor Report, 1956,* p. 17; idem, *Post Season Farm Labor Report, 1957,* p. 12; idem, *Post Season Farm Labor Report, 1958,* p. 14; idem, *Post Season Farm Labor Report, 1959,* pp. 19–20; idem, *Post Season Farm Labor Report, 1961,* pp. 33, 35; idem, *Post Season Farm Labor Report, 1962,* p. 29; [*Catholic Weekly,* June 11, July 23, 1950], *Saginaw News,* September 13, 1950 [September 17, 1950], clippings in Kern Papers; *DFP,* May 30, 31, 1948, October 16, 1951; Valdés, *Al Norte,* pp. 109–10, 157–58.

25. MMM, Report by State Director, 1958, Box 274, GMW Papers; MMM Annual Report, 1960, and Report of Projects, Box 2, MMM Papers; *Migratory Labor,* 1959, p. 198.

26. Michigan Churches work together . . . , n.d., Box 180, GMW Papers; MMM, Annual Report, 1956, Box 2, MMM Papers; Edith E. Lowery, "A Better Chance for Migratory Children," *American Child* 39 (January 1957): 11.

27. There is a wealth of material on the Michigan Migrant Ministry and its work over the years in Boxes 1 and 2 of the MMM Papers. See, especially, Annual Report, 1960, and Report of Projects in Box 2. See also MMM, Report by State Director, 1958, Box 274, GMW Papers. There is also some relevant material in the National Council of Churches, Division of Home Mission Papers, Box 10, RG 67, Presbyterian Historical Society, Philadelphia, Pennsylvania.

28. Valdés, *Al Norte,* pp. 110–11; *Migratory Labor in American Agriculture: Report of the President's Commission on Migratory Labor* (Washington, D.C.: Government Printing Office, 1951), pp. vii, 103, 134–35, 150, 157, 165, 174, 177; FPS, *Post Season Farm Labor Report, 1949,* p. 35; idem, *Post Season Farm Labor Report, 1957,* p. 31; idem, *Post Season Farm Labor Report, 1958,* p. 13; MESC, *Annual Report for the Fiscal Year Ending June 30, 1955,* p. 14; Inter-Agency Committee Minutes, April 20, 1954, Box 121, GMW Papers; Effland, "Federal Assistance Programs," pp. 63–64.

29. Information Paper on Migratory Farm Labor, Box 241, GMW Papers; Summary of Meeting of Inter-Agency Committee, October 25, 1957, Box 410, ibid.; Effland, "Federal Assistance Programs," pp. 63–68; James P. Mitchell, Interstate Recruitment of Agricultural Workers and Placement Policy, August 10, 1959, Box 26, Alvin M. Bentley Papers, BHL.

30. Effland, "Federal Assistance Programs," pp. 70–71; Douglas Fryer to Doctor ——, February 12, 1960, Box 305, GMW Papers; FPS, *Post Season Farm Labor Report, 1960,* pp. 6–7, 11; MESC Minutes, October 12, 1960, Box 8, Downs Papers.

31. FPS, *Post Season Farm Labor Report, 1961*, pp. 35–36; idem, *Post Season Farm Labor Report, 1962*, pp. 34–35.

32. Effland, "Federal Assistance Programs," pp. 123, 130.

33. Clinton M. Fair Memoranda to Williams, June 3, 1949, June 5, 1951, Committee on the Education, Health and Welfare of Migrant Workers to Williams, September 23, 1949, Williams to Johnston, October 12, 1949, Box 97, GMW Papers.

34. *Ann Arbor News*, August 13, 1949; Lawrence L. Farrell to Williams, June 6, 1951, Box 97, GMW Papers; Committee on Health, Education and Welfare Minutes, July 13, 1951, Statement of Johnston, October 7, 1952, Box 1, Johnston Papers.

35. Release, March 6, 1952, Box 471, GMW Papers; Williams to Kern, March 6, 1952, Box 73, ibid.

36. Study Commission, Areas of Committee Activity, April 29, 1952, Governor's Study Commission Minutes, September 30, 1952, Box 223, Thaden Papers; Recommendations of the Inter-Agency Committee for Consideration of the Governor's Study Commission [1953], Box 229, ibid.; Thaden and Johnston to Williams, December 22, 1952, Box 73, GMW Papers; Sub-Committee on Education and Child Labor Minutes, January 6, 1953, Box 1, Johnston Papers; Johnston to Larry Hansen, December 14, 1953, Box 97, GMW Papers.

37. Johnston and Thaden to Williams, January 19, 1955, Box 1, Johnston Papers; Governor's Study Commission Recommendations, January 1955, Box 418, GMW Papers; Johnston and Thaden to Williams, January 27, 1955, Box 149, ibid.

38. Williams to Merle L. Kerr, January 31, 1955, Mitchell to Williams, May 20, 1955, Box 149, GMW Papers.

39. Austin L. Pino to O. K. Fjetland, June 4, 1954, Box 223, Thaden Papers; Pino to Study Commission, March 22, 1955, Box 229, ibid.

40. *Ann Arbor News*, December 8, 1951.

41. *LSJ*, September 24, 1955, clipping in Box 20, BG Papers; Thaden to John Sweeney, October 14, 1955, Johnston to Sweeney, October 26, 1955, Box 149, GMW Papers; Valdés, *Al Norte*, p. 154.

42. Legislative Program, 1955, Box 430, GMW Papers; Frederick Tripp to John Reid, March 8, 1955, Williams to Mitchell, June 3, 1955, Williams to Johnston, December 6, 1955, Box 149, ibid.; "Michigan Inter-Agency Committee on Migratory Labor," n.d., Summary of Meeting of Inter-Agency Committee, October 25, 1957, Box 410, GMW Papers.

43. Williams to Johnston, December 16, 1955, Box 194, GMW Papers; Release, February 6, 1956, Box 471, ibid.; *LSJ*, February 4, 7, 15, 22, 24, March 4, 6, 28, 1956, clippings in Box 20, BG Papers.

44. Summary of Meeting of Inter-Agency Committee, December 13, 1957, Box 211, GMW Papers.

45. Preliminary Draft of Statement . . . , December 12, 1957, Box 5, Records of the Michigan Civil Rights Commission, Information Division, General Administrative Records of the Fair Employment Practices Commission, 1955–1963, RG 66-82-A, State Archives; Information Paper on Migratory Farm Labor, Draft, February 19, 1958, Box 241, GMW Papers; John T. Abernethy to A. W. Boles [1958], Abernethy to Fjetland, February 3, 1958, Box 244, ibid.; Abernethy Memorandum to Charles Brown, July 15, 1958, Box 410, ibid.; Johnston to Williams, February 24, 1959, Williams to Reporter, January 21, 1959, Recommendations of the Mid-American Conference on Migratory Labor, April 7–9, 1959, Box 274, ibid.; Williams Message . . . , April 14, 1959, Box 430, ibid.; August Scholle to Swainson, June 24,

1961, and enclosure, Frederick M. Mitchell to Williams, November 23, 1960, Box 17, JBS Papers; Lynn M. Bartlett to Swainson, July 11, 1962, Box 34, ibid.; *Migratory Labor, 1959*, p. 212.

46. MMM, Annual Report, 1962, Box 2, MMM Papers; Status of Agricultural Workers under State and Federal Labor Laws [April 1961], Box 229, Thaden Papers.

47. *LSJ*, April 19, 1961, *Ann Arbor News*, March 8, 1962, clippings in Box 20, BG Papers; MMM, Annual Report, 1961, Box 2, MMM Papers; *Migratory Labor,* 1961, pp. 181, 492; Francis J. Coomes Memo to Ferency, September 22, 1961, and enclosure, Mrs. Carl Gladstone to Swainson, April 3, 1961, Frederick Routh to Swainson, April 5, 1961, Scholle to Swainson, June 24, 1961, and enclosure, Richard L. Miller to Ed Winge, October 16, 1961, Box 17, JBS Papers; James H. Inglis to Miller, March 22, 1962, Box 34, ibid.

48. FPS, *Post Season Farm Labor Report, 1959,* p. 21; MESC, Report on Migrant Agricultural Worker Situation [1962], Box 34, JBS Papers.

49. Mitchell to Williams, November 23, 1960, Box 17, JBS Papers; James A. Browder to Swainson, June 28, 1962, W. J. Maxey to Swainson, August 21, 1962, Box 34, ibid.; FPS, *Post Season Farm Labor Report, 1953,* p. 24; idem, *Post Season Farm Labor Report, 1960,* pp. 15–16; Study Commission Minutes, May 27, 1952, Box 73, GMW Papers.

50. FPS, *Post Season Farm Labor Report, 1949,* p. 32; idem, *Post Season Farm Labor Report, 1950,* p. 3; idem, *Post Season Farm Labor Report, 1955,* p. 18; idem, *Post Season Farm Labor Report, 1957,* p. 14; idem, *Post Season Farm Labor Report, 1958,* p. 15; idem, *Post Season Farm Labor Report, 1959,* p. 20; idem, *Post Season Farm Labor Report, 1962,* p. 29; Joint Meeting of Governor's Study Commission and Inter-Agency Committee, October 20, 1954, Box 277, Thaden Papers; Summary of Meeting . . . , October 25, 1957, Box 410, GMW Papers; Heustis to Swainson, August 1, 1962, Box 34, JBS Papers.

51. Summary of Van Buren County Migrant Health Program [1955], Box 17, JBS Papers; Office of Education, U.S. Department of Labor, Report of Two Conferences on Planning Education for Agricultural Migrants, Box 416, GMW Papers; *Migratory Labor,* 1959, pp. 117–26.

52. Bay County Board of Education, Bay County School for Migrant Children, July–August 1956, Sam Rabinowitz to Charles Adrian, June 28, 1956, Box 180, GMW Papers; Sol Markoff to Rabinowitz, May 11, 1956, Box 1, Johnston Papers.

53. *Bay City Times,* June 27, 1956, clipping in Box 20, BG Papers; Bay County Board of Education, Bay County School . . . , 1956, Fjetland to Edwin F. Coffey, June 27, 1956, Box 180, GMW Papers; Ponitz to Curtis Catlin et al., July 18, 1958, Box 184, ibid.; *Migratory Labor,* 1959, pp. 185, 187–88; Thaden Statement, September 17, 1959, Box 228, Thaden Papers.

54. Ponitz to Catlin et al., June 18, 1956, Rabinowitz to Farrell, July 23, 1956, Box 184, GMW Papers; MESC, *Annual Report for the Fiscal Year Ending June 30, 1957,* p. 34; FPS, *Post Season Farm Labor Report, 1957,* p. 12.

55. Bay County School for Migrant Children, June 3–July 5, 1957, Box 274, GMW Papers; Summary of Meeting of Inter-Agency Committee, October 25, 1957, Box 410, ibid.; *Migratory Labor,* 1959, pp. 185–86; Michigan Youth Commission, Children and Youth in Michigan, A Report to Williams, March 1960, Box 307, GMW Papers; Bartlett to Swainson, July 11, 1962, Box 34, JBS Papers.

56. FPS, *Post Season Farm Labor Report, 1959,* p. 19; idem, *Post Season Farm*

Labor Report, 1960, p. 14; idem, *Post Season Farm Labor Report, 1961,* pp. 32–33; Keeler, July 7, 1961, Box 1, MMM Papers.

57. *DFP,* June 1, 1954; Joint Meeting of Governor's Study Commission and Inter-Agency Committee, December 17, 1954, Fjetland to Williams, March 20, 1956, Fjetland to Coffey, June 27, 1956, Box 180, GMW Papers; *Migratory Labor, 1959,* pp. 149–51, 156, 163–65, 171–76, 203–10; Paul Brohman to McNamara, February 20, 1962, Box 534, McNamara Papers; McIntyre to Swainson, August 14, 1956, Box 34, JBS Papers; FPS, *Post Season Farm Labor Report, 1954,* p. 13; idem, *Post Season Farm Labor Report, 1959,* p. 21; Thaden to Williams . . . , March 15, 1961, Box 229, Thaden Papers; *LSJ,* March 22, 1956, clipping in Box 20, BG Papers.

58. Williams "Exaugural Address," January 11, 1961, *Journal of the House of Representatives of the State of Michigan, 71st Legislature, Regular Session of 1961,* p. 46.

Chapter 8

1. Williams to Douglas, August 13, 1952, Williams to Robert F. Kearse, August 13, 1952, Box 490, GMW Papers, BHL; unidentified clipping [July 5, 1952], in Box 451, ibid.; McNaughton, *Mennen Williams,* pp. 229–31; Berthelot, *Win Some, Lose Some,* pp. 96–97.

2. Releases, September 29, 1955, April 27, 1956, Box 451, GMW Papers; Extracts from Williams Address, January 3, 1956, Box 426, ibid.; Berthelot, *Win Some, Lose Some,* pp. 57–58.

3. *New York Times,* June 3, August 19, 1956; *Detroit Times,* August 19, 1956, clipping in Box 456, GMW Papers; "Civil Rights" [1956], Box 494, ibid.

4. Democratic National Advisory Committee, Origin and Purpose, Draft, June 28, 1957, Box 508, GMW Papers; Williams to Harriman, October 31, 1957, Box 207, ibid.; Paul Weber Memorandum to Williams, November 14, 1957, Box 452, ibid.; Opening Statement by Williams . . . , January 31, 1959, Box 429, ibid.; McNaughton, *Mennen Williams,* p. 235.

5. Executive Office Release, November 18, 1957, Box 450, GMW Papers; Governor's Office, Memorandum to Governors' Conference— Civil Rights, December 2, 1957, Preliminary Draft of Statement, December 12, 1957, Box 5, Records of the Michigan Civil Rights Commission, Information Division, General Administrative Records of the Fair Employment Practices Commission, 1955–1963, RG 66-82-A, State Archives, Lansing, Michigan; *New York Times,* December 13, 1957.

6. Harriman to Williams, December 13, 1957, Box 238, GMW Papers; John Feild to Lester Markel, February 17, 1958, Box 5, RG 66-82-A; Katherine Shannon interview with John Feild, December 28, 1967, p. 34, transcript in Civil Rights Documentation Project, Moorland-Spingarn Research Center, Howard University, Washington, D.C.; *Fair Employment Practices at Work in Twelve States: A Report Prepared for the Conference of Governors of Civil Rights States* [1958], copy in Box 289, GMW Papers; *DN,* December 12, 13, 1957; McNaughton, *Mennen Williams,* p. 226. For the relationship of Williams's position on civil rights and his possible candidacy for the 1960 Democratic presidential nomination, see Victor Navasky Memorandum to Williams, September 10, 1959, Box 269, ibid.

7. Interim Sub-Committee of the Governors' Committee on Civil Rights Minutes, April 11, June 10, November 17, 1958, Box 5, RG 66-82-A; Governors' Committee on Civil Rights, A Summary Analysis of Experience of States Having

Civil Rights Jurisdiction over Housing, Public Accommodations and Education, April 1958, Box 269, GMW Papers; Opening Statement by Williams, January 31, 1959, Box 429, ibid.; *DN,* January 7, 1959.

8. Williams Statement, January 31, 1959, Box 429, GMW Papers; Statement Adopted at Second Conference of Governors and Civil Rights [January 1959], Box 5, RG 66-82-A; B. M. Joffe to Morris Adler, January 4, 1959, Box 4, Jewish Labor Committee Papers, ALUA; *DN,* January 31, 1959; *DFP,* February 1, 1959.

9. Interim Sub-Committee Recommendations, October 1959, Third Annual Conference Committee of Governors on Civil Rights, March 3–4, 1960, Summary of Proceedings, Third Annual Conference . . . , Summary of Principles Agreed Upon, Box 300, GMW Papers; Excerpts from Remarks by Williams, March 3, 1960, Box 452, ibid.

10. Williams Memorandum to Members of Midwest Governors Conference, February 16, 1960, Box 512, ibid.; Williams to John E. Amos, February 17, 1960, Goals for America, Suggested Policy Statement . . . , March 26, 1960, Release, March 27, 1960, Box 503, ibid.; Resolutions . . . adopted at Conference of Democratic Party of Michigan, May 6–7, 1960, Box 502, ibid.; Oral History Interview with G. Mennen Williams for the John F. Kennedy Library, April 27, 1960, p. 6, Box 103, GMW Non-Gubernatorial Papers, BHL.

11. Charles Brown Memorandum to Williams, n.d., Box 502, GMW Papers; Williams to Helen Berthelot, June 2, 1960, Box 34, Helen Berthelot Papers, BHL; Berthelot, *Win Some, Lose Some,* pp. 212–13; Herbert S. Parmet, *JFK: The Presidency of John F. Kennedy* (New York: Dial Press, 1983), p. 51.

12. Parmet, *JFK,* pp. 51–52; Summary of Washington, D.C., Meeting . . . , June 20, 1960, Confidential Report of Kennedy Meeting, June 20 [1960], Williams Memorandum to Adelaide Hart, June 21, 1960, Box 502, GMW Papers; Feild interview, pp. 30–32; Williams Interview, pp. 11–15, Box 103, GMW Non-Gubernatorial Papers.

13. John Murray Memorandum to Williams, June 21, 1960, Testimony by Williams, July 8, 1960, Box 502, GMW Papers. See also National Platform Resolutions to the Democratic Party Convention adopted at convention of Democratic Party of Michigan, May 6–7, 1960, ibid.

14. Brauer, *Kennedy and the Second Reconstruction,* pp. 35–37; Berthelot, *Win Some, Lose Some,* pp. 214–15.

15. Submitted by Swainson [July 3, 1962], Statement by Swainson, July 3, 1962, Executive Office Release, July 5, 1962, Box 33, JBS Papers.

Chapter 9

1. James K. Pollock, *Making Michigan's New Constitution, 1961–1962* (Ann Arbor: George Wahr Publishing Co., 1962), p. 68.

2. Roger C. Cramton, "The Powers of Michigan's Civil Rights Commission: A Problem in Constitutional Interpretation" [July 1964], pp. 18–19, Box 6, Tom Downs Papers, BHL; Michigan Coordinating Council on Civil Rights, Memorandum in Support of Proposal No. 1621, December 18, 1961, Box 1, Don Binkowski Papers, BHL.

3. See chapter 1.

4. Dunbar and May, *Michigan,* pp. 565–67; Albert L. Sturm, *Constitution Making in Michigan, 1961–1962,* University of Michigan Governmental Studies No.

43 (Ann Arbor: Institute of Public Administration, University of Michigan, 1963), pp. 27–28, 41–45, 47, 49, 55–56, 106–7, 114–16, 250, 258–60; Harold Norris, *Education for Popular Sovereignty through Implementing the Constitution and the Bill of Rights* (Detroit: Detroit College of Law, 1991), p. 398; Coleman Young, "Con-Con Evaluation" [1962], Box 5, Malcolm G. Dade Papers, Burton Historical Collection, Detroit Public Library, Detroit, Michigan.

5. See, for example, Robert Weisbrot, *Freedom Bound: A History of America's Civil Rights Movement* (New York: W. W. Norton and Co., 1990), passim.

6. Sidney Fine interview with Tom Downs, March 30, 1995, p. 32, transcript in BHL; Pollock Notes on Constitutional Convention Meetings, October 7, 1961, January 13, 1962, Box 8, University of Michigan Institute of Public Administration (hereafter IPA) Papers, BHL.

7. Dunbar and May, *Michigan,* p. 550; Article IV, Sections 2, 3, Constitution of the State of Michigan of 1963.

8. Bernard Schwartz, *Super Chief: Earl Warren and His Supreme Court* (New York: New York University Press, 1983), pp. 582–86; Stieber, *Politics of Change,* pp. 35–38; Dunbar and May, *Michigan,* pp. 550–51; *Michigan Statistical Abstract,* 8th ed., 1970, p. 544.

9. Pollock, *Michigan's New Constitution,* p. 66.

10. Sturm, *Constitution Making,* pp. 157, 294; Pollock Notes, November 11, 1961, January 20, March 3, 1962, Box 8, IPA Papers.

11. Proposals Nos. 1010 (October 12, 1961), 1014 (October 12, 1961), 1093 (October 25, 1961), Box 16, Michigan Constitutional Convention, 1961–62, University of Michigan Law School Library, Ann Arbor, Michigan; Committee on Declaration of Rights, Suffrage and Elections, Action Journal, October 12, 17, 19, 24, 25, 1961, Box 46, Alvin M. Bentley Papers, BHL; Pollock Notes, November 11, 1961, Box 8, IPA Papers.

12. Coordinating Council on Civil Rights, Steering Committee Minutes, October 31, 1961, and enclosed Draft of Proposal . . . , Box 3, Albert and Emma Wheeler Papers, BHL; Coordinating Council on Civil Rights, Memorandum in Support of Proposal No. 1621, December 18, 1961, and idem, A Proposal Added . . . to Article II, November 28, 1961, Box 1, Binkowski Papers; Proposal No. 146, Box 16, Michigan Constitutional Convention, 1961–62; Norris, *Education for Popular Sovereignty,* pp. 427, 428–29.

13. Hannah to William H. Combs, November 30, 1961, and enclosed "Civil Rights and the Michigan Constitution," Box 3, John A. Hannah Papers, Michigan State University Archives, Historical Collections, Michigan State University, East Lansing, Michigan; Rights Committee, Action Journal No. 19, November 30, 1961, Box 46, Bentley Papers; State of Michigan Constitutional Convention, 1961, *Official Record,* 1:742, University of Michigan Law Library.

14. Proposal No. 1621, December 8, 1961, Box 3, Wheeler Papers; Norris, *Education for Popular Sovereignty,* p. 429.

15. *Official Record,* 1:384–86, 389.

16. Pollock Notes, December 9, 1961, January 13, 1962, Box 8, IPA Papers; Coordinating Council, Memorandum in Support of Proposal No. 1621, December 18, 1961, Box 1, Binkowski Papers; Statement by Richard V. Marks, December 18, 1961, Box 1, American Civil Liberties Union, Ann Arbor–Washtenaw County Branch Papers, 1959–1967, Box 1, BHL; *DN,* December 19, 1961.

17. Pollock to Committee on Declaration of Rights . . . , January 11, 1962, Box 3, Wheeler Papers; Rights Committee, Action Journal No. 33, January 11, 1962, Box 46, Bentley Papers.

18. *Official Record*, 2:2888–89; Barrymore to Judd, December 11, 1961, Judd to Barrymore, December 16, 1961, Box 4, Dorothy Siegel Judd Papers, BHL; Rights Committee, Action Journal No. 34, January 12, 1962, Box 46, Bentley Papers.

19. Rights Committee, Action Journal No. 35, January 16, 1962, Box 46, Bentley Papers.

20. *Official Record*, 1:658, 739–52, 777–78; Dade to Mr. and Mrs. Charles G. Brown, February 20, 1962, Box 5, Dade Papers.

21. Pollock Notes, December 19, 1961, Box 8, IPA Papers; Rights Committee, Action Journal No. 36, January 18, 1962, No. 37, January 23, 1962, No. 38, January 24, 1962, Box 46, Bentley Papers; JLC, Civil Rights Newsletter, December 6, 1961, Box 17, Jewish Labor Committee Papers, ALUA; *DFP,* January 19, 1962; Thomas, *Rule 9,* pp. 64–66; Norris, *Education for Popular Sovereignty,* pp. 430–31; *Official Record,* 1:717.

22. *Official Record,* 2:2272, 2278–85, 2287.

23. Ibid., 2419–25, 2866–69, 2969–70, 3092–94.

24. Ibid., 2288–89, 2557, 2888–92, 2911–16; Judd to Barrymore, May 29, 1962, Box 4, Judd Papers.

25. Cudlip to Kauper, May 1, 1962, Box 8, William Byrnes Cudlip Papers, BHL; Kauper to Cudlip, April 4, 1962, Judd to Barrymore, May 29, 1962, Box 4, Judd Papers; Analysis of the changes made in Article I . . . , n.d., Box 2, Katherine Moore Cushman Papers, BHL. See also Kauper to Cudlip, April 4, 1962, Box 48, James Kerr Pollock Papers, BHL. Cf. Norris to Cushman, April 19, 1962, Box 3, Harold Norris Papers, BHL.

26. *Official Record,* 2:3088–92; Cushman, "Civil Rights in the New Constitution," January 28, 1963, Box 4, Judd Papers.

27. *DN,* March 10, 1963; Cudlip, "The Proposed Constitution Should Be Approved," *Detroit Lawyer* 31 (January 1963): 11.

28. Article II, Section 10, 1908 Constitution; *Official Record,* 1:467, 494, 525–27; Dade to Irma Steele, January 23, 1962, Box 5, Dade Papers; *Mapp* v. *Ohio,* 367 U.S. 642 (1961).

29. *DN,* March 10, 1963.

30. Harris to Wheeler, October 25, 1961, Wheeler to William Seabron, October 27, 1961, Box 3, Wheeler Papers; Sturm, *Constitution Making,* pp. 188, 294–95.

31. Coordinating Council, Steering Committee Minutes, October 31, 1961, Box 3, Wheeler Papers.

32. Wheeler to Martin, December 4, 1961, Wheeler to Hatcher, December 4, 1961, and enclosed "A Testimony . . . ," Wheeler to William O. Greene, December 26, 1961, ibid.

33. Henry Rowan to Wheeler, December 13, 1961, Wheeler to Rowan, December 21, 1961, Frederick Routh to Richard Emrich, December 7 [1961], Emrich to Henry Lewis, December 8, 1961, Wheeler to Hannah, n.d., Otis B. Smith to Wheeler, December 15, 1961, Wheeler to Greene, December 26, 1961, ibid.

34. Proposals Nos. 1522, 1523, December 5, 1961, ibid.

35. Martin to Wheeler, December 2, 1961, Wheeler to Martin, December 26, 1961, Wheeler to Greene, December 26, 1961, Wheeler to Pollock, October 28,

1961, Wheeler to W. B. Harvey, January 3, 1962, Pollock to Wheeler, January 3, 1962, ibid.; Pollock Notes, October 14, 1961, March 3, 1962, Box 8, IPA Papers.

36. Testimony of . . . Hatcher . . . , January 4, 1962, Proposal No. 1569, December 6, 1961, Box 3, Wheeler Papers; Wheeler Testimony . . . , January 30, 1962, Box 2, John B. Martin Papers, BHL; Committee on the Executive Branch, Action Journal No. 30, January 4, 1962, No. 43, January 31, 1962, Box 45, Bentley Papers.

37. Elliott, Supporting Statement . . . , n.d., Box 2, Martin Papers; Elliott to Pollock, February 15, 1962, Box 49, Pollock Papers; *Official Record,* 2:1921–22; Bentley to Alphonse N. Gaspard, March 20, 1962, Box 44, Bentley Papers; *DFP,* March 29, 1962.

38. Committee on the Executive Branch, Action Journal No. 44, March 5, 1962, Box 51, Pollock Papers; Weekly Digest–Public Information Office, March 9, 1962, Box 47, Bentley Papers; Young to Wheeler, March 7, 1962, Wheeler to Young, March 15, 1962, Box 3, Wheeler Papers; *DFP,* March 6, 1962; *DN,* March 6, 1962.

39. *Official Record,* 2:1921–22.

40. Ibid., 1929–30, 1933–34; *DFP,* March 29, 1962.

41. *Official Record,* 2:1924–28, 1941, 1945–46, 1950–52, 2200; Sturm, *Constitution Making,* p. 106; *DN,* March 29, 1962.

42. *Official Record,* 2:1954, 1976–89, 2004–5.

43. Ibid., 1989–2005, 2010; Joe Schore to Steering Committee, April 5, 1962, Box 56, UAW Fair Practices and Anti-Discrimination Department Papers, ALUA; Arthur G. Elliot, Constitutional Convention 1961–1962 Memo Books, March 29, 30, 1962, Arthur G. Elliot Papers, BHL; Pollock Notes, March 31, 1962, Box 8, IPA Papers; League of Women Voters of Michigan, Constitutional Convention Report No. 12, April 9, 1962, Box 30, League of Women Voters of Michigan Papers, BHL; *Official Record,* 2:2010–11; Sturm, *Constitution Making,* pp. 117–21; *DFP,* March 30, 31, 1962; *DN,* March 30, 1962; *Ann Arbor News,* March 30, 1962.

44. Pollock Notes (Ferrell Heady), March 31, 1962, Box 8, IPA Papers; Bentley to Marion K. Smith, April 4, 1962, Box 44, Bentley Papers; *DFP,* March 31, April 1, 1962; *DN,* April 3, 1962.

45. *Official Record,* 2:2186–88; *Convention Report: A Resume of Michigan's Proposed Constitution, 1962,* May 21, 1962, Box 2, Martin Papers.

46. *Official Record,* 2:2183–88, 2197–2200.

47. Ibid., 2743–44, 2756, 3118; Brake, "The Old and New Constitutions—A Comparative Approach," n.d., Box 8, Cudlip Papers; Norris, *Education for Popular Sovereignty,* pp. 453–54.

48. *Official Record,* 2:637, 762–63, 2781–82; Cushman, "Civil Rights and the New Constitution," January 28, 1963, Box 4, Judd Papers; Article VIII, Section 2, Article IX, Section 5, Michigan Constitution of 1963.

49. Article V, Sections 2, 20, 21, Article IV, Section 6, Michigan Constitution of 1963. See chapter 1.

50. *Official Record,* 2:3118; Sturm, *Constitution Making,* pp. 172–81, 252, 260–62, 285–87; Adelaide Hart and Tom Downs to Dade, January 23, 1963, Box 5, Dade Papers; Harold Norris, "A Case against Approval of the Proposed Constitution," *Detroit Lawyer* 31 (January 1963): 15–21.

51. Dunbar and May, *Michigan,* p. 574; unidentified clipping [January 5, 1964], in Box 4, BG Papers, BHL; Kelley Opinion, No. 4161, July 22, 1963, Box 2, Cushman Papers.

52. Kauper to Judd, January 20, 1964, Box 4, Judd Papers; Cudlip to Judd, January 7, 1964, Hannah to Judd, July 1, 1964, Box 5, Richard C. Van Dusen Papers, BHL; Cramton, "Michigan Civil Rights Commission," Box 6, Downs Papers.

53. Van Dusen to Judd, August 19, 1963, Box 4, Judd Papers; *Grand Rapids Press,* August 21, 1963, clipping in Box 427, GR Papers.

Chapter 10

1. Weeks, *Stewards of the State,* pp. 122–23, 125.

2. D. Duane Angell, *Romney: A Political Biography* (New York: Exposition Press, 1967), pp. 16–17, 40–63; James Jackson Kilpatrick, "Romney: Salesman on the Move," *National Review,* December 12, 1967, pp. 1374–77; Peirce, *Megastates,* p. 421; Winder, "Gubernatorial-Legislative Interaction," p. 148; William N. Hessler, "A New Face in American Politics," *Reporter,* March 1, 1962, pp. 26–27.

3. Angell, *Romney,* pp. 233–34; Selig S. Harrison, "Romney and the Republicans," *New Republic,* March 5, 1962, p. 27; Romney Statement, July 31, 1962, Box 225, GR Papers, BHL.

4. David R. Jones, "The Republican for 1968?" *New York Times Magazine,* February 28, 1965, p. 28; Charles A. Ferry, "George Romney Gone Bust," *New Republic,* January 25, 1964, p. 14; Hessler, "New Face," pp. 28–29; Stieber, *Politics of Change,* pp. 63, 79; Dunbar and May, *Michigan,* pp. 660, 662.

5. See Weisbrot, *Freedom Bound,* passim.

6. Romney Statement, July 31, 1962, Box 225, GR Papers; Romney, State of the State Message, January 10, 1963, Box 248, ibid.; Angell, *Romney,* p. 234; *DFP* [March 7, 1963], clipping in Box 427, GR Papers.

7. Romney Address, January 3, 1963, Box 239, GR Papers; Romney, State of the State Message, January 10, 1963, Box 248, ibid.

8. Governor's Message on Open Occupancy, February 25, 1963, Box 29, ibid.; *LSJ* [February 27, 1963], clipping in Box 427, ibid.; *DFP,* February 27, April 30, 1963; *LSJ,* February 7, March 16, 1963, *DN,* February 7, 28, March 25, 1963, clippings in Box 9, BG Papers, BHL; *DN,* February 9, 26, 27, 1963, DNSB 17, BHL; *DN,* March 15, April 11, 1963, DNSB 18.

9. Lynn W. Eley, "The Ann Arbor Fair-Housing Ordinance," in Eley and Casstevens, *Politics of Fair-Housing Legislation,* pp. 285–351; Jack Walker, "Fair Housing in Michigan," in ibid., pp. 346, 348, 377. There is a good deal of material on the Ann Arbor fair housing ordinance in Box 1 of the Eunice Burns Papers, BHL.

10. Fine, *Violence,* pp. 59–60; Provisions of the Greater Detroit Homeowners' [Ordinance], October 24, 1963, Box 54, Detroit Urban League Papers, BHL; Kelley Opinion No. 4195, in State of Michigan . . . Kelley, November 15, 1963, Box 43, ibid.; Lockard, *Toward Equal Opportunity,* p. 121.

11. Charles M. Tucker, "Negro Campaign Activities," December 1, 1962, Box 4, Richard C. Van Dusen Papers, BHL; Harold C. McKinney Memorandum to Romney, July 10, 1963, Box 315, GR Papers; Executive Office Release, July 26, 1963, Box 236, ibid.; [*LSJ,* July 2, 1963], [*DN,* July 3, 1963], clippings in Box 4, BG Papers.

12. Executive Office Release, July 17, 1963, Box 347, GR Papers; Release, August 8, 1963, Box 231, ibid.; *DN,* July 27, 1963, DNSB 18.

13. Some Thoughts on Proposed Conference . . . , July 8, 1963, Executive Office Release, July 17, 1963, Box 347, GR Papers; idem, July 26, 1963, Box 236, ibid.; Charles Orlebeke to Romney, July 31, 1963, Box 315, ibid.; *DFP,* July 27, 1963.

14. Romney to Kennedy, June 13, 1963, Box 29, GR Papers; Kelley to Romney, July 30, 1963, Box 3, ibid.; [*LSJ*], December 18, 1962, clipping in Box 4, BG Papers.

15. Release, June 13, 1963, Box 231, GR Papers; Kelley to Romney, July 30, 1963, Box 3, ibid.; *DFP,* July 27, 1963.

16. Romney to Magnuson, July 16, 1963, Box 231, GR Papers.

17. *DN,* March 12, 1963, DNSB 17; *DN,* June 22, July 13, August 2, 1963, DNSB 18.

18. Romney to FEPC, March 10, 1963, Romney to John Smith, June 10, 1963, Governor's Conference on Equal Employment Opportunity in Michigan, September 5, 1963, Box 347, GR Papers; Romney, Five Questions for the Employer Interested in Sound Personnel Practices [1963], Box 7, ibid.; Employer's Program of Action for Merit Employment in Michigan [September 1963], Box 2, Michigan Civil Rights Commission, Information Division, General Records of the Fair Employment Practices Commission, 1955–1963, RG 66-82-A, State Archives, Lansing, Michigan.

19. Zolton A. Ferency to Garland Lane, March 21, 1963, Box 66, JBS Papers, BHL; *DN,* December 10, 11, 13, 16, 18, 21, 1963, DNSB 18; [*Ann Arbor News,* December 11, 21, 1963], [*LSJ,* December 21, 1963], clippings in Box 4, BG Papers; Executive Office Release, December 20, 1963, Box 52, GR Papers; "Public Act No. 45," *Public and Local Acts of the Legislature of the State of Michigan Passed at the First and Second Extra Sessions of 1963,* pp. 58–59.

20. *LSJ,* August 21, 1963, [*LSJ,* January 2, 3, 1964], [*DN,* September 14, 1963], clippings in Box 4, BG Papers; *DN,* August 21, 22, 1963, DNSB 18.

21. Meeting with Governor Romney, Damon Keith and Civil Rights Groups [1963], Box 3, Albert and Emma Wheeler Papers, BHL.

22. Michigan CRC, *The Year of the Beginning: 1964 Annual Report,* pp. 5–6, Box 408, GR Papers; *DN,* January 1, 3, 1964; [*LSJ*], January 2, 3, 1964, Box 4, BG Papers; Executive Office Release, October 29, 1965, Box 135, GR Papers.

23. Marks Memorandum, January 16, 1964, Box 14, Detroit Commission on Community Relations Papers, ALUA.

Chapter 11

1. Michigan CRC, *The Year of the Beginning: 1964 Annual Report,* p. 6, Box 408, GR Papers, BHL; [*DN,* February 14, 1964], clipping in Box 4, BG Papers, BHL; *DN,* February 1, 1964, DNSB 18, May 23, 1965, DNSB 19, March 1, 1970, DNSB 20, BHL; *DFP,* April 19, 1964.

2. CRC, *1964 Annual Report,* p. 6, Box 408, GR Papers; Michigan CRC, *Report of Progress, 1965–1966,* Box 422, ibid.; Education Division, A Report on the Michigan Civil Rights Commission, April 22, 1965, Box 32, Records of the Michigan Civil Rights Commission: Administrative, RG 74-90, State Archives, Lansing, Michigan.

3. *DFP,* April 19, 1964; *DN,* April 26, 1964, DNSB 18.

4. CRC, *1964 Annual Report,* pp. 3, 6, Box 408, GR Papers; *DN,* January 3, 1964, DNSB 18; *Ann Arbor News,* January 4, 1964, clipping in Box 4, BG Papers.

5. CRC, *1964 Annual Report,* p. 3, Box 408, GR Papers.

6. Ibid., p. 6; Feikens et al. to Friend, March 21, 1967, Box 422, ibid.; Thomas E. Johnson Memorandum to Burton Levy, December 18, 1966, Box 4, RG 74-90; A. A. Banks to Romney, March 29, 1968, and enclosure, Box 1440, William G. Milliken Papers, BHL; Michigan CRC, 1968–1969 Budget Report, Box 901, ibid.;

Theodore E. La Marre, "American Indians and Their Problems in Michigan: An Overview," February 24, 1968, p. 2, Box 3, Records of the Civil Rights Commission: Executive Office, RG 87-6, State Archives; Michigan CRC Memorandum to Romney, October 28, 1965, Box 4, Joseph Kowalski Papers, ALUA; Feikens and Keith to Philip A. Hart, February 14, 1967, Box 59, John A. Hannah Papers, Michigan State University Archives, Historical Collections, East Lansing, Michigan; *LSJ,* October 8, 1967, January 14, May 31, 1968, clippings in Box 4, BG Papers.

7. CRC, *1964 Annual Report,* p. 7, CRC Newsletter, October 1965, Box 408, GR Papers; *DN,* June 12, 1964, DNSB 18; Michigan Civil Rights Commission, "An Overview" [1970], Box 70, Detroit Urban League (hereafter DUL) Papers, BHL; CRC Newsletter, January 1966, University of Michigan Law School Library (hereafter UMLSL), Ann Arbor, Michigan.

8. [CRC] to Civil Rights Subcommittee . . . , February 8, 1966, Box 2, RG 74-90; CRC to Mayors . . . , September 8, 1966, Box 3, ibid.; Gordin, "An Overview of the Problem in Michigan," April 20, 1966, Box 67, DUL Papers; Remarks by Gordin, January 16, 1967, Box 4, Horace Gilmore Papers, ALUA.

9. CRC Newsletter, April 1966, Box 20, Detroit Commission on Community Relations Papers, ALUA; Feikens and Keith to Albert Wheeler, February 2, April 4, 1966, Box 3, Albert and Emma Wheeler Papers, BHL. The reports and recommendations of the workshops are in Box 36, RG 74-90.

10. Max M. Horton to Romney, July 24, 1963, enclosing MESC, Older Worker Demonstration Project, a Study of Employability Factors of Selected Older Workers . . . in Lansing . . . , October 1961–April 2, 1962, June 1963, Horton to Romney, August 29, 1963, Box 408, GR Papers; Romney to Edward Shelley, September 27, 1965, Box 91, ibid.; Michigan Commission on Aging, A Report of the Governor's Task Forces on Aging [1964], pp. i, C 1–6, Box 16, Wilma E. Donahue Papers, BHL; "Public Act No. 344," *Public and Local Acts of the Legislature of the State of Michigan Passed at the Regular Session of 1965,* pp. 675–76; Legislation- -From Secretary of Labor Report, June 1965, Box 422, GR Papers.

11. CRC, Age Discrimination in Employment, November 1965, CRC, *Report of Progress,* CRC Newsletter, May 1966, *Aging in Michigan,* January 1968, Box 422, GR Papers; Michigan CRC, *How the Backlog Grew: Four Year Report of Claims, 1964–1967,* p. 11; idem, *Toward Equality: Two-Year Report of Claims Activity, 1968–1969,* p. 14.

12. Franklin DeWald to All Appointing Authorities and Personnel Officers, January 6, 1966, Box 422, GR Papers; *LSJ,* January 23, February 15, 1966, clippings in Box 9, BG Papers.

13. Inter-Agency Council Minutes, August 30, 1965, Box 422, GR Papers; MESC Minutes, January 5, 1966, Box 408, ibid.; Summary of Meeting, January 6, 1966, Box 422, ibid.; MESC, *Annual Report for the Fiscal Year Ending June 30, 1966,* p. 20.

14. MESC, *Annual Report for the Fiscal Year Ending June 30, 1968,* pp. 22–23.

15. CRC Newsletter, July 1968, UMLSL.

16. Minutes, January 23, May 12, 1964, Box 1, Records of Management and Budget: Women's Commission, RG 77-78, State Archives.

17. MESC, *Annual Report for the Fiscal Year Ending June 30, 1966,* pp. 31–32; Walter R. Greene, "Problems in Equal Employment Opportunity" [April 15, 1966], Box 40, RG 74-90; CRC Newsletter, July 1967, Box 422, GR Papers.

18. "Public Act No. 349," *Public and Local Acts . . . 1966,* pp. 604–5; DeWald to Mrs. John Finnegan, July 23, 1968, Box 4, RG 77-78; CRC Newsletter, September 1968, Box 422, GR Papers.

19. John Ferris to Wilbur Howard, October 24, 1969, Box 35, RG 74-90; Michigan CRC, *Toward Equality,* p. 4.

20. Ferris to Howard, October 24, 1969, Box 35, RG 74-90.

21. Gordin to State Senate, August 28, 1964, Box 17, Francis A. Kornegay Papers, BHL; Michigan CRC, *How the Backlog Grew,* pp. 11, 12, 13; idem, *Toward Equality,* pp. 14, 16.

22. Michigan CRC, *How the Backlog Grew,* p. 13; idem, *Toward Equality,* p. 17.

23. Gordin, "An Overview," April 20, 1966, Box 67, DUL Papers; Levy Memorandum to Gordin, August 31, 1965, Box 28, RG 74-90; Report and Recommendations of Workshops on Employment . . . , April 26–27, 1966, Box 36, ibid.; Report of Executive Staff . . . , July 1, 1966, Box 40, ibid.; Remarks by Levy, November 5, 1965, Box 19, National Association for the Advancement of Colored People, Detroit Branch (hereafter Detroit NAACP) Papers, ALUA; Feikens et al. to Friend, March 21, 1967, Box 422, GR Papers.

24. CRC Newsletter, August 1966, Box 422, GR Papers; *DN,* August 19, 1966, DNSB 20.

25. CRC Release, March 8 [1965], Box 17, Kornegay Papers; Statement by Gordin . . . November 19, 1964, Box 19, Detroit NAACP Papers; Report on Executive Staff Discussions, July 1, 1966, Box 40, RG 74-90.

26. Workshop on City Hall Equal Employment, Presented by Rita A. Scott, January 16, 1967, Box 4, Gilmore Papers; CRC News, December 22 [1964], Box 31, Detroit NAACP Papers.

27. A. D. Swift to Greene, May 11, 1967, Greene to Banks, May 15, 1967, Greene Memoranda to Gordin, June 21, November 29, 1967, Box 35, RG 74-90.

28. Martin E. Henner to Frank Linskey, August 25, 1967, ibid.; Henner to Greene, September 8, 1967, Box 11, ibid.

29. Greene Memorandum to Gordin, September 13, 1967, Box 11, ibid.; Staff Memoranda to Commission, August 9, September 20, 1968, Box 14, ibid.

30. "Our Experience with the Automobile Manufacturing Companies" [1967], Box 32, ibid.; Gordin Memorandum to Ben Segal, May 31, 1967, and enclosure, Box 11, ibid.

31. Gordin Memorandum to Commission, November 22, 1966, Box 4, ibid.; Gordin to Segal, May 31, 1967, and enclosure, Greene to Segal, July 10, 1967, Box 11, ibid.; Gordin Memorandum to Commission, July 25, 1967, Box 5, ibid.

32. Greene to Gordin, August 17, 1967, Box 20, ibid.; Gordin Memorandum to Commission, August 17, 1967, Box 11, ibid.

33. Gordin Memorandum to Commission, October 23, 1968, Box 21, RG 74-90; Gordin Memorandum to Commission, February 19, 1969, Box 15, Records of the Civil Rights Commission: Executive, RG 81-89, State Archives; Civil Rights Department Memorandum to Milliken, May 15, 1969, Box 905, Milliken Papers; CRC Newsletter, September 1968, UMLSL.

34. *DN,* January 1, 1964; Michigan State Advisory Committee to the United States Commission on Civil Rights, "Equal Opportunity in Job Training and Placement for Minority Youth in Michigan," First Draft, pp. IV, 13–24, Box 2, Dorothy Siegel Judd Papers, Grand Rapids Public Library, Grand Rapids, Michigan; Statement

of Gordin, June 30, 1964, Geraldine Bledsoe to Judd, October 21, 1964, Box 1, ibid.; William W. Layton to Judd, February 27, 1964, Box 6, Tom Downs Papers, BHL; MESC Minutes, October 27, 1965, Box 408, GR Papers. The July 1966 final draft of the youth employment study is in Box 2 of the Judd Papers in the Grand Rapids Public Library.

35. Gordin to State Agency Executives, July 20, 1965, Box 1, RG 74-90; Non-Discrimination Clause for All State Contracts, n.d., Box 4, ibid.; Gordin Memorandum to Commission, August 3, 1965, Box 5, ibid.; Gordin Memoranda to Commission, March 5, 15, 22, May 24, 1968, Box 13, ibid.; Staff Memorandum to Commission, November 1, 1968, Box 14, ibid.; Contract Compliance Program of the Michigan Civil Rights Commission [February 17, 1969], Box 901, Milliken Papers.

36. Kenneth W. Robinson to Wheeler, November 28, December 23, 1966, Box 3, Wheeler Papers; Remarks by Gordin, March 5, 1968, Box 13, RG 74-90; James McClung Memorandum to Gordin, January 28, 1969, and enclosure, Box 90, Milliken Papers; CRC Newsletter, November–December 1966, Box 20, Detroit NAACP Papers; CRC Newsletter, July 1967, Box 19, ibid.; CRC Newsletter, January 1967, Box 422, GR Papers. See chapter 15.

37. Remarks by Gordin, November 4, 1965, Box 19, Detroit NAACP Papers; *DN,* December 22, 1965, DNSB 19; CRC, *Report of Progress,* Digest of the Employment Distribution Study . . . , November 19, 1966, CRC Release, November 15, 1966, Box 422, GR Papers; CRC, Employment Distribution Study of the Construction Industry in Michigan, July 1966, copy in UMLSL; Gordin to Herbert Hill, May 5, 1967, Box 3, Wheeler Papers.

38. McClung Memorandum to Gordin, January 28, 1969 (and enclosure), Box 90, Milliken Papers; Remarks by Gordin, March 5, 1968, Box 13, RG 74-90; CRC Newsletter, November–December 1966, Box 20, Detroit NAACP Papers; CRC Newsletter, January 1967, Box 19, ibid.

39. Greene Memorandum to Gordin, January 7, 1967, Box 20, RG 74-90; Gordin to Romney, August 1967 (draft), Box 5, ibid.; Julian Cook to Milliken, January 29, 1969, enclosing CRC Annual Report, 1967–1968, Michigan Department of Civil Rights, Detroit, Michigan; Contract Compliance Program of the Michigan CRC [February 17, 1969], Box 901, Milliken Papers; CRC Newsletters, May 1968, June 1969, UMLSL.

40. Gordin Memorandum to Thomas Peloso, July 24, 1968, Box 11, RG 74-90; McClung Memorandum to Gordin, January 28, 1969 (and enclosure), Box 90, Milliken Papers; Contract Compliance Program of the Michigan CRC [February 17, 1969], Box 901, ibid.; Skilled Construction Tradesmen in Michigan, April 16, 1971, Box 902, ibid.

41. Arthur L. Johnson to Gordin, June 3, 1966, CRC Release, July 14, 1966, CRC Report on Detroit Area Hospitals, February 1967, Box 34, RG 74-90.

42. CRC Report on Detroit Area Hospitals, February 1967, ibid.

43. DeWald to Romney, December 20, 1963, Box 419, GR Papers; CRC Minutes, October 15, 1963, Box 14, ibid.; *MESC Messenger* 8 (February 1964), Box 6, Downs Papers; DeWald to All Appointing Authorities, January 14, May 12, 1964, Research Department, Michigan Civil Service Commission, A Study of Non-White Employment in the State Service, May 1964, Box 3, Dorothy Siegel Judd Papers, BHL.

44. Gordin to Commission, May 21, 1965, Box 92, GR Papers; Research Division, Michigan Civil Service Commission, A Follow Up Study . . . , June 1965, Box 20, Detroit NAACP Papers; *LSJ,* January 17, 23, 1966, clippings in Box 9, BG Papers; *DN,* January 17, 1966. There are copies of the nonwhite employment studies for 1966, 1967, and 1969 in Box 3, Judd Papers.

45. CRC, Michigan State Code of Fair Practices [1965], CRC, *Report of Progress,* Box 422, GR Papers; DeWald to CRC, May 24, 1966, Box 3, Judd Papers.

46. CRC Memorandum to CSC, February 22, 1966, DeWald to CSC, March 16, 1966, DeWald to Gordin, April 6, 1966, Box 3, Judd Papers; DeWald to All Appointing Authorities, July 14, 1966, DeWald to Milliken, May 15, 1969, Box 905, Milliken Papers; *DN,* June 7, 1966; *LSJ,* July 19, 1966, clipping in Box 9, BG Papers.

47. Louis Mezei to Gordin, July 19, 1967, Box 11, RG 74-90; Ernest Walleck to Members of Commission, January 15, 1968, Box 3, Judd Papers; DeWald to Milliken, May 15, 1969, Box 905, Milliken Papers.

48. Norval J. Trimke Memorandum to DeWald, April 1, 1968, Box 3, Judd Papers; DeWald to Milliken, May 15, 1969, Box 905, Milliken Papers; *DN,* November 21, 1969. See also Department Conclusions and Recommendations . . . October 1966–July 1971, August 1971, Box 905, Milliken Papers.

49. Workshop on City Hall and Equal Employment Presented by Rita A. Scott, January 16, 1967, Box 4, Gilmore Papers; Summary Report on Wayne County Survey [April 18, 1968], Box 6, RG 74-90; Department of Civil Rights to Milliken, May 15, 1969, Box 905, Milliken Papers.

50. Department of Civil Rights to Romney, May 31, 1968, Box 199, GR Papers; Department of Civil Rights to Milliken, May 15, 1969, Box 905, Milliken Papers; CRC, A Proposal to Study the Role of Organized Labor . . . [March 1969], Box 9, RG 74-90.

51. Department of Civil Rights to Milliken, May 15, 1969, Box 905, Milliken Papers.

Chapter 12

1. Rita A. Scott, "The Status of Equal Opportunity in Michigan's Public Schools," April 15, 1968, Box 18, Francis A. Kornegay Papers, BHL; Burton Levy Memorandum to Burton Gordin, August 31, 1965, Box 28, Records of the Michigan Civil Rights Commission: Administrative, RG 74-90, State Archives, Lansing, Michigan; Remarks by Damon J. Keith, January 29, 1967, Box 3, Records of the Civil Rights Commission: Executive Office, RG 87-6, ibid.; Gordin, "An Overview of the Problem in Michigan," April 20, 1966, Box 67, Detroit Urban League (hereafter DUL) Papers, BHL; Remarks by Gordin, October 19, 1966, Box 16, Richard McGhee Papers, ALUA; John Feikens et al. to Friend, March 21, 1967, Box 422, GR Papers, BHL.

2. Ira Polley Memorandum to State Board of Education, October 5, 1967, enclosed with Gordin Memorandum to Commission, November 16, 1967, Box 12, RG 74-90; CRC Newsletters, March 1967, January 1968, University of Michigan Law School Library (hereafter UMLSL), Ann Arbor, Michigan.

3. CRC, Vocational Preparation and Race in Michigan Higher Education [1966], UMLSL.

4. Michigan CRC, *How the Backlog Grew,* pp. 7–8, 22; idem, *Toward Equality,* pp. 7, 27.

5. CRC Newsletter, August 1965, Box 408, GR Papers; Michigan CRC, *Report of Progress, 1965–1966,* Box 422, ibid.; Fine, *Violence,* p. 50.

6. CRC, *Report of Progress,* Box 422, GR Papers; Gordin Memorandum to Commission, September 13, 1966, Box 3, RG 74-90; CRC, Annual Report, 1967–1968, Michigan Department of Civil Rights, Detroit, Michigan; *DN,* November 10, 13, 1966, DNSB 20, BHL.

7. Joint Statement—Michigan State Board of Education and Michigan CRC, April 23, 1966, Box 292, Michigan AFL-CIO Papers, ALUA; Polley to Superintendent, September 20, 1967, Box 11, RG 74-90; CRC Newsletter, October 1967, UMLSL; CRC, *Report of Progress,* Box 422, GR Papers.

8. "Public Act No. 127," *Public and Local Acts of the State of Michigan Passed at the Regular Session of 1966,* pp. 153–54; *DN,* June 24, 1966, clipping in Box 4, BG Papers, BHL; CRC, Annual Report, 1967–1968, Department of Civil Rights.

9. Keith Remarks, January 29, 1967, Box 3, RG 87-6; A. A. Banks et al. to Romney, March 29, 1968, enclosing CRC Annual Report for Fiscal Year 1966–1967, Box 1440, William G. Milliken Papers, BHL; CRC Annual Report, 1967–68, Department of Civil Rights.

10. Fine, *Violence,* pp. 9–10, 43–51.

11. Ibid., p. 48.

12. Ibid., p. 49.

13. Ibid., pp. 9, 50–51.

14. Ibid., pp. 52–56; Gordin, "An Overview," April 26, 1966, Box 67, DUL Papers; Department of Civil Rights Memorandum to Milliken, May 15, 1969, Box 905, Milliken Papers.

15. Michigan CRC, *How the Backlog Grew,* p. 7; idem, *Toward Equality,* pp. 6–7.

16. *DN,* June 1, 1964, DNSB 18, March 4, 1965, DNSB 19; [*Ann Arbor News,* June 3, 1964], clipping in Box 4, BG Papers; CRC Release, June 25, 1964, Box 19, Detroit Commission on Community Relations (hereafter DCCR) Papers, ALUA; Gordin to State Senate, August 28, 1964, Box 31, National Association for the Advancement of Colored People, Detroit Branch (hereafter Detroit NAACP) Papers, ibid.; Michigan CRC, *Year of the Beginning: 1964 Annual Report,* p. 9, Box 408, GR Papers; Sub-Committee on Public Accommodations, Citizens Committee for Equal Opportunity, A Report to the People of Detroit . . . , June 15, 1964, Box 1, Katherine Moore Cushman Papers, BHL.

17. CRC Newsletter, March 1965, Box 408, GR Papers; CRC News Release, March 8 [1965], Box 17, Kornegay Papers; *DN,* March 4 [5–7, 9], 1965, clippings in Box 4, BG Papers.

18. CRC Newsletters, July, August 1965, Box 408, GR Papers; *DN,* July 28, 1965, clipping in Box 430, ibid.; *DN,* April 10, 1966; CRC, *Report of Progress,* Box 422, GR Papers; Banks et al. to Romney, March 29, 1968, and enclosure, Box 1440, Milliken Papers.

19. CRC, *1964 Annual Report,* p. 9, CRC News Release, March 23 [1965], Box 408, GR Papers; CRC, *Report of Progress,* Box 422, ibid.; CRC Release, January 27, 1965, Box 19, Detroit NAACP Papers; CRC Newsletter, January 1968, UMLSL.

20. CRC, *1964 Annual Report*, p. 9, CRC Newsletter, May 1965, Box 408, GR Papers; idem, June 1966, January, July 1967, UMLSL; idem, July 1966, Box 22, Detroit NAACP Papers; Michigan CRC, *Toward Equality*, p. 7.

21. Banks et al. to Romney, March 29, 1968, and enclosure, Box 1440, Milliken Papers; *DN*, February 3, 1967, clipping in Box 4, BG Papers.

22. CRC News Release, March 23 [1965], CRC Newsletter, April 1965, Box 408, GR Papers; *DN*, March 24, 1965, DNSB 19.

23. Martin Henner to Gordin et al., September 1, 1966, Box 34, RG 74-90; Gordin Memorandum to Commission, September 8, 1966, Box 3, ibid.; CRC, *Report of Progress*, Box 422, GR Papers; Executive Office Release, September 21, 1966, Box 327, ibid.; Banks et al. to Romney, March 29, 1968, and enclosure, Box 1440, Milliken Papers; *DN*, September 21, 22, 1966.

24. Gordin Memorandum to Commission, March 27, 1967, and enclosure, Box 19, Detroit NAACP Papers; Henner and Alan Fox, Study of Patient Referrals in Nursing Homes in Wayne County, January 1967, Box 34, RG 74-90; *DN*, March 29, 1967, clipping in Box 4, BG Papers.

25. *DN*, January 5, 27, July 30, 1965; CRC Releases, January 4 [1965], January 27, 1965, Box 19, DCCR Papers; CRC Release, March 23 [1965], CRC Newsletters, February, March, August, 1965, Box 408, GR Papers; CRC, *Report of Progress*, Box 422, ibid.; David L. Good, *Orvie, the Dictator of Dearborn: The Rise and Fall of Orville L. Hubbard* (Detroit: Wayne State University Press, 1989), pp. 314–18. For a flareup of the bulletin board issue, see ibid., pp. 318–19.

26. Gordin Memorandum to Commission, July 2, 1964, Box 1, RG 74-90; Gordin to Commission, Weekly Report, October 23, 1964, CRC Release, December 28, 1964, Box 92, GR Papers.

27. Gordin Memorandum to Commission, July 7, 1964, Box 1, RG 74-90; Levy Memorandum to Gordin, August 31, 1965, Box 28, ibid.; Gordin, "An Overview," April 26, 1966, Box 67, DUL Papers; *DN*, April 26, 1964, April 10, 15, 1966; *Kalamazoo Gazette*, May 19, 1966, clipping in Box 4, BG Papers.

28. Agenda, August 3, 1965, Box 1, RG 74-90; CRC News Release, September 2 [1965], Box 408, GR Papers; *DN*, December 1, 1965.

29. CRC, *1964 Annual Report*, pp. 3, 10, CRC Newsletters, April, October 1965, CRC Release, May 6 [1965], Box 408, GR Papers; Gordin to Commission, Weekly Report, October 23, 1964, Box 92, ibid.; James L. Rose Memorandum to Gordin, A Report to the Michigan CRC, April 22, 1965, Box 32, RG 74-90; *DN*, April 26, 1964.

30. Rose Memorandum to Gordin, March 18, 1965, Box 1, RG 74-90.

31. Jack Walker, "Fair Housing in Michigan," in Eley and Casstevens, *Politics of Fair Housing Legislation*, p. 376; Feikens and Keith to Charles W. Kimball, September 22, 1966, Box 25, RG 74-90.

32. CRC to Builders et al., March 1966, Voluntary affirmative measures for the housing industry . . . [March 1966], Box 19, DCCR Papers.

33. *DN*, September 15, 1965.

34. Gordin Memorandum to Commission, October 17, 1965, Box 2, RG 74-90; CRC Minutes, May 24, 1966, Box 3, ibid.; CRC, *Report of Progress*, Box 422, GR Papers; CRC Newsletter, June 1966, UMLSL; CRC, Equal Housing Opportunities in Saginaw . . . , June 21, 22, 27, 1966, Box 19, Detroit NAACP Papers; Gordin to Herbert Hill, May 5, 1967, Box 3, Albert and Emma Wheeler Papers, BHL.

35. CRC, *Report of Progress,* CRC Newsletters, February, June 1967, Box 422, GR Papers; CRC, Equal Housing Opportunities in Jackson . . . , September 21, 22, 26, 1966, Box 4, RG 74-90; CRC News for Release, March 9 [1967], Box 5, ibid.; Olive R. Beasley Memorandum to Commission, February 23, 1968, Box 6, ibid.; CRC Newsletter, November–December 1966, UMLSL; Report and Recommendations from a Public Inquiry into the State of Race Relations . . . Pontiac, June 13–19, 1968, Box 35, BG Papers; *DN,* March 9, 1967; Sugrue, *Urban Crisis,* pp. 47–51.

36. Report on the Implementation of Recommendations by the . . . CRC . . . [1967], Box 6, RG 74-90.

37. Gordin to Hill, May 5, 1967, Box 3, Wheeler Papers; Report on Implementation of Recommendations [1967], Box 4, RG 74-90; William F. Dwyer to Rose, June 2, 1967, Box 5, ibid.; Beasley Memorandum to Commission, February 23, 1968, Box 6, ibid.; CRC, *Report of Progress,* CRC Newsletter, April 1967, Box 422, GR Papers; idem, January 1967, UMLSL; *DN,* April 26, 1966.

38. Eley, "Ann Arbor Fair Housing Ordinance," in Eley and Casstevens, *Fair Housing Legislation,* pp. 346–49.

39. Gordin Memorandum to Commission, December 7, 1965, Box 2, RG 74-90; Carl Levin Memorandum to Gordin, December 15, 1965, Box 18, ibid.; CRC, State Conference on . . . Housing, April 26, 27, 1966, Box 36, ibid.; A Summary of Fair Housing Ordinances in Michigan, March 31, 1968, Box 13, ibid.; CRC to Mayors et al., December 1966, September 1967, Box 19, Detroit NAACP Papers; Kelley Opinion No. 4585, August 4, 1967, Box 59, John A. Hannah Papers, Michigan State University Archives, Historical Collections, East Lansing, Michigan.

40. Meeting, Grosse Pointe Human Relations Board of Directors, March 1, 1966, Box 2, Grosse Pointe Committee for Open Housing Papers, ALUA; [CRC] to Residents of Grosse Pointe Woods, July 23, 1966, Box 25, RG 74-90; Blair Moody, Jr., to Feikens and Keith, September 21, 1966, Box 28, ibid.; Grosse Pointe Committee for Open Housing, Statement of Aims and Purposes, July 28, 1966, Box 7, Horace Gilmore Papers, ALUA; DUL, Department of Housing, Quarterly Report, July–September 1967, Box 63, DUL Papers; Cosseboom, *Grosse Pointe,* pp. 6–7, 9, 48–57, 63.

41. Fine, *Violence,* p. 60; Walker, "Fair Housing," pp. 373–74.

42. Fine, *Violence,* p. 59.

43. "September 17, 1965," Box 1, Rose Kleinman Papers, ALUA; Greater Detroit Committee for Fair Housing Practices, Operation Open Door, March 1965, Box 5, ibid.; DUL, Department of Housing, Second Quarterly Report, April–June 1965, Fourth Quarterly Report, October–December 1965, Box 63, DUL Papers; Greater Detroit Fair Housing, Inc., April 10, 1967, Box 70, ibid.; John J. Musial, Residential Trends in the Detroit Metropolitan Area, n.d., Box 34, DCCR Papers.

44. Address, March 24, 1965, Box 19, DCCR Papers; CRC, *Report of Progress,* Box 422, GR Papers; CRC Newsletters, March, June 1965, Box 408, ibid.; Mrs. Franklin W. Wylie Memorandum to Relocation Committee, October 19, 1966, Box 3, RG 74-90; CRC to Mayors et al., February 8, 1966, Box 25, ibid.; CRC, State Conference on . . . Housing, April 26, 27, 1966, Box 3, ibid.; Banks et al. to Romney, March 29, 1968, and enclosure, Box 1440, Milliken Papers; CRC, Annual Report, 1967–1968, Department of Civil Rights.

45. Gordin Memorandum to Commission, October 17, 1965, Box 2, RG 74-90; Wylie Memorandum to Members, October 19, 1966, Box 3, ibid., Gordin

Memorandum to Commission, April 15, 1966, and enclosure, Box 4, Records of the Attorney General: Civil Rights, RG 79-82, State Archives; CRC Newsletter, November 1965, Box 408, GR Papers; CRC Newsletter, December 1965, Box 19, Detroit NAACP Papers; *DN,* October 13, 1965, *LSJ,* October 1, 14, 1965, clippings in Box 4, BG Papers.

46. "Public Act No. 346," *Public and Local Acts . . . 1966,* pp. 649–61; Executive Office Release, November 2, 1966, Box 55, DUL Papers; CRC Newsletter, November–December 1966, UMLSL; CRC Newsletter, March 1967, Box 422, GR Papers; Dwyer Memorandum to Rose, May 2, 1968, Box 13, RG 74-90; CRC 1968–69 Budget Request, January 22, 1968, Box 901, Milliken Papers; Program Information, Michigan State Housing Development Authority, December 20, 1969, Box 1225, ibid.; Executive Office Release, July 29, 1970, Box 829, ibid.; untitled document [May 10, 1968], Box 32, Sander M. Levin Papers, ALUA.

47. CRC Newsletter, November 1965, Box 408, GR Papers; CRC Newsletter, December 1965, January, February 1966, April 1967, UMLSL; CRC, *Report of Progress,* Box 422, GR Papers; CRC to Mayors et al., January 1967, Box 19, Detroit NAACP Papers; Feikens to Editor New York Times, April 11, 1967, Box 2, RG 87-6; *DN,* January 22, 25, 1966.

48. Gordin to Ed Carey, November 16, 1966, Gordin to Commission, January 5, 1967, Rose Memorandum to Gordin, March 14, 1967, Box 4, RG 74-90; Julian Cook and John Dempsey to Robert C. Weaver, June 13, 1968, Gordin Memorandum to Martha Wylie et al., August 21, 1968, Box 7, ibid.; CRC Newsletter, March 1966, Box 422, GR Papers; *LSJ,* February 27, 1966, clipping in Box 9, BG Papers; Fine, *Violence,* pp. 58, 427–28.

49. CRC, *Report of Progress,* Box 422, GR Papers; CRC Newsletter, July 1967, UMLSL; CRC to Heads of Local Law Enforcement Agencies, June 27, 1965, Box 5, RG 74-90; CRC to Michigan Mayors et al., June 27, 1967, Box 19, Detroit NAACP Papers.

50. Michigan CRC, *How the Backlog Grew,* pp. 6, 12, 16–17; idem, *Toward Equality,* pp. 14, 20; Lockard, *Toward Equal Opportunity,* pp. 122–23.

51. CRC, *1964 Annual Report,* p. 10, CRC Newsletters, July, August, November 1965, Box 408, GR Papers; *LSJ,* December 28, 1964, *Ann Arbor News,* August 3, 1966, clippings in Box 4, BG Papers; *Ann Arbor News,* December 28, 30, 1964, September 1, 1965, clippings in Box 9, ibid.; *DN,* December 28, 1964, July 27, 1965, April 10, 1966; Eley, "Ann Arbor Fair Housing Ordinance," p. 348; *1964–1975 Michigan Civil Rights Commission Case Digest,* pp. 14–15, Box 668, Milliken Papers.

52. CRC Newsletter, October 1965, Box 408, GR Papers; CRC Newsletter, November 1967, Box 422, ibid.; CRC Newsletter, July 1967, UMLSL; CRC, *Report of Progress,* Box 422, GR Papers; *LSJ,* May 3, September 1, 30, 1965, July 1, 1967, *Ann Arbor News,* September 1, 1965, clippings in Box 9, BG Papers; [*LSJ*], September 1, 1965, clipping in Box 4, ibid.

53. CRC News for Release, December 22 [1964], Box 31, Detroit NAACP Papers; CRC Newsletters, August, October, November 1965, Box 408, GR Papers; Civil Rights Newsletter, February 1966, UMLSL; *DN,* August 29, September 4, October 1, 1965; *Beech Grove Investment Company* v. *Civil Rights Commission,* 380 Mich. 405, 412–16 (1968).

54. CRC Newsletters, January 1966, October 1967, UMLSL; 380 Mich. 405

(1968); *DN*, November 18, December 1, 1965, January 26, 1966; *LSJ*, April 12, 1968, *Ann Arbor News*, April 2, 1968, clippings in Box 9, BG Papers.

55. "Fair Housing Legislation," n.d., Box 54, DUL Papers; Equal Housing Opportunities in Jackson . . . , September 21, 22, 26, 1966, Box 4, RG 74-90; *DN*, April 23, 1966; *Michigan Official Directory and Legislative Manual, 1971–1972*, p. 99.

Chapter 13

1. Governor's Commission on the Status of Women Minutes, January 23, July 27, September 27, November 22, 1963, Box 1, Records of Management and Budget: Women's Commission, RG 77-78, State Archives, Lansing, Michigan.

2. Richard C. Van Dusen to Mildred Dunn, January 23, 1963, Van Dusen to Eleanor M. Tromp, February 25, 1963, Van Dusen to Lillian M. Comar, May 28, 1963, Box 347, GR Papers, BHL; Margaret Callam Goebel to Romney, October 28, 1964, enclosing Report of Governor's Commission on the Status of Women, Box 350, ibid.; *LSJ*, June 13, 1963, clipping in Box 31, BG Papers, BHL.

3. Governor's Commission Minutes, February 28, May 12, 1964, Box 1, RG 77-78; "Public Act No. 154," *Public and Local Acts of the Legislature of the State of Michigan Passed at the Regular Session of 1964*, pp. 145–47.

4. Report of Governor's Commission, pp. 2–7, Box 350, GR Papers.

5. Ibid., pp. 8–11.

6. Ibid., pp. 12–16.

7. Ibid., pp. 17–27.

8. Ibid., pp. 28–38.

9. Report of the New and Expanded [*sic*] Services Committee . . . , April 1, 1964, Betty Finegan to Members of Women's Commission, November 5, 1969, and enclosure, Box 4, RG 77-78; Paul H. Wileden Memorandum to Glenn S. Allen, September 10, 1964, Box 82, GR Papers; Background of the Day Care Committee, Michigan Youth Commission [1962], Day Care Committee . . . Revised Recommendation . . . , November 2, 1962, Box 38, ibid.; Report of the Governor's Commission, pp. 39–41, Box 350, ibid.

10. Report of the Governor's Commission, pp. 41, 43–44, Box 350, GR Papers.

11. Ibid., pp. 45–46.

12. Goebel to Romney, October 28, 1964, Box 350, ibid.; Status of Women's Regional Meetings, June 30, October 1, 16, November 5, 1965, Box 4, RG 77-78; Irma M. Liverance to Romney, November 15, 1968, in *Report of the Governor's Commission on the Status of Women, 1967–1968*, December 10, 1968, Box 35, Records of the Michigan Civil Rights Commission: Administrative, RG 74-90, State Archives.

13. Executive Office Release, November 22, 1967, Box 352, GR Papers; Michigan Status of Women Commission Report, November 1967, Box 7, RG 77-78.

14. Michigan Status of Women Commission Report, November 1967, Box 7, RG 77-78; Jerome R. Pikulinski to Louise Walker, November 15, 1967, Box 3, ibid.

15. "Public Act No. 187," *Public and Local Acts . . . 1967*, p. 248; Romney to John B. Forsythe, July 10, 1967, Box 196, GR Papers.

16. Davis to Anne Draper, November 1, 1965, and enclosure, Box 9, UAW Women's Department Papers—Dorothy Haener, ALUA; Oral History Interview of Carolyn Davis, July 23, 1976, pp. 158–59, Institute of Labor and Industrial Relations

of the University of Michigan–Wayne State University, Women and Work Program. The 20th Century Trade Union Woman: Vehicle for Social Change, Oral History Program, 1978–1979, BHL; Oral History Interview of Dorothy Haener, April 12, 1978, p. 62, ibid.; Gabin, *Feminism in the Labor Movement*, pp. 195–96.

17. *DN*, October 21, 1967.

18. "Public Act No. 282," *Public and Local Acts . . . 1967*, pp. 573–79; Governor's Commission Minutes, April 8, 1968, Box 1, RG 77-78; *Report of Governor's Commission, 1967–1968*, pp. 6–7, Box 35, RG 74-90; Romney to Wolfgang, August 15, 1968, Box 352, GR Papers; Stephen I. Schlossberg and Bernard F. Ashe to Leonard Woodcock and Ronnie Moran, May 23, 1968, Box 5, UAW Women's Department Papers—Haener.

19. [Finegan] Testimony at Public Hearing, August 19, 1968, *Report of Governor's Commission, 1967–1968*, pp. 6–9, Box 35, RG 74-90; Statement of . . . UAW, May 19, 1968, Box 18, UAW Women's Department Papers—Lillian Hatcher; Emily Rodolfsky to Reuther, March 3, 1969, Box 8, ibid.—Haener; Oral History Interview of Mildred Jeffrey, December 30, 1977, p. 73, Institute of Labor and Industrial Relations . . . , Oral History Program.

20. CRC Newsletter, February 1970, Box 905, William G. Milliken Papers, BHL.

21. "Public Act No.1," *Public and Local Acts . . . 1968*, pp. 7–8; *Report of Governor's Commission, 1967–1968*, pp. 4, 13, 14, Box 35, RG 74-90.

22. Governor's Commission Minutes, May 7, 1965, April 8, May 24, 1968, Box 1, RG 77-78; Franklin DeWald to Finegan, July 23, 1968, Box 4, ibid.; *Report of Governor's Commission, 1967–1968*, pp. 7–8, Box 35, RG 74-90; CRC, Annual Report, 1970–1971, Michigan Department of Civil Rights, Detroit, Michigan.

23. Governor's Commission Minutes, April 8, May 24, 1968, Box 1, RG 77-78; *Report of Governor's Commission, 1967–1968*, pp. 4, 16, 17, Box 35, RG 74-90; *Laws of Special Interest to Women in Michigan*, 1968, Box 53, BG Papers.

24. Michigan CRC, *How the Backlog Grew*, p. 11; idem, *Toward Equality*, pp. 14, 17; CRC, "Women in Higher Education" [1966], BHL; Governor's Commission, Six Month Report, May 1, 1968, Box 352, GR Papers; *Report of Governor's Commission, 1967–1968*, pp. 4, 5, 18–19, Box 35, RG 74-90.

25. Governor's Commission Minutes, April 8, May 24, 1968, Box 1, RG 77-78; Finegan to Commission Members [November 1967], Box 4, ibid.; Finegan to Organization President, August 25, 1970, Box 6, ibid.; *Report of Governor's Commission, 1967–1968*, pp. 4, 11–12, Box 35, RG 74-90.

26. Governor's Commission Minutes, April 8, May 24, 1968, Box 1, RG 77-78; Official Statement, Subcommittee Hearings on Equal Rights Amendment, May 6, 1970, Box 5, ibid.; *Report of Governor's Commission, 1967–1968*, p. 20, Box 35, RG 74-90.

27. Department of Civil Rights to Milliken, May 14, 1969, Box 905, Milliken Papers.

28. Theodore E. LaMarre, "American Indians and Their Problems in Michigan: An Overview," February 24, 1968, Box 13, RG 74-90. See chapter 6.

29. Hillman, *History*, pp. 47–52; Executive Office Release, June 3, 1964, Minutes of Governor's Commission on Indian Affairs, June 3, 1964, Findings and Recommendations, Governor's Commission on Indian Affairs, December 1965, Box 329, GR Papers; Romney to Mrs. Danny K. Welsh, April 12, 1966, Romney to Erwin T. Kirkwood, October 28, 1966, Box 152, ibid.

30. "Public Act No. 300," *Public and Local Acts . . . 1965,* pp. 576–77; Hillman, *History,* pp. 55, 65; Herbert Cameron to Lewis Beeson, February 8, 1965, Box 351, GR Papers; Executive Office Release, January 7, 1965 [1966], R. Bernard Houston to Romney, June 6, 1966, Box 329, GR Papers; Charles Orlebeke to John R. Winchester, September 1, 1966, Romney to Robert L. Bennett, May 16, July 25, 1966, Box 152, ibid.; Michigan Commission on Indian Affairs, 1970 Annual Report, p. 1, University of Michigan Library, Ann Arbor, Michigan.

31. Findings and Recommendations, Box 329, GR Papers; Cameron to Malcolm R. Lovell, January 13, 1965, Box 351, ibid.; Romney to Margaret C. Snoor, January 4, 1967, Box 183, ibid.; Romney to Mrs. J. Buck, March 4, 1968, Box 210, ibid.; Hillman, *History,* pp. 53–54; *LSJ,* October 22, 1967, clipping in Box 21, BG Papers.

32. Governor's Commission Minutes, June 3, July 18, 1964, March 6, 1965, Findings and Recommendations, Box 329, GR Papers; Romney to Richard Sullivan, April 1, 1968, Box 210, ibid.

33. LaMarre, "American Indians," Box 13, RG 74-90; Governor's Commission Minutes, June 3, July 18, 1964, March 6, 1965, Box 329, GR Papers; Russell Hendrick to Houston, May 31, 1967, Box 183, ibid.; Minutes of the Michigan Commission on Indian Affairs, August 10, September 28, October 22, 1968, in Hillman, *Minutes,* BHL; Hillman, *History,* p. 68.

34. Findings and Recommendations, Box 329, GR Papers; Romney to Herbert Hennings, May 1, 1967, Box 183, ibid.

35. Findings and Recommendations, Governor's Commission Minutes, July 18, 1964, Box 329, ibid.; Romney to Earl Russell, January 18, 1967, and enclosure, Romney to Willard J. Lambert, March 3, 1967, Box 183, ibid.; Michigan Commission Minutes, August 19, November 4, 1967, Hillman, *Minutes;* LaMarre, "Michigan Indians," Box 13, RG 74-90; Michigan Commission, 1970 Annual Report, p. 11.

36. LaMarre, "American Indians," Box 13, RG 74-90; Governor's Commission Minutes, August 29, 1964, Box 329, GR Papers; Michigan Commission, 1970 Annual Report, p. 8.

37. Michigan Commission Minutes, November 4, 1967, May 16, July 12, September 28, 1968, January 31–February 1, 1969, in Hillman, *Minutes;* Michigan Commission, 1970 Annual Report, pp. 8–10.

38. Hendrick Memorandum to Houston, May 31, 1967, Box 183, GR Papers; Cameron to Charles Orlebeke, March 12, 1968, Box 329, ibid.; Highlights of Request for Vista Volunteers, March 20, 1967, Box 340, ibid.; Orlebeke to Frank J. Dembinski, January 22, 1969, Box 210, ibid.

39. LaMarre, "American Indians," Box 13, RG 74-90; Governor's Commission Minutes, October 24, December 4–5, 1964, Box 329, GR Papers; CRC Weekly Report, October 31, 1964, Box 92, ibid.

40. Anderson Memoranda to Arthur L. Johnson, October 22, 1965, April 13, May 9, 1966, Box 33, RG 74-90; LaMarre, "American Indians," Box 13, ibid.; Burton Gordin to Mrs. Wright Brooks, February 20, 1967, Box 422, GR Papers; Michigan Commission Minutes, April 25–26, May 23–24, June 20–21, 1969, in Hillman, *Minutes;* CRC, Annual Report, 1989, Department of Civil Rights.

41. Hillman, *History,* pp. 69–70; CRC, Annual Reports, 1982–1983, 1983–1984, 1984–1985, 1989, Department of Civil Rights.

42. Orlebeke to Doris Seifert, May 27, 1963, Judson Perkins to Max Horton, May 16, 1963, Executive Office Release, September 25, 1963, Box 347, GR Papers; Thomas Roumell to Perkins, April 27, 1964, Box 346, ibid.; Romney to Ralf A.

Peckham, September 29, 1965, Orlebeke to M. W. Munns, February 1, 1966, Governor's Commission Minutes, October 12, 1965, Box 351, ibid.; Orlebeke, S. 71-Commission on the Employment of the Handicapped [1968], Governor's Commission Minutes, March 15, 1968, Box 328, ibid.; Barney Hopkins to Perkins, March 26, 1964, Box 237, Michigan AFL-CIO Papers, ALUA.

43. William Sheldon to Roland Lehrer, July 24, 1963, Box 250, Michigan AFL-CIO Papers; Governor's Commission, Summary of Acitvities for 1964–1965, July 8, 1965, Perkins to Roumell, January 15, 1965, Box 351, GR Papers; Orlebeke, S.71 [1968], Box 328, ibid.; Perkins to Commission, February 8, 1964, ibid.; Governor's Commission Minutes, November 17, 1967, Box 352, ibid.; *LSJ*, October 29, 1967, clipping in Box 14, BG Papers; MESC, *Annual Report for the Fiscal Year Ending June 30, 1966*, p. 22; idem, *Annual Report . . . June 30, 1967*, p. 27.

44. Romney, State of the State Message, January 10, 1963, Box 248, GR Papers; Dave Duncan Memorandum to Allen, October 9, 1968, Box 209, ibid.; Clarence Averill to Romney, January 21, 1963, Box 347, ibid.; Perkins to Romney [March 1964], Box 348, ibid.; Russell G. Albrecht to Romney, January 10, 1964, Romney to Albrecht, February 17, 1964, Box 6, Tom Downs Papers, BHL.

45. Duncan Memorandum to Allen, October 9, 1968, Inventory of Program Relationships [1968], Box 269, GR Papers.

46. MESC, *Annual Report for the Fiscal Year Ending June 30, 1964*, p. 26; idem, *Annual Report . . . June 30, 1965*, p. 9; idem, *Annual Report . . . June 30, 1966*, p. 22; idem, *Annual Report . . . June 30, 1967*, pp. 17–18, 27; idem, *Annual Report . . . June 30, 1968*, pp. 17, 21; [Ernest Walleck] to Chairman and Members, January 15, 1968, Box 3, Dorothy Siegel Judd Papers, BHL.

47. Peckham, Hiring Policy . . . April 1967, Ralph E. Cummins to Commissioners, February 27, 1966, Perkins to Romney, January 30, 1968, Box 328, GR Papers; Executive Release, June 3, 1965, Box 272, ibid.; Governor's Commission Minutes, September 8, 1967, Box 352, ibid.; Perkins to Burke L. Dailey, July 25, 1968, Box 420, ibid.; Joint Legisltive Interim Committee, Report to the Michigan Legislature, Regular Session of 1965, Workmen's Compensation, Box 53, BG Papers; "Public Act No. 317," *Public and Local Acts . . . 1969*, pp. 656–57.

48. A. N. Languis Memorandum to Allen, September 2, 1964, Languis to Mildred Otis, October 20, 1964, Box 348, GR Papers; President's Committee on Employment of the Handicapped, *Performance: The Story of the Handicapped*, p. 14, May 1966, copy in ibid.; Perkins to Frank D. Beadle, June 9, 1965, Box 351, ibid.; *LSJ*, January 21, 1966, *DN*, April 6, 1966, clippings in Box 14, BG Papers.

49. CRC Minutes, March 15, 1968, Box 6, RG 74-90. See chapter 16.

Chapter 14

1. J. Craig Jenkins, *The Politics of Insurgency: The Farm Worker Movement in the 1960s* (New York: Columbia University Press, 1985), pp. 131–33, 142–43.

2. *Training Activities in Michigan* 3 (July 1964): n.p., Box 82, GR Papers, BHL; *Report of Governor's Commission on Migrant Labor*, April 1965, pp. 11, 15, Box 325, ibid.; Michigan Migrant Ministry (hereafter MMM), Annual Report, 1964, Box 2, MMM Papers, BHL; Office of Economic Opportunity, *The Migrant and the Economic Opportunity Act*, n.d., Box 326, GR Papers; Michigan CRC, Public Hearing on Seasonal Farm Labor, August 25–26, 1968, Andrew Kramarz to Roy Fuentes, August 13, 1968, Box 325, ibid.; U.S. Senate Subcommittee on Labor and

Public Welfare, *The Migratory Farm Labor Problem in the United States,* 89 Cong., 2 sess., 1966, S. Rept. No. 1549, 24–25, 30–31, 57; idem, 92 Cong., 2 sess., 1968, S. Rept. No. 1006, 13–14, 18–19, 22, 25–26, 36, 55–56; *Year of Transition: Seasonal Farm Labor, 1965: A Report from the Secretary of Labor,* pp. 14, 20–21; Farm Labor and Rural Manpower Service Section (hereafter FLRMSS), *Post Season Farm Labor Report, 1968,* p. 20; Edgar Grant Johnston, "Migrant Workers in the State of Michigan," MASCD Issue Paper [1970].

3. *DFP,* August 17, 1969; *Year of Transition,* pp. 2, 6, 25, Appendix J; MESC, *Annual Report for the Fiscal Year Ending June 30, 1965,* pp. 25, 31; Romney to C. F. Powers, September 9, 1965, Box 351, GR Papers; Farm Placement Section (hereafter FPS), *Post Season Farm Labor Report, 1964,* pp. 9–10; idem, *Post Season Farm Labor Report, 1965,* pp. 6–7, 11; Farm Labor Service Section (hereafter FLSS), *Post Season Farm Labor Report, 1967,* p. 29; Johnston, "Migrant Workers"; Myrtle R. Ruel, "Sociocultural Patterns among Michigan Migrant Farm Workers," Rural Manpower Center Special Paper No. 2, July 1967, Box 905, William G. Milliken Papers, BHL; *LSJ,* December 30, 1965, *DN,* December 30, 1965, clippings in Box 20, BG Papers, BHL.

4. MMM, Huron County Report, 1964, Box 2, MMM Papers; *LSJ,* November 15, 1964, clipping in Box 20, BG Papers; Subcommittee on Migratory Labor of the Senate Committee on Labor and Public Welfare, *Manpower and Economic Problems: Hearings,* 91 Cong., 1 and 2 sess., 1970, Part 7-B, 4554; Michigan CRC, *Report and Recommendations on the Status of Migratory Farm Labor in Michigan, 1968,* Box 44, BG Papers; *DFP,* April 2, August 18, 1969.

5. R. Bernard Houston to Walter DeVries, June 21, 1964, and enclosure, Box 70, GR Papers; Michigan House and Senate Committees of Labor, A Preliminary Report on Migrant Labor Conditions in Michigan, November 1965, Box 352, ibid.; M. Juanita Walker to Lewis Knaggs, July 16, 1964, Legislative Service Bureau, *A Report on Migrant Labor in Michigan,* September 1965, pp. 28–29, Box 4, Sander M. Levin Papers, ALUA; Howard Jones to Executive Director, Michigan Migrant Opportunity, March 20, 1967, Box 22, ibid.; *DN,* July 14, 1965, DNSB 19, BHL; *LSJ,* July 14, 1965, clipping in Box 20, BG Papers; *Benton Harbor News- Palladium,* September 21, 1967, clipping in Box 352, GR Papers; Fuentes, "An Assessment of the Problems of Migrant Workers in Michigan," March 1, 1968, Box 6, Records of the Michigan Civil Rights Commission: Administrative, RG 74-90, State Archives, Lansing, Michigan; *DN,* August 27, 1968; *DFP,* August 17, 1969.

6. Fuentes, "Assessment," March 1, 1968, Box 6, RG 74-90; Legislative Service Bureau, *Migrant Labor,* September 1965, p. 14, Box 4, Levin Papers; *DFP,* April 2, 1969.

7. [*Chicago Daily News,* July 18, 1969], clipping, Milliken to Mrs. Thomas Gorman, August 4, 1969, Box 425, GR Papers; MMM, Annual Reports, 1968, 1969, Box 2, MMM Papers.

8. W. L. Mainland to Romney, January 15, 1963, Box 34, GR Papers; *Report of Governor's Commission on Migrant Labor,* April 1965, p. 7, Box 325, ibid.; *Second Report of Governor's Commission on Migrant Labor,* August 1966, p. 14, Box 352, ibid.; FPS, *Post Season Farm Labor Report, 1963,* pp. 28, 32; idem, *Post Season Farm Labor Report, 1964,* pp. 6–7; Subcommittee on Migratory Labor of the Senate Committee on Labor and Public Welfare, *Voluntary Farm Employment Service, Hearings,* 88 Cong., 1 sess., 1963, 205; MESC, *Annual Report for the Fiscal Year Ending June 30, 1964,* pp. 11, 15; Farm Labor Management Committee of

Michigan, Report of Committee for 1964 [February 1965], Box 18, Roger Craig Papers, ALUA.

9. *Voluntary Farm Employment Service*, p. 205; Harry H. Nye to Mainland, June 26, 1965, Box 4, Levin Papers.

10. *Report of Governor's Commission*, April 1965, p. 5, Donald R. Beaton to Fuentes, August 9, 1968, Box 325, GR Papers; Fuentes, "Assessment," March 1, 1968, Box 6, RG 74-90; Johnston, "Migrant Workers"; William R. Bennalack to Board of Supervisors . . . , July 31, 1968, Bennalack to Rebecca Super, December 6, 1968, Box 4, United Farm Workers Michigan Boycott Papers, ALUA; MMM, Annual Report, 1969, Box 2, MMM Papers.

11. *Report of Governor's Commission*, April 1965, p. 6, Box 325, GR Papers; *Second Report of Governor's Commission*, August 1966, p. 13, Box 352, ibid.; Johnston, "Migrant Workers."

12. "General Information," n.d., UMOI Newsletters, November 1968, March 1969, undated document, Box 905, Milliken Papers; MMM, Annual Reports, 1962, 1965, Box 2, MMM Papers; Release, March 19, 1965, James F. McClure to Theodore M. Berry, November 15, 1966, Box 3, ibid.; *Report of Governor's Commission*, April 1965, p. 9, Box 325, GR Papers; Fuentes, "Assessment," March 1, 1968, Box 6, RG 74-90; FPS, *Post Season Farm Labor Report, 1965,* p. 42; FLSS, *Post Season Farm Labor Report, 1966,* p. 46; *LSJ,* March 20, 28, 1965, clippings in Box 20, BG Papers; *Manpower and Economic Problems,* Part 7-B, 4541; *DN,* March 23, 1965, DNSB 19.

13. Romney to George B. Van Antwerp, February 23, 1968, Box 352, GR Papers; —— to Jack Carper, n.d., Box 30, Jewish Labor Committee (hereafter JLC) Papers, ALUA; Housing Component Project Narrative, n.d., Box 29, ibid.; Johnston, "Migrant Workers"; UMOI Newsletters, November 1968, March 1969, Box 905, Milliken Papers; UMOI Newsletter, August 1968, Box 6, Records of the Department of Agriculture, RG 78-107, State Archives; Harvey M. Choldin and Grafton D. Trout, "Mexican Americans in Transition, Migrant Employment in Michigan Cities," 1969, p. 42, BHL.

14. FPS, *Post Season Farm Labor Report, 1963,* p. 27; *Report of Governor's Commission,* April 1965, p. 8, Box 325, GR Papers; *Second Report of Governor's Commission,* August 1966, p. 10, Box 352, ibid.

15. Declaration of Grievances to . . . Romney, March 26, 1967, Release, March 30, 1967, untitled document signed by Alfaro, April 4, 1967, Box 326, GR Papers; Romney to Alfaro, October 2, 1967, Box 325, ibid.; *Michigan AFL-CIO News,* March 29, 1967, copy in Box 21, William Kircher Papers, ALUA; *DN,* March 27, 1967, DNSB 20; *LSJ,* March 22, 29, 1967, *Ann Arbor News,* April 5, 1967, clippings in Box 20, BG Papers.

16. Jenkins, *Politics of Insurgency,* pp. 144–62; *LSJ,* April 11, 13, 1967, *DN,* April 13, 1967, clippings in Box 20, BG Papers; Fuentes, "Assessment," March 1, 1968, Box 6, RG 74-90; WLK [Kircher] Memorandum to Files, March 29, 1967, Box 21, Kircher Papers; Carper to Albert Wheeler, May 16, 1967, Carper to Theodore Saches, May 17, 1967, Carper to Russell Smith, June 23, 1967, Carper to Burton Levy, July 5, 1967, Carper to Don Stevens, August 30, 1967, Carper to Benjamin Marcus, January 26, 1968, Carper to Emanuel Muravchik, March 10, 1968, Irving Bluestone to Carper, June 15, 1967, Walter Dorosh to Members . . . , July 25, 1967, Box 29, JLC Papers; Farm Workers Speech for Easter Demonstration [April 14, 1967], Box 40, ibid.; Carper to Detroit Branch NAACP, June 27, 1967, Carper to

Friend, August 23, 1967, Box 20, National Association for the Advancement of Colored People, Detroit Branch Papers, ALUA.

17. MCAFW Release, February 2, 1968, Carper to Wheeler, February 14, March 12, 1968, Carper to Dolores Huerta, March 7, 1968, Box 29, JLC Papers; Carper to Jack Conway, March 19, 1968, Carper to Joseph P. Swallow, March 19, 1968, Box 30, ibid.; Carper, Legislative Report, 1967–68 Session, Box 40, ibid.; *Michigan AFL-CIO News,* May 1, 1968, clipping in ibid.; *LSJ,* April 3, 1968, clipping in Box 20, BG Papers.

18. The National Advisory Commission on Civil Disorders had been established following the Detroit riot of July 1967.

19. Bennalack to Alfaro et al., December 8, 1967, Box 29, JLC Papers; Carper to Romney, April 12, 1968, Declaration of Grievances to . . . Romney, April 14, 1968, Carper Memorandum to Clement Kern et al., April 16, 1968, Carper to James Gonzales, April 30, 1968, Carper and Alfaro to Romney, May 17, 1968, Box 30, ibid.; Carper to Muravchik, March 10, 1968, Alfaro, Easter Sunday Rally, April 14, 1968, Farm Worker Speech . . . [April 14, 1968], Box 40, ibid.; *Michigan AFL-CIO News,* May 1, 1968, clipping in Box 21, Kircher Papers; William Whitbeck to Romney, April 12, 1968, Box 425, GR Papers; CRC Public Hearing . . . August 25–26, 1968, Box 325, ibid.; *LSJ,* April 14, 15, 25, 1968, clippings in Box 20, BG Papers; *DFP,* April 2, 1969.

20. MMM, Annual Report, 1968, Box 2, MMM Papers; Maurice Delgado to Friend, June 1968, Box 40, JLC Papers; Johnston, "Migrant Workers."

21. Al Applegate to Romney, May 13, 1964, Executive Office Release, June 4, 1964, Box 349, GR Papers.

22. *Report of Governor's Commission,* April 1965, p. 4, Box 325, GR Papers; *Second Report of Governor's Commission,* August 1966, passim, Box 352, ibid.

23. Executive Office Releases, October 2, 1964, May 7, 1965, Box 272, ibid.; Romney to Tompkins, August 21, 1964, Box 349, ibid. See, in particular, Migrant Labor Laws Passed in Michigan, May 1969, Box 12, Detroit Commission on Community Relations (hereafter DCCR) Papers, ALUA.

24. Helen Parks, Day Care Centers for the Children of Migrant Workers in Michigan, 1963, Box 4, Records of Management and Budget: Women's Commission, RG 77-78, State Archives; Legislative Service Bureau, *Migrant Labor,* September 1965, pp. 4–5, Box 4, Levin Papers; House and Senate Labor Committees, Migrant Labor Conditions, November 1965, Box 352, GR Papers; *Report of Governor's Commission on Migrant Labor,* April 1965, p. 15, Box 325, ibid.; Governor's Commission on Migrant Labor Minutes, September 2, 1964, Box 349, ibid.; Migrant Labor Bills, May 1969, Box 12, DCCR Papers.

25. Houston to Doris Beck, December 5, 1968, Box 33, Levin Papers; Migrant Farm Labor Hearing, Michigan CRC Presentation, August 26, 1968, ibid.; 1968 Summer Day Care Narrative, January 18, 1968, Box 29, JLC Papers; FLRMSS, *Post Season Farm Labor and Rural Manpower Report, 1969,* p. 44; *LSJ,* June 11, 1966, clipping in Box 20, BG Papers.

26. "Public Act No. 287," *Public and Local Acts . . . 1965,* p. 547; *Report of Governor's Commission,* April 1965, p. 15, Box 325, GR Papers; House and Senate Labor Committees, Migrant Labor Conditions, November 1965, Box 352, ibid.; Migrant Labor Laws, May 1969, Box 12, DCCR Papers; Fuentes, "Assessment," March 1, 1968, Box 6, RG 74-90; Legislative Service Bureau, *Migrant Labor,* September 1965, pp. 4, 5–6, Levin Papers; Johnston, "Migrant Workers."

27. Johnston, "Migrant Workers"; MMM, Annual Reports, 1967, 1969, Box 2, MMM Papers; Fuentes, "Assessment," March 1, 1968, Box 6, RG 74-90; *LSJ*, March 2, 1967, clipping in Box 20, BG Papers.

28. MMM, Annual Report, 1968, Box 2, MMM Papers; Beaton to Fuentes, August 9, 1968, CRC, Public Hearing, August 25–26, 1968, Box 325, GR Papers; Ira Polley to Beck, December 5, 1968, Michigan Department of Education, Migrant Program for 1969 Fiscal Year, December 19, 1968, Box 33, Levin Papers; CRC, *Status of Migrant Farm Labor, 1968*, pp. 11–12, Box 44, BG Papers; *LSJ*, September 2, 1966, March 2, 1967, clippings in Box 20, ibid.; FLRMSS, *Post Season Farm Labor Report, 1968*, pp. 35–36.

29. Johnston, "Migrant Workers."

30. Ibid.; FLRMSS, *Post Season Farm Labor Report, 1968*, pp. 35–36.

31. Johnston, "Migrant Workers"; CRC, *Status of Migratory Farm Labor, 1968*, pp. 11–12, Box 44, BG Papers; *LSJ*, August 26, 1968, clipping in Box 20, ibid.

32. Legislative Service Bureau, *Migrant Labor*, September 1965, Box 4, Levin Papers; UMOI Newsletter, August 1968, Box 6, RG 78-107; UMOI Newsletter, June 1969, Box 905, Milliken Papers; UMOI, Adult Education Program Narrative, n.d., Box 29, JLC Papers.

33. "Health Care for Migrant Families," *Michigan Health* 53 (January–February 1965): 22; *Report of Governor's Commission*, April 1965, p. 12, Box 325, GR Papers; H. L. Johnston, *Health for the Nation's Harvesters*, pp. 140–85.

34. Subcommittee of the Senate Committee on Labor and Public Welfare, *The Migrant Farm Labor Problem in the United States*, 88 Cong., 1 sess., 1963, S. Rept. No. 167, Appendix A; *Second Report of Governor's Commission*, August 1966, pp. 20–21, Box 352, GR Papers; Migrant Farm Labor Hearing, CRC Presentation, Role of State Department of Social Services, August 26, 1968, Houston to Beck, December 5, 1968, Box 33, Levin Papers.

35. "Health Care for Migrant Families," p. 22; Subcommittee on Health of Senate Committee on Labor and Public Welfare, *Migrant Health Services, Hearings*, 91 Cong., 1 sess., 1969, 73; FPS, *Post Season Farm Labor Report, 1964*, pp. 44–45; *Report of the Governor's Commission*, April 1965, p. 41, Box 325, GR Papers; House and Senate Labor Committees, Migrant Labor Conditions, November 1965, Box 352, ibid.; Douglas H. Fryer, "Solving Michigan's Migrant Worker Health Problems," *Michigan Hospitals* 4 (September 1968): 6–7; *Journal of the Michigan State Medical Society* 63 (1964): 813.

36. *Migrant Health Services*, pp. 73–74, 77; Michigan Department of Public Health, Report of the Governor's Task Force on Migrant Labor, Health Related Programs, August 4, 1969, Box 1226, Milliken Papers; Action to Aid Migrants: The Record, 1963–1968, Box 425, GR Papers; Johnston, "Migrant Workers."

37. Executive Office Release, May 7, 1965, Box 272, GR Papers; Legislative Service Bureau, *Migrant Labor*, September 1965, pp. 28–29, Meeting of Legislative, Agency, Agricultural Organization Representatives Concerned with Migrant Labor Problems, July 28, 1965, Box 4, Levin Papers; *Report of Governor's Commission*, April 1965, p. 14, Box 325, GR Papers; FPS, *Post Season Farm Labor Report, 1964*, p. 31; *DN*, July 11, 1965, DNSB 19; *LSJ*, July 13, 1965, clipping in Box 20, BG Papers; MESC, *Annual Report for the Fiscal Year Ending June 30, 1965*, p. 32.

38. "Public Act No. 289," *Public and Local Acts . . . 1965*, pp. 548–50; Legislative Service Bureau, *Migrant Labor*, September 1965, p. 28, Box 4, Levin Papers; CRC, Public Hearing, August 25–26, 1968, Box 325, GR Papers; Michigan

Department of Public Health, Statement Presented at CRC Hearing, August 26, 1968, Box 6, RG 74-90.

39. FPS, *Post Season Farm Labor Report, 1965,* pp. 28–29; idem, *Post Season Farm Labor Report, 1966,* p. 9; FLSS, *Post Season Farm Labor Report, 1967,* pp. 8, 40; FLRMSS, *Post Season Farm Labor Report, 1968,* p. 21; MMM, Annual Report, 1966, Box 2, MMM Papers; *Second Report of Governor's Commission,* August 1966, pp. 18–19, Box 352, GR Papers; Resume of Agricultural Labor Camp Licensing Program, November 1967, Box 425, ibid.; Johnston, "Migrant Workers"; Department of Public Health Statement, August 26, 1968, Box 6, RG 74-90; Fryer, "Michigan's Migrant Worker Health Problems," pp. 6–7; *DFP,* August 18, 1969.

40. Department of Public Health, Annual Progress Report, Agricultural Labor Camp Licensing Program, 1967, November 1, 1967, Box 421, GR Papers; Alvin E. Heustis to Executive Office, February 16, 1967, Box 325, ibid.; CRC, *Status of Migratory Farm Labor, 1968,* pp. 9–10, Box 44, BG Papers; *DFP,* August 18, 1969; "Public Act No. 157-1," *Public and Local Acts . . . 1968,* p. 244. See also Notes Taken by Senator Robert Richardson . . . , August 21, 1969, Box 425, GR Papers.

41. CRC, Public Hearing, August 25–26, 1968, Box 325, GR Papers; UMOI Newsletter, August 1968, Box 6, RG 78-107; Johnston, "Migrant Workers"; *DFP,* August 17, 1969.

42. "Public Act No. 44," *Public and Local Acts . . . 1965,* pp. 63–78; "Public Act No. 283," *Public and Local Acts . . . 1967,* pp. 579–80; Legislative Service Bureau, *Migrant Labor,* September 1965, pp. 20–21, Box 4, Levin Papers; Daniel W. Sturt, "Workmen's Compensation and Michigan Farm Employers," January 19, 1966, Box 12, ibid.; CRC, *Status of Migratory Farm Labor, 1968,* pp. 6–7, Box 44, BG Papers; *DFP,* August 18, 1969.

43. Sturt, "Workmen's Compensation and Michigan Farm Employers," February 1, 1968, idem, "The Rural Manpower Program in 1967," January 1968, Box 905, Milliken Papers; Barry Brown to Jack Dempsey, July 31, 1969, Box 1226, ibid.; Romney to Mrs. Ray Anderson, April 10, 1967, Box 302, GR Papers; *Report of Governor's Commission,* April 1965, pp. 20–21, Box 325, ibid.; FPS, *Post Season Farm Labor Report, 1966,* p. 9.

44. *Manpower and Economic Problems,* Part 7-B, p. 4556; "Public Act. No. 154," *Public and Local Acts . . . 1964,* pp. 145–47; "Public Act No. 269," *Public and Local Acts . . . 1966,* pp. 383–84; Sturt, Michigan's Minimum Wage Act of 1964, as Amended . . . , February 1, 1969, Box 905, Milliken Papers; FPS, *Post Season Farm Labor Report, 1964,* pp. 32–33; FLRMSS, *Post Season Farm Labor Report, 1968,* p. 27.

45. FPS, *Post Season Farm Labor Report, 1964,* pp. 32–33; idem, *Post Season Farm Labor Report, 1965,* pp. 8, 30; idem, *Post Season Farm Labor Report, 1966,* pp. 9–10, 32; FLSS, *Post Season Farm Labor Report, 1967,* pp. 7, 8–9; FLRMSS, *Post Season Farm Labor Report, 1968,* pp. 26–27; Michigan Department of Labor, Piece Rates Established by Wage Deviation Board, August 4, 1967, Box 326, GR Papers; CRC, Public Hearing, August 25–26, 1968, Box 325, ibid.; Michigan CRC, *1969 Report and Recommendations; A Field Study of Migrant Workers in Michigan,* CRC, *Status of Migratory Farm Labor, 1968,* p. 7, Box 44, BG Papers.

46. CRC, *Status of Migratory Farm Labor, 1968,* p. 7, Box 44, BG Papers; John T. Rhodes Memorandum to Ted Blizzard, August 4, 1967, Box 326, GR Papers; Brown to Dempsey, July 31, 1969, Box 1226, Milliken Papers; *DFP,* August 18, 1969.

47. Legislative Service Bureau, *Migrant Labor,* September 25, 1965, pp. 22–23, Box 4, Levin Papers; House and Senate Labor Committees, Migrant Labor Conditions, November 1965, Box 325, GR Papers; *DFP,* August 18, 1969.

48. Houston to Romney, September 18, 1964, Box 349, GR Papers; Executive Office Release, May 7, 1965, Box 272, ibid.; *Report of Governor's Commission,* April 1965, p. 17, Box 325, ibid.; Johnston, "Migrant Workers"; Houston to Beck, December 5, 1968, Michigan Farm Labor Hearing, CRC Presentation on August 26, 1968, Role of State Department of Social Services, Box 33, Levin Papers; *Migrant Services Directory* [1969], pp. 18–19, Box 1226, Milliken Papers; FLRMSS, *Post Season Farm Labor and Rural Manpower Report, 1969,* p. 44; Comparison of Recommendations . . . [1969], Box 34, RG 74-90.

49. Legislative Service Bureau, *Migrant Labor,* September 1965, pp. 17–18, Box 4, Levin Papers; Subcommittee on Migratory Labor of Senate Committee on Labor and Public Welfare, *Migratory Labor Bills, Hearings,* 88 Cong., 1 sess., 1963, p. 291.

50. *Migratory Farm Labor Problem,* pp. 30–31; "Public Act No. 234," *Public and Local Acts . . . 1966,* pp. 311–12; Michigan Welfare League Legislative Bulletin No. 10, August 13, 1966, Box 11, Wilma E. Donahue Papers, BHL; Kramarz to Fuentes, August 13, 1968, Box 6, RG 74-90; Legislative Service Bureau, *Migrant Labor,* September 1965, pp. 12–13, Box 4, Levin Papers.

51. "Public Act No. 288," *Public and Local Acts . . . 1965,* pp. 547–48; "Public Act No. 190," *Public and Local Acts . . . 1966,* pp. 216–17; Migrant Labor Laws, May 1969, Box 12, DCCR Papers; Legislative Service Bureau, *Migrant Labor,* September 1965, p. 12, Box 4, Levin Papers; Executive Office Release, July 22, 1965, Box 325, GR Papers.

52. "Public Act No. 160," *Public and Local Acts . . . 1966,* pp. 180–81; Michigan Welfare League Legislative Bulletin No. 10, August 10, 1966, Box 11, Donahue Papers; Johnston, "Migrant Workers"; Action to Aid Migrants: The Record, 1963–1968, Box 425, GR Papers.

53. Executive Office Release, October 27, 1964, *Report of Governor's Commission,* April 1965, p. 23, Box 325, GR Papers; *Second Report of Governor's Commission,* August 1966, pp. 22–26, Box 352, ibid.; Sturt, "Rural Manpower Center Program in 1967," January 1968, Box 905, Milliken Papers; *Manpower and Economic Problems,* Part 7-B, 4527.

54. *Report of Governor's Commission,* April 1965, p. 23, Executive Office Release, October 27, 1964, Box 325, GR Papers; *Second Report of Governor's Commission,* August 1966, p. 9, Box 352, ibid.; Executive Office Release, May 17, 1965, Box 272, ibid.; Action to Aid Migrants: The Record, 1963–1968, Box 425, ibid.; Johnston, "Migrant Workers"; FLSS, *Post Season Farm Labor Report, 1966,* p. 47.

55. CRC Minutes, April 5, 1968, Fuentes, "Assessment," March 1, 1968, Box 6, RG 74-90; MMM, Annual Report, 1968, Box 2, MMM Papers.

56. H. C. McKinney, Jr., Memorandum to Romney, May 6, 1968, Charles Orlebeke Memorandum to Romney, May 21, 1968, Box 17, RG 74-90.

57. CRC Release, April 5, 1968, Box 425, GR Papers; CRC, Public Hearing, August 25–26, 1968, Field Impressions of Project Staff [1968], Box 325, ibid.; MMM, Annual Report, 1968, Box 2, MMM Papers; Carper and Alfaro to Romney, May 17, 1968, Box 30, JLC Papers.

58. CRC, *Status of Migratory Farm Labor, 1968,* p. 2, Box 44, BG Papers; *LSJ,* August 23, 26, 1968, clippings in Box 20, ibid.; *DN,* August 27, 1968; MMM,

Annual Report, 1968, Box 2, MMM Papers; *Benton Harbor News-Palladium,* August 26, 1966, clipping in Box 325, GR Papers.

59. CRC, *Status of Migratory Farm Labor, 1968,* pp. 3–4, Box 44, BG Papers.

60. CRC, *1969 Report and Recommendations: A Field Study of Migrant Workers,* Box 44, BG Papers; Burton Gordin to Milliken, November 25, 1969, Box 905, Milliken Papers; Staff Memorandum to Commission, August 1, 1969, Box 904, ibid.; CRC Newsletter, August 1969, Box 903, ibid.; Information for Farm Labor Provided by the CRC [1968], Box 14, RG 74-90; CRC, Annual Reports, 1968–1969, 1969–1970, Department of Civil Rights.

61. CRC, Annual Reports, 1967–1968, 1969–1970, Department of Civil Rights; Walter R. Greene to Gordin, January 10, 1968, Box 21, RG 74-90; Staff Memorandum to Commission, May 17, 1968, Box 12, ibid.; Julian Abel Cook to Milliken, December 16, 1969, and enclosure, Gordin to Milliken, November 25, December 18, 1969, Box 905, Milliken Papers; *LSJ,* August 28, 1968, clipping in Box 4, BG Papers; *DFP,* August 20, 1969.

62. Milliken to R. Dale Ball, July 10, 1969, Final Report Governor's Task Force on Migrant Labor, October 9, 1969, CRC, Analysis of Report of Governor's Task Force, December 16, 1969, Cook to Milliken, December 16, 1969, and enclosure, Box 905, Milliken Papers; Executive Office Release, July 28, 1969, Box 1226, ibid.; Milliken to Levin, August 29, 1969, Box 33, Levin Papers; Comparison of Recommendations . . . [1969], Box 34, RG 74-90.

63. Milliken to Alton M. Shipstead, November 14, 1969, Conference for Area Councils on Migrant Labor, July 16, 1970, Governor's Task Force on Migrant Labor Recommendations— Implementation as of November 2, 1970, Box 905, Milliken Papers; Migrant Worker Position Paper Summary [1970], Box 625, ibid.; Release, July 16, 1970, Box 1226, ibid.; Milliken to Levin, August 29, 1969, Box 33, Levin Papers.

64. *Manpower and Economic Problems,* Part 7-B, 4548; Migrant Tour Report [August 1971], Box 34, RG 74-90; Johnston, "Migrant Labor."

65. *Manpower and Economic Problems,* Part 7-B, 4554; Johnston, "Migrant Labor."

66. *Ann Arbor News,* July 12, August 12, 1996.

Chapter 15

1. Burton I. Gordin, "An Overview of the Problem in Michigan," April 26, 1966, Box 67, Detroit Urban League (hereafter DUL) Papers, BHL.

2. Michigan CRC, *How the Backlog Grew,* pp. 6, 11; idem, *Toward Equality,* pp. 6, 14.

3. Michigan CRC, *The Year of the Beginning: 1964 Annual Report,* p. 3, Box 408, GR Papers; Gordin, "An Overview," Box 67, DUL Papers; *DN,* December 15, 16, 1964, April 27, 1965, DNSB 19, BHL; [*DN,* December 22, 1964], clipping in Box 4, BG Papers, BHL; Fine, *Violence,* p. 102.

4. Michigan CRC, *Year of the Beginning,* p. 8, Box 408, GR Papers, BHL; idem, *How the Backlog Grew,* p. 7; Staff Memorandum to the CRC, August 6, 1964, Box 39, Records of the Michigan Civil Rights Commission: Administrative, RG 74-90, State Archives, Lansing, Michigan; CRC to Local Mayors et al., August 24, 1964, Gordin Memorandum to CRC, February 10, 1965, Box 19, Detroit Commission on Community Relations (hereafter DCCR) Papers, ALUA.

5. CRC News for Release, September 21, 1964, Box 70, DUL Papers; CRC Minutes, September 22, 1964, Gordin Weekly Report to Commission, November 20, 1964, Box 1, RG 74-90; Thomas J. Peloso Memorandum to Gordin and Arthur L. Johnson, January 6, 1965, Box 26, ibid.; CRC Release, October 27, 1964, Box 19, DCCR Papers.

6. Peloso Memorandum to Gordin and Johnson, January 6, 1965, Original Agreement, Amended, April 22, 1966, Box 26, RG 74-90; CRC Minutes, April 21, 1966, Box 3, ibid.; CRC News, April 27 [1965], Box 31, National Association for the Advancement of Colored People, Detroit Branch (hereafter Detroit NAACP) Papers, ALUA; *DN*, April 19, May 23, 1965; *DN*, April 28, 1965, DNSB 19; Thompson, "Politics of Labor," pp. 110–11.

7. CRC, Report on Investigations of Law Enforcement Claims against the DPD, June 24, 1966, Box 19, Detroit NAACP Papers; *DN*, April 10, 1966; *DN*, June 28, 1966, DNSB 20.

8. [*DFP*, April 28, 1966], clipping in Box 434, GR Papers; *DN*, April 28, 1965, clipping in Box 4, BG Papers; *DN*, April 10, 1966.

9. CRC, Law Enforcement Claims, Box 19, Detroit NAACP Papers; CRC News Release, April 27 [1965], Box 31, ibid.; CRC Newsletter, June 1965, Box 408, GR Papers; *DN*, April 29, 1965, clipping in Box 4, BG Papers; Fine, *Violence*, pp. 14–15.

10. Gordin Memorandum to Commission, November 20, 1964, Box 1, RG 74-90.

11. Ibid.; CRC Newsletters, March, May 1965, Box 408, GR Papers; CRC, *Report of Progress, 1965–1966*, Box 422, ibid.; CRC Newsletter, June 1966, University of Michigan Law School Library (hereafter UMLSL), Ann Arbor, Michigan; [Burton Levy], "Law Enforcement and Civil Rights" [April 15, 1966], Box 18, Francis A. Kornegay Papers, BHL; Police Recruitment Project of Michigan, Inc., Final Project Report—June 1, 1967 through May 31, 1968, Box 13, RG 74-90; Workshop on Law Enforcement, CRC, Conference of Municipal Officials, January 16, 1967, Box 19, Detroit NAACP Papers; CRC, Master Copy of Final Budget . . . , January 6, 1969, Box 901, William G. Milliken Papers, BHL; *DN*, April 10, 1966.

12. Levy Memorandum to Gordin, August 31, 1965, Box 28, RG 74-90; A. A. Banks, Jr., et al. to Romney, March 29, 1968, enclosing report of the CRC for the fiscal year 1966–1967, Box 1440, Milliken Papers; Levy, "Law Enforcement and Civil Rights" [April 15, 1965], Box 18, Kornegay Papers; CRC Newsletter, June 1966, UMLSL.

13. Police Recruitment Project, Box 13, RG 74-90.

14. CRC Minutes, June 27, November 28, 1967, Box 5, ibid.; Gordin Memorandum to Commission, February 16, 1968, Box 12, ibid.; Gordin to Herbert Hill, May 5, 1967, Box 3, Albert and Emma Wheeler Papers, BHL; Levy to Edward N. Hodges, March 28, 1967, Richard S. McGhee to Levy, April 13, 1967, Police Recruitment Project of Michigan, Inc., Advisory Councils, June 1967, Box 17, Richard S. McGhee Papers, ALUA.

15. Gordin Memorandum to Commission, January 18, 1965, Box 1, Sander M. Levin Papers, ALUA.

16. Gordin Memorandum to Charles Orlebeke, March 5, 1965, Executive Order No. 1965-3, May 3, 1965, Box 327, GR Papers; Gordin to Clarence Schnipke, September 19, 1967, Box 11, RG 74-90; Fine, *Violence*, p. 172.

17. CRC Newsletter, August 1965, Box 408, GR Papers; Gordin Memorandum to Commission, July 21, 1967, Box 11, RG 74-90; Walter R. Greene Memorandum

to Gordin, May 14, 1968, enclosed with Gordin Memorandum to Orlebeke, May 14, 1968, Box 13, ibid.; Gordin Memorandum to Lucille Kapplinger, August 18, 1967, Box 17, Records of the Civil Rights Commission: Executive, RG 81-89, State Archives.

18. Michigan CRC, *Year of the Beginning,* p. 11, Box 408, GR Papers; Staff Memorandum to CRC, August 16, 1964, Box 39, RG 74-90; Report of Executive Staff Discussions . . . , July 1, 1966, Box 40, ibid.; CRC to Local Mayors et al., August 24, 1964, Box 19, DCCR Papers; CRC News for Release, August 27, 1964, Box 67, DUL Papers.

19. Gordin Memorandum to Commission, September 8, 1966, Box 3, RG 74-90; CRC's Role in Riot Control, June 28, 1967, Box 11, ibid.

20. Feikens to Gordin, September 1, 1966, Box 2, Records of the Civil Rights Commission: Executive Office, RG 87-6, State Archives; Gordin Memorandum to Commission, September 13, 1966, Box 3, RG 74-90; Workshop on Law Enforcement, Presented by Levy, January 16, 1967, Box 19, DCCR Papers; *LSJ,* January 16, 1967, clipping in Box 4, BG Papers.

21. McGhee to Levy, March 23, 28 (two documents), 1967, Box 17, McGhee Papers; Keith to Friend, March 21, 1967, Box 28, RG 74-90; Thomas E. Johnson Memorandum to Gordin, June 2, 1967, Box 5, ibid.; CRC Newsletter, June 1967, UMLSL; Johnson Memorandum to William Howard and Justice Moore, June 22, 1967, Box 4, Records of the Michigan Department of Civil Rights: Detroit Office, RG 80-17, State Archives.

22. Johnson Memorandum to Gordin, June 2, 1967, Box 5, RG 74-90.

23. Sidney Fine, "Chance and History: Some Aspects of the Detroit Riot of 1967," *Michigan Quarterly Review* 25 (Spring 1986): 403. For details of the Detroit riot, see Fine, *Violence,* passim.

24. Johnson Memoranda [*sic*] to Greene, August 16, 1967, Box 17, RG 81-89; CRC Newsletter, September 1967, Box 422, GR Papers.

25. Johnson Memorandum to Greene, August 16, 1967, Ruth Rasmussen Memorandum to Gordin, July 31, 1967, Box 17, RG 81-89.

26. Gordin Memorandum to Kapplinger, August 18, 1967, Box 17, ibid.; Albert Wheeler to Romney, October 4, November 13, 1967, Box 3, Wheeler Papers; CRC Newsletter, October 1967, UMLSL; CRC News Release, November 3, 1967, Box 59, John A. Hannah Papers, Michigan State University Archives, Historical Collections, East Lansing, Michigan; *LSJ,* October 18, 1967, clipping in Box 4, BG Papers.

27. Gordin Memorandum to Orlebeke, May 14, 1968, and enclosure, Box 13, RG 74-90; Johnson to Levy, December 27, 1968, Box 15, ibid.; [Ernest Walleck] to CRC, January 15, 1968, Box 3, Dorothy Siegel Judd Papers, BHL; CRC Memorandum to Romney, April 9, 1968, Box 4, RG 80-17; Fine, *Violence,* p. 402.

28. Fine, *Violence,* p. 401.

29. CRC Memorandum to Romney, April 9, 1968, Gordin Memorandum to Commission, February 16, 1968, Box 4, RG 80-17; Police Recruitment Project, Box 13, RG 74-90; Gordin Memorandum to Orlebeke, May 21, 1968, Box 17, ibid.

30. Statement to Governor by Michigan State Advisory Committee, April 1, 1968, Box 325, GR Papers; CRC Memorandum to Romney, April 16, 1968, Box 422, ibid.; CRC Memorandum to Romney, April 9, 1968, Box 4, RG 80-17; Gordin Memorandum to Orlebeke, May 21, 1968, Box 17, RG 74-90.

31. Gordin Memorandum to Orlebeke, May 21, 1968, Box 17, RG 74-90;

Gordin Memorandum to Commission, February 16, 1968, and enclosure, Box 4, RG 80-17.

32. Fine, *Violence,* pp. 411–12, 424; CRC Memorandum to Milliken, May 15, 1969, Box 905, Milliken Papers.

33. CRC Memorandum to Milliken, May 15, 1969, Box 905, Milliken Papers.

34. Fine, *Violence,* pp. 432, 441.

35. Ibid., pp. 441–44.

36. Ibid., p. 444.

37. Department of Civil Rights Memorandum to Milliken, May 15, 1969, Box 905, Milliken Papers; CRC, Annual Report, 1969–1970, Michigan Department of Civil Rights, Detroit, Michigan.

38. A Summary of Fair Housing Ordinances in Michigan, March 31, 1968, Box 13, RG 74-90; CRC Newsletter, November–December 1968, Box 70, DUL Papers; Fine, *Violence,* pp. 429–30.

39. CRC Newsletters, February, June 1968, UMLSL; Olive R. Beasley Memorandum to Commission, February 23, 1968, Box 6, RG 74-90; Cosseboom, *Grosse Pointe,* pp. 12–13, 17; *LSJ,* May 24, 1967, clipping in Box 9, BG Papers; *LSJ,* July 20, 1968, clipping in Box 4, ibid.

40. Fine, *Violence,* p. 430; Romney Special Message on Open Occupancy . . . , October 13, 1967, Box 17, RG 74-90; Romney to Donald E. Dresselhouse, November 17, 1967, Box 171, GR Papers; *LSJ,* October 20, November 26, 28, December 2, 22, 1967, *Ann Arbor News,* October 23, November 30, December 7, 1967, clippings in Box 9, BG Papers.

41. Executive Office Release, January 11, 1968, Box 266, Romney Message, March 28, 1968, Box 267, GR Papers; David Winder, "Michigan's Open Housing Legislation, 1967 and 1968," May 25, 1968, pp. 6, 9, Box 332, ibid.

42. Frank H. Abbott to Roger Craig, January 29, 1968, Robert Watts et al. to Craig, March 9, 1968, letters in folder 2, Box 1, Roger Craig Papers, ALUA; Lansing Legislative Memo, July 11, 1968, Box 27, Levin Papers; *LSJ,* January 4, 5, May 14, 19, 1968, clippings in Box 4, BG Papers; *LSJ,* April 5, May 13, 16, June 11, 20, 1968, clippings in Box 9, ibid.

43. "Public Act No. 112," *Public and Local Acts of the Legislature of the State of Michigan Passed at the Regular Session of 1968,* pp. 166–75.

44. CRC Minutes, December 19, 1967, Box 6, RG 74-90; Executive Office Release, June 11, 1968, Box 322, GR Papers; Lansing Legislative Memo, July 11, 1968, Box 27, Levin Papers; CRC Newsletter, November–December 1968, UMLSL; CRC, Annual Report, 1968–1969, Department of Civil Rights; *Jones* v. *Mayer,* 392 U.S. 409 (1968); Lockard, *Toward Equal Opportunity,* p. 119; Dye, *Politics,* p. 361; "Public Act No. 453," *Public and Local Acts . . . 1976,* p. 1708. Lockard and Dye erroneously assert that the 1968 Michigan law contained no exceptions.

45. Darden et al., *Detroit,* pp. 86–88.

46. "Public Act No. 189," *Public and Local Acts . . . 1968,* pp. 281–84.

47. "Public Acts Nos. 295, 344," *Public and Local Acts . . . 1968,* pp. 499, 664–67; CRC Newsletter, August 1968, UMLSL; Fine, *Violence,* p. 428.

48. Gordin to Hill, May 5, 1967, Box 3, Wheeler Papers.

49. David William Winder, "Gubernatorial-Legislative Interaction in Michigan" (Ph.D. diss., Michigan State University, 1982), pp. 151, 154–55. For white resistance to open housing in Detroit, see especially Sugrue, *Urban Crisis,* pp. 209–29.

50. CRC, Discipline and Suspension Policy and Practices in Michigan Public Schools, February 29, 1968, Box 3, Wheeler Papers; CRC Newsletters, February, April 1968, Box 422, GR Papers; CRC Newsletter, October 1968, Box 903, Milliken Papers; CRC, Annual Report, 1968–1969, Department of Civil Rights.

51. CRC, Annual Report, 1968–1969, Department of Civil Rights.

52. Fine, *Violence,* p. 434.

53. Ibid., p. 435.

54. Ibid., p. 434.

55. CRC, Annual Report, 1968–1969, Department of Civil Rights.

56. Department of Civil Rights, Memorandum to Milliken, May 15, 1969, Box 905, Milliken Papers.

57. See ibid. for the numerous memoranda that the Department of Civil Rights addressed to Milliken on May 15, 1969, regarding CRC activities in various civil rights areas within its jurisdiction.

Chapter 16

1. Civil Rights Commission, Annual Reports, 1969–1970, 1975–1976, Michigan Department of Civil Rights, Detroit, Michigan. There are copies of all the CRC Annual Reports cited in the notes for this chapter at this location.

2. Civil Rights Commission, Annual Report, 1975–1976.

3. Civil Rights Commission, Annual Reports, 1972–1973, 1973–1974.

4. "Public Act No. 220," *Public and Local Acts of the Legislature of the State of Michigan Passed at the Regular Session of 1976,* pp. 583–90; CRC, Annual Reports, 1975–1976, 1976–1977.

5. "Public Act No. 453," *Public and Local Acts . . . 1976,* pp. 1701–14; CRC, Annual Report, 1976–1977; Harold Norris, "A Perspective on the History of Civil Rights Law in Michigan," *Detroit College of Law at Michigan State University Law Review* (Fall 1996): 590–91.

6. "Public Act No. 153," *Public and Local Acts . . . 1978,* pp. 388–89; "Public Act No. 202," *Public and Local Acts . . . 1980,* pp. 512–14; CRC, Annual Reports, 1977–1978, 1992.

7. "Public Act No. 478," *Public and Local Acts . . . 1980,* pp. 2071–75; CRC, Annual Reports, 1979–1980, 1980–1981, 1986, 1990, 1992.

8. CRC, Annual Reports, 1980–1981, 1989.

9. CRC, Annual Report, 1989.

10. CRC, Annual Reports, 1970–1971, 1984–1985.

11. "Public Act No. 428," *Public and Local Acts . . . 1980,* pp. 1877–80; CRC, Annual Reports, 1980–1981, 1984–1985, 1986, 1989, 1991.

12. CRC, Annual Report, 1978–1979.

13. CRC, Annual Reports, 1972–1973, 1996.

14. CRC, Annual Report, 1992.

Bibliography

Manuscript and Archival Collections

Archives of Labor and Urban Affairs, Detroit, Michigan
      Association of Catholic Trade Unionists of Detroit Papers
      Olive R. Beasley Papers
      Civil Rights Congress of Michigan Papers
      Roger Craig Papers
      Detroit Commission on Community Relations Papers
      Ernest C. and Jessie M. Dillard Papers
      Alex Fuller Papers
      Horace Gilmore Papers
      Grosse Pointe Civil Rights Organizations Papers
      Grosse Pointe Committee for Open Housing Papers
      Mildred Jeffrey Papers
      Jewish Labor Committee Papers
      Edgar Johnston Papers
      Clement Kern Papers
      William Kircher Papers
      Rose P. Kleinman Papers
      Joseph Kowalski Papers
      Sander M. Levin Papers
      Donald Marsh Papers
      Richard McGhee Papers
      Patrick V. McNamara Papers
      Metropolitan Detroit Council of Churches Papers
      Michigan AFL-CIO Papers
      Michigan AFL-CIO, Lansing Office Papers

National Association for the Advancement of Colored People, Detroit Branch
Papers
Harold Norris Papers
Alex Pilch Papers
Walter Reuther Papers
William M. Seabron Papers
United Automobile Workers Fair Practices and Anti-Discrimination
Department Papers
United Automobile Workers Local 51 Papers
United Automobile Workers Political Action Department Papers, Roy Reuther
Files
United Automobile Workers Social Security Papers
United Automobile Workers War Policy Division Papers
United Automobile Workers Women's Department Papers
United Automobile Workers Women's Department—Dorothy Haener Papers
United Automobile Workers Women's Department—Lillian Hatcher Papers
United Community Services Central File Papers
United Farm Workers of Michigan Boycott Papers
Bentley Historical Library, Ann Arbor, Michigan
Paul Adams Papers
American Civil Liberties Union, Ann Arbor–Washtenaw County Branch Papers
Al Applegate Papers
Lynn M. Bartlett Papers
Alvin M. Bentley Papers
Helen Berthelot Papers
Don Binkowski Papers
Roscoe Osmond Bonisteel Papers
Eunice Burns Papers
Rollo G. Conlin Papers
Louis C. Cramton Papers
William Byrnes Cudlip Papers
Katherine Moore Cushman Papers
Detroit Urban League Papers
Wilma E. Donahue Papers
Tom Downs Papers
Arthur G. Elliott Papers
Lawrence Lewellyn Farrell Papers
John W. Fitzgerald Papers
Paul G. Goebel Papers
Robert J. Greene Papers
Adelaide Hart Papers
Philip Hart Papers
Woodrow Hunter Papers
Dorothy Siegel Judd Papers
Francis A. Kornegay Papers
League of Women Voters of Michigan Papers
John B. Martin Papers
Michigan Migrant Ministry Papers
William G. Milliken Papers

Harold Norris Papers
James Kerr Pollock Papers
Margaret Price Papers
George Romney Papers
George Romney Associates Papers
George Wahr Sallade Papers
Neil Staebler Papers
John B. Swainson Papers
Clark Tibbitts Papers
University of Michigan Bureau of Government Library Papers
University of Michigan Institute of Public Administration Papers
Richard C. Van Dusen Papers
Albert and Emma Wheeler Papers
G. Mennen Williams Papers
G. Mennen Williams Non-Gubernatorial Papers
Burton Historical Collection, Detroit Public Library, Detroit, Michigan
    Malcolm S. Dade Papers
Grand Rapids Public Library, Grand Rapids, Michigan
    Dorothy Siegel Judd Papers
Michigan State University Archives, Historical Collections, East Lansing, Michigan
    John A. Hannah Papers
Moorland-Spingarn Research Center, Howard University, Washington, D.C.
    Charles C. Diggs, Jr., Papers
Presbyterian Historical Society, Philadelphia, Pennsylvania
    National Council of Churches, Division of Home Mission Papers
State Archives, Lansing, Michigan
    Raymond C. Kehres Papers (RG 72-102)
    Records of the Commission on Aging (RG 66-77-A)
    Records of the Attorney General: Civil Rights (RG 79-82)
    Records of the Constitutional Convention of 1961–1962 (RG 62-24)
    Records of the Department of Agriculture (RG 78-107)
    Records of the Department of Social Services (RG 69-68)
    Records of the Department of Social Services: Commission on Aging (RG 69-24)
    Records of the Executive Office: Kim Sigler (RG 43)
    Records of the Executive Office: William Milliken (RG 88-269)
    Records of the Governor's Commission on Indian Problems (RG 65-47-A)
    Records of Management and Budget: Women's Commission (RG 77-78)
    Records of the Civil Rights Commission: Administrative (RG 74-90)
    Records of the Civil Rights Commission: Community Relations Bureau (RG 83-55)
    Records of the Civil Rights Commission: Executive (RG 81-89)
    Records of the Civil Rights Commission: Executive Office (RG 87-6)
    Records of the Civil Rights Commission, Information Division, General Administrative Records of the Fair Employment Practices Commission, 1955–1963 (RG 66-82-A)
    Records of the Michigan Department of Civil Rights: Detroit Office (RG 80-17)
    John F. Thaden Papers (RG 68-69)

State Historical Society of Wisconsin, Madison, Wisconsin
Wilbur J. Cohen Papers

U.S. Government Documents

Employment: 1961 Commission on Civil Rights Report. Washington, D.C.:
Government Printing Office, n.d.

Fair Employment Practices Committee. *Final Report, June 28, 1946.* Washington,
D.C.: Government Printing Office, 1947.

*The 50 States Report: Submitted to the Commission on Civil Rights by the State
Advisory Committees.* Washington, D.C.: Government Printing Office, n.d.

*Hearings before the United States Commission on Civil Rights: Hearings Held in
Detroit, Michigan, December 14, 15, 1960.* Washington, D.C.: Government
Printing Office, 1961.

*Migratory Labor in American Agriculture: Report of the President's Commission
on Migratory Labor.* Washington, D.C.: Government Printing Office, 1951.

To Secure These Rights: The Report of the President's Committee on Civil Rights.
New York: Simon and Schuster, 1947.

U.S. House of Representatives. General Subcommittee on Education of the
Committee on Education and Labor. *Problems of the Aged and Aging:
Hearings.* 87 Cong., 1 sess., 1962, Part 2.

———. Special Subcommittee on Labor, Committee on Education and Labor.
Equal Employment Opportunity: Hearings. 87 Cong., 1 sess., October 1961,
Part 1; 87 Cong., 2 sess., January 1962, Part 2.

U.S. Senate. Committee on Labor and Public Welfare. *The Migratory Farm Labor
Problem in the United States.* 89 Cong., 2 sess., 1966, S. Rept. 1549.

———. Committee on Labor and Public Welfare. *The Migratory Farm Labor
Problem in the United States.* 90 Cong., 2 sess., 1968, S. Rept. 1006.

———. Committee on Labor and Public Welfare. *Migratory Labor Bills: Hearings.*
88 Cong., 1 sess., 1963.

———. Subcommittee on Health of the Senate Committee on Labor and Public
Welfare. *Migrant Health Services: Hearings.* 91 Cong., 1 sess., 1969.

———. Subcommittee on Labor and Management Relations of the Committee on
Labor and Public Welfare. *Migratory Labor: Hearings.* 82 Cong., 2 sess., 1952.

———. Subcommittee on Labor of the Committee on Labor and Public Welfare.
Age Discrimination in Employment: Hearings. 90 Cong., 1 sess., 1967.

———. Subcommittee on Migratory Labor of the Committee on Labor and Public
Welfare. *Manpower and Economic Problems: Hearings.* 91 Cong., 1 and 2
sess., 1970, Part 7-B.

———. Subcommittee on Migratory Labor of the Committee on Labor and Public
Welfare. *Migratory Labor: Hearings.* 86 Cong., 1 sess., 1959, Part 1.

———. Subcommittee on Migratory Labor of the Committee on Labor and Public
Welfare. *Migratory Labor: Hearings.* 87 Cong., 1 sess., 1961.

———. Subcommittee on Migratory Labor of the Committee on Labor and Public
Welfare. *Migrant Health Services: Hearings.* 90 Cong., 1 sess., 1967.

———. Subcommittee on Migratory Labor of the Committee on Labor and Public
Welfare. *Voluntary Farm Employment Service: Hearings.* 88 Cong., 1 sess.,
1963.

———. Subcommittee on the Problems of the Aged and Aging of the Committee on Labor and Public Welfare. *The Aged and the Aging in the United States: Hearings.* 86 Cong., 1 sess., 1959.

U.S. Indian Claims Commission. *Final Report.* August 13, 1946, September 30, 1978.

Year of Transition: Seasonal Farm Labor, 1965: A Report from the Secretary of Labor. Washington, D.C.: Government Printing Office, 1966.

State Government Documents

Farm Labor and Rural Manpower Service Section. *Post Season Farm Labor Report, 1968.*

———. *Post Season Farm Labor and Rural Manpower Report, 1969.*

Farm Labor Service Section. *Post Season Farm Labor Reports, 1966, 1967.*

Farm Placement Section. *Post Season Farm Labor Reports, 1949–1965.*

Journal of the House of Representatives of the State of Michigan, 1949–1968.

Journal of the Senate of the State of Michigan, 1949–1968.

Michigan Civil Rights Commission. *Annual Reports, 1968–1996.*

———. *How the Backlog Grew: Four-Year Report of Claims Activity, 1964–1967.*

———. *Toward Equality: Two-Year Report of Claims Activity, 1968–1969.*

Michigan Commission on Aging. *Aging in Michigan, 1961–1969.*

Michigan Commission on Indian Affairs. *1970 Annual Report.*

Michigan Employment Security Commission. *Annual Reports . . . , 1949–1962.*

Michigan Official Directory and Legislative Manual.

Public and Local Acts of the Legislature of the State of Michigan . . . 1949–1980.

State of Michigan Constitutional Convention, 1961. *Official Record.* 2 vols.

Interviews

The Civil Rights Documentation Project, Moorland-Spingarn Research Center, Howard University, Washington, D.C. Transcripts of interviews with John Feild, Richard V. Marks, and George Schermer.

G. Mennen Williams and Nancy Quirk Williams Oral History Project, 1980–1982. Interviews by Ruth Wasem and Ruth Bordin. Bentley Historical Library, Ann Arbor, Michigan. Transcripts of interviews with Geraldine Bledsoe, Tom Downs, Alfred B. Fitt, Adelaide Hart, Jane Hart, Wade McCree, Horace Sheffield, Otis Smith, and Nancy Quirk Williams.

Institute of Industrial Relations, University of Michigan and Wayne State University. Women and Work Program. The 20th Century Trade Union Woman: Vehicle for Social Change. Oral History Program, 1978–1979. Bentley Historical Library, Ann Arbor, Michigan. Transcripts of interviews with Carolyn Davis, Dorothy Haener, Lillian Hatcher, and Mildred Jeffrey.

Interview with G. Mennen Williams for the John F. Kennedy Library, April 27, 1960. Transcript in Box 103, G. Mennen Williams Non-Gubernatorial Papers, Bentley Historical Library.

Sidney Fine interviews with G. Mennen Williams, December 1964, and Tom Downs, March 30, 1995. Transcripts in Bentley Historical Library.

Newspapers

Detroit Free Press, 1948–1968
Detroit News, 1948–1968
Detroit News Lansing Bureau Scrapbooks, 1948–1966, Bentley Historical Library
Michigan Chronicle, 1948–1968
New York Times, 1948–1968

Dissertations and Other Unpublished Material

Anderson, Clarence W. "Metropolitan Detroit FEPC." M.A. thesis, Wayne State University, 1947.

Dillard, Angela Denise. "From the Reverend Charles A. Hill to the Reverend Albert B. Cleage, Jr.: Change and Continuity in the Patterns of Civil Rights Mobilizations in Detroit, 1935–1967." Ph.D. diss., University of Michigan, 1995.

Effland, Anne B. "The Emergence of Federal Assistance Programs for Migrant and Seasonal Farmworkers in Post–World War II America." Ph.D. diss., Iowa State University, 1991.

Hillman, James R. "The Michigan Commission on Indian Affairs—The Early Years: The Governor's Study Commission on Indian Problems, 1956–1958." MS, Wayne State University, 1979.

Stevenson, Marshall Field, Jr. "Points of Departure, Acts of Resolve: Black-Jewish Relations in Detroit, 1937–1962." Ph.D. diss., University of Michigan, 1988.

Stuckman, Noel W. "Some Economic Aspects of Increasing Cucumber Yields in Michigan." MS, Department of Agricultural Economics, Michigan State University, 1959.

Thompson, Heather Ann. "The Politics of Labor, Race, and Liberalism in the Auto Plants and the Motor City, 1940–1980." Ph.D. diss., Princeton University, 1995.

Tillery, Tyrone. "The Conscience of a City: A Commemorative History of the Detroit Human Rights Commission and Department, 1943–1983." Detroit Human Rights Department [1983].

Wigderson, Seth Mark. "The UAW in the 1950s." Ph.D. diss., Wayne State University, 1989.

Winder, David William. "Gubernatorial-Legislative Interaction in Michigan." Ph.D. diss., Michigan State University, 1982.

Published Books and Articles

Achenbaum, W. Andrew. *Shades of Gray: Old Age, American Values, and Federal Policies since 1920.* Boston: Little, Brown, 1983.

Angell, D. Duane. *Romney: A Political Biography.* New York: Exposition Press, 1967.

Ashmore, Harry. *Civil Rights and Wrongs: A Memoir of Race and Politics, 1944–1994.* New York: Pantheon Books, 1994.

Ball, John M. "Changes in Sugar Beet Production in Michigan." *Papers of the Michigan Academy of Science, Arts, and Letters* 45 (1960): 137–44.

Barnard, John. *Walter Reuther and the Rise of the Auto Workers.* Boston: Little, Brown, 1983.

Becker, Robert W., et al. "Correlates of Legislative Voting: Michigan's House of Representatives, 1954–1961." *Midwest Journal of Political Science* 6 (November 1962): 384–96.

Berger, Morroe. *Equality by Statute: The Revolution in Civil Rights.* Rev. ed. Garden City, N.Y.: Doubleday, 1967.

Berthelot, Helen Washburn. *Win Some, Lose Some: G. Mennen Williams and the New Democrats.* Detroit: Wayne State University Press, 1995.

Beyle, Thad, and J. Oliver Williams, eds. *The American Governor in Behavioral Perspective.* New York: Harper and Row, 1972.

Blumrosen, Alfred W. "Antidiscrimination Laws in Action in New Jersey: A Law-Sociology Study." *Rutgers Law Review* 19 (Winter 1965): 189–287.

Brauer, Carl M. *John F. Kennedy and the Second Reconstruction.* New York: Columbia University Press, 1977.

Buffa, Dudley W. *Union Power and American Democracy: The UAW and the Democratic Party, 1935–1972.* Ann Arbor: University of Michigan Press, 1984.

Clifton, James A. "Michigan's Indians: Tribe, Nation, State, Racial, Ethnic or Special Interest Group?" *Michigan Historical Review* 20 (Fall 1994): 93–152.

Cosseboom, Kathy. *Grosse Pointe, Michigan: Race against Race.* East Lansing: Michigan State University Press, 1972.

Craig, Richard B. *The Bracero Program.* Austin: University of Texas Press, 1971.

Cudlip, William B. "The Proposed Constitution Should Be Approved." *Detroit Lawyer* 31 (January 1963): 7–11+.

Darden, Joe T., et al. *Detroit: Race and Uneven Development.* Philadelphia: Temple University Press, 1987.

Densmore, Frances. *A Study of Some Michigan Indians.* Anthropological Paper Number 1. Ann Arbor: University of Michigan Press, 1949.

Dunbar, Willis F. *Michigan: A History of the Wolverine State.* 3rd rev. ed. by George S. May. Grand Rapids, Mich.: Eerdmans, 1995.

Dye, Thomas R. *Politics in States and Communities.* Englewood Cliffs, N.J.: Prentice Hall, 1969.

Eley, Lynn W., and Thomas W. Casstevens. *The Politics of Fair- Housing Legislation: State and Local Case Studies.* San Francisco: Chandler, 1968.

Feild, John G. "Hindsight and Foresight about FEPC." *Buffalo Law Review* 14 (February 1964): 16–21.

Fenton, John H. *Midwest Politics.* New York: Holt, Rinehart and Winston, 1966.

Ferry, Charles A. "George Romney Gone Bust." *New Republic,* January 25, 1964, pp. 12–15.

Fine, Sidney. "Chance and History: Some Aspects of the Detroit Riot of 1967." *Michigan Quarterly Review* 25 (Spring 1986): 403–23.

———. *Frank Murphy: The New Deal Years.* Chicago: University of Chicago Press, 1979.

———. *Violence in the Model City: The Cavanagh Administration, Race Relations, and the Detroit Riot of 1967.* Ann Arbor: University of Michigan Press, 1989.

Fuller, Richard C. *George Romney and Michigan.* New York: Vantage Press, 1966.

Gabin, Nancy F. *Feminism in the Labor Movement: Women and the United Auto Workers, 1935–1975.* Ithaca: Cornell University Press, 1990.

Golden, Mrs. James R. "The Migrant Problem in Michigan." *American Child* 39 (January 1957): 7.

Good, David L. *Orvie, the Dictator of Dearborn: The Rise and Fall of Orville L. Hubbard.* Detroit: Wayne State University Press, 1989.

Halpern, Martin. *UAW Politics in the Cold War Era.* Albany: State University of New York Press, 1988.

Harrison, Selig S. "Romney and the Republicans." *New Republic,* March 5, 1962, pp. 17–27.

"Health Care for Migrant Families." *Michigan's Health* 53 (January–February 1965): 22.

Hessler, William N. "A New Face in American Politics." *Reporter,* March 1, 1962, pp. 26–29.

Higbee, Jay Anders. *Development and Administration of the New York State Law against Discrimination.* University, Ala.: University of Alabama Press, 1966.

Hill, Herbert. "Twenty Years of State Fair Employment Practices Commissions: A Critical Analysis with Recommendations." *Buffalo Law Review* 14 (February 1964): 22–69.

Hillman, James R. *A History of the Michigan Commission on Indian Affairs, 1960–1977.* Clinton, Ohio: Hillman Publishing Co., 1984.

———. *The Minutes of the Michigan Commission on Indian Affairs, 1956–1977.* Canal Fulton, Ohio: Hillman Publishing Co., ca. 1990.

Hodges, Edward N. "The Negro's Future through Fair Employment Practices." *Negro History Bulletin* 26 (October 1962): 16–18.

Horne, Gerald. *Communist Front? The Civil Rights Congress, 1946–1956.* Rutherford, N.J.: Farleigh Dickinson University Press, 1986.

Jenkins, J. Craig. *The Politics of Insurgency: The Farm Worker Movement in the 1960s.* New York: Columbia University Press, 1985.

Johnston, Edgar Grant. "The Education of Children of Spanish-Speaking Migrants in Michigan." *Papers of the Michigan Academy of Science, Arts, and Letters* 32 (1946): 509–21.

———. "Migrant Workers in the State of Michigan." MASCD Issue Paper [1970].

Johnston, Helen L. *Health for the Nation's Harvesters: A History of the Migrant Health Program in Its Economic and Social Setting.* Farmington Hills, Mich.: National Migrant Worker Council, 1985.

Kersten, Andrew E. "Jobs and Justice: Detroit, Fair Employment, and Federal Activism during the Second World War." *Michigan Historical Review* 25 (Spring 1999): 77–101.

Kilpatrick, James Jackson. "Romney: Salesman on the Move." *National Review,* December 12, 1967, pp. 1372–83+.

Konvitz, Milton R. *Expanding Liberties: Freedom's Gains in Postwar America.* New York: Viking Press, 1966.

Kornhauser, Arthur. *Attitudes of Detroit People toward Detroit: Summary of a Detailed Report.* Detroit: Wayne State University Press, 1952.

———. *Detroit as the People See It.* Detroit: Wayne State University Press, 1952.

Laikin, Judith. "What Made the Mess in Michigan?" *Reporter,* March 31, 1960, pp. 33–35.

La Palombara, Joseph. *Guide to Michigan Politics.* East Lansing: Michigan State University Press, 1960.

LeBreton, Betty Lou, and Preston P. LeBreton. *The Michigan State Fair Employment Practices Act.* University of Detroit Institute for Business Services Research Bulletin No. 103. Detroit: University of Detroit, 1956.

Lockard, Duane. *Toward Equal Employment Opportunity: A Study of State and Local Antidiscrimination Laws.* Princeton: Princeton University Press, 1968.

Lowery, Edith E. "A Better Chance for Migratory Children." *American Child* 39 (January 1957): 4, 11.

Manis, Jerome G. *A Study of Migrant Education: Survey Findings in Van Buren County, Michigan, 1957.* Kalamazoo: Western Michigan University Press, 1958.

Marks, Richard V. "The Catalytic Role of Governmental Human Relations Agencies." *American Journal of Public Health* 55 (April 1963): 615–18.

McCree, Wade H., Jr. "The Negro Renaissance in Michigan Politics." *Negro History Bulletin* 26 (October 1962): 7–9+.

McNaughton, Frank. *Mennen Williams of Michigan: Fighter for Progress.* New York: Oceana, 1960.

Meier, August, and Elliott Rudwick. *Black Detroit and the Rise of the UAW.* New York: Oxford University Press, 1979.

Moreno, Paul. *From Direct Action to Affirmative Action: Fair Employment Law and Policy in America, 1933–1972.* Baton Rouge: Louisiana State University Press, 1997.

Norgren, Paul H., and Samuel E. Hill. *Toward Fair Employment.* New York: Columbia University Press, 1964.

Norris, Harold. "A Case against Approval of the Proposed Constitution." *Detroit Lawyer* 31 (January 1963): 15–21.

———. *Education for Popular Sovereignty through Implementing the Constitution and the Bill of Rights: A Collection of Writings.* Detroit: Detroit College of Law, 1991.

———. "A Perspective on the History of the Civil Rights Law in Michigan." *Detroit College of Law at Michigan State University Law Review* (Fall 1996): 567–601.

Obermann, C. Esco. *A History of Vocational Rehabilitation in Michigan.* 5th ed. Minneapolis: T. S. Dennison, 1968.

Osofsky, Gilbert. *The Burden of Race: A Documentary History of Negro-White Relations in America.* New York: Harper and Row, 1987.

Parmet, Herbert S. *JFK: The Presidency of John F. Kennedy.* New York: Dial Press, 1983.

Peirce, Neal R. *The Megastates of America: People, Politics, and Power in the Ten Great States.* New York: Norton, 1972.

Pilling, Patricia L. "Segregation: Cottage Rental in Michigan." *Phylon* 25 (Summer 1964): 191–207.

Pollock, James K. *Making Michigan's New Constitution, 1961–1962.* Ann Arbor: George Wahr Publishing Co., 1962.

Rabinovitz, Sam. "Michigan Migrants and the NLCC." *American Child* 39 (January 1957): 7, 9.

Reichley, James J. *States in Crisis: Politics in American States, 1950–1962.* Chapel Hill: University of North Carolina Press, 1964.

"The Right to Equal Treatment: Administrative Enforcement of Antidiscrimination Legislation." *Harvard Law Review* 74 (January 1961): 526–89.

Routh, Frederick B. "Supplementary Activities for State Governments Seeking to Prevent Discrimination." *Buffalo Law Review* 14 (Fall 1964): 148–50.

Sarasohn, Stephen, and Vera Sarasohn. *Political Party Patterns in Michigan.* Detroit: Wayne State University Press, 1957.

Sawyer, Robert Lee. *The Democratic State Central Committee in Michigan, 1949–1959: The Rise of the New Politics and the New Political Leadership.* Ann Arbor: Institute of Public Administration, University of Michigan, 1960.

Schermer, George. "Effectiveness of Equal Opportunity Legislation." In *The Negro and Employment Opportunity: Problems and Practices,* ed. Herbert R. Northrup and Richard L. Rowan, 67–84. Ann Arbor: University of Michigan Press, 1965.

Schwartz, Bernard. *Super Chief: Earl Warren and His Supreme Court.* New York: New York University Press, 1983.

Sladek, Edward F. "Vocational Rehabilitation in Michigan." *Journal of the Michigan State Medical Society* 54 (August 1955): 952–53+.

Smith, Beverly, Jr. "Soapy, the Boy Wonder." *Saturday Evening Post,* November 9, 1957, pp. 25–27+.

Staebler, Neil. *Out of the Smoke-Filled Room: A Story of Michigan Politics.* Ann Arbor: George Wahr Publishers, 1991.

Stieber, Carolyn. *The Politics of Change in Michigan.* East Lansing: Michigan State University Press, 1970.

Stolberg, Mary M. *Bridging the River of Hatred: The Pioneering Efforts of Detroit Police Commissioner George Edwards.* Detroit: Wayne State University Press, 1998.

Sturm, Albert L. *Constitution Making in Michigan, 1961–1962.* University of Michigan Governmental Studies No. 43. Ann Arbor: Institute of Public Administration, University of Michigan, 1963.

Sturt, Daniel W. "The Federal Minimum Wage Law and Michigan Farm Employers." Rural Manpower Center Mimeograph No. 7. Department of Agricultural Economics, Michigan State University, February 1, 1969.

Sugrue, Thomas J. *The Origins of the Urban Crisis: Race and Inequality in Postwar Detroit.* Princeton: Princeton University Press, 1996.

Thomas, Norman. *Rule 9: Politics, Administration, and Civil Rights.* New York: Random House, 1966.

Valdés, Dennis Nodín. *Al Norte: Agricultural Workers in the Great Plains Region.* Austin: University of Texas Press, 1991.

Weeks, George. *Stewards of the State: The Governors of Michigan.* Detroit and Ann Arbor: Detroit News and Historical Society of Michigan, 1991.

Weisbrot, Robert. *Freedom Bound: A History of America's Civil Rights Movement.* New York: Norton, 1990.

"Welfare State in Trouble." *US News and World Report,* February 13, 1959, pp. 49–51.

Williams, G. Mennen. *A Governor's Notes.* Ann Arbor: Institute of Public Administration, University of Michigan, 1961.

INDEX

422

Titles in the Great Lakes Books Series

Deep Woods Frontier: A History of Logging in Northern Michigan, by Theodore J. Karamanski, 1989

Orvie, The Dictator of Dearborn, by David L. Good, 1989

Seasons of Grace: A History of the Catholic Archdiocese of Detroit, by Leslie Woodcock Tentler, 1990

The Pottery of John Foster: Form and Meaning, by Gordon and Elizabeth Orear, 1990

The Diary of Bishop Frederic Baraga: First Bishop of Marquette, Michigan, edited by Regis M. Walling and Rev. N. Daniel Rupp, 1990

Walnut Pickles and Watermelon Cake: A Century of Michigan Cooking, by Larry B. Massie and Priscilla Massie, 1990

The Making of Michigan, 1820–1860: A Pioneer Anthology, edited by Justin L. Kestenbaum, 1990

America's Favorite Homes: A Guide to Popular Early Twentieth-Century Homes, by Robert Schweitzer and Michael W. R. Davis, 1990

Beyond the Model T: The Other Ventures of Henry Ford, by Ford R. Bryan, 1990

Life after the Line, by Josie Kearns, 1990

Michigan Lumbertowns: Lumbermen and Laborers in Saginaw, Bay City, and Muskegon, 1870–1905, by Jeremy W. Kilar, 1990

Detroit Kids Catalog: The Hometown Tourist, by Ellyce Field, 1990

Waiting for the News, by Leo Litwak, 1990 (reprint)

Detroit Perspectives, edited by Wilma Wood Henrickson, 1991

Life on the Great Lakes: A Wheelsman's Story, by Fred W. Dutton, edited by William Donohue Ellis, 1991

Copper Country Journal: The Diary of Schoolmaster Henry Hobart, 1863–1864, by Henry Hobart, edited by Philip P. Mason, 1991

John Jacob Astor: Business and Finance in the Early Republic, by John Denis Haeger, 1991

Survival and Regeneration: Detroit's American Indian Community, by Edmund J. Danziger, Jr., 1991

Steamboats and Sailors of the Great Lakes, by Mark L. Thompson, 1991

Cobb Would Have Caught It: The Golden Age of Baseball in Detroit, by Richard Bak, 1991

Michigan in Literature, by Clarence Andrews, 1992

Under the Influence of Water: Poems, Essays, and Stories, by Michael Delp, 1992

The Country Kitchen, by Della T. Lutes, 1992 (reprint)

The Making of a Mining District: Keweenaw Native Copper 1500–1870, by David J. Krause, 1992

Kids Catalog of Michigan Adventures, by Ellyce Field, 1993

Henry's Lieutenants, by Ford R. Bryan, 1993

Historic Highway Bridges of Michigan, by Charles K. Hyde, 1993

Lake Erie and Lake St. Clair Handbook, by Stanley J. Bolsenga and Charles E. Herndendorf, 1993

Queen of the Lakes, by Mark Thompson, 1994

Iron Fleet: The Great Lakes in World War II, by George J. Joachim, 1994

Turkey Stearnes and the Detroit Stars: The Negro Leagues in Detroit, 1919–1933, by Richard Bak, 1994

Pontiac and the Indian Uprising, by Howard H. Peckham, 1994 (reprint)

Charting the Inland Seas: A History of the U.S. Lake Survey, by Arthur M. Woodford, 1994 (reprint)

Ojibwa Narratives of Charles and Charlotte Kawbawgam and Jacques LePique, 1893–1895. Recorded with Notes by Homer H. Kidder, edited by Arthur P. Bourgeois, 1994, co-published with the Marquette County Historical Society

Strangers and Sojourners: A History of Michigan's Keweenaw Peninsula, by Arthur W. Thurner, 1994

Win Some, Lose Some: G. Mennen Williams and the New Democrats, by Helen Washburn Berthelot, 1995

Sarkis, by Gordon and Elizabeth Orear, 1995

The Northern Lights: Lighthouses of the Upper Great Lakes, by Charles K. Hyde, 1995 (reprint)

Kids Catalog of Michigan Adventures, second edition, by Ellyce Field, 1995

Rumrunning and the Roaring Twenties: Prohibition on the Michigan-Ontario Waterway, by Philip P. Mason, 1995

In the Wilderness with the Red Indians, by E. R. Baierlein, translated by Anita Z. Boldt, edited by Harold W. Moll, 1996

Elmwood Endures: History of a Detroit Cemetery, by Michael Franck, 1996

Master of Precision: Henry M. Leland, by Mrs. Wilfred C. Leland with Minnie Dubbs Millbrook, 1996 (reprint)

Haul-Out: New and Selected Poems, by Stephen Tudor, 1996

Kids Catalog of Michigan Adventures, third edition, by Ellyce Field, 1997

Beyond the Model T: The Other Ventures of Henry Ford, revised edition, by Ford R. Bryan, 1997

Young Henry Ford: A Picture History of the First Forty Years, by Sidney Olson, 1997 (reprint)

Detroit Kids Catalog: A Family Guide for the 21st Century, by Ellyce Field, 2000

The Sandstone Architecture of the Lake Superior Region, by Kathryn Bishop Eckert, 2000

Radical Education in the Rural South: Commonwealth College, 1922–1940, by William H. Cobb, 2000

Expanding the Frontiers of Civil Rights: Michigan, 1948–1968, by Sidney Fine, 2000

BAKER COLLEGE OF CLINTON TOWNSHIP
34950 LITTLE MACK AVENUE
CLINTON TOWNSHIP, MI 48035

1. Most items may be checked out for two weeks and
   renewed for the same period. Additional restrictions
   may apply to high-demand items.

2. A fine is charged for each day material is not returned
   according to the above rule. No material will be issued
   to any person incurring such a fine until it has been paid.

3. All damage to material beyond reasonable wear and all
   losses shall be paid for.

4. Each borrower is responsible for all items checked out on
   his/her library card and for all fines accruing on the same.

DEMCO